Praise for *Overcoming Evil*

"Staub has written a superb book that has excellent scholarship and well-conceived practical suggestions for preventing massive intergroup violence and for developing reconciliation if it occurs. It is an extraordinary book of heart, as well as fine scholarship. I recommend it highly for all leaders and citizens who seek a more peaceful world, as well as for social scientists who wish to be informed of the best thinking in this area."

—Morton Deutsch, Professor Emeritus of
Psychology and Education, Teachers College, Columbia University

"*Overcoming Evil* offers readers a front row seat to witness Ervin Staub's wisdom and expertise gained from three decades of research and thoughtful engagement with the problem of evil. He wrote *The Roots of Evil* with refreshing clarity. With *Overcoming Evil*, he has raised the bar and spells out a set of principles and values necessary for transcending evil and building peaceful societies. From training those in positions of power to become 'constructive leaders,' to developing communities of 'active bystanders,' Staub shares with readers cutting edge research that shows how to create what he terms 'structures of prevention and reconciliation.' Staub leaves the reader with no doubt that it is possible to prevent the cycles of violence that so often repeat themselves historically. If you care about building and *sustaining* peace in the aftermath of mass violence and genocide, read this book from cover to cover. You will want to stand up and applaud the ethical clarity and profound insights in this extraordinary work of scholarship."

—Pumla Gobodo-Madikizela, Former Member,
South Africa's Truth and Reconciliation Commission, and author of
A Human Being Died That Night: A South African Story of Forgiveness

"In a fitting capstone to Ervin Staub's remarkable career, *Overcoming Evil: Genocide, Violent Conflict, and Terrorism* addresses the psychology of man's inhumanity to man. Leavened by his own personal experience and field work in countries ravaged by genocidal struggle, Staub's book covers the range of political violence, from terrorism to ethnic cleansing, exploring and illuminating the dark corners of man's psychology that permit ordinary people to commit such extraordinary evil. Not merely an academic exercise, the book provides pragmatic guidance for resolving the seemingly intractable conflicts that beset contemporary society."

—Jerrold M. Post, Director, Political Psychology Program,
George Washington University, and author of *The Mind of the Terrorist:
The Psychology of Terrorism from the IRA to al-Qaeda*

"*Overcoming Evil* is a remarkable book. Many works on conflict focus on the destructive element of the forces at hand, a task at which this book succeeds admirably. Both authoritative and personal, the volume gives us a profound understanding of the nature, sources, and dynamics of violence, building on over thirty years of the author's research and analysis on the topic. However, Ervin Staub has given us a volume that takes us beyond understanding the costs of destruction, slaughter, and war. It also shows us the way out. *Overcoming Evil* gives the reader in-depth instruction on how to stop the violence. Focusing particularly on prevention, it makes the case for the power of the individual (the active bystander), as well as the power of groups, nations, and international leaders, to intervene in order to reverse escalating hostility or to halt conflict that has already broken out. This is a book of hope and action, and will be a valuable addition to the libraries of scholars and practitioners alike."

—Pamela Aall, Vice President for Domestic Programs,
Education and Training Center, U.S. Institute of Peace

"The leading author on genocide has turned his analysis to address the question of how to prevent it. The work is deeply personal, analytically penetrating, and tactically broad. It deserves a wide readership, from those who make policy to those who are bystanders to unfolding events."

—I William Zartman, Jacob Blaustein Professor Emeritus,
Paul H. Nitze School of Advanced International Studies,
Johns Hopkins University.

"Staub has done it. In a single volume, he has given us illuminating, multidisciplinary analysis of the causes of mass violence and terrorism, their impacts, and most important, the steps we can take collectively toward prevention. The extraordinary scope and depth of this book makes it essential reading for everyone who cares about peace and building a humane world."

—Michael Wessells, Professor, Program on
Forced Migration and Health, Columbia University

Overcoming Evil

Other Books by Ervin Staub

Positive Social Behavior and Morality, Vol. 1.
Personal and Social Influences. 1978

Positive Social Behavior and Morality, Vol. 2.
Socialization and Development. 1979

Personality: Basic Aspects and Current Research. Edited, 1980

The Development and Maintenance of Prosocial Behavior:
International Perspectives on Positive Morality.
Co-edited, with Daniel Bar-Tal, Jerzy Karylowski and Janusz Reykowski, 1984

The Roots of Evil: The Origins of Genocide and Other Group Violence. 1989

Social and Moral Values: Individual and Societal Perspectives.
Co-edited, with Nancy Eisenberg and Janusz Reykowski, 1989

Patriotism in the Lives of Individuals and Nations.
Co-edited, with Daniel Bar-Tal, 1997

The Psychology of Good and Evil: Why Children, Adults and Groups Help and
Harm Others, 2003

The Panorama of Mass Violence: Origins, Prevention, Reconciliation and the
Evolution of Caring and Active Bystandership. 2011, forthcoming

Overcoming Evil

Genocide, Violent Conflict, and Terrorism

Ervin Staub

OXFORD
UNIVERSITY PRESS
2011

OXFORD
UNIVERSITY PRESS

Oxford University Press, Inc., publishes works that further
Oxford University's objective of excellence
in research, scholarship, and education.

Oxford   New York
Auckland   Cape Town   Dar es Salaam   Hong Kong   Karachi
Kuala Lumpur   Madrid   Melbourne   Mexico City   Nairobi
New Delhi   Shanghai   Taipei   Toronto

With offices in
Argentina   Austria   Brazil   Chile   Czech Republic   France   Greece
Guatemala   Hungary   Italy   Japan   Poland   Portugal   Singapore
South Korea   Switzerland   Thailand   Turkey   Ukraine   Vietnam

Published by Oxford University Press, Inc.
198 Madison Avenue, New York, New York 10016

www.oup.com

Oxford is a registered trademark of Oxford University Press, Inc.

Library of Congress Cataloging-in-Publication Data
Staub, Ervin.
Overcoming evil : genocide, violent conflict, and terrorism / Ervin Staub. — 1
p. cm.
Includes bibliographical references and index.
ISBN 978-0-19-538204-4
1. Conflict management. 2. Genocide. 3. Violence. 4. Aggressiveness.
5. Social groups. I. Title.
HM1126.S73   2010
303.6'9—dc22
2010031253

9 8 7 6 5 4 3 2 1
Printed in the United States of America
on acid-free paper

For Vera, Dora, Noah, and Rory: may you live in a peaceful world

Preface and Acknowledgments

This book represents the evolution of my approximately 32 years of engagement with research, scholarship, work in real-world settings, and publications on violence between groups and its prevention. It is informed by my earlier and continuing work on altruism and helping behavior. I also extensively draw on the work of others. I describe in this book the principles or influences I consider important in understanding the roots of violence, and both principles and practices relevant to preventing violence between groups and bringing about reconciliation.

I wrote this book to advance scholarship but also very much to promote practical efforts in prevention and reconciliation. To prevent group violence we need people who will engage, with each other, with leaders, with the world. We need people who develop concern and caring and who act, or exert influence on their countries to act, on behalf of other people, sometimes in their own countries, sometimes near to home in other countries, sometimes in distant lands. I hope this book will increase not only knowledge, but also concern about people belonging to varied groups, and their welfare. Both are needed for effective engagement by citizens, secular and religious communities, members of the media, government officials, leaders of all kinds, nongovernmental and international organizations and nations. All of them can become "active bystanders" and help prevent mass violence. Even the power of individual actors is substantial. Even in large organizations, it is individuals who determine passivity or action—especially if they join together.

The genesis of my own concern and motivation, both to develop caring and helping, and to understand and prevent genocide and other mass violence, came from my early life experiences in Hungary, first under Nazism, then Communism. I will briefly mention these experiences. We change as a result of our engagements, and my concern and motivation has greatly expanded as I was doing this work.

Knowledge develops progressively, and I want to thank the many people who have greatly advanced the fields the book covers. Many of them are named in the text, and more are cited in the book's endnotes and references.

I am deeply grateful to Laurie Anne Pearlman, a clinical psychologist and trauma specialist, my collaborator on work in Rwanda, Burundi, and the Congo. Her research and theories have seeped into and become intertwined with my thinking, especially in the realm of trauma and healing. As my wife she has been completely supportive of my commitment to, and engagement and preoccupation with, the matters this book addresses. Lori Handelman of Oxford University Press has been an excellent, supportive editor.

I am also deeply grateful to people who read all or part of drafts of the book and made very useful comments. Daniel Bar-Tal, Jerrold Post, Roger Smith, Adin Thayer and William Zartman, all outstanding experts on and/or practitioners in the various topics I discuss, read all of the book. Laurie Pearlman and Johanna Vollhardt read parts of the book, Gerry Caplan, Catherina Newberry and Karen Murphy read the brief history of the Rwandan genocide and the violence in the Congo in Chapter 3, and Jack Rosenblum and Daniel Staub read Chapters 1 and 2. Many people sent me useful materials, in particular Bert Ingelaere on Rwanda and Rafi Nets-Zehngut on the Israeli-Palestinian conflict.

Part of the book is about our work in Rwanda on healing, reconciliation, and the prevention of new violence in that country, work that later expanded to Burundi and the Democratic Republic of the Congo. While this is only perhaps a fifth of the book, it has special meaning to me. I am grateful to people in Rwanda who invited us, worked with us, helped facilitate our work, and by accepting us and showing their appreciation, encouraged us. They include Charles Murigande, who among other important leadership jobs was foreign minister of Rwanda and who invited us to Rwanda; Aloisea Inyumba and Fatuma Ndangiza, the first and second executive directors of the Unity and Reconciliation Commission; Jean de Dieu Mucyo, the justice minister; Romain Murenzi, the minister of education during our early years there; and Alphonse Bakusi and Alphonsine Mutabonwa, who worked with us and assisted us in varied ways. A few of the many others we worked with include Michel Kayitoba, Anne Abiuseli, Frank Kobukyeye, Antoine Zurayisire, Athanase Hagengimana, Athanase Mugabe Dusabe, and Solange Shengero. I also want to thank U.S. Ambassador Margaret McMillian, and of USAID Rwanda its head and later ambassador Henderson Patrick, and Kim Pease.

I am grateful to the Amsterdam-based film and television producer George Weiss, who wanted to do a television series with me, *Hate in Ten Lessons*, based on my book *The Roots of Evil*, to help prevent mass violence everywhere. When Laurie Pearlman and I invited him to come instead to Rwanda to work with us in developing educational radio programs to promote healing, reconciliation, and violence prevention, he enthusiastically shifted direction. He created an organization, Radio La Benevolencija Humanitarian Tools Foundation, which produces in collaboration with us an ongoing media education"campaign," featuring a variety of regular weekly radio programs. We started in Rwanda and then expanded to Burundi and the Congo. He and the team working with him developed this work in many ways, including "grassroots projects" that directly involved members of many communities as active bystanders that turn the radio program content into daily practice.

Others who have been an important part of the educational radio projects and their expansion include Anneke van Hoek, George Weiss's associate from the start; Suzanne Fisher and Marie Coutin, who have been the organization's producers, respectively, in Rwanda and the Congo, in charge of creating the programs; and Johan Deflander, the organization's producer in Rwanda and then in Burundi. Local writers and journalists prepared the programs, local actors performed them, and local staff provided the infrastructure for them and increasingly assumed leadership roles. A few of them are Albert Nzamukwereka, Charles Rukundo, Perpetue Mukahigiro, Jean Karambizi, André Musagara, King Ngoma, Fidéle Mpabwanimana, Innocent Dunya Byavulwa, Enack Makunda, and Aimable Twahirwa.

Rezarta Bilali and Johanna Vollhardt, former students in the doctoral program I founded and directed in the Psychology of Peace and Violence at the University of Massachusetts at Amherst, and recent (2009) Ph.D.s, joined Laurie Pearlman and me and since 2005 have been working on the educational content of our radio project projects. Adin Thayer, who has worked in varied settings in Africa on peace building, joined us later. Terri Haven was part of this group for a period of time. Alexandra Gubin, Ph.D., and Vachel Miller, Ed.D., graduate students at the University of Massachusetts at the time, assisted us in our early work in Rwanda. Wilton Dillon was my closest collaborator in organizing the conference that inspired us to go to Rwanda. Frank Ochberg in varied ways supported our work in Rwanda. I am grateful to all of them.

Our work in Rwanda and East Africa was supported by successive grants to me and Laurie Pearlman from the John Templeton Foundation, the Dart Foundation, the University of Massachusetts at Amherst, the United States Institute for Peace, and U.S. Aid for International Development, with a small grant also by a private donor, and by grants to LaBenevolencija from the Netherlands, Belgium, the Swedish Foundation Sida, and the European Union. I greatly appreciate their help.

I am grateful to the University of Massachusetts at Amherst, and in particular to the Department of Psychology, for making it possible for me to engage with many projects in the outside world. Some of them are briefly described in this book, and others can be found on my Web site, http://www.ervinstaub.com. I also want to thank the many wonderful colleagues at the International Society for Political Psychology; the Society for Research on Peace, Conflict and Violence; and the Association for Genocide Scholars. While I have been a member of the major professional associations in psychology for many years, these smaller societies have been especially important communities for me. Their members have done groundbreaking work on the topics of this book. Many of them, and others as well, have inspired and supported me in this work over the years. And special thanks to Macs, the first active bystander in my life, whose courageous actions on behalf of me and my family when I was a young child have been a lifelong inspiration for me.

Contents

Overcoming Evil

1

Introduction: I

Origins, Prevention, Reconciliation

I sit on a chair in a field in Rwanda, with a lovely view of hills all around, at the edge of a large group of people from the local community. There is canvas stretched over our heads, which protects most but not all of us from the sun. There are not enough benches and chairs, so some people are standing. Children play near us. I am here to attend the weekly community meeting, called the *gacaca*, at which local people elected to serve as judges lead the community through a process of establishing who was killed and what other crimes were committed during the genocide. They then try people from their community who are accused of perpetrating these acts. If there are gradations among the horrors of different genocides, the one in Rwanda is near the top, with people killing neighbors and even family members. My translator sitting next to me, a young journalist in her regular job, is a survivor of the genocide.

I have long studied the origins of genocide and mass killing to learn the answers to some questions that can guide us in the prevention of genocide and other mass violence. What leads to intense violence between groups? How does the motivation to harm others develop, and how are our inhibitions about killing people lost? How can we prevent the evolution of conflict into violence, and too often into indiscriminate murder? What is required for reconciliation, after violence between groups has taken place, so that new violence is averted, or for reconciliation before significant violence has occurred between hostile groups, so that violence is prevented? How can groups develop peaceful, harmonious relations?

I am addressing these and related questions in this book following many genocides and mass killings in the twentieth century. Although the number of violent conflicts in the world has declined, still very great violence exists between groups early in the twenty-first century. This includes recent violence in Sri Lanka, ongoing violence in Darfur in the Sudan, in the Democratic Republic of the Congo, in Northern Uganda, in Iraq, in Afghanistan, between Israelis and Palestinians, lesser violence between groups in Nigeria and South Sudan, 9/11 and terrorist violence in many places, and more.

It is imperative that we learn about the prevention of violence, since conditions in the world create continuing and perhaps increasing danger of violence. These conditions include cycles of intense competition for and crises in energy, in food supply, in clean water, and in the price of materials essential for industrial production; recessions and financial crises with one in 2007–2010 reaching a magnitude that created the potential for worldwide economic collapse; and technological and cultural changes occurring at a rapid pace. All of them have great political and social consequences, especially, but not only, in poor countries. They deeply affect the material and psychological well-being of individuals and create the potential for groups to turn against each other.

There are many forces external to us and within us that can turn us, as individuals and groups, against others. But like individual human beings, groups and nations are capable of constructively engaging with each other and addressing their conflicts and grievances without lapsing into the horrors of mass violence, be it genocide, mass killing, protracted and violent conflict, or terrorism. Like waves created by rocks thrown into water, the effects of such violence expand. Beyond many deaths, they create cycles of retaliation. They wound survivors psychologically, with long-lasting effects. They also wound and change perpetrators of violence, and they change passive bystanders who witness them and do not attempt to stop them. They affect children both directly, as they are victimized or witness the violence against their group or by their group, and indirectly, as they are raised by adults deeply affected. Mass violence in one society often expands to neighboring countries, and not infrequently it ends in the defeat of perpetrators, and much suffering by their group.

This book is about understanding the forces that lead groups and their individual members to turn against others violently. It is about how we can learn not to yield to these forces, how we can tame them and find alternative, peaceful ways to deal with them. It is about preventing violence by developing practices, ways of being in the world, and creating cultures, institutions, and societies that enable groups to live in harmony and peace. Harmony and peace do not mean the absence of differences in interests and in visions of how to live life. They do mean developing attitudes, orientations to the "other," norms and institutions that enable groups to address their differences in respectful and effective ways. The challenge is to learn to turn toward rather than against each other and to jointly address difficulties of life and diverse and opposing interests.

The book is also about caring and helping. In the midst of great violence, some individuals endanger themselves to help others, as when they attempt to save lives during a genocide. Groups also often make significant sacrifices to help, sending food supplies and other forms of humanitarian aid, providing expert knowledge, whether in agriculture or institutional development, and at times sending soldiers to save people from violent circumstances. Such actions are examples of *active bystandership*. They can expand and increasingly become early actions by individuals and institutions that help prevent mass violence from occurring.

However, witnesses and bystanders, both within and outside a society, often remain passive. Their passivity allows the evolution that leads to extreme violence; their actions are essential in prevention. I will later discuss the many reasons that individuals and groups remain passive. At the extreme, they are so absorbed in their own lives that they hardly notice what is being done to another, especially a devalued other. I encountered an example of this when, during a visit to give a lecture at a German university in 1987, I asked my hosts to arrange a meeting for me with a group of Germans who were at least teenagers during the Nazi era. The meeting was scheduled for 2 hours; it ended when I had to leave 4 hours later. These now older Germans could not keep away from talking about their highly satisfying experiences as teenagers during the Nazi era. They were part of a community, spending time in recreational camps with other teenagers, sitting at campfires, singing songs.[1]* This is consistent with historical accounts of Germans' increasing satisfaction with their lives under Hitler.[2] The persecution of the Jews during the 1930s was not part of the consciousness of my informants. They had difficulty recapturing anything they noticed at the time, although this persecution was highly public. After a while, one of them remembered a warning to his father, who rented out rooms, not to rent to Jews.

In this book I hope to develop understanding that can be used to inspire and guide active bystandership for the prevention of violence and the promotion of reconciliation between hostile groups. If we were all active bystanders, even to a limited degree, both doing what we can and influencing other people—our neighbors, the media, our leaders—so that they take appropriate action, we could prevent most group violence. A central aim of this book is to give readers, whether they are individual citizens, members of civic groups and religious organizations, members of the media, or leaders, *information* that can lead them to notice the need to respond, and *principles* to follow as active bystanders. I will also describe *practices* that apply these principles, and hope that readers will generate and creatively apply additional practices in taking action to prevent violence and promote harmonious relations within and between groups.

---

* The numbers in the text refer to citations in endnotes, for example, the number 1 above. Endnotes are listed at the end of each chapter. After the last chapter there is a reference list that gives the full reference for every citation. Readers not concerned with citations or references to sources can ignore the numbers. On occasion, when there is some text in an endnote, I indicate this with a star * next to the number that refers to the citation.

Forms of Mass Violence Addressed in This Book

I use *mass violence* as a summary term for genocide and mass killing, but I occasionally use it to refer to all the forms of intense group violence I address, including persistent, violent conflict and terrorism. Research studies, books, and scholarly and popular articles are usually about one or the other of these forms of violence. However, there are commonalities, or at least significant overlap, in the influences that lead to them, and in ways to prevent them.

In terms of who are the perpetrators and victims, genocide and terrorism are often the opposites of each other. The people who become the perpetrators of genocide are usually those who have historically devalued, excluded, and discriminated against members of another group. Those who are devalued and suffer discrimination tend to become the victims. But some of those who belong to or identify with groups that experience devaluation, exclusion, discrimination and political repression, are people who become terrorists. And it does happen that when a less powerful group gains power, particularly if they gain it through revolt and violence, they perpetrate mass killing, or genocide, as in Cambodia.

What we know and learn about the origins and prevention of one type of group violence can inform our understanding of other types. For example, we know how people in small groups influence each other as the group moves toward or engages in violence especially from the study of terrorism (combined with psychological research in university settings). This knowledge is relevant to leadership groups and other small groups in all forms of group violence.

Extreme violence means extreme suffering. In the Holocaust, Jews were lined up at huge pits and shot to death. Millions of them were transported to killing centers, made to undress, told that they would be taking showers, and then gassed to death. Millions of people belonging to other groups, including Gypsies, Poles, and Russians, were also killed in the same period. In the genocide of the Tutsi people in Rwanda, Hutus went into their Tutsi neighbors' houses to kill them. Tutsis were stopped and killed at roadblocks. They were killed in churches and schools where they gathered, hoping for safety, and they were hunted down in fields and forests. The primary method was "cutting" people, a Rwandan term, by machetes. In persistent, violent conflict, groups can go on killing each other for many years, with their members living in mistrust, fear, and enmity, as in the Israeli–Palestinian conflict. In terror attacks, people are killed as they go about their everyday affairs.

Genocide and mass killing are, perhaps without exception, the outcome of an evolution of progressive increase in hostility and violence. While some observers describe some mass violence as volcanic[3], or suddenly erupting, its evolution was most likely there, just not noted. I will describe this evolution in detail.

The perpetrator of genocide and mass killing is usually a government and its agents, but it can also be one group in a society that turns against another. The victim is usually but not always a minority group. The group in power can be the minority perpetrating mass violence against the majority.

In violent conflict that is protracted and intractable, in that it has resisted resolution,[4] the violence is mutual, although not necessarily equal in magnitude. As the conflict persists, it tends to become the central focus for each group, or a whole society, and in the lives of its members.[5] Preventing conflict from degenerating into intractable conflict is important in its own right. It is especially important for the prevention of mass killing and genocide, which are not infrequently an outgrowth of protracted conflict.

Terrorism is also usually violence committed by people who act as members of a group against people they identify as members of another group. However, it is most often violence by the weak against the strong, violence that is indiscriminate in its target. The aim of terrorists is usually to create fear and influence societal values, politics and the relations between groups. The targets may include the military and government officials, but violence against civilians is a central element. Although people often engage in this type of violence in response to repression, limited rights, and in general real and at times imagined grievances, it also arises when a minority responds to what they believe is a threat of violence by the majority. What political psychologist and terrorism expert Jerrold Post calls "ethnic-nationalist-separatist" terrorism[6] comes about, in his view, from a minority believing that the majority wants to eliminate them. While indiscriminate violence against civilians creates horror, the motivation of some terrorists is to serve their group, and their groups sometimes see them as altruistic.[7]

While terrorism is most often perpetrated by the weak, government-inspired and military death squads in Latin America in the 1960s to 1980s, and continuing after that in some places like Colombia, can also be considered terrorists. Some governments also instigate and support terrorism aimed at enemies who are too strong or whom it would be politically unwise to attack directly.

I address terrorism in this book because it is an important form of violence between groups, a vitally important contemporary issue, and has had an important role in the Palestinian–Israeli conflict, which is a primary example I use to illustrate violent conflict. One hardly needs to stress its contemporary relevance, with the many examples of terrorist attacks in this century. Some of the more sensational ones include September 11, 2001 in the United States; 2002 in Bali; 2004 in the Madrid train stations; the London transit bombing in 2005; the many suicide bombings in Iraq and Afghanistan, not only in a kind of war against the United States but also between the groups in the society; and over 160 people killed and several hundred injured in Mumbai in 2008. An article by a group of experts on counterterrorism notes the "....political ascendancy of fundamentalist terrorism-using groups, such as Hamas and Hezbollah;

the emergence of the global Salafi Jihad movement inspired by Al-Qaeda; the specter of the acquisition and use of weapons of mass destruction...."[8]

While terrorism is ancient—it has been and still is perpetrated by varied groups—given its relevance today, I focus on the origins and avenues to prevention of contemporary Islamic terrorism perpetrated and inspired by Al-Qaeda, as well as Palestinian terrorism. Among the influences leading to terrorism, I will examine the role of actions by some of its victims, Egypt in an earlier period, the United States, and Israel. Occasionally, I will refer to other recent examples, such as Northern Ireland.

War between nations is not a focus of this book. But there is overlap in the influences leading to the violence I explore and those leading to war.[9] In addition, the nature of war is changing, involving small groups, guerillas, or militias as in the Congo. The fighting between Palestinians and Israelis has been a type of war.

This book does not focus on, but has relevance to, situations in which governments and leaders for political reasons kill, or create practices that lead to the death of, large numbers of people in their own countries, belonging to *varied* groups. This is often referred to as state terror—I prefer to call is mass killing. The sociologist Paul Hollander estimates that under communism 100 million people were killed by their own governments.[10] Many people were killed in right-wing dictatorships in Latin and Central America. While I do not focus on such cases in this book, many of the influences I discuss have a role in such mass killings.

To illustrate this, let's briefly consider communist violence. Like genocide, it was to a significant extent shaped by ideology. As in genocide, those identified as enemies of the utopian vision of the future that the ideology proclaimed were intensely devalued. There were sharp lines drawn between groups, in this case primarily on the basis of political views and affiliation, not on the basis of race, ethnicity, or religion—although these sometimes were intermixed with political categorization. Victims of genocide could not change their group membership, and often this was also true of those victimized by communist governments: People could not change the fact that they came from backgrounds of wealth and privilege or had some relationship to the past regime. Even the children of such people were regarded as enemies. However, the designation of enemies in the case of communism was not as fixed as in genocide. Former comrades were often designated as traitors and enemies, and sometimes people regarded as belonging to an enemy group, such as former factory owners, could gain good standing through their loyalty to the regime.[11] In past writing, I have described what took place in communist Cambodia, Khmer killing Khmer, as "autogenocide"[12] But in addition to Khmer, ethnic minorities were also the targets of killing, fitting the Genocide Convention designation of genocide (see Chapter 4). In this case the extreme violence against varied groups qualified as multiple genocide.

In some cases of relatively indiscriminate state violence, for example, under Idi Amin in Uganda, and Joseph Stalin in the Soviet Union, individual pathology of the leaders may have also been involved. But even then, the ability of these leaders to gain power and remain in power was part of a societal process.

A question at times explicit, but central even when implicit in this book, goes beyond prevention as a response to conditions that threaten mass violence. It is whether and how it is possible to create conditions that would make such a threat unlikely to arise. Can there be social transformation in societies—that is, transformation of culture, institutions, and the psychology of individuals and the group—leading to an inclusive sense of community and caring about others, so that in difficult times people turn toward and join with, rather than against, each other? And transformation in the international system so that nations truly care about what happens to people in other countries, not only at times of natural disasters and after violence but also preceding and during violence? Can such inclusive caring develop in "postconflict" societies, after violence between groups? While the violence intensifies preexisting negative views, fear, and hostility, which make mutual acceptance and caring highly challenging, the chaos and upheaval also create fluidity in which change is possible. Exploring reconciliation after violence is one major topic of this book.

The Primary Aims of This Book

My first aim is to describe what I see as the central principles of or primary influences leading to intense violence between groups, with attention to variations in them in the case of different types of violence, and in particular situations. The kind of "difficult life conditions" in a society, their psychological consequences, the ideology they give rise to, the material or psychological bases of conflict, cultural characteristics that tend to contribute to violence, past relations between the groups, the behavior of bystanders, all of which have a role in group violence, can all vary. As an example of variation in past relations, in the Holocaust, the genocide against the Jews, there was no real, material conflict between the Jews and ethnic Germans. In the case of the genocide in Rwanda, there was a history of conflict and a civil war. I will give an overview of the principles later in this chapter and then describe them in depth, with examples, in Part I of the book.

It is always a combination of influences that leads to mass violence, and while many of the central influences are often present, there can be variation in them, as well as in their particular manifestation. In one case, difficult life conditions can be mostly economic deterioration; in another case, great social change and disorganization. There are also less central influences, which apply more to particular cases of mass violence. For example, modernity and bureaucracy[13] were proposed as important contributors to the Holocaust. They did have a role, but it was less as instigators or motivators of the violence and more in its implementation. Technology and bureaucracy were involved to some extent in Nazi German propaganda against Jews, and more in their segregation and transportation to death camps, and the operation of the death camps themselves. In the Netherlands, the Germans were helped in finding, gathering, and transporting Jews to concentration camps by the well-developed Dutch bureaucracy. The Dutch were not hostile to Jews, but they kept good records, including records of Jewish residents. When Dutch officials were instructed to assemble lists of Jews, they followed their orderly habits, and using these records, prepared the lists for the German occupiers.[14]

But while radio broadcasts had a role in the genocide in Rwanda, they were not a necessary condition for it, and there was little modernity involved in the machete killing of people there. The nature of the state, which has been historically centralized and hierarchical, increased the possibility of genocide, but such a state organization was not particularly modern and had existed for some time. Bureaucracy was involved to a limited degree in the creation and use of identification cards for Hutus and Tutsis. In Cambodia, modernity and bureaucracy had little role. Most people were killed directly, at close range: When the victims were not Khmer, they were easy to identify.

The principles I will stress are those that I consider common to most instances of mass violence. In considering the origins of genocide and mass killing in *The Roots of Evil* and other earlier publications,[15] I did not identify, but now I consider highly important, a past history of victimization of a group and the resulting psychological woundedness. I deemphasized there the role of leaders, because their role had been overemphasized, as if mass violence were simply a matter of leadership, not a societal process. I stressed instead the roles of followers and bystanders. In this book, I further expand the discussion of the crucial role of bystanders. However, leaders are of great importance, and I focus on them as well. In my earlier writings, I gave greater emphasis as starting points of group violence to difficult life/societal conditions of varied kinds than to the role of conflict. In this book, I stress both as starting points. And I substantially expand the principles I discussed in my past writing on terrorism.[16]

Another primary aim of the book is to describe central principles, as well as avenues to or practices of violence prevention, and of reconciliation after as well as before violence, with attention to variations in which central principles and practices may be most relevant to specific situations. Many of the primary principles of prevention or reconciliation, such as developing constructive ideologies, positive orientations to the other group, creating constructive communities/groups that people can join in place of ideological movements, as well as practices to bring them about, are relevant to most situations. I will give an overview of the principles and practices later in this chapter, and I will then discuss them in detail, with examples, in Part II of the book.

An important variation that must be considered in applying principles and practices is culture. Culture includes a group's shared beliefs, values, perceptions, understanding of the world and ways of interpreting events, and its norms or the behavior that is expected of its members. Knowledge of and sensitivity to culture is especially important for outsiders who want to help with prevention and reconciliation. For example, the concepts of reconciliation and forgiveness, which many consider an aspect of reconciliation, receive more emphasis in certain religions and cultures than others. Forgiveness, especially, may find more resonance in a predominantly Catholic society like Rwanda than in some other societies.[17] The substantial success of the truth and reconciliation process in postapartheid South Africa was probably helped by an aspect of traditional South African culture, Ubuntu, which emphasizes community and inclines people to forgiveness. While justice seems universally important, cultural characteristics and practices shape what will satisfy people's need for justice. A justice process like the *gacaca* in Rwanda, where groups of judges elected by the population were in charge of trying defendants in front of their local communities, would be more difficult to introduce in a society without cultural roots in such a practice.

I have learned about cultural variations in field settings, ranging from Rwanda to the aftermath of the Rodney King incident. In the latter case, a couple of police officers in Los Angeles beat Rodney King as he lay on the ground after a car chase, while other police officers stood by watching. Subsequently, I was asked to prepare a program for the training of police officers in the State of California to reduce the use of unnecessary force by the police. Working with the police, I have learned the extent and nature of loyalty dictated by police culture. It makes officers reluctant to step in and redirect a situation when a fellow officer becomes increasingly hostile and aggressive toward a civilian; this passivity, and support for their fellow officer (e.g. complicity), allows the aggression to unfold. Working for change must be guided by understanding of and sensitivity to culture. A central aspect of the program I offered was to train officers to become active bystanders to each other. In addition to skills in positive bystandership, this requires fostering a change in thinking, so that a fellow officer's attempt to redirect a developing interaction would be seen as good teamwork, as supporting rather than opposing a comrade.

General Principles and Specific Circumstances

The International Crisis Group assesses and analyzes particular conflict situations and offers advice on responses to them. Its director, Gareth Evans, sees the understanding of the specifics of a conflict, both the exact conditions and the personality of important actors, as crucial to preventive action. Evans says that in "trying to understand the dynamics of particular situations ...(for) sorting between those situations which are combustible and those which are not ... you need detailed, case by case analysis, not making assumptions on the basis of experience elsewhere, or what has gone before, but looking at what is under your nose, right now."[18]

But people who work in field settings do not start from scratch. They are guided in their assessment of a situation by principles that are part of their individual (or institutional) theory, explicit or implicit, of what causes violence and how it can be prevented. This theory directs what they look for. If it is effective, their theory will be open enough to allow extension or revision based on the actual situation.

Explicitly identifying a broad range of principles makes it possible to use them, test them, and revise them. An analysis of the specific situation can identify what combination of principles and practices is relevant and how they need to be applied. One needs to do this in all "interventions," including public education. My associates and I have been applying the general principles I am describing in this book in conducting seminars and workshops in Rwanda, and in developing educational radio programs in Rwanda, Burundi, and the Congo. For educational radio we created "communication messages," brief statements of the general principles. (They include messages related to psychological trauma derived primarily from the work of my associate Laurie Anne Pearlman).[19] The messages are used to guide writers and journalists as they weave educational material into the radio programs. Before introducing the messages, we analyze and consider the specifics of the situation. We then decide which principles, as represented in communication messages, are especially relevant to the situation in that setting (e.g., Rwanda, Burundi, or the Congo), and at the time a particular program is created.

For example, in Rwanda life conditions have been improving. However, the government does not permit open expression of varied views, and the restriction on free speech has increased preceding an upcoming election in August 2010. Therefore, a message that stresses the absence of pluralism as a contributor to violence and the value of pluralism in prevention receives more emphasis than some other messages.

Psychology, Culture, and Structures

The structures of a society are its institutions, its laws, and its policies. Culture, structure or the way institutions are set up and operate, and the psychology of individuals and groups are related but far from identical. They all have a role in the origins of violence and must be addressed in prevention. Structural inequality is one main source of conflict. There can be economic inequality, one group poorer and with less access to resources and opportunities. This may be due to current discrimination, to a history of past discrimination that diminished a group's capacity for effective participation in society, or to a group culture, for example, limited acculturation by an immigrant group. Difference in the economic situation of Catholics and Protestants in Northern Ireland was one source of the violence between them.[20] A related inequality is in power and influence, various degrees of exclusion of groups from political participation, or repression of political activity in general. The psychological impact of these inequalities is magnified by economic or other societal problems.

Societal practices, laws, and rules can also deprive groups of the freedom to use their language, to practice their religion, even to have a cultural life. Culture shapes structures, and they can join in their destructive roles. During the Holocaust, more Jews were killed in European countries with both stronger preexisting anti-Semitic beliefs, a matter of culture, and institutions that discriminated against Jews, a matter of structure.[21] Group violence is also more likely in societies with autocratic or authoritarian governments.[22] Certain child-rearing practices, used not only by parents but by institutions such as schools, also contribute to group violence.[23]

Democracies, especially "mature democracies,[24] are less likely to engage in mass killing or genocide against their own people or wage war against other democracies.[25] But democracies do conduct wars against nondemocratic countries, and not always defensive ones. For example, the United States has engaged in both small wars, such as attacks on Panama and Grenada, and large ones, such as those in Vietnam, Iraq, and Afghanistan. Democracies also support repressive dictatorships and autocratic systems, in the case of the United States countries such as Saudi Arabia, Egypt, Iran under the Shah, Guatemala, El Salvador, and South American dictatorships in earlier decades. They do so even when autocratic countries perpetrate mass violence, such as British and American support for Indonesia at the time of mass killings there, and American support for Saddam Hussein's Iraq in the 1980s even when it used chemical weapons against both Iraqi Kurds and Iran. As we shall see, repression contributes to terrorism, and support for repressive systems has been one of the motivators of terrorism against the United States. Eliminating such support, a policy change, is an aspect of prevention. Finally, especially at this time in European democracies with large Muslim immigrant populations, it is relevant to mass violence that "although majoritarian democracies largely eliminate explicit forms of discrimination, they also result in political, cultural, and economic inequalities and hierarchies.".[26]

However, within mature democracies, there is little mass violence. Thus, democratization, especially when accompanied by decreasing inequality and power differences, is a significant avenue to prevention. But a prerequisite for free elections, power sharing, and creating the institutions needed for a functioning democracy is that individuals at least begin to develop beliefs, values, and attitudes that accept and support such institutions and practices.

I will discuss change in structures and cultures. But I will stress proximate influences in preventing violence, that is, how people think and feel. Changes in these are prerequisites for changing structures. George Mitchell, the former Senate Majority Leader, was a major actor in resolving the long-lasting conflict in Northern Ireland and in January 2009 was appointed by the Obama administration to serve as special envoy for the Israeli–Palestinian conflict. Mitchell

said about conflicts: "They are created, sustained, conducted by human beings....
[and] they can be resolved by human beings."[27] While institutions of society
that maintain or help prevent violence, like other institutions, have to a significant degree a life of their own, they are created, maintained, and can be changed
by people.[28] To change institutions, and even to be able to resolve practical issues
between groups, people have to change.[29] Many changes in people had to
precede the creation of policies of affirmative action in the United States, which
by reducing inequality and leading to more contact between groups improved
group relations.

Change in many people is a change in culture. We can think of culture as the
"personality of the group." Culture ranges from beliefs about what is considered
just and unjust, moral and immoral, to how to raise children. It shapes the
thoughts and feelings of its members in response to events. The institutions of
society both express and help maintain culture. To create schools with equal
treatment of students belonging to different groups, or a justice system that
does not favor one ethnic group over another or the wealthy over the poor,
requires changes in people's psychology. In turn, the changed institutions shape
attitudes, beliefs, worldviews, and behavior.

Thus, in this book my primary focus is on people, the psychology of the individuals that make up groups, and of their leaders: their needs, worldviews, attitudes toward other people, feelings of threat, fear, hostility, caring and empathy
for others or lack of these emotions, their woundedness as a result of past
history, and other psychological conditions that are the proximate, direct sources
of violence and peaceful relations. *The focus will be on how social conditions
affect people and, joining with culture, give rise to psychological reactions that shape
choices and actions.* It will be on experiences or processes that can bring about
change, for example, helping people heal from past victimization, develop
positive attitudes toward others, and fulfill important psychological needs
constructively.

Positive changes in groups of people enable them to build good institutions,
which in turn shape individuals and the culture in a continuous cycle. For
example, in schools in authoritarian societies teachers are listened to but cannot
be questioned, and there is little discussion in class. This shapes the excessive
respect for authority that is one of the influences contributing to mass killing or
genocide. Changing this aspect of how teachers and schools operate can lead to
more appropriate respect for authority and lessen obedience to destructive
authority.

Thus, while changes in people are essential, institutions must also change.
Without that, psychological change can be ephemeral. New events can undo
changes in attitudes, or progress in healing psychological wounds after violence.
Good institutions will address the needs of the people, with more equal access to
resources, equal treatment of children in schools, equal respect for members of
different groups.

Motives for Violence

Group violence rarely if ever has a single, specific cause. It is the outcome of a combination of influences that leads to an unfolding, an evolution that involves changes in individuals, groups of people, and whole societies. The more of these influences are present, the more likely they lead to violence. The motives that arise out of these influences are usually manifold.

Psychologists have identified two main classes of motives by individuals using violence: to cause hurt or harm, or to accomplish other goals-expressive or hostile violence and instrumental violence. Among the sources of the former are a negative view of the target, hostility and anger. In the case of the latter, aggression or violence often serves to achieve a practical goal, like a child pushing away another child wanting that child's toy. Sometimes in group relations the term used for competition over instrumental goals is real or *realistic conflict*. This refers to material or quasi-material goals, such as gaining land, scarce resources, possessions, power, and influence. Instrumental violence by groups can also have psychological goals, like affirming identity or values and ways of life, or fulfilling an ideology, such as racial purity (as in the Holocaust), complete social equality (as in Cambodia), or Hutu power (Rwanda). The followers of an ideology may come to see any and all means as acceptable in acting against a group they believe stands in the way of the ideology's fulfillment.

Motives of hostility, the desire to harm, and achieving instrumental goals, whether material or psychological, are often intertwined. Hutus, in killing Tutsis, acted out of hostility, the desire to protect themselves, the desire to maintain their dominance and fulfill the ideology of Hutu power, the desire to take the land and possessions of Tutsis, possibly the desire to make up for past humiliations, the desire to be a good member—to not be ostracized and punished by their group for not participating—and more. Conflict between groups is often (although not always) instrumental at the start, but especially as it turns violent it becomes also psychological, and the violence increasingly expressive or hostile. This can be the case in defensive action against a group seen as a danger to one's own.

In summary, group violence is a method or tool to fulfill varied motives and goals. For example, Luca Ricolfi,[30] a sociologist at the University of Turin, identified four waves of suicide bombing in the Middle East up to 2003 and suggested different motives for each. These ranged from inducing foreign troops to leave Lebanon, to keeping the first *Intifada* against Israel alive and inhibiting further peace attempts, to disrupting the peace process, to enhancing the influence of Hamas within the Palestinian community during the second *Intifada*. Rucolfi focuses on instrumental goals, but his own research and analysis indicate that intense hostility toward Israel is a core motive, and the instrumental goals have become intertwined with this hostility.

It is difficult to disentangle the exact motives and their relations to each other. As I will suggest in the next chapter in discussing evil, even the perpetrators themselves may not truly know their motives. It is possible, however, to identify the influences that give rise to motives for group violence; these influences, their psychological and social impact, and the evolution leading to extreme violence will be my focus.

Overview of This Book and Its Conception

The substance of this book is presented in two parts. Since understanding the origins or roots of mass violence and the influences that lead to it is crucial for knowing how to prevent it, the first part is primarily about how violence between groups comes about. The second part focuses on principles and practices of violence prevention and on group reconciliation that averts (new) violence and enables people who have lived in hostility to lead peaceful and harmonious lives. Chapters 1 and 2 introduce the book. The rest of Chapter 1 provides an overview of the conception and content of this book, including the principles of the origins of violence and the principles and practices of prevention and reconciliation. Among the topics in Chapter 2 are early and late prevention, the costs of mass violence, and concepts of evil and goodness.

Part I begins with Chapter 3, in which I discuss the nature of conflict between groups and provide brief histories of the cases that will be the primary examples. The subsequent chapters in Part I examine in detail the origins of mass violence. In addition to looking at what happens both in whole societies and in small groups, I also discuss the kind of individuals who get involved in mass violence, especially in terrorism. One chapter considers the psychological effects of violence on all parties: survivors, perpetrators, and bystanders.

The principles of and approaches to both prevention of violence and reconciliation will unfold in Part II. To be effective, the work of prevention must create awareness of the conditions that lead to violence, increase the ability of members of a society to resist them, as well as their ability and that of external bystanders to prevent the development of such conditions and when they exist generate constructive responses to them. In Part II, I also address psychological healing or recovery after violence—especially social or group healing, without which new violence is more likely. Part II also describes our work on reconciliation in Rwanda, Burundi, and the Congo.

Overview of Key Principles and Practices

In the following I summarize key points about the origins and prevention of group violence and reconciliation. Chapter numbers identify primary chapters on these points.

The Origins of Violence

- Persistent conflict between groups, often a combination of material and psychological conflict, is an instigator of or a starting point for the evolution of group violence. It is not conflict itself that is the problem, but the inability to resolve it. As conflict persists, as it leads to psychological changes and the emergence of violence, it is transformed and can become increasingly intractable. The psychological elements of the conflict—for example, harboring mistrust and negative views of the other, while seeing one's cause as just and one's action as moral—make the conflict difficult to resolve (Chapter 3).

- Difficult societal conditions, such as economic deterioration, political disorganization, or great social/cultural change; the confusion and chaos they create; and their psychological effects are also instigators of or starting points for the evolution of mass violence (Chapter 4).

- The evolution of violence that war represents can lead to extreme violence against either the enemy in the war or an internal group, and/or war can be a cover in the context of which mass killing or genocide can take place against a group that is not the opponent in the war (Chapter 4).

- Difficult life conditions, intense conflict, and war can create threat and fear, and they can frustrate universal or basic psychological needs in whole groups of people. Under these conditions some members of the group will be open to, tend to follow, join, or even seek leaders who address their psychological needs (even if they can't address their material needs) by turning the group against another. In this life context, individuals turn to their group, or a new group, often an ideological movement, to fulfill needs for security, identity, a feeling of effectiveness and control over events, connection, and a meaningful understanding of the world. The leaders and members of such groups frequently scapegoat some previously devalued group or blame their opponent in a conflict. Especially when the culture has certain characteristics, leaders and followers tend to create what is for them a hopeful vision of societal arrangements and human relations (an ideology), but that also identifies enemies who must be "dealt with" to fulfill the ideological vision (which makes the ideology destructive) (Chapter 5).

- Individuals and groups change as a result of their actions. Harmful actions tend to start an evolution of increasingly harmful and violent actions. They change the perpetrators, who justify their actions by devaluing members of the other group, and progressively exclude them from the moral and human realm. They change social norms and institutions. There is a reversal of morality: killing members of the targeted group becomes right and moral. With "steps along a continuum of destruction,"[31] a group or society can move toward extreme violence (Chapter 6).

- A variety of elements in the culture, social structure, and political system join with instigating conditions to make group violence more likely. They include a history of devaluation of a group, which can become the target of scapegoating and/or be identified as an ideological enemy; excessive respect for authority; a monolithic society that limits what can be said in the public domain; and past victimization and group trauma that have created psychological injuries. These become central to the group's "collective memory" and identity, and they lead to "defensive" and at times hostile violence. An authoritarian political system is another significant contributor (Chapter 8).
- Passivity is common both among "internal bystanders" and "external bystanders," outside groups and nations. Their passivity encourages destructive leaders and perpetrators. In a culturally monolithic or politically autocratic society, where public opposition is especially difficult, internal witnesses or bystanders, members of the population who are neither perpetrators nor victims, are especially likely to remain passive (Chapter 7).
- The background or instigating conditions for terrorism include real but also sometimes imagined grievances, difficult life conditions, conflict between dominant and subordinate groups and injustice, repression, as well as great social changes. The impact of the latter is enhanced in traditional/repressive societies that make it difficult to process change. The experience of dislocation due to migration is another background condition. These conditions can intensely frustrate basic psychological needs (Chapter 4).
- The psychological and social processes that take place in small groups of people, the commitment to ideology and comrades that develops, as well as acceptance and support of terrorists by members of their surrounding community, contribute to the evolution of terrorist violence (Chapter 6).
- Terrorists have usually been small in number. This is also true of contemporary Islamic terrorists, especially relative to the number of Muslims in the world. Some researchers have pointed to the role of social influence in terrorism—friends, relatives, teachers, and organizations that draw people in. But what activates these initiators? Why does an organization that influences people to engage in terrorism come into being? People become terrorists as a result of social conditions and social context, an ideology, their personal history and how it shapes their personality, the influence of associates and the dynamics of a group process, and the evolution and change in individuals and a group under the influence of an ideology and their own actions. Some people

who become terrorists have in the course of their personal history developed values and beliefs that lead to identification with a group or with ideals the person sees as needing protection. Others have had a painful history of victimization or loss, whether experienced personally, or as a group member, or both, which frustrates basic needs and can lead to openness to fulfill them in destructive ways (Chapter 9).

- Group violence has powerful, harmful impact on survivors but also on perpetrators and even passive bystanders. This can include in survivors an intense need for self-defense as well as a desire for revenge, and in perpetrators the refusal to accept responsibility and blaming the victim. When not addressed, these effects make continued or renewed violence more likely (Chapter 10).

Prevention and Reconciliation

Understanding the origins of group violence makes it possible to engage intelligently in prevention, including early prevention. The following is a brief summary of important principles and practices of prevention:

- Early efforts by influential parties to respond to conflict, providing "good offices," bringing parties together, and facilitating dialogue can help resolve crises and prevent the development of intractable conflict. Successful resolution of crises needs to be followed by addressing the underlying material, structural, and psychological issues (Chapter 13).
- Early societal responses to difficult life conditions can increase people's material as well as psychological security, give them a sense of belonging, and affirm their identity and connection to others. Poor societies do not have the wherewithal for material responses, like the huge government bailouts and stimulus expenditures, including expanded unemployment benefits, that occurred in the United States and other developed nations in response to the economic crisis that began in 2007. They need help by outside parties. Still, even in poor societies, societal responses can create a sense of community and join people rather than turn them against each other (Chapter 13).
- Developing a positive orientation toward the "other" (in place of devaluation), and toward human beings in general, makes it possible to take others' perspective and feel empathy with them. The focus by members of groups in conflict or facing difficult life conditions on their own suffering, need and injuries, and the inability to consider the situation and suffering of the other is an important contributor to ongoing hostility and violence. Leaders, the media, schools, members of the community, clergy, and outsiders, by their words and actions, can *humanize* people who have historically been devalued. They can enhance awareness of

the needs of all groups. Significant *contact* across group lines, especially in working together for shared goals, helps to overcome devaluation and enhance openness to the other Dialogue is an important form of contact and an avenue for overcoming devaluation, developing trust, and resolving practical issues. Dialogue and negotiation, which often require the involvement of neutral outsiders, "third parties," can prevent conflict from becoming intractable. Peace education can prepare the ground for changes in collective memories, so that the groups' conflicting views of the history of their relations do not prevent peace (Chapters 14 and 16).

- The creation of a *constructive ideology*, a positive vision that is inclusive and embraces all groups, can provide hope for people in difficult times. In conflict situations, its creation requires dialogue between leaders within each group and between groups. Information, dialogue, and other types of preparation in the population can create a readiness for constructive solutions, without which positive leadership tends to be resisted. Creating an inclusive vision that joins all subgroups of a society in working together for a better future, addressing real problems, with help by outsiders if needed, will make violence less likely (Chapter 15).

- Moderating respect for and obedience to authority and developing pluralism, a society in which varied views can be expressed and all groups have access to the public domain, help prevent violence. Public education, including radio and television programs, which model pluralism, democratization and active bystandership, and nonpunitive child rearing that allows children a voice, can all contribute to these goals (Chapters 12, 13, 15, 16, and 22).

- The availability and creation of *constructive groups* in society that join rather than divide people, whether community groups, religious groups, or ideological movements, can constructively fulfill basic psychological needs in difficult times and make it less likely that people will join destructive ideological movements (Chapter 15).

- Active bystandership is essential to prevent the evolution of violence and to bring about all the outcomes and processes required for prevention. It can be inspired by the words and example of individuals, whether leaders or citizens, by external bystanders as they engage with potential internal bystanders, and by many of the processes listed here. It requires expansion of the boundaries of "us," and/or inclusive caring for those outside one's group, and moral courage. The latter can be developed through positive child rearing, and generated through support that people provide each other. When action by internal bystanders is especially difficult and dangerous, action by external bystanders is crucial (Chapter 18).

- Healing by historically victimized and traumatized groups is an aspect of prevention; healing by survivors as well as perpetrators and bystanders is important in reconciliation. It requires the right kind of commemorations; a person-to-person community approach that enables people to listen and respond to each other sensitively; and creating awareness of the impact on the group of past victimization or other group trauma. Healing can enable perpetrators and their group to acknowledge the harm they have caused and show regret and empathy. This in turn can create openness by survivors to the beginning of reconciliation (Chapters 16 and 19).

There is substantial overlap in the principles and practices of prevention and reconciliation. The following emphasize what is primary for reconciliation:

- Reconciliation can be advanced by establishing the truth about past history, about past relations, and about the actions of each group that have harmed the other group. Since the truth is often complex, each group having its own truth, this is a demanding and difficult process (Chapter 20).
- Establishing the truth can be a step toward creating a shared view of history, in place of conflicting views. To do that requires dialogue, compromise, changes in each group's collective memory, the acceptance both that the other has a different view of history and of a less than complete agreement about the past (Chapter 20).
- Reconciliation also requires justice, which has different aspects: punishment; perpetrators and/or society providing compensation to the victimized group; perpetrators helping to rebuild society; the restoration of relationships (restorative justice); and a justice system that makes future impunity unlikely (Chapter 20).
- Forgiveness, letting go of hostility and anger toward and increasing acceptance of harmdoers, and even more importantly of their group, contributes to reconciliation. But the ideal in reconciliation is *mutual* acceptance (Chapter 19).

The following activities and processes contribute to both prevention and reconciliation between hostile groups both before and after violence:

- On the basis of our work in Rwanda, Burundi, and the Congo, I have come to believe that helping victims, perpetrators, and passive members of the perpetrator group to understand the influences that lead to violence creates, by itself, some degree of healing and openness to the other group. It can also diminish the power and create resistance to the influences that lead to violence. Understanding how violence can be prevented and hostility overcome can motivate people to participate in building a society that fulfills the material and psychological needs of all people (Chapters 12 and 16).

- It is essential to create institutions, such as high-level offices in foreign ministries, with the people serving in them having the direct responsibility not only to gather information that indicates the probability of violence at particular places, but also to initiate preventive action. They can collaborate with each other, the United Nations, and the nongovernmental organizations to mobilize nations as well as individuals (Chapters 17, 18, and 22).
- Leaders must be trained from areas where conditions indicate the probability of violence, and from bystander nations, so that they understand the roots of violence, the possible avenues for its prevention, and develop relevant skills and the capacity to work with each other across group lines (Chapter 18).

With regard both to origins, as well as prevention and reconciliation, we need to focus on both the influences that are "external" to people and the internal ones, the psychology of individuals and groups that are the immediate, proximal causes of violence. Developing constructive rather than destructive responses to instigating conditions is of great importance. People can only resist the impact of instigating conditions, destructive leadership, and the changes in themselves in the course of a psychological and social evolution if they have alternatives, constructive responses available that fulfill basic material and psychological needs.

While individual and group psychology is central, so is the creation of positive cultures, structures, institutions, and political arrangements. These include a fair justice system, schools that care about the welfare and education of all children, the development of civic institutions and a civic culture necessary for democracy, media that present information in a balanced and positive manner, and equitable economic development.

The Primary Examples of Group Violence in This Book

The primary examples I will use in the book to illustrate principles and practices are the following: the Israeli–Palestinian conflict; the genocide in Rwanda; the violence in the Democratic Republic of the Congo (and the work my associates and I have been doing in Rwanda, Burundi, and the Congo on healing, reconciliation, and the prevention of renewed violence[32]); terrorism perpetrated or inspired by Al-Qaeda; and suicide terrorism by Palestinians. The Holocaust, the genocide against the Jews by Nazi Germany, will be another important example. I will write about Dutch–Muslim relations as well, which has relevance to the relationship and prevention of violence between Muslim minorities and the original populations in many European countries.

I will also refer, less extensively, to the genocide in Cambodia, the genocide of the Armenians, and the mass killing (disappearances) in Argentina (the origins of these, together with the Holocaust, I discussed in detail in *The Roots of Evil*). I will also refer to the mass killing and ethnic cleansing in Bosnia, the "troubles" in Northern Ireland, the mass killing or genocide in Darfur, and race relations in the United States.

One of the challenges in addressing prevention and reconciliation in the cases I selected is that most of the primary ones are ongoing and constantly changing. As an example, let's briefly consider events in the Palestinian–Israeli conflict since 2005. Israel unilaterally withdrew from Gaza, after which Palestinians groups, especially Hamas, which does not recognize and has aimed to eliminate Israel as a state, shot thousands of rockets into Israel from Gaza. Hamas won the Palestinians elections in 2006, and in response for a period Israel withheld taxes it collected and the U.S. and the European Union withheld aid. The split between the two major Palestinians groups, Hamas and Fatah, intensified and in 2007 Hamas attacked Fatah in Gaza and took over Gaza. Israel and Egypt began to blockade Gaza, over time creating significant scarcity.

Israeli Prime Minister Ariel Sharon became severely ill. The first of two prime ministers who followed became active in behalf of peace, but mainly just before he left office; the second one was in office only for a short time. Hamas rockets into Israel were followed by a truce. While it is unclear who broke the truce first, in 2008 Hamas refused to renew the truce. Israel responded with a major military incursion into Gaza, which led to much destruction and the loss of many lives. In 2009 a conservative government under Benjamin Netanyahu came into power. Hamas and Fatah began to negotiate to heal their rift, but they made little progress. All along, Israel continued to build settlements in the West Bank, on territory which in a two-state solution to the conflict should go to the Palestinians. After a relatively hands-off approach by the Bush administration, initial attempts by the Obama administration to exert influence on Israel and Arab countries had little success. After further pressure Israel stopped some settlement building, but not all that the United States and the Palestinians demanded.

There was little violence between February 2009 and mid 2010. Better trained Palestinian police improved the security situation in the West Bank, and as a result Israeli practices making Palestinian travel in the area difficult became less restrictive and economic activities in the West Bank have increased. However, there has been no progress toward peace. Both sides have refused to negotiate at various times over the years. Israel often insisted that first terrorism must stop. This time Palestinians insisted that first all settlement building must stop.

After continued pressure by the Obama administration indirect talks, with George Mitchell as the intermediary, began in May 2010.

Soon after this, a group of activists, on ships initiating from Turkey, attempted to break the blockade on Gaza. When Israeli soldier boarded one of them in their attempt to stop them, supposedly they were attacked. They shot and killed 9 people and injured others, with resulting calls to stop the blockade. The blockade had a variety of aims, but one likely aim was to turn the population against Hamas and remove it from power. As in other places I will discuss, such efforts at "regime change" often do not work and may backfire. While there can be no absolute principles about this, a more constructive practice would often be to engage with regimes, aiming to change their policies.

The quite different cases of group conflict and mass violence in this book will help us examine the generality of the principles and practices I describe. In working in real-world settings, I have found such an approach useful. But organizing this book around principles may create some difficulty for readers who want to get a coherent picture of particular cases. To get a full picture of, for example, the origins of the Palestinian–Israeli conflict, avenues to its resolution, and reconciliation, readers will have to find the relevant material in varied chapters. A detailed index will help. In addition, in the concluding chapter I return to the primary examples, to review what is needed in each case for prevention or reconciliation at the time of this writing.

Notes

1 See Staub, 1989
2 Craig, 1982
3 Albright and Cohen, 2008
4 Coleman, 2006; Kriesberg, 1998a, b
5 Bar-Tal, 2000a, b
6 Post, 2007
7 Victoroff, 2009b
8 Kruglanski et al., 2008
9 Staub, 1989, 2006b
10 Hollander, 2006
11 Ibid.
12 Staub, 1989
13 For both, see Bauman, 2000; for bureaucracy see Hilberg, 1961
14 Ibid, Staub, 1989
15 Staub, 1989, 1996
16 Staub, 2003b, 2007a
17 Staub, 2005a
18 Evans, 2008; Lund, 2009
19 Pearlman, 2001; Pearlman & Saakvitne, 1995
20 Cairns & Darby, 1998
21 Fein, 1979
22 Rummel, 1994, 1999
23 DeMauss, 2008; Grille, 2005
24 Staub, 1999b

25 Rummel, 1994, 1999

26 Rouhana, in press

27 Mitchell, 2008

28 See also Wolpe and McDonald, 2008

29 See Deutsch, Coleman, & Marcus, 2006; Kelman, 1990, 2007; and many others

30 Ricolfi, 2005

31 Staub, 1989

32 See Staub, 2000, 2006a; Staub & Pearlman, 2001, 2006, 2009; Staub, Pearlman, & Bilali 2008, 2010; Staub, Pearlman, Weiss, & van Hoek, in press.

2

Introduction: II

*Early and Late Prevention, the Costs of Violence,
Evil and Goodness*

I wrote in the *The Roots of Evil* that "the Holocaust had been described as an incomprehensible evil. This view, it seemed to me, romanticized evil and gave it mythic proportions. It discouraged the realistic understanding that is necessary if we are to work effectively for a world without genocides and mass killings and torture." Over the last decades there has been substantial progress in coming to understand the roots of genocide and mass killing. But understanding origins is easier than prevention, which requires understanding origins as well as principles and practices of prevention and specific complex situations, the willingness to act, and collaboration among divergent actors often with conflicting interests.

Late Prevention and Early Prevention

The focus in preventing mass violence has been on late actions, addressing crises and halting violence, which of course is of utmost importance. Its primary means have been sanctions or military action. But the willingness to act is still greatly limited, even when violence needs to be stopped. In Rwanda, just one example of this, no one took preventive action even though there were concrete warnings, such as an ongoing civil war, intense hate speech spread through radio, and the repeated killings of Tutsis. Even when the genocide was in progress, and the whole world watched, the U.S. government, the United Nations, and other parties were vacillating about what to call it and tried to avoid action. Such behavior is all too common.[1]

Government officials are usually focused on many matters and are guided by a narrowly defined national interest. They may pay little attention to violence at faraway places. Irwin Cutler, the former justice minister of Canada, described a brief after-dinner speech he gave to the justice ministers of G8 (Group of Eight industrialized countries) about the mass killing or genocide in Darfur when it had been in progress for some time. Four of the ministers afterwards expressed their appreciation, saying that they knew nothing about it.[2]

But while there is a history of much passivity by the international community, which I will discuss in Chapter 7, there has been more action in recent years. Gareth Evans has noted that while new conflicts and violence have emerged, many old ones have died down. He and others have suggested as likely reasons the death of colonialism and its diminishing aftereffects, the end of the cold war and less support for dictatorial systems and proxy wars, and more engagement by the international community. Evans said, "UN diplomatic peace-making missions rose from four in 1990 to fifteen in 2002; peacekeeping operations rose from ten in 1990 to seventeen in 2005, and generally with much broader protective mandates. And beyond the United Nations, a number of regional organizations, individual states, and literally thousands of NGOs have played significant roles of their own.".[3] Many individual actors have also been engaged, which is how our work (described in Chapters 12 and 16) started in East Africa.

But with regard to the decline in conflicts, the news is complex. The Human Security Center[4] reported that new conflict onset between 2000 and 2005 remained higher than it was in the 1970s and 1980s. Terrorism increased in the first decade of the new century, and there was huge loss of life in recent cases of mass violence, such as the Congo, Rwanda, and Darfur. Extraordinary diplomatic efforts, unified sanctions, or military intervention when needed in late prevention is still rare. Halting violence requires costly measures or unified effort by the international community. But some countries are usually unwilling to pressure the parties involved. Russia with the Serbs during the violence in Bosnia, China with Sudan in relation to Darfur, the United States with Israel and Arab countries with Palestinians are recent examples. Nations don't usually work well together in a coordinated response.

With regard to terrorism, much of the focus has also been on late actions, using force, killing or capturing terrorists.[5] Even separating terrorists from populations that support them, which as terrorism expert Louise Richardson[6] has stressed is important in prevention, and reeducating captured terrorists to prevent renewed violence by them[7] are examples of late prevention.

However, in the last couple of decades effort to help groups reconcile after violence, and transitional justice processes, a summary term used for truth commissions, trials, work to repair the material and moral effects of violent conflict and human rights abuses, and at times for anything that helps rebuild society,[8] have become more common. Part of their aim is to prevent renewed violence. There are practical, grassroots efforts at many places addressing reconciliation. Many communities in Africa have been reintegrating child soldiers—who were often led by the group that enticed or abducted them to kill members of their own communities.[9]

Reconciliation is important, but what we need most is early prevention. Preventive diplomacy, which I will discuss, can be relatively early, but more often it comes late and by itself does not address the conditions that lead to violence. However, the willingness of the international community to act early, when there is only a *probability* of violence, even if it is shown by reasonably well-established indicators which I will describe, is still very limited.

This unwillingness to engage when there is uncertainty about whether violence will develop is a serious mistake. As I will illustrate later in this chapter, prevention is much less costly than violence and its aftermath. Addressing violence-producing conditions in a society, working to resolve conflict, and transforming the relationship between hostile groups can be more effective when leaders and most of the population are not yet committed to violence. It can avert the great disruptions and suffering that often result. Even if extreme violence would not develop, addressing significant societal problems would improve the relations between groups and the lives people lead.

While the focus in the political world and in genocide studies has been on what I call late prevention, there has been substantial *study* of practices that can be used in early prevention.[10]* For example, there is extensive research on the positive effects of contact and its use in real-world settings, such as joint projects like rebuilding houses, and on its combination with conflict resolution and transformation such as members of hostile groups engaging in dialogue. An increasing number of organizations such as the U.S. Institute for Peace, the U.S. Holocaust Museum, and institutions around the world are concerned with prevention, including early prevention. Both advancing knowledge and stimulating practical efforts at early prevention are among the goals of this book.

Many components of the international community can serve prevention: the United Nations, the European Union, regional organization such as the African Union, individual nations, and many nongovernmental organizations (NGOs). But David Hamburg, a former president of the Carnegie Foundation, notes, "the U.N. and its partners don't usually have a mandate in situations of previolence prevention. This is a serious deficiency."[11]

George Will, the columnist and TV commentator, mocks the notion of an international community. He sees the belief that there is such a thing as naïve. He notes glaring failures of community response, for example, the U.N. Security Council, which "could not even bring itself to say that North Korea's launch (of a missile in April 2009) violated the resolution against launches."[12] In a similarly pessimistic (or to some, realistic) vein, Leslie Gelb, past president of the Council of Foreign Relations, does not believe that persuasion will get leaders to yield to others' influence. In his book *Power Rules*, he stresses the importance of using one's position and resources to get others to do what they don't want to do; he also notes that the United States is still the predominant power in the world.[13]

Power is important, but it has many elements, including the power of friendship, persuasion, example, education, and cooperation.

There is no question of the challenges. But as the historian Michael Beschloss wrote in a review of *Power Rules*, Gelb's view "might understate the importance, for instance, of American support for 'good' Western values of human rights, democracy and market economics that emboldened millions of Eastern Europeans in 1989 to revolt against Soviet hegemony."[14] Of course, the revolt was due not only to U.S. support for such ideals, but to intrinsic dissatisfaction with the system. But they revolted peacefully, and successfully. The United States has often played a negative role,[15] but at times it had powerful positive influence, and one way to renew U.S. power and influence is through constructive, moral leadership.

My hope and belief is that groups and their members can find ways to address their self-interest constructively, partly by moderating their expectations, and partly by working in cooperation with others. This is possible to do, I believe, whether that self-interest is focused on acquiring material resources, on gaining influence; its greatest challenge may be addressing opposing ideologies. My hope and belief is that it is possible for Israel and the Palestinians to create a shared, constructive vision for their future, for Rwanda to increase pluralism and political participation, for advocates of tolerant and peaceful versions of Islam to shift it away from its recent separatist and jihadist tendencies, for the United States to stop supporting repressive dictatorships, and for developed countries to help the economic development of poor nations, for example, by opening currently restricted markets to their agricultural products.

People need to satisfy basic material needs, but their satisfaction ought to be in the context of the constructive satisfaction of basic, universal, psychological needs. It is the latter that brings the greatest contentment and happiness. For people to appreciate the importance of these needs, and for societies to make possible their constructive satisfaction requires changes by institutions, societal climates and values, and individuals. Moving in that direction is an aspect of prevention.

What, How, and Who

In prevention, early or late, we need to consider what, how, and who. First, what do we need to accomplish, that is, what outcomes must be achieved to make violence less likely? In early prevention these include economic development, with practices that reduce inequality rather than enriching already privileged groups; promoting democracy by building civic society; just social relations; positive attitudes toward members of other groups; and healing from wounds inflicted by victimization. Following what, comes a mixture of what and how: how do we move toward these desired outcomes, what activities are needed, such as humanizing the other and contact to create positive attitudes toward the other? These aspects of prevention require knowledge, as well as experimentation to advance knowledge. The most difficult part, however, is how to bring about the required practices or activities. Without the ability to do so, just describing desirable outcomes and practices has little value.

This leads to the question of *who*. Prevention requires people who are motivated and effective, who have developed the necessary knowledge and skills, and who are in positions to engage in the activities required. Their motivation can be enhanced by the actions of citizens, and by roles in organizations that focus responsibility on them to act. (See Table 23.1 in Chapter 23 for more on the "how" and the "who.") Parties external to the societies that are at risk of group violence are crucial in late prevention. They are also important in early prevention, although this has to be done in collaboration with internal actors. By their words and actions external actors can help people in a society see the humanity of members of minority groups at risk, and contribute to the motivation of internal actors and their belief that they can take effective action.

To prevent violence, to address in constructive ways the conditions and influences that give rise to it, requires the joint efforts of many constituencies. Citizens have an essential role in this. Commitment and action by nations and by NGOs can be stimulated by the interest, concern, and demand for action by citizens. Some authors argue that evident concern by citizens makes leaders of bystander countries feel free to act. Active engagement by many citizens can mobilize governments, businesses, and NGOs. It can lead the media to play a constructive role. Citizens can influence governments and international organizations to create institutions, some of which I will describe and propose, that have the responsibility to note danger signals around the world and initiate preventive actions. In the same spirit, the U.S. Genocide Prevention Task Force report (see later discussion) calls on the American people to build a permanent constituency for the prevention of genocide and mass atrocities. It points to the huge coalition that has gathered to advocate for the prevention of genocide in Darfur. That coalition is unprecedented. It has been effective in bringing attention to Darfur and probably influenced the International Criminal Court to indict Sudan's President for Crimes against Humanity and War Crimes in February 2009. While this led to short-term retaliatory actions, limiting humanitarian aid, contrary to the expectations of many the violence soon diminished and conditions improved in Darfur.[16]

We will consider in Part II of the book the constructive actions that nations can take to prevent mass violence. We will also consider the power of single individuals and small groups to take constructive action. We will consider ideas for developing an international system that leads external actors and internal actors to cooperate in preventive efforts worldwide. While it will take time to create an effective system of prevention, in the meantime there can be many successes through less comprehensive action.

The Costs of Violence: Material, Psychological, Moral

The concerns of this book are relevant to all members of societies in which social conditions and cultural characteristics create a significant potential for group violence, as well as for societies with ongoing violence between subgroups. But they are also significant for the rest of the world. One reason is moral, since the human suffering created by such violence is incalculable. Consider the life of just one person, a woman in Rwanda whose husband and children were killed, who was raped, and whom the perpetrators intended to kill. She survived, regaining consciousness in the midst of a large pile of dead bodies. Difficult as her life became, she adopted young children whose parents were killed in the genocide. And she now works on healing her community. This is a real person, and there are many others like her.

The moral obligation to prevent such suffering is evident. In addition, when such violence takes place in a society, it often spreads and involves whole regions. The genocide in Rwanda, in which an estimated 800,000 people were killed, had a central role in leading to the violence in the Congo, which since 1996 has led, according to a Newsletter of the U.S. Holocaust Museum in October 2008, to the death of 5.4 million people through killing, starvation, and disease. At this writing, this violence in still ongoing.

The economic effects of group violence are also huge and widespread, in clearly identifiable terms such as the loss of productivity, physical and social infrastructure, and the costs of humanitarian aid and reconstruction. Intervention in ongoing violence is especially costly. Michael Lund describes comparisons between the actual costs of prevention in vulnerable societies which then did not experience violence and intervention, estimates of the cost of prevention in other cases, and the costs and estimated costs of violence. The peacekeeping in Macedonia cost $255 million; the estimated cost of a 2-year conflict was $15 billion.[17] Lund cites an assessment that "lists the costs of the countries in conflict as military and civilian death, disease (HIV/AIDS, malaria), physical destruction, population displacement, high military expenditures, capital outflows, policy and political breakdown, psychological trauma, and landmines. The costs to other nations during and after conflicts include refugees, humanitarian aid, reconstruction aid, disease, increased military expenditures and tasks such as peacekeeping, reduced economic growth, illicit drugs, and international terrorism .... Africa's two dozen internal wars in 23 countries from 1990—2005 are calculated to have cost $18 billion, which could have gone to ..." help these societies in health, education, and many other ways.[18]

Extreme violence between ethnic, religious, racial, political, and ideological groups also has profound psychological and social effects. It can diminish the well-being of whole populations for generations. The moral meaning of the violence and the apparent lack of caring by passive bystanders, both internal and external, contribute to the corrosive impact of extreme group violence.

Evil and Goodness

I define morality as *principles, values, emotional orientations and practices that maintain or promote human welfare.* Evil is the extreme of immorality; I use the word to refer to the varied forms of intensely harmful actions this book addresses. Intractable conflict is not by itself evil: it is unfortunate, sad, and tragic that parties in a conflict cannot resolve their differences and therefore many people die, and that the lives of people revolve around conflict, violence, and fear, usually for decades or more. But often in the course of intractable conflict there is indiscriminate killing, and at times a horrific endpoint, genocide.

My purpose in using the word *evil* is to point to the extreme effects of certain actions, the harm they cause. By *evil* I mean human destructiveness. I use the word primarily to refer to actions that create great harm, are not in the service of self-defense, and are not commensurate with provocation. Evil can take obvious forms, such as indiscriminate killing. But it can also come in the form of many small acts of persistent wrongdoing, such as parents or peers consistently hostile and aggressive toward a child, or people persistently diminished and harmed through verbal attacks and discrimination. Such acts frustrate basic psychological needs, and as their effects accumulate they destroy dignity, self-worth, and the ability to trust others. They sometimes lead to violence by the people so treated.

One difficulty in judging evil is that violence is not evil if it is necessary self-defense. Ending violence committed by Germany during World War II required both self-defense and the defense of Germany's victims. Terrorism requires defense. Extreme repression can sometimes be addressed only through violence. However, even necessary defense of self and others can turn into evil action when it creates harm that is not commensurate with the danger or harm done. Another difficulty is that those who act violently often claim self-defense, and they may believe that they are acting to defend themselves, even when violent self-defense is not necessary.

Considering the behavior of an individual or group as evil is a matter of judgment, easier to make in at least some cases of extreme destructiveness. Contrary to the claims of some philosophers and psychologists who write about morality, this judgment cannot be based *only or primarily* on the intentions of actors, especially their stated intentions. They themselves may not know what internal psychological or outside forces lead them to their actions, and if they do, what they say may not express their motives but provide justifications for them. They may incorrectly perceive the need for self-defense or act with unnecessary violence in the name of self-defense. They may be guided by ideals and visions that aim to benefit their group or to improve the world but may have developed the belief that any means are acceptable to serve these.

The judgment of evil in the perspective I present does not accept cultural relativity, the notion that we cannot judge actions in other cultures because they have developed their own values, beliefs, and ways of life. I encountered an extreme example of this view one year in a large undergraduate lecture course I taught, "The Psychology of Good and Evil." In a question-and-answer period at the beginning of the semester, students in the class argued that the action of a mother who spanked her young child, with the intention of teaching her not to run out into the busy road just outside their house where she could be killed, after the child did so twice, was aggressive and wrong. However, they also argued that we cannot judge the actions of Nazi Germany, because they had their own values, culture, and way of life.

At the start, evil is the action, not the person or the group. But individuals and groups change as a result of their actions. Victims are increasingly devalued, and violence intensifies as it continues. Destructive actions can become increasingly normal and probable, a characteristic of a system, a group—or a person. In such cases, we can regard the society, group, or individual actors as evil. Slavery was an evil system. Individuals who live in and act according to the dictates of such a system can vary, some acting with maximum cruelty, some with maximum kindness within the framework of the system. The more the actions of individuals are in opposition to the norms of a destructive system, the more we may consider them examples of goodness. Extreme wrongdoing by individuals can be the outcome of extreme circumstances, with severe punishment or even the danger of being killed for refusing to harm others. Judging the actions of such persons is much more challenging than judging the actions of those who initiate or willingly engage in destructive action. Judging actions at the extremes of wrongdoing or opposition to it is easier than judging those in the middle of this continuum.

Judging acts as good and evil requires a consideration of intentions, the nature of the acts, their probable consequences, their actual consequences, the degree of environmental pressure on a person to act, and even their effects on the actors' further behavior. It requires a consideration of universal principles (such as the sanctity of life and justice) and the principles of utilitarianism, the greatest good for the greatest number. By these considerations genocide, killing a whole group of people (for a formal definition see Chapter 4), would always be judged evil. What about terrorism? The indiscriminate killing of civilians points to a judgment as evil.

But sometimes people called terrorists act against a repressive and violent system. Sometimes they are supported by the population they come from. The actors often believe they are acting altruistically on behalf of their group. We would not consider violent actions by small groups of individuals against the Nazi system in Germany to be terrorism, especially actions directed against buildings, the military, and officials, or if we do, we would consider them terror- ism for a good cause. The atomic bombs dropped on Nagasaki and Hiroshima killed huge numbers of civilians, but these actions are difficult to judge, because by bringing war to an end they may have saved even more lives. Some people consider them evil, others do not. While evil and goodness carry significant meanings, they require care in application.

Can passivity, not responding to others' suffering, allowing it to continue, also be considered evil? In certain instances, yes.[19] Consider someone watching a child drown in what for an adult would be shallow water, and doing nothing. Or the world's inaction at the time of the genocide in Rwanda. It was evident that a genocide was taking place, and it might have been halted with even a limited military force,[20] and possibly stopped without fighting simply by the presence of a moderate-sized force, even 10,000 soldiers. If actions can be evil, under certain conditions so can inaction. This does not mean that the many decision makers involved are evil, but the outcome of their decision not to act had extremely harmful consequences and was evil. The culture or system they were part of, and/or the members of the communities coming to watch the lynching of black people in the United States, photographs showing their smiling, happy faces, may also be considered evil.[21] On the other hand, individu- als who endangered their lives to rescue Jews or Tutsis or Armenians or other designated victims of genocides were heroic. But not engaging in heroism is not evil.

Just as individuals and systems can change and move toward evil actions, they can also move away from them. The conditions, the values, the psychology of individuals and groups that lead to evil actions can change. New leadership can create new visions, policies, and practices. A different system can evolve. Apartheid in South Africa was an evil practice deeply rooted in society, but South Africa is already a very different country. Germany looked as evil a coun- try as one could imagine during World War II, but within a few decades after the war, it became a well-functioning democracy that has peaceful, cooperative relations with its neighbors and has asked for forgiveness in words and by some of its actions.

Political theorist Hannah Arendt, watching the trial of Adolf Eichmann in Jerusalem, coined the term *the banality of evil*.[22] Eichmann was in charge of the assembly and transportation of Jews to concentration camps. Arendt saw in Eichmann a bureaucrat doing his job, interested in his career, obeying authority. Arendt responded to what she thought many people believe, and perhaps she did, that evil actions are performed by evil people who are extraordinary, who possess at least a distorted form of specialness. This was probably what inspired writers of recent books to refer to "ordinary" people as perpetrators of genocide.

But the notion that immorality and evil is or has ever been anything other than the outcome of ordinary psychological, social, and political processes, enacted by ordinary people, in ordinary groups, is a romantic but misleading, false notion. Extreme violence by groups is the result of the coming together of such processes in a problematic way. Each process is "normal," common in individuals and groups, such as the human tendency to divide people into "us" and "them," a crucial element in people turning against others, or to respect and follow people in authority. But as they join and evolve, these processes can create the extremes of devaluation, hostility and violence. What is extraordinary is the resulting actions, and their outcome. What may also seem extraordinary is that the evolution that leads to this outcome is allowed to unfold by witnesses. However, this is also ordinary, both in how common it is and in the psychological processes and social forces that lead to passivity In summary, *social and psychological forces can overwhelm or subvert moral principles and moral emotions.*

As they respond to certain conditions, human beings—individuals, groups, and their leaders—at times foster, or at least allow, the unfolding and evolution of these processes, until it reaches the extraordinary outcome of evil. *But extreme violence is not inevitable; understanding how it comes about cannot mean accepting or excusing it.* Along the way, people make choices. It is more possible to choose *early* to turn away from engagement with groups and activities that can end in great violence, before people are transformed by a guiding ideology, by devaluation, and enmity toward their victims, before their vision of what is moral is reversed, killing the designated victim or enemy becoming moral for them. This is even true of turning away from passivity as witnesses/bystanders. They also undergo a transformation in the course of changes in their group or society. Still, as observers of a destructive process, they can retain a moral perspective that makes opposition and preventive action possible. This is easier for external than internal bystanders.

The consideration of both acts and the influences that lead to them makes it possible to see the acts as immoral or evil, while still seeing the humanity of the actor—at least in most cases. But there is a seeming paradox in talking about evil in this book, since the preceding discussion makes it clear that there are no firm rules of judgment, and I stress not judgment but knowledge, understanding, and positive action. *However, extreme violence usually is evil, and the word or concept can focus us on the actions and outcomes we need to stop, that must be resisted and opposed.*

The opposite of evil is goodness.[23] Goodness is also the outcome of ordinary human psychological and social processes, part of everyone's potential, such as valuing human life, the capacity for empathy and feeling of responsibility for others' welfare. The prevention of violence and reconciliation require the cultivation of these processes. Like evil, goodness can evolve and become part of a person or a system.

Goodness refers to actions that bring substantial benefit to individuals, or to whole groups of people. Not all helpful or kind acts represent goodness; some are too limited, others while they have social value are performed to gain benefit through reciprocation or social rewards. Like evil, goodness comes in more and less dramatic forms, such as a heroic act that saves someone's life, or persistent actions that produce great benefit over time. The actions of rescuers are often both heroic and persistent, such as hiding people from perpetrators for long periods of time. But small nonheroic acts can add up, producing great benefits. Consistent acts of kindness by neighbors toward a child badly treated at home, by a relative caring for a sick person for a long time, or by people persistently working for positive social change are also examples of goodness.

So are acts by nations that produce significant benefit to others. Sometimes these acts arise out of pure motives, such as the desire to help people in need. At other times they are the result of mixed motives, as in the case of the Marshall Plan by which the United States helped rebuild Europe. The Plan created great benefit, but its motives included the desire to stop the spread of communism and probably also to avoid a repetition of the end of World War I, when a humiliating peace treaty and subsequent social problems in Germany contributed to the rise of Nazism. But persistent efforts to prevent violence can be motivated in part by enlightened self-interest and still qualify as goodness in my view.

Knowledge Base for This Book

While preventive action, especially early prevention, is still limited, there is diverse and very active scholarship in the interrelated fields I address. There is a huge literature on genocide, both on the general topic and particular instances, especially the Holocaust and Rwanda. This literature includes my own work on mass violence.[24] Terrorism has long been studied, but its study greatly expanded after 9/11. There is an enormous literature on conflict, intractable conflict, conflict resolution, conflict prevention, and transformation. There is a very large literature in psychology on intergroup relations, prejudice, overcoming prejudice, and other relevant topics. This book is not a review of the existing literature, but it is informed by knowledge in these fields, both explicitly referring to it and implicitly drawing on it.

Social and political psychologists such as Robert Jay Lifton, Herbert Kelman, Ed Cairns, Daniel Bar-Tal, Gavriel Salomon, Morton Deutsch, Jerrold Post, Martha Crenshaw, Israel Charny, James Waller, Vamik Volkan, Peter Coleman, Jack Dovidio, Roy Baumeister, Ari Nadler, and *many* others have focused *primarily* on the psychology of individuals and groups. In contrast, sociologists, political scientists, historians and conflict specialists, such as Helen Fein, Barbara Harff, Robert Melson, Michael Lund, Ben Kiernen, Herbert Hirsch, R. J. Rummel, Roger Smith, Frank Chalk, Samuel Totten, Richard Hovanissian, Vahakan Dadrian, Gregory Stanton[25*] and *many* others have focused *primarily* on history and the role of institutions and political systems. Researchers on terrorism have come from many realms. In terms of both scholarship and practice, understanding and preventing violence must have multidisciplinary and multifocused approaches. The research reflects that. This book attempts some integration of it, and application to prevention.

My Research and Field Experiences

In addition to scholarly sources and my own research and writings, the knowledge base of this book includes my engagement and work in applied settings, and with people affected by violence and working in these settings. What gives rise to or can prevent violence is complex, not "observable" in a direct way, and knowledge has to be derived from many sources. Inspired by an invitation to speak at a conference about how we know what we know in this realm, I will describe some of my personal knowledge base for writing this book. I have already referred to a few of my experiences in real-world settings in Chapter 1.

My strong motivation for this work comes from my early experience, surviving the Holocaust as a 6-year-old Jewish child in Hungary. This did not provide me with knowledge of how such violence comes about or can be prevented. But after I received a Ph.D. at Stanford and began to teach at Harvard, my *motivation* to study related questions emerged. I did learn some important things, though, from my early experience. While my family and I were surrounded by danger and by hostile or passive people, some endangered themselves to help us, and others.[26] There are active bystanders even in the most dangerous situations.

I began to learn what is relevant to the topics of this book through my early work, which for nearly 15 years focused on empirical research in university settings, and "field research" in life settings on the origins of caring, helping, and altruism. I studied what leads people to respond, to be active bystanders, and what leads them to remain passive when they witness others' need and distress. I also studied how children can become caring and helpful. One of the important things I learned is that people who have developed feelings of responsibility for others' welfare are more likely to help, especially if this sense of responsibility is combined with a feeling of competence or empowerment.[27] Although it has to be applied cautiously, empirical research about helping and aggression by individuals can help us understand the behavior of people in groups.

I began to study the origins of genocide and mass killing in 1979. My earlier work pointed me to the role of passive bystanders in allowing the unfolding of increasing persecution and violence, and of active bystanders in inhibiting this evolution. I came to understand how, when people are faced with the immediate need of a person in an emergency such as sudden illness or an accident, a combination of circumstances and their own characteristics can lead them to relinquish responsibility, even to turn away, rather than help. As I began to study genocide, I thought that a combination of forceful circumstances, culture and evolving group climate, and the changes these create in them can lead people to stand by passively as a subgroup of society, an identified scapegoat or enemy, is harmed more and more.

Based on the study of instances of genocide and mass killing, I developed a conception of their origins and tested it by applying it to further instances. As part of this work, I studied the history and culture of each society in which the violence had taken place, including past relationships between groups, as well as current societal conditions and the political situation. I also considered relevant research and theory in psychology and from the developing field of genocide studies. The instances I examined in detail included the Holocaust, the genocide of the Armenians, the autogenocide and genocide in Cambodia, and a mass killing, the disappearances in Argentina. I later wrote, in less detail, about the origins of the mass killings in Bosnia and the genocide in Rwanda.[28]

I also applied elements of the conception to different realms.To prepare my testimony as an expert witness at the Abu Ghraib trial of Sergeant Davis, I studied in detail what happened there.[29] I accepted the invitation to be an expert witness because I thought it was important for the judge and jury to understand how the conditions that existed at Abu Ghraib and the actions and inactions of superiors influenced the military guards' actions. At Abu Ghraib, lack of supervision and control by superior officers, their passivity in the face of actions by untrained or minimally trained guards, such as keeping prisoners in cells naked, allowed the violent behavior we have seen in the photos to unfold. The spread to Abu Ghraib of extreme interrogation techniques that were authorized by the government and specifically by Defense Secretary Donald Rumsfeld for detainees at Guantanamo Bay, and intelligence officers directing the guards to "soften up" inmates for interrogation, also had an important role. Frustration and anger created by mortar attacks on the prison and inmate rebellions also had a role.

My most extensive work in an applied setting has been in East Africa, especially Rwanda. Laurie Anne Pearlman, a trauma specialist, and I developed, and in the course of our work progressively refined, an approach to psychological recovery and reconciliation. Starting in 1999, we conducted trainings, seminars, and workshops in Rwanda with facilitators of groups working in the community, members of the media, community leaders, and high-level national leaders. This was followed by the development, in collaboration with George Weiss and Anneke van Hoek of Radio LaBenevolencija, a Dutch NGO, of radio programs to promote healing and reconciliation in the population. A primary component of this public education campaign has been a radio drama, broadcast since early 2004, about two villages in conflict. This public education program expanded to Burundi in 2005 and to the Congo in early 2006. I will describe in Chapter 12 the "Staub-Pearlman" approach to reconciliation, its use in Rwanda and our evaluation of its effects, and in Chapter 16 the use of this approach in radio programs and its effects shown in evaluation research.[30]

I learned a great deal just from going to and being in Rwanda. I learned about the terrible impact of the genocide on survivors. I also learned about their grace.

Although Rwandans were abandoned by the world and felt pain and anger about it, they welcomed us. They appreciated that we cared enough to be there and our intention to help, our understanding of their situation, and that we stayed and persisted in our work.

Another application of my work came in response to a request by administrators of the city of Amsterdam after the journalist Theo van Gogh was killed by a Muslim man in 2004. This was followed by the burning of Muslim schools, mosques, and churches. I developed proposals to improve Dutch–Muslim relations so that terrorism in the Netherlands would be less likely.[31] These proposals, applied to the local context, can also be useful in other European countries with large Muslim populations. They are embedded in the material of this book.

Before preparing the proposals, I had meetings with and gave talks to the city administrators. The concern of some of them was palpable. One man asked: "Are we sitting on a powder keg?" According to a report by the assistant city administrator at the time, which I will describe in Chapter 14, the proposals were applied in a number of significant ways.[32] But his report also suggested that more extensive engagement with potential actors/stakeholders—such as different segments of the city administration—would have led to more use of the proposals. There were divisions in the city administration about how pressing the need was and what approach to take in addressing group relations. The acceptance of the proposals was greater after I prepared a manuscript describing them,[33] and greater among the people I met with personally.

Outsiders working on prevention and reconciliation in complex real-world settings must engage with local parties in ways that help each party understand and take seriously the other's perspective. System change requires extensive and continuing engagement among potential actors. One limitation of our seemingly very successful work in Rwanda was that we did not continue our seminars/workshops for sufficient time with national leaders. We moved to a new focus on public education through radio and had limited human and financial resources. These are ever-present issues for people working in the field of prevention and reconciliation.

In 2005 and 2006, I went to New Orleans to work with a local organization, the Southern Institute for Education and Research, associated with Tulane University, to respond to the psychological impact of Hurricane Katrina. On the basis of our work in Rwanda I developed a conceptual approach, and Lance Hill, the Institute's director, and his associates developed a workshop using the approach to address the psychological aftereffects of both the natural disaster and the lack of appropriate help for many of the poorer residents of the city. The workshop aimed to promote healing and racial reconciliation. We conducted a training to try out the approach, and now it is increasingly used by the Institute and others in New Orleans and its environs.[34]*

I learned a great deal working with children, with teachers who had hundreds of years of collective experience, and with their schools to create school and classroom environments that reduce aggressive behavior and promote caring and helping. I have also done work assessing harassment, intimidation, and bullying by students in schools. It was clear in the course of this work that while many teachers deeply care about children, they are often passive bystanders to bullying and intimidation. So are fellow students most of the time.[35]

In 2006–2007, Sharon Tracy and Susan Wallace of Quabbin Mediation, an organization in Western Massachusetts, and I developed a program to train students as active bystanders. In 2007, we trained eighth- and tenth-grade students and local police officers to be trainers. Joint teams of students and police officers then trained over 600 students, eighth and tenth graders in two middle and high schools, in active bystandership. An evaluation study showed that in comparison to control schools where students did not receive the training, the schools in which such training occurred saw an over 20% decline in harmful actions directed by students at each other.[36] This is an ongoing project with new trainers working with new groups of students, and experimenting with the application of the "training active bystanders" curriculum to adult settings. People can learn ways to be positive bystanders and gain power to create positive change in many environments.

I have also learned a great deal from audience responses at my talks. In 1995 I gave a lecture in Belgrade, the capital of Serbia, to about 500 people, soon after the North Atlantic Treaty Organization (NATO) bombing of Serb artillery positions that had shelled Sarajevo brought an end to the violence in Bosnia. I had learned by then that it does not work to presume to tell people why their group has acted in certain ways. I therefore talked about the origins of violence between groups, using examples from other contexts and inviting the audience to apply the conception I described to their own situation. Extremely heated discussion, shouting, and anger followed, not toward me, but between groups in the audience holding different views. Opposing groups shouted at each other across the large hall. The most intense argument was about their own role as bystanders. What did they know or not know about the actions of their government and the paramilitary groups in Bosnia? Some supported these actions. Others said they did not know. Some said it was all on CNN, which did not broadcast in Serbia but could be picked up from broadcasts in neighboring countries. Still others argued that CNN could not be believed. (The translator sitting next to me did his best to tell me what people were saying).

During this visit it became evident to me how important outside support is for people who oppose their group's destructive course. After the talk I was invited by one such group to meet with them. I listened to them and expressed my appreciation for what they were doing. While resistance in the course of the evolution of violence is often limited, in the former Yugoslavia it gathered momentum, encouraged I believe by the rare international reaction that halted the violence. After little action for 3 years, the NATO bombing of Serb artillery positions led to the Dayton peace accord. The people I talked to were later part of the coalition of students, workers, and farmers who engaged in nonviolent action. Tractors, cars, and demonstrators in Belgrade blocked the streets; a national strike brought everything to a halt. They succeeded in ousting Milosevic, which was followed by democratic elections.

I also spent some time in Medellin and Bogota, Colombia, in 1997, giving talks and meeting with people involved in varied ways with the violence among guerrillas, the military and right-wing paramilitaries. About 50% of all kidnappings in the world took place at that time in Colombia. Everyone in Bogota who could afford it had armed guards either outside or inside their home, whether a private house or an apartment building.

I became friends with a person who some years before had been kidnapped on her way to a class at the University where she was a student. She was kept in an isolated hut in the countryside, alone with two male guards, until the kidnappers received a substantial ransom from her family. Years later, she was still deeply traumatized. I also visited the newspaper *El Colombiano* in Medellin. On the day of my visit, on two adjoining pages, the newspaper described, with extensive quotes from interviews, the perspectives of the guerrillas and the paramilitaries—what they wanted, what their views were. They were doing what newspapers need to do but rarely do, providing the public with reliable information about the perspectives of the parties to a conflict. Possibly because some parties did not like their balanced reporting, their offices were bombed several times. Up to that time they suffered only limited damage. Active bystandership has its risks, but it is crucial for the creation of a well-functioning society.

I have also learned from diplomats during question-and-answer periods after my talks at conferences on genocide prevention, organized by the U.S. State Department, and on the prevention of radicalization, organized by Homeland Security, and when I conducted brief workshops for CIA Africa analysts. At one meeting I had an exchange with a Rwandan diplomat who was in the audience about the value of including extreme groups in negotiations, which added to my perspective on this. I discuss this later in the book.

My awareness was raised by my involvement with a faculty group appointed by the President of Brown University to address that institution's responsibility in relation to racism. The University was started in part with money earned through the slave trade. My experience at Brown has further engaged me with the question of how might later generations address the past. This is important because, as we shall see, past victimization and unhealed wounds shape society and can contribute to later violence.

I have learned a great deal in interviews with the media, as I answered questions that led me to new thoughts or to gathering new information. In a television program on Canada's history channel in December 2007, I applied my understanding of the origins of mass violence to the killing by the Japanese army of 150,000 to 300,000 civilians in Nanking, China, in 1937, what is now known as the "Rape of Nanking." I briefly discuss this massacre in the book.

I was on another Canadian television program together with Romeo Dallaire, the former Canadian general who was the head of U.N. peacekeepers in Rwanda—we will encounter him later in the book. There and at other times I was exposed to his perspective on events in Rwanda.

In an interview in Sweden in April 2008 the journalist was especially concerned about an event that was the object of public discussion there at the time. Why did Swedish soldiers, on a joint U.N. mission with French soldiers in the Congo, remain passive when they witnessed the French torture a Congolese they captured? I saw solidarity with other soldiers on a shared mission, the Swedish and French sharing a common identity as Europeans and becoming even more "us" for the duration of the mission, and devaluation of the Congolese as important reasons. I will discuss in Chapter 15 how creating a common, overarching identity can inhibit violence against another group. But here is an example where such an overarching identity contributed to violence by increasing passive bystandership.

I learned something else while working with the media in the course of taping an interview for *20/20*. My interviewer tried to get me to say, returning to it again and again, that *the cause* of international passivity to the Rwandan genocide was racism. My view, that it may have been one element, but that bystanders have been passive in many instances of mass violence, was clearly not satisfactory. In the program they used those of my statements that came closest to what they tried to elicit from me, and then presented a former politician who has never studied genocide and presumably has never been to Rwanda—who made the points they wanted to make.

In Rwanda, the favorite explanation for the genocide was that it took place because of bad leaders (which is *one* of the influences) and ignorance. But the roots of genocide are complex, and it is not easy for people who have experienced it to know why it has happened. They can confirm or disconfirm, however, whether particular influences were present in their country. I described to many groups in Rwanda the conception of the origins of violence that I present in detail in this book, giving examples from other countries. After this, with one exception that I will describe, participants were able to apply the conception to Rwanda.

While studying the history and culture of a country and the population's beliefs and attitudes from books is useful, experiencing life there can expand understanding. My conception of genocide suggests that excessive respect for authority is one element of culture that makes group violence more likely.[37] It is widely believed, and my experience confirmed it, that this is a characteristic of Rwanda, together with a tendency not to express contrary views publicly. Moreover, in conversations some Rwandans would say that Hutus and Tutsis lived together in harmony before 1994, when leaders turned the Hutus against the Tutsis. A conversation I had with a Hutu woman started this way, but as it progressed, it became clear, and we came to agree, that even apart from obvious matters such as discrimination, recurrent killings of Tutsis, and a civil war, under the surface of everyday relations there was tension and hostility.

The Genocide Prevention Task Force

As one more way of introducing the book, I will describe elements of the report by a Genocide Prevention Task Force, chaired by Madeleine Albright, former secretary of state, and William Cohen, former defense secretary, issued in December 2008.[38] Discussing this valuable report and divergences between its perspective and mine will help to further show the book's orientation to the origins and prevention of mass violence.

The report calls the prevention of genocide and mass atrocities a U.S. national and global imperative. It identifies as a core challenge the task of persuading leaders of the urgency of this imperative. One of its primary contributions is the recommendation to create a new interagency task force in the U.S. government to assess dangers and initiate preventive action, which I will discuss in Chapter 18, and to allocate significant funds for work on prevention. Sadly, the world-wide economic crisis and ongoing wars lessen the impact of this report.

The report calls on the president to make the prevention of genocide and mass atrocities a U.S. priority. It calls on the secretary of state to work with other governments and concerned parties to create a formal network for prevention. It calls on the United States to help NATO, regional organizations such as the African Union, and NGOs to build the capacity for prevention. Part of the value of the report is its acknowledgment that there are only very limited U.S. (and international) resources or programs directly related to early prevention of genocide or atrocities. Responsibility among agencies is diffused. The United States, other countries, and international agencies focus on stabilizing coun-tries after conflict, not on preventing genocide and atrocities. The report states that improving the record of the international community in genocide preven-tion must begin with the "frank acknowledgment that for too long, too many nations and international institutions have found it too easy to avert their gaze from mounting signs of the most grievous peril to human life until too late."

The U.N. Security Council has often been unable to act in crisis situations because permanent member nations on the council have often vetoed action due to economic relations or other ties. The report calls for working with and making prevention a joint purpose with other governments and international institutions. It asks the U.S. government to engage in robust negotiation with permanent members of the Security Council to reach an agreement on the "non-use of the veto in cases of genocide and mass atrocities." It proposes that unless three permanent members are against it, all should support resolutions for actions, or abstain from voting. However, Roger Smith, a leading genocide scholar, notes that this is simply a way for France, Britain, and the United States to overcome the veto power of Russia and China, and "there is no way that it would be adopted."[39]

The report notes that arguments about definitions of what is genocide often slow response or lead to no response. Consistent with my perspective, it calls for approaching the prevention of genocide and other atrocities together. It calls for the establishment of institutions within the U.S. government to be charged with assessing the risk of violence in particular settings, early warning, and prevention. It calls for the involvement of citizens.

The report notes the great potential of the United States, given its wide-ranging diplomatic representation and influence in the world, to prevent genocide and mass atrocities. It acknowledges, however, that the U.S. government's customary operation, its default mode, is to respond after rather than before violence, and that national interest and other considerations have in the past led to no response when both moral and humane considerations, and even a consideration of the costs of inaction in financial terms, should have led to action. As one example, it mentions the dispatches of Ambassador Henry Morgenthau from Turkey, describing the horrific violence against the Armenians in 1915, and the lack of a U.S. response because at that point the United States wanted to remain neutral in World War I.

The Task Force report is concerned not only with prevention, but early prevention. It discusses, among approaches to early prevention, economic development that is equitable, improves the conditions of people, and reduces group differences; democratization, building civil society, and developing its institutions; and effective security forces that don't become tools of mass violence. The report also stressed eliminating impunity for violence and influencing how leaders operate. All these are important, and I will address them to in the book to some degree, the last one to a substantial degree.

The report's focus is on the "structural" conditions that lead to violence and the need to address them. But it does not consider *how* to create the desirable conditions, for example, economic development that reduces the difference in power and wealth between groups. The report notes ideologies as one contributor to genocide, but not their crucial role or how to address them in prevention. It pays no attention to characteristics of cultures which, when they are present, combine with social conditions that initiate, in my terminology, psychological and social processes that can lead to an evolution of increasing hostility and violence. As I have already noted, while changing structures is of great importance, changing beliefs and hostile attitudes and relationships, and addressing psychological woundedness and feelings of vulnerability arising from past history are among the preconditions for the readiness and willingness of people to change institutions/structures. The report does mention, however, developing positive skills and relationships between leaders belonging to hostile groups, an issue I will discuss in detail.

The report stresses the role of leaders. Prevention should address both the *"underlying causes of conflict and the means and motives of leaders."*[40] In addressing the latter, the report's focus is on positive and negative inducements—again, an instrumental focus. But addressing the leaders' thoughts, feelings, psychological needs, and worldview is of great importance as well.

By stressing the underlying causes of conflict, the report does *imply* the role of the population. I regard the population, as followers and bystanders, as crucially important. When initiating or instigating conditions for violence are present, usually there are some people who will advocate scapegoating and destructive ideologies that turn a group against another. It is the inclination of some part of the population to follow them that turns these advocates into leaders. It is the readiness to accept them that turns the rest of the population into passive bystanders. Prevention requires addressing these psychological and social inclinations, so that the population will resist destructive leaders, take action to halt the progressive evolution of destructiveness, and turn to positive leaders.

Invitation to Readers

In 1996 the *New York Times* had a conference on the Internet called "Bosnia: Uncertain Road to Peace." I was the moderator of a section on "Healing and Reconciliation." Anyone could enter the discussion, and many participants added well-informed and useful ideas.[41] Knowledge of and practice in prevention and reconciliation are just developing, and we need the experience and help of all of us. I invite readers to suggest, on the basis of the material in this book and their own experiences, ways to promote prevention and reconciliation, both in specific instances and in relation to group violence in general. With supervision by faculty members, advanced graduate students in relevant fields will read, summarize, and integrate suggestions; post their summaries on the Web site; and, when appropriate, write professional articles about them, so that these contributions will advance the scholarship and practice of the prevention of mass violence and reconciliation. Such articles would be posted on the Web site as well. There is a great deal of collective wisdom among us, and my hope is that our Web site will provide an effective means of harnessing the wisdom that readers of this book wish to share. Readers can post suggestions on the blog http://overcomingevil.wordpress.com

Notes

1 See Power, 2002
2 Cutler, I. 2009
3 Evans, 2008; see also Fein, 2007
4 Human Security Center, 2006. P.4.

5 Kruglanski et al., 2008; Sageman, 2004, 2008

6 Richardson, 2006

7 Horgan and Braddock, 2010; Kruglanski, et al., 2008

8 http://www.ictj.org/en/tj/

9 Wessells, 2007

10 In most articles and books the focus has been on what leads to genocide or other mass violence. This has also been the emphasis in much of my early work—see Staub, 1989, 1996. However, for some writings on early prevention, see Staub, 1999b, 2003a and our work on reconciliation in East Africa such as Staub, 2001, 2005a, 2006a, 2008a; Staub & Pearlman, 2001, 2006, 2009; Staub et al., 2005, 2010. Some of the many valuable recent good books on genocide are Fein, 2007; Jones, 2005; Kiernan, 2007; Straus, 2006; and terrorism Post, 2007; Richardson, 2006; Sageman, 2004, 2008; Victoroff & Kruglanski, 2009, Horgan, 2009.

11 Hamburg, 2007. p.148

12 Will, 2009

13 Gelb, 2009

14 Beschloss, 2009

15 See Staub, 2000, and Chapter 7 in this book

16 Sudan: Cooperation better, U.N. Finds. The New York Times, July 18, 2009, p. A6, by Reuters.

17 Lund, 2009, Notes #1 and # 2, p. 308.

18 Ibid, p. 308

19 Staub, 1999c

20 Des Forges, 1999

21 Ginzburg, 1988

22 Arendt, 1963

23 See Staub, 2003, Chapter 1.

24 Staub, 1985, 1989, 1996, 1998, 1999b, c, 2003a, b, 2006a, b. See also references on work on reconciliation.

25 I mention in these lists some people who are well-established, important contributors to these fields, not the huge numbers of excellent younger people. I refer to the work of many of them in the book.

26 Staub, 2002

27 For overviews, see Staub, 1978, 1979, 2003a, 2005c, Staub & Vollhardt, 2008

28 Staub, 1989, 1996, 1999a, b, 2003a

29 Staub, in pressb

30 We described this work in many publications: Staub, 2000, 2006a, 2008a, c; Staub & Pearlman, 2001, 2006, 2009; Staub, Pearlman, & Bilali, 2008, 2010; see also Staub, in pressa

31 Staub, 2007a

32 de Lange, 2007

33 Staub, 2007a

34 The name of this workshop is Stormbridge. For a power point presentation of if go to http://www.suno.edu/Colleges/Social_Work/community.html, select

"Social Work" at the bottom left of the screen, then select "In the community," and then Stormbridge.

35 Staub, 2003a, especially chapters 15 and 16. See also chapters 19 and 20.

36 Quabbin mediation and Ervin Staub, 2006; Staub, Tracy, and Wallace, in press

37 See Chapter 8, and Staub, 1989

38 Albright & Cohen, 2008—I will also refer to this as the Task Force report

39 Roger Smith, personal communication, May 2009

40 Task Force report. P.36. Italics in the report

41 http://www.nytimes.com/specials/bosnia/forums/digstau.html

Part I
The Origins of Mass Violence

3

The Sources of Conflict between Groups and Primary Examples

Conflict between groups can be over material or psychological issues. Conflicts that start over material issues usually become psychological as well.

As conflicts remain unresolved, they can become violent, persistent and intractable, and sometimes lead to mass killing or genocide.[1] *

Conflict, defined as opposing desires, needs, interests, and goals of individuals and groups, is unavoidable in human relationships and may therefore be regarded as natural. Awareness of conflicts and bringing them into the open, for example, inequality between subgroups in a society, even have positive potential, making it possible to constructively address them. However, conflict can become persistent and intractable, resisting attempts at its resolution and resulting in increasing hostility and mutual violence. Conflict between groups can also become one of the starting points or "instigating conditions" that over time evolve into mass killing or genocide, or into terrorism.

My purpose in this chapter is not to discuss in detail the origins, management, and resolution of conflict between groups, topics about which there is a huge literature.[2] My main purpose is to identify major sources and some properties of group conflict as a background to later chapters in which I describe the starting points for the evolution of violence, with difficult conditions of life in a society and conflict the primary ones, and to chapters in Part II in which I describe the prevention of violent conflict and reconciliation between hostile groups. Later in this chapter I will introduce the cases of violence that will serve as primary examples in the book. In most of them, conflict had an important role.

Material Sources of Conflict

Power and Opportunity

Conflict between groups can arise over *competition for power and opportunity*—who is to rule and to have what accompanies power, including access to wealth and the opportunity to generate wealth. Conflict of this kind can occur in any society where political parties and factions vie for power and influence. It becomes especially dangerous when the divisions involve ethnicity, religion, or race; when there is a history of great differences in power and wealth; and when there is a past history of violence between the groups. Conflict between such groups may not be only or primarily about who dominates in the political, military, and economic realms but also about domains of values, ideology, religious beliefs, customs, and ways of life. Conflicts in these domains have to do with identity and cultural existence.

Differences in power, privilege, and wealth can persist a long time without giving rise to active conflict. But when the less privileged group perceives them as due to injustice, contention intensifies. This change in perception sometimes results from worsening conditions of life in a society, from increased discrimination, or from changes in the world that alter a group's perception of its own situation, seeing now as unjust what it had previously accepted as customary and normal. The latter circumstance may partly explain the greater demand among Muslim minorities in European countries for rights, equal treatment, and respect for their identity. What may also intensify a group's perception of injustice are the many modes of communication today that enable people to compare themselves not only to real others but also to images of wealth and the good life. Intense feelings of frustration due to relative deprivation and powerlessness may result. As Evelin Lindner, a psychologist, medical doctor, and an originator of "humiliation studies," suggests, it may also be that values (or as I see it, at least ideals) of equality are becoming more dominant in the world, resulting in the experience of humiliation for those lower in traditional hierarchies[3] and fueling their demand for equality and better treatment.

Sometimes greater demand is the result of *improved* conditions that lead to hopes and expectations that remain unfulfilled. This is indicated by the J curve of revolutions,[4] the observation that revolutions tend to start after the lessening of repression. In Hungary, for example, the lessening repression by the communist government, accompanied by the removal of land mines and barbed wire at the border that sealed off the country, created expectations of greater change. This change did not materialize, which led to the revolution of 1956.

The improved condition of a group can bring, however, significant benefits. In Northern Ireland, the improved economic situation of the Catholics under British home rule helped to prepare the ground for the resolution of the long-standing conflict in that country.[5] But demands by less privileged groups for greater rights and access to societal resources are often resisted by the more powerful and lead to counter-reactions by them, such as repression and violence. A cycle of reciprocal actions can end in intense violence, even genocide.

Those in power usually resist demands for change partly because they don't want to give up privilege. But their resistance also arises because ideologies have developed that make the group's privileged position seem right. According to some research, members of a majority are more willing to act to improve the situation of people who are disadvantaged than they are willing to give up some of their own advantage.[6] They are also more likely to support social change when they are led to perceive their advantage as illegitimate.[7] In interactions between members of more and less privileged groups, both in experiments at universities with students and in field work with naturally existing groups, those with less privilege had greater desire to talk about power. Those with more privilege were more interested in talking about communalities than differences between groups. But when they were led to perceive their group's advantage as illegitimate, they became more interested in addressing differences in power.[8]

Research starting with the French psychologist Serge Moscovici has shown that when members of a minority group consistently express a viewpoint, they can influence the majority. This is not an easy task, since *legitimizing ideologies* that serve to justify existing privilege are common. They are beliefs or visions that describe, and affirm the rightness of, the existing social arrangements between groups and the position that groups and their individual members occupy in the world. They are an important category of ideologies, which I define as beliefs or visions of social arrangements and the nature of relationships that are considered right, desirable, or ideal, whether they exist at the time or not. Ideologies can specify the right relationship not only between groups and among humans in general, but also between human beings and God. While legitimizing ideologies affirm the status quo, ideologies often provide a vision of something to be attained. People absorb and hold legitimizing ideologies to varying degrees. Those with power usually believe in them more. But since legitimizing ideologies become part of the culture, those with less privilege also absorb them.

Social psychologist James Sidanius and his colleagues[9] identified a personal disposition, a *social dominance orientation*, that is associated with the desire to maintain the current social order, and especially the system of hierarchy within it. Another conception identifies the interest in maintaining the social order as system justification.[10] While social dominance theory focuses on variation in individuals'tendency to justify the system of dominance in their society, system justification theory is concerned with how people justify whatever exists, be it social dominance or economic practices that contribute to, say, global warming. Like ideologies in general, legitimizing ideologies motivate people, whether to justify dominance or other aspects of systems. University education lessens a social dominance orientation, but students who study subjects associated with privilege (law, business) retain more of this orientation. The difference between them and students who study topics like philosophy or social work is greater at the end of college than at the beginning.[11]

For many people, the belief that the world is just also provides a justification of the reasons why some people suffer or have less. This belief offers psychological protection; if the world is just, and I am a good person, I won't suffer.

Unfortunately, "just-world" thinking contributes to "blaming the victim"—that is, derogating those who suffer and seeing them as deserving their suffering, either because of their actions or because of their very nature, because of who they are. Research shows that this happens especially if people believe that the suffering will continue. People hold just-world beliefs to a different extent. Those who believe more in a just world also believe more that those with less privilege or who are poor deserve their situation.[12]

A related psychological process that justifies privilege is the powerful human need for cognitive consistency. To believe that people who have more are better than those who have less, and therefore that they deserve their privilege, creates balance in our thinking. Legitimizing ideologies and these psychological processes justify the condition of less privileged groups by establishing negative views of them, that is, by devaluing them.

In the face of unjust social arrangements, members of a disadvantaged group will sometimes try to gain redress for their grievances. Failing in that, they may see the use of force as their only alternative. Mob violence, for example, often follows failed attempts by a community to get redress. It can be a planned strategy, but it can also be spontaneous, often in response to an event that activates the readiness in people that has been created by those grievances. An event of that type is forceful police action following unsuccessful community attempts to improve the behavior of the police toward community members.[13] Often members of a group are unaware of, or unwilling to acknowledge, their group's responsibility for creating grievances, such as when Boston police officers, during a training workshop I conducted, expressed incomprehension and anger that residents in certain neighborhoods threw beer bottles at them from their windows. A thoughtful assistant superintendent of the Boston police present at the workshop described to them bad past police conduct in those neighborhoods that had created anger toward the police.

Groups and their members may at times perceive injustice that does not in fact exist and may use that perception, or the presumed hostile intentions of another group, as reason and justification for their actions. Mob violence can arise out of such imagined or trumped-up grievances, as occurred well into the twentieth century with the lynching of thousands of black Americans who were accused of some crime, often an alleged sexual approach to a white woman. Sometimes these lynchings were initiated by white business owners who wanted to get rid of black competition.[14] Mob violence can also be organized and directed by authorities, as in the case of Kristallnacht, the destruction of Jewish property and the first significant mass killing and incarceration of Jews in Germany in November 1938.

A group's use of force in response to injustice, imagined or real, often sparks greater violence in return. The use of force even in legitimate self-defense, but especially as retaliation or vengeance, creates cycles of violence, as in the Palestinian–Israeli conflict, in the course of which often the level of violence increases. In the civil war in Cambodia, both parties perpetrated many atrocities. After its victory, the Khmer Rouge proceeded to mass killing on a large scale: genocide.

Material Resources

Sometimes the initial source of conflict is over *material resources*, such as land and water rights. Nusseibeh, a Palestinian philosopher who has been an important member of the Palestine Liberation Organization, writes: "The Jew seeks space to continue living, while the Arab defends his space to the death."[15] At times the "conflict" over material resources simply means that one group wants something another group has. Evolutionary psychologists note that "Darwin displayed a keen awareness that men used warfare as a means of capturing women and reproductively relevant resources such as food, tools, and territory." Conquest of territory and of peoples used to be part of the customary relations among groups and nations. At times the conquerors would exterminate the whole group, at other times only its male members, incorporating the women and children into their group.[16]

Such genocides have been referred to as "routinized,"[17] killing conquered people a normal operating procedure. The violence could be seen as instrumental, in the service of the group's goals, but also involving a differentiation from "us" and protecting the group from later threat by this other. While not routinized as such killings were in earlier times, what may be regarded as an "ideology of conquest" was still widespread during the colonial period, allowing and leading to the killing of large numbers of people, such as the Germans killing all Hereros in Africa early in the twentieth century.[18]

In recent times, violent conflict over material resources often takes place within societies or countries. Internal conflicts are nothing new: in Europe, princes used to fight each other over territory, spoils, and power. In cases of great harm done to indigenous peoples, such as the natives of North America or of various South American countries, whites wanted the land of these groups for settlement or for development of its natural resources.[19] The devaluation of these groups allowed this, and ideologies related to development and legitimacy promoted it. Historical study might show whether there was also a relationship between difficult life conditions and more harmful actions against indigenous groups. At the time of slavery, if we think of that time as conflict, the struggle was over material resources of the most extreme kind—one group claiming the right to the bodies, the existence, and labor of members of another group.

Governments planning genocides often try to gain the support of the people by transferring to them or allowing them to take the property of a victimized group. This happened to Jewish property in Germany and in German-occupied countries. The Belgian leaders in exile appealed to Belgians, as an essential step in resistance to the Nazis, not to take over Jewish property.[20] In Rwanda, Hutus were allowed to loot the property of Tutsis being killed (see Chapter 9 on perpetrators).

In the twenty-first century, material interests in oil and other essential resources can have an important role in relations both between and within countries. When they do, "resource competition," arising from conflict over land and scarce resources that are needed by two or more parties, or from just plain greed, normally combines with other influences in leading to mass violence. Concern about access to oil or other scarce resources possessed by a country that engages in violence against one of its subgroups also contributes to passivity by bystander nations.

The Psychological Bases of Conflict

Group conflict can also be highly psychological, that is, it can be over "resources" such as security, which is both a material (involving bodies and property) and a psychological issue, and identity: who is good, worthwhile, deserving and accepted. Does a group, especially a subgroup in a society, have a right to its own, separate identity, and is its identity acknowledged or denied by others? These concerns are expressed by groups as they demand the right to practice their religion, or use their language, as Albanians did in Kosovo, or demand equal treatment and an end to discrimination in schools and in the justice system. Groups may ask for and demand greater autonomy in the territories they occupy. These demands for the affirmation of belief, values, and identity, and for recognition and access, challenge the existing social arrangements and the dominant groups. As conflict persists, devaluation, mistrust, and the experience of threat increase, reducing the willingness to compromise.

Group identity, as social psychologists have proposed, can be seen as the result of categorization (who we are and who they are), identification (defining oneself and others as belonging to particular groups), and social comparison (people evaluating their worth relative to others in terms of the standing of their group).[21] Identity is at least partly defined by culture, consisting of customs—what people eat and how they dress, how they express feelings—and of beliefs and values—what is just and how children ought to behave and how to raise them. People have multiple identities, shaped by their roles as parents, as workers, as members of a society and citizens of a country, and so on. They can shift from one identity to another, and they can integrate their identities in different ways. But for many people, important identities are fixed: They cannot choose their membership in an ethnic or racial group, and in most religions/countries it can be extremely difficult to shift religious identities or to escape the identities that others may impose on them. As members of an identity group come together around shared beliefs, as commitments to ideology and group intensify, these types of identities become increasingly fixed.

William Zartman, a conflict researcher and practitioner of conflict resolution, and his associate Mark Anstey write "In countries such as Zimbabwe, South Africa and Malaysia....Ethnic tensions may be less over differing customs, rituals or values, more over how these are translated into access to or distribution of economic resources such as land, business ownership or jobs. In Kosovo ethnic conflict has been translated into a sovereignty issue. In Kenya ethnic tensions...over distribution of power...."[22] Zartman and Anstey believe that identifying with particular groups helps people fulfill important needs for protection, participation, power, and privilege.

I will focus in this book on another set of needs that overlap with these. They include identity and connection. Group identity often becomes important in response to difficult life conditions or conflict, when as we shall see, people shift from an emphasis on who they are as persons (although this emphasis is less in "collectivist" societies) to their membership in groups, as a way to fulfill important needs. However, at times the groups that most satisfy their needs are not their original religious, ethnic, or other identity groups, but ideological movements in which people from different groups join, influencing the identity and choices of each individual.

As another origin of conflict, difficult conditions of life in a society lead one group to blame or scapegoat another group for the societal problems. Thus, the "conflict" is the result of the psychological effect of social conditions—that is, the frustration of basic material and psychological needs. I will discuss in the next chapter the psychological and social processes that difficult life conditions and conflict give rise to that provide psychological protection and hope, but that make harming another group more likely.

Conflict that looks material, such as conflict over territory, can be to a significant extent psychological. The territory may not even be needed as living space and may have no natural resources. But the groups find it difficult to compromise because the territory is part of both groups' identity, of their definition of who they are, and because of the fear and mistrust they have developed for each other.

Conflict that may start over material resources also becomes psychological if it persists. Over time the psychological aspects can become even more powerful than the material ones. Persistent conflict is a difficult social-life condition, and as such it frustrates basic needs. An important psychological development that occurs as a conflict resists resolution, intensifies, and becomes violent is that each group sees itself as good and its cause as just, and the other group as bad, unjust, and immoral. Whether the actual conditions, the rights and wrongs, are in imbalance, or both groups are responsible, usually the psychology of the groups is similar, and their beliefs about the rightness of their cause and the responsibility and immorality of the other are mirror images of each other. Persistent and violent conflicts, like the Israeli–Palestinian conflict, are characterized by such psychological developments.

A usual element in the mirror image is each group's sense of its own victimization. Opinion surveys in the Israeli–Palestinian conflict show that members of each group see their own actions as justified, although this tendency is stronger in the Palestinians. Neither side sees its violent acts as terrorist. Both sides believe, however, that the international community is hostile to them and sees their actions as terrorist but applies this judgment less to the actions of the other side.[23]

Some Properties of and Variations in Views of Conflicts

Theorists differ in what they see as some of the central properties of, and the motivations and goals in, group conflict.[24] Some see ethnic conflict as driven by material interest and calculation. Others see it as arising from passion, love, and hatred, which lead to biased perceptions. I see an important distinction between instrumental motivation of the members and leaders of groups, whether ethnic, religious, or political, and a complex mix of psychological, ideological, and emotional motivations. But many in this field see various degrees of both types of motives at work. While their relative importance varies, the two types of motives are often highly intertwined. Extreme violence serving material self-interest becomes possible because of psychological, ideological, and emotional forces and processes, which serve as a background for them. Another variation is in seeing leaders, as opposed to group processes, as having especially important roles in group conflict. Here again, both are important. Without effective management and resolution of these forces/motives, conflicts between groups can become intractable and destructive.

Ethnic, religious, or politically based conflict can be "balanced" in that *(a)* the two parties are similar in power, and *(b)* they harm each other and suffer at the other's hands about equally. Or it can be imbalanced *(a)* between more and less powerful groups, a situation that has been referred to as asymmetry, for example, dominant and subordinate groups in a society, and with *(b)* one party harming the other to a substantially greater extent. In either case, persistent conflict that does not yield to resolution can be an important contributor to—and instigating condition for—the evolution of violence into mass killing or genocide. This was the case in Argentina, conflict leading to the "disappearances," in Turkey where the Armenians' demand for more rights and autonomy was a background to genocide, in Rwanda, and in other cases.

However, there was no actual conflict between Germans and Jews living in Germany at the end of World War I. There was anti-Semitism in Europe in general and Germany in particular. Societal prejudice, combined with personal prejudice by leaders and important public figures and then more intensely by Hitler, with the relative well-being of Jews in Germany, and with the blaming of

Jews—without any basis—for the loss of World War I, and with racial theories in Europe and other elements gave rise to the Nazi view of a profound conflict between German and Jews. The difficult life conditions in post–World War I Germany further inclined the population to scapegoat the Jews and accept an ideology in which the Jews were the enemy.

Ideology is an important element in existential conflicts, those in which a group perceives another group as a threat to its survival—whether physical survival or as a group. According to one study, a perception among Israelis of a "collective Palestinian threat to harm Israelis and destroy Israel"[25] has made them unwilling to compromise. Those who saw the conflict as a "zero sum" situation, believing that anything that is beneficial to the other group is harmful to their own group, were especially unwilling to compromise. Such an orientation to another group is an aspect of what I have called an "ideology of antagonism." On the other hand, Israelis who had empathy for Palestinians showed more willingness to compromise.

In sum, important reasons for conflicts becoming intractable, resisting resolution, include the development of negative attitudes toward the other and mistrust, seeing one's group as moral and right and the other as immoral, and ideologies that emphasize conflicting interests and define the other as an enemy. These make compromise over material issues extremely challenging. Violence, once it begins, adds to the intensity of these forces and to intractability. Proponents of "dynamical systems" theory suggest that even when there is improvement in relations, without dismantling these forces maintaining conflict, which they call "attractors," the system will return to equilibrium, which is the state of conflict. They suggest that in addressing conflict one must focus not on the pattern of behavior, but on the elements comprising the pattern.[26] This book is consistent with such thinking; changes in attitudes toward the other and in other psychological elements, and in ideologies, are crucial both to resolve conflict, and to inhibit a group from turning against another under difficult life conditions.

Conflict between groups within a society is also affected by outside groups and the international system. Both the passivity and complicity of "external bystanders" and the context of events matter. British interests and behavior affected the relationship between Arabs and Jews between World War I and 1948. Iraq's mass killing of Kurds in the 1980s occurred in the context of its war with Iran and the support for Iraq by outside parties. A context for mass killing in Indonesia was the hostility between Western countries and the Soviet Union. In many instances of mass violence, the international context has some role.

Summary

Conflict between groups can be one starting point for violence. Conflict can be over material resources, such as land or water rights, or over power and privilege. Conflict also often has psychological components, with each side wanting its identity acknowledged and respected, and competition about whose values and visions for life (ideology) will dominate. Sometimes the conflict is primarily about these psychological needs and issues. Material conflict over time often becomes increasingly psychological. As conflict persists and becomes intractable and violent, negative views of the other party, as well as mistrust and fear, intensify. The members of groups in violent conflict can come to see their existence as threatened. Other psychological elements consist of groups in intractable conflict seeing themselves as right and moral, and the other group as responsible for the conflict, violent and immoral.

Primary Examples of Mass Violence

I will next describe several cases of significant violence between groups, past or ongoing. One case, Dutch–Muslim relations, serves as an example of the *potential* for violence in European societies between the original population and Muslim inhabitants. In many but not all cases, the violence evolved from prior conflict. What follows are relatively brief historical accounts of events leading up to and during the violence, and if the violence has ended, after the violence. Many books have been written about most of these cases. I give here limited accounts of their history, which I expand in later chapters as necessary, to exemplify principles of the origins of violence, ways to address hostility and conflict and prevent violence in general and in the cases I discuss, and methods to promote reconciliation.

A caveat: When groups are in conflict, or when there has been mass violence, history is usually contested. The parties involved have different views of how the violence came about. They emphasize their own injuries and pay less attention to the injuries of the other party. While I hope to provide accurate and unbiased pictures, an objective history is difficult to create, especially in the eyes of members of the groups and their sympathizers. Attempts at unbiased narratives are rarely seen as unbiased. Ethan Bronner, who has reported for many years on the Israeli–Palestinian conflict for *The New York Times*, has noted that in e-mail messages to him both sides condemn him for the manner in which he describes their story.[27] Divergent views are powerfully demonstrated in letters to the *New York Times* in response to its columns or articles about the conflict. The following are excerpts from two letters in response to a column about Israeli fears that Iran is developing and may use nuclear weapons against it:

> ... What other country had had to endure multiple nonstop calls for its extinction from the time of its birth and extending into its seventh decade? What other country is continually vilified for human rights violations by

farcical displays in the United Nations often by undemocratic, totalitarian regimes that brutalize their own citizens....

And the other letter:

> ... So Israel contemplates a pre-emptive strike on Iran. Thus Israel decimates the infrastructure of Lebanon in 2006, the civilians of Gaza in 2008, and now threatens Iran... [28]

Both events, and even more their interpretation—who started it, and did what and why—are often contested in cases of violence between groups. This is also true in the case of Rwanda, to some extent even about events leading up to the genocide, but especially about subsequent events and the nature of the current government and its actions.[29] An important element in reconciliation is coming to a complex truth, and to the extent possible moving toward a common or shared view of history.

Hutus and Tutsis and Genocide in Rwanda

In 1994, there was a genocide in Rwanda. Estimates vary, but about 700,000 to 800,000 Tutsis and about 50,000 moderate Hutus were killed by Hutus in 100 days. There has been a history of conflict between these groups, and that conflict had an important role in the evolution of the psychological and societal bases for extreme violence.[30]

In 1994, the minority Tutsis represented about 14% of the population in a country of 8 million people. Hutus comprised about 85% of the population, and Twa 1%. All three groups speak the same language and have the same religion. The differences between Hutus and Tutsis are complex. Group identities were constructed based on occupation, class, power, and to an unknown extent, ethnicity. Hutus were primarily farmers, Tutsis primarily bred cattle, but this specialization was not rigid. The main distinction was power and social status. For centuries, the country was dominated and ruled by Tutsis, with a Tutsi king, although some of the king's advisors were Hutu. Hutus could in theory become Tutsis, if they accumulated enough cattle. While this was probably a rare occurrence, it may have had important psychological meaning. In part of the country, specifically the northwest, Hutus were relatively dominant.

The colonial powers entered Rwanda in 1884, first the Germans, and from 1916 to 1962 the Belgians. My experience in Rwanda was that most Tutsis believe there was little conflict between the groups before colonialism. But Catherina Newbury, a longtime student of Rwanda, describes significant social inequalities,[31] and Mahmoud Mamdani describes some violence near the time of the arrival of the colonial powers.[32] However, under Belgian rule the difference between the two groups was emphasized, and the dominance of the Tutsis was greatly enhanced. The Germans and the Belgians saw the Tutsis, who tend to be tall and handsome by Western standards (and even more were stereotyped that way), as European/Western looking. The Belgians propagated the view that Hutus and Tutsis are different races.[33]* They did what colonial powers have done in many places, which is to have a segment of the local population, in this case Tutsis, rule in their behalf.

Under the direct rule of Tutsis, the Hutus' work situation, freedom, and economic condition all greatly deteriorated. In 2001, I interviewed in prison a number of accused perpetrators of the genocide, including the justice minister of Rwanda during the genocide, Agnes Ntamabyariro. Before I had a chance to say anything, she said to me: 'The reason for the genocide was slavery." She continued, "The slavery of the Hutus under the Tutsis." She claimed that she was against the killings and tried to stop them. Like her, none of the accused I interviewed took responsibility; even a man who "confessed" only admitted witnessing killings, not perpetrating them.[34]* But a Rwandan court in early 2009 sentenced the former justice minister to life in prison for her role in the genocide, including the distribution of weapons and ordering the assassination of a Tutsi prefect (regional administrator).[35]

The Belgians introduced an ideology that had highly destructive effects. A Belgian priest wrote a "white paper" in 1916 proclaiming that Hutus and Tutsis were racially different. Drawing in part on existing cultural myths, it described the Hutus as the original inhabitants of the area, and Tutsis as coming there from Ethiopia in the sixteenth century, conquering the local population. Under the Belgians, racial segregation, as well as identity cards, stamped Hutu and Tutsi were introduced.

The claim of biological difference, which first served to elevate Tutsis,[36]* was used against them after 1959. At that time, the Hutus violently revolted against the Tutsis. Perhaps due to the spirit of the times that supported independence movements and human rights but also anticipating Hutu dominance, both the Church, which in the course of history became closely tied to the government,[37] and the Belgians switched sides and supported Hutu dominance. The country became independent under Hutu rule in 1962. A long period of discrimination, persecution, and violence against Tutsis followed.

There were mass killings in the early 1960 and 1970s, and occasional killings of Tutsis at other times. During these periods of violence many Tutsis left Rwanda and became refugees in neighboring countries. Usually the killings of Tutsis in Rwanda followed internal political upheavals,[38] and incursions by Tutsis from neighboring countries, especially Uganda. Scholars note that internal upheavals, both before, during, and after colonial rule, could be unrelated to group differences, the result of power struggles between elites within the same group. However, leaders, themselves hostile to the other group, could and would use ethnic differences to promote their power and position.[39] As I will later discuss, I see leaders in such situations acting not only out of instrumental motives, but also because of the psychological effects of the existing conditions on them.

Tutsi refugees in neighboring countries could not get citizenship. Even in Uganda, where Tutsis fought with and helped the now longtime president Yoweri Kaguta Museveni gain power, who promised them citizenship, they were ultimately denied it.[40] And the Rwandan government did not allow Tutsi refugees to return to Rwanda. These were people without a homeland.

In 1990, a primarily Tutsi group, made up of children of refugees and some Hutus who were dissatisfied with the repressive system in the country, entered Rwanda from Uganda and began an armed attack, using the name Rwandan Patriotic Front (RPF). Their stated goal was to gain the right of exiles to return and to move the country toward democracy. A civil war began. While it was fought, new political parties were created. For the first time in Rwandan history there was open, intense, and hostile political contest. The intense competition between the parties, added to the civil war, created insecurity for both Tutsis and Hutus.[41]

A stalemate in the fighting in 1993 led to the Arusha peace accords, which would have given Tutsis a substantial role in the government. However, after the civil war began, a Hutu power ideology, which had roots in the revolution of 1959, was propagated. It proclaimed the dominance of Hutus as its goal. As an extension of the ideology, the *Hutu Ten Commandments* were created, which derogated Tutsis and advocated violence against them. There was extensive propaganda and hate speech against Tutsis in the media. Radio Milles Collines (which began broadcasting with funding from Christian Democratic International)[42] became infamous for its messages of hate, even directing killers where to go to kill once the genocide began.

The genocide was in preparation, according to what an informer told General Romeo Dallaire, the head of U.N. peacekeeping in Rwanda, well before the plane of Rwanda's president was shot down on April 6, 1994, killing him as well as the president of Burundi. A number of leaders of the "hard-line" anti-Tutsi faction of Hutu politicians were also on the plane. Immediately after the president's plane was shot down, the group that took power initiated the genocide, at its very start killing moderate Hutu leaders who might oppose it, including the prime minister. That the genocide was in preparation is also indicated by its organized nature as it unfolded, with lists of people to be killed first, and emissaries sent to local communities by the government that assumed power to initiate the killings. The wide-ranging participation of the population in the violence again Tutsis was easier to bring about because the president was killed and the Hutu government claimed that the RPF was responsible.[43]

The killing was done by parts of the military, by militias composed mainly of young men, the *Interahamwe*, and by Hutu members of the community. People killed neighbors, and in many mixed families even family members. Some people killed their own children whose other parent was Tutsi. People killing others with whom they had ongoing relationships led us to call what took place the "intimate genocide."[44] This tragic and traitorous "intimacy" is shown in the story of one of our Rwandan research assistants. Neighbors came into her home at the beginning of the genocide and killed the men in the family, her father and brothers. Then other neighbors came in and wanted to kill the women, but the neighbors who killed the men stopped them from doing it.

Much of the killing was methodical, performed day after day like work in the fields. Groups of Hutu men killed Tutsis at roadblocks, or those gathered at schools and churches, where sometimes in the past Tutsis found refuge from violence. Another way the genocide was "intimate" is that much of the killing took place close up, person to person, by machetes. Local residents were at times joined, encouraged, and supported in the killing by soldiers and the Interahamwe. Women were often raped before they were killed or kept as sexual slaves. While some bishops and priests tried to save Tutsis, many of them supported the genocide, handing over their parishioners or even directly participating in the killings.

Meanwhile, the whole world abandoned the Tutsis. The international community did nothing, except that early in the genocide, with killings all around, many countries sent their military, which evacuated their own citizens and left. This told the perpetrators that they didn't need to worry about external intervention. The genocide was finally stopped by the RPF, which resumed fighting and defeated the Hutu army.

France, which had a long relationship with Rwanda as a French-speaking country, supported the government all along, helping it militarily from the time the RPF invaded in 1990. Just before the complete victory of the RPF, France sent troops to Rwanda, supposedly to save lives. It did save some Tutsis, but it also helped most of the perpetrators, including the leaders, escape into Zaire (since 1997 the Democratic Republic of the Congo, or DRC). They were allowed to leave with all their arms, not only light arms, but substantial weapons of many kinds. They also took all the funds in the government's possession. According to the journalists and authors Linda Melvern and Stephen Kinzer, and other commentators, saving their allies was the true purpose of the French force.[45] Many Hutus who were not perpetrators also left. The Hutu leaders pressured civilians to follow them, and they presumably feared Tutsis because of the intense propaganda against them, because they expected retaliation for the genocide, and perhaps because of violence against civilians by the RPF (see below). Over 1.5 million people left.

In Zaire, the international community that did nothing to save the Tutsis responded to the genuine humanitarian emergency of the refugees by a massive aid effort.However, the camps were ruled by former perpetrators, who sold food and other supplies the camps received, using the money to buy more weapons. They conducted raids into Rwanda, killing more Tutsis, extending the genocide, and presumably intending to invade and retake the country. The international community continued providing humanitarian aid without addressing this widely recognized problem.

Violence against Hutu Civilians and Rwanda Fighting in the Congo

The RPF, even in exile, before it entered Rwanda, created an ideology of unity. It proclaimed that the divisions between Hutus and Tutsis were artificially created by colonialists, and that there are no Hutu and Tutsis, only Rwandans. It attempted to make a joint cause with Hutus against the government and attract Hutus into its ranks. Their invitation was answered by a few Hutu leaders unhappy with the government policies and practices, but not by the population. Even after the genocide began, the RPF called on members of the government army and the Interahamwe to change sides. Only a very small number of the latter did so.[46]

The description by Mahmood Mamdani, a scholar of African Studies, of what happened as the RPF gained territory during the civil war, before the genocide, shows the evolution of distrust by the RPF. "Every time the RPF captured a new area and established military control, the population fled." The peasants, who were "predominantly Hutu showed no enthusiasm at being liberated." Mamdani writes that "from recognizing that the peasants distrusted them to a distrust of peasants, a sort of mutual distrust, was but a short step." The RPF shifted from their "initial expectation of a relationship of political tutelage..."[47] Instead of trying to get the population on its side, it encouraged them to leave, and then used violence against civilians, especially starting with an RPF offensive in 1993. Consistent with later discussion of reciprocity in human relations, there seemed to be a cycle of actions and reactions.

I will write much more about the genocide in the course of the book. Here I will discuss the killing of Hutu civilians during and after the genocide which must also be addressed for reconciliation. While there is independent research about this, for example, by Human Rights Watch led in Rwanda by Allison Des Forges, a longtime Rwanda scholar, both she and others, like Gerald Prunier, an Africa scholar, refer to the Gersony report. The report was commissioned by the *United Nations High Commissioner for Refugees* (UNHCR) as a refugee survey, but it reportedly described widespread killing of Hutu civilians by the RPF. The United Nations "decided to suppress it, not just in the interests of the recently established Rwandan government but also to avoid further discredit to itself. The U.S., and perhaps other member states, concurred...largely to avoid weakening the new Rwandan government."[48] Neither of these authors has seen the report; their information about it came from confidential sources. Prunier does report a conversation with Gersony.[49]

After the RPF stopped the genocide and established a government, the new Rwandan army was given the name Rwandan Patriotic Army (RPA). RPF remained the name of the movement's political party. According to the Gersony report between April and September 1994, the RPF and then RPA killed between 25,000 and 45,000 people. The report by Human Rights Watch describes people killed at meetings convened by authorities, or by soldiers going from house to house. At times, before they killed people, they interrogated Tutsi survivors and sometimes Hutus who seemed trustworthy, sometimes the people whom they suspected, about these people's actions during the genocide. The Human Rights Watch report also mentions instances when the RPF killed Tutsis, as well as Hutus who were trying to save Tutsis.[50] Prunier describes a second wave of killings, smaller in number and more focused and selective, in his view aimed at people who constituted a potential elite.[51]

After the RPF established a government, the real power was in the hands of Tutsis, especially of those who returned from Uganda as part of the RPF. However, the government was mixed, Tutsi and Hutu. All potentially active bystanders—Hutu members of the government, perhaps hoping to maintain a "unity government," the United Nations and the United States, probably due to guilt for inaction during the genocide (or just the general tendency for caution and inaction), and human rights organizations—remained silent. When more killings took place in April 1995 at Kibeho, a camp of internally displaced people the government wanted to disband, where the RPA fired at the people gathered on a large field, some Hutu government ministers resigned.[52]

Bert Ingelaere, a Belgian researcher, writes in referring to the RPA killing civilians after it stopped the genocide and fought infiltrators from the Congo, that because it was difficult to "distinguish infiltrators from civilians, the RPA gradually resorted to brutal counter-insurgency strategies."[53] Much of the killing of Hutu civilians within Rwanda took place as the RPF fought to stop the genocide, when the difficulty of separating perpetrators from civilians was just as great. However, as the accounts indicate, this does not explain all the killings. In some places intellectuals and community leaders were separated from a larger group and then disappeared. Des Forges describes instances when people were gathered and all of them, including women and children, were killed.[54]

In Prunier's judgment the killings, and in general the practices of the RPF, resemble "neither genocide nor uncontrolled revenge killings, but rather a policy of political control through terror."[55] He sees a group that wants to rule over an intimidated, passive Hutu peasantry. Some other analysts also see the government as cold bloodedly doing what is in their interest.[56]

There is a tendency, however, among political scientists, students of international relations, even sociologists, and diplomats to focus on power, and not give proper weight to psychological motives. While they see the role of anger and the desire for revenge to some degree, they give limited weight to the continuing experience of threat, fear, vulnerability, and mistrust. Fear and revenge can join. Power in the form of political control can be in the service of protecting oneself and others from harm and gaining a sense of security.

Difficult as it is to establish what people did, it is even more difficult to infer their motives. Appropriately, Prunier attempted to do that from a pattern of actions. However, he wrote that the primary targets killed in what he presents as the second wave included the family and friends of genocidaires, as well as old members of the political party that was the origin of Hutu power ideology. This suggests that both revenge and eliminating a threat were likely parts of the motivation. What the motives were is important, because it says something about the possibility of reconciliation and of a harmonious society. What combination of policy was involved, versus the difficulty of separating genocidaires from civilians, or the initiative by young Tutsi soldiers most of whose relatives who lived in Rwanda were killed? But even if Prunier is right in his assessment of motives, which would limit hope for a harmonious, equitable future, as leaders and a group come to feel secure and established, motivation can change.

After asking for help from the international community against the genocidaires on its border and receiving none, General Kagame warned that Rwanda would have to take action alone. In spite of international agreements that refugees are not allowed to settle near the border of the country they left and then conduct armed actions against that country, nothing was done. Rwanda took action in 1996. The timing may have had to do with the continued attacks and threat by former genocidaires and their ongoing training to fight, and attacks on the Banyamulenge in the Congo, Congolese Tutsis of Rwandan origin. The Banyamulenge were fighting back, with Rwandan help, and then fighting with Rwanda once the RPA invaded.

Beyond fighting against the Interahamwe and the remnants of the genocidal Rwandan army, the war expanded to the overthrow of the President of Zaire, Mobutu. There was strong sentiment against a corrupt Mobutu among the leaders of the countries in the region, propped up by Western countries, in particular the United States as part of its cold war policy of containing communism, and by France. So moving against Mobutu and supporting Laurent Kabila's insurrection against his rule had strong African support.[57*]

A third wave of killings of Hutus took place in 1996–1997, in the course of the fighting that followed the entry of the Rwandan army into Zaire. The number of people killed has not been established; Prunier estimates it as over 200,000. The United Nations set up an inquiry, but this was supposedly hindered and the United Nations gave up.[58] Refugee camps were attacked and the people in them were killed. To what extent the Rwandan army decided to fight the genocidaires by a scorched earth policy, and to what extent this was part of revenge, is unclear. However, according to Filip Reyntjens, a Belgian law scholar, special units of the RPA in 1997 went deep into the Congo to kill civilian refugees who moved from the border into the interior.[59] At the same time, however, Rwanda was repatriating many Tutsis. According to an UNHCR report, 834,000 Hutu refugees were resettled back into Rwanda during the same period.[60]

A small number of soldiers were tried and sentenced for the killings in the first wave. But beyond that no societal processes were set up to address the killings of Hutus. As I will suggest, wounds of the past tend to fester; they can become a "chosen trauma" and affect future actions and group relations for a long time. Truth, acknowledgment, and healing from trauma and justice are essential for Tutsis in the wake of the genocide. But the injuries and losses of Hutus must also be addressed, as a matter of justice and healing, both of which further reconciliation. This will also make it more likely that Hutus can honestly engage with their group's actions in perpetrating genocide.

Violence against Civilians in War and Retribution by Victims

Both reciprocity in human relations and the need for self-defense are powerful forces. They lead groups not to draw distinctions between the actual perpetrators and other members of an extremely violent group. This is understandable from a psychological perspective, and even to some extent from a practical standpoint. Extreme violence, such as genocide, arises out of a societal or group process. Many members of a genocidal group are implicated in some way— although not all members. In addition, often the violent group represents continuing danger. As I will discuss this, past victimization inclines a group to "defensive violence" even when there is little danger. None of this makes violence by victims or opponents that extends to nonviolent members of violent groups right or acceptable, but it is a tragic reality. It reemphasizes the importance of prevention.

Contrary to just-war principles, much of the time opponents in a war also draw only limited distinctions between soldiers and civilians. In World War II the Germans bombed enemy cities. The Allies extensively bombed German cities. Only one of these bombings became famous, and infamous: the firebombing of Dresden that destroyed the city and killed a large number of people. While earlier estimates were much larger, recent estimates of the number of people killed are between 25,000 and 45,000. This was done in February 1945, near the end of World War II, although some argue it still had significant military value.[61] Another example is the atom bombs dropped on Hiroshima and Nagasaki. This is presumed to have saved lives by ending the war. But whatever their military value, these acts show disregard for the lives of noncombatants. The same is true when the United States uses drones to kill *presumed* terrorists, or Taliban in Afghanistan or Pakistan, with civilians nearby who are also killed.

An example of retaliation by victims is the expulsion of Germans from Eastern and Central European countries starting near the end of the war and continuing afterwards. The number of people expelled is estimated between 12 and 14 million. A variety of German commissions have been set up to establish the number of German deaths in the course of this. One of them after 5 years of work provided the West German government in 1974 with the estimate that 630,000 Germans died, but substantially over 1 million more were missing.[62] Some estimates of the dead and disappeared are higher.[63] Germans were killed by the Soviet Army, died in Soviet or Polish camps or in transit, and were killed in Czechoslovakia and Yugoslavia. About 200,000 were taken as forced laborers to the Soviet Union. These findings were not published for 15 years, until 1989, so that relations between Germany and Poland, where many died, would not be disrupted. While the expulsions began earlier, Britain, the United States, and the Soviet Union agreed to them at the Potsdam conference between July 17, 1945 and August 2, 1945. Perhaps, as some sources claim, Britain and the United States did this so that the expulsions would be conducted in a humane manner, or perhaps accepted it as a given. Polish messenger Jan Karski, who reported in the West about the extermination camps, told President Roosevelt in 1943 that Polish reprisals were inevitable.[64]

We must protest when people respond with unnecessary violence to harm done to them, however great. But the most effective way to avoid retributive violence is to prevent extreme violence in the first place: to learn to create the conditions that make it unlikely and to be willing to take the necessary actions, and/or enable people to resist the power of conditions that lead to it, both of which are the focus of this book.

A paragraph from Prunier's 1995 book is prescient. "Only the death of the real perpetrators will have sufficient symbolic weight to counterbalance the legacy of suffering and hatred *which will lead to further killings if the abscess is not lanced....*This is the only ritual through which the killers can be cleansed of their guilt and the survivors brought back to the community of the living. ... If justice does not come than death will return."[65] In his view, justice had to come speedily to avoid this. Not only did it take a long time to come—the International Criminal Court set up for Rwanda was very slow to begin its work—but new dangers for the Tutsis arose.

Justice is important, but it is rarely swift. Punishment is necessary, but even as a form of justice, ideally is it not primary in reconciliation and building peace. Many perpetrators of the genocide in Rwanda receive mild sentences relative to the nature of their crimes but have to work to rebuild society. What would likely have limited retributive violence is the involvement of the outside world *before, during, and immediately after* the genocide. Any effort to prevent the violence beforehand, engagement and preventive actions by outsiders during the genocide, or even in response to the continued danger from Hutu genocidaires afterward, would have created a connection to the rest of the world. It would have said to Tutsis, you are not alone. Immediate and powerful acknowledgment of the suffering and help for survivors would also have helped. Nonetheless, given what actually has happened, Rwanda does need the complex truth and a societal process that addresses all the violence that has taken place.

Many of the perpetrators of the genocide in the Congo survived the first war of 1996–1997 and remained there. They continued for several years to infiltrate into the north of Rwanda and attack Tutsis there. In the Congo the actions of the militia created and led by former genocidaires, the FDLR (increasingly over time its members included Hutus too young to have been perpetrators during the genocide), have contributed greatly to violence and deaths. I'll describe this situation in the next section.

By the end of the 1990s the government successfully stopped the infiltration and resettled refugees. It introduced enlightened policies, such as free elementary education and nondiscrimination in admission to schools and universities. It has energized the country, which shows significant economic progress. One of our colleagues working on our educational radio projects, Adin Thayer, wrote from Rwanda in February 2008:

> They (the government) are expropriating without compensation land from some members of the elite, and redistributing it free to the landless, in 5 hectare parcels. (It is) astonishing to me, this socialist act at the hand of a leader pushing capitalism and competition as hard as he can.... Here in the capital there's definitely a feeling of energy and forward motion.

The government continued to proclaim the ideology of unity that the RPF has advocated all along. This is a positive ideology, to overcome the divisions of us and them, but its uses after the genocide have been problematic. It is accompanied by disapproval of identifying people as Tutsis and Hutus and talking about the relationship between the groups. But these are powerful psychological, social, and group identities. For a period of time, people used coded language, referring to perpetrators, survivors, and returnees. Over time people became somewhat freer to refer to Hutus and Tutsis.

However, the government has regarded speech it does not approve of as "divisionist" and has been claiming the continued presence of "genocidal ideology." It is understandable that the government does not want to allow hate speech, which was one impetus to genocide. But this ideology, policy, and laws introduced in 2002 making divisionism a crime and in 2008 making "genocidal ideology" a crime, without clear definitions of these terms, limit free discussion and Hutu voices. They make the history of the groups' relations difficult to address and inhibit the discussion of current societal issues. They limit press freedom and political opposition. According to one newspaper report, "In the past three years, Rwandan officials have prosecuted more than 2,000 people, including political rivals, teachers and students, for espousing 'genocide ideology' or 'divisionism.'"[66]

Filip Reyntjens wrote that the current Rwandan government destroyed civil society.[67] While all aspects of life, including civil society, were devastated in the course of the genocide, in my experience a great variety of local organizations have developed afterward, although not political ones. But the government did make the functioning of certain organizations difficult, such as an independent human rights organization with Hutu personnel, whose officials then left the country.[68]* So did some Hutu members of the postgenocide government who had little power and some Tutsis, including high-level politicians, who felt restricted by current policies or feared retribution for opposing them or attempting to create a more democratic system.[69]

The complexity of the current situation in Rwanda is shown by the world's reactions. Development specialists admire the country and Kagame's leadership. In 2007 the "index of African Governance, which seeks to quantify the performance of African governments, named Rwanda as the continent's most improved country over the last five years."[70] The hope generated by the government has inspired enough Rwandans to engage in successful entrepreneurial activities to bring about strong economic development. There has been support by other countries and by many individuals whose imaginations have been captured by the combination of the horror of the genocide and Rwanda's emergence as a country of stability, vision, and growth.

However, some claim that only a small percentage of the population benefits from this growth—which unfortunately is common in a suddenly developing economy. Human rights organizations as well as scholars also accuse the government of problematic human rights practices, judging it severely.[71] The reasons include past violence against civilians, limitations of democracy, and actions against political opponents going back to before the 2003 presidential elections. At that time the parliament, which was appointed, not elected, ruled that the major opposition party cannot participate in the elections. Its candidate for president, a Hutu who was a former prime minister in the postgenocide government, then campaigned as an independent but had difficulty getting exposure.

This was an election the international community, including financial donors Rwanda relied on, pressured Rwanda to hold. There was as yet little psychological recovery or reconciliation, or the kind of civic institutions that prepare people for democracy. Imagine, moreover, a situation in which some German Jews who had survived the Holocaust returned to the country and managed to take over the government. How would they feel 9 years after the Holocaust about Germans regaining power? Even a moderate Hutu and his party resuming power could have led to what has happened in other countries at such times: the resurgence of violence and insecurity.

Kinzer[72] notes that many Rwandans given the background of authoritarian rule and the chaos that accompanied the introduction of new parties just before the genocide, with awareness of still intensely hostile feelings between groups, welcomed the strong hand of Kagame and his government. This was also my experience during visits to Rwanda, including the time before that election. However, this may be a limited view, since is it difficult to hear Hutu voices and perspectives. Moreover, it is reasonable to expect that with distance in time from the genocide, the government would become less authoritarian. But as I will note, in moving toward new elections in 2010 the opposite has happened.

In addition to differing in focus on economic development versus issues of democracy and judgments about the current political situation, differences in perspectives about Rwanda also have other sources: who authors talk to (those who extensively talk to the president tend to be impressed),[73] their level of familiarity with the country, whether it is a snapshot visit and exposure, or deep familiarity not only with Kigali but with the countryside, which is rare; and even what was their initial exposure and sympathy. Some scholars, aware of the repression of Hutus before 1959, had Hutu sympathies.[74] While they struggled with the genocide perpetrated by Hutus, reaching a balance can be difficult. Others were exposed to Rwanda first through the genocide, which led to Tutsi sympathy. I am one of these people.

In working in Rwanda, I found the limitation of press freedom and public voices problematic, but I also found individuals in the government committed to healing, reconciliation, and building a good society for everyone. It is a challenge to bring together all one's experiences about Rwanda, including the varied views of it, into a coherent picture and to make informed and wise judgments. But it is important for reconciliation and peace to try to establish the complex truth, engage with the moral meaning of events, and address them constructively.

What is a both moral and constructive perspective to take on Rwanda? What do the government and the people need to do to create a peaceful country in terms of the elements of reconciliation that I will discuss in Part II, such as truth, acknowledgment of past actions, justice, collective memories, and shared history? The past has to be addressed. But the judgments about policies and practices in the aftermath of the genocide need to have a broader perspective. Culture is slow to change. Democracy requires civic institutions. Rare is a speedy transformation from autocracy to democracy. Rwanda has long been authority oriented in culture and centralized in structure. While many local officials are still appointed, so that their primary allegiance is to the central government, there have also been elections of local officials.

For Tutsis after the genocide power as a small minority must feel, and may be, essential for security. Bert Ingelaere, who studied the experience of Hutus and Tutsis in the countryside reported in 2009 that, perhaps surprisingly, in the period after 2000 and especially after 2005, the feeling by Hutus that they had political representation increased greatly. This is consistent with the return of some members of FDLR militias from the Congo, which I will discuss, who do so in part because of the changing views of Rwanda they hear from their relatives inside the country. Not surprisingly, the feeling that they have political representation was even greater for Tutsis, starting in 1994 when the RPF established the postgenocide government. But Tutsis also experience living in a hostile social environment with Hutus who are untrustworthy.[75]

If one considers Rwanda in relation to other, more repressive countries, the level of distress and disapproval by some Western organizations and individuals of policies, which began soon after the genocide, may seem the result of a perhaps idealistic but unrealistic belief and hope that a country that has suffered a genocide should and would move to pluralism and democracy. But countries after great violence face tremendous challenges. Genocide has profound psychological and social impact. It creates psychological wounds and insecurity in survivors that shape their perceptions and actions. While some perpetrators asked for forgiveness as a justice process progressed, some at least in part to receive reduced sentences and be accepted back into their communities, many others showed little regret or sympathy for their victims. While some survivors granted forgiveness in words to former killers they live next to, as yet few could grant them in their hearts.[76] The denial of the genocide that some Hutus who live outside the country still engage in[77] must also have powerful impact.

Gerald Caplan, a genocide scholar, wrote with regard to Rwanda: "Besides justice, democracy, truth and reconciliation, there are the equally daunting goals of peace, ending impunity, healing, forgiveness, national unity, harmony, short-term relief, longer-term reconstruction and development. And all of these are to be acted on by a new government that does not enjoy universal support and that depends on human and financial resources that are minuscule and infrastructure that barely exists."[78] An example of the challenges Rwanda faces is the occasional murder of Tutsis who are to appear as witnesses before the *gacaca*, the community justice process trying perpetrators of the genocide.

Reconciliation is as yet far from exact science; the ideology of unity is an ongoing experiment in reconciliation. Unity is a worthwhile goal, but it is questionable that it can be dictated. It needs to evolve. Some research suggests that a larger identity is accepted more by people who have a double identity, as members of both the larger group and a subgroup of society.[79] The complexity in Rwanda is great. Intense emotions have been generated by people hearing and giving testimonies about the killings of Tutsis in the recently completed *gacaca* justice process.

I noted earlier the varied perspective on Rwanda. Perspectives also shift, as in the case of Gerard Prunier, an Africa scholar, whose book in 1995 was the first report on the genocide, with strong sympathy for Tutsis. But in a generally excellent book in 2009 he expresses strongly negative views of the RPF and the current government. This is apparently due to a combination of factors, including the violence by the RPF and RPA against civilians, the feeling that he received misleading information, what he saw as objectionable government practices, and perhaps negative Rwandan government reactions to some of his writings. But his attitude is often expressed indirectly, the way he interprets events, which can strongly shape readers' attitudes. For example, he writes about a massacre of Tutsis in the Congo at the Garumba refugee camp that it "finally gave the *hard line Tutsi camp what it considered to be a decisive justification* (my italics) to resume hostilities" in the Congo. But one can see a massacre as a *reason* for Tutsis, sensitized by genocide, to respond. At another place, again in relation to Rwanda's actions in the Congo, he writes about Kagame: "He presented the West with a very convincing storyboard: prevent a supposed genocide of the Banyamulenge (Tutsis in the Congo) and remove the border threat created by armed elements of the former genocidaire Rwandese governments."[80] But these threats were real. Interpreting events must be done with care to reach a reasonable truth.

With substantial stability in Rwanda as I write this in 2010, it would have seemed possible for the government to allow increased pluralism, open discussion in the public sphere in a civil manner, and increased political activities. Unfortunately, the opposite seems to be happening, presumably motivated by the elections scheduled for August 2010. According to reports by recent Western travelers to Rwanda I talked to, as well as Human Rights Watch and media,[81] there are increased tensions. Among their sources is restriction on political activity. Human Rights Watch reports that new political parties, which require a license, have difficulty obtaining one. According to its report, even children can be accused of genocidal ideology, their parents receiving jail sentences. The government in 2010 denied a work visa to a representative of Human Rights Watch.

The government allows, as the gacaca is ending after years of this justice process, that people report further crimes that took place during the genocide. This has led to denunciations, often for monetary compensation for property supposedly taken or damaged. There were grenade attacks in busy places in the capital, which the government attributes to genocidaires, or others hostile to the government, including high ranking military officers who have recently been accused of anti-government activities and have fled the country. They in turn accuse the government to be the source of the attacks, presumably to increase the belief in the population of the need to reelect President Kagame, to maintain stability and security.

A complicated matter relates to a Hutu woman who returned to Rwanda to run for President after living outside the country for many years, Victoire Ingabire. She was accused of genocidal ideology and detained. While according to some reports her crime was making statements that many Hutus were also killed during the genocide, and that justice for all is important, according to others she had connections before returning to groups denying the genocide.[82]

These are complex events, involving complex processes, but there is a pattern of actions limiting critical voices and political opposition. Rwanda is not alone in repressing political competition, especially before elections. Ethiopia has severely repressed political opposition in moving toward elections in 2010. It is still psychologically understandable for the Rwandan government to try to limit Hutu political activity. But it is also dangerous. Denying public space and political activity for about 85 percent of the population can intensify group divisions and hostility, contrary to the unity the government proclaims it wants to achieve.

Moreover, Tutsi opposition to government policies and actions also appear to be increasing.

I will discuss the cases that serve as examples all along, including Rwanda. Here in addition to a brief historical account I have attempted to provide likely psychological motivations, in addition to power motivations that are usually stressed, (and still existing hostility to Tutsis), of current policies and practices in Rwanda. These motivations are certainly still present in 2010. However, as I will show, people change as a result of their actions, and earlier actions often lead to a psychological and social evolution, leading to continuation and intensification of earlier practices. This may be the case in Rwanda, as those in power justify to themselves reasons that they must remain in power. Rwanda receives substantial support of varied kinds from other countries, in particular the U.S. and the U.K. I will discuss the role of "external bystanders" at length. Outside parties are good friends only if they exert influence to move a country they support in a positive direction. Although the international community discredited itself in the eyes of Rwanda's current leaders during—and after—the genocide, this can and ought to happen in relation to Rwanda.

Violence in the Congo

The story of the violence in the Democratic Republic of the Congo (DRC), renamed from Zaire, is in part a continuing story of Rwanda. Kinyarwanda speakers have lived for a long time in the Kivus, near the border with Rwanda. Their relations to local tribes began to deteriorate after 1937, when the Belgians started to move Rwandans from their overpopulated country into the much less populated Kivus, to work in agriculture and in the mines, about 85,000 over a period of two decades. The situation of the Rwandese in the DRC was difficult because they lacked citizenship and firm property rights, and because of enmity by local tribes. This had to do with both landownership, which in this country poor in spite of it natural resources has long been contested between local tribes and then with those of Rwandan origin, and the related ability to exploit rich natural resources.[83] The Mobutu government was first friendly to Kinyarwanda speakers, which contributed to hostility to them. But later policies of the system were hostile to and disempowered Congolese of Rwandan origin, and also divided and created hostility between and even within local ethnic groups.[84] All this contributed to the widespread violence that followed. However, Mobutu welcomed the Hutu refugees in 1994; enmity turned progressively against the Tutsis.

After Laurent Kabila came to power in 1997, there was great and increasing confusion. There were economic problems, and inflation greatly increased. The violence among various parties continued. The Mayi Mayi militias fought against the Rwandan army and Tutsi supported militias, presumably for nationalistic reasons.[85] All "of 1997 and early 1998 were filled with a monotonous litany of attack and counterattacks, by shadowy armed forces..."[86] Part of this fighting was a rebellion against the government.

The Rwandese had very substantial influence in the government, as advisors and as a military presence, which was unpopular among substantial segments of the leadership and the population. In 1998 Kabila decided to expel his Tutsi advisors and the RPA. The FDLR, because they were seen as needing support and therefore especially loyal, were progressively included in the Congolese military. A new war began, as the Rwandan army again entered the Congo, fighting against government forces and the former genocidaires.

In addition to the fighting between Rwanda, and the Congolese army and genocidaires, and between varied ethnicities, the tremendous violence in the Congo that a variety of authors have referred to as Africa's world war also was an outcome of hostility among the countries in the region and rebellions against these countries. Rebel groups fighting their countries used the Congo as a base. Some countries supported rebel groups against other countries they were hostile to, while fighting rebel groups hostile to them. Uganda and Burundi joined the war on the side of Rwanda, while Zimbabwe, Angola, and Namibia on the side of the government of the DRC, each fighting for its own, complex reasons.[87]

The various parties supported militias, some of which fought on the side, others against the Congolese government, and against each other. The general insecurity also led to the emergence of local militias, mainly ethnically based. Rwanda and Uganda, who have been allies, became increasingly hostile to each other, with battles between their troops. Prunier[88] sees this as due to differences in their vision of the kind of government they wanted to see in the Congo. He and others also see it as conflict over the exploitation of natural resources. But consideration of human psychology, human feelings, suggests that past resentments probably added to the conflict. Tutsi refugees fought with Museveni and helped him come to power in Uganda. He promised them citizenship and then reneged.[89] And to start their invasion of Rwanda in 1990 many Tutsis who were part of the Ugandan military simply left, taking military equipment with them.

For the members of the Congolese army and the many militias, brutal violence and looting became normal. Prunier writes about the "disintegration of a 'rational' war (perhaps meant ironically) into myriad 'privatized' socially and economically motivated subconflicts."[90] This seems an especially appropriate description of what was happening in the Kivus, with nine guerilla movements and many local militias.

Most of the fighters, including members of the army, did not receive regular pay. Looting, mining, and selling valuable minerals (often to Western companies) was a way to maintain themselves and finance their continuing fight. Taking minerals from the Congo was private looting by the militias, and some of the foreign militaries fighting there such as Uganda, but it was coordinated by the government as a way to finance the war by Rwanda. Civilians became the object of much of the violence, since the fighters took food and other means of livelihood from them. In fact, the fighters sometimes maneuvered around each other to avoid direct military confrontation.

After several earlier efforts a peace agreement was reached. The foreign parties either lost the support of their population, lost interest, or lost the need to fight. For example, Angola, one of the main participants in the war, stopped its involvement when Jonas Savimbi, the head of the main rebel group in Angola, UNITA, was killed in February 2002. By the time the peace agreement was signed among all the parties, including the main militias, in December 17, 2002, about 3.5 million people have died, probably about 90% from disease and malnutrition as both the import and the production of food have greatly declined in the course of the war.

Continued Fighting in the Kivus

Many more people died as the fighting among militias in the Kivus continued. The violence had to do with ethnicity, with competition for rights, with the exploitation of natural resources, with local and national political power, and with the psychological effects of the difficult conditions and war. At one point the enmity of the local population led Hutus and Tutsis of Rwandan origins to form a coalition, fighting against indigenous groups. This coalition collapsed when a law in 2006 gave citizenship to Congolese Hutus but not Tutsis.[91]

An Oxfam report in 2008[92] based on 60 focus groups in 30 communities in the Kivus, described a great deal of violence perpetrated on the population by the national army, militias composed of or led by former genocidares, local militias, and a militia of Ugandan origin. All groups committed rape, not only of women but often children and occasionally men as well. They took property and sometimes tortured and killed people. In many communities the FDLR and members of the national army were described as the main perpetrators. In the chaos, civilians also committed violent acts. Members of the communities described the large U.N. peacekeeping force as not helpful. It stayed on the main roads and was not seen where the violence took place.

The media and other outsiders have focused on material interest, the exploitation of Congo's natural resources, as the primary motivation in the fighting, more than on the divisions between groups and the political and psychological bases of the many-sided conflict. A document by the United States Holocaust Museum states: "A key aim of almost all the combatants was control of eastern Congo's vast natural resources, which include diamonds, gold and coltan, a mineral used in cell phones and other electronic equipment. A UN Panel concluded in 2002 that 'criminal groups linked to the armies of Rwanda, Uganda and Zimbabwe and the Government of the Democratic Republic of the Congo ... have built up a self-financing war economy centered on mineral exploitation."[93]

An article in the *New York Times* in November 2008 described a renegade colonel of the Congo army, who with his brigade maintained control of a mountain with tin mines. He taxed workers in the mine, those who carried the tin to collection points, and anyone who used the roads leading to and from the mines. The government, occupied with the violence in the region, supposedly did not have the wherewithal to remove him so that a company that bought rights to the mine could work there. But the article suggested that the colonel could do this because of his government connections.[94]

Laurent Kabila was assassinated in January 2001 and was replaced by his son Joseph Kabila. After the withdrawal of foreign armies, from 2003 to 2006 there was a transitional government. Leading up to elections in 2006 many political parties were established, with a great deal of political (and military) infighting. There was hate speech and violence, but the elections themselves, won by Kabila, were described by international observers as fair. However, the fighting did not stop. A policy to absorb members of the militias into the army broke down, and since the army had not enough structure and discipline, those who were absorbed, accustomed to violence, contributed to the army's violence. There was little attempt, not surprisingly given the conditions, to reintegrate fighters into their communities. This is an important aspect of stopping violence and reconciliation. I will return to it repeatedly.

There had been several formal agreements calling for a cease fire, voluntary demobilization of combatants, and a peace process, all of which were supported by the United States and the African Union. One journalist wrote that there was also a declaration of "normalization of relations between Congo and Rwanda, the disarming of Rwandan Hutu rebels, including some perpetrators of the 1994 genocide, and ending Rwandan support to Nkunda and his Tutsi rebels ... (however, the guarantors of these agreements) ... delegated responsibility for enforcement to the UN Mission in the Congo. (They did not have) the courage to press Rwanda or Congo to respect their commitments."[95]

In contrast to some of these reports, Rene Lemarchand, a longtime researcher on this region in Africa, identified ethnic differences ("contested identities") as a highly significant source of violence.[96] This is consistent with my view. The Congolese have long seen those of Rwandese origins as foreigners, and they were the object of violence under Mobutu before 1996. But ethnic antipathies came to be primarily directed at Tutsis. Because of the two wars Rwanda initiated and was involved in, many Congolese blame Rwanda, led by Tutsis, for the chaos and violence in their country. The militia led by Hutu genocidaires, the FDLR, aligned itself with the Congolese government and fought against Rwanda. The Hutu civilians who came into the Congo as refugees after the genocide also sympathized with the Congolese. As a result, they are accepted, while ethnic Tutsis are ostracized. This acceptance is in spite of the extreme violence of the militias led by the former genocidaires, perhaps because there are indications that much of this violence has been directed against Tutsis.

Mobutu who earlier was hostile to the Rwandese in Zaire welcomed the Hutus in 1994, including the genocidaires. Even after Laurent Kabila, who used the genocidaires to fight for him, various leaders kept helping or maintaining alliance with the FDLR. The FDLR has become a professional, trained army, with regular salaries paid to the soldiers. Although it represents no immediate danger to Rwanda, both in real terms and psychologically this group represents a threat to the Tutsi living in the Congo, and potential danger to Rwanda. After the war of 1998–2202 ended, Rwanda asked both MONUC and the Congolese army to deal with the FDLR, but these were neither willing nor capable to do it.[97]

Laurent Nkunda, a Tutsi born in the Congo who fought with the RPF, was later a general in the Congolese army and then started a rebellion, renewed this rebellion in 2008, claiming he was protecting Tutsis. Lemarchand believed he had a following because of his protection of Tutsis at a time when their insecurity was great and also because he showed concern about minority rights, including the rights of Twa, a very small minority.[98] However, troops under Nkunda's leadership have repeatedly engaged in atrocities for which he was indicted by the International Criminal Court.

After more than a decade of violence, insecurity, disease, and starvation in the Eastern Congo, in late 2008 hundreds of thousands of people were again refugees or new refugees. However, in January 2009, Nkunda was arrested while he was in Rwanda, leading his militia to dissolve. According to one author, the arrest was motivated by "the release of a UN report documenting Rwanda's close ties to the warlord, and concluding that he was being used to advance Rwanda's economic interests in Congo's Eastern hinterlands."[99] After his arrest, Rwanda and the Congo joined in fighting the militia of the former genocidaires[100] and in the following weeks, the violence diminished and some refugees began to return.[101] But the FDLR remained powerful, with about 6000 fighters.[102] After the Rwandan army withdrew, they went on a rampage of violence.

During the fighting, and renewed action by the Congolese army against the FDLR, rapes that had been widespread before became more frequent again. Nicolas Kristof, the *New York Times* columnist, described in a 2010 column two instances in which an "extremist Hutu militia" killed members of a family and raped both the adult women and a child. They took daughters from both families with them, "presumably to be turned into 'wives.'" These girls have not been seen since.[103]

While a number of reports indicate that Rwanda has participated in the exploitation of the Congo's natural resources, first directly, then increasingly through proxies and business relations, this was not the likely initial motive for Rwanda's involvement in the Congo. The psychological, political, and security situation of the Tutsis, and their leaders in 1998, when Rwanda started the second war in the Congo, was that of a small minority ruling a large majority that just tried to exterminate them, with some of those who did this still killing Tutsis in the Congo and infiltrating into Rwanda, and supported by Congolese.

However, the initial aims of Rwanda may have expanded, including perhaps the conquest of territory in the Congo.

Although many groups have been involved in the violence in the Congo, the Congolese blame primarily Rwanda. Even though Rwanda had reasons for the second war, they were not as pressing as in the first war. It conducted this war with ferocity, killing civilians.[104] Kristof in a somewhat oversimplified but effective manner sums up the current situation: "This is a pointless war—now a dozen years old—driven by warlords, greed for minerals, ethnic tensions and complete impunity. While there is plenty of fault to go around, Rwanda has long played a particularly troubling role in many ways, including support for one of the militias."[105] Reconciliation between Rwanda and the Congo, both between the governments and the people, would advance peace. The collaboration between the two governments in fighting the FDLR may have been a significant first step in that direction.[106]

The Rwandan genocide was one source of the persistent and intense violence in the Congo. The long rule of Mobutu and the ethnic hostilities it engendered was another. The poverty of huge numbers of people was still another. Relations between and within countries in the region was still another. But the psychological effects of upheaval, chaos, deteriorating economic conditions, and the war itself, combined with divisions between local groups, was a further important cause. I will discuss such conditions and their effects in subsequent chapters, as well as avenues to reconciliation and peace.

The Israeli–Palestinian Conflict

This is a conflict that started with competition for land needed as living space, between Jews who established the state of Israel in 1948, and Palestinians who have long lived in the area, many of whom became refugees in 1948. The conflict, involving core life issues even beyond living space, such as existence and identity, fast became violent, intensely psychological and intractable. The increasingly negative view of the other, mistrust and fear, ideologies and reciprocal violence have blocked the resolution of the conflict. As social and political psychologist Herbert Kelman wrote, when the core of a conflict involves both groups needing, wanting, and identifying with the same land as living space, group members are likely to see the conflict as existential, as well as "zero-sum," meaning that only one party can win.[107]* Feeling their lives and identity threatened, group members identify more deeply with their group.

While ancient Israel occupied the territory that came to be called Palestine, in the nineteenth century there was only a small Jewish community in Palestine. More Jews came around the turn of and early in the twentieth century, escaping persecution and pogroms in Russia and the Ukraine. During the 1930s Jewish refugees came from Nazi Germany. After the war, survivors of the Holocaust came in larger numbers. Jews came to Palestine because it was a place that they could go to at times when no one accepted them, because of their emotional connection to the ancient Jewish state of Israel, because they were moved by the Zionist dream of the creation of a homeland for Jews, and because this dream was greatly intensified by the horrors of the Holocaust. The Arabs who had lived in the area for many centuries became concerned even before World War II about the fact that Jews bought land in Palestine from absentee landlords and about the prospect that a Jewish homeland would be in time established there.

Palestine and other areas where Arabs lived were ruled by the Ottoman Empire for a long time. During World War I, Britain tried to enlist Arabs in the fight against the Ottoman Empire and made promises of independence in exchange for help. With the defeat of the Ottoman Empire in the war, Britain occupied the area. Its policies did not help the situation.[108] During and after the war, Britain also made promises to Jews, as well as secret agreements with the French, that were contrary to the promises it made to Palestinians. The Balfour declaration in 1917 talked about the creation of a Jewish homeland in part of the territory of Palestine. In 1936–1939 there were Arab revolts against the British, violence between Arabs and Jews, and massacres of Jews by Arabs.[109] Later, in response to these local tensions and to gain Arab support in the fight against Nazi Germany during World War II, Britain instituted a boycott of immigration for Jews. After the War, Britain captured at sea and interned on Cyprus Jews who attempted to get into Palestine, most of them people who just survived German extermination and labor camps.

The British left Palestine in April 1948, partly driven out by increasing confusion and violence, including terrorist attacks. Irgun, a Jewish organization often identified as a terrorist group, bombed the King David Hotel, which was a British headquarter. Meanwhile, the cycle of violence between Arabs and Jews continued. An Arab league-sponsored liberation army cut off Jewish communities from each other. Arabs blockaded the road leading to Jerusalem, which led to fighting to open the road for Jewish convoys bringing food and medical supplies to the city. In the course of the fighting, about a month before (and perhaps contributing to) the invasion of Arab armies, there was a massacre of the inhabitants of Deir Yassin, an Arab village near Jerusalem, by fighters of Irgun and another Jewish group. Estimates are that between 107 and 120 people were killed. In retaliation, medical personnel who were part of a convoy going to the Hadassah hospital in Jerusalem were killed.

After Israel declared its statehood in May 1948, five armies of neighboring Arab countries attacked it. The better prepared and organized Jewish Israelis won the war. The original Arab hostility to the existence of a Jewish state was enhanced by the humiliation of losing a war against this small state. Before, during, and after the war, about 700,000 Palestinians left their homes. They did this for many reasons: the massacre at Deir Yassin created fear; the fighting around their villages created fear and danger; they were expelled or were intimidated or induced to leave by the Israeli military, they followed the example of Arab leaders and elite who left; apocalyptic Arab broadcasts and accusations that those who stayed were traitors;[110] and in some areas because they were told by the Arab armies to leave until these armies defeated the Israelis.

For a long time the official view in Israel, and in the world, was that Palestinians left because the Arab leaders told them to leave, assuring them that the war would be short and they could soon return. But revisionist Israeli historians, led by Benny Morris,[111] have established that while it was only one of the reasons for leaving, many Palestinians left because of Israeli actions. Using loud speakers, leaflets, threats, and force, people were induced to leave (see further discussion in Chapter 20). In a later book, Morris writes[112] that expelling Arabs was never part of the Zionist agenda, and that at first some Jewish leaders, like the mayor of Haifa and Golda Meir, desperately wanted them to stay. But once the Palestinian exodus began, Israel used varied means to encourage it and even to force Palestinians to leave. Whatever their reasons for leaving, many of the Palestinians who left became permanent refugees, living in refugee camps. With the exception of Jordan, no Arab countries gave them citizenship, preferring instead to use them as pawns against Israel.

During the 1948 war, the Arab leaders talked about pushing the Jews into the sea. This remained a continuous theme. For many years, there were terrorist attacks on Israel, and later suicide bombers killing civilians. In 1964 the Arab states established the Palestine Liberation Organization (PLO), with the aim of eliminating Israel. The PLO soon became an authentic Palestinian organization, organizing violent attacks on Israel as well as on international targets; these were terrorist attacks in that most of their victims were civilians. Before the 1967 war, in an 18-month period, there were 120 attempts at sabotage within Israel by Palestinians, bombing water pumps, setting up land mines, and killing many people.[113]

Nasser, the President of Egypt, persistently talked about eliminating the alien Israeli state and attempted to unite Arabs in this cause. In 1967 he had the United Nations remove its international peacekeeping force from the Sinai. Egypt closed the Straits of Tiran to all ships flying an Israeli flag and moved about 100,000 of its troops to the Israeli border. All this created great fear and concern in Israel, which in turn attacked Egypt's air force. In the course of the war that followed, Jordan attacked Israel. Israeli leaders recognized before the war that occupation of the West Bank and Gaza, administered by Jordan, would not benefit Israel, but with great initial success in the war and in the heat of victory, they proceeded to occupy these areas.[114] Israel also occupied the Golan Heights, which belonged to Syria, another participant in this war, and from which there were frequent artillery attacks on Israel.

Israeli rule over these territories and over Palestinians was often harsh and oppressive. There were two Palestinians uprisings, or *Intifadas*, of significant duration. The first occurred between the late 1980s and early 1990s.

The second one began in September 2000 and officially ended in February 2005 when the leaders of Israel and the Palestinian authority proclaimed an end to the violence.[115] Suicide bombing became a frequently used means of attack on Israelis, in buses, marketplaces, restaurants, and weddings, making people unsafe everywhere. There were also a few Jewish terror attacks, the most infamous by Baruch Goldstein, an American medical doctor who was a settler in Hebron, a primarily Arab city. In February 1994 he entered a mosque and, with a machine gun, killed 29 people and injured 125. He was affiliated with Israeli organizations, led by the Israeli-American rabbi Meir Kahane and then by his son, that aim to restore the biblical state of Israel. Just as many Palestinians honor suicide bombers as martyrs, some settlers and ideologically aligned Israelis honor Baruch Goldstein. His attack led to riots in Hebron and to attacks on Jewish communities in Arab countries.[116]

In spite of the violence, the focus for many Palestinians slowly and progressively became not the destruction of Israel, but the creation of their own state. A major breakthrough occurred in 1993, when after secret negotiations, in the Oslo agreement the PLO came to recognize the existence of Israel and was recognized by Israel as the representative of the Palestinians. A Palestinian Authority was created, which was to administer parts of Gaza and the West Bank, and prevent terror attacks.Israel was to progressively transfer territories in the West Bank to Palestinian control The parties also established a framework to work out outstanding issues between them. As Herbert Kelman suggested, this interim agreement may have been the best possible at the time.[117] However, it did not address the most central issues, such as the status of the refugees of 1948, whether their return or compensation for the land they lost when they left; the status of Jerusalem and of Palestinian East Jerusalem, a city which is the capital of Israel and to which Palestinians are also strongly committed as their future capital; the creation of a Palestinian state and the borders between the two states, and related to this the status of settlements that Israel had been building for many years in the West Bank and Gaza; and control over holy sites of Muslims and Jews in Jerusalem.

There was opposition on both sides to the Oslo agreement, and with crucial practical issues unresolved, each side proceeded with actions that undermined the agreement. The terror attack by Baruch Goldstein took place just five month after the agreement. In February and March 1996 Hamas, which had gained support after the signing of the Oslo Accords, conducted suicide bombings in Israel that killed fifty-seven Israelis.[118] Terror attacks by Palestinians, especially Hamas, killed substantially more Israelis in the years immediately after than before the agreement.

Israel continued to build settlements in the West Bank and Gaza, on land that has been assumed would be part of a future Palestinian state, and some on land that has been privately owned by Palestinians. They are separating communities from each other and interfere with the creation of a viable Palestinian state.

The continued building of settlements may be the result of multiple motives. They provide places for Jews to live, often with attractive houses substantially less expensive than those in Israel proper, giving people an economic incentive to move there. They separate Palestinian communities from each other, presumably intending to increase the security of Israel. They also serve the ideological vision of intensely religious settlers to recreate the greater Israel of ancient times.

The building of settlements continued under different parties and prime ministers. The opposition to stop building them, and to substantive steps toward peace, has at times been intense. In 1995 when Yitzhak Rabin, a former war hero and the prime minister of Israel, was making significant progress in engagement with the Palestinians and was apparently ready to give up territories and remove settlements, he was killed by a religious Jew. However, when Ehud Barak, another prime minister, was ready to make concessions for peace, Israelis appeared ready to accept it, but close to an agreement, the longtime PLO chairman Yasser Arafat changed his mind. His reasons have been a matter of speculation.

The Oslo agreement set up a substantial degree of self-rule by Palestinians under the Palestinian Authority. However, the Authority became increasingly corrupt, its leaders taking money provided as aid for the Palestinians, and it failed to establish effective services for the people. Under its president, Yasser Arafat, and his movement, Fatah, the Authority allowed little political freedom. It did not create effective state structures, thereby limiting the development of political and civic life.

The PLO has been an umbrella organization, with Fatah its most powerful group. When the PLO finally recognized Israel's right to exist, Hamas, an organization with a strong Islamic religious orientation, refused to follow suit and engaged in suicide attacks and other violence against Israel, which Arafat and Fatah either could not or did not want to control. A branch of Fatah under Arafat's control also engaged in suicide attacks, contributing to Israeli mistrust of Arafat. Hamas started out as an effective community organization, providing services to people that the Palestinian Authority did not. It was initially supported by Israel as a way to counterbalance Fatah. Like the support by the United States for Muslim fighters against the Soviet Union in Afghanistan, which I will later discuss, this is an example of how supporting groups as a proxy against an enemy can misfire. Rather than negotiating an agreement that would have enhanced the status of Fatah, and then Palestinian president Mahmoud Abbas, in 2005 Israel unilaterally withdrew from Gaza.[119] Attacks by Hamas were credited by many Palestinians with bringing about the withdrawal.

The following January, in 2006, Hamas won the Palestinian elections and became the ruling party. In response, Israel stopped delivering the taxes it collected for the Palestinians, and the international community stopped providing aid.[120] The United States insisted on the elections, but it was in the forefront of refusing to deal with Hamas after it won. Individuals and groups need psychological space to change. They resist change if they see it as humiliating, as showing weakness, or as acknowledging defeat. This is especially so in societies where honor and receiving respect is a primary value. It would have been worth seeing whether, after gaining power, some degree of acceptance and engagement by Israel and the international community would have begun to change Hamas.

Fatah and Hamas have become not only political opponents but enemies. Perhaps this is the result of divergent backgrounds. Fatah is rooted in the West Bank, which between 1948 and 1967 was under Jordanian rule. Hamas is strong in the Gaza strip, which was under Egyptian rule during the same period, with those who became Hamas leaders influenced by the Muslim Brotherhood,[121] an Islamist organization involved in terrorism. It may also be that Fatah, which started as a terrorist organization, learned terror's limitations in accomplishing its aims. Different circumstances in the West Bank and Gaza may also contribute to their differences. Gaza is a greatly overcrowded refugee area, where life is more difficult than in the West Bank. In any case, the conflict between the two groups culminated in June 2007, with Hamas attacking the offices and killing the leaders of Fatah in the Gaza strip. Following this, Israel and Egypt—which dislikes Hamas' Islamist orientation—established a boycott of Gaza. The Palestinian president Mahmoud Abbas appointed a new government, without Hamas, but this government had no authority in Hamas-held Gaza.

There are also divisions in Israel. Its complicated political environment usually requires a coalition of parties to govern, which normally includes parties that favor the creation of greater Israel and resist giving up settlements. The divisions between and within Israelis and Palestinians, the competing ideologies (of greater Israel; of the elimination of Israel), and mutual fear and mistrust, understandable in terms of past history and current circumstances, make resolution of the conflict particularly difficult. Israel experienced several wars, many terror attacks and suicide attacks. Israeli cities experienced rocket attacks by Iraq at the time of the Persian Gulf War in 1991 and later by Palestinian groups. For a long time Israel has experienced the unrelenting hostility of the Arab countries that surround it, including calls for its extinction. Saddam Hussein paid the families of suicide bombers. In recent years Iran has denied the Holocaust and has threatened to eliminate Israel.

For a long time Palestinians have lived in refugee camps. Since 1967 they have lived under Israeli control, often in poverty, with limited rights. Their houses have been searched without warrant, and sometimes destroyed when family members were known or suspected to have engaged in anti-Israeli attacks. Palestinians have had difficulty receiving permits to build houses, and when they build them without permits, they can be demolished. They have received only limited protection from police when their olive trees are torn out or even when they are attacked by settlers while working on their fields. They are stopped and often have to wait for long times at checkpoints, and they have to take circuitous routes to get to their workplaces and other locations. Palestinians not involved in fighting have been killed during the *Intifadas*, and in the course of attacks on real and suspected terrorists. To protect itself against terror attacks, Israel has built a wall, which separates Palestinian communities.

The Palestinian–Israeli conflict has become a rallying point for many Arabs. The conflict itself, and strong U.S. support for Israel, while Palestinians continue to live difficult lives, has contributed to radicalizing Arabs and has become an organizing tool of Muslim fundamentalists and jihadists.

The violence has continued. In the years following Israel's withdrawal from Gaza, various Palestinian groups, primarily Hamas, shot thousands of rockets into Southern Israel. When in December 2008 Hamas refused to renew a cease-fire agreement, Israel attacked Gaza, first with airplanes and then with a ground invasion. Many civilians were killed, and many buildings were destroyed. The situation could have become what William Zartman has called a "hurting stalemate"[122] a condition that motivates parties to negotiate when neither party can gain the upper hand. But a new conservative Israeli government elected in 2009 has focused on the threat to Israel by a potentially nuclear Iran, has resisted calls to stop building settlements, and stated as an intermediate goal, before focusing on a state, the need to strengthen the economic situation of Palestinians. Then under U.S. pressure it stopped building some settlements and expressed its acceptance of the idea of a Palestinian state. With continued U.S. pressure, indirect negotiations, with George Mitchell as intermediary moving back and forth between parties, began between Fatah and Israel in May 2010. But new elements often appear in the relationship between these parties that inhibit progress, this time the killing of people by Israeli forces on a boat that attempted to breach the blockade of Gaza.

Arab states, concerned that the radicalization of their youth might under-mine their traditional and dictatorial rule, have become interested in promoting peace. The leaders of Arab countries, which are primarily Sunni, are also concerned about the growing influence of Iran, a Shiite Persian country that supports both Hamas and Hezbollah, an anti-Israeli military group in Lebanon. Under the influence of Saudi Arabia, the Arab League has come forward with a peace initiative. It offers acceptance of the state of Israel and normal ties with Arab countries, in exchange for agreement on a Palestinian state, Israel with-drawing to its pre-1967 border (which means the abolition of settlements or agreeing with the Palestinians to exchange some territories), and a just but as yet unspecified resolution of the issue of Palestinian refugees.

The enmity that is usually in the forefront between Palestinians and Israelis appears to wane during periods of little violence and when there is an advance in the peace process. There are moderates on both sides, and even some leaders of Hamas, while unwilling to say they accept Israel's existence, spoke at various points about a lasting truce.[123] However, if Israel and Fatah reach a peace agreement, without including Hamas its implementation will be highly challenging. Hostility, fear, and ideologies have led both sides to act unwisely, and repeatedly so over the years. The peace agreement that Yasser Arafat refused, in 2000, would have given the Palestinians almost all the territory they claimed for their state. Israeli leaders have maintained an occupation that created great suffering for Palestinians, and through the settlements, even in East Jerusalem, and other practices, established realities on the ground that make the creation of a Palestinian state more difficult.

Both Palestinian needs and rights, and Israel's security, its future well-being, and even survival, require peace. As Tony Blair said: "The absolute priority is to try to give effect to what is now the consensus across the international community— that the only way of bringing stability and peace to the Middle East is a two-state solution."[124*] Later chapters will explore how groups in general, and in this case in particular, can work out their differences and move beyond conflict. Persistent engagement, dialogue, psychological healing and a constructive ideology are among the essential elements for the psychological changes required in both leaders and the population to make an effective peace agreement. Reconciliation aimed at resolving the negative views and fear of the other is essential for forging a lasting peace. Resolving this conflict would eliminate one source of attraction to terrorism in Islam.

There is great "asymmetry," as many call it, between Palestinians and Israelis, differences in power and in the conditions of their lives. The challenge is that while Israelis know and believe in their superior power, due to their past woundedness, the hostility of the Arab world, and threats by Iran, they also feel greatly threatened, and thus there is a double asymmetry in how the two sides perceive their situation.

Still, both before and after (and if) a separate state is established, the more the lives of Palestinians improve, the more chance of a lasting peace. New hope in this regard comes from reports from the West Bank of greatly improved security in 2009, due to new, well-trained, and effective Palestinian police,[125*] and improved economic activities under the leadership of the prime minister, Salam Fayyad. He has a doctorate in economics and is a former official of the International Monetary Fund. New investment from outside and new businesses inside have begun to transform life in the West Bank.

Pluralism and free expression are essential to create the space in which opposition to hostility and violence can grow. It is difficult, however, given the climate in their communities, for Palestinians to express favorable views toward Israel and advocate peace. While Israel is a pluralistic country with varied media, there has been decreasing acceptance of public expressions of views favorable to Palestinians and advocating peace, and at times police interference with demonstrations. Some groups and individuals have begun a kind of oversight of academics, with intimidation through public censure of those who express such views. All this makes the role of external bystanders even more important.

Relations between the Dutch and Muslims in the Netherlands

Another conflict that is less "classic" in its properties but that embodies many of the complexities of our modern age, including terrorism, is between Muslim minorities in European countries and the original populations in those countries. I will focus on the situation in the Netherlands, but the analysis can be applied, with consideration of local circumstances, to other European countries with large Muslim minorities. Some of these nations have suffered significant terrorist attacks. The violence in the Netherlands was somewhat limited, but it gave rise to concern about more. Focusing on Dutch–Muslim relations gives us an opportunity to consider early measures to improve group relations and prevent violence from escalating.

Many Muslim men, primarily from Morocco and Turkey, came to work in the Netherlands in the 1950s and 1960s. Their labor was needed during the economic boom that followed the war, particularly in low-paying, low-status jobs. It was assumed that they would eventually go back home. Instead, they brought their families to the Netherlands. By the 1970s the economic conditions changed, and their jobs disappeared. Uneducated and unskilled, they were not qualified for jobs in the developing technological economies. As a result, many in this older generation, especially the Moroccans, have been living on social support provided by the state.[126]

These groups have maintained their Muslim religion and close group ties. However, roles and relationships within the group are strongly affected by the conditions of their lives and surrounding culture. They are an impoverished minority in a society and culture very different from their own. The fathers, without jobs and often not speaking the language, have lost their traditional authority in the family. Young boys used to gather in groups and harass store owners and people on the street. This behavior and the involvement of some, especially Moroccans, in criminal activity, as well as the Muslim treatment of women and the social support and services the society provides to many of the immigrants, have created resentment and hostility by the Dutch. Prejudice and discrimination challenge the Netherlands' long tradition of tolerance. The Muslim minorities resent the prejudice and discrimination, and find some of the practices of Dutch society, such as open sexuality and homosexuality, highly objectionable.[127]

Two elements have added a dimension to this low level but potentially significant conflict. One is the increase and projected increase in the Muslim population. It is clear that even with limiting immigration, which most European countries now do, the proportion of Muslims in the population will grow because of the high birthrate in the Muslim groups. The other issue is terrorism, both actual and potential. Both groups fear it. Muslim groups know that if a terrorist attack occurs, they will be blamed for it as a group, prejudice and discrimination will increase, and violence against them will likely follow.

In fact, prejudice and discrimination did increase in the Netherlands following 9/11 and other Muslim terrorist attacks, especially the Madrid and London bombings. In addition, in the fall of 2004, Dutch journalist Theo van Gogh was killed in Amsterdam. He and Hirshi Ali, a Somali refugee woman who became a member of the Dutch Parliament and was an outspoken critic of the treatment of women in Muslim societies, made a TV film together. The film, *Submission*, criticizing the treatment of Muslim women, started with an image of the back of a woman with text from the Koran written on it. This outraged many Muslims. A man who belonged to a group that was developing plans for terrorist action killed van Gogh, leaving a note on his body that said Hirshi Ali would also be killed. In a normally peaceful society, this act precipitated about 800 violent attacks in the following months—the burning of mosques and Muslim schools, as well as churches.

According to one author, "Many of Europe's guests have overstayed their welcome. They live on the seam: the old world of Islam is irretrievable and can no longer contain their lives; the new world of modernity is not fully theirs. They agitate against the secular civilization of the West, but they are drawn to its glamour and success."[128] But there are large Muslim minorities now in many European countries, and they are there to stay. The question is how to help them accept and adapt to the countries they live in, and to be accepted in them.

The conflict in the Netherlands and other European countries seemingly has three dimensions: power, wealth, and access; identity; and values and ways of life. The last one is based on differing ideologies, deeply set democratic values versus deeply set religious beliefs. However, many young Muslims are attracted to aspects of Western culture and values, and Muslim religious views and traditional cultural practices in general, and in Europe, are the object of discussion and reformulation. And European countries can take steps to improve the economic, social, and psychological situation of Muslim minorities, increasing the willingness of their members to adapt to their societies, especially if they are not required to abandon their identity as Muslims. This adaptation has been better in the United States, which has a well-established Muslim population with little conflict between it and other groups (although I will later discuss a few young men joining violent or jihadist groups). Such developments can also help prevent the radicalization of Muslims—and of the Dutch, since much of the violence after the killing of van Gogh was against Muslim property—so that individuals leading normal lives will not embrace extreme beliefs and ideologies that create a readiness for violence.

Terrorism by Al-Qaeda and Palestinian Terrorism

There has been terrorism in many places in the course of history. One realm of terrorism that I focus on in this book is that by Al-Qaeda, or groups loosely associated with Al-Qaeda. This includes groups that may have been inspired by Al-Qaeda or may have little connection with the original Al-Qaeda, but we now call them or they call themselves Al-Qaeda. Another realm is Palestinian terrorism, especially the more recent kind, suicide terrorism, which I will discuss extensively in later sections. Both types of terrorism have become great challenges in our contemporary times.

There was research and theory about the roots of terrorism before 9/11, and much more since then, and we have some understanding of how it originates and a reasonable understanding of how it spreads.[129] With regard to prevention, a primary focus of the U.S. government after 9/11 has been to eliminate terrorism by eliminating terrorists, but this approach does not address the conditions and influences that lead to and maintain terrorism.

Terrorism often arises out of conflict. Differences in power, and repression by a government or powerful group, are one instigator of it. Sometimes a weaker party begins to use terror to fight for real, or imagined, or ideologically driven causes. Palestinian terrorism arose from conflict over territory, identity, and existence, and transformed into suicide terrorism under occupation by Israel. Central in the creation of Al-Qaeda have been people who practiced terrorism in Egypt, a predominantly Muslim country with a secular government that repressed political freedom in general and Islamic movements in particular. This repression created opposition and hostility and radicalized groups. The Muslim Brotherhood, a religious Islamist organization that was not allowed to operate, gave rise to terrorism against the state. The terrorist groups that arose killed foreign tourists, in order to reduce the state's income and damage its standing in the world.[130]

When the Soviet Union invaded Afghanistan, a Muslim country, to support its communist government, people came from many Muslim countries to take up arms against the Soviets. Many Egyptian terrorists were among them. Their fight was supported and largely financed by the United States, through Pakistani agencies. When the Soviet Union, exhausted by fighting, left the country, many of those who fought them remained.

Imagine these mostly young and some middle-aged men at the end of the fighting in Afghanistan. They just won a war against a superpower. They were helped by another superpower, with money and weapons, but they were the fighters—and the victors. Imagine, for example, the situation of the Egyptians. Do they go back to Egypt, to live underground, very likely pursued by the government for their earlier activities?

Terrorism has been described as motivated by "cause and comrades." You fight to fulfill your cause and increasingly also to live up to your commitment to fellow fighters. Here were men who fought together. They had financial support from Osama bin Laden, a member of a rich Saudi family, and from other contributors. And while they didn't have specific goals, as they had in fighting to get the Soviets out of Afghanistan, they had a cause: Islam.

Earlier they were guided by an ideology that inspired them to violent jihad (struggle) against, and for the overthrow of governments in Islamic countries, the "near enemies," that did not practice the religious laws, the *sharia*, and that therefore did not live up to the ideal of an Islamic state. The Egyptian terrorist fought for this ideal. But the ideology evolved and shifted focus to the "far enemies," nations that supported repressive and non-Islamic governments in Muslim countries and in their view acted to hold back Islam, harmed Muslims around the world, and spread values antithetical to Islam. America was a prime far enemy. These Islamic fighters had defeated one of the far enemies—now they turned to the other, the United States. (I will discuss their ideology and its evolution in Chapter 5.) Over a number of years, they attacked U.S. properties and citizens and people associated with the United States, causing great damage and the loss of many lives, for example, the U.S. embassy in Nairobi, Kenya, the U.S. warship *Cole*, the World Trade Center in 1993, and on September 11, 2001 again the World Trade Center and the Pentagon.

Was there any conflict between them or Islam and the United States? They apparently thought so. Was this only in their imagination? Is it that the United States as a rich country and great power invites envy and is an attractive target for people looking for an enemy? Perhaps more to the point is that the United States has had an important role in generating technological, economic, and cultural changes that have spread around the world, these changes greatly affecting people in traditional countries, frustrating powerful psychological needs.

But while terrorism against the United States did not arise out of conflicts as clearly identifiable as those that spawned Palestinian terrorism or the terrorism in Egypt, it had a basis in real conflict, or at least an understandable perception of harm done by the United States. The United States has been supporting repressive Muslim governments. It has long supported Egypt financially and politically. Israel and Egypt have usually been the largest recipients of U.S. financial aid. The United States has also been a staunch ally of Saudi Arabia, which is firmly and repressively ruled by its huge princely family. It helped to overthrow a government to bring the Shah of Iran into power, and then supported that Shah's repressive regime, with its feared secret service and jails. It has supported Israel in its conflict with the Palestinians. It has not been a wise bystander in that conflict and has not exerted all the influence it might to bring about peace.

Another issue has been U.S. policy toward Iraq. The United States supported Iraq in the war against Iran. When Iraq later invaded Kuwait, the United States went to war against Iraq. Then the United States established a boycott of Iraq and *maintained* it in spite of the great suffering it created for the Iraqi population. Advocates of the continuing boycott disputed the harm it had been causing— and to the extent they acknowledged it, they insisted that Saddam Hussein was responsible. However, Louise Richardson[131] gives a detailed account of the significant deprivation and loss of lives, especially children's lives, that resulted from the boycott.

Some time after the withdrawal of the Soviet army from Afghanistan, many Muslim fighters moved to the Sudan, where Osama bin Laden joined them. Out of this community arose Al-Qaeda. From the Sudan, some of the group and its leaders returned to Afghanistan and established camps to train fighters to use terrorism. The new terrorism that followed pointed to grievances and had a guiding ideology. However, an additional impetus for the creation of Al-Qaeda may have been the search by a large group of men for a way to live their lives, for finding continued purpose and goals to pursue. These men showed commitment by going to fight the Soviet army. They had spent years fighting, they had not lived "normal" lives for a long time, and for all of them, not only the former terrorists among them, it would have been difficult to return to what they had been doing before. Fighting can become a way of life. The guerrillas in Colombia started with an uprising on behalf of the poor and powerless. But then fighting became a way of life for them, continuing for a half a century, their true cause seemingly lost.

Islamic terrorism, outside Palestine-Israel, has evolved since the 9/11 attack on the United States and the subsequent "war on terror." From the start, Al-Qaeda was decentralized. In many guerrilla or terrorist movements, a central leader has a crucial role, and when that leader is captured or killed, the movement collapses. This was the case with guerrillas/terrorists in Peru and Kurdish rebels in Turkey. In contrast, Al-Qaeda was set up, from the start, not to have such reliance on a leader. It followed the model, in Jerrold Post's phrasing,[132] of a corporation, in which managers can be moved into higher leadership roles. In addition, many independent cells have been organized, or inspired by Al-Qaeda, or have self-generated. Forensic psychiatrist and terrorism expert Marc Sageman coined the term *leaderless jihad* to describe the activities of such decentralized terrorist groups.

An example of the emergence of terrorist cells is found in the small groups of young men who seemed to be part of their societies, had education and opportunity, and who have engaged in terrorist actions in Great Britain and elsewhere. Sometimes they acted autonomously, at other times with limited outside support from Al-Qaeda "central" or other parties, with no clear, specific aims other than destruction. While destructive ideologies often lead to the development of specific aims, they can also lead to violence against "enemies" without specific goals beyond that. They can be guided by a belief that one's group, or the world in general, will be better if the enemies are harmed or destroyed. Or they can have idealistic but unrealistic aims that do not seem directly connected to their actions, such as establishing a Caliphate, recreating an Islamic regime that includes many if not all the Islamic countries.

There have been some positive developments. An important aspect of prevention is to decrease support for terrorists in the populations they are part of and claim to serve.[133] This decrease in support can be a naturally occurring development. A 2008 study reports an "extraordinary drop in support for Islamist terror organizations in the Muslim world over the past five years."[134] Many Muslims seem to have turned away from the intense and often gruesome terrorist violence, such as decapitating hostages and videotaping this act for later public viewing on television. They also turned away because many Muslims were among the terror victims. Another development: Excluding the violence in Iraq and in Afghanistan, which arises partly from civil war and partly from wars against the United States as an outsider and occupier, there has been a substantial decrease in worldwide terror. One study of terrorist attacks over 10 years, up to mid 2007, concludes that from 2004 there has been a decline of 65% in the number of attacks and 90% in fatalities.[135]

Nonetheless, the future is unclear. The war against terror, with leaders and members of Al-Qaeda killed, and even lessening of popular support, can for a while intensify commitment from already committed members, and even create new sympathizers. Bruce Hoffman, the author of *Inside Terrorism*, notes that Al-Qaeda is still highly active.[136] In Afghanistan and Pakistan both the Taliban, which is both a social/religious and military movement and a terrorist organization, and Al-Qaeda have been resurgent. In 2007 Al-Qaeda intensified its efforts to recruit new people to its cause, releasing a video every 3 days.[137] Well-established terrorist organizations, other than Al-Qaeda central, still exist, with horrific attacks such as that in Mumbai in November 2008 in which 10 gunmen killed over 160 people and injured several hundred. This attack apparently originated from Pakistan, by a terrorist organization that has organized similar attacks in the past. Lashkar-e-Taiba, the Army of the Pure, like Al-Qaeda, was established by the people who fought against the Soviet Union in Afghanistan,[138] and some consider it an Al-Qaeda affiliate.

There have been arguments about which source of terrorism, Al-Qaeda or "leaderless jihad," is more important.[139] But as the United States and others fight terrorism, the types of organizations and groups that Al-Qaeda has given birth to have multiplied. There is still Al-Qaeda central, even if many of its leaders have been killed. There are regional groups that claim to be or are loosely associated with Al-Qaeda, such as the one in Yemen which inspired and outfitted with a bomb the young man who attempted to blow up an airplane over Detroit in December 2009. There are local groups, sometimes referred to as "homegrown," inspired by Al-Qaeda ideology, and also by identification with people killed by the United States, especially civilian casualties in the course of attacks on terrorists or the Taliban. Occasionally there are individual actors, such as Major Hasan of the U.S. army, who killed 13 people and wounded 31 others at Fort Hood, Texas, and a Muslim convert Abdulhakim Mujahid Muhammad who is accused of having shot two soldiers in Little Rock and "claims to have been driven to violence by the actions of the U.S. military abroad."[140] There is the Taliban. And there are independent terrorist groups, some connected to Al-Qaeda, such as the one that is responsible for the attack on Mumbai. Genuine prevention remains a burning issue.

Extending this threat has been the support that individual states give to groups that fight for a cause and use terror as a strategy. They use these groups as proxies in fighting wars. Iran and Syria have been supporting Hezbollah and Hamas. Pakistan has supported terrorist groups in a war against India, in particular in Kashmir. Lashkar-e-Taiba is one of these groups. It is reported to have had close ties to Pakistani intelligence.[141] In addition to direct support, because of connections to terrorists or their ideologies, or preoccupation with internal matters, some countries have ignored terrorists—until they themselves become targets. This has been true of both Saudi Arabia and Yemen.

To address these challenges requires addressing the conditions that generate terrorism and support for terrorists, such as the Israeli–Palestinian conflict and the conflict between India and Pakistan over Kashmir. These conflicts, the belief by each side that its cause is just, and in the case of Palestinians their relative powerlessness all make it possible for actors to see themselves as soldiers fighting wars in behalf of their group, even as they kill civilians. Preventing terrorist violence also requires the international community to work with the states that support the violence, and sometimes engage in proxy wars through terrorist groups. The tools of prevention described in Part II, which include engagement between parties, contact, dialogue, the creation of constructive ideologies, and addressing difficult life conditions, real conflict, and repression, should also include engagement with states that support or tolerate terrorism. Engagement, negotiation, and developing positive relations to such states should be primary in prevention, but sometimes targeted economic sanctions (focusing on leaders), and in extreme cases military force that creates conditions for effective negotiation can be necessary.

The Holocaust: The German Genocide against the Jews

The history of the Holocaust is well known, and much of it will also emerge in the course of the rest of the book.[142]* But a very brief summary of its basic events is warranted here. After Germany lost World War I, and after great political chaos, economic problems, and other difficulties of life, the Nazis came to power in 1933 and soon established a dictatorship. The Nazi regime immediately killed or jailed many opponents and began the persecution of Jews. Ultimately it killed about 6 million Jews during World War II.

The great majority of Jews were killed in factories of death, specially constructed for this purpose, with the infusion of gas into large rooms where people were told they were going to take a shower. Others starved to death while working as slave laborers. People were also killed in many other ways: lined up naked and shot at huge ditches that they were forced to dig, forced into trucks where the carbon monoxide created by the exhaust was redirected into the trucks, and killed with lethal injections into the heart. The Nazi regime also perpetrated genocide against the Gypsies or Roma people and killed millions of Russian prisoners of war, millions of Poles, and others.

Notes

1 Such brief statements introduce most of the chapters in the book. Some of them are revisions of "communication messages" I and my associates have developed to briefly summarize for writers in Rwanda, Burundi, and the Congo the educational content to be included in radio programs. The messages are based on my previous work, especially *The Roots of Evil*, and an early brief version of this book, as well as on work on trauma by Laurie Pearlman and her associates (see Pearlman, 2001; Pearlman & Saakvitne, 1995; Saskvitne et al., 2000). They formalize the "Staub-Pearlman approach" we developed in earlier work in Rwanda. A first, brief version of communication messages we developed in collaboration with LaBenevolencija, a Dutch NGO that produces the programs and its director, George Weiss. The second version from which some of these statements are drawn I developed in collaboration with Laurie Pearlman, Rezarta Bilali, Johanna Vollhardt, and Terri Haven.

2 See, for example, Anstsey & Zartman, in press; Deutsch, 1973; Deutsch, Coleman, & Marcus, 2006; Hamburg, 2007; Horowitz, 2008; Kelman & Fisher, 2003; Kriesberg, 1998a,b; Lund, 2009; Staub & Bar-Tal, 2003

3 Lindner, 2006, 2008

4 Davies, 1969

5 Cairns and Darby, 1998

6 Lowery, Chow, & Crosby, in press

7 Iyer, Leach, & Crosby, 2003

8 Saguy, Dovidio, & Pratto, 2008

9 Sidanius & Pratto, 1999

10 Jost, Banaji, & Noek, 2004

11 Sidanius, Pratto, Martin, & Stallworth, 1991

12 Lerner, 1980; Lerner & Simmons, 1966; Rubin & Peplau, 1973

13 Staub & Rosenthal, 1994

14 Ibid.

15 Nusseibeh, 2007

16 Buss, 2009

17 Smith, 1999

18 Kiernan 2007

19 Totten, Parsons, & Charney, 1997

20 Fein, 1979

21 Tajfel, 1978; Tajfel & Turner, 1979

22 Anstey & Zartman, 2010, p.12

23 Shamir & Shikaki, 2002

24 See, for example, discussion by Horowitz, 2008

25 Maoz & McCauley, 2005, p.82

26 Vallacher, Coleman, Nowak, Bui-Wrzosinska, 2010

27 Bronner, 2009

28 The first letter is by Jerry Rapp, the second by Anne Remley, The New York Times, May 26, 2009, p.16

29 Lemarchand, 2009; Prunier, 2009

30 des Forges, 1999; Mamdani, 2001; Melvern, 2004; Prunier, 1995; Straus, 2006

31 Newbury, 1998

32 Mamdani, 2001

33 According to David and Catherina Newbury, 2000, both Africa scholars, it was the members of the Tutsi aristocracy who fit that stereotype. In my experience, even Rwandans, who claim they can tell who is Tutsi and Hutu, make mistakes in identifying each other. In one of our seminars a Tutsi assistant explained to us at the end of the first couple of days the somewhat negative reactions of the group to one of its members as the reactions to a Hutu suspected of having been involved in the genocide. It turned out he was a Tutsi.

34 This changed later when confessions could lead to reduced sentences.

35 http://www.rnw.nl/internationaljustice/tribunals/ICTR/090121-justice-minister

36 Most scholars use the designation Hutu and Tutsi, without the plural s. However, depending on the context in the sentence this can be awkward in English and like many journalists, I use the plural terms.

37 Newbury & Newbury, 2000

38 Straus, 2006

39 Newbury, 1998

40 Mamdani, 2001

41 Ingelaere, 2009c

42 Jones, 2006

43 Straus, 2006

44 Staub & Pearlman, 2001

45 Kinzer, 2008; Melvern, 2004

46 Des Forges, 1999

47 Mamdani, 2001, p. 186, 188, 189

48 Des Forges, 1999, p.726

49 Prunier, 2009

50 Des Forges, 1999

51 Prunier, 2009

52 Ibid.

53 Ingelaere, 2008, p.31

54 Des Forges, 1999

55 Prunier, 2009

56 Lemarchand, 2009; Reyntjens, 2004

57 Prunier, 2009, writes that Kabila who once led a rebellion against Mobutu was put forward as the head of a Congolese insurrection. Newbury, 1998, writes as if Kabila was the leader of an ongoing insurrection.

58 Prunier, 2009

59 Reyntjens, 2009; see also Prunier, 2009

60 The state of the world's refugees, 1997-1998, quoted in Prunier, 2009

61 Packer, 2010

62 Rummel, 1998

63 For an overview of varied reports and references see http://en.wikipedia.org/wiki/Flight_and_expulsion_of_Germans_during_and_after_WWII#cite_note-Overmans_1994-132

For an estimate based on English sources see Rummel, 1998, 1999

64 Rummel, 1998

65 Prunier, 1995, 354-355

66 Gettelmen, 2010b

67 Reyntjens, 2004

68 I met with officials of this group, and at least in their interaction with me, they seemed concerned with the fair treatment of both Hutus and Tutsis.

69 Sebarenzi, 2009

70 Kinzer, 2007

71 Ibid. See also Lemarchand, 2009; Prunier, 2009; Human Rights Watch, 2010

72 Kinzer, 2008

73 Gourevich, 1999, 2009, Kinzer, 2008

74 See Ingelaere, 2009b and Prunier, 2009 for discussion of some of these points

75 Ingelaere, 2009c; see also Sebarenzi, 2009

76 Gourevitch, 2009; see also later in this book.

77 Clark and Kaufman, 2009

78 Caplan, 2009

79 Dovidio, Gaertner, & Saguy, 2009

80 Prunier, 2009, p. 332.

81 Human Rights Watch, 2010; Gettelmen, 2010b

82 For the first statement see Gettelmen, 2010b; for the second, Caplan, 2010

83 Austeserre, 2008

84 See Prunier, 2009, for a detailed discussion of the complex situation in Zaire/the DRC

85 Personal communication from Catherina Newbury, February 2010

86 Prunier, 2009, p. 174

87 Ibid

88 Ibid

89 Mamdani, 2001.

90 Prunier, 2009, p. 225

91 Austeserre, 2008

92 Oxfam, 2008

93 United States Holocaust Memorial Museum Alert, October 2008

94 Polgreen, 2008

95 Campbell, 2008

96 Lemarchand, 2008

97 Prunier, 2009.

98 Lemarchand, 2008; Gourevitch, 2009

99 French, 2009

100 Gettlemen, 2009, January 25

101 Gettlemen, 2009, March 4

102 International Crisis Group Report, 2009, May 11

103 Kristof, 2010

104 Prunier, 2009

105 Kristof, 2010

106 Gourevitch, 2009

107 Kelman, 2007. Kelman, a professor at Harvard, spent many years bringing Israelis and Palestinians together in "problem solving workshops," starting at a time when officially the two groups would not talk to each other.

108 Gerner, 2003

109 Morris, 1989, 2004, 2008a

110 Ibid.

111 Ibid.

112 Morris, 2008a

113 Remnick, 2007

114 Segev, 2006

115 MidEastWeb, retrieved May 2009. Other sources give larger numbers of people killed.

116 http://www.palestinefacts.org/pf_1991to_now_israel_hebron_shooting_1994.php

117 Kelman, 2007

118 US History Encyclopedia: Israeli-Palestinian Peace Accord. http://www.answers.com/topic/oslo-accords.

119 Goldberg, 2009

120 Ibid.

121 Post, 2007; Smith & Myre, 2007

122 Personal communication, February 2009

123 Carter, 2009

124 Ibid. Former British Prime Minister Tony Blair was appointed Middle East envoy working on behalf of the US, Russia, the UN and the EU.

125 However, a September 14, 2009 article in *Newsweek* by Kevin Peraino, ("Palestine's new perspective") suggests that the newly trained police, under the leadership of the prime minister, uses overly forceful, repressive means to create order.

126 Staub, 2007a

127 For more extensive discussion of these matters and relevant references see Staub, 2007a

128 Ajami, 2009, quoting Caldwell, 2009, in a review of his book.

129 Crenshaw, 1995; Post, 2007; Sageman, 2004, 2008; Richardson, 2006; Victoroff & Kruglanski, 2009 and many others

130 Sageman, 2004; Wright, 2008

131 Richardson, 2006

132 Post, 2007

133 Richardson, 2006

134 Zakaria, 2008, p. 37

135 Ibid.

136 Scoliano & Schmitt, 2008

137 Kruglanski et al., 2008

138 Weiner, 2008

139 Scoliano & Schmitt, 2008

140 Dickey, 2010, p. 35

141 Ibid.

142 I applied my earlier conception of the origins of genocide to the Holocaust in great detail in Staub, 1989

4

Instigating Conditions
Starting Points of Mass Violence

Difficult life conditions, group conflict, and war create threat and uncertainty, and they frustrate basic, universal, psychological needs. They are instigators or starting points that can begin an evolution to mass violence such as genocide or mass killing.

Group Violence, the United Nations, and the International System

Genocides and mass killings are not easily distinguishable, especially since the U.N. definition of genocide is confusing, identifying genocide as "acts committed with intent to destroy in whole or in part, a national, ethnical, racial or religious group."[1] The Genocide Convention does not appropriately clarify the meaning of "in part," that is, when killing *some* members of a group is genocide and when it is not. The definition is also incomplete in that it does not include the killing of political groups as genocide. Political scientist Barbara Harff calls this politicide.[2]

Many other definitions of genocide have been offered.[3]* Although similar to the U.N. Genocide Convention's definition, they do differ in some important details. For example, Helen Fein, one of the originators of the field of genocide studies, defined genocide as "sustained, purposeful action by a perpetrator to physically destroy a collectivity directly or indirectly, through interdiction of the biological and social reproduction of group members, sustained regardless of the surrender or lack of threat offered by the victim."[4] My definition is closest to hers: it is genocide when *a government or some group acts to eliminate a whole group of people, whether by directly killing them or creating conditions that lead to their deaths or inability to reproduce.* In contrast to genocide, I see mass killing as "killing (or in other ways destroying) members of a group without the intention to eliminate the whole group, or killing large numbers of people" without a focus on group membership.[5]

In the U.N. Genocide Convention, the intent to destroy has great importance. In my definition, the focus is on "acts," not on stated intentions. Perpetrators can create a system that leads to the destruction of a group, without stating or even explicitly considering the intention to destroy the group. As I have already written, perpetrators of evil often justify their acts, even to themselves. They can engage in "defensive" killings that can eliminate a whole group, without elaborating their intention to do so.

The influences leading to genocide and mass killing are similar. As the psychological orientation and system that lead to violence develop and as violence progressively increases in magnitude, it is impossible to know what will be its most extreme form, a genocide or "only" mass killing. Therefore, in studying origins, we must look at the origins of mass violence in general. With regard to prevention, we must also focus on the prevention of group or mass violence in general, rather than of genocide in particular. True prevention is early, before intense violence occurs. Halting already occurring intense violence, and especially stopping an already ongoing genocide, requires coordinated measures by nations, and usually military force. Since nations are reluctant to contribute their soldiers to such a force, even if they slowly come to an agreement to use force, by the time they act, huge numbers of people will have already been killed.

The United Nations has produced many resolutions, conventions, and principles to protect human rights, to protect individuals from harm inflicted on them because they are members of particular ethnic, religious, racial, or political groups or for other unjustified reasons. In addition to the Genocide Convention, it has produced the Convention against Torture, the Universal Declaration of Human Rights, the Convention on the Rights of the Child, the Convention on the Elimination of Discrimination against Women, and others. I will discuss in Part II an especially important principle for the prevention of mass violence adopted by the United Nations: the responsibility to protect. The declaration of principles and the conventions have created a climate in which policies and practices that are in conflict with human rights are held unacceptable. However, widespread violence against people and widespread abuse of their human rights have continued, ranging from genocide, to torture, to sexual trafficking that keeps women in sexual servitude. For all its efforts to introduce principles and conventions on human rights, the international community has remained unprepared to act in response to these human rights violations.

This has many reasons, one of which is that some countries, even major powers, have so far refused to ratify some of the conventions. For example, the United States has not ratified the Convention on the Rights of the Child. An apparent reason is worry by some influential people that this gives the government a right to interfere with how families raise their children. While after many years the United States has ratified the Genocide Convention, it did so "reserving the right to decide whether, when and how, the Convention on Genocide can be applied to itself."[6] This reduces the meaning of ratification. Nations, especially powerful ones, do not want other countries to have a reason, or justification, to interfere in their affairs, including violence they may engage in within their borders. But other countries can think, if the principles don't apply to them, why should they apply to us?

There are also no enforcement mechanisms. There are not even systems to appropriately assess an increase in the potential for violence, to provide convincing and effective early warning. Even less do we have effective systems to activate preventive actions in response to conditions that tend to lead to violence. The international community has done little about early prevention and has no effective systems to respond to already occurring violence.

With regard to genocide, the moral pressure the Genocide Convention creates is clearly not enough to bring about action. But the focus placed on genocide has also given rise to an originally unexpected problem. Governments and people in general seem to pay little attention to mass violence unless it is proclaimed a genocide. A mere mass killing pales in significance—in the eyes of the world, but not in the suffering of victims.

An example of these issues is Darfur, where "Arabs" supported by the central government have been attacking, killing, and raping "Africans." The U.N. International Commission of Inquiry concluded in 2005 that victims and perpetrators may have identified themselves as members of different groups but were not *objectively distinct* enough for the violence to qualify as genocide.

> The various tribes that have been the objects of attacks and killings (chiefly the Fur, Massalit and Zaghawa tribes) do not appear to make up ethnic groups distinct from the ethnic group to which persons or militias that attack them belong. They speak the same language (Arabic) and embrace the same religion (Muslim). In addition, also due to the measure of intermarriage, they can hardly be distinguished in their outward physical appearance from the members of tribes that allegedly attacked them.[7]

The Commission recommended that the International Criminal Court consider Darfur as a case of crimes against humanity. While the United Nations and the international community have done little to stop the violence, the Court indicted the President of Sudan in 2009 on that basis.

In summary, since the influences leading to genocide and mass killing cannot be distinguished, and since the definition of genocide in the Genocide Convention is problematic, we must act on the basis of indicators that some form of group violence is likely to happen. What its form might be not even the perpetrators know, since their motivation and goals evolve progressively.

What are the indicators of likely group violence? My core conception of the origins (and prevention) of hostility and violence between groups is schematically presented in Table 4.1 (and in more detail in Table 17.1 in Chapter 17). The chapters in Part I describe the influences and processes that give rise to and

Table 4.1 The Origins and Prevention of Violence between Groups

A: Starting points

Difficult life conditions–economic deterioration, political disorganization, great social changes

Conflict between groups

War, revolution

Consequences of these starting points:

    The frustration of basic psychological needs

    Individuals turning to a group for identity and support

    Scapegoating

    (Destructive) ideologies

B: History, culture, and current practices

Elements Contributing to Violence (←):	*Elements of Prevention* (→):
Devaluation of the Other	Humanizing the Other
Destructive, Exclusive Ideology	Constructive, Inclusive Ideology
Unhealed Wounds	Healing of Past Wounds
Uncritical Respect for Authority	Moderate Respect for Authority
Monolithic Society	Pluralism (Structures; Processes)
Unjust Societal Arrangements	Just Social Arrangements
Passive Bystanders	Active Bystanders

C. Continuous processes

The evolution of harm doing (changes in perpetrators, bystanders, institutions, social norms, and culture)

The role of leaders

The role of followers

Self-interest as a motivation

Source. Revised from Staub, 2006a.

maintain hostility and violence, including genocide, together with how these are manifested in our primary case examples.

The conception of the origins I present here is probabilistic. A number of these elements are often present in societies without leading to mass violence. The more elements are present, the greater their intensity, and the fewer the opposing influences that can prevent violence, the greater the likelihood that intense violence will evolve.

Universal (Basic) Psychological Needs: Their Frustration and Fulfillment

Difficulties of life in a society are important starting points for, or instigators of, group violence. They include severe economic problems—especially economic deterioration, rather than just poverty—political disorganization (intense and hostile competition between different parties vying for power, especially without a stable political system, stable government, or established power relations, for example, at a time when a society begins to move from an authoritarian system to a more democratic one), or great and rapid societal/cultural change, I refer to these as *difficult life conditions*. I use a single label for these different societal problems because of similarities in their psychological (and resulting social) impact. When problems develop in a society, a number of the difficult life conditions often arise or develop together and create threat, danger, and societal chaos, profoundly affecting people's experience. Each of these conditions, and even more their combinations, powerfully frustrate basic psychological needs in whole groups of people.

Frustrated needs are not direct instigators of group violence. But they tend to give rise to shared psychological reactions and social processes, such as members of a group scapegoating another group for life problems, adopting destructive ideologies, and joining ideological movements. These satisfy basic needs to some degree, but turn groups against others, and are elements of the evolution of the psychological/social bases of violence. Not every member of a group reacts the same way, and I will later discuss some differences between individuals that shape their reactions. But social conditions are powerful, and especially when the culture has certain characteristics, it becomes likely that there is a substantial vanguard that begins to initiate an evolution toward violence.

Before I discuss the nature of difficult life conditions in more detail, I want to both consider their impact on basic needs and examine these needs in relation to other psychological constructs. All of the conditions I listed, and the societal chaos they entail, create uncertainty and the experience of threat and fear. The psychological needs I have proposed they frustrate[8] are basic, universal needs that all human beings possess, which means they must be part of our shared genetic makeup. As evolutionary psychologists might suggest, they have become adaptive functions, because when they are fulfilled, they make survival more likely.[9]

One of these needs is for *security*, for the feeling that we (including important people in our lives, such as our families and our group) will not be harmed and that we will be able to provide for ourselves the necessities of life. The need for security has to do with both our physical and psychological security. Difficult life conditions and the behavior of other people can threaten our physical/material well-being. But even when this is not the case, our psychological need for safety, for not being diminished, disrespected, and humiliated, can be profoundly frustrated. Another need is for *effectiveness and control*, to feel and be effective and have control over important events and goals, such as protecting ourselves from harm or achieving positive aims. In difficult times, people often feel helpless. They do not know what to do, and feel they cannot assure their own or their family's safety. They may be unable to make a living or build a future. They lose hope about the possibility of fulfilling the visions they have held for their lives.

Another need is for *positive identity*. We all want to feel good about ourselves, to feel that we can respect ourselves and have other people's respect. In difficult times our need for self-respect and dignity are threatened or frustrated. When we cannot protect ourselves and our families, cannot make a living, cannot achieve important goals, or when we experience devaluation and discrimination because we are members of some group, the need for a positive identity is greatly frustrated. These needs are interconnected in the sense that the same conditions can frustrate the need for security, for feelings of effectiveness and control, and for a positive identity, and some of the same conditions and experiences can fulfill all these needs.

Another need is for positive *connection to other people*—individuals and groups. In difficult times people often focus on their own needs. At the time they most need connection and support, people become disconnected from each other. This leads to an intense search for connection, and the turning to groups that can provide it. People also need *autonomy*, the ability to make their own choices. Under difficult social conditions choices are limited, and without the ability to fulfill them, they are also meaningless.

Another basic need is for *comprehension of reality*, to understand the world, and one's own place in it. This overlaps with what is sometimes referred to as worldview. Human beings like novelty and change that are limited and manageable. But the social disorganization or chaos that is an aspect of difficult life conditions frustrates the need for comprehension. It challenges our understanding of reality or worldview. Great changes in the world also make our own position and role in the world uncertain. At its most basic level, comprehension of reality involves knowing both how the world operates and what one's position is in the world—how to act in one's various roles, in relationships, as a group member, and so on. At an advanced level, comprehension involves meaning, the sense of purpose in one's existence. Psychologist Abraham Maslow, in his theory of the hierarchy of human needs, considered meaning as the most advanced need.

Great social changes, as well as great changes in people's own lives—such as when a young Muslim man moves from a Muslim country to Europe—especially without appropriate support and shared sense making, can frustrate several needs, especially the needs for identity, comprehension, and effectiveness and control. Under novel conditions people have to relearn how to accomplish their goals. Their need for positive identity and belonging/community may also be frustrated, as people have to adjust to a changing world and find new ways to develop or maintain positive connections.

People also have a powerful *need for fairness or justice*. This may be a basic psychological need. It may also be a by-product of other needs, such as identity, connection, and effectiveness. Injustice diminishes people. It creates disconnection between those who get more or less than their fair share. It also frustrates the need for effectiveness and control, since it means that people have difficulty reaching the outcomes they work for or may not be able to reach them at all. Injustice also affects comprehension of reality, or worldview. Poverty in a society may exist for a long time without creating violence. But lasting poverty combined with the experience of discrimination and the perception that another group has privilege that one's own group does not often becomes a significant source of group conflict, as people come to experience relative deprivation as injustice.

Finally, another important psychological need is the need for *transcendence* of the self. This is a need to go beyond concern with and focus on the self. "Forms of transcendence include experiencing connection with nature, the universe, or spiritual entities, devoting oneself to the welfare of others or working for significant social change."[10] Although even very young children may experience *states* of transcendence, in the form of absorption in some activity, as a *need* transcendence becomes especially relevant and powerful *when basic needs have been fulfilled*. However, unfulfilled basic needs can lead to *pseudo-transcendence*. They can motivate people to relinquish a burdensome self, and fulfill other basic needs by giving themselves over to causes, beliefs, and movements.[11] The two forms of transcendence can look the same, but the focus of one is going beyond the self, of the other escaping the self and its circumstances. Turning to and giving oneself over even to destructive ideological movements can be motivated by genuine transcendence, based on the belief that one's people and group need one's help. Or it can be pseudo-transcendence, a response to one's unfulfilled needs.

These universal psychological needs are powerful. They press for satisfaction. They can be fulfilled constructively: When a child is loved and well cared for, the child will feel secure, feel good about himself or herself, and connected to other people. In tough times, these psychological needs can become unfulfilled or frustrated. For example, research showed that when during the difficult economic period beginning in 2007 parents lost their jobs, their children were strongly negatively affected not by having less, but by the fact their parents became preoccupied, unavailable, irritable, and hostile.[12] On the other hand, harmonious relations within a society, a sense of community and mutual support, can help fulfill most basic psychological needs even in difficult times. They strengthen identity, fulfill the need for connection, and provide a positive comprehension of reality. But while many families and immediate communities provide such experiences, many societies do not create social conditions and climates that help fulfill psychological needs of the population even in good times, much less in difficult times.

Destructive fulfillment of basic needs is a crucial element in leading to mass violence. One form of this is fulfilling needs in ways that harm other people. A child, an adult, or members of a group can gain a feeling of effectiveness, and a positive identity, by elevating themselves over others through dominance, force, and violence. As they do so, they may create a worldview, a way of understanding life, in which the use of dominance and force are right. The fulfillment of a psychological need is also destructive when it interferes with the fulfillment of another need. While the people who join in harming others feel more connected, their actions disconnect them from the group they harm. They often create disconnection within their own ethnic or religious group as well. In Rwanda, the first people who were killed in the genocide were Hutus seen as potentially opposing the genocide. But later people were also killed due to past personal conflict or enmity. Harming others also reduces security. It makes the group that was harmed more dangerous, as they (and the rest of the world) may respond with violence. To defend against that, violence against others often intensifies.

In summary, every need, and combinations of needs, can be fulfilled constructively or destructively. Constructive actions address the conditions that frustrate needs and provide satisfaction for them in ways that connect people, rather than turn them against each other. Destructive fulfillment reduces uncertainty and satisfies some needs but usually interferes with the fulfillment of other needs. It also potentially or directly harms other people and creates reactions by others that harm the self.

As a more elaborate example, aggression can reduce uncertainty and helplessness in difficult times (e.g., joblessness, scarcity). It can give people at least a temporary sense of security, make them feel effective, and strengthen their identity by elevating them over others. It can create connection among those who aggress together, and it can help develop an understanding of the world as one in which aggression can achieve important ends. Effective group aggression increases unity within the group and establishes dominance in relation to others. However, it creates disconnection from those who are harmed; it is harmful to the victims; it often leads to retaliation, if not by the victims, then by the rest of the world; it psychologically transforms and often wounds the perpetrators; and it usually does not address the social conditions that have frustrated material and psychological needs.

A human needs conception originally became influential with Maslow's work.[13] As noted, his conception of human needs was hierarchical: To fulfill a higher need, according to him, first lower needs have to be fulfilled. In contrast, I believe that all the needs I described are present from a very early age, and most are present in rudimentary forms even in infants. They are all important, although security may be primary, and a genuine need for transcendence may become important when other needs are fulfilled.[14]* They all play a role in the evolution of mass violence. Some others, such as J. W. Burton, Herbert Kelman, and Joseph Montville, have also stressed the importance of human needs, using a somewhat different conception of them to explain why group conflicts arise and are difficult to resolve.[15] Others[16] have proposed the quest for personal significance as a human need or aspiration to explain the motivation of terrorists.

Human needs also have important roles in prevention and reconciliation. As Laurie Anne Pearlman and her associates have shown, traumatic experiences in general, and victimization through violence in particular, frustrate psychological needs.[17] Healing from victimization requires the constructive fulfillment of needs, as does the prevention of group violence and reconciliation. Societies that successfully fulfill the material needs of their population, and enable them to fulfill their psychological needs constructively at least to a moderate degree, are likely to be harmonious and peaceful.[18]

Basic Needs and Personal Goals

As I describe conceptions of the origins and prevention of mass violence, and of reconciliation, I draw on micro-theories I have developed to explain important social phenomena, such as altruism and violence. One of these is the *theory of basic needs* and their constructive and destructive satisfaction that I just described. Another is a *theory of personal goals.*[19]

While we cannot get rid of basic psychological needs, socialization and experience can shape and vary their form, manifestation, modes of satisfaction and even intensity. Put another way, these needs are shaped by the culture, of the larger society and particular families, by experience in schools and with peers, and by individual inclinations. On the cultural level, for example, researchers have distinguished between individualist societies, which emphasize greater separation between the individual and the group and more focus on autonomy, and collectivist societies, which focus more on connection to the group and on valuing the goals of the group.[20] The former are primarily Western societies, the latter Eastern and African societies, which include Rwanda and Islamic countries. The need for autonomy is intensified in Western, individualistic cultures, making the need for connection more difficult to fulfil. The need for connection is strong in collectivist societies, making it more difficult to fulfill an individual's need for autonomy, since autonomous decisions create separation from others.

With socialization and experience, basic needs develop into personal goals. In some children the need for effectiveness may come to be primarily expressed and fulfilled through intellectual activity, in others in art or in sports, in still others in friendship and social relations. Identity may also be shaped in different ways.

Its focus may be about becoming a good person—good husband, father, a responsible and caring individual. For others being an effective person, perhaps good at making money, or at fixing things, or at having good judgment may become especially valued and important to the sense of who they are. For one person the need for connection may be habitually fulfilled by having fun with others, for another by helping, for a third by receiving help, for still another by being embedded in a community.

Values, which are beliefs about what is desirable, and attachment to desirable outcomes or personal goals, develop out of basic needs: being a moral or caring person, helping people (which may fulfill identity, effectiveness, connection, worldview and transcendence), or achievement (which may fulfill effectiveness, identity, and others). The values and the outcomes associated with them come to vary in their importance. The result is that each person has a hierarchy of goals, of valued outcomes. But such a hierarchy is relatively loose, not static or fixed. We respond to circumstance. Different values and goals will be called forth on the beach, at work, and when we face someone else's need. Circumstances *activate* particular goals, raising their importance in our current hierarchy, while lowering the importance of others. When a value/goal is low in a person's hierarchy, circumstances have to be especially powerful to activate it and make it dominant.

There are important applications of these principles to mass violence. As an example, let's consider mid-level leaders, either in a government that is moving toward increasing hostility toward some group, or in a bystander nation. The culture they are part of, the ideology that is propagated, the direction given by high-level leaders, their embeddedness in a system that demands loyalty, and their concern about their careers can all activate, that is, raise in importance, personal goals which dominate and preempt moral concerns or caring. As a result, they will not resist the increasing hostility, or the passivity of their governments. Prior training can make leaders aware of these dynamics, and especially combined with other training experiences I will discuss, can lead to more active bystandership by them.

There has been much discussion in psychology of the existence of "multiple selves" within the individual that lead him or her to different actions under different circumstances. Psychiatrist Robert Jay Lifton has suggested that the Auschwitz doctors could make "selections," sending many people directly to the gas chambers, and participate in direct killings (for example, through injections into the heart), yet remain loving and caring to their families, because they developed a separate Auschwitz self.[21] An alternative explanation I have proposed is that they had intensely different attitudes toward their families and toward Jews.[22] In addition, the circumstances at the camp and in their homes would activate very different need/value/goal combinations. However, long-term engagement with intense violence would have also affected their capacity to love people close to them.

Basic Needs and Other Psychological Processes:
Threat, Uncertainty, and Mortality Salience

The original frustration-aggression hypothesis, proposed by a group of scholars at Yale in the 1930s, stated that frustration—the inability to fulfill goals, or more specifically the interruption of behavior that aims to fulfill goals—leads to hostility and aggression. Over time experimental research has shown that frustration can lead to aggression, but it does not inevitably do so.[23] In the conception I am presenting, *neither difficult life conditions, nor the resulting frustration of material and psychological needs, leads directly to group violence. Instead, the psychological effects and social processes they give rise to can begin an evolution that over time leads to extreme violence.*

Being attacked is an even stronger and more consistent source of aggression. Social psychologist Thomas Pettigrew summarized the view that threat to a group, collective threat and the fear it generates, is a core influence in intergroup violence.[24] These can lead to actions—by Israelis, Palestinians, the United States after 9/11—in the course of which groups can abandon their deeply held principles, such as respect for the rights and lives of people, especially those seen as "them," outside the group. Not only actual attack, but the belief that someone *intends* to harm or attack you, has been found to increase aggression toward the potential harmdoer.[25] For us humans, ideas, beliefs, what we imagine and fear will happen, have very great force. The effects of real, or expected and feared material and psychological losses are great—of land, jobs and livelihood, a stable, normal life, ideals to live by. In violent conflict territory, power, influence, image, and prestige can be lost.[26] The loss of territory is not only material, since groups often see the territory on which they live as part of who they are. Both actual attack and the expectation of it frustrate basic psychological needs, for security, and identity and effectiveness if people fear they cannot protect themselves or will suffer loss and humiliation.

In Rwanda, a significant economic downturn, a history of Tutsi dominance before 1959, violence against Hutus in neighboring Burundi by the minority Tutsis who ruled that country, and a civil war in which a mainly Tutsi rebel army successfully fought against the Hutu government, created uncertainty and fear. This was enhanced by politicians and the government with propaganda that claimed that Tutsis would take away the property of Hutus, and kill and subjugate them if they won the war. Such fear was also created in Germany toward the Jews, and toward intended victims in many countries, even in cases, such as Germany, when the target group had no power and no hostile intentions.

Uncertainty, not knowing, not being able to predict events, greatly threaten the fulfillment of material and psychological needs. People often don't know whether they will be physically safe, will have food and shelter, or will be degraded and humiliated by the conditions of life or by other people. They don't know if they will be able to take effective action to protect themselves or accomplish important goals. Change, unpredictability, and chaos challenge their understanding of reality and their place in the world.[27]

Such a climate makes destructive need satisfaction more likely. It leads people to think about other groups in terms of stereotypes, to see them as homogeneous, to strip them of their individuality and humanity. They turn these other groups into categories—Jews, Bosniaks (the term used for Bosnian Muslims)— and apply derogatory terms to them, such as cockroach (as Tutsis were called). Threat and fear also lead people to be less trusting, more suspicious. In collective threat people share these thoughts and feelings with each other, which confirms, maintains, and strengthens them. They also become less open to information that contradicts existing negative beliefs about another group. Moderate uncertainty, novelty, and complexity can be appealing. Intense uncertainty is aversive. But even low-level uncertainty is aversive when it has to do with the impact of a changing and difficult world on the ability to protect and provide for oneself and one's family and to fulfill important goals.

Scarcity, physical threat, the frustration of basic psychological needs can remind people of their mortality. Cultural anthropologist Ernest Becker[28] has proposed that human beings are unable to accept their mortality. In his view much human violence, for example, human sacrifice that in earlier times was practiced in many societies, had to do with the illusion of immortality and attendant feeling of power that people gained through power over the lives of others.

A contemporary theory in social psychology, terror management theory, has built on this idea. According to it, cultural worldviews, the beliefs and values of their group, provide people with meaning and purpose, something greater than oneself, and protect them against existential anxiety. These worldviews can be secular, or they can be religious. People who feel they are valued members of their group or society will have high self-esteem, which protects them from anxiety related to their awareness of mortality. Others who hold different worldviews, or in some way challenge one's own, threaten the capacity to manage anxiety.[29]

Research shows that "mortality salience," reminding or asking people to contemplate and write about their death, or describe what thoughts death gives rise in them or what will happen to them physically when they die, has wide ranging effects. It increases prejudice against groups other than one's own. It also leads people to report stronger belief in, or stronger readiness to defend, cultural beliefs and symbols.[30] According to proponents of this theory, religion may be an especially strong buffer against existential anxiety. In one study, Christian fundamentalists and non-fundamentalists were exposed to passages from the Christian Bible that were contradictory to each other. The authors describe the belief that "the Christian Bible is error free and literally true" as an essential tenet of Christian fundamentalism.[31] Afterward, in completing sentences, fundamentalist Christians made more reference to death and death-related thoughts than did non-fundamentalists. In another study, Islamic students approved more of a martyrdom attack by another student, and expressed more willingness to join the cause, when they were led to think about their own mortality.[32] Psychologist Tom Pyszczynski and his associates summarize a variety of research as showing that "in the face of elevated concerns about death, people are more prone to dehumanizing, vilifying, and supporting the killing of worldview-threatening others."[33]

Threat to life, which is presumably activated by deeply thinking about one's death, is a profound threat. But it is unclear as yet to what extent the effects of mortality salience are different from other significant threats to security, or even to identity, or realistic threats to existence without direct reminders of death.[34*] We don't know the relative impact of people thinking about death or facing actual threats of various kinds in the real world.

In addition, people differ in how they respond to mortality threat. This is consistent with the theory, which suggests that in response to such threat people will defend their worldviews, and worldviews vary. Conservatives and liberals respond differently. People can respond positively to the ingroup, which carries their values, after mortality threat; American students made greater charitable contributions in support of American projects. In another study when people were reminded, after thinking about death, of compassionate, caring values of their own religion or culture, they were less likely to express negative attitudes and to support violence against outgroups.[35] This is consistent with the evident power of leaders and the media to orient people to threat and to shape both the extent people experience threat and their reactions to it. People also have this power in relation to each other.

I have proposed in response to Becker's original ideas that vulnerability to reminders of mortality, in particular in real life, may be greater in people who struggle with life, who feel less able, less effective, whose basic needs have been unfulfilled.[36] In a relevant study, older people who functioned better in cognitive and social realms were less affected by reminders of death than older people who functioned less well.[37] Confident, secure people, reasonably satisfied with their lives, and with their ability to fulfill basic needs, may be less vulnerable to reminders of mortality and perhaps to imagined (or possibly event to actual) threats in general.

Threat leads people to find safety in groups. As we shall see, as a group they tend to scapegoat others and turn to destructive ideologies, which are new beliefs and worldviews, often connected to and arising from old ones. These reactions reduce uncertainty and feelings of vulnerability, and at least temporarily fulfill basic needs, but also lead people to turn against others. They can be starting points for the evolution of group violence.

Humiliation and the Multiplicity of Influences in Group Violence

Severe losses, bad treatment by others—anything that diminishes identity, self-respect, and dignity—can lead to the experience of shame and humiliation.

So can powerlessness, especially if seen as imposed by others. Shame and humiliation have been suggested as important in contributing to group violence. Genocide scholar Adam Jones quotes Thomas Friedman, the *New York Times* columnist: "If I have learned one thing covering world affairs it is this: the single most under-appreciated force in human relations is humiliation."[38] Evelin Lindner, an originator of humiliation studies, defines humiliation as "... the enforced lowering of a person or group: a process of subjugation that damages or strips away pride, honour, and dignity. To be humiliated is to be placed .... in a situation that is markedly at odds with one's sense of entitlement ... (it is a situation that forces) ... the victim into passivity."[39] Robert Jay Lifton wrote: "Humiliation involves feelings of shame and disgrace, as well as helplessness in the face of abuse at the hands of a stronger party."[40]

Shame is especially destructive because, as sociologist Thomas Scheff wrote, it is an emotion that is difficult to acknowledge and talk about, but unacknowledged, it exerts a powerful influence.[41] Scheff and Lindner distinguish between shame that is the result of a person's own actions, and humiliation that is due to the actions of others. A child may feel shame when unable to fulfill a task, and humiliation as a result of unfavourable comparison by others. But shame and humiliation are deeply connected. People tend to believe that others see them as less, as incompetent, in the wake of mistakes or failures, or see them as morally deficient when they don't live up to certain standards. While moderately positive self-concepts may provide a buffer against these beliefs, feelings of superiority may exacerbate them. Individuals, groups, or nations that pride themselves on their power and superiority react strongly when events disconfirm their beliefs about themselves or their image in others' eyes.[42]

Shame and humiliation give rise to the motivation to reassert identity and dignity, often by violent means. This may be especially so in cultures that prize honor. Injuries—real or imagined—at the hands of another group can give rise to the motivation for revenge. Revenge seems a response to some combination of loss and humiliation. Soldiers in war who commit atrocities, such as killing civilians or raping women, have sometimes suffered significant losses to their unit not long before it. This was true of U.S. soldiers who killed a large number of civilians in My Lai during the Vietnam War.[43] Revenge is often an important motive for terrorist actions. Louise Richardson[44] describes how members of the Irish Republican Army responded to the killing of a comrade, or a relative, with fury and retaliatory violence. When it is possible to regain by constructive means what has been lost or when compensatory gains occur to reverse losses[45] and fulfill basic needs, violence becomes less likely. However, regaining what has been lost in destructive ways, such as through violence, contributes to the evolution of violence.

According to Lindner, humiliation is the result of hierarchical arrangements in society, with people above and below. Humiliation arises partly from the awareness in people who are "below" of their subordinate role and the lack of respect they have been enduring, once values of hierarchy are replaced by values of human rights and equal dignity. In Lindner's view this has been happening around the world—although she correctly implies that much of it so far is an ideal rather than reality. But people now are often aware, when it is happening, that these ideals of equality and dignity are violated. Humiliation also partly arises from the shame of people Lindner calls "subalterns," those below in the hierarchy, for having admired those above them and acquiesced to their superiority. "The cruelest behaviour may ... be exhibited by .... subaltern actors attempting to 'cleanse' themselves of inferiority and elite-admiration."[46]

Lindner suggests that it is because of the desire or need to make up for humiliation that genocide victims are often "dehumanised and humiliated, before being exterminated." "The Rwandan genocide of 1994 offers an intricate and gruesome catalogue of practices aimed at destroying victims' dignity. The most literal way to achieve this was to cut the legs of Tutsis (whose 'superiority' was symbolised by their average greater height), or to sever the Achilles tendon so they would be forced to crawl. These actions not only shortened Tutsi bodies, but 'cut them down to size' in a metaphorical sense, obliterating the source of their alleged arrogance."[47] For other likely reasons for such actions, see Chapter 9 on perpetrators.

The experience of humiliation can arise in response to events or conditions, or it can be instigated. Lindner refers to humiliation-entrepreneurs. Just as leaders can be in the vanguard of scapegoating and creating ideologies, so they can remind the group of humiliating experiences and instigate anger, rage, and the desire for revenge, as they did in Rwanda. In contrast she and others point to South Africa and the leadership of Nelson Mandela as an example of constructive, humane ways of addressing past humiliation, through cooperation rather than retribution.

Conditions that are intensely humiliating can have multiple effects. They can frustrate all basic needs, create threat, feelings of injustice and/or relative deprivation, and make people feel aware of their mortality. They can make people feel greatly endangered and helpless to protect themselves, the hallmarks of trauma. Under humiliating conditions, it is difficult for people to fulfill their goals. It is this aggregate that gives humiliation its motive force.

Theory and research in psychology and other social sciences attempt to identify specific psychological and social processes that underlie human behavior. But it is unlikely that a single process ever causes or appropriately accounts for group behavior such as genocide, violent conflict, or terrorism. Threat and fear, diminishing others or being diminished, past victimization and the wounds it leaves behind, and other factors jointly lead people to mistrust the intentions of another group, to be unwilling to compromise in order to resolve conflict, and to turn against others.

But there are circumstances in which a single factor has a particularly powerful role. When humiliation has that role, gaining power and influence, or simply inclusion and having a voice, can prevent violence. This was the case in South Africa after the shift in power to the black majority, the powerless and humiliated becoming powerful. But what happens after a shift depends on varied factors. In Rwanda, after power shifted to the Hutus in 1959, they engaged in discrimination and violence against Tutsis. The additional conditions required for the prevention of violence, such as healing from past victimization, confidence by Hutus in their new power, as well as positive leadership, did not exist.

To the extent repression is humiliating, people in Arab countries are humiliated by their own governments. To the extent discrimination and prejudice create the feeling of being a "subaltern" and on the outside, many Muslims in Europe are likely to feel humiliated. Being dependent on material and social support from the government may add to humiliation. Being needy and receiving help from others who devalue you diminishes your feelings of effectiveness, dignity, and self-worth.

Understanding and gaining a perspective on how their circumstances have developed, and understanding the inherent complexity of their situation due to migration, religious difference, and the psychological impact of terrorism on their host populations, can be temporary steps in normalizing the psychology of Muslim minorities. Many of them entered their host countries as migrant laborers; their leaders could help them appreciate the host countries' current kindness in providing material support. Inclusion, acceptance, and empathy by European governments, and Europeans in general, can help reduce the social, material, and psychological difficulties that Muslims face. Beyond words, significant practical efforts are required to enable immigrants and their descendents to acculturate in their new countries, without having to give up their identities. Both conditions that fulfill basic material and psychological needs and reconciliation are required for the reestablishment of dignity and positive relations.

Types of Difficult Life Conditions

Poverty is often referred to as a source of group violence. However, in Barbara Harff's statistical analysis of the causes of genocide, poverty was not one of the contributing conditions.[48] Except perhaps when extreme, poverty may not create by itself the psychological consequences that start the evolution toward extreme violence. But substantial *inequality* in resources can lead to hostility between groups and then to violence. It is a significant component of conflict. Poverty, inequality, and lack of opportunity also tend to make people more vulnerable to incitement to violence.

Scott Straus[49] looked at the relatively small variation in the time of the onset of the genocide in Rwanda in different regions of the country and found that it did not have an earlier onset in poorer areas. Nor did he find that poorer people were more likely to participate in killing. However, they were likely to be among those who killed the most people, to be the especially violent, those he called the "thugs."

While poverty may not have a substantial direct influence, my studies of cases of genocide and mass killings indicate that *deteriorating* economic conditions have often been present before mass violence. In the years preceding the Rwandan genocide, the price of both coffee and tin, the country's primary exports, greatly decreased in the international markets.[50] Psychological adaptation is a powerful force, and people can live with having relatively little for long periods of time. But economic deterioration frustrates both material needs and the psychological needs of whole groups of people for security, effectiveness, and identity. People worry that they will be unable to take care of themselves and their families.

Economic deterioration has many components. It usually includes unemployment. In some cases it includes hyperinflation, money losing value at a tremendous rate. A loaf of bread may cost five times as much as it did the day before. In Germany during the depression in the late 1920s and early 1930s there was hyperinflation. Money that bought dinner for a family one day may not even buy a cup of soup the next day. Tent cities rose up. Economic problems intensify the relative deprivation that less privileged groups may experience in normal times. They also intensify resentment, when members of a devalued minority, such as Tutsis, Jews, or Armenians, are seen as well off, whether that perception is based on reality or stereotypes. A group of Rwandan killers interviewed by journalist Jean Hatzfeld often referred to the wealth of Tutsis—their cows and other possessions.[51]

In working in Rwanda we found that people focus on poverty as *the* difficult life condition. However, it is economic *deterioration* that is significant, as represented by unemployment, depression, inflation, and an increase in the poverty of already poor people. And it is only one of the difficult life conditions. Political disorganization, as well as great and rapid societal changes, including changes in technology, culture, and ways of life, are also important. All of these conditions can create great uncertainty and insecurity.

Different types of life problems in a society often occur together. Every possible one was present in Germany before the Nazis gained power. Germany's defeat in World War I had a great impact on the German people, on their identity and self-concept as members of a nation that was proud of its strength and power. This impact was magnified by leaders who hid from the population that the war was being lost. It was also magnified by the huge number of German soldiers killed during the war (as were soldiers of other countries) and by the trauma of the soldiers who returned after fighting endless and futile battles as armies moved back and force over the same terrain.

A peace treaty was imposed on Germany that many Germans experienced as humiliating and that created material difficulties. Soon after the war, the Kaiser abdicated, and a revolution overthrew the monarchy and established a democratic republic, which in a strongly authoritarian country experiencing great life problems was at odds with the preference of many people for a leader with strong authority. While autonomy is an important need, when people are not accustomed to its exercise, the absence of clear guidance in difficult times, under chaotic conditions, can be frustrating.

A worldwide depression also strongly affected Germany. France, a historical enemy, dissatisfied with the rate of postwar reparation payments by Germany, occupied the Ruhr industrial district, a further humiliation. In response, the Germans sabotaged industrial production, which increased economic problems. Many political movements that emerged strongly opposed the republic. Militias were fighting each other. The conflict between the Nazis and Communists was especially intense.

The combination of different components of difficult life conditions, often with additional elements such as war or civil war, was also present in many other countries where mass killing or genocide have taken place, such as Cambodia, Turkey, Rwanda, the Congo, and others. I've already mentioned the economic deterioration that occurred in Rwanda when the price of its main exports, tin and coffee, greatly declined in world markets. But in addition, in one of the most densely populated countries in the world and with increasing over-population, there was increasing competition for land ownership. There was unemployment. There was a civil war, with some engagement by outside parties, such as support by France for the government. In a country not accustomed to political freedom, new political parties emerged, with fierce competition among them. Some parties split into more moderate and more ideologically extreme Hutu power–oriented branches.

As part of their vying for power, some of the parties created youth branches, providing young men with material support as well as a sense of community in these difficult times. It was some of these groups, especially the youth group associated with the ruling party and with an extreme Hutu power party, that were later transformed into the militias, the Interahamwe, that became one of the primary killers in the genocide.[52]

Societal Change and Personal Dislocation

Let us examine in greater detail the significant psychological and social impact that great societal changes, even of a positive kind, can have on a population. In Germany, as the revolution changed a hierarchical, authority-oriented country from a monarchy to a free-spirited republic, many political parties emerged, including extreme radical ones, with intense competition among them. This conservative society also saw the emergence of great social and cultural free-dom at this time: Homosexuality became more open and visible, and expression-ist art emerged. In Rwanda, after the 1990 invasion by the Rwandan Patriotic Front (RPF), the multiparty system that emerged in 1991 added to the civil war and serious economic problems to create uncertainty and fear and to frustrate basic needs. For the first time in a historically authoritarian country people could make political choices. But the competition and hostility between the parties were intense. A speech by a political leader associated with the ruling party that later became infamous as an instigator of genocide incited people not only against Tutsis but also against a competing, more moderate political party. In Germany, Rwanda, and elsewhere, the social and political disorganization added to people's feelings of threat and fear.

Scott Straus argues, both on the basis of his interviews with killers in prison and on the basis of his study of Rwandan history, that violence against Tutsis— in 1961, 1963–1964, and the early 1970s—was always in response to internal social disorganization and uncertainty, created by shifts in power and thus unstable social conditions. But on occasion it was also associated with incursions by Tutsis from neighboring countries, refugees who left in response to earlier violence or their children, a source of threat and anti-Tutsi feelings.

Political changes in a society affect people both because of the impact of change and because of the conflicts and competition for power they often generate. As a result, transitions from an autocratic to a democratic system, from a one-party to a multiparty system, as well as transitions that occur when a country gains independence from a colonial power, are times of danger. New institutions are needed and old ones need to be transformed. Often the party still in power or having just gained power allows only limited democracy. There is uncertainty as well as unfulfilled hopes and expectations. If the dominant party practices at least informal power sharing, if instead of discrimination it promotes access of less privileged groups to jobs and education, if it allows at least some degree of pluralism, the society can move toward increasing democracy.[53]

The psychological impact of uncertainty and societal disorganization would be especially great in countries where people have been accustomed to and developed a dependence on strong authority. This was the case in Rwanda, Germany, Turkey, and Cambodia. Overly strong respect for authority makes mass violence more likely. Its prevention requires addressing the uncertainty and insecurity associated with transitions in power. It requires social systems and cultures in which human connections, and institutions and responsive policies, help limit the challenging psychological effects of change.

Even without violence, all basic needs can be frustrated by great political changes, as well as by changes in technology, moral values and standards of behavior, and relationships between different groups, including between men and women. Even "good" changes can be difficult as they challenge identity and worldview. In the United States, a free, individualist society, feminism, a move toward greater equality for women, with more expansive views of their nature, rights, and roles in the family, workplace, and society, required substantial adjustment by individuals and society, an adjustment still ongoing. Men and women had to relearn both who they are and how to effectively relate to each other. They had to adjust their understanding of the world. Many men began to do housework, which given their earlier role definition was difficult for them. They had to learn to live with working and professional women, who were more independent and assertive, and to spend more time with their children. Even people who see feminism and the changes it brought as good had to learn to adapt to it.

The same has been true of changes in civil rights and the improved position of African Americans in the United States. One consequence is more interaction between whites and blacks, in the course of which, research finds, many white people work hard at not appearing prejudiced. Presumably it is because of this effort that their interaction with black people is often exhausting for them, cognitively and emotionally. As new standards of conduct develop, it takes time and experience for new ways of behaving to become natural and habitual.

Adapting to great change is always challenging, more so in cultures with firmly established traditions and roles. In the Congo it is difficult to find work and to manage everyday affairs. Women seem to handle the chaos and difficulty better, which may create hostility in men. The difficulties have been apparent for Muslim minorities living in more gender equalitarian societies, for Europeans living with substantial Muslim minorities, and for Iranians during the modernization and Westernization programs that occurred under the Shah. For many Muslims—and religious people of other faiths—some of the changes in the contemporary world are contrary to deeply held religious or moral values. While Europeans see the restrictions on women's lives in Muslim families as wrong, Muslims see the sexual mores in the European societies as perversions.[54] The challenge of social change is greater when, as with the Shah's programs, they occur in a highly traditional country and under a repressive system.

While certain orderly culture changes, for example, increase in pluralism, ultimately serve the prevention of violence, great and especially sudden changes can instigate violence. Probably a secondary but still important reason for Islamic hostility toward the United States is that the United States is a primary source of great social changes, in technology as well as in culture, arts, and morality. This creates hostility both because change is difficult to handle and because some of these changes are seen as corrupting.

When people move to another country, even in large enough numbers to have their own community, the family and group dynamics are usually changed in their new situation. Among Muslims moving to the Netherlands or other European countries, the young, the next generation, are greatly affected. They have seen the helplessness of their fathers, who often lost their jobs as economies in their adopted country changed and who live on social welfare. Their parents are outsiders in this different world. Often they are the parents' translators and guides.

Vamik Volkan is a psychiatrist who has worked on resolving group conflicts in many settings. On the basis of 150 interviews in Kuwait after its liberation from the invasion by Iraq, Volkan wrote about fathers who were humiliated by Iraqi solders. Whether this happened in front of their children or when the children were absent, they did not talk about it to their children, but distanced themselves in an effort to hide or deny their sense of shame. "Frustrated by the distant and humiliated fathers who would not talk to their sons about the traumas of the invasion, they (the sons) linked themselves together and expressed their frustration in gangs."[55] They engaged in gang activities not known in Kuwait before that. In the Netherlands, young boys, mainly Moroccans, roam the streets in shifting combinations, going into stores and taking property, harassing and sometimes beating up passersby.[56] I see the experience of Moroccan boys in relation to their fathers as psychologically similar to those in Kuwait. Groups of other youths provide them with the connection and identity so badly needed during this time of development.

The above analysis has relevance to young Muslims in the Netherlands as well as in other European countries. Their family dynamics, their own role in their families and their relationship both to their group and the larger society, all seem affected. As members of the second generation, many may be reasonably acculturated but not truly accepted. They experience devaluation and discrimination as youths and young adults. This makes it difficult for them to develop their identity and positive connections to their group and to the host society, and it limits their feelings of effectiveness. As a result, they are open to potentially destructive ideas and connection to groups that help them fulfill basic needs. Young people are more likely to join destructive ideological movements that lead to violence against other groups. They often have a role in terrorism, as well as genocide.

In 2007 journalist Shiv Malik published an article about Mohammed Siddique Khan, regarded by some as the main suicide bomber in the London subway attacks.[57] Based on interviews with many people who knew Kahn, including his own brother, Malik writes that Kahn was considered a "well-integrated, middle class Briton." He was middle class, but apparently not well integrated. His parents came from Pakistan, he knew little of their lives there, spoke their language poorly. He was disconnected from his roots and from British culture and society. He progressively developed a strong connection to Wahhabi Islam, the extreme form of Islam practiced in Saudi Arabia, and to its worldview and to people who propagated it. The changes in the life of his family and his experience with living between different worlds opened him to a movement that provided him with identity, connection, and understanding of the world. It also created a psychological orientation, an attitude toward Britain, in which terrorism became a possibility. In my exploration of different reasons that people are attracted to terrorism, he is primarily an example of what I call a "lost soul," secondarily a "respondent," affected by his negative experiences (see Chapter 9).

In his book *Leaderless Jihad*, Marc Sageman has analyzed the public material available on about 500 people who participated in terrorist actions. His sources included the media, trials and trial transcripts, and the Internet. The people were members of what he calls Al-Qaeda central, and its offshoots, what he calls the Al-Qaeda social movement. Of this group 60% "joined a terrorist organization while living in a country in which they did not grow up. An additional 20 per cent were the sons ... or grandsons ... of Muslim immigrants to the West."[58] Altogether, 84% were dislocated, whether alone or with their families.

Sageman starts his book with a case study of the man accused and convicted of abducting *Wall Street Journal* reporter Daniel Pearl. The man was big, strong, intelligent, and charming. He was born in London of Pakistani parents, 5 years after his family moved there. He later described persistent racist attacks by his peers, being rejected and called names such as a "Paki bastard." When he was 13 years old, his family moved back to Pakistan for 3 years, where he also felt on the outside. His frustrated needs for identity and connection, as they combined with later experiences, became building blocks for his turn to terrorism.

Conflict as an Instigator of Mass Violence

In Chapter 3, I discussed the various sources of group conflict. Here I will probe them further and review ways that persistent conflict is an instigator for mass violence.

First, competition for resources, whether material or psychological (security, identity, whose values to live by), can by itself lead to violence—although it is especially likely to do so through the other influences described below, such as devaluation, and ideologies that elevate a group's rights and claims. Second, conflicts between groups frustrate basic needs, especially if the conflicts are persistent. Violent conflicts create uncertainty, threat, and fear and intensify negative views of the other group. But they can also affirm one's identity as a group member and one's connection to the group, fulfilling basic needs—often in a destructive way. Third, persistent conflict usually creates social and political changes, and often creates economic problems as well. In other words, it creates difficult life conditions, for one or both parties. This is the case in active conflict between dominant and subordinate groups, as well as in other conflicts.

Difficult life conditions, by intensifying already existing conflict, enhance its instigating potential for violence. Material issues are heightened, and the other is blamed more. While difficult life conditions and conflict can each separately instigate conditions, in combination they are powerful instigators of the psychological and social processes that can lead to the evolution of extreme violence.

Structural conflict, such as unjust social arrangements and discrimination, or repression, can be an instigating condition for either party. A dominant group may scapegoat the less privileged group in response to difficult life conditions or act to defend its status and position. The less privileged group may respond to discrimination and bad treatment. Contact between groups in conflict can be limited, or skewed by structural arrangements. Not knowing each other makes it easier for people to devalue each other.

"Conflicts" in which one group wants land or other resources that belong to another group have led to the destruction of some indigenous peoples (whether through actual violence, or creating conditions that lead to disease and starvation). In some such cases, material interests were the primary instigators.[59] But very frequently the role of material interests in conflict that evolves into mass killing or genocide is deeply intertwined with psychological needs and motives. Possessing material goods contributes to feelings of safety, and more so in difficult times. Control over resources contributes to safety, feelings of effectiveness (and control or power), and affirms identity.

While greed is a common human characteristic, it is constructed to a substantial extent out of psychological elements and is shaped by culture and experience. Behavior that appears to be motivated by greed often has other psychological roots. Robert Frank, an economist, has proposed that a core human motive is to do better than others.[60] A psychoanalyst who had many clients from Wall Street found that, more than money, their motivation was to do well, and better than others, for which pay was a measurable sign.[61] This is consistent with the finding that doing worse than others, relative deprivation, affects people more than simply having little.[62] Doing worse materially, in either position or prestige, can be humiliating. Doing worse relative to others with whom we habitually compare ourselves can lead to intense comparison distress.[63]

The cooperation of the population and the involvement of some direct perpetrators in mass violence are enhanced by the opportunity to take over the property of the victims. This was true even in communist countries, where people moved into the apartments of those who were executed or imprisoned in labor camps. A U.S. consul in Turkey wrote at the time of the genocide of the Armenians: "A crowd of Turkish women and children follow the police about like a lot of vultures and seize anything they can lay their hands on and when the more valuable things are carried out of the house by the police they rush in and take the balance. I see this ... every day with my own eyes."[64] There will be more detail on such behavior in Rwanda in the chapter on perpetrators.

Governments, corporations, and groups of people have taken actions that severely impacted indigenous groups. We don't know whether in such cases difficult life conditions had some role, because past research has not explored it. The destruction of the Ache Indians in Paraguay and violence against Native Americans in the United States were certainly shaped by self-interest, as well as by a colonial ideology and attitudes of superiority and special rights over local people. The influences I will later describe in detail had significant roles, such as devaluation, the absence of pluralism (at least in the sense that such groups didn't have a voice in the public domain), and some form of ideology, including sometimes a "development ideology" that stresses the value and rightness of developing land and natural resources, and/or a "legitimizing ideology" that stresses the superiority and therefore special rights of the dominant group.

As shown in my description of the genocide in Rwanda, conflict between Hutus and Tutsi had an important role in leading to violence and then to genocide. This was conflict over power, wealth, and resources. It was also the persisting effect of past conflict, the subordination, hard work, and deprivation of Hutus during the Belgian colonial era. It was also a conflict of identities, again rooted in the past, in Tutsi dominance and the Belgians elevating Tutsis, not only in power and influence but also as having greater worth, as being more attractive and intelligent, as a superior race. The conflict greatly intensified as in turn Hutus discriminated against and engaged in repeated mass killings of Tutsis. It intensified further after the Rwandan Patriotic Front entered the country from Uganda, a civil war began, and Hutus again started to kill Tutsis living in Rwanda.[65]

Analyses of mass violence since 1945 show that conflicts between dominant, more powerful groups, and subordinate, less powerful and poorer ones, have been an important source of them.[66] A minority ruling over a majority, an inherently conflictual situation, is also a contributor to mass violence.[67] This condition exists now in Rwanda, increasing the importance of reconciliation and of policies and practices that reduce the danger of new violence.

Conflict of varied kinds has a role in the relationship between ethnic Dutch and Muslim minorities. One is a conflict over resources, as the state provides substantial support for Muslim families, schools, and other organizations. Another has to do with discrimination against Muslims. Still another is a conflict of ideologies, worldviews, and ways of life. The Dutch believe that Muslims hold views that are incompatible with a liberal democratic system. They resent that Muslims turn to and are often guided by religious authorities in Muslim countries, rather than identifying with Dutch society.

Many Muslims regard homosexuality as a perversion, and open sexuality as contrary to the way men and women ought to relate. Both are accepted and respected in the liberal Dutch society. The Dutch regard the subservient role and limited freedom of women in Muslim families and society as contrary to their values, ways of life, and laws.[68] Forced marriages of girls are unacceptable to the Dutch. So is, of course, the murder of girls who are seen as having dishonoured their families through relations, sexual or otherwise, with men outside the group. While I am not aware of this in Holland, it has been reported elsewhere in Europe. Research has shown that the Dutch would like Muslims to assimilate, to absorb Dutch mores completely, rather than to be integrated, to be connected both to Dutch society and culture and to their own. Muslims, in contrast, would like to be integrated, which is true generally of Muslim minorities elsewhere in Europe, but believe that the Dutch think they want to be separate from Dutch society.[69]

Many observers note that Islam has shown itself adaptable to varied contexts. This may be easier in countries such as the United States and Australia, which are traditionally countries of immigrants, than in Europe. Differences between Muslims and local inhabitants are often also due to culture and class. In the Netherlands, Turkish Muslims are better adjusted, with higher employment and lower crime rates, than Moroccans.[70]

U.S. Muslims are educated and economically well off, while the majority of European Muslims have come from rural areas and have little education. Many U.S. Muslims are descendents of earlier immigrants. Prior to 9/11 there have been no major problems in the United States between Muslims and other inhabitants.

In Europe, there is a movement to create a European Muslim culture. Muslim clerics and other leaders have made proclamations about the need for greater equality for women within Islam.[71] Still, Muslims wanting to maintain their identity and values, while living harmoniously with the dominant group in primarily secular Christian societies, at a time of anxiety about jihad and terrorism, is a challenge for both parties. Their host societies are greatly concerned about the intrusion of Muslim values and practices. The Bishop of Canterbury's suggestion in 2008 that perhaps family matters in the Muslim community could be adjudicated in family courts guided by sharia, Muslim religious law, brought a great outcry.

Conflict is a natural part of life, both between individuals and groups. The existence of the right institutions, especially democratic ones, can help in the peaceful resolution of conflicting goals, enabling people to live together in reasonable harmony. However, when important aspects of conflicts are not addressed or successfully resolved, increasingly frustrated basic needs, the beginning of violence, and intensifying mistrust and hostility make the conflict increasingly intractable.

The Local Context

It is important for prevention of group violence to look at conflict and hostility not only between groups as wholes but also in local, specific contexts. Political scientist Severine Autesserre describes as a significant component of the intense violence in the Congo local disputes over the ownership of land required to secure material existence, intensified by the desire to acquire the rich natural resources that are part of the land.[72] That many of these conflicts involve people belonging to different ethnic groups, including Congolese originally from the Congo and those of Rwandan origin, and the conflict between Hutu and Tutsi, contributes to ongoing violence. Historian Omar Bartov,[73] in analyzing the way genocide against the Jews was perpetrated in the town of Buczacz, in Poland, describes the complex history of relations between Jews and other local inhabitants, Poles and Ukrainians. Envy, prejudice, and past violence against Jews all had a role in the enthusiastic participation of the local population in the killing of Jews, even more extensive than the wide-ranging participation of Hutus in Rwanda in killing Tutsis.

Counterterrorism expert David Kilcullen[74] brings the analysis of the local to the emergence of guerrilla movements at various places around the world, what might be regarded as local terrorist networks. He has lived and worked alongside villagers in West Java and has been involved in Afghanistan and Iraq, advising both Secretary of State Condoleezza Rice and General Petraeus. He stresses the importance of fighting terrorism both at the global and the local levels.

He describes how Al-Qaeda takes over communities. Its members move there, marry, start businesses, and once they are established and trusted, recruit fighters. When they are attacked by outsiders, for reasons of loyalty, excitement, and pride the local people fight with them. Presumably, local people are also affected by their circumstances, such as poverty, the absence of education that would provide them with an expanded vision of the world, and lack of skills and opportunity to improve their lives. These make them vulnerable to ideological influences, which in Pakistan and Afghanistan are advanced by madrassas, a significant number of which teach an extreme form of Islam and jihad.[75] The Taliban also protect the poppy fields, which provide many people with their livelihood, and help them take the poppy to market.

Effective "counterinsurgency" requires security, both in the sense of alternative livelihoods and in terms of the presence of security forces. Kilcullen suggests it requires long-term engagement with the community and alliance with its leaders, and helping populations to develop the capacity to defend themselves. The elements of prevention I describe in Part II of the book are also applicable to such contexts, including constructive visions that offer hope.

War and Revolution as Contributors to Mass Violence

War has some of the same psychological effects as the other difficult life conditions. Especially when a nation is losing a war, basic needs will be frustrated—in the population, but initially even more on the part of the leadership, who may be most aware that the war is being lost. However, when leaders hide from the population that the war is being lost, the shock of the loss and its psychological impact, as in Germany after World War I, can be especially great.

In war usually at least some rules of law are suspended, and the rules of war take over. Unfortunately, people rarely follow just-war principles, which proclaim that only defensive war among combatants is just and that civilians must not be harmed. In the absence of their influence, violence easily expands. Inherent in the intense violence of war is speedy progression along a continuum of destruction (see Chapter 6). Even greater and crueler violence, such as genocide, becomes easier and more likely. Mass killing or genocide not infrequently takes place during some type of war. War can be an instigating condition, giving rise to the psychological reactions and social processes that lead to genocide against the opponent in the war, usually jointly with cultural and other influences. The civil war in Rwanda was an instigating condition for the genocide in this way, creating threat, fear, and frustrating basic needs.

But genocide during war is not necessarily against the enemy in the war. Turkey during World War I and Germany during World War II perpetrated genocide against a third party. As violence evolves, it relatively easily spreads in new directions. War makes genocide more likely against a group that is a scapegoat, or an ideological enemy, or against whom there are grievances due to past conflict. War also creates a cover, making mass killing less evident and in the chaos of war bringing less reaction by bystanders.

The actions of Palestinians and Israelis can be categorized as war. The Palestinians engage in violence that is within their means as a people without an army: terror, suicide bombings, and the killing of civilians. The Israelis respond to these violent acts not as criminal behavior that comes under the review of the justice system, but as acts of war. Without establishing through due process who is responsible for Palestinian violence, the Israelis destroy the houses of suspected terrorists, imprison many people, and sometimes attack hostile parties such as leaders of Hamas or known terrorists. In this process, they kill civilians, sometimes in large numbers, such as during the attack on Gaza in 2008–2009.

The view of the French scholar Jacques Semelin of the "politicization of war" adds another explanation for how war contributes to genocide. In the French revolution during the late eighteenth century, there was mass conscription. For the first time, a whole nation was at war, not just the nobility and an army of their servants, as it had usually been. Under the doctrine of national sovereignty, the state enlisted every citizen's involvement. From then on, increasingly the rest of the population was to give support to its fighting soldiers, by making weapons, maintaining the economy, and spreading propaganda against the enemy. In World War I, all the resources of the countries that were fighting were mobilized, and all their people served the war effort. This made it possible, in Semelin's view, for the "distinction between combatants (armed or not) and non-combatants... to disappear."[76] As a result, all civilians in countries at war became military targets, explaining in part the huge increase in civilian casualties in war from the beginning to the end of the twentieth century. By attacking civilians, the enemy would try to break the material and moral resolve of the country.

In Semelin's view this politicization of war also led to political and cultural mobilization against minorities, or "foreign elements" presented as enemies within. Massacres in Paris in September 1792 at the time of the French revolution were the result of the fear of invasion combined with "the dread of a counter-revolutionary conspiracy."[77] He writes that during World War I such fear of internal enemies gave rise to the most extreme violence against civilians.

The enemy on the outside is linked to an enemy within. The hostility against a group that already developed before a war "proceeds in war to find a solution."[78]

Consistent with this argument, Turkey claimed that its violence against Armenians was the result of Armenian sympathy with and support for the Russian enemy in World War I. The Tutsis in Rwanda were seen as allied with the RPF, fighting against the Hutu government army. Often, however, the group identified as the internal enemy is different from the external enemy. Fear of and hostility toward an enemy in the war may generalize to a group that has been the object of devaluation and hostility and seen as a danger to one's group and identified by ideology as an enemy. Enmity toward the Soviet Union during World War II intensified Nazi and German hostility to Jews, because the Nazis connected Jews to communism from the start, talking about the Jewish-Bolshevik enemy. The extermination of the Jews began after the early German losses in the Soviet Union.

War represents an evolution of violence that can expand to devalued groups, especially if they are identified as ideological enemies. It can provide a cover for violence against them. A psychological element in this expansion can be the mistrust and fear of such groups, enhanced by vulnerability to external enemies. A real element at times, however, is that such groups, badly treated in their society, do sympathize with and when possible provide help to the enemy. For example, Ukrainians, Lithuanians, and others who were part of the Soviet Union but felt occupied by it sympathized with and helped Germans during the war.

However, the expanded involvement of the population in war may have only a secondary role in the rise of civilian casualties. In earlier times conquerors sometimes killed whole civilian populations. During the 30-year war in Europe in the seventeenth century, for example, huge numbers of civilians were killed. And the increase in civilian casualties in the course of the twentieth century had to do as well with increasingly powerful weapons, including aerial bombardment, as in the case of the fire bombing of Dresden.

In addition to conventional war, revolution, a different kind of war, can also make genocide more likely. Revolutions often arise out of conflict—inequalities between groups or political repression. Political scientist Robert Melson identified the defeat of old regimes through revolution, and great difficulties of or the collapse of the regimes that arise in their place, as important sources of genocide.[79] Usually in these cases all the instigators of violence are present: difficult life conditions with economic problems, political confusion and disorganization, group conflict, and the violence of the revolution. In place of a stable social order, there is societal chaos, and often a failed state. In addition, revolutions are guided by ideologies that identify enemies, an especially important contributor to group violence; legitimizing ideologies of the old order and revolutionary ideologies clash.

Weak or Failed States

Many students of mass violence see such violence taking place in "failed states." Difficulties of life persist and intensify when states lack effective institutions of government, and if civic institutions, institutions in the population that regulate life and create community, are weak or absent. While genocide can evolve in strong states under certain conditions that have characteristics I will later discuss, state failure makes mass violence more likely.

One consequence of the absence of effective state institutions is insecurity. Military and police are often perpetrators of violence. The absence of effective law enforcement also allows and invites both individual violence and violence among subgroups of the society. Establishing lawfully acting and effective police and military is crucial. Conditions under the Palestinian Authority have improved when they trained an effective police force, and restrictive practices by Israel have diminished. The Palestinian prime minister has started to build state institutions, in preparation for a Palestinian state coming into existence.

The Congo, certainly its Eastern part, where violence and chaos rule, manifestly lacks effective state institutions. In the many years of Mobutu's dictatorship, and since, no such institutions have developed. There is no effective justice system; crimes go unpunished. Since the state is absent, it does not collect taxes. Private parties collect tolls on roads on which cattle farmers take their cattle to market, with competition among such "tax collectors."[80] Corruption is widespread, taking many forms. Important government positions are given to people to gain their support for the government, or as a result of bribes, rather than on the basis of their expertise. A wealthy trader managed to buy the position of president of the provincial assembly of South Kivu, but he cannot read any documents, since he is illiterate. Many high-level officers in the army are former warlords, many of whom are known for severe human rights violations.[81]

Corruption extends to judges, who normally extort a percentage of the property they give to the party in a civil suit that bribed them more. They send a percentage of their take up the line to higher officials, a practice known as the "elevator." Corruption is widespread in the army. Officers in the continually expanding army, as members of militias are incorporated into it, steal even the money for supplies and food, and in turn soldiers use their arms to rob people in the villages and towns where they operate.[82] Thus, corruption creates insecurity. The lack of effective state institutions and corruption create a moral climate in which people look out for themselves and their families, and join groups to satisfy material and psychological needs that act without respect for laws or concern for the common good.

In a failed state, where people experience uncertainty, threat, and the frustration of basic needs, enmity based on group differences intensifies. Consistent with my views, Rene Lemarchand notes that ethnic polarization is central to the crisis in North Kivu, the Eastern region of the Congo where most of the violence has taken place. Hostility toward Tutsis is especially strong, and they are excluded from representation in government structures.[83]

Current approaches to address state failure only minimally consider the role of psychological factors. An invitation to a program at the Woodrow Wilson Center in 2009 on "Preventing and Rebuilding Failed States" said the following:

> To address fragile and failed states, it is becoming accepted that sustainable peace and development is achievable only through multi-dimensional "whole of government" strategies that treat underlying as well as immediate drivers of instability and state weakness... . So far, the specifics of whole-of-government, integrated, "3-D" (development, diplomacy and defense) strategies and other holistic ideas like "civil-military cooperation," "smart power," and "human security" have not been spelled out.[84]

The specifics of addressing people's attitudes toward each other, their thoughts and feelings about the past relationships between their groups and about a joint future, and ways to constructively fulfill basic needs also must be spelled out.

Summary

The starting points, or initial instigators, of intense group violence are usually either difficult life conditions in a society—economic deterioration, great political instability and confusion, great societal change—or group conflict. Revolution and war can also be starting points. War is a context in which genocide becomes easier and more likely. Each of these instigators, and especially combinations of them, can give rise to feelings of uncertainty, threat, fear, loss, and humiliation and deeply frustrate universal or "basic" human needs—for security, positive identity, feelings of effectiveness and control, positive connection, autonomy, and a comprehension of reality. In turn, these psychological states—feelings, thoughts, and frustrated needs—give rise to psychological and social processes that turn a group against another and/or intensify antagonism. The lack of effective institutions of the state and civil society makes this process more likely.

Notes

1 United Nations, 1948, Article 2

2 Harff, 2003; Harff & Gurr, 1990

3 See Chalk and Jonassohn, 1990, p. 23, and Raphael Lemkin, 1944, p. 79, the man who coined the term genocide and whose intense commitment and perseverance led to the adoption by the U.N. of the genocide convention.

4 Fein, 1993b, p. 24

5 Staub, 1989, p. 8

6 Report of the U.N. International Commission of Inquiry, 2005, p. 129

7 Staub, 2006

8 Staub, 1989, 1996, 2003a

9 Buss, 2009

10 Staub, 2003a, p. 59

11 Ibid, p. 60

12 DeAngelis, 2009

13 Maslow, 1955, 1971

14 See Staub 2003b, Chapter 5, for a discussion of these matters and and more detailed discussion of basic needs.

15 Burton, 1990; Kelman, 1990; Montville, 1993

16 Kruglanski, Chen, Dechesne, Fishman, & Orehek, 2009

17 McCann & Pearlman, 1990; Pearlman & Saakvitne, 1995. See also Staub, 1998; Staub & Vollhardt, 2008

18 Staub, 2003a

19 Staub, 1978, 1980

20 Triandis, 1994

21 Lifton, 1986

22 Staub, 1989

23 Dollard, Doob, Miller, Mower, & Sears, 1939

24 Pettigrew, 2003

25 Epstein & Taylor, 1967

26 Midlarsky, 2004

27 See also Hogg, 2007

28 Becker, 1975

29 For a review of the theory, see Pyszczynski, Greenberg, Solomon, Arndt, & Schimel, 2004; See also Pyszczynski, Rothschild and Abdollahi, 2008

30 Ibid.

31 Friedman & Rholes, 2007, p. 795

32 Pyszczynski, Abdollahi, Solomon, Greenberg, Cohen, & Wise, 2006

33 Pyszczynski, Rothschild, & Abdollahi, 2008, p. 319

34 In studies of mortality threat, there are comparison groups in which people are asked to think about other aversive events, such as future university exams. This does not have the same effects, but this is a threat of much lesser magnitude.

35 See Pyszczynski, Rothschild & Abdollahi, 2008 for a brief overview of these studies.

36 Staub, 1989

37 Presented at the meetings of the Society for Personality and Social Psychology in February, 2006, Tampa, Florida.

38 Jones, 2006, p. 268

39 Lindner, 2008; see also Lindner, 2006

40 Lifton, 2003, p. 103

41 Scheff, 1994

42 Staub, 1989; see also Baumeister, 1997

43 Staub, 1989

44 Richardson, 2006

45 Midlarsky, 2004

46 Lindner, 2008

47 Ibid.

48 Harff, 2003

49 Straus, 2006

50 Des Forges, 1999; Staub, 1999b

51 Hatzfeld, 2003

52 Des Forges, 1999; Mamdani, 2001; Staub, 1999b; Straus, 2006

53 Hamburg, 2007; Lund, 2009.

54 Staub, 2007b

55 Volkan, 2004, p. 83

56 Germert, 2004; Germert & Fleisher, 2005

57 Malik, 2007

58 Sageman, 2008. p 67

59 Totten et al., 1997

60 Frank, 1985

61 Thatcher Green, personal communication, June 2009

62 Gurr,1970

63 Staub, 1978

64 Quoted in Jones, p. 264.

65 Des Forges, 1999, Mamdani, 2001

66 Fein, 1993a

67 Harff, 2003

68 Staub, 2007b

69 Ibid. See also Kruglanski et.al., 2008

70 Staub, 2007b

71 Ibid.

72 Austesserre, 2008

73 Bartov, 2003

74 Kilcullen, 2009

75 Mortenson & Relin, 2007

76 Semelin, 2007, p. 134

77 Ibid, p.135.

78 Ibid, p. 185

79 Melson, 1992

80 Reyntjens, 2009

81 Lemarchand, 2008

82 Hochschild, 2009

83 Lemarchand, 2008

84 http://www.wilsoncenter.org/index.cfm?topic_id=1411&fuseaction=topics.
event_rsvp&event_id=535471

5

Psychological and Societal/Group Processes That Arise from Instigating Conditions

In response to difficult life conditions, individuals tend to turn to existing or newly created groups for the fulfillment of basic needs such as security, identity and connection.

National, ethnic, or religious groups, or ideological or other groups that arise and that people turn to in difficult times, tend to scapegoat and create destructive ideologies, and choose and follow leaders who are in the vanguard of this.

Motives to defend or gain power, status, and wealth or to combat repression, discrimination, and inequality can also lead to conflict, hostility, and violence; especially under difficult life conditions, they can join with motives to fulfill basic needs.

Shifting from a Personal to a Group Identity

The identity of every person, to a smaller or greater extent, is rooted in one or more groups. We absorb the beliefs and values of groups and to a varying extent identify ourselves as members of tribes or ethnic, religious, national, or other groups. At the same time, we also experience and identify ourselves as separate persons, more so in Western individualist than in Eastern or African collectivist cultures.

However, in response to difficult life conditions, societal chaos and insecurity, group conflict or war, individuals turn increasingly to groups. Their identity shifts from a more individual identity to a more group or collective identity, from being a separate person to being a group member. People then see events much more from the perspective of its meaning for the group. This view of a shift to group identity is suggested by influential theories of group relations in social psychology and by related research, and it is evident from observing what happens in societies that experience the instigating conditions I described in the previous chapter. As people identify with and more actively engage with groups, they gain feelings of security, connection to others, and effectiveness. Their worldview is strengthened or the group offers a new comprehension of reality.

Social identity theory, developed by the British psychologist Henri Tajfel, and his student John Turner, focuses on how people categorize themselves, how they identify with groups, and how they compare their groups to other groups.[1] Just as we categorize everything (for example, objects by color, size, utility), so we categorize ourselves and other people as members of groups. As we categorize ourselves as members of a particular group, we adopt the identity of that group. We emphasize similarities within the group, and differences with other groups, whose members we see as similar to each other. We compare our group to others, and we are motivated to enhance the difference in favor of our group, to elevate our group relative to others. When we do that, we feel better about ourselves, we enhance our self-esteem, which the theory views as a core motivation for identification with groups. As I see evidence from relations between groups, especially under instigating conditions, we often do this in destructive ways, by devaluing other groups or actually diminishing them through power and force.[2]

As we categorize other people as members of "outgroups," we see them less as individuals. We apply the stereotype we hold of the group to its individual members. Our beliefs about the group tell us what to expect of its members. If we have a strongly negative view of the group, we apply that to its individual members.

Since we apply our views of our group to ourselves, it is important for us to see our group in a positive light. The norms and beliefs of our group tell us how to behave, what beliefs to hold, what our views of the world should be. Social psychologist Leon Festinger has proposed, and both observation and research have confirmed, that our understanding of the world develops through mutual influence among people. In his footsteps many others have emphasized that our knowledge of the world, and our certainty about what is true and false, is based on social consensus.

Especially under difficult life conditions people need groups. A great deal of research has shown the positive value of the "ingroup": people feel more positively toward ingroup than outgroup members, see them as more trustworthy, and are more helpful toward them.[3] People turning to and identifying with groups is crucial to understanding intergroup relations. But different psychological theories suggest different reasons why people need groups: to protect or gain self-esteem, to reduce uncertainty, to reduce fear in response to real threat, to protect against existential anxiety and awareness of mortality, or to deal with humiliation.

From my perspective, a prime motivation for people turning to groups is that membership, whether in an immediate community, an ideological movement and group, or a larger symbolic group such as a nation, helps to fulfill basic needs. As part of a group, people who feel diminished by events and their impact on them can give up an individual self that has become burdensome and regain a more positive identity. The strength and power of the group also helps them regain feelings of effectiveness and control over events, as well as physical and psychological security. The group provides them with connection. The ideology a group develops provides a new understanding of reality. Humiliation, threat, fear, and uncertainty all frustrate basic needs, and all can be eased as these needs get fulfilled at least to some degree through belonging to groups.

Political scientists Ted Robert Gurr and Barbara Harff propose that identification with a group is greater when there are shared characteristics among people, such as language, religion, history, or territory. It is also likely to be greater when there is more cohesion in the group, greater unity between elites and the collective, between the leadership and the people.[4] In groups that are the objects of discrimination, more internal cohesion provides better psychological protection.[5]

But in difficult times cohesion often diminishes, leading people to turn to new groups. In response to societal chaos and insecurity—or discrimination and other bad treatment—people often turn to ideological leaders and movements. Such groups can have mixed membership. The Bolsheviks included people from many nationalities and ethnic groups and different religions. Al-Qaeda's members are Muslim, but they come from many nationalities. Still, groups that emerge in difficult times, whether primarily ideological or oriented to power, wealth, and security, are often organized along already existing group divisions. In the Congo, in the midst of tremendous chaos, violence, and insecurity, groups that are fighting each other are primarily organized along ethnic lines, even as they are focused on material needs, conflict over land ownership and access to rich natural resources, as well as political power.[6]

As identity shifts, what increasingly matters is the collective, and what is important is what the collective sees as important. A separate perspective becomes increasingly difficult to maintain. When people undergo such a shift in identity, what happens to their group can become more important to them than what happens to them individually. In one study, women in Rwanda who after the genocide felt that they personally had not received justice but that other women did, felt better about the justice system than those who felt they received justice but women in general did not.[7]

Evelin Lindner suggests that when people identify with their group, they experience humiliation not only for themselves but on behalf of their group. From my perspective, what happens to the group can frustrate the need for a positive identity, dignity, and justice. Lindner quotes a 20-year-old Palestinian woman she worked with when she was a psychological counselor in Egypt from 1984 to 1991.

My father wants me to study, get married, and have a life. But I cannot smile and laugh and think of a happy life, when at the same time my aunts and uncles, my nieces and other family members face suffering in Palestine. This suffering is like a heavy burden on me. I cannot smile and laugh. I feel their suffering in my body. Sometimes I cannot sleep. ...I obey my father and try to concentrate on my studies. But I do this only because I respect my father. If he were not there, I would go to my homeland, get married and have as many sons as I could have, and educate them in the right spirit. I would be overjoyed to have a martyr as a son, a son who sacrifices his life for his people. I feel that suicide bombers are heroes, because it is hard to give your life. I want to give my life. I want to do something. I cannot just sit here in Cairo and watch my people suffer. Their suffering eats me up. I feel so powerless, so heavy; sometimes I can hardly walk. The burden crushes me. What shall I do?

Lindner has also worked with young Palestinian men who had similar feelings. She writes: "Whenever I counselled these young and bright people I was aware that they were vulnerable to being recruited by leaders who could instrumentalize their ability for empathy and use them for acts of destruction."[8]

The shift to collective identity helps in the formation or strengthening of groups in difficult times. But it also makes it easier for people to turn against others, even neighbors and former associates, who belong to another group. As they see their neighbors not as individuals but as group members—as Tutsis or Hutus, as Palestinians or Jews—they can change in their eyes into ethnic or class enemies. They can become scapegoats, immoral opponents, a threat to their group, or ideological enemies.

Many who study terrorism share this perspective. They see collective identity as the "most constructive framework for understanding terrorist psychology and behavior."[9] One direction of research on reducing stereotyping has been to find ways to *individuate* people, so that they are looked at as persons rather than as group members.[10] However, in hostile group relations, when many people are involved, the group as a whole has to be humanized and/or the boundaries of "us," the "ingroup," have to be expanded. An important element in preventing mass violence is to extend the ingroup to "them" or create inclusive caring that applies to "them."

When people are divided into groups even on trivial bases, they immediately identify to some degree with their group and favor its members. This happens in research when people are told they were put into a group with others who assemble dots on a page in similar ways, or who have similar aesthetic preferences, or even when they are randomly assigned to groups. In the real world, people divide themselves into groups based on more substantive considerations, with identification enhanced by past history or current conditions. It has been found in a number of real-world conflicts—such as between Catholics and Protestants in Northern Ireland, between people on the left and those on the right who supported the repressive dictatorship of Pinochet in Chile, and among

Bosnians[11]—that people who identify with their own group more tend to forgive the other group less.

By contrast, identification with various ethnic or racial subgroups in South Africa in 2001 was not associated with intolerance toward other groups. These identifications were positively associated with identification with South Africa as a nation.[12] I will later discuss the value of such dual identification. But for that to come about, the conditions of the society at the time are important. Most likely during apartheid black or "colored" South Africans identified themselves with their group and not very much with their country. By 2001, a dual identity[13] was psychologically possible.

Social identity theory focuses on the context of people's lives as the crucial influence in shaping group identity. But context needs to be broadly interpreted. Identification with the group is affected by circumstances that individuals and the group face, by privilege or lack of it, ethnicity, and so on. Children's identity can be shaped so that their collective identity is central to who they are. This shaping happens not only through direct guidance but also through life experience.

One example of such identity development is children identifying with parents who have worked for the rights or independence of a minority and suffered as a result. Jerrold Post suggests that some terrorism arises as children carry on the cause of their parents and grandparents.[14] Another example is identification with a group that suffers from discrimination or persecution. Various individual characteristics also affect the degree and type of identification with groups. The need for certainty and strong respect for authority—an authoritarian personality—would lead to greater need for membership in a tight-knit group with strong leaders.

Deindividuation, a loss of one's sense of separateness or individuality due to wearing a uniform, being part of a crowd or mob, in general being anonymous and not easily identifiable, makes violence against other people easier. Shifting from an individual to a collective identity may have a similar effect. In research, people wearing masks were more aggressive toward others.[15] Warriors in a society who paint themselves before battle are more violent.[16] The loss of individuality is likely to weaken one's personal morality, as well as inhibitions and self-control.

The shift to group identity can be especially fast, and identification with a group intense, when there has been a history of hostility and violence between groups. Past violence such as mass killing creates a rift, like a fault line in the earth, which can reopen. It also makes such violence more conceivable. In this, it is like what happens after a suicide in a family: Once the possibility enters people's awareness, suicide, which may have been inconceivable before, is now conceivable, and it is more likely to happen again in that family. New threat, whether real or imagined or manipulated by leaders, can lead to a shift to collective identity and also turn people's attention to what has happened to their group in the past—or what their group has done in the past.

The use of the principles and practices of prevention and reconciliation that I will describe in Part II, such as understanding the influences leading to mass violence and their impact, healing, and significant contact between groups, can provide inoculation against some of the harmful effects of past group violence. These practices make it less likely that people will look at those outside their groups as members of a (devalued) category rather than as human beings. Becoming aware of the effects of the past, of the psychological woundedness and chasm it has created, can contribute to reducing these harmful effects.

The Nature of Groups and the People Who Join

As a group becomes more important to people, their views and beliefs are shaped more strongly by it. Social reality is always defined jointly with other people, but more so in difficult times. With the uncertainty and insecurity associated with difficult times, conflict and war, people seek others similar to themselves. These others may be similarly threatened, or members of the same group, or hold similar beliefs. In experimental research people under threat of receiving electric shocks preferred to be in the company of people facing the same threat.[17] Under threat and uncertainty people also tend to become more conservative, their thinking becomes less complex, and they have less tolerant attitudes.[18] As they join with others, they can strengthen these tendencies in each other.

Group identification is a potent and effective way to resolve uncertainty.[19] But as people increasingly identify with a group and jointly develop an understanding of the meaning of events—and ways to deal with them—they are increasingly less likely to have an independent perspective. How can our views, including our extreme responses be wrong, if they are confirmed by everyone around us? This uniformity increases the destructive potential of groups.

According to current wisdom people identify more strongly with groups that have clear boundaries, are homogenous, whose members have common goals and a sense of shared fate. Social psychologist Donald Campbell and his student Marylinn Brewer have called the combination of such group characteristics "entitivity."[20] When members agree what the group is about, who belongs and who does not, and how members are to relate to each other and the world, the sense of being a group and the satisfaction associated with that will be strong, especially in difficult times. Michael Hogg, also a social psychologist, sees groups that have been called extreme or totalistic as having such characteristics, as well as intolerance for dissent and strong hierarchy within the group. Members of such groups tend to assume that the group has an underlying immutable essence, perhaps due to biology or genetic origin.[21]

Under difficult life conditions many people are drawn to groups that not only have a strong entity but also an ideology—a vision and a cause. As I will show later in this chapter, destructive ideologies have a very important role in leading to mass violence. The groups that people turn to and identify with can be their nation, their ethnic or religious group, or an ideological (political) movement. They can be preexisting groups that people are already members of, or new groups that arise, that people create. These are not necessarily violent groups at the start, but for reasons of structure and ideology, they have the seeds of violence in them, and their characteristics and ideology change and evolve over time. While the creation of extreme groups usually begins in response to external conditions, internal processes, and leaders and members, move groups to become more polarized, more extreme. For example, in order to gain influence in terrorist groups (and in leadership groups), members advocate positions in line with the group's direction and ideology, but that are more extreme.[22]

Such groups fulfill basic needs, except that they limit autonomy. However, in difficult times, autonomy may be subordinated to other needs. Moreover, people with high autonomy needs would be less likely to give themselves over to strongly hierarchical groups, except perhaps as leaders. Neither would people who hold values or an ideology that conflicts with those of the group. In collectivist societies people feel embedded in their original group and might be less likely to create new groups at odds with the society. When people are members of ethnic, racial, or religious groups that are in conflict or the object of enmity, it is very difficult for them to stray from allegiance to those original groups.

The modern world with its complexity, its constantly changing values and roles, its many choices about who to be and how to live, represents a challenge for us human beings. How do we fulfill our needs in this ever-changing and flexible universe? Children who are raised with certainties, for example, orthodox forms of religiosity, or who grow up in inflexible societies and homes that do not provide opportunities to experiment and learn to live with change, would be especially impacted by the chaotic nature of the world we live in. People with such backgrounds develop characteristics that in difficult times make "totalistic" groups especially attractive to them. Among them are authoritarian individuals, who are comfortable in a system with clearly defined hierarchy, and for whom uncertainty and threat represent a special challenge.[23] Authoritarian tendencies overlap with or give rise to the need for a precise vision of reality, for closure. Change would also be difficult for people whose basic needs have not been appropriately fulfilled earlier in their lives. I will later discuss in more detail "self-selection," personal characteristics that make it more likely for people to join potentially destructive groups.

Hogg and his associates[24] have done a number of studies which showed that when people feel uncertain, they identify more with extreme rather than moderate groups. The uncertainty in these cases was limited in nature, induced by having people think about their own characteristics that they are uncertain about, or by engaging them in difficult tasks where they could not judge the outcome of their efforts. Extremity was also limited, related to groups advocating either more moderate or more extreme responses to student issues at Australian universities. Greater uncertainty led people to shift their preference from moderate to extreme groups, and to be willing to engage in more extreme actions.

But not all groups that advocate causes are extreme or totalistic. For example, some groups working to advance feminism, guided by their ideology, insisted on equitable rather than hierarchical relations among members.[25] Groups in which children or adults were brought together to work cooperatively have resulted in more cooperative behavior among participants and more positive behavior toward outsiders.[26] I will later discuss the creation of "constructive" groups or communities as among the approaches to preventing group violence. There are varied examples of such groups, with people working together for combined individual and group goals. At their best they can be inclusive in their membership, have equitable internal relations that make space for discussion and disagreement, advocate inclusive ideologies with positive goals, and promote positive attitudes toward outsiders. Such groups fulfill basic needs constructively. We need to experiment with creating and maintaining such groups and conduct research to evaluate the effects of membership in them.

Scapegoating, Beliefs, and Ideologies

The leaders to whom the group turns or who emerge in difficult, chaotic times or in the course of group conflict are often in the vanguard of scapegoating, of identifying another group as responsible for the difficult life conditions or conflict. They are also in the vanguard of developing ideologies, visions of a better future for their group or for the whole world. Again, by ideology, I mean visions of social arrangements in the society or the world, and of relationships between people. Ideologies that are created in difficult times serve to provide hope for the group. But when the ideology also identifies some group that stands in the way of its fulfillment, an enemy, it becomes what I call a *destructive ideology*. Life conditions, group conflict, and culture create an openness or receptivity to leaders who advocate scapegoating and destructive ideologies.

Turning against the scapegoated group or ideological enemy can begin an evolution of increasing violence, of steps along a continuum of destruction. The destructive need satisfaction this process provides harms the group intrinsically, as it becomes psychologically and morally less healthy, as well as extrinsically through retaliation from others (boycotts, military actions) and loss of respect and exclusion from the moral community.

People turn to or follow leaders who advocate scapegoating and destructive ideologies not only because of frustrated needs but also because of a desire for solutions to their problems. The sources of their societal problems are complex and difficult to understand, and the solutions that effectively address severe life problems in a society are difficult to identify, agree on, and institute, and they require patience to take effect. In contrast, the "solutions" that the group and its leaders espouse speedily address, at least to some degree, the psychological needs frustrated by instigating conditions. People are especially likely to turn to scapegoating and destructive ideologies when the cultural conditions I later describe are present, including historical divisions between groups. It requires strong, visionary, positive leadership, guided by a constructive ideology, to prevent people from turning to such solutions.

Blaming or scapegoating another group diminishes a feeling of responsibility for life problems and thereby helps maintain a positive identity. I and my group are not responsible for the difficulties and losses. At a time when they feel helpless and unable to control their destinies, scapegoating also gives people a feeling of potential effectiveness, believing that as they "deal with" the scapegoat, conditions will improve. It helps them "understand" the reasons for the problems—they arise because of what this other group has been doing, or even because of its nature, the very being of its members. This understanding is often false, hence it is scapegoating, but as people scapegoat together they affirm its truth for each other. Their joining in scapegoating also fulfills the need for connection. In similar ways, ideological movements help to satisfy all frustrated basic needs. They create a new, hopeful understanding of reality, a feeling of effectiveness, affirm identity, and create positive connection within the group as people join in working for the ideology's fulfillment. When hostility toward another group develops in response to legitimate grievances, scapegoating and ideology foment further hostility in the aggrieved group.

Ideologies are among the most important influences leading to mass violence, especially genocide. A guiding ideology seems always present. The ideology that a group and its leaders tend to adopt or create can be a vision for the future of the group, for the society the group is part of, and sometimes for the whole world—what I have called a *better world ideology*. Ideologies can be relatively general and abstract in specifying societal arrangements and relationships among people. But usually goals are derived from them that are more specific and guide action. As a means of achieving the better world, the worldwide utopia they promote, or achieving a better life for the group, which nationalistic ideologies or ideologies of superiority promote, ideologues are often increasingly willing to do extreme harm to a designated enemy of the better future. Alexander Solzhenitsyn wrote:

> To do evil a human being must first of all believe that he is doing good ... The imagination and the spiritual strength of Shakespeare's evildoers stopped short at a dozen corpses. Because they had no ideology.
>
> Ideology—that is what gives evil-doing its long sought justification and gives evildoers the necessary steadfastness and determination. This is the

social theory which helps to make his acts seem good instead of bad in his own and others' eyes.

That is how agents of the Inquisition fortified their wills: by invoking Christianity; the conquerors of foreign lands by extolling the grandeur of their Motherland; the colonizers by civilization, the Nazis by race; and the Jacobins (early and late) by equality, brotherhood and the happiness of future generations.[27]

The role of ideology in mass killing in the modern age has been pervasive. Solzhenitsyn, who won a Nobel Prize for his writing on the Soviet Gulags, was especially concerned with communist violence. Communist countries identified many and varied groups of enemies, based on their past as owners of the means of production, as officials in past regimes, as educated people, as people showing or presumed to be resistant to communist practices such as collectivization, and as people whose past experiences in living in or dealing with capitalist countries made them class enemies. The children and other relatives of such people were not spared from identification as enemies. Communists killed many they deemed a threat, they worked and starved people to death in prison camps, and they created conditions that, sometimes intentionally and sometimes unintentionally, killed huge numbers of people. For example, the Khmer Rouge killed

....those who were regarded as corrupted by their education, class, or employment—civil servants, doctors, lawyers, soldiers, and teachers were identified and eliminated...The killings of soldiers' wives and children is also to have occurred frequently. A Khmer Rouge slogan advanced the maxim that "Their line must be annihilated down to the last survivor."[28]

Various versions of this directive have been used many times in history, even as early as in the period of the Old Testament, for example, in Deuteronomy where God commands the Israelites to "utterly destroy" various groups.[29]

There is an oft-cited talk by Himmler to German SS officers about their sacrifice in killing Jews, the great hardship this placed on them, which they must bear for the higher cause. Later generations will glorify them for it.[30] Paul Hollander shows through quotes from communist authors and argues persuasively that the Communists believed the same. While the personalities of leaders like Stalin and Mao contributed to the widespread killings and brutality, the culture of the communists imbued perpetrators with the feeling that all is justified for the higher good. "...everything that corresponded to the interests of the revolution and communism was moral. That is the morality with which hostages were executed ....concentration camps were built, and entire people's forcibly relocated." And further, "Bolshevism shares the feeling expressed by a character in Dostoevsky's *A Raw Youth*: It doesn't matter if one has to pass through filth to get there as long as the goal is magnificent. It will be washed off, it will be smoothed away afterward."[31]

Some scholars have differentiated between ideological and other types of genocides, based on what they see as the primary motivations leading to them. Roger Smith describes the ends that genocides aim at as revenge, conquest, gain, power, and purification/salvation. He distinguishes among the following types of genocides:[32]

- *Retributive genocide.* While some genocides are primarily retributive, he sees retribution as playing a role in most genocides, mainly as rationalization, as a way of blaming or scapegoating the victim.
- *Institutional genocide.* Genocide used to be part of warfare; it was routinized. No decision had to be made; it was part of how war was conducted. The practice of genocide as part of conquest ended in the West by the late medieval period, although it reemerged in the religious passions of the Crusades. It continued until later in the East, but for the last 500 years genocide has not been associated with conquest. (But see my earlier comment about the role of an "ideology of conquest" in the colonial era.)
- *Utilitarian genocide.* This was especially prominent as part of colonization. It had to do with the domination and exploitation of indigenous peoples, taking their land and using their labor.
- *Monopolistic genocide.* This type of genocide has to do, according to Smith, with "who belongs, who is to have a voice in the political society, what is to be the basic shape of the community, what should its purposes be?" (p. 7). In contrast to most genocides before the twentieth century, which were external, most since then have been internal, within the boundaries of a country that perpetrates it. Smith sees their most frequent source as "the struggle for the monopolization of power" (p. 7).
- *Ideological genocide.* Smith sees most genocides as not ideological, not an instrument "for the restructuring of society according to some blueprint of the mind" (p. 8), although when they were ideological, they were especially devastating.

It is rare for modern genocides to have had a single, dominant motive. However, I do see ideologies as a significant influence in them. The approach of this book is to consider the *influences* that give rise to mass violence, both external (difficult life conditions, conflict) and internal psychological ones. The varied types of modern genocides that Smith, Helen Fein[33] and others identify arise in my view from a number of usually overlapping influences, with overlapping avenues to their prevention. Some influences seem always present—such as devaluation of the group that becomes the victim and a destructive ideology. However, there can also be specificity. Certain influences can be especially important in particular situations, such as self-interest in the genocides ("utilitarian") of indigenous peoples. Life conditions and the experiences they create may frustrate certain needs especially intensely. Understanding the specific influences, for example, both the nature of those intensely frustrated needs and the content of the ideology that the group has adopted in response to them, can be helpful in developing appropriate preventive approaches.

Destructive ideologies often have a seemingly positive element, a vision of a better future, at least for the group, sometimes for all humanity. The nature of this positive element varies. The Khmer Rouge in Cambodia had a vision of total social equality among all members of the society. Often the vision is nationalism. One type of it is the desire by a people to create a state of their own. Another potentially more destructive type, as in the Turkish ideology of pan-Turkism that contributed to the genocide of the Armenians, is to enhance the nation's power, influence, and greatness. The ideas in such nationalism, and indeed in any similarly destructive ideology, usually involve elevating a group or country relative to others, and overcoming enemies who stand in the way.

In the Hutu Power ideology in Rwanda the positive element and the negative one, dealing with an enemy, joined. The ideology identified as the ideal future a world without the existence of the enemy group. The focus on power would put the genocide into Smith's monopolistic category, but as we shall see other influences and motives were also at work. Which group has power remains an important, although underground issue in Rwanda; the experience of shared power would be important for reconciliation. When conflict between groups is over land or power, preventive efforts must not only address identity, dignity, and other psychological issues but also deal with the material issues.

A frequent aspect of the nationalistic impulse is to hark back to a time when the country was successful and powerful, with a vision to recreate past greatness, whether it was actual or is exaggerated. This was true of Turkey, which was a great power for a long time but by the middle of the nineteenth century was regarded as the "sick man of Europe."[34] The Khmer Rouge, in addition to advocating social equality, was also nationalistic. Cambodia was once an important regional power, and the Khmer Rouge had a vision of recreating its greatness. Historian Ben Kiernen regards the reference to antiquity as a common characteristic of genocidal ideologies. Ideology is also important in intractable conflict: in Israel, its focus is recreating the Greater Israel of ancient times.

When ideologies and leaders harken back to the past, they often refer either to national greatness as a model for the future, or to the wounds the group or country has suffered, or both. Stalin, for one, portrayed Russia as "a routine victim of history."[35] I will later discuss past victimization and woundedness, and their uses by leaders, as important contributors to mass violence.

In Rwanda a focus on the past has been through the belief, propagated by the Belgians, that the Hutus were the original inhabitants, while the Tutsis were alien, a different race that moved to the region around the sixteenth century.

This intensified the "us and them" division between the two groups. Religious fundamentalism also embraces a yearning for the past, a return and adherence to long ago created religious texts and strictures. Islamic fundamentalism, for example, yearns for the recreation of the caliphate and the Umma, a worldwide Muslim society, and a worldwide community of Muslims.

Another common element Kiernen proposes is a focus on agriculture, on the effective use of the land and the taking of others' land. Land can be precious as a living space or as a means of growing food to maintain life. It is also a source of status and power. The focus on land, on who has it and how it is cultivated, had a role in both Cambodia and Rwanda. In Rwanda, an extremely densely populated country, competition for land as a scarce resource was significant. Land ownership is also important in the Congo. The Nazi ideology included the notion of *Lebensraum* or living space, probably influenced by colonialism and the feeling of Germans, with little colonial conquest in their history, that they had been deprived of its benefits. The concept of *Lebensraum* asserted the right of Germany to more land, which required expansion.

A third common element in genocide in Kiernen's view is nationalistic expansionism. Expansionism may lead to genocide, or be a by-product of or evolve out of genocide. The Khmer Rouge, in addition to its violence within Cambodia, engaged in attacks on Vietnam. Expansionism may aim at recreating the greatness of the country, a common element of ideology. It may represent an evolution of violence beyond its genocidal aim. Or the genocide may be perpetrated in the context of war that aims at expansion. That said, while land and expansion seem important aspects of materially based group conflict, they only occasionally seem *central* in genocide.

Extreme nationalistic ideologies often give rise to the goal of purifying the group by eliminating alien elements. Seemingly paradoxically, utopian ideologies that advocate a better world for all humanity also often insist on purifying the group. The former aim to get rid of those not belonging to the group by race, ethnicity, or religion, the latter to get rid of those who because of their background and past affiliations are deemed not willing or capable of supporting or living by the ideology. But these two ways of identifying enemies are often intertwined, as they were in Germany, Cambodia, and elsewhere.

It is possible to blame one group for past problems and to identify another as standing in the way of a better future. However, there is usually a convergence, the scapegoated group identified as the ideological enemy. At other times initial scapegoating does not seem as important, but as an ideological enemy is chosen, it is at least implicit that the group is responsible for past problems of the society or that it stands in the way of the fulfillment of the ideological vision and is responsible for lack of progress in fulfilling it. The Khmer Rouge in Cambodia identified various internal groups as enemies, including Vietnamese and Chinese immigrants whom they regarded as historical enemies, as well as other minorities.

Leaders and Followers

Contrary to my views, political scientist Benjamin Valentino has argued against the role of widespread scapegoating in mass violence, which he regards as the result of a small group of people intent on violence taking hold of the machinery of the state. They attract followers inclined to violence; such people are presumably present in all societies and can be activated.[36] This latter point was also proposed by John Steiner, who conducted several studies of former SS members and suggested that some people are *sleepers*. They are not violent under normal conditions, but certain social conditions activate their inclination to violence. He writes: "Extreme deprivation coupled with powerlessness at one end of the spectrum and the assumption of considerable power, causing elation or ecstatic joy on the other, tend[s] to produce the necessary conditions and thereby passions which activate the sleeper."[37]

Some people appear to have a direct inclination to violence that is activated under certain conditions. Many others seem to possess characteristics and inclinations, such as an insecure self, strong respect for and need for guidance by authorities, and the difficulty of tolerating uncertainty, that can lead people in difficult times to enter into movements and groups that over time become violent. On the surface, then, they seem inclined to violence, even if for many violence is the outcome of their evolution. The same characteristics and inclinations make them receptive to leaders who scapegoat and offer destructive ideologies.

Initially, scapegoating is not necessarily widespread; it often starts with a small proportion of the population. Usually those who blame some group have a public forum; they are part of the elite, or a group that is gaining influence partly through scapegoating and the ideology they offer. Scapegoating spreads because of the presence of instigating conditions and the history of devaluation of the group that becomes the scapegoat.

A destructive ideology is also usually propagated, initially, by a small group. Inherent in the concept of a destructive ideological *movement* is that it can start with a limited group. This was the case in Germany, where out of many movements and political groups in the late 1920s and early 1930s three dominant rival ideologies emerged, Nazism, Socialism, and Communism. They were in competition until the Nazis came to power. Once in power they created a totalitarian dictatorship. Over time, in part due to effective economic policies, they became popular, and most Germans came to support them.[38]

Intellectuals in Germany, as well as in other countries, often had a role in creating, supporting, and elaborating destructive ideologies. In Argentina, they advocated anti-communism and the protection of the religious traditions of the country. The Khmer Rouge leaders were themselves students in Paris, intellectuals of a sort, when they created their ideology out of a joining of many intellectual strands and past practices. These included communist ideology, the example of violence against supposed opponents in communist countries, the ideology and practice of terror in the French revolution, as well as the history of Cambodia when it was a great regional power based on advanced agricultural practices.

While only a segment of the society is usually in the vanguard, extreme mass violence is very much a societal process. In some analyses leaders scapegoat and point to enemies out of self-interest, in order to gain followers. This is often true; it happened repeatedly in Rwanda. But it is not the whole story. Even Gordon Allport, a brilliant psychologist, described Hitler this way in the middle of the last century.[39] It is quite clear, however, that Hitler was also guided by his personal experiences of failure, by his experiences in World War I and Germany's loss of the war, by social conditions, and by his intense anti-Semitism. While many Germans were certainly less anti-Semitic, historically German anti-Semitism was strong, and it remained part of the deep structure of the society.[40] This precondition was sufficient for many to be attracted to Hitler's anti-Semitism, and for others who turned to him in response to difficult life conditions not to be turned away from him. Those who were more anti-Semitic moved into leadership positions.[41] Others accepted Hitler, and still others did not have enough motivation to act on behalf of a group that they had learned to devalue.

Catherine Newbury notes that in Rwanda the whole other group was repeatedly blamed and identified as the enemy, for actions that a particular segment of the group was responsible. In the 1959 revolution not only powerful Tutsis were the enemy, who were the source of discrimination against Hutus, but all Tutsis. During the civil war not only the RPF fighters, but again all Tutsis. And during and immediately after the genocide not only Hutu genocidaires but all Hutus.[42] But this is not likely to be only political calculation; it is a division into us and them and hostility toward "them," which given past history is either present in the population or can easily be evoked.

However, an explanation of mass violence by any one influence is inadequate. Author Daniel Goldhagen[43] saw the Holocaust as the result of "eliminationist anti-Semitism." In his view this special form of anti-Semitism was characteristic of the German population. In the context of difficult life conditions, which Goldhagen does acknowledge as a background, this intense devaluation of the Jews was sufficient for Germans to become "willing executioners."

Leaders may scapegoat *in part* to gain followers, and construct ideologies out of many elements. But the beliefs and actions of leaders, followers, and passive bystanders usually have deep roots in the group, in a combination of difficult life conditions or group conflict, their impact, and the group's culture and historical experience. Nonetheless, leaders and followers often have partly different motivations. They do not hold ideology to the same degree. In Rwanda, the leaders were guided more than followers by Hutu power as an ideology.[44] Potential followers often seek leaders they can follow, and once part of a group, they don't want to deviate from the group. Maintaining power and influence is often, as it seemed in Rwanda, a strong additional motivation for leaders.

There is a two-directional influence between leaders and followers/populations that I discuss at a number of places in the book. For example, the influence of followers was shown after the elections in Iran in June 2009, when Ahmadinejad was declared the winner. Many people believed that Mir Hossein Moussavi won and that the election was stolen from him. They wanted change in Iran and defied the authorities, demonstrating in huge numbers. Government forces fired at them and killed many people. Moussavi himself was part of the original Islamic revolution, served as prime minister, and after 20 years away from public life returned to run for president, believing that the country needed a new direction. But he wanted to give it a new direction within the existing political framework and by following the established rules. He was not a radical. Yet as his followers braved the authorities, he was transformed, moving out in front of them, endangering himself, ready to be a martyr.[45]

Leaders, Instigation, and the Population

The leaders and the people are both affected by the group's situation, by difficult life conditions, and persistent group conflict. In difficult times people look for leaders who promise fast and easy solutions. It is unlikely that Hitler, or the Khmer Rouge, or advocates of Hutu power in Rwanda would have gained influence as they did, had the times not been so difficult, conflictual, and chaotic. In turn, leaders respond both to their own and the group's psychological needs, as well as the need for group cohesion in the face of instigating conditions. However, new leaders who come to power after a revolution or other shift in leadership may be especially affected when things don't go well in the society they now rule.[46] Difficult social conditions may challenge their position, ideology, identity, and belief in their competence.

While there is synchronicity between leaders and the group created by the conditions that surround them, power is usually an additional motive for leaders. Raphael Ezekiel[47] studied white supremacist groups in the United States and found that the leaders were very interested in power. Everyone has some need for efficacy and the feeling of control over important events in his or her life. But in many leaders this need develops into a desire for power over other people. In the case of destructive leaders, the ideology or worldview they shape may justify both their desire for power and their belief in violence as a means of both maintaining power and furthering their cause. This was true of Hitler, Stalin, Mao, as well as the Khmer Rouge.

In Rwanda and elsewhere the leaders' motivation to maintain power and privilege in the face of Tutsi challenge was intertwined with their strong negative views and fear of Tutsis. The genocide started when the president's plane was shot down, during a cease-fire and before the Arusha accords were executed. The agreement gave substantial, almost a dominant role to the Tutsis in the government to be created.[48] For some Hutu leaders, it was intolerable that such a devalued, feared, and (for the architects of the Hutu Ten Commandments) hated group would again have substantial power.

Leaders usually interpret the meaning of events for the population. One author offers the concept of "crisis framing" and suggests that this is what Milosevic did in Yugoslavia, thereby shaping the attitude of the population.[49] Events can be framed so that they create or intensify hostility. Using propaganda, intense devaluation and hate speech,[50] and such framing of events, leaders prepare the population for violence. David Hamburg writes that "Incitement is a hallmark, and perhaps prerequisite, of genocide. Every modern case of genocide has been preceded by a mass media propaganda campaign directed by political leaders...(who)...take advantage of predisposing elements and cultural myths, then skilfully work on them to incite their population to genocide."[51]

A destructive ideology that both identifies enemies and advocates action against them is an aspect of instigation. Speeches by leaders, the media, and educational institutions can all be their carriers. In the realm of terrorism, mosques have been identified as important. This is probably because they provide a forum both for authorities whose ideas carry special weight, and for the recipients to discuss those ideas. Ideas become powerful when they develop into a shared consensus with like-minded people. Islamic schools or madrassas had also been considered important purveyors of terrorism. But while many of them teach a fundamentalist form of Islam, and some of them preach jihad, most of them are apparently not direct sources of terrorism.

However, Greg Mortenson, the mountain climber who stumbled into a village in Pakistan and subsequently spent many years building schools in the region, especially for girls, writes about some madrassas that do inspire their students to fight. He found many madrassas and mosques that rich Saudis have built in the region. The Saudis have been guided by and have promoted a severe form of Islam, Wahhabism. Mortenson says, "Many of their schools and mosques are doing good work to help Pakistan's poor. But some of them seem to exist only to teach militant jihad,"[52] and many of their students become Taliban fighters or jihadists.

An important tool of recruitment is the Internet. Young Muslims looking for identity and meaning in their lives can connect with each other and with groups on the Internet. They can find social connections in chatrooms and on the Web sites of radical groups, which have recruitment drives on the Internet,[53] where they adapt their messages for the different groups they try to reach. For example, Hezbollah has a Web site with downloadable games for children.[54]

Incitement by leaders, combined with hostile actions of individuals and the group, can also generate hate. Once hate develops, it does not remain under the leaders' control. It is maintained by ideology and can grow into people's identity. When groups that have lived in antagonism, hostility, and mutual violence, as in the Israeli–Palestinian conflict, begin to move toward peace, hate often flares up. Haters may feel desperate about the potential disconfirmation of their beliefs, identity, and ideological vision or fear that the objects of their hate will get away without punishment and continue to endanger them.

Leaders can move people by changing their political course, especially if they do so with full commitment. Often, however, they change their course half-heartedly. For example, Palestinian leaders, after the Oslo accords, continued to use hate speech about Israelis in talking to their own people. Palestinian text-books continued to present highly negative images of Jews. Israelis continued to build settlements and exercise harsh control over Palestinians. There was a destructive terrorist attack by an Israeli, and many Palestinian terror attacks. The actions of each group reinforced enmity within its own group and in the other group toward it.

Research and experience have led many observers to believe that people who hate, as well as people committed to extreme ideologies, true believers, are very difficult to change. But that does not mean impossible. At the very least the rest of a group, whose passivity and compliance support haters, can change. In Part II, I will discuss influences and experiences—for example, humanizing the other, contact, and constructively fulfilling basic needs—that can change enablers, and even some of the haters themselves.

Instigators, Other Leaders, and Perpetrators

Psychologist David Mandel differentiates between instigators, other leaders, and perpetrators. He considers instigators as "critical for the origination of an act of collective violence, whereas a perpetrator—usually one of many—is critical for its execution." While perpetrators are interchangeable, instigators are not. He sees instigators as "serving a catalytic role in the development of collective violence."[55] He considers Himmler, for example, who was a very high-level member of the Nazi government and a major architect of the Final Solution of the Jewish Question, as a perpetrator not an instigator, because it was Hitler who "commissioned" the plan to exterminate the Jews.

His analysis of Hitler's evolution shows, however, how interconnected the evolution of an instigator is with his environment. Hitler suffered a powerful injury to his self-concept when, imagining himself a potentially great artist, he was not accepted into the Academy of Fine Arts in Vienna. This injury was enhanced by what I have called "comparison distress,"[56] as his only friend and roommate, a musician, was accepted into the Vienna Conservatoire. Hitler later successfully shifted from a focus on an individual, personal identity as an artist to a collective identity of a deeply committed and nationalist German. He was then devastated when Germany lost World War I. He could not believe that his great country could suffer such defeat and was open to the scapegoating of Jews that was part of right-wing political movements in Germany. Earlier, when he lived in Vienna, he was exposed to the intense anti-Semitism of that city and its mayor. But Hitler wrote in *Mein Kampf*[57] that it took time for him to absorb and make his own the way the right-wing groups in Germany vilified Jews. He proceeded, however, to vilify them more than anyone.

While most who begin to instigate develop their destructive aims over time, some may be, as William Zartman suggests, ready to be "a crystallizing agent" who acts when he sees a situation in which people are "vulnerable to his blandishments ... like loose tinder lying around (that) only excites pyromaniacs, it does not create them, they must pass by and see the opportunity."[58] Both in some people who help others, and people who harm others, inclinations they have developed through prior experiences can be activated by powerful social conditions. I have referred to this in helpers as "spontaneous helping,"[59] when their personality prepares people to respond without an elaborate process of decision making, whether to catch a falling child from a window or to hide a persecuted member of a group.

In the case of Hitler, we know that to whatever extent his anti-Semitism was shaped by right-wing groups after the war, it was already intense in *Mein Kampf*, his autobiography and description of political ideology published in 1925 and 1926. According to author Richard Rhodes, an adjutant wrote down in 1935 that Hitler told his closest associates: "Out with them from all the professions and into the ghetto with them; fence them in somewhere where they can perish as they deserve while the German people look on, the way people stare at wild animals."[60] This was 2 years after the Nazis came to power with the persecution of the Jews well underway.

In addition to difficult life conditions, real conflict, and their psychological impact, both a "prejudiced consensus and propaganda"[61] are important in leading to mass violence. As a result of past evolution in attitudes and actions, members of groups can be strongly inclined to act violently against others without direct and current instigation. Hamburg notes, for example, that in 1867 in Queensland, Australia, "a newspaper urged 'a war of extermination' against aborigines. Even without totalitarianism and organized incitement by state authorities, ethnic extermination was a common theme in the nineteenth century."[62] At various times this was also the case in the United States with regard to Native Americans.

Instigators' motivations and actions are part of both a larger group process, and the mutual influence in a small leadership group. Even in the case of Hitler, his interactions with other Nazi leaders, and the responses of the population, are likely to have shaped his decision to "commission" genocide. The Nazis were surprised by the population's passive acceptance of their early anti-Jewish policies and were influenced by the population when it took anti-Jewish actions ahead of them. For example, businesses refused to pay Jews for holidays, claiming that they did not have the right attitude toward labor.

We usually have little information about the internal processes among genocidal decision makers. Minutes exist from the 1942 Wannsee conference of 15 high-level Nazi administrators who designed the "final solution of the

Jewish question," but this was a conference dealing with the execution of a decision that had already been made, and its minutes were an edited document. We do know a little about high-level decision making in other situations. Social psychologist Irving Janis studied a number of decisions that high-level leaders have made with disastrous consequences. He noted the strong social pressures that develop in many different kinds of groups, ranging from heavy smokers who try to quit to presidential advisers, to maintain friendly relations in the group. He called the resulting process "groupthink," a deterioration of mental efficiency, reality testing, and moral judgment that results from pressures within the group.[63]

One of his examples was the 1961 decision by President John F. Kennedy and his advisors to launch an invasion of Cuba, which ultimately resulted in the Bay of Pigs fiasco. Once an opinion in favor of the invasion was formulated in the group and seemingly accepted by Kennedy, others mostly did not question it, or if they did, they were discouraged to do so. Robert Kennedy acted in a role that Janis called self-appointed mind guard, privately pressuring Arthur Schlesinger, the historian who was part of the decision-making group, not to raise more questions about the planned invasion, since the president had made up his mind and it was time for everyone to support him. Only later did several members of the group say that they did not think the Cuban people would rise up to support the U.S.-backed invasion, a basis for the decision to invade with a small force.

Not only in society in general, but within a small group of leaders as well, an evolution takes place. Their decision to engage in violence against others, including genocide, is the result of this evolution. Knowledge that can create awareness by leaders of their own group processes may lead some to express practical and moral concerns that can shift directions. The training of leaders to understand the origins of group violence, and the destructive evolution both in society and in small groups as an aspect of it, is important for prevention. Prevention must also address the population, the difficult conditions in societies and their impact, and "prejudiced consensus" and other characteristics of culture/society.

The Ideologies in the Primary Cases in the Book

The Power of Ideas

The power of ideas in human life is enormous. Powerful ideas are not just thoughts: They have great emotional power and they affect behavior. People can be killed on the basis of ideas and customs even in the absence of a coherent ideology or "higher ideals." Consider the following extreme ideas and actions: Infants who are considered imperfect are put out to die or killed (as in Sparta, among other instances); widows are burned alive on wood pyres (in India) or cast out of the group to starve or freeze to death (some native American tribes); violence between different branches of the same religion, such as Catholics and Protestants, or Shiite and Sunnis; people who have religious ideas slightly different from the traditional ones are killed as "heretics"; and children are killed by one parent because the other parent is a member of another ethnic group. In Rwanda, where some people killed their own children during the genocide, several different motives may have contributed to their actions: In addition to coming to see the children as the "other," they may feared for their own lives if they did not kill the children of mixed marriage, or they may have feared that other people would kill the children in a more horrible way. Ideologies that lead to mass killing, genocide, terrorism, or to war, and that can bring about the death of many millions, are manifestations of a more general principle: the power of ideas, and ideals, in human life.

Ideas and ideals embodied in cultural customs are not simply intellectual constructions. They carry great emotional force. That is why many African families maintain the practice of clitorectomy, female circumcision, even after they have come to live in the West, or why some Muslims engage in the honor killings of girls in Western countries. Ideas, thoughts, and beliefs, and the strong emotions they generate, shape people's lives and guide their actions. Over time the practices they generate can become everyday matters, group norms. The emotional force reemerges if the norm is breached. This is even true of great violence. Ideologies that lead to self-sacrifice, "martyrdom," genocide, or terrorism, carry both passion and commitment, and the actions they lead to can become group norms.

At times ideas and feelings, based on old practice or newly emerging, can spread fast. When people gather, for example, in crowds or mobs, there can be a contagion of emotion. Some information or ideas emerge and give rise to feelings which intensify as they spread quickly throughout the group. This was the case in lynch mobs and other violent crowd behavior.[64] The same can also happen in smaller groups—large mobs often start with small groups. Under extreme conditions, intensely difficult life conditions or threat to the group, ideas and associated emotions may move speedily through channels of communication, increasing the effectiveness of leaders or a vanguard to exert influence.

Ideas, ideals, and ideologies can lead people to kill for them and to sacrifice their lives to live up to them. Early Christians endured terrible deaths; they preferred to be thrown to the lions rather than give up their faith. Soldiers in wars have thrown themselves on machine gun placements to fight the enemy and save their comrades—presumably, like terrorists, acting for both cause and comrades. At the ruins of Chichen Itza in what is now Mexico, there is a large field on which, according to historians, the ancient Mayans had athletic competitions, supervised by the king. At the end, the captain of the victorious team was decapitated, with his cooperation, by the captain of the losing team. This allowed him to go directly to heaven, instead of going through the many steps that according to Mayan belief were required to reach heaven.[65]

Terrorists and suicide bombers have become heroes in many communities. We used to find the idea of someone "voluntarily" giving up his or her life difficult to grasp. But the aforementioned examples show that this is not uncommon. More than for a widow in India going to her painful death as dictated by societal standards, an act of suicidal self-sacrifice that can provide feelings of positive identity, admiration by and connection to one's community or at least one's comrades, a feeling of effectiveness, and the belief that one's death contributes to a better world for one's group (and sometimes brings honor and material gain to one's family) can have significant attraction. While some suicide bombers, for example, Tamils in Sri Lanka, are not religious, many Muslim suicide bombers are religious. If you add the belief that you are pleasing God, fighting the enemy by suicide becomes even more attractive.

The power of ideas, and of an ideology, was evident in a training we conducted with national leaders in Rwanda. As I described earlier, after they stopped the genocide and assumed power, the new leaders of the country created an ideology of unity: There are no Tutsis and Hutus, only Rwandans. When we discussed, among the influences leading to genocide, that of one group devaluing the other, they said in 2001, 7 years after the genocide, "But there are no groups in Rwanda." The ideology of oneness was not adopted just to influence the population; the leaders had come to deeply hold it themselves. It took intense and extensive discussion before the president of Ibuka, the umbrella survivors' organization, said, "Even if we are not genetically different, we are socially different." And later, another high-level leader said, "I wonder what they (Hutus and Tutsis) say about each other when they are in their houses." A couple of the busy leaders were out of the room during this discussion, attending to some business. When they returned, it took time for them to catch up with this shift in the group.

German Nazi Ideology

Germany is one case where scapegoating and aspects of ideology were deeply intertwined. German ideology had a number of elements. One of them was the superiority of certain races, in particular Aryans—and the Germans were seen as more Aryan than any other group—over other races. The Nazis came to regard getting rid of Jews, the lowest race in their view, as improving not only the German race but all of humanity. Another element was the Germans' right to more living space—more territory. Germany had a right to take territory in the East. Another was the leadership principle, which involved complete obedience to the leader, Adolf Hitler.

One of the Nazis stock slogans was "the Jews are our misfortune." Jews were blamed for the loss of World War I, in which they "stabbed Germany in the back"[66] Hitler also blamed them for the start of World War II, even though Britain and France declared war after Germany, following a takeover of Austria and parts of Czechoslovakia, invaded Poland. Hitler even blamed the German army's defeat at Stalingrad on the Jews.[67]

A core aspect of Nazi thinking was the *Volk*, which can be translated more or less as "a people," or the German people as a community. The Nazis gave the concept of *Volk* mythic meaning and power. The Germans I interviewed in 1987 powerfully spoke of the satisfaction and joy they felt in being part of a community. Historian Thomas Kuehne[68] has described the value Germans placed on comradeship and their practice of it. In the military, living together, fighting together, killing partisans and Jews together in Eastern Europe and even dying together were made special by comradeship. Together comrades could kill, commit atrocities, and as members of the group could relinquish individual responsibility. Mutual support and warm feelings toward each other within the group gave them a sense of their own humanity. Although not all in the military succumbed to the culture of comradeship, those who did not were still under the power of the norms of conduct it created. Kuehne believes that comradeship extended beyond the military to the larger German society. Its basis and source of power was the emphasis on the *Volk*, on Germans as part of a single, special community.

Kuehne described camps, widespread during the Nazi era, both military and civilian, where much was done to strengthen comradeship. Everyone was expected to participate in group activities and to conform. The group turned against those who kept themselves apart from comrades and the community. Somewhat surprisingly and paradoxically, given the authoritarian focus and submission to authority demanded of Germans, a kind of ritualistic rebellion by a group of comrades against authority, at least one with a low-level authority such as a sergeant, was part of camp life. This was seemingly a way of strengthening comradeship. Comradeship was likely to increase the power of the group in creating conformity, for example, in the case of reserve police on the Eastern front who were sent to kill Jews, which I will later discuss.

Members of small groups often develop strong ties. Many authors write about the strong comradeship that develops in the military. Terrorists are assumed to be motivated by their commitment to both cause and comrades. The ideology and practice of comradeship as Kuehne described seems to have intentionally strengthened these ties, based on German culture and Nazi ideology.

A further element of Nazi ideology has been referred to as a biomedical view. The Nazis believed that different groups, the Jews in particular, were biologically different. Jews were regarded as biologically inferior, diseased, a cancer on the body of Germany. The cancer had to be removed to heal the patient, Germany. It was perhaps due to this aspect of the ideology that many medical doctors were involved in the Holocaust.[69]

Ideologies are usually constructed from many elements, often elements of the group's culture. In *The Roots of Evil*, I described the elements out of which

Nazi, Khmer Rouge, Turkish, and Argentine ideologies were constructed. For example, the elements out of which Nazi ideology arose included the strongly authoritarian German culture, Nietzsche's writings distinguishing superior human beings and the common masses, German anti-Semitism, Germans feeling left behind and yearning for expansion as other European countries became colonial empires, racial ideologies sweeping Europe, and eugenic thinking and practice—improving the genetic makeup of the group—that had become popular both in the United States and in Europe early in the twentieth century.

Ideology in the Rwandan Genocide

In relatively rate instances, as in the case of Rwanda, the positive element of an ideology is submerged in the negative. The Hutu power vision, as it was elaborated in the Hutu Ten Commandments published in 1990,[70] with its spirit expressed in widespread propaganda, came to assert that to create a better life for Hutus they had to sever ties with Tutsis. Implicit in the document was the aim to get rid of Tutsis. Tutsi women were presented in an especially harsh manner, as seducers of Hutu men who were to be protected from them by Hutu women. The intense hostility expressed toward Tutsi women was at least partly responsible for the fact that in the course of the genocide Tutsi women were not only raped but also often mutilated.

Scott Straus found in his research on perpetrators that many of them did not know the Hutu Ten Commandments. Those who did (or admitted it) were the especially violent killers. But those who did not know about the document were still exposed to its substance through speeches and radio programs intensely hostile to Tutsis.

The primary positive element in Hutu ideology was to elevate the Hutus—by getting rid of Tutsis. Was there some other positive element as well? Economist Philip Verwimp of Belgium has analyzed the speeches of Habyarimana, the president/dictator of Rwanda until his plane was shot down in April 6, 1994. Habyarimana wanted to make Rwanda self-sufficient in its food supply. He stressed that important exports of Rwanda, coffee, tea, and fur, were the result of peasant labor. He idealized a peasant society, "glorified" the peasantry, and pictured himself a peasant. He reintroduced communal labor, people working for the community, as part of this idealization of the real work of the peasants—the free labor benefiting the state. But however positive this vision might have appeared, Verwimp believes that the ideological elevation of the peasantry was one of the influences leading to genocide. He wrote:

> ....only the Hutus were real peasants in Rwanda; the Tutsis were the feudal class, closely associated with colonialist occupation...a peasant society does not tolerate the existence of non-peasants, in the same way as a communist society does not tolerate the existence of a capitalist class..."[71]

Some other genocidal regimes, in particular the Khmer Rouge in Cambodia, also idealized agriculture and those who worked the land.[72] As it is often the case, an ideology is often constructed from elements of a society's past, especially as it was at a time of past greatness. Cambodia was once a wealthy, powerful country, in part due to its agricultural techniques and production. The Khmer Rouge ideology defined total social equality (combined with a nationalistic ideology) as an equality of peasants working the land. The uses of the ideology were both destructive and self-destructive: After their takeover the Khmer Rouge destroyed the industrial-technological infrastructure of the country as they forced everyone to move into the countryside and work the land. The idealization of the peasants intensified differentiation between groups in both societies.

Ideologies in the Israeli–Palestinian Conflict

The creation of Israel was motivated by a nationalist ideology, born of Jewish persecution in Europe. It represented a benevolent form of nationalism, the desire to create an independent state or nation. A less benevolent form is to enhance power and influence in relation to other nations. While the Zionist ideology was the former, the nation was established on territory already inhabited by Palestinians and involved a takeover of Palestinian land, at first by buying land from Palestinians.

Ideology of another kind became especially important after the occupation of the West Bank and Gaza. One persistent influence on Israeli policies has been the vision of greater Israel, recreating the Israel of ancient times. A movement advocating the creation of greater Israel, *Gush Emunim*, segments of the Israeli public, especially many (but not all) very religious Jews, and some of the political parties have been reluctant to give up the West Bank because of their determination to create a greater Israel. *Gush Emunim*, the Movement of the Faithful, is committed to recreating the original land of Israel, and not giving up any of the territory that God gave to Israel. In a country that has always required a coalition government, even small parties committed to such a vision and purpose have had significant influence. The creation of the settlements, a substantial obstacle to peace with the Palestinians, has been motivated partly by this ideology and partly by the belief that the settlements increase Israel's security. While some settlers have gone to live in the settlements because of available, less expensive, and attractive housing, many of them have gone there to hold the territory for a greater Israel. Added to these ideologies is Israel's very strong focus on security. While security is essential, such focus can also develop into an ideology, shaping group relations. I consider both Israel's and Rwanda's approach to security as "defensive superiority."

On the Palestinian side, and generally the Arab side, the ideology has been more like that in Rwanda, the positive submerged in the negative. For a better life for Palestinians (and Arabs in the area), the Jewish state (and perhaps the Jews as well) had to be eliminated. Such a simple view can regarded as an ideology because it envisions a restructuring of the social world, in the hope of creating a better world, at least for Palestinians and/or Arabs in general. At this time only a segment of the Palestinians and Arabs may hold this view, but even today it is perhaps a substantial segment.

Hamas, formed during 1987–1988 at first primarily as a social service organization that was initiated by the leaders of the Muslim Brotherhood of Egypt, stated as its short-term goal the removal of Israeli forces from the occupied territories and as its long-term goal "the creation of an Islamic state in all of Palestine." One article in the group's charter says that "Giving up any part of the homeland is like giving up part of the religious faith itself"[73] Suicide terrorism was driven partly by this ideology, and partly as a response to Israeli occupation and practices in the occupied territories, as well as the resulting humiliation of and difficult life conditions for the Palestinians.

But enmity to Jews is at the core of Hamas. The Charter blames Jews for all the evils of the world in the past century and before:

> With money they ignited revolution in all parts of the world...they are behind the French Revolution, the Communist Revolution ....They are behind the First World War in which they destroyed the Islamic Caliph and gained material profit...They created the League of Nations so they could control the world through that organization. They are behind the Second World War...forming the United Nations and Security Council...in order to rule the world through that organization....[74]

Some of these ideas are derived from Arab leaders from before the time Israel was established. In 1943, in response to an approach by President Roosevelt, King Sau'ud of Saudi Arabia said that he was prepared to meet anyone of any religion "except (repeat except) a Jew." And the not especially radical prime minister of Jordan, Samir Rifa'i, said of the Jews, "they were responsible for starting two world wars..."[75]

The beliefs of extreme ideological groups are very difficult to change. But among Palestinians, Fatah was originally committed to the destruction of Israel and has changed over the years. Some among Hamas expressed a willingness to establish a lasting truce, which could begin a positive evolution. And the attitudes of the Palestinian population have shifted with events. In 2006 and 2007, for the majority of Palestinians reality came to dominate over ideology and anger. In a number of polls they said they would accept a two-state solution and favored negotiation to bring it about.[76] The polls in 2007 were also affected by the conflict between Fatah and Hamas. There have been further great changes since then, with increased enmity and violence between Fatah and Hamas, and especially severe conditions in Gaza as a result of boycott and isolation. In March

2008, a poll found that Palestinian support for violence was the greatest it had been in the past 15 years, and a majority opposed continuing peace negotiations.[77] The Israeli attack on Gaza late in 2008 in response to Hamas shooting rockets into Israel further changed the situation. But past shifts indicate that with the right conditions attitudes for a peace settlement can develop.

Ideology consists of ideas and ways of thinking, which often become passionately held beliefs with strong emotional commitment. When Israel unilaterally pulled out of Gaza in 2005, some of the settlements in Gaza were demolished in preparation for the pullout. Given their passionate belief that God gave that land to the Jews, some settlers refused to leave. They faced the army and were forcefully removed. While involvement in violent and traumatic events, whether as victim or witness, has created trauma among many Israelis, these settlers subsequently showed positive mental health and no significant trauma symptoms. They engaged in confrontation, guided by their principles, and were not psychologically harmed by it.[78]

Like many Israeli settlers, members of some evangelical Christian groups strongly believe in the creation of a greater Israel. Many evangelicals passionately believe that the Messiah will return when the Jews have recreated greater Israel. (Many evangelicals also believe, however, that once that happens all nonbelievers, including Jews, will die a terrible death.) There is strong support in some evangelical groups for Israelis maintaining and expanding settlements and recreating greater Israel.[79] (See also the discussion of bystandership in Chapter 7.)

Ideologies thus can generate powerful commitment and an overriding motivation to work for its fulfillment. Fulfilling the goals derived from the ideology can become a higher purpose. Fanaticism means that some goals become so dominant that they override all other goals and lead to the use of any means in their fulfillment. Religions as ideologies—a particular view of God and a way of life and commitment to create a world faithful to this view—as well as communism, Nazism, and other utopian ideologies have led people to sacrifice everything, including their lives, for their fulfillment. Unfortunately, all too often, they have led to an even greater willingness to sacrifice other people's lives.

Threat, Ideals, and the Ideology of Contemporary Al-Qaeda Terrorism

Ideologies often develop progressively, as ideas, theories, and actions build on each other. Communism evolved out of the writings of Marx and Engels, was developed further by Lenin, and was shaped by the writings, proclamations, policies, and actions of the leaders of the Soviet Union and increasingly of other communist countries as well.

A foundational ideological text for Egyptian terrorists, which then inspired Al-Qaeda, was written by Sayid Qutb, while in an Egyptian jail. A leading intellectual of the Muslim Brotherhood, he was later executed by Nasser's government, on an apparently trumped-up charge that he planned to overthrow the government. Qutb wanted to return Islam to its fundamentals. His ideas were expanded by one of his disciples, Faraj, who was the head of the *Jihad Organization* in Cairo that killed President Anwar Sadat, and then by others, including Ayman al-Zawahiri, who is regarded as Osama bin Laden's second in command.[80]

In the *Battle for God*, author Karen Armstrong[81] provides a history of fundamentalism in the three religions of the Book—Judaism, Christianity, and Islam. She describes its origins in the fourteenth century and regards it as a revolt against modernity as manifest in Western civilization. In our conceptualization, it is best seen as a response to great societal changes that lead people to turn to what they regard as well-established fundamentals. Armstrong sees it as a reaction to threat and fear—the fear of losing one's faith and of changes in the core aspects of life that support people. At the extreme, it can be seen as a fear of annihilation of one's beliefs, culture, and way of life—which for some people might become fear for their existence.

The reality is that Western civilization *has* changed the world. Some religious people have reacted to these changes by focusing on abstract ideals, and fortifying their identities, based on a literal interpretation of their scriptures and adherence to doctrines set long ago. The psychological needs that motivate people's return to fundamentals, both abstract ideals and the concrete practices that embody them, underlie the rise of fundamentalism in the United States in the late twentieth century, but they have exerted an even greater influence in Muslim societies. Many Muslim societies have remained highly traditional but have been invaded by profound changes in culture, technology, and communication.

Research by social psychologist Ian McGregor and his associates[82] has shown that people turn to abstract ideals and become more extreme in their views when they experience threat, even if the ideals and views have nothing to do with the nature of the threat. The threat in the research was created by giving rise to uncertainty in personal dilemmas about academic studies (should I stay in engineering or major in art?) or about relationships (shall I stay with or leave a boyfriend?). In response, people became more extreme in their views about abortion, about terrorists, and about groups other than their own. Their religious commitment increased. They supported the war in Iraq more. All these effects were stronger in people who had high self-esteem and who in McGregor's view had an approach personality, that is, they were people who move toward things. Uncertainty and frustration can lead people to turn more intensely to ideals and principles, and against people who represent a threat to them.

Qutb has spent time in the United States and returned to Egypt frustrated and disillusioned. In his writings he expanded concepts advanced by other Muslim thinkers, describing the world at the brink of a precipice. One reason was the current state of Islam, whose original teachings he believed had been corrupted. Other reasons that Qutb cited were communism and capitalism, which both dehumanized men. It is Islam, and only Islam, that can address human needs other than the material ones and create the proper relationship between God and man. In existing Muslim societies, life is not based on submission to God, as it should be. Education, one form of Jihad, is inadequate to address the problem, given the power of the forces aligned against the recreation of true Islam. The only available avenue is jihad by the sword, led by a vanguard. Qutb's thinking influenced those who became terrorists in Egypt. It was expanded by Faraj, who focused further on "infidel leaders" within the Muslim world who strayed from the path of Islam, on fighting the "near enemy," the existing Muslim governments.

In the aftermath of the fight against the Soviet Union in Afghanistan, there was competition among ideological views. One influential ideological thinker and leader, who was a teacher of and inspiration to Osama bin Laden, Azzam, was killed in 1989. The ideological focus has shifted to the "far enemy." Contributing to the shift was the first war against Iraq in 1991, and especially upsetting to Osama bin Laden, the presence of U.S. troops in Saudi Arabia, the land with the two holy cities of Mecca and Medina. The overthrow of the democratically elected Islamic party in Algeria was another grievance. While Osama bin Laden's declaration of war in 1996 focused on jihad against the leaders of Saudi Arabia, by 1998 the focus shifted to the United States, to a war against all Americans.

Muslim leaders were now seen as pawns of global powers, who were the main obstacle to the creation of a worldwide Islamic community, the Umma, and the recreation of the Caliphate, an Islamic government with political unity and the leadership of the whole Muslim world. The main culprit was seen as the United States, and the West in general.[83] Jerrold Post quotes from an Al-Qaeda operations manual, which provides both instructions and inspiration to undercover operators, with elaborate quotes from religious texts as justification for the actions it describes:

Islamic governments have never and will never be established through peaceful solutions and cooperative councils. They are established, as they (always) have been,
> by pen and gun
>> by word and bullet
>>> by tongue and teeth.[84]

Al-Zawahiri wrote in 2001:

...the Jewish-Crusade alliance, led by the United States, will not allow any Muslim force to reach power in any of the Islamic countries....we concentrate on the following:

1. The need to inflict maximum casualties against the opponent, for this is the language understood by the west, no matter how much time and effort such operations take.
2. The need to concentrate on martyrdom operations...[85]

The Encyclopedia of the Orient identifies the goals of the Al-Qaeda ideology to "radicalize existing Islamic groups and create Islamic groups where none exist," to "advocate destruction of the United States which is seen as the chief obstacle to reform in Muslim societies," and to support Muslim fighters in Islamic countries.

In Marc Sageman's view, radical Islamists see themselves fighting, in my terminology, for a "better world." They "blame Western values of greed and moral decadence as sources of corruption," and see the West "engaged in an apocalyptic war against Islam."[86] In his view, terrorists want to be heroes in this fight of good against evil. In my perspective, a terrorist group provides people with a community, and terrorist actions fulfill needs for effectiveness and identity. As one terrorist said: "An armed action proclaims that I am here, I exist, I am strong, I am in the field, I am on the map."[87]

An ideological shift of potential significance near the end of the first decade of this century is a turn away by some terrorists from violent jihad. One of these people is Dr. Fadl, whose writings have been a major ideological blueprint for the use of violence by Al-Qaeda. His book, *The Compendium of the Pursuit of Divine Knowledge*, provided justification to kill. But a new book, written in an Egyptian prison, renounces and denounces the use of violence. A group of other jihadists now in Egyptian prisons also have shifted in their thinking. They claim that they were misled and were manipulated to use violence, which brought them much suffering and brought no gain for Islam.[88]

A possible influence leading to this change in Fadl's thinking was his animosity to Al-Zawahiri. He had a history of conflict with him and accused him of changing the content of his book *The Compendium*. Another possible influence on all the prisoners is the personal losses they refer to. A still further influence may have been dialogue with them. Egypt's Grand Mufti Aheikh Ali Gomaa was involved in this dialogue. He is an advocate of moderate Islam, who believes that "there is no conflict with democratic rule and no need for theocracy ... and Muslim women ... should have equal standing with men." He said: "I began going into the prisons in the nineteen nineties...We had debates with the prisoners, which continued for more than three years. Such debates became the nucleus for the revisionist thinking."[89] He notes that it is very difficult to move terrorists, and their reexamination of their views is important progress. In addition to the new book by Fadl, leaders of the Islamic Group imprisoned in Egypt wrote a series of pamphlets in which they explain the revision in their thinking.

The Islamic Group had already called for an end of armed action in 1999, clearly to no effect. The impact of an ideological shift by a group of terrorists and an intellectual leader may be limited, for a number of reasons. These people are in prison, and Al-Zawahiri and other Al-Qaeda leaders claim that what they say is the result of coercion. The Grand Mufti is "hated" among Islamists for his views.[90] His views are presumably partly shaped by the political conditions in Egypt, a country with a secular government that has suppressed Islamist movements. This reduces his credibility among Islamists.

Still, while violence evolves, as I will show, so reactions that inhibit violence can also evolve. Other voices, including Islamic scholars, are advancing moderate interpretations of Islam. They point to the quotes from Islamic texts that Al-Qaeda uses to justify its actions as distorted or taken out of context. A more moderate "European Islam" is also evolving.[91] There are an increasing number of voices that advance a form of Islam that is more open to a constructive vision of peaceful coexistence with other religions.

Ideologies of Antagonism

A negative perception of and orientation to another group can develop into what I have called an ideology of antagonism. Such an ideology "identifies the other as a threat to the well-being, security, and even survival of one's group..." The group sees not only the other as its enemy, but sees itself as the enemy of the other. When a group holds such an ideology, harm suffered by the other group becomes a source of satisfaction. The ideology may include a "...belief that superiority is required for security and a wish to diminish, subdue, and in extreme cases exterminate the enemy."[92] The content of such an ideology is the relationship itself; us and them are enemies.

The differentiation between us and them, differences in values and beliefs, negative views of the other, conflict and differences in interests, and violent acts by the other toward one's group as well as by one's group toward the other can all contribute to the evolution of this ideology. It can develop out of opposing nationalisms or opposing ideologies. For example, for communists, to eliminate the oppression of the workers, capitalism had to be eliminated, which meant eliminating capitalists. An ideology of antagonism creates a bias against another group that makes it difficult to realistically evaluate the other's intentions and actions. It further reduces nations' or groups' normally weak ability to critically evaluate their own actions. It creates resistance to constructive actions that might resolve real conflict. An ideology of antagonism seems to have characterized Hutus in Rwanda and seems present in at least some segments of Palestinians and Israelis.

Much of my discussion so far about how people turn against others has been about the influence of social conditions and conflicts of interest, and/or instigation by leaders who are themselves affected by social conditions and conflict. But devaluation, hostility, and violence are also the result of culture, and of education, socialization, or direct training of children and adults. I will write about these when I discuss cultural influences in Chapter 8.

Summary

Groups and their members tend to respond to difficult life conditions and group conflict by fulfilling basic needs in destructive ways—ways that over time lead them to harm others and that in the long run also harm them. This is more likely to happen in societies with certain characteristics. In response to these conditions, identity tends to shift from experiencing oneself as an individual, a separate person, to being a member of a group. At the same time, other people outside the group are also seen less as individuals and more as group members. The leaders who emerge or to whom the group turns, and their followers, join in scapegoating another group for life problems. In the case of group conflict, they blame the other group for the conflict, the inability to resolve it, and violence. They adopt or create destructive ideologies, visions of a better life but with some group identified as an enemy that stands in the way of the ideology's fulfillment.

Notes

1 Tajfel, 1978; Tajfel & Turner, 1979, 1986
2 Staub, 1989
3 For a review of some of this research see Dovidio, Gaertner, & Saguy, 2009
4 Gurr & Harff, 1994
5 Tajfel, 1982
6 Autessere, 2008
7 Lillie, 2004
8 Both quotes are from Lindner, 2008
9 Post, 2007
10 Fiske, 2004
11 Cehajic, Brown, & Castano, 2008; Noor, Brown, Gonzalez, Manzin, & Lewis, 2008; see also Cairns, Tam, Hewstone, & Niens, 2005
12 Gibson, 2006.
13 see Dovidio et al., 2009
14 Post, 2007
15 Zimbardo, 1969
16 Waller, 2007
17 Schachter, 1959
18 For a review of some of the relevant research, see Pettigrew, 2003
19 See also Hogg, 2007
20 Brewer & Pierce, 2005

21 Hogg, 2007

22 McCauley, 2004

23 Suedfeld and Schaller, 2002

24 Hogg, 2007

25 See Hogg, 2007 for a discussion of this

26 Lippitt & White, 1943; see also Staub, 1979

27 Solzhenitsyn, 1973, pp. 173-174

28 Chalk & Jonassohn, 1990, p. 404

29 Kiernan, 2007, p.3

30 Quoted in Staub, 1989

31 Hollander, 2006. The page number for the first quote is xlvi, for the second, xlvii.

32 Smith, 1999

33 Fein, 2007

34 See Staub, 1989

35 Kiernen, 2007

36 Valentino, 2004

37 Steiner, 1980, p. 431

38 Craig, 1982.

39 Allport, 1954

40 Staub, 1989

41 Abel, 1938

42 Newbury, 1998

43 Goldhagen, 1998

44 Straus, 2006

45 Karim Sadjadpour of the Carnegie Foundation for Peace, a political analyst of Iranian origin, describing this transformation on "Fresh air," on 6/23/09

46 Melson, 1992

47 Ezekiel, 1995, 2002

48 Mamdani, 2001; Straus, 2006

49 Oberschall, 2000

50 Volhardt, Coutin, Staub, Weis & Deflander, 2007

51 Hamburg, 2007, p. 33-34

52 Mortenson & Relin, 2007

53 Kruglanski, et al. 2008; Sageman, 2008

54 Weimann, 2006; see also http://www.usip.org/fellows/reports/2004/0513_weimann.html

55 Mandel, 2002, p.260 and 262

56 Staub, 1978

57 Hitler, 1925

58 Zartman, 1989, p. 11

59 Staub, 1978

60 Rhodes, 2002, p. 36

61 Hamburg, 2007, p. 35

62 Ibid, p.20

63 Janis, 1972, 1973

64 Staub & Rosenthal, 1994

65 The Ball Court. Quoted in Moffatt, 2008

66 Hilberg, 1961; Staub, 1989

67 Friedlander, 2007

68 Kuehne, 2009, 2010

69 Lifton, 1986

70 des Forges, 1999

71 Verwimp, 2004, p. 3

72 Kiernen, 2007

73 Quoted in Post, 2007, p. 176

74 Quoted in Post, 2007, pp.176-177

75 Both quoted in Remnick, 2008, p. 72

76 For a variety of poll results, see http://www.pcpsr.org/survey/polls/2006/p22ejoint.html

77 Wright, 2008

78 Hobfoll et al., 2007

79 Hagee, 2007

80 For overviews of the development of Al Qaeda ideology, and the ideology itself, see Kressell, 2007; Post, 2007; and Sageman, 2004

81 Armstrong, 2001

82 McGregor, 2006; McGregor, Gailliot, Vazquez, & Nash, 2007; McGregor, Haji, Nash, & Teper, 2008

83 Kressell, 2007; Post, 2007; Sageman, 2004

84 Post, 2007, p. 201

85 Al-Zawahiri, 2001

86 Sageman, p. 80, 81

87 Post, Sprenzak, & Denny, 2003, p. 183

88 Wright, 2008

89 Ibid, p. 42

90 Ibid.

91 See Staub, 2007b, and later in the book for more discussion of it.

92 Staub, 1989, p. 251

6

Learning by Doing in Individuals and Groups
The Evolution of Extreme Violence

Individuals (and groups of people and whole societies) learn by doing; they change through their actions (or through their passivity) in either negative or positive ways.

Hostility and violence by groups as individuals and groups change as a result of their actions.

Extreme violence by groups does not suddenly burst forth. Not only are the influences I identified present, but there is a progressive evolution in attitudes and actions that can become evident and be assessed if one looks at historical continuity over time. This means that the world can observe and note what is happening in a society, which provides the opportunity to halt the evolution. While the social conditions I described already indicate the danger of mass violence, it is this evolution—as manifested in scapegoating, the creation of destructive ideology, increased devaluation, discrimination, the beginning of violence, changing societal standards, and the creation of institutions that serve and promote persecution and violence—that signal the increasing need for prevention and reconciliation.

Changes in Individuals and Groups as a Result of Their Actions

As discussed in the previous chapter, scapegoating and a destructive ideology (that arise in part from a history of devaluation of others and other cultural characteristics) lead a group and its members to turn against another group. As some members of the group (or through institutionalized discrimination the whole group) begin to harm members of the other group psychologically, spiritually, economically, and physically, they justify their actions by seeing the other in a more and more negative light. The scapegoated group, the ideological enemy, becomes increasingly devalued. Negative views and enmity may be propagated in literature, art, and the media, by the words and actions of public figures, and the way members of the group talk about them and to them.

An evolution also takes place in the course of group conflict. As conflict remains unresolved, as it intensifies, and especially as it becomes increasingly violent, people in both groups feel threatened and fearful. They come to believe that the other group wants to take away what they have, and even destroy them physically. This can happen even in a country with great power, as occurred to a fairly significant extent in the United States after 9/11. Circumstances combined with past history created such fears among Hutus in Rwanda, Jews in Israel, and among Palestinians. Hate speech by leaders, in the media, and by the public in general intensify devaluation and fear and add to the justification and increased devaluation that follow harming people. Together, they create and foment hate. Hate consists of an intensely negative view of others, usually based on beliefs that they are morally bad and/or represent a profound threat to oneself and/or one's group because of their actions or because of their very nature. Such intense negative emotions make the suffering and even death of the other desirable and satisfying.[1]

Harmful actions and violence lead to more harmful actions and greater violence. A learning process is involved in this evolution. People learn by doing and change, for better or worse, as a result of their own actions. Harming other people can lead some to feel guilty, to apologize, and to attempt to make amends for their actions. One of my students reported in a paper he wrote for a class that in high school someone he regarded as a friend stole a substantial amount of money from him. He badly beat up this "friend," but then felt so guilty about having done so that he committed himself to never acting violently, a commitment that he wrote he has lived up to. But under the conditions I described, violent actions are likely to be followed by justification, which makes more violent action probable.

As members of another group are harmed, individuals change, norms and standards of conduct of the group change, and institutions change or are created to serve violence. These may include changes in the justice system (so that harmful actions against the "enemy" group are not punished) and changes in laws that deprive members of the other group of their rights, exclude members of the group from the government and military, or alter the way children belonging to the group are treated in schools. Yvette Ragasuguhanga, a Tutsi survivor of the Rwandan genocide, described the "homework" assigned to her on the first day of school. At the start of the school day the children were told to stand up separately in one of two groups—Hutu children or Tutsi children. Because she did not know which group she belonged to, she was berated and shamed. She was told the next day she had to explain to the class what a Tutsi is.[2]

As the evolution progresses, changes in societal beliefs and norms of conduct make acceptable and even normal previously inconceivable actions against the victim group. Old institutions are transformed or new ones are created that administer affairs related to the group, including confiscation of their property, and that in general serve to perpetuate discrimination and violence against them. Paramilitary groups are created to serve as agents of violence, including mass murder.

The "steps along a continuum of destruction" consist of both a psychological and a behavioral evolution. Negative views of the other expand, until devaluation becomes so intense that the "other" is excluded from the human and moral realm. Accompanying moral exclusion, or as a further evolution after moral exclusion, there is often *a reversal of morality*. Killing, eliminating this particular group and its members, comes to be seen as the right, moral thing to do. Killers may come to see themselves as fulfilling the higher ideals of their ideology. Such evolution has been evident in instances of genocide whether in Turkey, Germany, Cambodia, Rwanda, or elsewhere. The evolution can be speeded up and intensified by a variety of influences or slowed down and brought to a stop by other influences. Early prevention is intended to bring this evolution, progression, or continuum to an early halt, and ideally to start a positive evolution.[3*]

This evolution has a role in the huge number of violent rapes in some settings, such as the Congo. But the transformation of people in the course of the evolution of violence does not automatically reverse itself when the violence is brought to an end. Sexual violence during the civil war in Liberia became normal; one survey found that 75% of women had been raped. After the fighting ended, raping women and young girls, many of them very young, has continued. Nicholas Kristof wrote that "it has been easier to get men to relinquish their guns than their sense of sexual entitlement."[4] I will later discuss how former perpetrators continue to devalue their victims and remain committed to their ideology, which interferes with reconciliation.

Experimental research, while sparse, also shows how violence evolves. In the famous studies of social psychologist Stanley Milgram on obedience to authority[5], participants who had the role of teachers were told to increase the level of electric shock they administered each time a "learner" made a mistake. In this study, and other replications, between 60%–65% of the teachers continued to increase the shock level and administer even the strongest shocks, which the shock machine indicated were highly dangerous. A smaller but substantial percentage did so even when they could hear the learner shouting in pain in the next room. When the teachers were told to hold a learner's hand on the shock machine, 30% of participants still administered the strongest shock. While at no time did the learner, part of the staff of the research study, actually receive the shocks that the participants thought they were administering, participants believed that the shocks and the learner's pained reactions were real.

Many participants who administered the strongest shocks questioned along the way what they were doing, but when the experimenter insisted, they continued. One likely influence in creating such "obedience to authority" was the gradual, stepwise increase in shocks. A similar teacher-learner setup when people in the role of teacher were *not* instructed to increase the level of shock clearly showed learning by doing, as they did so on their own when the learner made repeated mistakes. These latter studies did not test whether people would administer very intense shocks.[6]

Psychologist Albert Bandura and his associates[7] have conducted a study that shows both that devaluing people leads to harming them more—while a positive evaluation leads to harming people less—and that doing harm evolves. In this study three-member "supervisory teams" received information to evaluate the quality of decision making by decision-making teams. The task of the supervisory teams was to punish members of the decision-making teams when they made bad decisions. Before they began this process, supervisors overheard on an intercom, presumably accidentally, the experimenter and a research assistant talking about the characteristics of the decision-making teams as shown on questionnaires that these teams supposedly completed. The supervisors in the dehumanized group overheard comments about the decision-making teams that they were "an animalistic, rotten bunch." The supervisors in the humanized group overheard about their teams that they were perceptive and understanding. In a third, neutral group, supervisors did not hear any comments.

The first time that the supervisors shocked the decision makers, there was no difference in the level of shock administered, but then the three groups diverged. Although in all groups the decision makers made the same decisions, in the dehumanized group the supervisors administered stronger and stronger shocks over time, with an average level of seven out of ten. The decision makers in the humanized group received the least amount of shock. Those in the neutral group were in the middle. In addition, sometimes the supervisors were told that the intensity of the shocks was based on their individual decision, at other times on average levels set by their teams. When responsibility was shared this way, or diffused, they set higher levels of shock.

The evolution of violence also takes place in intractable conflict, in a parallel fashion in both (or all) groups involved in the conflict. As the conflict persists, it gives rise to societal beliefs that social and political psychologist Daniel Bar-Tal has called an "ethos of conflict."[8] This ethos helps maintain commitment to the group's cause. It includes beliefs about the morality of the group and the justice of its cause, and the immorality of the other group and its responsibility for the conflict, as well as about what is required to create security for the group, and about the need for unity and patriotism. The ethos of conflict "helps people adapt and cope with their threatening and difficult situation, but also feeds the violence."[9]

Persons, Roles, and the Structure of Organizations

People change or evolve also because of the roles they enter in a system that perpetuates harm toward others. A person who goes along with what the system asks, such as boycotting Jewish stores, has a small role, although the influence of many people who go along this way is great. All involvement in a system of perpetration shapes people, with greater involvement shaping people to a greater degree.

Psychologist James Waller's[10] story of a German man provides a compelling example of this. Franz Ziereis, whose father was killed in World War I, joined the German army as an 18 year old and remained in it for 13 years. After that, in 1936, he accepted a job as a training officer in the Waffen SS and joined the Nazi party. This was the military arm of the SS, but the SS also ran the concentration camps, and in 1939 he became the commander of one of them, Mauthausen. He participated in the shooting of prisoners, and to practice his marksmanship, he would randomly shoot at new transports of prisoners when they arrived at the camp. He admitted to frequently driving the vans in which carbon monoxide was routed back into the passenger area to kill Jews, and he participated in the beating and execution of "scores of prisoners." He was rewarded over the years with increasingly high rank in the SS.

Waller aims to show that perpetrators are ordinary people. As I will later show, for example, in the discussion of the Stanford Prison Study, there is self-selection in who enters what roles. In the case of Ziereis, it is likely that the early loss of his father at a time when his country experienced loss, confusion, and chaos greatly affected him, and that his father having been a soldier contributed to his attraction to the military. Those who enter into roles that lead them to become perpetrators are "ordinary" people, but often have characteristics that predispose them for these roles and make their evolution in them easier.

The structure of organizations they enter, the way roles are defined in them, and the actions required in them socialize people. The training and indoctrination they receive in these organizational roles also shape them. The SS received intense training in loyalty, obedience, and submission to the organization and its leaders. Marriage partners had to be approved by superiors.[11] Indoctrination and special training are normal in the military, paramilitary, and terrorist groups, and in the training of torturers. The Greek torturers during the dictatorship of the colonels in the 1970s were made to endure cruel treatment, including severe physical abuse, as a way of increasing their submission to authority and obedience.[12] People in such groups are also led to engage in violence, which both furthers their evolution and ties them more to the group. Some members of the Rwandan militias, the Interahamwe, were made to kill as part of their indoctrination into the group.[13] Under some conditions alternative groups that are available can fulfill important needs and limit attraction to groups that move people to perpetration. However, some people may be attracted specifically to such hierarchical, intensely ideological groups, and perhaps to their potential or actual violence. And sometimes people enter groups that only later become aggressive in ideology and action.

Principles of Change in the Evolution of Violence

Initial acts of doing harm can be a response to threat or harmful actions, they can result from past devaluation—judging others as bad—and discrimination, and from instigation, scapegoating and a destructive ideology. As people change as a result of their actions, what are the principles by which change takes place? I already suggested that people need to justify their actions and do so by devaluating those they have harmed. But why is this? One reason is the human need for *cognitive consistency*, demonstrated by a great deal of research in social psychology. This is a need for our varied thoughts and actions to be reasonably consistent, rather than at odds with each other.

As Germans increasingly appreciated the better life the Nazi government created for them in the 1930s, they increasingly came to like Hitler.[14] Since Hitler intensely disliked the Jews, this motivation for consistency would have led Germans to derogate Jews more. Given such motivation, their own actions—obeying the Nazis, avoiding Jewish stores, severing relations with Jews, or harming Jews—would require that they see them in a more negative light and believe that they deserve to suffer. Following harm done to others, cognitive consistency, a motivation that normally exerts its influence automatically and without awareness, can lead to a cycle of devaluation and further wrongdoing. This principle also makes is easier to harm scapegoats and ideological enemies. Another principle that contributes to the evolution of violence is *habituation or adaptation*. Humans get accustomed to what frequently happens. The usual becomes normal. When certain levels of discrimination and violence are widely practiced, people habituate or adapt to it, which makes it easier for them to move to a new, higher level.[15] People not only come to see what *is* as normal, but as the philosopher Hume wrote, they come to see the familiar, what is, as morally good. Lawrence Kohlberg, a psychologist who studied morality, also wrote about the change from *is* to *ought*, the familiar becoming the right thing in people's minds.

A related notion is *status quo bias*, people's tendency to stick "with opinions and practices from the past."[16] In one study with a large number of Americans who closely matched the U.S. census, people were told about the use of stress by U.S. forces when questioning suspects in the Middle East. The practices using stress, actually torture, were listed. When a sentence was added saying, "This kind of stress interview is not new; according to some reports, it has been used for more than 40 years in the U.S. military,"[17] support for and justification of the use of these practices increased substantially among the study's participants. This was true regardless of their party affiliation, be it Republican, Democrat, or Independent. In the researchers' view, the likely reason for this response is that people "equate existence with goodness in a relatively intuitive, automatic manner."[18] The findings are consistent with *system justification theory*, another approach to explain why people accept and approve of what is in existence—seeing it as fair and legitimate.[19] Both the status quo bias and system justification suggest that once a certain level of discrimination and violence against people is established, people would accept it, justify it, consider it right.

Another principle or common, widely held psychological tendency that contributes to the evolution of violence is one I mentioned in Chapter 3: *belief in a just world*. If the world is just, people who suffer must be getting what they deserve.[20] Both perpetrators who inflict harm, and witnesses or bystanders to harm, appear to be influenced by just-world thinking. A further principle is *reinforcement*. When an action is followed by something that is satisfying, people are more likely to perform that action again. Aggressive actions can make people feel powerful and superior, and they can create connections among those acting together as comrades in a shared cause. As they are seen to fulfill the "higher values" of an ideology, as they create coherence, as they contribute to the fulfillment of basic needs, actions are reinforced. Fairly often in cases of mass violence perpetrators also gain materially, another reinforcement.

Diffusion of responsibility is also important.[21] A great deal of research shows that people help someone in need less when other people are present, or when conditions focus responsibility for helping on other people who are present, such as a person in a leadership role or someone with a medical background. If a person is alone facing someone's need, or if other people are present who focus responsibility on him or her, this person is more likely to help. But individual characteristics also matter. People who feel personally responsible for other people's welfare help more[22] even when someone else is also there.[23]

The study by Bandura and his associates showed that when participants believed that the decisions of members of supervisory teams were averaged—which would presumably make each of them both feel and appear to others less responsible—each person decided to harm others more. The conditions for diminished individual responsibility often exist in real life, when individuals participate in or execute group decisions, or when each person is one among many bystanders who witness harm done to other people. Bandura suggested that under certain conditions, for example, when others are dehumanized, people *morally disengage*.[24] Their usual moral values and constraints are not applied. Moral disengagement is accomplished through some of the processes I described, such as diffusion of responsibility and belief in a just world.

In my view, over time as part of an evolution of doing harm, people tend to exclude members of the victim group from the moral realm, from the realm of those to whom moral considerations apply.[25] In Helen Fein's terms, they exclude them from the universe of moral obligation.[26] Moral exclusion is an outcome of extreme devaluation. But there is a further step in the psychological/moral evolution, what I have called the *reversal of morality*, when killing members of a group becomes the right thing to do. As part of the evolution such changes in morality often extend beyond its primary, initial objects to other groups.

Psychologists in their research (and theory) tend to pit principles, or psychological processes, against each other, to determine which one operates. This is useful, even crucial, to advance knowledge. But as individuals or groups act in the real world a number of processes, such as those I described, can operate at the same time. Although depending on the exact conditions, one or another principle or process may predominate, thoughts, feelings, and actions can be the result of multiple processes.

Leaders and the Population in the Evolution of Violence

Mass violence is furthered by psychological, ideological, and other influences that support each other and move the evolution forward. Usually elements of a destructive ideology develop further as actions are taken against the victim group. The goals derived from the ideology become more extreme. Leaders and the media describe the target group as a threat, often because they truly believe this, and also because they want to influence the population. Hate speech facilitates the evolution.[27]

In Germany Jews were excluded at first from jobs in the government and military and later from other jobs. Laws were passed identifying and separating them from the community. They were pushed to sell their businesses (for little money), and if they did not do so their businesses were later taken away from them. They had to wear yellow stars as identifying signs, and there was increasing violence against them. In leaders' speeches, the media, and literature, Jews were represented as a great threat, with old Jews depicted as seducers of young girls and the existence of Jews as a cancer in the body of the German people. Germans were admonished not to have relations with Jews. In schools, pseudo-science was used to show that Jewish children were physically different from ethnic German children, by measuring their heads and facial features[28]

Discriminatory actions initiated in the population contributed to the evolution of violence against Jews. The unilateral decision of businesses not to pay Jewish workers for holidays led to the creation by the Nazi government of new regulations to catch up with these actions.[29] The ideology and the goals set to fulfill it became increasingly more destructive, until the government initiated the "final solution of the Jewish question," the extermination of the Jews. Such euphemisms help make it easier for bystanders to remain passive and for perpetrators to engage in violence. Killings in Rwanda came to be referred to as *umuganda*, which designates the traditional communal work; chopping up men as "bush clearing"; and killing women and children as "pulling out the roots of the bad weeds."[30]

Increasing dehumanization by words, or by the conditions created, is a usual, "normal," aspect of the evolution. It can be a natural evolution, as well as intentional, to achieve instrumental goals. As Daniel Bar-Tal suggested, one of these goals in group conflict is to increase commitment by people, to strengthen them so that they tolerate deprivation in the fight of "good against evil." Another goal, in genocide, is to make it easier for perpetrators to do their "jobs." In Nazi extermination camps, being starved, with extremely bad conditions for hygiene, inmates looked less than human. When the head of the Treblinka extermination camp was asked after the war why the extreme brutality, he said that it made it easier for the guards to do what they needed to do.[31] Such systems also allow personal inclinations for brutality to emerge and evolve.

What is the relationship between emerging or changing public outlooks and the acts, gestures, and decisions of political leaders? As discussed in the previous chapter, societal conditions—difficult life conditions and conflict—impact both the population and the leaders. They give rise to powerful needs, both material and psychological. I have noted the tendency to see leaders as only manipulating the population for their own ends. But leaders are also affected by social conditions—not necessarily the same way as the population, since people are affected differently as a function of their role in society. At least in part, leaders or people who emerge as leaders act out of their own needs, as they scapegoat, create destructive ideologies, and the like. But even to the extent they manipulate to gain followers, to retain or gain influence, they are aware of the experience of the population, in part because they are also impacted. Both their awareness of what is happening to the population and the shared experience enables leaders to speak to people's concerns and psychological needs. So the population and leaders join.

As part of the evolution of violence, leaders change as a result of what they say and do, but as I have noted, they also change because of the responses to their words and actions, including actions by the community. German businesses not paying Jews for holidays and the government's codifying of this action in laws changed the norms and institutions of the society. The Serb population's response to a nationalistic address by Milosevic about the role and importance of Kosovo encouraged him in actions that led to the violence in the former Yugoslavia. In Argentina at the time of the disappearances, because of terrorism, other difficult life conditions, and societal chaos, the population initially supported the military and paramilitary groups allied with them that were abducting people—whom they tortured, and often killed.

The Evolution to Genocide: Reason, Attitudes, and Emotions

In writings about the origins of genocide, some authors, following rational choice theory, have proposed that perpetrators make a rational choice, a conscious, calculated decision to address practical problems, to fulfill political and social aims, by deciding to eliminate a group of people. One author, Benjamin Valentino, sees genocide as the result of a strategic choice by elites to accomplish policy goals that are extreme or radical, when other means have failed or seem ineffective.[32] Rational choice has also been proposed as a source of terrorist actions. Terrorism can be a tool for weak parties to gain dignity, rights, and practical benefits, and it can qualify as a rational choice. However, as with genocide, there are powerful emotional and attitudinal forces at work. In addition, as terrorism expert Martha Crenshaw[33] has noted, the goals that terrorists pursue are often so impractical that it is difficult to see them as rational.

The choice of genocide becomes possible only when many of the conditions that I have described and will describe exist and lead to both a psychological evolution—frustrated needs, devaluation, hostility, destructive ideology, exclusion of the other from the moral realm, and on the part of some of the perpetrators, hate—and the evolution of harmful actions. Enmity in Rwanda was evident in the decades before the genocide, where sometimes the central government, which set up a system of discrimination, had to stop the killing of Tutsis by local people in the provinces.[34] Ben Kiernen noted the strong emotions that are displayed in violence. He and many other historians regard emotion and "irrational" motivation important. One of them, McMullen, writes: "*anger* gives the most, and most long lasting, force to our actions."[35]

Psychological and social forces and defensive and hostile motivation are therefore a background for decisions based on instrumental motives, practical reasons, and "rational choice" to exterminate a whole group of people. The hostility unites leaders and followers, and it may come to characterize much of the group. Leaders are likely to initiate systematic mass killing or genocide when they see readiness in people's feelings and attitudes toward the potential victim. This readiness may be increased by past mass killing, a history that creates a chasm between groups and a mindset in which mass killing is seen as a possibility. In the case of repeated mass killings, as in Rwanda, such violence becomes to some degree normalized. Both perceptual/conceptual elements and emotions tend to have powerful roles. Given past history new threat or conflict immediately gives rise to intense feelings. Thus, even when instrumental motivation for mass murder has a significant role, prevention requires addressing the underlying psychological and social forces that make genocide a conceivable instrument to bring about desired outcomes. Prevention is crucial not only for victims but also for perpetrators. The not so rational choice they make usually causes them great future losses.

Some recent German historians have begun to describe the decision to exterminate Jews as a rational decision, made for practical reasons by officials in the government and in areas occupied by Germany in Eastern Europe. These officials wanted to ensure a food supply for Germans at a time of great scarcity and create territory needed for German settlers or Germans who were made homeless in the war. The historian Saul Friedlander[36] challenges this questionable view.

He points to Hitler, the architect and decision maker, as responsible. Although Hitler was the prime "instigator," as I have noted genocide is very much a societal process. There was reciprocal influence between Hitler, fellow Nazis, and the population—followers and bystanders.

Ideologies become more destructive in the course of their evolution and are embraced by more people. As they evolve and gain influence and power, people in varied roles, or who assume varied roles, will be affiliated with it. They include leaders, intellectual contributors to the ideology, functionaries of different kinds, violent promoters of its goals, and in the end direct perpetrators of mass violence. People serving different functions may be part of smaller groups working together, such as administrators of schools, members of government units, or members of paramilitary groups.

Some may not belong to the movement but still execute its aims. In Nazi Germany, some of the medical people who participated in the euthanasia program in the late 1930s, which involved the killing of mentally ill, mentally deficient, physically handicapped, or homosexual Germans, were such people. So were people working for the railroads that carried Jews to concentration and extermination camps. Often the whole population is complicit, as people adhere to the increasingly harmful standards of action toward the victim group. In Germany, this included boycotting Jewish stores, severing relations with Jewish friends, discriminating against Jewish employees, and taking over Jewish businesses and apartments. In Rwanda, a very large number of people participated in the killings.

The participation of many in the population in varying roles, and the passivity (and complicity) of bystanders, furthers or allows the evolution of violence. People did protest the "euthanasia" killings of mentally deficient, physically handicapped, and some other categories of Germans, which brought the official program of killing to an end. Could the German people not have stopped the persecution of Jews because the Nazis' commitment to that was greater? The killing of Germans to improve the race, which came first, suggests that they were strongly committed to that, and protests did stop it. One known effort to protect Jews within Germany, when German women married to Jews congregated in front of government buildings to protest their husbands' deportation, was successful. Some of the men who had already been taken to Auschwitz were even brought back from there.[37] This success has been attributed to the government not wanting to move against German women in the midst of the war. But we don't know what the government's reasons were, nor do we know what its response would have been to popular opposition to the deportation of Jews, because no significant protests against the persecution of Jews occurred. The different response to the euthanasia program may have been due to different attitudes toward the victims, Germans and relatives in one case, Jews in another. It may also have to do with what seems to be a pattern: Populations go passively along as a group is increasingly persecuted, and only when their killing begins do some people, usually a small minority, attempt to save lives.

The evolution of violence may span long time periods, intermingled with periods of quiet. For example, in Turkey, there was large-scale mass killing of Armenians in 1895–1896, by troops assembled by the Sultan for this purpose. The genocide of the Armenians that took place primarily in 1915–1916 occurred under a new regime, which in 1908 overthrew the monarchy and created a republic. It took place during World War I, with Turkey already losing battles in the war. The degree of historical continuity can be substantial, as long ago practices against the target group are introduced again. In Germany, beginning in the late 1930s, the Jews were forced to wear a yellow star for identification, reviving a practice that was introduced in Europe in the fifth century.

Cultures retain memories of historical events, including a group's own actions toward another group. Orientation toward another group can become part of the deep structure of a society.[38] In Rwanda, there was intense devaluation of Tutsis and discrimination against them after the Hutu rebellion in 1959. People were required to continue to use identity cards, created by the Belgians, which designated them as Hutu or Tutsi. There were periodic mass killings of Tutsis, for example, in the early 1960s and early 1970s, with killings of smaller numbers of people at other times. After the entry of the Rwandan Patriotic Army from Uganda in 1990 and the beginning of the civil war, there were killings of Tutsi peasants. There was hate speech in the press and on radio, in particular on Radio Milles Collines. At the time of the genocide this radio station directed Hutus where to go to kill Tutsis. Advocates of the Hutu power ideology created the Hutu Ten Commandments, inciting people to violence against Tutsis.

Stages, Evolution, and Denial of Genocide

Gregory Stanton, a former diplomat and genocide scholar/activist, has proposed that genocide develops in stages. He described eight stages: "classification (us versus them), symbolization (e.g. yellow stars, blue scarves), dehumanization (vermin, traitor), organization (hate groups), polarization (eliminate moderates), preparation (expropriation, disarmament of victims, concentration, training and arming killers, trial massacres), extermination (genocide), and denial."[39]

We best think of such stages as points along a progressive and continuous evolution toward genocide. To the extent they can be identified as separate points, they can serve as markers of how far the evolution has progressed and of the level of the danger of genocide. They may also help identify appropriate preventive actions. However, many of the processes identified in these stages are present for substantial periods, during several of the stages, often to increasing extents. They are intermingled, several of them present at the same time. Dehumanization, for example, happens early but increases over time. Organization and preparation have many elements that progressively build on each other and move a society along the continuum of destruction. But sometimes the organization is limited, as in Cambodia, where the "autogenocide" began immediately after the victory of the Khmer Rouge in a civil war. "Trial massacres" can be trials to see how the population responds, but they often are the outcome of the evolution up to that point, without necessarily an intentional plan for further violence. But they change individuals and the society and make greater violence probable—sometimes at a substantially later time.

The points along a continuum are primarily descriptive; some of them are also causal. However, since individuals and groups change as a result of their actions, change or progress in the evolution or "stages" indicates an increased probability of further movement toward extreme violence. The value of identifying change and where a group is along the continuum as predictor will greatly increase, however, if we consider them together with the presence of influences that give rise to genocide that I describe in this book, such as group conflict, destructive ideology, or justification of harmful acts (See Tables 4.1; 17.1).

Denial is an important phenomenon. Perpetrators and members of their group often deny that genocide has taken place. But for various reasons, such as prejudice against the victim group, perhaps in rare instances a misguided idealistic belief that such terrible things don't happen, and at times because of inducement by perpetrator groups, some outsiders—individuals, groups, and nations—have also denied the existence of particular genocides, such as the Holocaust, the genocide of the Armenians, and others. In probably the most infamous case of denial, Turkey has paid scholars and donated money for professorships, and threatened to break off relations with countries, to get them to deny that a genocide took place and/or to adopt and propagate the official Turkish position that Armenian deaths occurred in the context of removing hostile Armenians from a region where they could have done harm to Turkey during World War I.

Enmity can also lead to denial. Some people in the Congo deny the genocide in Rwanda. They blame Rwanda for their problems and see Rwandan actions in the Congo as motivated by material interest, that is, the exploitation of the Congo's mineral wealth, with the claim of genocide merely a cover. Similarly, some Palestinians and other Arabs and Muslims sympathetic to them—such as the President of Iran—have questioned and denied the reality of or extent of violence against Jews in the Holocaust. Denial has a powerful emotional impact on victims/survivors, and while Palestinians' denial is presumably due to their suffering in the course of their conflict with Israel, it interferes with the conflict's resolution.

Denial hinders healing by survivors, for whom the truth and acknowledgment of their suffering is of great importance. It frustrates the group's need for security, as well as identity, which is in part shaped by great suffering. Instead of empathy, denial expresses contempt and points to victims as liars. It prevents the perpetrator group from accepting responsibility for its actions and addressing the cultural and psychological elements in the group that led to them. It can maintain both devaluation of the victims and elements of the ideology that led to the violence, increasing the danger of new violence. All this makes reconciliation less likely.

Another summary of the progression toward genocide provides a matrix, a combination of influences and steps or actions on what I regard as a continuum moving toward genocide. A detailed specification of what conditions and actions are indicators of increasing danger is important for agencies responsible for early warning and activating responses Some of the elements in the matrix are described as stable or long term, such as persistent cleavages between groups and a history of elites using repression to hold power. They are often present early in the continuum. Others are "medium-term indicators," such as dehumanization and blaming target groups for difficult life conditions, or dismissal of their members from civil service jobs. Still others are short-term indicators, which appear later in the process leading to genocide, such as the prevention of food distribution to the target area or the assassination of political leaders.[40]

Other Considerations Related to the Evolution of Violence

Loss of External and Internal Constraints

Leadership is important both in the rules that leaders set and in the constraints that they lift. After Japan invaded China during World War II, Japanese soldiers killed probably between 150,000 to 300,000 people in Nanking.[41] They killed indiscriminately and with great cruelty, smashed infants on the ground, and raped and gang raped women whether they were young girls or grandmothers, often mutilating and killing them afterward. Earlier fighting by the Japanese in China and Korea was characterized by violent treatment of the population. In addition, potential inhibitors to violence were removed before the Japanese army reached Nanking. Hirohito, the emperor, agreed to the army's proposition to remove the constraints of international law on the army's conduct, thereby offering impunity and providing implicit sanction for violent conduct. The standards of conduct already developed, the army's proposition and the emperor's "ruling" partly explain why officers did not act to inhibit the violence.

The Japanese invasion was the result of a nationalistic ideology of expansion and conquest. Being part of the military at war, engaging in what may be called "required violence," would already bring about the kind of changes that make greater violence easier. Along the way to Nanking, the soldiers engaged in atrocities, including unjustified killing of civilians, although not nearly on the scale of Nanking. In the fighting before reaching Nanking, the Japanese army encountered intense resistance by the Chinese army. The Japanese had an extremely negative view of the Chinese. Soldiers who were at Nanking described later the animal labels they applied to the Chinese, such as "ant" and "sheep." On the one hand, this labeling made cruelty against the Chinese easier. On the other hand, the strong resistance by these lowly beings, and the number of Japanese soldiers killed during this combat, must have infuriated Japanese soldiers. There are descriptions by former soldiers and military historians of how the killing of comrades enrages soldiers, who want to punish the enemy. The violence in Nanking became a community event, and anger, group pressure, and conformity, and even competition in who could do more killing (including reported competition in target shooting at people) all probably joined in leading to the massacre.

Another psychological force in the frenzy of violence in Nanking may have been the heady feeling of great power without constraints. When those doing harm reach a point that they feel they can do with people's bodies whatever they want, without external restriction and having lost the usual internal moral constraint and inhibition, they can gain a sense of great power. Such unrestrained exercise of power may be especially satisfying for people who live in a culture of restraint, like Japan at the time, where strong social controls regulate behavior.

Social psychologist Roy Baumeister has suggested that some of the perpetrators of great violence are sadistic and gain satisfaction out of the suffering of their victims.[42] He does not assume that they start out that way; they may become that way as they engage in violence. Sadism on the part of some people may be an outcome of learning by doing, a result of the satisfaction gained as they lose inhibition and exercise unrestrained power over others.

The Semai of Malaysia provide an example of temporary loss of external controls, without apparent internal controls. The people in this very peaceful society never engaged in violence. When conflict within the group arose, the community discussed it until it was resolved. Then, in the 1950s, the men were lured, with promises of rewards, to join British army units fighting communists. With war unknown to them, the men acted, perhaps in response to the killing of some of their fellow kinsmen, with unrestrained and, according to some reports, bloodthirsty violence.[43] "They had strong social controls, but not the personal capacity to regulate aggressive feelings and behavior.... On their return home, they reverted to their peaceful ways."[44]

Consistent with my discussion of perpetrators refusing to accept responsibility, the Japanese government up to the present day questions the accounts of the "rape of Nanking" and minimizes the amount of violence there. Similar to Turkey in relation to the Armenian genocide, they acknowledge that some people were killed but greatly minimize the number. Their statements claim that what happened there was not extraordinary to war. Unless they are confronted with overwhelming evidence and an international community unified in proclaiming the truth of their violence, perpetrators usually persist in denial.

The Continuity of Hostility and Violence

Sometimes there is a seemingly sudden flare-up of violence between groups; it looks like there was no evolution. People often express surprise that groups that have lived peacefully together suddenly turn against each other. But in these cases, there has often been significant past division between groups, including hostility and intense violence. In the former Yugoslavia, for example, Serb, Croats, and Muslims lived together peacefully under authoritarian communist rule. However, in addition to hostility and violence between them at various times, during World War II several hundred thousand Serbs were killed by a fascist Croatia allied with Nazi Germany, with the Croats supported by Bosnian Muslims.

As communism collapsed, the Yugoslav economy significantly deteriorated, and the different parts of Yugoslavia began to separate and proclaim independence, the psychological consequences of such a past reemerged. The impact of these conditions was intensified as Croatia, after declaring independence, began to take actions that were reminders to the Serbs of the mass killing they suffered during the war—using the Croatian flag from that time and moving Serbs out of positions in the army. This would reactivate trauma and psychological wounds, and generate fear and anger.

Both my analyses of cases in *The Roots of Evil* and elsewhere, as well as Barbara Harff's[45] statistical analyses, indicate that past mass killing or genocide is one of the predictors of later mass violence. Mass violence creates a *chasm* between victims and perpetrators that can be reopened. It also becomes part of the history and psychology of both groups that can lead them to violence in response to threat from any source, and perhaps in response to conflict as well. Again, suicide in a family is a relevant analogy. It increases the likelihood of later suicides in that family. Something that was unthinkable becomes conceivable. Without healing and reconciliation, under certain conditions past violence makes new violence more likely.

The view that groups live together as a community and suddenly violence emerges is a surface view. In Rwanda, people we have interviewed in the community in the course of developing radio programs to promote healing and reconciliation would say, 'We were living together peacefully, and then the leaders told us to go and kill Tutsis. That is when the problems began.' This denies or ignores the ongoing devaluation, discrimination against, and occasional mass killing of Tutsis after 1959. In one of these conversations, a Hutu respondent described a funeral of a Tutsi the day before the killings began. Members of the community came together at the funeral, as usual. However, as I probed this notion of a peaceful community, she mentioned that as the killings started the very next day, some people dug up the man just buried and hacked the body to pieces. It is difficult to imagine such action without intense feelings of hostility.[46*] The conversation led her to say that people can have cordial relations on the surface but continue to mistrust each other.

People may think of members of another group as friends, or drinking partners. But just as a person can shift from seeing herself as an individual to seeing herself primarily as a Hutu, so the perception or categorization of friends, seemingly even spouses or children in a mixed marriage, can undergo a dramatic shift. Seeing this person primarily as a Tutsi can evoke very different feelings. Hutu killers whom Jean Hatzfeld interviewed described this distancing, this shift to seeing former neighbors or drinking partners as Tutsi and therefore suspected, envied, devalued, and perhaps hated(see Chapter 9, on perpetrators).

In the course of the research evaluating our radio programs in Rwanda, participants did talk about the increasing tension and hostility that preceded the genocide. In spite of this, during the first year of the program, they reported that the genocide itself was unexpected and a surprise to them.[47] Given that the evolution is usually gradual, that people habituate even to small-scale mass killing, apparently the beginning of large-scale killing is a surprise, perhaps for most parties—victims, bystanders, and even perhaps for many perpetrators. The ability to foresee where an evolution can lead seems a potentially important motivator of preventive actions.

Reciprocity in Hostility and Violence

Reciprocity is a powerful guide to human behavior. We help those who have helped us, especially if we believe that they *intended* to benefit us, and we harm those who have harmed us, especially if we believe that they meant to harm us.[48]In intractable conflict, this reciprocation of harmful actions facilitates the evolution of violence.

When an individual or group engages in violence, the victims can be helpless. But if they are in a position to do so, they tend to strike back. They may believe that they must strike back in order to stop the other from attacking them further—that only force will convince the other to stop their violence. Psychologist Michael McCullough suggests that our ancestors, living in groups, engaged in aggressive self-defense (or revenge) in order to stop violence against themselves, as well as to stop witnesses to the violence from harming them.[49] It is true that not responding to aggression often encourages more and greater aggression, whether in the case of bullying in schools, or other individual or group violence. But it is also the case that aggressive responses can lead to cycles of aggression. Using excessive force in self-defense, which is then perceived as attack by the original aggressor, is especially likely to generate further aggression.

Others' actions can lead to strong emotional reactions. Positive action can lead to liking, affection, and gratitude. In contrast, harmful actions can lead individuals and groups to feel diminished, injured, lowered in status, insecure, and angry. They may try to reestablish their dignity in their own and others' eyes by aggression. They often want revenge. Revenge or vengeance is more than self-protection or just punishment, which can be an appropriate means of self-defense and can prevent future attacks. Instead, it aims to create suffering, at least as great as and often greater than one's own. Revenge can become a well-established norm in a society. Blood feuds used to be common in human societies: Families responded to a murder—or even to an accidental killing—by killing a member of the killer's family, which then responded with killing, in a continuous cycle between families that sometimes lasted for centuries.[50]

Neta Oren and Daniel Bar-Tal,[51] looking at both psychological reactions and actions, see the violence between Palestinians and Israelis as a response to each other that occurs in continuous cycles. It was a form of reciprocity when after the exodus of Palestinians during the 1948 war, partly voluntary and partly forced, there was a primarily forced exodus of Jews from Arab countries to Israel. While the desire to go to a Jewish homeland, and fear of persecution probably entered for many, expulsion was the immediate cause of their departure. Those who left mostly had to leave their possessions behind.[52] However, in contrast to the Palestinians, a large percentage of whom have remained in refugee camps or lived in occupied territories ever since, these Jews found a home in Israel.

There are many examples of reciprocity in violence. In 1953 a young Israeli mother and her two children were killed by Palestinians. In response, Ariel Sharon led a commando that killed 69 Palestinians. Terrorist attacks increased in 1954 and nearly doubled in 1955. When Sharon was prime minister, in 2002, without the approval of his cabinet, he ordered the bombing of Gaza city, which killed one Hamas leader and many civilians and wounded many others. This action broke down negotiations for a cease-fire that were progressing well, and resulted in retaliatory attacks by Hamas.[53]

In November 2008 during a cease-fire, Israel entered Gaza to destroy a tunnel it believed was to be used to abduct soldiers. The days following this Palestinians fired mortar shells and rockets into Israel. Israel then closed down commercial crossing, severely limiting the entry of basic goods into Gaza. In other instances, Hamas shot rockets into Israel, with Israel immediately retaliating, followed by the use of larger rockets by Hamas.

Luca Ricolfi,[54] who analyzed internal relations between Hamas and the Palestine Liberation Organization, saw less reciprocity, as violence by one side often did not immediately follow violence by the other side. However, reciprocity can sometimes be immediate and direct, and at other times follow a "bank account" model.[55] In ongoing friendly relationships, good actions may be stored, as in a bank account—and reciprocal kindness may be hoped for, expected, and drawn on in times of need. The same is likely true of hostility and violence between groups that have ongoing hostile relations: Hostility and anger may be stored, leading to delayed responses. Moreover, like other individual and group behavior, violence is multi-determined. Ricolfi showed that the level of Palestinian violence toward Israelis has also been affected by the rivalry between

Hamas and Fatah. Suicide bombing against Israelis increased when one side or the other wanted to enhance its influence in the Palestinian community.

Reciprocity, striking back and revenge, is evident in the actions of terrorists and in the responses to them. I have previously cited Louise Richardson's[56] example of an Irish Republican Army (IRA) member who, enraged when one of his comrades was killed, swore revenge. President George W. Bush promised that the perpetrators of 9/11 would be found and punished. In practice, this meant that many of them were killed; others, including innocent people caught up in the subsequent war on terror, were imprisoned, some in 2010 still in prison in Guantanamo and elsewhere. There are important differences between self-defence and appropriate punishment, and revenge and indiscriminate lashing out after one's own suffering and loss. The challenge is for justice to prevail.

In their reciprocal actions people respond not only to actions but also to intentions. In research, when participants learn that another who has not harmed them yet intends to administer stronger rather than weaker shocks to them as part of their interaction in the context of a study, they proceed to administer stronger shocks to this person.[57] In intractable conflict, each group assumes that the other has negative intentions and plans negative actions, so each group "responds" to defend itself. Such assumptions are strengthened by continued statements of hostility, for example, by Hamas toward Israel.

Part of the "security dilemma" is to know the actual danger, to accurately assess the other's intentions. It is for this reason that groups take seriously when hostile intentions toward it are suggested by another group's internal processes. Leaders often talk to their groups in one way and the rest of the world in another way. But the other party keenly looks for what leaders say to their group, draws conclusions about their intentions, and responds accordingly. Groups also draw conclusions about the other's intention when they see that children are taught in schools to derogate them.

All these factors have influenced the Palestinian–Israeli conflict. Arafat, in particular, was famous for saying things in Arabic that were different from what he said in English. In Rwanda, during the cease-fire surrounding the Arusha accords, the anti-Tutsi parties were training militias, advocating against Tutsis, and collecting weapons. According to some combination of real information and rumor, the Rwandan Patriotic Front engaged in a number of practices during this time to weaken the government and strengthen its army.[58] The actions of both parties may have been due to mistrust and hostility, the intention to gain full control—and to knowledge of the other's actions and reciprocity. What each side does internally can increase or reduce the other side's perception of threat and danger. Leaders can reduce conflict and hostility by what they say to their own people; groups can reduce it by their internal actions.

In the course of an escalating cycle of violence, each party focuses on the other's actions. It sees responses to its own violence as violence by the other, requiring a response. Due to anger, the desire for revenge, the desire to teach the other a lesson and thereby stop its violence, and due to the evolutionary spiral of violence, the response is often disproportional to the initial act of violence. Israel suffered great violence by terrorism at home and abroad. Abroad there were numerous hijackings of Israeli commercial airliners. In the 1972 Olympics in Munich, 11 Israeli athletes were killed by a militant organization allied with Fatah. At home, suicide bombings at markets, in buses, restaurants, weddings and religious ceremonies led to many deaths and injuries, and the experience of terror. Israel systematically attempted to control such violence, and the two Palestinian uprisings or Intifadas, by using repressive measures such as imposing curfews, destroying the houses of Palestinians, setting up roadblocks, holding Palestinians in detention, assassinating Palestinians identified as terrorists or leaders of terrorists groups, building a wall to separate the occupied territories from Israel, and building settlements that served this among other goals.

The retaliatory actions of Israel have often created more harm than the initial acts it suffered, as indicated by the greater number of Palestinian deaths during the various phases of the conflict. The Palestinians started the second Intifada by throwing rocks, injuring people and destroying cars. Israel responded by shooting with live ammunition, killing people,[59]* followed by Palestinian escalation and the killing of Israelis. One Web site, the MidEastWeb, which in a timeline of the second Intifada describes many violent actions by both sides, lists 828 Palestinians and 112 Israelis killed by 2004.[60]

More people were killed in both sides in subsequent years. Many of the suicide attacks on Israel were initiated from Gaza. The unilateral Israeli pullout from Gaza in 2005 did not stop the violence. Various groups, primarily Hamas, shot thousands of rockets into Southern Israel from Gaza. This created constant fear and disrupted lives, although it killed only a small number of people. Israel responded by an attack on Gaza in late 2008 that killed about 1600 people.

While there were a variety of factors in South Africa that contributed to the white rulers' willingness to relinquish apartheid, including moral ostracism, boycotts, and the denial of loans by the international community, the behavior of the African National Congress was important. Former South African journalist Benjamin Pogrund wrote: "When the ANC decided in 1961 to switch to armed resistance, it adopted a policy that there would be no killing of white civilians. The decision had partly to do with the belief in Mahatma Gandhi's philosophy of non-violence, and was partly strategic: The ANC accepted that if it targeted white civilians it would confirm their fears of being swept into the sea by the black majority and this would harden their resolve to hold on to power. The ANC's approach was proved correct: Only a few attacks on whites took place over the decades, and this was a significant factor in persuading whites that it was safe to end apartheid."[61]* In contrast, suicide bombing by Palestinians creates fear and terror and solidifies hostility by Israelis. Perhaps it is a combination of some of these factors, and the past woundedness of both groups, that create the mistrust and suspicion which according to Pogrund is much greater than it was in South African society.

A recent large experimental study expanded the usual "prisoner's dilemma" game, in which individuals, in interactions with another person, can behave cooperatively or competitively. Cooperation in the prisoner's dilemma means that a person chooses a smaller gain, so that his or her opponent also has a reasonable gain. Competition or defection means that a person chooses to have a larger gain, which either reduces the gain or leads to a loss for the opponent. In this version of the game there was also the additional option of "costly punishment," losing one unit to make another person lose four. In the prisoner's dilemma participants usually respond to each other's choices. The participants, 104 Boston college students, played a total of more than 8000 rounds. Overall, players who did not punish or punished the least made the most money, while those who punished the most made the least money. Those who did not retaliate when an opponent punished, even if the opponent did this repeatedly, did better than those who retaliated.[62]

In the prisoner's dilemma there is a limited mode of interaction. While punishment or retaliation can lead to cycles of harmful behavior in real-life contexts, appropriate self-defense might not. We found in a study of children's interaction in their classrooms that children who *engaged in moderate defensive aggression but did not initiate aggression* were recipients of little aggression and many positive actions from other children. Children who initiated aggression tended to engage in varied forms of aggression and were the recipients of substantial aggression and other negative behavior.[63]

Sometimes responding to slight hostility or aggression by positive action may be the most effective self-defense. But active self-defense in response to violence is justified and is often necessary to stop greater violence. Sometimes the use of force by groups suffering persistent and intense repression, with no one coming to their aid, seems essential in fighting for their rights and perhaps ultimately for their lives. Forceful response that is appropriate to the provocation and is primarily defensive, or at least limited in scope, is more likely to induce cooperation. Initiating dialogue and other peaceful gestures at the same time can limit violence, create an opening for the resolution of conflict, and induce positive reciprocity. So can the involvement by constructive bystanders. I will have more to say about these processes in Part II.

The Evolution in Small Groups That Perpetrate Group Violence

Much of the analyses so far have focused on societal conditions and influences. However, a great deal of violence is planned or perpetrated by small groups of people. This is especially true of terrorism. How are such groups formed, and what happens among the people who are in real, tangible contact with each other as they turn to violence? How do people adopt an ideology? What happens as they work together to fulfill the ideology and goals derived from it, or together engage in harmful actions against others? People in groups shape each other's perception of the world, interpretation of events, and commitment to the cause. They also develop strong commitments to each other. What forges this commitment?

Researchers have written about psychological and social processes that take place in small groups. Their work is relevant to perpetrator groups. One process they identified is "group polarization,"[64] the tendency of groups to move to positions that are more extreme than the average initial position of those who make up the group. Both groups that become terrorist[65] and mobs that turn violent[66] manifest this principle.

Some people who become terrorists start with political engagement. They have concerns and grievances, which they try to address by political action. For example, members of the German terrorist group the Baader-Meinhof gang started with participation in demonstrations and protests against nuclear policies. Such actions often do not bring results. Both in reaction to this failure, and in competition for influence in the group and for gaining leadership roles, some members advocate more extreme views. With more extreme views, with the risk of extreme actions shared and therefore everyone becoming less responsible and perhaps less frightened, and with learning by doing, the group can progressively change. Along the way, moderate members may drop out.

In many groups, mutual influence is increased by a variety of other psychological and social processes. One of them is contagion, the spread of feelings among group members. Contagion is especially likely to occur when there is a shared perception of wrongs and a shared vision of how to correct them. It is also likely to occur when people outside the group respond negatively to its ideology or actions. Once young people engaged with the Nazi movement in Germany, even before Hitler came to power, their commitment increased in response to others' disapproval or opposition to them.[67]

Another principle is deindividuation, the loss of a sense of individuality and separateness, accompanied by a decreased regard for the power of traditional social and personal norms. In research, people wearing hoods were more punitive, and their punitiveness increased more over time.[68] Anything that shifts people from a sense of their individual identity, such as wearing uniforms or other clothes that hide identity, or being in a crowd or a member of a close-knit group, is likely to create deindividuation. Deindividuation reduces the restraint of conscience, of personal values, and increases conformity to other group members and new group norms, even if these violate conventional standards. Being a member of a collectivist society may itself involve some degree of deindividuation.

Under difficult social conditions, or for people who are struggling because of their life circumstances and psychological states, the abandonment of the self and the giving of oneself to a group can bring relief and substantial satisfaction. It may be experienced as a falling away of limitations and restrictions in identity, rules, and relationships. It can result in a feeling of oneness and wholeness. This can happen both in destructive groups and in "good groups," which have the goal of self-development or positive social action. It can strengthen commitment to the group and the people in it.

As this happens, in small ideological groups, both cause and comrades become very important. It has become a widely shared view that terrorists in particular act for both cause and comrades. They are usually part of small groups, and they share danger and enemies. While some terrorists are part of and supported by their communities—as have been Palestinian suicide bombers at times of more intense conflict with Israelis—other terrorists are separated from their communities and are each other's only support. Even those who remain less committed to the group's vision or actions, if they remain in the group and as time passes are increasingly embedded in it, would have to have substantial moral (and physical) courage to separate from or oppose the group.

But not only terrorists are affected by embeddedness in, loyalty to, and conformity with their group. The same processes affect decision-making groups of many kinds. I mentioned Irving Janis's concept of *groupthink*, and one of his examples, how this affected the decision that John F. Kennedy and his advisors made in the Bay of Pigs invasion of Cuba.

In another example of group commitment, historian Christopher Browning wrote about one of the reserve police units sent to the Eastern front behind the German army to round up and kill Jews.[69] In Browning's description, during the first roundup, the officer in charge gave anyone in the unit permission not to participate in the killing if that individual found it too "demanding" to shoot unarmed Jews, men, women, and children. No person asked to be relieved of this duty. A number of them later claimed that they did not shoot this first time.

Although the commanding officer gave permission not to participate, the members of the unit were still part both of the larger system of the German military and of their immediate group. Even the meaning of the permission must be questioned—their leader was unlikely to make that offer if he had thought that most of the group would avail itself of it. For the individual men, to publicly step back would have meant to acknowledge that they were not tough enough for the job, or loyal enough to their comrades, or that they cared about Jews. If any of them did not want to shoot that first day, they lacked strong enough values and the moral courage to say so. In contrast to the later claims of reluctance by some of them, Daniel Goldhagen[70] wrote that reports of this group's behavior the first day showed enthusiastic engagement in the killings. At any rate, they all speedily accustomed themselves to this "task" and became full participants in killing.

These reserve police had experienced the increasing devaluation and persecution of Jews in Germany. Like many Germans they probably became devoted to the Nazi regime. They were part of a semi-military unit that by that time must have become a small community. Richard Rhodes, who traced the history of such "Einsatzgruppen,"[71] believes that by the time they started their duties as killers they had experienced, in my terminology, substantial evolution. As Rhodes describes, they had started their operations in the wake of the German army's advance by promoting pogroms by the local populations, in countries like Latvia and Lithuania. They organized locals into militias, and freed prisoners, who in some cases beat large numbers of Jews to death in the town square, while the town people watched and often cheered them on. Such experiences had to contribute to their own evolution.

As an example of the power of commitment to the group, Ariel Merari, a prime terrorism researcher, described the hunger strike by IRA prisoners in a Belfast prison in 1961. Ten Irish nationalists killed themselves this way when their demand to be recognized as political prisoners rather than common criminals was refused by the British government. He points to the overwhelming motivation that these people must have had, given the very painful experience of slow death from starvation. It took them from 50 to more than 70 days to die. "Their mothers, wives and priests begged at least some of them to stop."[72]

Merari believes that their actions demonstrate the influence of the group on its members. They were part of a group contract they could not break. The pressure increased and the possibility of opting out decreased with the death of each person in the chain. Louise Richardson, also stressing the power of the group, believes that once the first hunger striker died, the others felt compelled to continue out of loyalty to their comrade.[73]

A small, relatively stable group, especially one that separates itself from the rest of the society, which members of extreme ideological movement do—until and unless the ideology becomes more mainstream—has great power over its members. Part of this power lies in the group's ability to fulfill psychological needs. Such group influence manifests itself in many settings: among groups of killers in Rwanda, in German Einsatzgruppen, among villagers in Poland who turned against their Jewish neighbors,[74] and presumably in leadership groups that move societies and terrorists toward violence.

While the power of the group is great, there are individuals who at times are able to resist this power. In addition to having strong moral values, the way a person's identity is constructed may make this resistance possible. I have proposed that people develop different types of selves: disconnected, autonomous, connected, and embedded.[75] Being disconnected limits both the group's influence on people and their caring for other people in the group. Having developed autonomous selves, people tend to focus on their own needs and goals; they tend not to be deeply connected to the group and are able to separate from it. Those with embedded selves are deeply connected to the group and have trouble separating from it. People with connected selves are connected to and value the group and other people, but they can also separate themselves and make their own decisions when the group goes contrary to their values and needs. However, the balance of the power of the group and the influence of personal character-istics can vary depending on the exact circumstances. Other characteristics, such as moral values, join with the way identity is constructed in influencing behavior.

The Formation of Groups Inspired by Al-Qaeda

Small groups involved in perpetration can be created by authorities or formed by physical proximity, past relationships, or ideology. As we'll see in Chapter 9, the group of killers Jean Hatzfeld studied in Rwanda were friends before they started to kill together. The initial followers of Hitler, inspired by his speeches, were likely to entice others to come to Nazi meetings. Once the Nazis were in power, groups of perpetrators, such as killing units, were organized by authorities. However, self-selection and selection by the authorities based on individual characteristics still had some role.

Al-Qaeda was formed by past terrorists and fighters against the Soviets in Afghanistan. It was, from the start, a decentralized organization. It had a cen-tral leadership but independent units. Even the central leadership was set up so that people could be easily replaced. The initial membership, dispersed around the world, was made up of people trained at Al-Qaeda training camps in Afghanistan. But increasingly, new groups have emerged and acted locally, killing people in the subways and buses in London and on trains in Madrid.

Consistent with the research of Martha Crenshaw, Jerrold Post, Ariel Merari, and others, Marc Sageman[76] found that the formation of these groups was based on relationships—for example, through countries of origin and family relations. About half of the people arrested as members of Islamist terrorist groups in France came from the same place in Algeria; members of a group arrested in Montreal grew up together in the suburbs of Algiers; members of another group in Amsterdam came from the same region in Morocco; those who perpetrated the Madrid bombings came from the same city in Morocco; and the British terrorists were children of Pakistani immigrants from the same region in Kashmir. Often one person or a family immigrated, and relatives and friends followed. People who engage with ideologies and groups that move them toward terrorism turn to and involve others they know and trust.

When connections and thereby trust were established, local groups could get help from the original Al-Qaeda. The British Pakistani terrorists received train-ing and guidance. They included those who planned in the summer of 2006 to hijack and blow up 20 U.S. bound airplanes—one of 70 plots that were discov-ered, according to the head of the British Secret Service.[77]

People also got involved through student associations at universities and at mosques, and through friendship, which sometimes started as accidental rela-tionships, or as roommates sharing an apartment. Muhammed Atta and some of the other 9/11 terrorists shared an apartment in Hamburg. Some met as members of a soccer team. Many such people in European countries were members of youth gangs. Before the training camps were destroyed in 2001, sometimes young men decided to go together to get training in Afghanistan.

As in the case of Muslim immigrants to the Netherlands,[78] these young men have experienced a combination of dislocation as a result of their family's move to Europe or their own move as immigrants or students, and a combination of devaluation, exclusion, and discrimination as the "other" in their new countries. Members of the second generation have often experienced disconnection from their own families, who remained rooted in their old culture. Even if they returned to the country of their families, they continued to feel as strangers.

To what extent their circumstances have frustrated their basic needs would depend on their specific situation, such as family relations, friendships, and jobs. What they do about it would depend on their associations to other people, the situations they chose to enter or happened to encounter, and their personality. Many of the local terrorists groups started through exposure to "radical" mosques and student associations. While circumstances and group processes play a powerful role in an individual's radicalization, since only a small number of people become terrorists, personality obviously matters. People may go to a fundamentalist mosque or ideological student association simply to connect with people or because of the reputation of the place. However, even the former can be affected by their environment.

Muslim student associations, mosques, and other groups can provide connection and identity. They can also shape worldview and ideology. Many members of the terrorist cells had not been strongly religious, if at all. Their associations strengthened their identity as Muslims and their embrace of a form of their religion that promotes enmity to non-Muslims and the West and belief in jihad by the sword. In part this happened by having their attention focused on violence against Muslims in Bosnia, Chechnya, or other places. Anyone would or should feel empathy for the suffering of Muslims at such places, and outrage about the violence against them. For some, the empathy and outrage arose from watching films, reading about it, or hearing imams or fellow students talk about it. In this process people shape each others' perceptions and views, and some of them enter the kind of group process I described earlier, leading to increasing commitment to ideology, to action, and to each other.

The personal evolution of an individual terrorist is shown in the story of the convicted killer of Daniel Pearl, the reporter for the *Wall Street Journal*. As mentioned previously, his early experiences of exclusion in England, and disconnection when his family moved back to Pakistan for 3 years, may have laid the groundwork for becoming a terrorist. But other, later developments also contributed to his evolution. He was admitted to the London School of Economics, where he joined an Islamic Society. There he was exposed to people, literature, and films that influenced him. A strong influence was the violence against

Bosnian Muslims, especially the mass murder at Serebnica. He felt increasing identification with and empathy for Muslims who suffered. He joined a charitable organization, Convoy of Mercy, and helped bring supplies to Bosnia. He felt this was not enough and went to receive training in the Al-Qaeda camps in Afghanistan. He was sent to India to free Muslim prisoners, by kidnapping tourists and exchanging them for the prisoners. He was caught and spent 5 years in prison. Later he was accused of, tried, and found guilty of killing Pearl.[79]

Summary

People "learn by doing," and they change as a result of what they do. Individuals and the whole group change as they begin to harm members of another group. They justify their actions by increasing devaluation of that group and by coming to believe that moral and humane values that protect people's well-being do not apply to members of the devalued group. This evolution may end in a reversal of morality, killing the other becoming the right thing to do. A psychological and behavioral evolution—steps along a continuum of destruction—can lead to extreme violence. Perpetrators may be motivated by their commitment to cause (ideology and enmity to the other) and comrades. Leaders emerge and evolve as they respond to the group's (and their own) needs, as well as serve their own interests, promoting scapegoating and destructive ideologies.

Notes

1 Staub, 2005b; Sternberg & Sternberg, 2008

2 Ragasuguhanga, 2008

3 The French scholar Jacques Semelin, in his book Purify and Destroy, questions my use of the concept of a continuum of destruction in The roots of evil. In his view the word continuum suggests "an inescapable progression that would necessarily go from event a to event b, ...For that reason the concept of a 'process' is preferable to that of a 'continuum' since the former implies the idea of a dynamics that is liable to change, slow down or speed up, in short not a scenario foretold...." p. 325. However, this is a misunderstanding of the concept as I originally described it. I hope the preceding discussion clarifies it.

4 Kristof, 2009, p. A27

5 Milgram, 1965, 1974

6 For example, Buss, 1966; see also Staub, 1989

7 Bandura, Underwood, & Fromson, 1975

8 Bar-Tal, 2000

9 Staub & Bar-Tal, 2003, p.726

10 Waller, 2007

11 Staub, 1989

12 Haritos-Fatouros, 2003

13 Des Forges, 1999

14 Craig, 1982

15 Helson, 1964

16 Crandall et al., 2009

17 Ibid, p. 3

18 Ibid, p. 7

19 Jost, Banaji, & Noek, 2004

20 Lerner, 1980; Lerner & Simmons, 1966

21 Latane & Darley, 1970

22 Staub, 1974, 1978, 2003a

23 Schwartz & Clausen, 1970

24 Bandura, 1999

25 Staub, 1989; see also Opotaw, 1990

26 Fein, 1979

27 Vollhardt, Coutin, Staub, Weiss, & Deflander, 2007

28 Staub, 1989

29 Hillberg, 1961

30 Mamdani, 2001

31 Sereny, 1974

32 Fein, 1993b, 1999; Valentino, 2004

33 Crenshaw, 2000

34 Straus, 2006

35 Quoted in Kiernen, 2007

36 Friedlander, 2007

37 Dori Laub, in a talk at a conference on rescuers, Yale University, May 8, 2009

38 Staub, 1989

39 Stanton, n. d.

40 The author of this matrix prefers not to be identified.

41 Chang, 1998

42 Baumeister, 1997

43 Dentan, 1968

44 Staub, 1989, p. 54

45 Harff, 2003

46 Nick Valentino, another scholar in this field, has suggested that perhaps this was done for symbolic reasons. Personal communication, November 2009

47 Paluck, 2009a; Staub & Pearlman, 2009

48 Mauss, 1954; see also Staub, 1978

49 McCullough, 2008

50 Daly & Wilson, 1988

51 Oren & Bar-Tal, 2007

52 Aciman, 2009

53 Pettigrew, 2003

54 Ricolfi, 2005

55 Staub, 1978

56 Richardson, 2006

57 Epstein & Taylor, 1967

58 Straus, 2006

59 Some Israelis I talked to in 2010 claimed that the Palestinians also carried Molotov cocktails, which are inflammable and when thrown can create great damage.

60 mideastweb.org/second_intifada_timeline.htm

61 Pogrund, 2007. Benjamin Pogrund was the last editor of the *Rand Daily Mail*, the last antiapartheid newspaper in South Africa before it was closed down. He lives in Israel, and until 2010 directed the Yakar's Center for Social Concerns that aims to promote peace between Israelis and Palestinians

62 Dreber, Rand, Fudenberg, & Nowak, 2008

63 Staub & Feinberg, 1980

64 Moscovici, & Zavalloni, 1969, and many other references since then

65 McCauley, 2004; Sageman, 2004

66 Staub & Rosenthal, 1994

67 Merkl, 1980

68 Zimbardo, 1969

69 Browning, 1992

70 Goldhagen, 1998

71 Rhodes, 2002

72 Merari, 2005, p.443

73 Richardson, 2006

74 Bartov, 2003

75 Staub, 1993

76 Sageman, 2008

77 Ibid.

78 Staub, 2007b

79 Described in Sageman, 2008, based on varied sources.

7

Internal and External Bystanders

Their Passivity, Complicity, and Role in the Evolution of Violence

Passivity by witnesses/bystanders affirms the perpetrators and facilitates the evolution of doing harm.

The behavior of bystanders is crucial in allowing mass violence to evolve or inhibiting its evolution. This is true of both members of a population who are not perpetrators or intended victims, who I call internal bystanders, and outsiders including nations, international organizations, nongovernmental organizations (NGOs), civic groups, and even individuals outside a country, who I call external bystanders. I define bystanders as witnesses who are in a position to know what is happening and to take action. I say "position to know" because witnesses often do whatever they can to not notice and to avoid knowing even what is right in front of their eyes.

Inhibitors of Bystander Action

An example of bystander behavior comes from one of my naturalistic research studies.[1] We had a young Harvard student collapse, again and again, on a quiet street in Cambridge, Massachusetts, when a passerby was approaching him about 50 yards away. We studied a variety of influences that may affect whether a person helps, such as the passerby approaching on the same side of the street or on the other side (more helping occurred on the same side), and whether the student as he collapsed grabbed his knee or his heart (more helping occurred when he grabbed his heart if he was overweight, less helping if he was in very good shape).

When bystanders passed by on the other side of the street and noticed the young man collapse, some of them immediately rushed over. Others looked, slowed down, and after a while walked across the street to the collapsed student. Sometimes they acted so slowly that others helped before they made up their minds. Some moved on without helping. But a powerful phenomenon also appeared that we did not expect. Some passersby after a single glance never looked back, and sometimes at the next corner they turned and walked away from the scene.

Something similar happens when groups suffer. Bystanders may be in a position to know about this suffering but avoid knowing, perhaps so that they don't have to get involved. The Genocide Prevention Task Force report notes that often governments actually resist learning about grave risks of genocide and mass atrocities. "Officials want to avoid getting involved in a complex and difficult situation requiring hard choices, or want to protect their principles from accountability for failures....it is easier to deflect charges that one should have known but was never informed than that one knew but chose not to respond."[2]

Internal bystanders tend to be passive in the course of the evolution of increasing harm done to victims. In the face of difficult life conditions or group conflict, they need connection to their group. As an evolution toward violence progresses, it is difficult to act in opposition to their group on behalf of people who have usually been devalued in the society and whom therefore most people have learned to devalue. The combination of the effects of difficult life conditions and past devaluation creates a *cultural tilt* against the victimized group— or the enemy in a conflict. As they go along and act as if everything was normal, people become complicit.

In addition to prior devaluation and the impact of instigating conditions on people, there are other inhibitors of action. One of them is pluralistic ignorance: Everyone may remain silent, so that no one knows the extent to which other people oppose the ideology and harmful, violent actions. Another is diffusion of responsibility among the many people who witness what is happening.[3*] In addition, certain people may be seen as responsible for taking action, such as opposition political leaders, further reducing feelings of responsibility by citizens. Often these processes unfold under autocratic and violent governments, which do not tolerate opposition. The cost of active bystandership, whether potential ostracism, physical danger, or both, helps to maintain and reinforce passivity. The feeling of powerlessness on the part of individuals, and the difficulty in joining together when an authoritarian system limits communication and freedom of assembly, can be added inhibitors.

The passivity and complicity of bystanders affirms the perpetrators. When the Nazis introduced anti-Jewish measures in Germany, they waited to see the reactions of the population. But nothing happened to discourage them–at home or internationally. If anything, they were encouraged—at home by community passivity and actions. Outsiders'actions also encouraged them, such as when the U.S. track team at the 1936 Olympics removed Jewish runners so as not to offend their Nazi hosts, or when at a meeting of the community of nations in Switzerland, most countries decided not to accept Jewish refugees from Germany.[4] Linda Melvern described how the initiators of the genocide in Rwanda waited, in the first week, to see the reactions of the international community and were emboldened when there weren't any.[5]

Some actions by bystanders cannot be considered just passivity, but represent a degree of participation or active complicity. When so directed by the Nazis, Germans avoided shopping in Jewish stores.[6] Many Germans began under Nazi rule to cross the street when they saw Jews who had been their friends. I consider such bystanders "semi-active participants" in the evolution of violence. When the genocide started in Rwanda, Western countries sent troops that gathered their own citizens and then left. They were also not just passive bystanders. Their actions sent a powerful message to the killers that they could do as they wished.

The passivity, seeming acceptance, and complicity by bystanders confirm perpetrators in their belief that what they are doing is acceptable, even right. Passivity also reinforces the passivity of other bystanders. The lack of concern and inaction of each person says to all others that there is no reason for concern and action. In the course of the evolution of doing harm, passive bystanders change. Even at the start, reactions to the suffering of a group is less than to an individual, perhaps because we can imagine more the experience, and therefore empathize more with a single individual. When people are shown the picture of a single child in need, their empathy is greater than when they are shown the picture of a number of similarly looking children in need. In addition, to lessen their own empathic distress and feelings of guilt, bystanders tend to distance themselves from the victims. This can be done consciously, but it is mostly automatic. Like perpetrators, they tend to justify the victims'suffering by devaluing and blaming them. The progressive evolution of harmful actions makes it possible to get accustomed to them and see them as normal, reducing reactions to the next step in the evolution. As bystanders are transformed, some join the perpetrators.[7]

Uncertainty and fear of the other group are also inhibitors of bystander action. How does one know that this group is not out to destroy one's own group— including one's family and oneself? Herbert Kelman,[8] writing about the Palestinian–Israeli conflict, describes internal conflict within each group among those who are willing to take risks for peace, and those who believe that making peace with the other group is impossible. While some in Israel are driven by an ideology of greater Israel, others fear Palestinians and the elimination of the Jewish state. There is also approach/avoidance conflict. When decision about making peace is near, those willing to act for peace become ambivalent, afraid that the arrangements under consideration will jeopardize their existence. The definition of reality by leaders, by the media, and by external bystanders, and internal communication within the other group may create or intensify uncertainty and fear. However, they also have the potential to lessen uncertainty and fear.

The influence of other people in the evolution of violence, including their passivity, is also shown in circumscribed situations such as in the Stanford Prison Study (described in detail in Chapter 9) and at the Abu Ghraib prison in Iraq. Those in charge did not set rules that might have inhibited the guards'abuse of the prisoners in these situations. For the most part, neither superiors nor fellow guards took action when they saw the abuse. Their passive bystandership allowed the evolution of increasing abuse.

In both situations there were also influences that made abuse more likely. At Abu Ghraib interrogators used forceful, abusive techniques, which provided a model for the guards. They also encouraged guards to use force and humiliation to "soften up" prisoners for interrogation.[9] In the Stanford Prison Study the superintendent set no rules for the guards to follow and the instructions he gave them could incite forceful action.[10] In addition, one of the guards started to act aggressively toward prisoners in the first evening and was increasingly abusive. This created a competitive situation with the other guard on the same shift, who tried to match him, and contributed to a culture of increasing aggressiveness.

Research studies found, and real-life situations have shown, that through their words, actions and example, or passivity people strongly affect each other. When in one study a number of people, collaborators of the experimenter, said that lines of obviously different length were the same length, the unknowing participant in the study also said, close to 40% of the time, that they were the same length, even though there were no consequences of disagreeing.[11] In Stanley Milgram's obedience experiments, participants complied with instructions by administering what they believed were intense shocks. Christopher Browning also claimed that the conformity and compliance with the group had an important role in the behavior of German reserve police who were sent to the Eastern front, behind the German army, to kill Jews.[12] In many situations, as in the case of one bystander's interpretation of an emergency situation affecting the behavior of another bystander,[13] people's perception and judgement of events, and their actions, are affected by others'perspectives and actions. People can exert powerful influence on each other. By defining the meaning of events and appropriate behavior, and by their example, people can increase passivity, conformity, and compliance, or generate opposition and action.

The Possibilities of Opposition and Nonviolent Resistance

I will discuss active bystandership in Part II of the book, but I want to briefly consider the possibility of resistance here. There is always variation in people's attitude toward violence against another group. Human beings are never uniform: Variations in temperament, in child rearing, and in individual life experience create variations in personality and morality even among people in the same society. Even in small nontechnological societies with a great deal of uniformity in life, around 45% show the modal personality that characterizes the group, the rest deviating from it to varying degrees.[14] Some people are likely to disagree as their society moves toward or engages in violence. Will they express opposition or remain passive?

Even under a repressive government, when the harm is inflicted on people the group identifies with, bystanders are motivated to act. In Germany, when physically and mentally handicapped and some other categories of Germans were being killed in a eugenics program aimed to improve the race, euphemistically named a "euthanasia" program, relatives, lawyers'groups, and leaders of the Catholic Church spoke out. While the killings continued for a while on a much smaller scale, the official program was terminated. Nonetheless, this program was part of the steps along a continuum of destruction. The Nazis later used personnel and techniques in extermination camps (such as gas to kill people) that were initiated in this program.[15]

Another example is Serbia. As I mentioned in Chapter 2, there were groups that opposed the nationalistic ideology and actions of the government and the violence it incited. The Serbs did not live under a brutal dictatorship; they could talk to each other and join in opposition. There were demonstrations in support of democracy and against war in 1991, 1992, and 1993. In 1998, students formed an organization to promote democracy by nonviolent means. Joined by workers, they opposed the Milosevic government by speaking out, and more importantly by nonviolent demonstrations in which hundreds of thousands of people participated. In the end, long convoys of buses and cars blocked the streets. They succeeded in ousting Milosevic.[16] It is highly likely that the views of these actors were affected, and that they were emboldened by, the preceding actions of the international community to stop Serb violence.

Often nonviolent movements that attempt to create change have to do not with a country engaged in or moving toward violence, but simply with repressive systems. Such systems are one source of terrorism, and of guerrilla warfare, or of violent revolutions that, even if they succeed, often give rise to new repression. When, however, the system is changed by nonviolent means, the new system is much more likely to be democratic.[17] Well-known examples of nonviolent movements that have created change are those led by Gandhi in India and Martin Luther King, Jr. in the United States. But there are many cases of transition from an authoritarian system to democracy that involved nonviolent movements—in the Philippines in1986, Chile in 1988, Ukraine in 2004, and the collapse of communism. In earlier times as well there was nonviolent resistance, such as Egyptians liberating themselves from the British, or resistance to the Shah of Iran.

Merriman and DuVall write[18] that nonviolent movements use "protest and persuasion (with rallies and marches), noncooperation (such as economic boycotts and strikes) and intervention (such as sit-ins and civil disobedience)." They also use communication with their supporters to mobilize them, and with outsiders to gain their support. The age of the Internet makes communication easier (although with the danger that people interact on the Internet in place of real action). These movements stress common values and inclusiveness, providing at least aspects of a constructive ideology (see Chapter 15). Such movements need and deserve support by external parties.

Passivity—and Complicity—by External Bystanders

The psychological and behavioral evolution of the group toward violence is supported by the passivity of internal bystanders and external bystanders. External bystanders at times act to halt already significant violence, as did the international community in the wars in the former Yugoslavia, the British in the extremely violent civil war in Sierra Leone, or the United Nations when it authorized missions for East Timor.[19] While in the last decade U.N. engagement has increased, much of the time the international community has remained passive, at times complicit in violence, and when it acted it normally did so after a long period of intense violence. Usually outside groups and nations don't have to fear speaking out, as do people in a repressive country. Early expressions of disapproval and nonmilitary actions might inhibit the evolution of violence, with limited cost.

Traditionally nations have not regarded themselves as moral agents. This may be slowly changing, with international human rights conventions that are creating a body of international law that imposes moral obligation on nations. But historically, afraid of the costs involved in engagement, focused on their own concerns and interests, guided by principles of nonintervention and a narrow definition of national interest, most countries have remained passive in the face of mass violence. Everybody ignored warnings, for example, by Human Rights Watch that there was impending violence in Rwanda. The United Nations ignored information that Roméo Dallaire, the commander of its peacekeepers in Rwanda,[20] received from an informant indicating that arms had been accumulated and a genocide was planned. It did not give him permission to look for and destroy the arms before the genocide and to intervene once the genocide began. When eight Belgian peacekeepers were killed, all but 250 of the peacekeepers were ordered to leave Rwanda, as intended and hoped for by the killers. (In spite of his orders, Dallaire kept 200 more peacekeepers there.) When they left, the genocidaires immediately proceeded to kill Tutsis gathered around the places where the peacekeepers were stationed.

While any neutral observer could see the killings in Rwanda as genocide, the United States resisted calling it a genocide. As I mentioned before, countries now avoid the obligation to take action by not defining mass violence as genocide. Moreover, perpetrator groups, to prevent intervention by bystanders, can create uncertainty and confusion about what is happening in their country. The U.N. Security Council respectfully listened to the representative of the genocidal

Rwandan government claiming that what was happening was a continuation of the civil war.

If huge numbers of people, in this case hundreds of thousands of them, are being killed, should help depend on how we choose to label the event? Even if the international community genuinely believes that a civil war is taking place, and that historical enemies are fighting, mechanisms must be created to intervene if there is large-scale killing of the civilian population. When the Council finally decided to return peacekeepers to Rwanda, the Pentagon and the United Nations haggled over how much the Pentagon would charge for equipment to lease to the peacekeepers while 10,000 people a day were killed.

There are prior examples that knowing that genocide is taking place does not necessarily lead to action. After everybody knew about the gas chambers at Auschwitz, with planes flying within 30 miles from the camp to bomb factories, the Allies refused to divert a single plane in order to bomb the railroad to the camp.

Many countries are not only passive but complicit to varying degrees. Some continue with business as usual, maintaining diplomatic, commercial, and other relations with a government and nation as it is progressing along a continuum of violence. Many U.S. corporations as well as corporations of other nations were busy conducting business in Germany during the 1930s. Currently, many violent groups maintain themselves and generate funds to buy arms by dealing in drugs or exploiting natural resources. Corporations around the world, including those in the United States, buy minerals from such groups in the Congo, helping to maintain the fighting there.

France supported the Rwandan government and military with arms and training when the Rwandan Patriotic Front (RPF) entered Rwanda from Uganda in 1990. This may have been due to the RPF entering from an English-speaking country and France wanting to maintain a Francophile government. It may also have been due to a friendship between the French President Mitterand and the Rwandan President Habyarimana. France continued its support, without raising any objections when in the course of the following years Tutsi peasants were repeatedly massacred. When the RPF defeated the government, France also helped the perpetrators escape to Zaire, with their arms and money.

Countries protect perpetrating nations due to commercial interests, a history of friendship, or current relationships among leaders. Russia tried to prevent actions against the Serbs during the wars in the former Yugoslavia. China has been unwilling to support actions in the Sudan by the United Nations aimed at stopping the genocide in Darfur, presumably because the Sudan is an important supplier of oil for China. A slight shift in policy by China emerged in 2008, perhaps because the Olympics in Beijing was approaching and people used that opportunity to create pressure on China. Countries often do not even express their disapproval to a violent regime, which is the most minimal and still potentially effective action they could take, with their silence encouraging perpetrators.

The words and actions of influential outside groups can also encourage harmful policies. Many evangelical Christian groups support the building of the settlements in the West Bank. Some claim that they give their support because of their love of Israel. But there is usually a subtext, the belief that the recreation of biblical Israel is necessary for and will lead to the return of the Messiah. This is accompanied by the belief that upon the return of the Messiah, Christians will go to heaven, and nonbelievers, like Jews, will suffer a terrible death. Although Jews don't believe this notion, the settler movement opportunistically accepts evangelical Christian support. This support for Israel not giving up occupied territories, for the settlement movement and its expansion, is multifaceted—ideological, moral, religious, and financial. Christian ministers write books,[21] delegations go to Israel, and money is collected and donated at Church rallies. But the expansion of the settlements makes the resolution of the Israeli–Palestinian conflict much more difficult, if not impossible. It is hard to understand how the settlers and their supporters inside and outside Israel imagine the future. Can they foresee anything but hostility and violence if Israel retains the West Bank, or large portions of it?

The lack of appropriate influence on Israeli policies by the U.S. government, the closest friend of Israel, is also bad bystandership. All administrations since Lyndon Johnson's have correctly and publicly stated that they consider the building of settlements on occupied land illegal, and a significant obstacle to peace.[22] An important part of the Oslo agreement that Israel did not fulfill was stopping the building of settlements. Some U.S. Presidents have exerted positive influence on Israel, such as Jimmy Carter demanding that Israel return all of Sinai to Egypt, which made the Camp David accords and peace between Israel and Egypt possible. But no administration has exerted sufficient influence to stop Israel from building settlements. The resistance is especially strong to stop expanding settlements through "natural growth," to accommodate the families of increasing size living in them. Early demand by the Obama administration to stop building settlements met with resistance. With continued pressure, Israel agreed to stop building certain kinds of settlements for a limited time. With the United States as Israel's best friend, American leaders have the greatest potential to persuade Israeli leaders to change harmful policies.

A powerful lobby for Israel, the American Israel Public Affairs Committee (AIPAC), seems to intimidate members of Congress—and apparently presidents as well. George H. Bush "was holding up $10 billion in loan guarantees Israel desperately need to build housing for Russian émigrés till Bush got an assurance that the loans would not fund settlements. Alas, in the end, Bush folded on the issue."[23] Peace-oriented Israeli leaders don't necessarily like AIPAC policies and actions. When Yitzhak Rabin came to Washington for the first time as Israel's prime minister, "he summoned AIPAC's leaders to a closed-door meeting at the Madison Hotel in which he accused them of steering Israel into a needless confrontation with the White House."[24] A newer small Israel lobby, calling itself J Street, supports peace oriented actions by the United States.

Even worse bystandership has been practiced by Arab countries, as well as non-Arab Muslim countries such as Iran. In the course of many years they have instigated, rather than attempted to halt, violence by Palestinians. They have supported the terrorist actions of Hamas and Hezbollah, although in recent times it is primarily Iran and Syria who have done so. So did Iraq under Saddam Hussein, who offered $20,000 for the family of each suicide bomber.

Frequently outside groups materially and psychologically support violent movements in a country, including terrorism. Sometimes they see violence as serving the legitimate rights of a group they identify with. Perhaps this was true of Muslim countries that supported Palestinians. But their support continued long after it became clear that the reciprocal violence with Israel creates desperate conditions for Palestinians and interferes with a resolution. Irish Americans presumably also felt they supported fighting for legitimate rights as they provided financial support for the Irish Republican Army.

Groups and individuals in Saudi Arabia and other countries have provided support for jihadist terrorists. This support is presumably based on shared views about Islam and shared antagonism against nonbelievers—and perhaps toward the West in general. The support is not only financial. It is also ideological, including education in religious schools that propagate views that motivate potential fighters.

On the rare occasions when outside nations have responded to mass violence, they have done so after much violence has occurred, as in Bosnia. The bombing by the North Atlantic Treaty Organization (NATO) of Serb artillery positions not only inflicted damage but finally demonstrated to the Serb leaders that the rest of the world was taking their actions seriously and would not tolerate them further. The later NATO attacks to stop the violence in Kosovo were also late responses to a long developing situation. Because it came when violence had already become intense, and because of the unwillingness to use ground troops, the level of air bombardment of Serb targets, including the city of Belgrade, was extensive and highly destructive. Military interventions could usually be avoided with committed early efforts at prevention, but they become necessary when intense violence is in progress.

An example of the short-sightedness of the international community was shown in Cyprus. There after 1974 the so-called Green line physically separated the Greek and Turkish communities for 29 years. Peace was maintained by the Green line, which was closed, and by U.N. peacekeepers. But there were also peacemaking/reconciliation efforts, especially dialogue between citizens, that were initiated, financed, and supported by the United Nations and the international community. Interested citizens met between the two zones, in spite of potential or actual disapproval by their communities. In these meetings people could build relationships and discuss the issues of interest between the two groups.

When after 29 years the wall was opened, there was great excitement and much visiting. This has diminished, and now a substantial amount of the traffic between communities consists of Turks going to work into the more economically advanced Greek area of the island, which is part of the European community. The evident inequality of the two groups in conflict maintains hostility. However, external support for meetings and for peace building has stopped.[25] In a cold peace, without reconciliation, negative attitudes remain. Change in the conditions of the groups, or new leadership, can give rise to new violence.

In recent decades, *after* mass violence, there is often substantial humanitarian aid provided to those harmed or dislocated by the violence. Such aid is costly, often difficult to deliver, and has increasingly put humanitarian aid workers in harm's way, as combatants respect their safety less and target them more. It is also inadequate. It comes after many deaths and great suffering, and it is usually insufficient for the existing need. Sometimes it is highly problematic, as after the Rwandan genocide, when the genocidaires who escaped into the Congo used the aid as a means to continue their violence against Tutsis in Rwanda and in the Congo.

As another example of passive bystandership and complicity, I want to mention the agreements with Germany in the 1930s that allowed it to annex parts of other countries—for example, the Sudetenland that was part of Czechoslovakia. They contributed to the evolution of German aggression that led to World War II. Neville Chamberlain, the British prime minister, believed he was saving peace in Europe by caving in to Hitler's demands. But agreeing to his demands and accepting the German takeover of parts of Czechoslovakia and Austria were followed by the occupation of Poland (which Germany divided with the Soviet Union). At this point England and France declared war on Germany.

Winston Churchill opposed these agreements and believed that had he been prime minister of England at the time, he would have stopped German expansion and prevented World War II—and the Holocaust—by creating a powerful coalition that either would have intimidated Hitler or led to his assassination by the German military.[26] While Churchill's opposition to Chamberlain's actions at the time is historical fact, the rest is conjecture on his part. A conjecture on my part is that Churchill would have been a much more effective negotiator with Hitler, who was very aggressive in his manner, shouting at and intimidating people. Churchill was not easily intimidated.

The United States as a Bystander

Occasionally, the United States has been a very positive bystander. A prime example is the Marshall Plan that helped to rebuild Europe after World War II.

It was motivated by some combination of altruism and enlightened self-interest in creating a peaceful Europe and making the spread of communism less likely. The United States tends to help in natural disasters, such as a famine in Somalia or an earthquake in Haiti. The United States led NATO to intervene and stop Serb violence in Bosnia and later in Kosovo.

However, the United States has engaged in many interventions, "bystander actions," that were *not* humanitarian. The United States helped with or directly overthrew elected governments, whether by military means or CIA subversion, and supported governments that kill their people. In Guatemala in 1954 U.S. marines overthrew the government. This was followed by decades of repression, with military governments engaging in mass killings as they were fighting guerrillas. In Chile, the United States helped overthrow Allende, the elected president. Mass killing under military rule followed. In Iran, the United States helped overturn the government and install the Shah of Iran, whose brutal rule prepared the way for the revolution of the Ayatollah Khomeini and the current system. In El Salvador, the United States for a long time supported those in power with substantial financial and military aid, in spite of many killings by the military and by death squads allied with or created by the government. It only began to change course as a result of the outrage that followed when it was established that a group of nuns and a priest, who the government claimed were killed by guerrillas, were actually killed by government soldiers.[27]

Over several decades up to the 1990s, in a number of South American countries, in the course of so-called counterinsurgency campaigns, large numbers of people were killed. Many of the military officers who instituted and executed these policies had been trained by the United States at the infamous School of the Americas. The United States continues to support repressive regimes around the world, in particular in Arab countries like Saudi Arabia and Egypt. I suggested earlier that repression is one of the societal origins of terrorism. The United States' support for these repressive countries, including substantial financial aid to Egypt, the sale of military equipment to both Egypt and Saudi Arabia, and good relations with their governments, which help maintain their credibility and power, is one source of hostility toward the United States by Al-Qaeda and those sympathetic to it. It is one of the reasons that Al-Qaeda has shifted from the near enemy, governments in Islamic countries that they regard as untrue to Islam, to the far enemy, especially the United States.

I am stressing the U.S. role as an intervener/ bystander for several reasons. One is that given its great power, negative actions by the United States have substantial consequences. Another is that the United States could be a powerful leader of the international community in positive bystandership. This is true even in the wake of the war in Iraq, when U.S. power, credibility, and moral standing have been greatly diminished. The United States still has great power, and credibility and moral standing can be rebuilt. A third reason is that as an American I am concerned with the harm my country does and the good it can do.

The passivity and actions I described have been, unfortunately, the way great powers often behave. One observer, referring to U.S. actions, has coined the term "superpower syndrome."[28] But these actions are not expressions of core U.S. values. The Carter administration was true to these values when it spoke out and acted against brutality in South American countries, including the disappearances in Argentina. The Carter policies contributed to the impetus for the establishment of democracies in South America. Other presidents, however, have been less concerned about human rights and lives. We have often been hypocritical. President George W. Bush's proclamation that we love freedom—and that terrorists hate us because of that—is not credible to a world that sees the United States supporting regimes that allow their people no freedom.

The United States' great potential for positive leadership has important implications for Americans as citizens. Our research has shown that people who love their country can greatly vary in the nature of their patriotism. The patriotism of some may be characterized as "my country right and wrong." They are highly averse to criticizing their country and therefore support even destructive policies. They feel protective of their country's culture—for example, dislike that the Japanese play baseball, an American sport. I called them "blind patriots." The research found that such people inform themselves less about current events. Others, in contrast, say that because they love their country, they must speak out when it acts contrary to humane considerations, moral values, or its own essential values. They believe in their own (and by implications their country's) responsibility for the welfare of other human beings. I called them "constructive patriots."[29]

Constructive patriots would want the United States to be a positive, constructive bystander. Bystanders need to exert influence not only with opponents but also and even especially with friends. Countries listen more to friends than to enemies,[30] particularly friends they are dependent on. In recent times, the United States has effectively promoted peace in Northern Ireland. But while some of our presidents have constructively engaged in "good offices," mediating between the parties, it has not done enough in the Palestinian–Israeli conflict. It has accepted continued Israeli occupation of the West Bank and Gaza and the building of settlements, has not engaged enough with Palestinians, and under the second Bush administration, it did little to advance peace. Hopefully, the constructive engagement that was started by the Obama administration will continue.

Summary

In the face of escalating violence, witnesses or bystanders usually remain passive, due to past devaluation of the victims, pluralistic ignorance, diffusion of responsibility, the definition of the meaning of events by leaders and the media, and feelings of powerlessness and fear. The passivity and often at least some degree of complicity of bystanders make the perpetrators of violence believe that what they are doing is right. To protect themselves from empathic distress, bystanders who remain passive distance themselves from the victims, and like perpetrators they come to justify the harm to the victims and their passivity by devaluing the victims more. External bystanders, outside nations and groups, also usually remain passive. Internal and external bystanders are often complicit, continuing with business as usual. Sometimes external bystanders actively support perpetrating governments.Positive, constructive actions by bystanders are crucial in the prevention of group violence.

Notes

1 Staub & Baer, 1974
2 Albright & Cohen, 2008. p. 47
3 See Latane & Darley, 1970, for the initial formulation of the concepts of pluralistic ignorance and diffusion of responsibility. See Myers, 2010, and Staub, 1978, for discussion of relevant research.
4 Staub, 1989
5 Malvern, 2004
6 Staub, 1989
7 See Staub 1989, and especially on this last point, also Lifton, 1986
8 Kelman, 2007
9 Staub, 2010b; Zimbardo, 2007
10 Zimbardo, 1989
11 Asch, 1956
12 Browning, 1992
13 Staub, 1974, 2003a
14 Konner, 1978
15 Lifton, 1986; Staub, 1989
16 Ackerman & DuVall, 2000
17 Merriman & DuVall, 2007
18 Ibid, p. 3
19 Albright, 2008
20 Dallaire, 2003
21 Hagee, 2007
22 http://www.cmep.org/documents/settlements.htm
23 http://www.philipweiss.org/mondoweiss/2006/07/did_the_first_p.html
24 Frankel, 2006
25 Modenos, 2008
26 Melson, 2008
27 Staub, 2001
28 Lifton, 2003
29 Staub, 1997a; Schatz, Staub, & Lavine, 1999
30 Fein, 1994

8

Cultural/Societal Characteristics That Make Hostility and Violence More Likely

A history of devaluation of and discrimination against a group increases the likelihood of violence against that group.

Past victimization and unhealed psychological wounds tend to lead to vulnerability and seeing the world as dangerous, and this can lead to unnecessary "defensive" violence and sometimes to hostile violence.

A monolithic society with an excessive respect for authority makes it more likely that people will follow leaders that move the group toward increasing hostility and violence.

Past enmity usually leads to seeing the other group as responsible for conflict and violence, which makes increasing violence more likely.

Extreme instigating conditions, persistent difficult life conditions, and conflict can give rise to what I have described so far: destructive psychological and social processes and violence. But in a society that possesses certain characteristics, it is more likely that instigating conditions give rise to the evolution of the psychological and social bases of violence and to violence itself. This chapter describes these characteristics and their role in mass violence. I have already mentioned the role of devaluation, woundedness that results from past experience, and other psychological conditions and attitudes that contribute to violence. Here I examine them in depth and discuss them as characteristics of whole cultures/societies.

Us and Them, Historical Devaluation, and Discrimination

A past history of division between groups, with lines drawn between "us" and "them," and a history of devaluation or negative images of "them" are cultural/societal characteristics that make later violence against "them" more likely.

In difficult times it is the historically devalued group that is likely to become the scapegoated group and the ideological enemy. The psychological differentiation between us and a devalued them is often accompanied by social differentiation, such as discrimination, that bars the devalued group from equal access to societal resources and promotes social injustice in general.

What are the sources of division, devaluation, and discrimination? One of them is simply the existence of varied ethnic, religious, or racial groups in a society. It is common wisdom among genocide scholars[1] that "plural societies," especially if there are significant "cleavages" between groups, are more likely to experience genocide. Cultural differences between groups and political or economic inequality associated with them are both the outcome and a source of devaluation. An important issue for prevention is to overcome cleavages and move toward just relations between groups.

As I have already discussed, human beings have a strong tendency to divide people into "us" and "them." The human mind naturally categorizes, along many dimensions—small and big, short and tall, intelligent and unintelligent, kind and unkind, and us and them. Our evolutionary heritage seems to have prepared us to identify ourselves as members of groups. At the very least, groups help people survive by providing protection and increasing effectiveness in accomplishing material goals, such as finding food, building shelters, fighting animals, and dealing with other physical dangers. Membership in groups also helps fulfill basic psychological needs.

When people are divided into groups for research purposes, even when they are told that it is on as superficial a basis as how they group dots on a page, they immediately begin to treat each other differently. They start to favor their group in dividing available resources. This happens even when they know that they are randomly assigned to groups.[2] Becoming "us" leads to a preference for us over "them." It also makes it easier and more likely for us to devalue them. How much greater is the force of such tendencies when we are members of groups that we are deeply committed to, and if the other group is seen as a threat to our own?

While I focus on persistent cultural/historical divisions into us and them and the devaluation of "them," this capacity or tendency to speedily categorize people as "other" is very much apparent between individuals. Much of individual violence takes place in families, and one way to understand it is that in response to certain events, a wall goes up, a disconnection develops, and the other person becomes a "them." While this can happen over a period of time, it can also happen suddenly. In groups also, under difficult life conditions, when there is no natural target for scapegoating, some subgroup of society can become a "them," its target. As conflict with a previously friendly group emerges, they can be blamed for it.

What I call devaluation has been given many different names, with similar meanings, such as dehumanization, delegitimization,[3] or prejudice (which includes connotations of power in relation to the devalued group). There is a paradox in that a devalued group can be seen as having certain positive qualities, but these become a detriment in the eyes of those who devalue them, who envy and resent their good qualities. This was the case with Tutsis who tend to be tall and attractive, although more in stereotypes of them than reality. They were primarily cattle breeders and historically wealthier, in contrast to Hutus who were primarily farmers. Their material well-being, probably exaggerated at the time of the genocide, after a history of discrimination, was also resented.

Tutsis were seen as sly and untrustworthy. They were inconvenient—in an overcrowded country, their land was needed for the children of Hutus, who probably realistically believed that it was not possible to live on the small parcels of land that would result from subdividing their property among their children. Scarcity, the need for and competition for resources, is not uncommon in leading up to group violence, but devaluation, ideology, and other elements shape what people do about it. In the context of the ongoing Rwanda civil war, leaders and the media also propagated beliefs that the Tutsis would appropriate Hutu property, make Hutus do forced labor again, and even intended to kill all Hutus.[4]

There are different types of devaluation, with different potential consequences. Another group and its members can be seen as *less intelligent or lazy*. This perception is probably the least likely to lead to group violence directed at them. Or they can be seen as parasites who exploit one's own group, or as generally *immoral*. This form of devaluation of Jews started very early in the Christian era. The likely initial impetus for the devaluation of Jews was the need of the early Christians to separate and differentiate themselves from their origins in Judaism, to establish a separate identity and the superiority of their way of worshipping God.[5] Over time discriminatory policies against Jews were created in Europe that prohibited them from owning and working the land, or from practicing certain professions. They were, however, allowed and even encouraged to practice banking and commerce because Christians were prohibited from handling money. They became wealthier, were disliked for it, and were seen as exploiters.

Another group can also be seen as a *threat*, as *dangerous* to oneself and one's group. Often seeing a group as immoral and a threat go together, with the strongest potential for violence against the "immoral" and "dangerous" group. These views need not have a basis in reality. The Jews were law-abiding citizens who did not represent a threat to Germany, but the Nazis believed it and intensely propagated this belief.

Open and crude forms of prejudice have become much less acceptable in the United States and Western European countries, and researchers have begun to study subtle forms of prejudice and stereotyping. A great deal of research has assessed levels of prejudice by comparing the speed with which people associate words describing positive or negative qualities with white and minority faces. Associating negative words faster and positive words slower with minorities indicates prejudice and is expressed in various behaviors. Some researchers have used the term *infrahumanization* to denote research findings that devalued people, minorities that are the object of prejudice, are believed to have less of the advanced or uniquely human emotions and qualities, such as empathy, love, and aesthetic appreciation. Moreover, after a group is harmed, its members are less likely to be seen as having such qualities.[6]

While subtle forms of devaluation can intensify under instigating conditions, in the kinds of violence discussed in this book even at an early point in the evolution of hostility and violence devaluation usually ranges from reasonably open to blatant and extreme. In place of expressing subtle prejudice, such as not looking at black members of a mixed group, making somewhat more negative evaluations of minority candidates for a job, or even trying hard not to seem prejudiced, devaluation is often openly expressed. Members of devalued groups are often called animal names.

The danger to a devalued group increases when its members do reasonably well in a society, materially or in terms of their status (usually because a combination of external conditions and internal culture has led to skills and capacities that make them needed and successful in spite of their social situation). The Jews in Germany, the Tutsi in Rwanda, and Armenians in Turkey are all examples of devalued groups doing relatively well—and ultimately becoming victims. The negative view of the group makes it difficult to tolerate its success and gives rise to envy, resentment, and further devaluation.

Case studies of mass violence show that there had been divisions between groups and the group that became the victim was seen in a negative light.[7] The experimental research by Albert Bandura and his associates, discussed in Chapter 6, showed that just overhearing a negative statement about strangers, which described them as a rotten bunch, led participants to give stronger electric shocks to them. When a group is devalued, there are many derogatory comments made about its members, or the group as a whole.

In Darfur, "Arab" militias, at times supported by Sudanese military helicopters and/or by soldiers, have been attacking black Africans, killing them, raping women, burning down villages, and driving away their inhabitants. To understand the situation there, the U.S. State Department authorized in 2004 an Atrocities Documentation Survey. A total of 1136 refugees in Chad were interviewed in 22 settlements. An analysis of their statements by sociologists John Hagan and Wenona Rymond-Richmond[8*] showed that when the attackers shouted more intense racial epithets at their victims, they were more violent. Some examples were: "You donkey, you slave, we must get rid of you," "You blacks are not human. We can do anything we want to you. You cannot live here," "We kill our cows when they have black calves—we will kill you too," "You blacks are like monkeys. You are not human," "All the people in the village are slaves; you make this area dirty, we are here to clean the area." A few of these epithets also point to one source of the devaluation—a history of slavery, the memory of which lingers in the culture.

Clearly derogation is associated with violence. It could be that more intense devaluation caused greater violence by the attackers in Darfur, but the findings cannot convincingly establish this. It could also be that when the violence was greater, the perpetrators were justifying their actions to themselves by shouting these statements. The research findings also showed that when Sudanese troops and Janjaweed militias acted together, violence was greater. In these cases the presence of the other group may have instigated both more devaluation and more violence. These attacks were not on rebels. The majority of them took place away from areas where the rebels operated.

Genocide scholar Maureen Hiebert[9] differentiates among three types of devaluations: a group seen as outsider or foreign, or seen as less than fully human, as subhuman or animals (pagans, savages, infidels, vermin), or seen as a threat to one's own group. She sees the second type as necessary to enable perpetrators to engage in violence against the victims. But she sees the third type, threat and especially mortal threat (which others have called existential threat), as motivating violence, as leading "elites to initiate, and society to accept, genocidal policies."[10]

It makes sense that the belief that the other is bent on your destruction would have special motivational force, and some Israelis and Palestinians, and Hutus before the genocide, have apparently held such beliefs. But as the study by Bandura and his associates shows, devaluation can lead to violence without the other being able to harm us. And of course groups can be perceived as a threat when in actuality they are not. They can be scapegoated for societal problems or made into ideological enemies even if initially they are not seen as a threat, especially a mortal threat. Further research is needed on what types of devaluation leads to violence under what conditions, and especially how devaluation originates and how its nature changes.

Empathy and a related form of it, sympathy, which includes the desire to improve the situation of a person in distress, are two primary reasons that we care about and help others and do not harm others. But we neither empathize nor sympathize with those we regard as immoral or as enemies, hostile and dangerous to ourselves or our group. We also feel less empathy for people geographically distant from us. Similarity is an important basis for empathy, and we probably assume that they are less similar to us. With such people, we probably take an "observer" perspective. Observing what is happening to others gives rise to less empathy than imagining what it is like for them, or what it would be like for us, to be in their situation.[11] When we dislike or feel hostile to people, we may even feel good when bad things happen to them.[12] There are exceptions. Some rescuers of Jews in Nazi Europe were anti-Semitic but had strong moral principles and believed that no one should be treated as the Jews were.[13]

By 2007, there were more than 600 reports of intense abuse of Iraqis by American soldiers.[14] Civilians not involved in fighting were killed, including the family of a girl who was then raped and also killed. Americans certainly hold values that normally prohibit harming people. But attitudes toward Iraqis, seeing some as terrorists, lumping them together as enemies, or simply not "seeing" them, may explain the very limited public outcry about and media attention to these abuses. Our attitudes toward a group affect our concern about their members' welfare and our judgment of our conduct in relation to them.

Devaluation and discrimination increase the potential for violence not only toward but also by devalued groups. In Europe, where local terrorist groups emerged, Muslims feel much more devalued and discriminated against than do Muslims in the United States, where they are better integrated, with less radicalization of Muslim youth.[15] Many Europeans see Muslims in a highly negative light, with values and practices contradictory to their own, alien to Europe, untrustworthy, hostile, and fanatical. They believe that Muslims want to remain separate. Muslims in the Netherlands, at least, report that they want to be integrated, although not assimilated—to be part of their country but also to retain their Muslim identity.[16] However, many Muslims in Europe do report very strong religious identification, even stronger than those in Muslim countries, and young Muslims see themselves as part of a separate community. This may be due to their need for community in the midst of cultures/religions different from their own. It may also be due to lack of acceptance and limited interaction between groups. Muslims are largely separate in everyday life—in where they shop, go for entertainment and sports—involved in political life only to a limited extent, and discriminated in housing and employment.[17]

European Muslims feel both unaccepted and devalued, and they devalue Europeans.[18] They see them as immoral—selfish, arrogant, greedy, and violent. These feelings and attitudes can become, and have been, under instigating conditions at home, or in response to instigation from the outside by terrorists or other radical influences, starting points on the road to terrorism.

The Origins, Persistence, and Role of Historical Devaluation

Race and ethnicity, that is, genetically based physical differences between groups and differences based on culture—in religion, values, beliefs, practices, skills, and political ideology—can all be powerful dividers. What is important is the perceptions and meanings of these differences that develop, and the uncertainty and fear about what the other is like and how the other might act. Differences in perceptions and attitudes may give rise to societal practices such as discrimination that lead to poverty or low status for some groups, or deprive them of legitimacy (such as not having citizenship).

Even if low status is partly the result of group differences in skills required for success in that society, but especially if it is the result of having been badly treated or exploited, it is usually justified by devaluation, which maintains or increases discrimination. The negative beliefs about black people in the United States, for example, were maintained and intensified as their bad treatment had to be justified—in a country that had adopted the dignity and equal rights of all people as core principles.[19] Everything possible, including the Bible, was used to establish that black people were not human the way white people were and therefore such principles did not apply to them.

Religion has been an especially important divider.[20] While all religions advocate love, they believe with varying intensity that their God, and their way of worshiping God, is the only right way. Many religions derogate and often persecute those who worship God in a different way. People who stop following the dictates of their religion are excluded from the group and often persecuted as well. All religions traditionally, but Muslims especially, have been extremely harsh with those who convert from Islam to another religion.

Religions that are closest to one's own can be the targets of the harshest views. This has been the case with Christian anti-Semitism. It increased in intensity as Jews resisted efforts to convert them, thereby refusing to acknowledge the superiority of Christianity. The persecution of early Protestants was a reaction to their deviation—heresy, a kind of treason—from the already established identity and beliefs of Catholicism, as well as to their challenge of already existing structures, the Catholic Church, and the role of priests as crucial intermediaries between people and God. In the ideological realm in general, small differences or deviation can led to intense hostility. The Bolsheviks hated the Mensheviks, whose ideology was very similar to their own.

Christianity, Judaism, and Islam, with their long histories, have many sacred texts and have accumulated many doctrines and doctrinal interpretations. As a result, there can be great variation in the dominant ideology of the religion in different locations and different historical periods. All of the religions have texts that exemplify and foster enmity and violence toward outsiders or those accused of not living up to the rules or true meaning of the religion, as well as texts that foster cooperation and love.[21]

Under difficult conditions, or in the face of hostility or conflict based on religion, people are likely to identify more with their religion. They also tend to turn to a more extreme, fundamentalist religion. A danger in European countries is that in response to difficulties of life Muslim minorities may turn to a more fundamentalist, and currently more militant, Islam.[22] These difficulties include dislocation and a resulting disorganization in culture and community life, prejudice and discrimination, and economic problems. Self-imposed or externally created obstacles to acculturation, to acquiring and using the habits and skills of one's new country, may keep people in the interstices of two cultures, frustrating both material and psychological needs. This enables fundamentalist or militant Muslim leaders inside or outside Europe to move people to more extreme and combative religious views by offering ideals, identity, and community.

A certain level of devaluation of and discrimination against a group can become normal in a society, but changes in the world can lead to an increased perception by the group that this is unjust. Access to information may create awareness of greater equality and fairness in other societies. National or international values may change, for example, as a result of new international conventions and laws articulated by the United Nations. Or under difficult life conditions the situation of a less privileged group can worsen, or devaluation and discrimination—or the perception of them—may increase.

Devaluation and discrimination thus can be starting points for both the evolution of increasingly harmful actions against, and for demands for change as well as hostility and violence by, the badly treated group. However, grievances and demands are often disregarded, and more forceful demands are met by force, in an increasing cycle. Violent conflict, genocide, and terrorism can all evolve out of this explosive mix of harmful actions and reactions.

When the more powerful and privileged group is a minority, especially when the group rules a country, mass violence is more likely.[23] The majority is more likely to perceive inequality as unjust, and its demands for equality are likely to be perceived by the minority as more threatening. However, in many well-known instances of genocide and mass killing, such as Germany, Turkey, Cambodia, Bosnia, and Rwanda, the powerful group in the society, which became the perpetrator, was the majority.

Devaluation is central to the ability to harm members of another group. Some form of split between groups and devaluation has been present in all cases of genocide and mass killing that I know of. In Cambodia, one of the divisions was between those who ruled the country from the cities and the people in the countryside who worked the land often owned by people in the cities. This division between city dwellers and peasants became central to the Khmer Rouge ideology. On winning the civil war the Khmer Rouges emptied the cities, driving the people into the countryside and making them work the fields. Their vision of equality was for everyone to be a peasant.

In Germany the Jews, while quite assimilated at the end of World War I, had suffered a long history of devaluation, discrimination, and violence against them. At the end of the nineteenth century there was enough anti-Semitism that the central aim of a party represented in parliament was to overthrow the laws that created greater equality for Jews.[24] Anti-Jewish feelings increased in the course of the evolution of hostility and violence. A survivor of Auschwitz, later an editor of a major newspapers in Israel, said in an interview: "In the winter, when it was very cold, when they literally exterminated people by means of hard labor, I remember doing backbreaking work, the foreman sitting above us with a truncheon he used to beat us, shouting:'Dirty Jews, for 2,000 years you calculated and calculated, but you still miscalculated.'"[25]

The Tutsis and the Armenians were both greatly devalued and discriminated against, and they were the objects of intense violence preceding the genocide. In writing about Rwanda, Scott Straus argues that hate did not drive the genocide. He speaks out against the frequently articulated reference to "ancient tribal hatred" in reports by the Western media about violence between groups in Africa and elsewhere. This is appropriate; even intense devaluation does not create mass violence by itself.

But what many of the 210 perpetrators whom he interviewed said is surprising, and not credible: "the overwhelming majority of the perpetrators in the sample reported (that they had) positive attitudes toward their Tutsi neighbors before the genocide."[26] A large percentage of responses to questions about relations with Tutsis before 1994 and after the 1990 invasion were categorized as "good," "very good," "truly good" "more than 100%," "we were friends," "we shared," or "we intermarried." Strauss did find that the local leaders of the killings, and those who were the most violent, who did most of the killing, "had fewer preexisting ties with Tutsis and tended to look unfavorably on them."[27] Nonetheless, instead of negative attitudes, Straus sees *collective ethnic categorization* as a major influence on participation in the killings. This is a division between us and them on the basis of ethnicity. This is consistent with my view, that in response to difficult life conditions or conflict people shift to a group identity and identify members of "outgroups" by their group membership. This takes place in every type of group violence, including terrorism. Under the existing conditions, Hutus came to see neighbors, friends, and even relatives not as individuals, as human beings, but as Tutsis.

However, in spite of what the Hutu perpetrators said, most likely they had negative attitudes toward Tutsis before the genocide. Calling Tutsis cockroach and snake was common. Children heard this in their homes, the devaluation handed down to them. Their teachers identified them as Hutu and Tutsi at the beginning of the school year and thereafter had them stand up in their separate groups at the beginning of each day. Tutsis had also been discriminated against for years. Starting in 1959, there were repeated mass killings and extensive propaganda against them. The civil war and the way that leaders used it created fear of Tutsis. It would, in short, have been a psychological miracle not to hold negative views and attitudes toward them. Perpetrators may have reported positive feelings about Tutsis because of a desire, as in other genocides, to make their actions appear as due to the orders of authorities.

Hate would have been a likely component of at least some Hutus' feelings toward Tutsis. One group of researchers defined hatred as "...an extreme and continuous emotion which rejects a person or a group in a generalized and totalistic fashion."[28] As I have suggested, such an emotion is rooted in and develops out of intensely negative views of others. They found in three surveys in Israel, over a period of time, that hate is a primary source of political intolerance, of the disapproval of another group's participation in political life. Hate was more important than fear and anger, or even perceived threat, its power especially great among less "sophisticated" persons.

In contrast to the United States, where relations are predominantly peaceful and open expression of prejudice against African Americans and other groups in most contexts is not acceptable, in Rwanda, before the genocide, Hutus could say derogatory things to Tutsis to their face. Having done so, people went on socializing and drinking beer together.[29] Devaluation was the ground of people's experience in many cases of mass violence; it was the customary way of seeing the other.

But even perpetrators who had confessed and were sentenced had good reason to minimize their negative feelings toward Tutsis. By doing so, and by emphasizing the pressure on them of authorities and their peers, they could diminish their moral culpability not only in others' eyes but also in their own. In spite of this, many in a group of killers Jean Hatzfeld interviewed did express derogatory views of Tutsis.[30] This was probably because they were asked to talk about the attitudes of people in general toward Tutsis, not about their own attitudes.

Teaching Devaluation: Education, Socialization, Indoctrination

Devaluation can result from differentness, from exploitation and its justification, from difficult life conditions, conflict, and scapegoating. But it is also handed down through education, socialization, and training. The words and actions of political leaders, authorities in the workplace, teachers, and parents can all teach a negative view of and hostility toward members of another group. So can literature and the media.

A woman who later became a civil rights activist described the transformation of her racial attitude. At a young age her favorite playmates were the children of her family's black servants. At age 7 she had a birthday party, to which these playmates were not invited. She threw a temper tantrum and her parents allowed her to have a separate party for them. By the time she got to Wellesley College and was assigned a black girl as a table mate for meals, she was outraged.[31] The Mundurucu head hunters in Brazil trained their boys from a young age to attack other villages. In their language, the word *outsider* also means enemy. German children in schools, and in the Nazi Youth organization, the Hitler Jugend, were taught that Jews were anatomically different, a lower race, and immoral, an enemy.[32]

Muslims receive socialization into devaluation and ideology in some madrassas, from imams in particular mosques, and the Internet. Many radical organizations provide "information" and instruction on the Internet.[33] Hezbollah's Shiite youth movement teaches the ideology of "radical Iranian Islam" to tens of thousands of youth ranging in age from 8 to 16. According to an Egyptian newspaper, the group's objective is "to train (a) high calibre Islamic generation of children who would be willing to sacrifice themselves for the sake of Allah."[34] Hamas trains kindergarten children. On a TV program, they were shown in camouflage suits, carrying plastic rifles and performing military exercises.[35] Both children and adults can be trained in devaluation and hostility—or guided to see others' humanity and develop inclusive caring.

In summary, divisions into us and them that result in the devaluation of *them* often have long historical continuity. Devaluation can be based on differences in, and collective categorizations by, race, ethnicity, religion, power and wealth, or other dimensions. It can be the result of naturally occurring conditions. But once it develops it is usually taught and then fostered through education and socialization. Unless it is counteracted in ways I will discuss in Part II, it will be handed down through the generations. It is often accompanied, maintained, and exacerbated by discrimination of the devalued group. It usually increases in intensity in difficult times, as it joins with other influences such as scapegoating, ideology, and competition for scarce resources. It is a central source of hostility and violence. Certain forms of it—seeing the other as morally bad or as dangerous to one's own group—and the situation in which a devalued group is doing relatively well in society, have especially great potential to lead to increasing hostility and violence against the devalued group.

Those who hold more negative views and feelings toward this group will tend to be in the vanguard, but the shared devaluation by others of the group provides a basis for their leadership and actions. Devaluation does not mean hate. But it can, and for many perpetrators, even bystanders, and members of groups in conflict, it does become hate as they justify violent actions or passivity, or are affected by the other's action, and change psychologically. After violent actions against others, fear of retaliation also intensifies a negative view of them.

Past Victimization, Suffering, and the Existence of Unhealed Psychological and Social Wounds

Past group experiences with violence, and their continuing impact, make it more likely that under certain conditions a group will perpetrate violence against others. Past victimization often (but not always) gives rise to posttraumatic stress disorder (PTSD), as well as to more complex trauma responses. It also gives rise to other psychological effects of victimization that are especially important from the standpoint of their contribution to group violence. Having been subjected to great violence makes people feel vulnerable. As devaluation and discrimination are followed by violence, against which people cannot defend themselves because they face others with much greater power, they tend to feel that something must be wrong with them and their group. Their experience makes them feel diminished. The world, other people, especially other groups and their members, look threatening and dangerous. Mistrust of other people and fear make it difficult to resolve new conflict or to respond to a new threat in a manner commensurate with the actual threat. Believing that they need to defend themselves, members of the group may strike out in the face of new conflict or threat, even when forceful self-defense is not necessary. They then become perpetrators.[36]

It is reasonable to assume that Germans, who experienced a long series of traumatizing events, with the great loss of lives in World War I, loss of the war, severe economic problems, and internal political conflicts, experienced group trauma. The same may be assumed about the Hutus. They had experienced victimization from both the Belgians and the Tutsis whom the Belgians led to rule on their behalf. The Hutus were designated as an inferior race, diminished, and victimized by the conditions of their lives.

There are many examples of the victimization of people under colonialism, which had to have a significant role in subsequent events. A combination of colonial exploitation of natural resources and intense devaluation led to great violence against Africans. As historian John Higginson wrote: "Almost all the European protagonists in the colonial engagement believed the myths of African savagery and prepared for the consequences of this belief with an armed plan to impose law and order."[37] In the Congo, under King Leopold of Belgium during the late nineteenth and early twentieth century, Africans were forced into hard labor, mainly to harvest rubber. If they tried to avoid or escape it, horrible punishments were imposed on them, such as cutting off their arms. Huge numbers of Congolese were killed during this period. However, there was also substantial resistance, with powerful rebellions, both by African soldiers and the population. This resistance was brutally put down by the Belgian military.[38]

Without healing, that can be partly naturally occurring, partly the result of intentional processes, the psychological woundedness of a group can persist. It can be transformed and become part of the group's culture. It can be reactivated by new events. In the Congo intervening experiences, including the long dictatorship of Mobutu, provided no opportunity for group healing. While the aftereffects of the genocide in Rwanda, war and societal disorganization, were the direct initiators of violence in the Congo, the historical experience of victimization and woundedness, and of responding to threat with force, may be additional cultural roots of its widespread nature.

Colonialism, victimization, and woundedness probably also left their mark in Darnah, a city in Libya that Italy invaded in 1911 and ruled brutally, with concentration camps, deliberate starvation, and mass executions. The population dropped from 1.2 million to about 800,000 by 1933. Here again, there was local resistance, for 20 years, which the Italians destroyed in the end. The leader of this resistance, who also spread a strict version of Islam in the region, is still a greatly admired hero. There has also been more recent resistance against the current regime. Local rebels called themselves the Libyan Islamic Fighting Group, which were attacked by government helicopters in the mid 1990s.

As in every instance of group violence, many elements join. In addition to past victimization, fighting, and resistance, there have been bad economic conditions in this part of Libya, with substantial unemployment and apparent aimlessness among the young people in the city. People have seen the images of devastation in the war in Iraq presented daily by Al-Jazeera television (which the American media does not cover). They identified with the Iraqis and responded with outrage. A disproportionately high number of young men from Darnah went to fight against the United States in Iraq. A very high percentage of them volunteered to become suicide bombers.[39] The brother of one of the "martyrs" said: "...He was right to go. We see people getting killed for nothing. I used to think about going myself,"[40] which he said he could no do since he was the only support for his family. There was also a local mosque involved, at which many of the young people who went to Iraq had gathered. There were local recruiters, who attracted and organized these young men and send them to Iraq in small groups.

A historical/collective memory specifically related to the United States may also have had a role in the high number of young men willing to fight in Iraq. During the Barbary Wars of the early 1800s, a U.S. expeditionary force went to the region and to this specific city to fight pirates who had overtaken many American ships and abducted people for ransom. This fight, against Americans, with at least initial successes, is part of the city's heroic memory. A group's stories of heroism—another example is of the "martyred" Palestinian suicide bombers—give rise to new heroism.

It is not only members of a victim group who are wounded. Their actions also wound perpetrators. Their psychological woundedness is not identical to that of survivors and certainly has a different moral meaning. However, their tendency to deny their responsibility and continue to devalue and blame their victims, partly to avoid shame and guilt, makes new violence by them probable. Their former victim is still to blame—even for the perpetrators' own violent actions. Internal bystanders, passive members of the perpetrator group, are also psychologically changed, wounded by the harm their group has done and by their own passivity. (See Chapter 10 for a more detailed discussion of the psychological consequences of violence on all the parties—victims, perpetrators, and bystanders.)

Harsh Child Rearing, Family Systems, and Their Effects

There are a number of authors who account for group violence by the effects of punitive child rearing, which especially in its harsher form, over a long period of time, is a powerful form of victimization. I regard it as *one* important influence, that becomes especially important when it is widely practiced in a society.

Societies vary in the treatment of children. In many societies physical punishment is considered normal, and many children are harshly and punitively treated. But even in the United States, where physical punishment has become less acceptable, at the beginning of this century 97% of parents reported that they smacked or spanked 4 year olds, and 40% that they regularly hit 13 year olds.[41] Many children are sexually abused, or physically harmed to the extent that it constitutes abuse.

As mentioned previously, Benjamin Valentino[42] suggests that mass violence results when a small group inclined to violence takes over leadership of a country, joined by individuals prone to violence who in his view can be found in every society. John Steiner[43] proposes a "sleeper effect," that certain conditions activate an inclination for violence in individuals who have been normal members of society. Valentino and Steiner do not directly talk about the role of child rearing in creating these tendencies in individuals, but others do.

I discuss at length harsh child rearing in Germany in *The Roots of Evil*. I see the effects of harsh child rearing as similar to the effects of victimization on groups of people. It makes children feel vulnerable and see the world as hostile. Kenneth Dodge, a psychologist, and his associates found in a series of studies that boys who are harshly treated become aggressive. They also found that aggressive boys see other people as hostile. What other boys see as accidental harm—for example, when playing soccer, a boy tries to get the ball from another boy and kicks him in the process—aggressive boys see as intentional. They see retaliation as the right response.[44] Depending on their circumstances, children who are badly treated can also withdraw or get depressed.

Richard Rhodes suggests, on the basis of research by a sociologist with a large number of violent criminals, that intensely violent individuals have been both victimized and have received coaching in violence.[45] Violent parents often not only model aggression but also encourage aggression toward other people. Or some other person guides a young person who is harshly, violently treated to strike back. As they begin to do so, they discover that aggressive actions protect them from harm and give them power over others. The violence of prior victims then evolves, increasing in intensity and in the breadth of targets. In my perspective, in addition to providing protection, it (destructively) fulfills their need for security, for effectiveness, for a positive identity and often also for connection—to a subgroup of other violent individuals.

The more punitive is child rearing in a society, the more there are individuals who are inclined to violence. Because anger and hostility toward punitive parents is dangerous, children learn to displace these feelings to other targets. Their feelings, and their inclination for violent self-defense, can be channeled by leaders who depict outside groups as hostile, which requires self-defense.

Psycho-historian Lloyd de Mause (2008)[46] and psychologist Robin Grille[47] see harsh family relations, authoritarian family systems, and harsh child rearing as having pervasive roles in group violence. Grille described a wide-ranging study of rural family life and child rearing conducted in the 1930s in 300 Yugoslav villages.[48] Most of the people lived in extended households, with a patriarch ruling over the families of his sons. Everybody owed absolute obedience to him. Women were completely subordinated. In many households women had to stand behind their husbands while they ate. Young boys could order the women around. Women were regularly beaten by their husbands—beating a woman was part of being a real man. Such lack of respect for women is a characteristic of rape-prone societies.[49] An authoritarian family system with male dominance and adverse relationships between men and women, including violence, was the background to the huge number of rapes by Serbs of Muslim women in Bosnia and the policy of raping women as a means of violence against the group as a whole.

Harsh treatment of children is part of authoritarian child rearing that creates strong respect for authority. It tends to limit people's ability to think for themselves and to use their critical consciousness—their own judgment. It also limits their ability to feel empathy. I will later discuss experiences that can help people heal, turn toward others, and give rise to "altruism born of suffering," a transformation of painful experiences into a source of empathy and altruism.[50] However, harsh child rearing is only one influence contributing to group violence. In the presence of instigating conditions and a societal evolution toward violence, many people who have not been harshly treated can also get involved.

Strong Respect for Authority, Obedience, Compliance, and Fear

When a society's culture, belief system, socialization of children, and institutions promote overly strong respect for authority, it makes violence under difficult life conditions more likely. Difficult life conditions or group conflict for extended periods of time are conditions under which strong respect for authority develops, as powerful authorities provide security and group cohesion is important for survival. The Germans have experienced many wars, and this is one explanation for the origins of the strong respect for authority in German Prussian culture. Lasting authoritarian rule is likely to have a similar effect. Strong respect for authority is maintained by hierarchical social arrangements, where officials oversee and maintain control over people at various levels in society.

Having been raised by parents who demand obedience and provide authoritarian guidance, in difficult times people are more likely to turn to authoritarian leaders. So, too, in a culture that greatly respects those in authority—not because of who they are and what they do, but because of their position of authority—leaders are less likely to face questioning and opposition when they promote and advocate scapegoating, destructive ideologies, and harmful policies and practices. People are less likely to be active bystanders in the course of the evolution of doing harm to others. When leaders direct people to violence, they are more likely to be obeyed. But even in less authority-oriented societies, in times of threat, insecurity, and crises people look for strong leaders and may question little where they lead. One example of this was the behavior of people in the United States after the 9/11 terrorist attacks.

The societies that I use as examples of mass killing or genocide in this book have been characterized by strong respect for authority. With regard to Germany, in the middle of the nineteenth century a French historian wrote that the lead motive of the German is obedience to those in authority.[51] Advice to German parents on child rearing used to stress how to break children's will, at an early age, so that they would obey those in authority.[52] The strong respect for authority was one reason that many Germans had difficulty accepting the Weimar republic after the overthrow of the monarchy. It did not help that the overthrow happened in the midst of intensely difficult life conditions. The *Fuhrerprinzip* (leadership principle) in the Nazi ideology, which demanded unquestioning obedience to the leader, Hitler, embodied this cultural orientation.

Rwanda has been a communal and authority-oriented society, in culture, social arrangements, and the way children are treated in school. It requires conformity and compliance from its people. In working in Rwanda over the years I have experienced this orientation in a number of ways. In our seminars we managed to create an atmosphere in which people felt free to engage in discussion—and even sing and dance. Perhaps being outsiders made this easier. When in one of our early seminars a local associate, a psychiatrist, gave a lecture, the participants were completely passive and did not ask him questions. In another instance, after I interviewed a number of people in prison accused of perpetrating genocide, I asked my interpreter whether he believed one particular prisoner's story. He said he did, and he told me why. I gently described a couple of reasons why I did not believe the prisoner. He proceeded to talk after that as if he had never believed him either. Not expressing contrary views may contribute to social harmony in small, close-knit communities, but this becomes problematic when speaking out is important for the social good.

Authorities have long been powerful in Rwanda, and their power was reinforced by German and Belgian colonialists, and afterwards. This is partly because of culture, and partly because of structure—that is, Rwanda's hierarchical social institutions. Rwanda had administrators at many levels, in most villages starting with someone in charge of every 8 to 10 households. There was a cultural practice of community labor, and while the exact requirements for the work that people did changed over time—earlier work was for local chiefs, later work for the government, presumably benefiting the country—on the whole people obeyed and did what the authorities required of them. Ninety-one percent of the killers whom Straus' interviewed said that they had never disobeyed authorities. This had to be an exaggeration. Even in an authority-oriented society people find ways to evade authority. In Rwanda some peasants at various times have avoided compulsory labor. In 1980 when the price of coffee fell, peasants uprooted state-owned coffee bushes. Under the current government many people did not go to *gacaca* trials, which were required by law and by the authorities.[53] But all this does not negate the strong tendency in Rwanda to obey authorities, and the power of authorities to move people to action.

Straus argues that it was not a culture of obedience but compliance with pressure that was of special importance.[54] Perpetrators were made to believe that killing Tutsis became the law, and they were pressured by many parties—the central government, local officials, some of the military, the Interahamwe, and those Hutus who already began to kill. Groups of such people went from house to house and demanded that at least one person join in the killing. In this perspective, people acted out of fear, since disobedience would have led to punishment and even death.

As we have seen, conformity and compliance can have important roles in people's behavior. But usually many influences join in leading to violence, as they have in Rwanda. While strong pressure can create compliance, authority orientation in a culture, and authoritarian personality as an individual characteristic, makes compliance more likely and can lead people to *follow* rather than simply comply with authorities. Moreover, claiming that they had to obey authorities is usual for perpetrators, as a way to disclaim their responsibility. As I have noted, devaluation and hostility are strongly indicated by earlier killings of Tutsis that sometimes started locally, with people so intensely engaged that at times the central government had difficulty stopping the violence. While their relative contribution may not be possible to determine, antagonism toward Tutsis, the intensification of hostility by life conditions, the civil war, hate speech, an authority orientation that led people to respond to the call for violence, compliance out of fear, and learning by doing all seem important contributors to participation in the genocide.

Daniel Goldhagen has argued that the German people rather than complying, due to their intense, "eliminationist" anti-Semitism, were willing participants in the Holocaust and were Hitler's willing executioners. He writes, "If a large segment of a group, not to mention the vast majority of its members, opposes or abhors an act, then the social psychological pressure would work to prevent, not to encourage, individuals to undertake the act."[55] But in an autocratic society the leaders and media dominate the public space, so that people don't know what others believe, and if the society is also authority oriented, people to tend to be strongly influenced by leaders.

The initial focus on the role of authority in mass violence came from a large study that a group of researchers after World War II and the Holocaust conducted on the authoritarian personality. In response to criticism of their research methods, there has been much change in research strategies over the years. The accumulated research points to a set of seemingly coherent characteristics of authoritarian individuals. Some of these have to do with the way these individuals think. Social psychologists Peter Suedfeld and Mark Schaller[56] summarized this in the following way. Authoritarian persons tend to be close minded, rigid, and categorical in their thinking. They look at the world in black-and-white terms. They tend not to consider alternative possibilities. They have a "low need for cognition—(they do not enjoy thinking)."[57] They have a high need for closure, for reaching conclusions, and to do so, they dismiss contradictory ideas. These authors suggest that such simple, in contrast to complex, thinking can have different consequences depending on their context. They suggest that such thinking might have characterized some rescuers in the Holocaust who helped people in response to requests by authorities such as priests or community leaders.

However, authoritarian persons also have other characteristics. They tend to perceive the world as dangerous. This tendency can be activated and intensified by leaders who present some group as a threat, or as a danger due to characteristics of that group that they claim will contaminate their own group. Authoritarians tend to be submissive to and obedient to people in authority, but are inclined to be aggressively dominant and punitive toward those below them in a hierarchy, toward people with little power or those outside their group.[58] I use the concept of *authority orientation* to focus on strong respect in a society for authorities and the tendency to follow their guidance. Both this and widespread development of authoritarian personalities in a society contribute to group violence.

In societies that promote strong respect for authority, children are usually raised by adults who set rules with little or no explanation, demand and enforce unquestioning obedience, and punish deviation from rules or disobedience. This can happen in the home, as well as in schools. In such restrictive environments children learn not to express, and even become unaware of and uncomfortable with, their feelings.[59] This also makes empathy by them less likely.

In highly hierarchical societies, disobeying authorities has harsh consequences. In totalitarian societies, no deviation in the political domain is acceptable. The respect for authority that is likely to develop is intertwined with fear of the consequences of deviating from the dictates of authority. But since families can be authoritarian even when a society is less so, in most societies there are individuals with an authoritarian orientation. Even in a democratic society, like the United States, some parents raise children by setting rules without explanation and demanding unquestioning obedience, which promote respect for— and fear of—authorities.[60] People learn to be part of and come to prefer hierarchies, where their role in the hierarchy is clear, obeying those above them and expecting to be obeyed by and tending to act punitively toward those below them.

In looking at Stanley Milgram's research on obedience, the focus has been on the many people who obeyed a researcher and administered increasing electric shocks to another person. But many people did not obey and at some point refused to administer shocks. Those with a more authoritarian personality were more likely to continue to obey and administer the strongest shocks. People whose moral reasoning stressed personal responsibility obeyed less.[61]

Strong respect for authority, which characterizes some people in most societies and many people in authority-orientated societies, is one of a variety of influences that make mass violence more likely. People with strong authority orientation are more likely to turn to and *join* potentially destructive ideological movements in response to instigating conditions and as a way to satisfy needs.

Cultural tendencies are deeply set and slow to change. For the Rwandan writers and journalists who write our radio programs promoting reconciliation, we have provided training in the conception I am describing. They engaged with it and apparently embraced it. But in the course of writing episodes of the educational radio drama, they at times reverted to the representation of characters in terms of the existing culture. They overemphasized the role of the "bad leader" provoking hostility and violence, in contrast to followers and bystanders, and presented behavior toward authorities with the customary cultural subservience. Changing cultural orientations requires extensive relearning. Over time, as we worked with editing and reworking each episode of the radio drama, the writers' orientation changed. The radio drama, which has continued to broadcast since 2004, brought about a change in listeners' orientation to authority by the end of its first year. I will later describe its content and the evaluation of its effects.

A Monolithic Society with Lack of Pluralism

Another cultural/societal characteristic that adds to the likelihood of group violence is the absence of pluralism. This has two aspects: *(1)* only a limited range of beliefs and values can be expressed in the public domain, and/or *(2)* some groups (usually less privileged groups and or those who become the scapegoat or ideological enemy) are excluded from the public domain and public discussion.

The limitation in public discourse makes opposition in the course of the evolution of violence less likely. The absence of wide-ranging discourse about what is happening in the society, including the destructive processes that leaders propagate and the society is engaged in, helps maintain "pluralistic ignorance." People don't know what others think and feel, making it more difficult to decide that what is happening is wrong and to join in opposing it. The feeling of powerlessness by each person to affect societal processes combined with the inability to join together contributes to passivity. An important element in creating active bystandership is for people to find ways to join. To initiate this, as described in Part II, requires both moral courage and ingenuity. It is becoming easier in the Internet age—which is why authoritarian systems often attempt to censor the Internet. Both an authority-oriented culture and an autocratic political system make pluralism less likely.

Autocratic and Democratic Political Systems, Traditional/Repressive Societies, Violence and Terror

Overly strong respect for authority can be a matter of culture and societal institutions that guide it and perpetuate it. But it can also be the result of the political system. An autocratic system can shape culture and create strong respect for authorities. It has the power to force the compliance or obedience of large segments of the population. It can create adoration or worship of leaders. In the Soviet Union, an effective cult of personality led people to worship Stalin, and a dead Lenin, to such an extent that even when their crimes of mass killing became known, many continued to worship them.

Genocide and mass killing,[62] as well as state terror[63]—large-scale violence by governments against their own population—have been much more likely to occur in authoritarian/autocratic systems. Political scientist R. J. Rummel summarizes information about the huge numbers of people that have been killed in such systems. He proposes a "power principle," according to which the more power elites and governments have, the more they can act arbitrarily to fulfill their desires, and the more they "will make war on others and murder foreign or domestic subjects."[64] In such systems, state failure is more likely to lead to genocide.[65]

Such systems limit or eliminate pluralism. Political opposition, or devalued minorities, are not allowed a public voice or participation in public processes. It is dangerous for them to speak on their own behalf and for others to speak on their behalf. Domestic disagreements and conflicts are managed by repression or violence. When the authoritarian rule is by a minority, it is likely to feel endangered by the subordinate majority, which leads to more repression, generating more hostility. Repression by an autocratic system generates terrorism. Studies show a relationship between the absence of civil liberties and terrorism.[66] In the case of terrorism in South Africa against the apartheid system, in Iran against the Shah, and in Egypt, civil liberties and political expression were greatly limited. But as with revolutions, terrorism is less likely when repression is especially intense, as it was in the Soviet Union or Nazi Germany.

Societies that are both traditional and repressive make it difficult for people to handle the tremendous changes in the modern world in technology, knowledge, culture, and mores. Even when governments set up barriers to them, these changes seep into societies in this age of globalism and communication, but lack of freedom in engaging with them makes it difficult for people to integrate them into their lives. The columnist Thomas Friedman[67] described the terrorists of September 11, 2001 as educated young men from middle-class families in the Arab world who went to Europe for more education. The narrowness of the experience and worldview they grew up with clashed with the complex, modern world they encountered in Europe. Added to that was their encounter with the marginality, lack of respect, and the resulting frustration of needs for identity and connection that Muslims experience in Europe. These young men joined local prayer groups or mosques, where they became radicalized. They went off to Afghanistan, where they received training in Osama bin Laden's training camps.

Great social changes are difficult for everyone, but they would be more so in highly traditional and both politically and culturally repressive countries, for example, Saudi Arabia. The lack of past experience in effectively engaging with and integrating change would make adjustment to countries with very different cultures and religion especially challenging. But only a small minority of young men from Arab countries who went to Europe became terrorists. Their associations, with particular mosques and with certain people, influenced them. Their earlier life experiences, in their families of origin and with peers, and the kind of people they became, must have also been important.

The route to terrorism I just described is indirect. But repressive systems also have more direct effects. They create opposition, which gives rise to ideological movements, as in the case of Egyptian terrorists I discussed earlier. Governments can also attempt to shift anger and hostility away from themselves to outsiders. They direct their people's attention away from political repression, and repression by tradition, and from difficult economic conditions that have led to unemployment by young people even in some oil-rich countries, to blame instead the values, culture, and policies of the West.

One of the usual aims of terrorists is to create a reaction. Even if the reaction is increased repression, the terrorists, it is believed, interpret it as a success, since it presumably converts more people to their cause. In the short run at least, the reaction often does not benefit the terrorists' cause, but it can have long-term beneficial consequences, especially if governments overreact. In Argentina, in the 1970s terrorists attacked buildings, government officials, military officers, and other targets. They claimed to seek greater justice for the poor. Their actions led to a military takeover—a frequent occurrence in Argentina at the time. The military and paramilitary groups kidnapped and tortured many people, the so-called disappearances, including people they regarded as simply left leaning, or who worked for social change or to help the poor. They killed perhaps as many as 30,000 people. This does not look like success. However, as they were losing support, they occupied the Falklands, starting a war with Britain for islands that had little value but that they claimed belonged to Argentina.[68] They lost the war, lost power, and a stable democracy was created in the aftermath.

Political psychologist Jeff Victoroff[69] lists a number of instances in which terrorism contributed to change: in bringing about the independence of Israel, ousting the Shah of Iran, overthrowing the apartheid system in South Africa, and others. Terrorism in these cases worked in combination with other influences, for example, in South Africa, actions by both external and internal bystanders. In these successful instances the terrorists' focus was primarily military and state targets, rather than civilians, which helped to gain the support of the population and external parties. While outright terrorist victory is rare, terrorism often ends when the terrorists' goals and interests are included in the political process. Psychologist Clark McCauley[70] argues that terrorist violence may be associated with political progress 50% of the time.

But this requires a shift in the terrorist group. The complexity of "success" is shown in the case of the Palestinians. While terror attacks have brought attention to their cause, and may have led to negotiation with Israel and the creation of the Palestinian Authority, the unwillingness by at least some segments of the Palestinian community to make political accommodation, combined with continued violence against civilians, has greatly limited improvement of their situation. Political success often requires a shift from extreme ideologies and actions to moderation.

Democratic, open political systems, especially "mature democracies,"[71] are less likely to give rise to mass killing and genocide. But democracies have not been free of terrorism. Democratic systems implicitly promise people the ability to bring about change, to address grievances. But change is difficult and the promise is often not fulfilled. They also implicitly promise that individuals and groups can improve their lives. But minorities often face difficult conditions economically, in their status and rights. Moreover, when groups are in an inferior position, imagined grievances can add to real ones and become enlarged by motivated leaders.

There have been opposing arguments about the likelihood of terrorism in democracies versus nondemocratic systems. One argument is that democracies make it possible for citizens to address their grievances by nonviolent means. A contrary argument is that freedom of speech and organization, combined with the unwillingness of democracies to limit civil liberties and use harsh measures, makes terrorism more likely.

Some of the research has found more terrorism in democratic countries. But democracies differ in important ways. One researcher, Quan Li[72] has studied the relationship between varying aspects of democratic societies and transnational terrorism, that is, terrorism from outside, or from inside a country against foreign targets. Studying terrorism in 119 countries between 1975 and 1997, he found that greater participation by citizens in the democratic process is associated with less terrorism. On the other hand, "institutional constraints," checks and balances among the branches of government that inhibit effective public policies, is associated with more terrorism. In such a system decision making and action are more difficult, the grievances and concerns of citizens are addressed less, and taking action against terrorist acts is more cumbersome. Li also looked at different types of governmental systems and found that proportional representation, in which all segments of the population are represented in the government and differences have to be worked out, is associated with less terrorism than a majoritarian (the winner takes all, one party wins and rules) or a mixed system.

The representation of all segments of the population in the government and effective political decision making with a government responsive to citizens are conditions under which people are likely to feel that their country lives up to the promise of democracy. Citizen participation suggests this. Autocracies lack genuine citizen participation (people may be pressured to vote, but their vote is a sham). They tend to inhibit terrorism through repression, but unless repression is highly effective, it may not overcome the hostility it generates. Terrorism, a war in which everyday people are often the primary victims, can be the unfortunate result.

Unjust Social Arrangements

Throughout this book I stress the role of unequal social arrangements, of differences in power, wealth, influence, and access to resources and institutions, as sources of conflict and violence. These differences are usually maintained by discrimination and justified by devaluation. I have also discussed conditions that make the less privileged group aware that these differences are unjust, and that thereby give rise to active conflict.

Conflict can be useful if it leads to constructive engagement and positive change. At times a past history of inequality and discrimination, or limited acculturation by large immigrant groups such as Muslims in European countries, contributes to groups' inability to use society's resources, even if legally these are now accessible to them. Society needs then to take action to enable and empower people to use these resources, so that inequality will be reduced. Reducing inequality and addressing unjust social arrangements are important elements in the prevention of violence.[73]

Other Important Cultural Characteristics

Group Beliefs

One group's beliefs can contribute to harmful actions against another group. They include ethnocentricity, the tendency to see one's group as better than others and using this to justify power and dominance, ideologies, and in particular the legitimizing ideologies[74] I discussed in Chapter 3 that further justify differences in power and wealth.

Because legitimizing ideologies are cultural values, beliefs and preferences that are widely propagated in society, less powerful groups may be socialized into them as well. For example, support by working people in the United States for Republican policies that benefit wealthy individuals has been explained as the result of the belief that since the United States is a society of opportunity, they will benefit from these policies in the future. Those who are wealthy have used the opportunities available to everyone, and so can working people. But contrary to the long-held belief about social mobility in the United States, more people do better than their parents in Denmark, Austria, Norway, Finland, Canada, Sweden, Germany, Spain, and France than in the United States.[75]

Together with structural arrangements, such as the nature of the justice system, schools, the police, and financial and other institutions, widely held societal beliefs maintain differences in power, wealth, and rights. However, legitimizing ideologies only work up to a point. As noted, when people come to see differences between groups as due to unjust social arrangements, anger, hostility, and violence often follow.

Daniel Bar-Tal[76] has stressed the role of societal beliefs in perpetuating group conflict, with his primary referent the Israeli–Palestinian conflict. These beliefs are about the past, who did what to whom; about the present, who is right or wrong, moral or immoral; and about the future, who wants peace and how to bring it about. Societal beliefs at times of conflict make the world predictable and comprehensible, create coherence and unity, and energize the group fighting for its goals. But the "ethos of conflict" they create, which strengthens identity and maintains a sense of the group's rightness, also contributes to continuing violence. Group narratives about the past, including collective memories and chosen traumas, may also be seen as group beliefs.

Group Self-Concepts

While the tendency for ethnocentrism may be universal, still there are differences in what I call group self-concepts, which are shared beliefs by people about their groups. Some groups see themselves as especially superior to others, others have more modest views about themselves, and some have a low-self-concept.

In individuals and in groups, both very low and very high self-concepts can contribute to aggression. Some individuals with low self-esteem may respond to perceived threat with aggression that increases feelings of effectiveness and strengthens identity. And Roy Baumeister has argued and has shown in research that individuals with high self-esteem are likely to be aggressive in response to events that might disconfirm their positive view of themselves.[77] I see this as especially the case with a particular type of high self-esteem, involving feelings of superiority and pride that hide fragility or vulnerability.[78] Individuals and groups with such self-concepts will have trouble with losses and reversals, which injure their pride and challenge their views of themselves. This has been confirmed by research in schools with bullies who have high self-esteem but difficulty tolerating anything that challenges their view of themselves.

As in individuals, and for similar reasons, low self-esteem can contribute to violence by groups. But groups with a self-concept of superiority may also respond intensely to misfortune and loss. This seems to have been the case with Germany, a country with great pride in its military and economic accomplishment, and its culture and way of life, before the disasters of World War I and all the misfortunes that followed. I have mentioned that groups that have suffered losses in well-being, influence, territory, or in other ways tend to harken back to past greatness. They then create ideologies that project a vision of renewed greatness. This was true of Turkey, where the young Turks, the party that in 1908 overthrew the monarchy, propagated a pan-Turkish nationalist ideology. It was true of Cambodia, where the Khmer Rouge harkened back to the Cambodian empire of Angor Vat.[79]

Americans tend to have a very positive group self-concept. Difficulties in the country are often blamed on some "other." At various times over the years, the Japanese and the Chinese have been blamed for economic downturns in the United States. After 9/11, except by some scholars and in small segments of the population, there has been little exploration of U.S. actions that might have understandably caused anger at the United States in the Islamic world. Anger does not justify mass killing, but to improve one's relationships requires awareness of one's effects on others.

Constructively dealing with the frustration of the need for a positive group self-concept is an important challenge. It is easier to address this frustration when groups develop moderate self-concepts in place of feelings of inferiority or superiority. Valuing oneself, seeing one's virtues, but also one's faults and limitations, enables both individuals and groups to better deal with the inevitable challenges of life and of an increasingly complex world.

A Past History of Violence and Cultural Memory

In many genocidal societies, there is a history of resolving conflict between groups by violence.[80] Indeed, one of the predictors of mass killing or genocide is past mass killing or genocide.[81] This is one reason why reconciliation and prevention after past violence are so important. Even defensive violence, as in the Congo against King Leopold's soldiers, is likely to provide a historical/cultural memory and base that makes aggression in later times more likely. As I noted, the fighting in Libya against Italy, the earlier fighting against the United States, and the way these events are held in group memory, may have encouraged young men to fight against the United States in Iraq. Case studies also suggest that extensive individual violence in a society may also make group violence more likely under difficult social conditions. For example, in spite of its image as a paradisiacal society before the events that moved it toward genocide, in Cambodia there was substantial aggression between individuals.[82] Children in families where there is violence learn that violence is an appropriate and even normal mode of addressing conflict. Individuals, and whole groups, can learn the same through their experience in their societies.

Rape in Violence between Groups

In many cases of group violence—in Nanking in China by the Japanese, in Bosnia, in Rwanda, and in the first decade of the twenty-first century in the Congo and in Darfur—rape has been widespread. Even when there is no group violence, rape is frequent in many societies. Its occurrence is an expression of culture. Peggy Sanday, an anthropologist, described rape-free and rape-prone societies.[83] A primary difference between them is the degree of respect or disrespect in the culture for women, and the corresponding relationship between men and women.

Similar to other kinds of violence, a division between us and them, and the attitude toward the other—disrespect or devaluation—is a significant contributor to rape. In many societies the culture makes men feel superior and gives them psychologically, and at times legally, the right to treat women as property. The differential valuing of males and females is also expressed in the parental preference for boys and the selective killing of newborn girls in many societies. In the contemporary world, killing is replaced by selective abortions.[84] In some societies, husbands hitting women is considered so normal that many men do it and don't even regard it as violence.[85]* Rape is an extension of this orientation to women.

Some practices associated with rape are similar across widely different societies. Sanday describes one form of rape in some simple societies that are "rape prone," with young men roaming outside their villages and getting sexually initiated by raping women they encounter. She describes groups of young men in Philadelphia looking for women and raping them.

In group violence, men are the primary victims of killing. They are the fighters, the dangerous enemy. In earlier history, often in the course of group violence, all men in a group were killed, and the women distributed as spoils among the victors. However, the rape of women, and keeping women in sexual slavery, has also been common. Often women who are raped are also injured by violence against them and sometimes killed afterwards. Both were widespread in Nanking as well as Rwanda.

Rape can be a byproduct of violence, such as Soviet troops raping women as they advanced against the German army in World War II, including women in countries they just liberated. Widespread rape of women is also often an aspect of the evolution of violence. In Argentina as the disappearances and killings of people were in progress, some young paramilitary and military officers roamed the streets in their cars, picking up women, raping them, and at times killing them.[86]

But violent rape is sometimes an intentional policy used by groups as a weapon, as an aspect of civil war and mass violence. It harms the women physically and emotionally, and sometimes it is used to spread HIV infection. It reduces the cohesion and functioning of victim groups by impregnating women and infusing the group with the perpetrators' genes, shaming and humiliating the men who are powerless to protect the women, and in many societies leading to the exclusion of the women who had been raped, as they are seen as degraded and damaged.

The Absence of Connection to Other Countries

Another condition that contributes to the likelihood of mass violence is a state's isolation. Barbara Harff,[87] in analyzing many instances of mass violence, found that it was more likely to happen in the absence of economic connections to other countries. Significant connections of other types are also likely to matter. Social isolation makes violence more likely both by individuals—for example, spouse abuse happens more in isolated families—and by groups. When groups are isolated, their psychological situation is affected, and they lack outside social control.

Connections to other countries can provide support and give leaders and the people some hope in difficult times. They may make a country more concerned about others withdrawing from beneficial and necessary relationships, and about what others will think of and how they would react to the country's actions. In the case of both Israel–Palestine and Northern Ireland, connection to outsiders and the searchlight of the community of nations focused on them are likely to have inhibited even greater violence. Of course, if other countries are complicit, for example, continue with extensive trade in spite of violence against a minority, as the United States and others did with Germany during the 1930s, connections can strengthen violence.

Socialization Revisited

The cultural characteristics I have discussed are transmitted to children partly in an automatic manner, just by the way the society operates, how adults behave, what they say not as instruction to children but as part of everyday life, and how they guide children to behave. This may be called *natural socialization*. There is powerful learning about divisions when in Rwanda children have to identify themselves in school as Hutu or Tutsi. There is powerful learning about attitudes toward women when children see that women must do whatever they are told, that they are beaten, and that they must even obey young boys, as Serb culture in the early twentieth century has been described.[88]

Such naturally occurring learning also takes place when certain ideas and behaviors are so frequent that they become normal in a society. Jerrold Post suggested in 2007 that such normalization of suicide terrorism has occurred in Palestinian society. Whereas earlier suicide terrorists required indoctrination after they volunteered, and careful supervision so that they wouldn't change their minds, in his view Palestinian society has become so suffused with the ideas and examples of suicide terrorism that indoctrination and supervision have become unnecessary. A person can volunteer one day and be on a suicide mission a day or two later.[89] All that is required is instruction in how to carry and detonate a bomb. However, the great decline in suicide terrorism later in the decade suggests that something so extreme may not become quite so embedded in a society.

The transmission of societal woundedness and chosen trauma also occurs naturally to a large extent. Parents describe their painful experiences or those of their own parents. Or children learn in many indirect ways that their parents had suffered greatly, even if the parents don't actually talk about what has happened to them. Research on children of Holocaust survivors has found that the resulting "knowing but not knowing" has especially deleterious effects. The adults' woundedness can be expressed in overprotectiveness of the child or can result in children learning to be overly protective of parents and to refrain from expressing contrary views or anger that might upset them. Some victimized people become harsh, victimizing people in their own families.

Strong respect and obedience to authority also develop, at least in part, through natural socialization. Parents set rules in an absolute manner, without explanation. The rules must be obeyed without questioning. This is more likely in a society, or in a sub-culture, that is highly authority oriented. But explicit teaching of ideas and values is also important. In communist countries, such as Hungary where I lived until the age of 18, children were taught that capitalism and capitalists were bad. There is widespread teaching of hostility to the West in Islamic schools, in Pakistan, Saudi Arabia, and elsewhere. The devaluation of subgroups in a society is often directly communicated, in literature, in the media, as well as by adults, and as a result peers (see Chapter 22 on positive socialization).

Summary

In the presence of certain characteristics of cultures or societies, instigating conditions are more likely to lead to psychological and social reactions that lead to violence. One of these characteristics is a history of devaluation of and discrimination against a group. Another is a past history of victimization of a group, which makes its members feel vulnerable and the world look dangerous, as well as harsh treatment— victimization—of children as part of their socialization. Autocratic/ authoritarian societies, social inequality and injustice, past use of violence by the group, and certain group beliefs and group self-concepts, shaped by historical experiences or current social conditions, are also among the cultural characteristics that can contribute to violence.

Notes

1 Fein, 2007, Hiebert, 2008

2 Brewer, 1978; Tajfel, Flamant, Billig, & Bundy, 1971

3 Bar-Tal, 2000

4 desForges, 1999; Hatzfeld, 2003; Straus, 2006

5 Staub, 1989

6 Castano & Giner-Sorolla, 2006

7 Staub, 1989

8 Hagan & Rymond-Richmond, 2008. As noted in chapter 4, in Darfur people who identify themselves as Arabs and black Africans, have the same language and are seemingly identical in physical characteristics.

9 Hiebert, 2008

10 Ibid, p. 333

11 Aderman & Berkowitz, 1970; Stotland, 1969

12 Staub, 1971a

13 Oliner & Oliner, 1988

14 Zimbardo, 2007

15 Sageman, 2008

16 Staub, 2007b

17 Kruglanski et al., 2008

18 Pew Global Attitudes Project, 2006

19 Staub, 1996

20 Kressel, 2007

21 Ibid.

22 Staub, 2007b

23 Harff, 2003

24 Staub, 1989

25 Shavit, 2008

26 Straus, 2006, p. 128

27 Ibid, p. 129

28 Halperin, Canetti-Nisim, & Hirsch-Hoefler, 2009

29 Hatzfeld, 2003

30 Ibid.

31 Colby & Damon, 1992

32 Staub, 1989

33 Sageman, 2008

34 Quoted in Kruglanski et al., 2008. p.116

35 Ibid.

36 Staub, 1998; Staub, Pearlman, Gubin, & Hagengimana, 2005

37 Higginson, 2008, p.8

38 Ibid.

39 Peraino, 2008

40 Ibid, p. 30

41 See www.childjustice.org/docs/leach2001.pdf

42 Valentino, 2004

43 Steiner, 1980

44 Dodge, Bates & Pettit, 1990; Dodge & Frame, 1982

45 Rhodes,1999

46 deMause, 2008

47 Grille, 2005

48 Erlich, 1966

49 Sanday, 1981

50 Staub, 2005c; Staub & Vollhardt, 2008; see also Chapter 22

51 see Staub, 1989

52 de Mause, 2008; Miller, 1983

53 Waldorf, 2007

54 Straus, 2006

55 Goldhagen, 1998

56 Suedfeld & Schaller, 2002

57 Ibid, p.74

58 Altemeyer, 1996

59 Miller, 1983; Staub, 1989

60 Baumrind, 1971

61 Kohlberg & Candee, 1984

62 Fein, 1993, 2007

63 Rummell, 1994

64 Rummel, 1994, p 2

65 Harff, 2003

66 Krueger & Maleckova, 2003

67 Friedman, 2002

68 Staub, 1989

69 Victoroff, 2009

70 McCauley, 2008

71 Staub, 1999b

72 Li, 2005

73 Staub, 2007b

74 Sidanius & Pratto, 1999

75 New York Times, July 13, 2007

76 Bar-Tal, 2000, 2007

77 Baumeister, 1997

78 Staub, 1999a

79 Staub, 1989

80 Ibid.

81 Harff, 2003

82 Staub, 1989

83 Sanday, 1981

84 Jones, 2006

85 This has been described by participants, both men and women, in the workshops of Men's Resources International, a U.S. NGO, conducted in Rwanda and

Burundi in September 2007. Personal communication by Adin Thayer, one of the workshop leaders

86 Staub, 1989
87 Harff, 2003
88 Erlich, 1966
89 Post, 2007

9

Perpetration and the Perpetrators

The general social conditions, the immediate circumstances and their psychological effects, the characteristics of individuals that lead to self-selection or selection by authorities for certain roles, mutual influence in small groups, and learning by doing and the evolution of violence all contribute to perpetration.

In order to understand perpetrators of violence, one needs to understand the societal conditions that give rise to perpetration. One also needs to understand individual life experience and people's immediate circumstances. People who in their own lives have experienced victimization will, under certain conditions, be more likely to become perpetrators. So are people who are members of an ideological movement or group, or are connected to its members. In subsequent sections I discuss some conditions in people's lives and the proclivities in some individuals that make them more likely to become perpetrators.

Some of the material in this chapter is drawn from interviews with perpetrators themselves. But getting reliable information in this way is challenging. Even if they are willing to be interviewed, for many reasons, including often an ongoing justice process, perpetrators are likely to deny what they have done, or at the very least justify their actions and deny their responsibility. They blame victims, claiming that their actions were defensive, or they assign responsibility to superiors, claiming that they were ordered to do what they did and had no choice. It is true that sometimes there is great pressure on people to participate in violence, or they may have experienced great pressure. However, sometimes it is evident even from what perpetrators say that they were guided by ideology, by a sense of rightness, by devaluation, anger, and hate, and that they had been fully committed to their actions and even proud of it afterwards. They may be driven by a commitment to their beliefs and thus don't want to or find it difficult to maintain a false front during the interviews, and/or have the need to unburden themselves. Some may simply be ready to tell the truth.

The Direct Perpetrators

Local Processes, Killing, and Raping in Rwanda

I will primarily draw here on two projects. In one of them, Scot Strauss, in a doctoral dissertation later published as a book, interviewed 210 men imprisoned for their part in the Rwanda genocide, as well as a smaller number of local people in various communities around Rwanda, many of them officials. The prisoners he interviewed all pled guilty and have been sentenced. I integrate his findings and conception at various places in the book, but I note some of them again here. In another, heartrending book, Jean Hatzfeld[1] gives a close-up picture of a group of perpetrators and an accessible picture of the genocide in Rwanda. He interviewed the perpetrators in prison, as well as people in the community where they lived and killed. Rwanda is a very hilly country, and most of these men lived on the same or nearby hills. These mostly young men had been close to each other for many years—drinking beer together, playing soccer, and associating with a couple of older men who were then part of their killing group. Hatzfeld refers to them as the Kibungo gang. This section is also informed by interviews I conducted in prison with a small number of accused perpetrators in Rwanda, my past research on perpetrators, and other information about the situation in Rwanda and perpetrators.[2]

Genocide is assumed to be intentional and usually a policy set and directed by the government. But most genocides are not orderly, and they don't unfold uniformly from location to location. They often develop in response to many influences, environmental and psychological, which create social processes that can be chaotic. Straus[3] describes regional variation in Rwanda in the way the widespread killing of Tutsis came about, all within a few weeks after the president's plane was shot down. He writes about tipping points, how the influences accumulated until they tipped the balance toward mass violence against the Tutsis.

However, while specifics varied, there was an overall pattern. Usually local leaders emerged, at times the people already in official positions, at times other members of the local elite. Determining leadership sometimes involved inter-Hutu conflicts and power struggles among local elites. It is unclear to what extent these struggles were due to party politics, personal ambitions and competition for power, or differences in the attitude toward Tutsis and toward killing them. What is clear is that the local elites, already in place or emerging, directed people to kill. They were supported, and at times instigated, by outside actors such as members or emissaries of the central government, members of the military or of the Interahamwe. Sometimes an additional instigator was already occurring violence—the burning of Tutsi houses or the killing of Tutsis in a neighboring community.

At least in some locations there were "moderates" not inclined to the violence, including officials like burgomeisters (mayors). They were intimidated and, fearing for their own safety, usually changed direction. If there had been contrary influences, the violence in such localities might not have taken place. In some if not all settings, early action by the international community, even if not directly within that village or town, could have created sufficient contrary influence on local leaders and inhabitants to inhibit the killings. Instead, one of Hatzfeld's interviewees described seeing white soldiers come and leave with nuns who lived in the community, everyone realizing that the outside world was not going to interfere.

Hatzfeld interviewed the group of killers individually and confidentially. He was aware that perpetrators say things to protect and justify themselves. But he believed that what they said was more trustworthy because they were part of a group and the whole group agreed to talk to him, they were already sentenced so that what they said would not hurt them, and they expected to spend time in prison so that they would not see the outside world for some time. He did not get anywhere when he asked an interviewee what he did during the genocide. The killers began to talk only after Hatzfeld accidentally slipped in French into a grammatical form that refers to the plural you (*vous*). Then they responded to questions about what they, not as individuals but the gang—and also people in the community—did and thought, and became progressively more open in the interviews. While some of them started with imaginary, made-up stories—for example, about great battles between them and Tutsis rather than about the one-sided killings of people trying to take refuge in the marshes—in the course of the interviews they came to say amazing things, with the ring of truth. (There was one area of the country in which Tutsis did powerfully resist. But the determined killers continued to attack, in increasing numbers. In the end, out of about 50,000 Tutsis in this region, about 1000 survived.)

The genocide began on April 7, 1994, and arrived in the commune of Nyamata, which consists of a number of villages, on April 11. After that the men from the area started each day at the soccer field, directed by leaders, people they referred to as intimidators; from there they went into the marshes to kill Tutsis looking there for refuge. Everybody had to be there, with some weapon. Mostly they had machetes, but some preferred clubs, and a few even used bows and arrows. Then off they went, to do the day's labor. At first, and later occasionally, members of the Interahamwe militia or soldiers who came from the outside went with them, but most of the time it was just the local people. The local leader of the Interahamwe, the only one sentenced to death, was also interviewed.

Some did the killing eagerly and enthusiastically, and others were laggards, at least at first, which could have been out of ambivalence or laziness. But day after day, after a plentiful breakfast, including beef taken from the Tutsis and beer, they went off to kill. Everyone in this group of friends participated. For most of the perpetrators, the killing was fun; if not at first it soon became so.[4] There was excitement and even frenzy associated with the "work," with bragging about who had done more killing.

A female witness from the community said: "[At the end of the day] ...they returned with tired but laughing faces, tossing out jokes to one another, as in seasons of bumper harvests. It was clear from their manner that they were leading an exciting life."[5] One of the men had a Tutsi wife. He was accepted as part of the group. The rule was that the Tutsi wives of Hutus in good standing, partly due to being materially well off, would be spared if their husbands were diligent in killing Tutsis.

A main theme of the killers interviewed by Straus was the pressure on them to participate. In his view this pressure, not an authority orientation or a culture of obedience to authority but fear of the consequences of not participating, was the powerful, direct influence that led most of the killers to participate. But following the authority of leaders and rules was also evident. There had been a history of community labor in the country. Most killers reported that they had participated in these, as expected. The killing took on the character of community labor. In addition, the perpetrators claimed that "they joined attacks because it was the law."[6] Communication by the authorities made them believe this.

But there was also direct pressure, face-to-face mobilization, first by leaders, then by killers going from door to door, demanding that at least one person from each household join them. Part of the pressure was social influence: it was both a communal activity, and people wanted to oblige others, Some said that if a person did not participate, he would be accused of being an accomplice and could be killed. Others said, however, that people who did not fully participate were just fined by the authorities, or that it was possible to refuse to participate if they paid a fee, which could be negotiated. The killers Straus interviewed claimed that they did not have the money, or that even if one paid, one would be accused of being an accomplice and of hiding Tutsis.

While the men Hatzfeld interviewed said that they started the killing when directed by the authorities, one of them told of a different beginning. The Saturday after the president's plane was shot down everyone was in church for choir practice, Tutsis and Hutus. On Sunday, at the service, the Tutsis were not in church. The men got their machetes and went after them.

After the daily killing, the men Hatzfeld interviewed went looting, for anything and everything. With so much to take, there was no quarrel about who got what, except for Tutsi land, over which they argued. Women were very much involved in looting, although with rare exceptions, they didn't participate in killing. "Still," one of the men, Adalbert, said, "if a women happened to come upon some Tutsi children in an abandoned house, that was different" (p. 110). The men reported that most of their wives were supportive of what they were doing, but one or two worried about it, and one of them was greatly upset by her husband's actions, refusing to have sex with him. The wife of one of the men, Marie-Chantal, described the women as very supportive: "I don't know of any wife who whispered against her husband during the massacres. Jealous wives, mocking wives, dangerous wives—even if they did not kill directly they fanned the burning zeal of their husbands. They weighted the loot, they compared the spoils. Desire fired them up in those circumstances."[7]

Some who in the marshes encountered a Tutsi who was a friend or acquaintance may have moved on to another victim, leaving this one to the comrade coming behind. This was similar to some of the "kindness" that SS guards in concentration camps showed toward Jewish victims. A little kindness was acceptable, since it did not change the fate of the victims. However, some Hutus took special pleasure in killing acquaintances, and some looked to kill particular people against whom they held a grudge. Some killed fast, doing their job efficiently, and some took pleasure in making their victims' death more prolonged and painful.

One witness, a woman in the community who had a Tutsi husband, described an occasional spectacle. A man who may have tried to pass for Hutu, who was rich before, or whom someone disliked because of an old quarrel would be brought back and taken to the marketplace.

> The killers would call everyone to watch. All the women and children would gather to watch the show. There were people still carrying drinks, or nurslings on their backs... [Here Hatzfeld has a sentence describing the brutal violence against the person that followed.] ...They wanted them to last. They wanted the audience to learn from these torments. Shouts would rise from all sides. These were raucous village jamborees, quite rare and quite popular."[8]

And another female witness, also not a prisoner, said: "All the little children saw public killings.... The oldest, over twelve or thirteen, could even participate sometimes.... They went off with the dogs to nose out the fugitives in their hideouts. That was what they did during all those weeks with no school, no games, no church. Along with looting."[9]

No Tutsi in the area who was found was spared—no one on the hill hid a Tutsi. One nurse, leaving the maternity hospital where the Tutsi residents were about to be killed, smuggled out a Tutsi infant as she took her own children. But a couple of Hutus who spoke against the killings were themselves killed.

As other witnesses reported to Hatzfeld, this group of men harassed Tutsis before the genocide. One of the older members was deeply and vocally hostile to Tutsis, and another older member killed one in an earlier attack on Tutsis. Although the men were directed by the local authorities, the judge and the burgomeister, and respect for and fear of authorities and occasional visits to the area by Interahamwe groups and soldiers influenced them, they were also deeply hostile to Tutsis, making frequent negative references to them.The perpetrators said that while on the one hand they lived as neighbors—resenting things about Tutsis, such as their cattle trampling on their fields, but still getting along—on the other hand they were constantly exposed to Hutu hostility toward Tutsis. The one killer sentenced to death, because he had a part in the preparation of the genocide, said he was exposed to "the stories old folks told us at home about unpaid forced labor and other humiliations of that period, and ... the awful things happening to our brothers in Burundi,"[10] this referring to the mass killings of Hutus by the minority Tutsis who ruled Burundi, resulting in an influx of Hutu refugees escaping Burundi. He also heard many radio programs about "major problems between Hutus and Tutsis."[11]

While the authorities initiated and activated the killings, difficult life conditions in Rwanda, a history of conflict, and preexisting attitudes made many participants, certainly in this group, willing participants. In fact, most of them did the "work," the "cutting" as they euphemistically referred to it, enthusiastically. This group of killers supported each other and reinforced each other's commitment and determination. The principles of learning by doing, and commitment to the completion of a goal that had become important to them, make it understandable why these perpetrators became so committed that even as the Rwandan Patriotic Front was approaching, they eagerly went on with the killing, wanting to finish the job before they took refuge in the Congo. In this they were similar to the Nazis, who used trains badly needed to carry supplies to the front to transport Jews to extermination camps, and who continued with the killing of the Jews as enemy armies were approaching, with the war lost and Germany collapsing.[12] It is similar also to the Soviets, who even while their army was fighting desperately for survival against advancing German armies used their resources to resettle ethnic groups from one part of the country to another.[13]

Hatzfeld contrasts the pain, confusion, and struggle of survivors, whom he interviewed for an earlier book, with the seeming normalcy and lack of distress of the killers. In discussing the topic of regret, some of them did acknowledge the impact of what they had done. One of them, Jean-Baptise, talked about his dreams: "I see again the people killed with my own hand. When that happens, every single detail of blood and terror come back: the mud, the heat of the chase, the colleagues....Only the cries are missing. These are silent killings, which are slow but are as dreadful as before."[14] This man is unusual, perhaps, in that his killings may have been motivated partly by wanting to save his Tutsi wife. While some expressed regret, none of them said anything that showed empathy for the victims. And one of them, Elie, said: "In the prison and the hills, everyone is obviously sorry. But some of the killers are sorry that they did not finish the job. They accuse themselves of negligence rather than wickedness."[15] Perhaps he was also talking about himself.

Hatzfeld sees the killers as calmly detached and their egocentrism as the most impressive facet of their personalities on display, "overpowering in all of them." While they blamed others, "the Hutu government, the Interahamwe, possibly even whites and Tutsis," "they place themselves at the center of a swirl of activity ... focus only on themselves in the story, then and now ... worry only about their own fates and essentially feel no compassion for anyone but themselves." When in the interviews they discussed the theme of regret, "not one of them spontaneously mentions the victims....their instinctive reaction is to dwell on their personal losses and hardships."[16] This was so even though, after their initial silence, they talked more freely—in contrast to Hutus in the countryside, in their community, who were silent.

One part of the picture is that these men had the times of their lives. They killed people they disliked, or even hated, if not as individuals then as members of a group. As I believe and as they said, they stopped seeing the Tutsis they killed as individuals, except perhaps those they especially disliked or liked previously. Their mundane, everyday work on the fields was forgotten. Most of them killed with abandon: They ate and drank as they never had, had sex as they wished with women they were going to kill as well as with their wives, and they looted and felt rich and believed in a wonderful future. They were freed from the constraint of morality and the law; the authorities, usually oppressive, gave them a free hand and approved of what they were doing. Some priests supported them; some who were Tutsi were killed. The community stood behind these men. Religion and God, according to their own testimonies, were essentially forgotten.

They supported each other as a group while they killed; they exchanged stories and shared good times. In prison, they remained comrades. Who they were in prison, and in their interviews, was probably partly the result of their connection to each other. They reinforced each other's views and encountered no contrasting points of view. Hatzfeld writes that they had never seen a Tutsi survivor. Although judging from my experience in Rwanda, some of the prison personnel had to be survivors, they may not have engaged with the perpetrators as survivors.

Their stories support much of what I have written in this book, about devaluation, the role of authorities, the support within a small group and by a larger community, and the reversal of morality with regard to killing members of a victim group. It shows that material interest had a role, but seemingly not a primary role. It also shows the kind of frenzy created in some people by unbridled power over other human beings, of the loss of the normal constraints by morality (and normal societal constraints).

Hetzfeld's account also shows the harmful transformation in personality that accompanies such submergence in violence, like self-absorption and lack of empathy. This is another part of the picture: deep personal changes as well as psychological wounds that result from perpetrating violence. A number of research studies have found that soldiers who have killed in combat have more posttraumatic stress disorder than others equally exposed to combat who have not killed. Most of these studies were done with Vietnam veterans. Those who killed tended to dissociate at the time of the killing, a disconnection between events, experience, and consciousness. One form of this is the experience of looking on from the outside, as if the person was an observer, not the agent doing the killing. Such dissociation can defend against, "shut down or minimize feelings associated with the act of killing."[17] Even frenzied activity in the course of killing can be a kind of defense against feelings. Killing in war was also associated with lower level functioning in later life, more mental health symptoms, and violence.

Dissociation at the time of the violence may minimize distress, guilt, and other negative emotions. It can lead to continued dissociation,[18] creating a separation between oneself and one's actions and the feelings they may give rise to. Such disconnection from one's experience and feelings interferes with healing. Especially with repeated killings, and then being called to account for it, feelings may in general be inhibited, giving rise to a flatness of emotions (see also Chapter 10).

In other research on perpetrators, Charles Mironko,[19] a Rwandan-born researcher, suggests that for many people who participated in killing, fear had a strong role. He conducted 110 interviews in prisons with people who pleaded guilty of participation. Mironko recognizes that in the course of years in prison, certain common stories may have developed, but he believes that his interpretation is based on elements of stories that are unlikely to have been created. The primary element is that the killers acted in groups.

He writes about the cultural roots of *igitero*, a group response to danger. Originally its meaning was to assist people under attack, but its meaning and use have been transformed. He draws on historical sources to say that in the 1959 riots in which Hutus killed Tutsis, *ibitero* (the plural of *igitero*, and in this case meaning killing by groups) was common, and it has been used ever since as the practice of assembling attackers. He points to many interviews in which the prisoners described the killing they participated in as *igitero*, a group of people going together to kill. Of the 110 interviewed, 92 described their actions as part of a group, giving many details including the names of others in the group.

He writes that *igitero* has sometimes been "misidentified as spontaneous rioting and as selective political violence."[20] But actually, these were organized groups of attacking mobs, consisting of between 20 and 50 people. The organization was done by local officials, in a system set up by Habyarimana's ruling party long before the genocide. By organizing people in such attack mobs, the authorities ensured the participation of many people. In Mironko's view coercion by local leaders was central. He writes: "It seems from their own statements that their fear of immediate injury—physical, political, social—at the hands of local leaders already in power (i.e., other Hutu) was at least as great as, if not greater than their supposedly natural propensity for obedience (as Prunier argues) or fear of a future restored Tutsi monarchy, or domination at the hands of the RPF (as Mamdani suggests)."[21] However, when there is a predominant tendency in a group, fear need not be for one's life, but that by deviating from the group one is diminished in the eyes of others and ostracized.

In their accounts the killers talked about their victims in both devaluating terms, and in a distant, objectifying manner. Many of them automatically referred to *hunting* down Tutsis as if this was a normal, natural activity. They often talked not about Tutsis but about cockroaches. Mironko notes that they used euphemisms, such as hunting, talked about their actions in the third person, and in a "flat, unemotional voice," and like Hatzfeld noted showed lack of regret and "no trace of remorse."[22] The author is uncertain whether this showed true lack of remorse, or grief or trauma.[23]*

While the perpetrator accounts focused on the pressure to participate, some of what they said and survivors' accounts indicate initiative, excitement, and even enjoyment by them. One survivor, Immaculee Ilibagiza, described how, while a friend of her brother Damascene was away trying to arrange for a boat to take Damascene to Zaire and that way to save him, the friend's brother went to a group of killers to betray him. He "...offered my brother to wash his clothes before he left for Zaire. Damascene stripped down to his underwear, and Simoni took his clothes (he later confessed that he'd wanted my brother to feel ashamed and humiliated before he died). After he'd taken his clothes, Simoni called Damascene into the living room, where dozens of killers were waiting for him. They fell on my brother...." She described how they tortured him before killing him, trying to find out from him where she was hiding—presumably to rape and kill her.[24]

Ilibagiza, who was hidden during the genocide in a small bathroom with six other women, one day heard the chanting of killers outside the house. To the consternation of the other women she looked out through a small hole in the curtain. She saw a large group of people who "...whooped and hollered ....They chanted a chilling song of genocide while doing a dance...kill them, kill them, kill them all...a baby snake is still a snake...let none escape...." It wasn't the soldiers or the militiamen who were chanting. "...these were my neighbors, people I'd grown up with and gone to school with—some had even been to our house for dinner."[25] A BBC team interviewing people reported one person saying: "The hatred was deeply imbedded so anyone who saw a Tutsi killed them. That is why we left our homes and went from one area to another."[26]

Mironko writes that many of the interviewees referred to intense pressure to participate. But these other reports do not reflect this. Some of what is said in the transcripts represents local myths, such as "The so-called Tutsi and Hutu lived together like brothers and sisters." The reports that much (although not all) of the killing was perpetrated in groups are consistent with Hatzfeld's interviews and are convincing. After all, it would be dangerous for one or two people to find and kill a group of Tutsis. And structures from past history, in this case group labor and killing groups, tend to be re-created for use.

It is difficult to apportion the balance of influences and motives that led the killers to their actions. This is partly because people justify their actions and partly because, as is often the case in genocide, there were multiple influences and presumably motives. Again, devaluation of victims, the experience of threat from an enemy, sometimes hate of this other, scapegoating, an ideology, respect for and following authorities, obedience to authority, fear of authorities, conformity, and the hope of material gain (the property of those who are killed) all seemed to be present. Often killers—like the rest of us in everyday life—may only vaguely know why they are doing what they are doing.

Especially when many influences are active, people who get involved can become enthusiastic killers over time. Although the influences that affect perpetrators (and bystanders) lead to "ordinary" psychological processes that subvert moral values and inclinations, they don't eliminate moral responsibility. But true prevention requires, and the crucial challenge is, to prevent the conditions from arising that lead to the beginning of such violence. Another challenge is to raise children and help people develop in ways that make it unlikely that they initiate or join movements and actions that lead to such violence, that they resist, and work to counteract, the influences that lead to them.

Killings and Rapes in the Congo

Rwanda invaded the Congo first in 1996 to fight former genocidaires who escaped to the Congo and in incursions into Rwanda killed Tutsis. They then helped Kabila's rebels overthrow the dictatorship of Mobutu. It invaded again in 1998; the war that followed until 2003 involved the armies of neighboring countries. Many militias were formed, including former genocidaires, militias created by Rwanda and Uganda, and local militias that emerged partly because of insecurity, partly to exploit the natural resources of the country, partly due to land conflicts, and other reasons. Violence intensified again in the fall of 2008, it diminished in early 2009, but it continues, with many fighting groups.

All of them, including the government military, kill people and rape women and young girls. Even U.N. peacekeepers have been accused of raping women. The former Hutu genocidaires are perhaps the worst perpetrators. The rapes they perpetrate are especially brutal, physically damaging the victims.[27] As our thinking about the evolution of violence suggests, when people engage in violence, they change. After well over a decade of fighting in the Congo, perpetrating violence, and being its target, violence is the only life many members of these militias know. Raping women seems to have become normal for them. What the groups led by former genocidaires do to women in the Congo is reminiscent of what genocidaires did in Rwanda, where they raped Tutsi women and often mutilated their victims.

The nature of this violence against Tutsi women in Rwanda may have been the combined result of the attitude toward women in this patriarchal society, where husbands hitting wives is common, the devaluation of Tutsis, the special hostility toward Tutsi women created by the Hutu Ten Commandments, and the genocide as an overall context. The commandments gave a sexual shape to the denigration of Tutsi women, describing them as vile seducers of Hutu men. All this may have contributed to Hutu wives not objecting when their husbands, in the midst of killing Tutsis, also raped the women,[28] perhaps considering it revenge as well as reward for the men's hard labor. Having killed, raped, and mutilated in Rwanda, and having engaged in violence in the Congo ever since, facing all the hardships and enmity that have accompanied this violence, without a real home, supporting community, and the opportunity to create a different life, would maintain and increase these men's hostility and the need to affirm their effectiveness and power. Their actions in the Congo contributed to making rape "normal," to create a culture of rape among all the fighting groups, including militias that have been integrated into the Congo army. They, too, have been fighting for over a decade, and the discussion of the evolution of violence is relevant to them as well.

The women in the Congo have become more vulnerable in the course of history. While the society has long been highly patriarchal, before the colonial era if a woman was badly treated by her husband, she could go to her brother's home and stay there until the husband agreed to some reasonable resolution of their situation. This arrangement began to break down during colonial times, with women losing the power to protect themselves.[29] Moreover, not only forced labor and violence but also rape was widely practiced in King Leopold's time. His private army of black conscript soldiers under white officers would march into a village and hold the women hostage, to force the men to go into the rainforest for weeks at a time to harvest lucrative wild rubber. "The women taken during the last raid... are causing me no end of trouble," a Belgian officer named Georges Bricusse wrote in his diary on November 22, 1895. "All the soldiers want one. The sentries who are supposed to watch them unchain the prettiest ones and rape them."[30] And as I have argued elsewhere, the deep structure of culture often remains for very long periods. The difficult life conditions in the Congo and the inability of many men to find work may also contribute to rape. Women seem better able to deal with the chaotic situation psychologically, and men's need to maintain their status in relation to women may contribute to their hostility and violence toward them.

In an interview study by Ingaelere and his associates,[31] 101 FDLR fighters who returned to Rwanda said that much of the sexual violence takes place during fighting, gang rape is common, sometimes even infants are raped, and often alcohol is involved. However, such actions are not simply the result of immediate conditions–women are also kept in sexual slavery. The nature of gender relations has an important role, the dominance of men. Women are seen as weak, submissive, as second class citizens. The FDLR fighters also express or imply that it is a generally held belief that man, especially soldiers, need (and have a right) to sex. They also feel that they live in a world where the most powerful prevail.

Over time, sexual violence has become normal, and there is an apathy about it in the population—most likely in part born of a feeling of powerlessness. Also, violence evolves not only in that it becomes more intense and extends to more victims, but also in that more people become violent. Rape by civilians has increased substantially in recent years. Characteristics of the culture and relations between men and women, chaos and confusion, and the frustration of men without work and their general powerlessness all seem to have a role in leading men to use force this way.

Some of the violence against women may also express hostility toward an ethnic group, and it may serve as a means of intimidating and harming that group. While information about who is raped is limited, a Human Rights Watch report in late 2007 claims that at times the intent of those who raped was "to terrorize communities into accepting their control or to punish them for real or supposed links to opposing forces." The report also says that in areas where Congolese Rwandophones of Hutu ethnicity lived, "FDLR combatants [the groups made up or led by former genocidaires] caused little disturbance to local life."[32] The FDLR fighters also said that rape is sometimes used as a means of war.

In sum, many influences may be at work in the widespread rape of women and girls in the Congo. They include the need by men to reestablish culturally established superior identity as men and to regain a sense of power; the evolution of violence; the general chaos and normlessness that lead fighters to feel that they can take what they want, whether it is the food of local people or forced sexual relations with women they see in the fields or find in houses they invade; the cultural background of rape and the development of a current culture of rape; in the case of former Hutu genocidaires the ideology they brought with themselves and their earlier practices; and the use of rape as an instrument to intimidate and harm the enemy.

As for the fighting itself, many commentators have stressed as its cause the role of natural resources. They tend to ignore the many other influences I have described: the historical legacy of King Leopold of Belgium, the genuine need of Rwanda to defend itself from former genocidaires, the psychological effects of the Rwandan genocide, the general insecurity, the evolution of violence, and the hostility toward Tutsis. Reciprocity is also an influence: Violence by each group fuels violence by the others. Our analysis of mob violence[33] showed that it usually starts with politically engaged people who respond to grievances of their community that remain unaddressed. However, soon a second wave appears, and people use the ensuing chaos to loot. Similarly, the motives I just listed were probably significant at first. Since then the varied additional motives I discussed are likely to have become important, with many new actors, not only for rape but for violence in general. Lack of opportunity, and lack of power to accomplish ordinary life goals, makes fighting and taking natural resources the only meaningful "work" available. But the original motives may also persist, especially when they are kept active by threatening circumstances.

Impunity, the absence of punishment, has a role in the continued rapes. The government in 2006 passed a Law on Sexual Violence, which is only slowly beginning to be known by the population, and may slowly begin to have an effect. Educational radio programs about gender relations, respect, the traumatic effects of violence would be helpful. Thinking at the community level, since it is unclear when and if the government will engage in serious educational efforts or enforcement, the law could be used as a tool for community discussion of gender relations and a starting point for new gender norms. Discussion within the community, perhaps with facilitators trained from within the community by local agencies, may reduce civilian rape.

Whole communities could attempt to initiate dialogue with fighting groups. In my studies of genocide and mass killing I found that under certain conditions when individuals who are potential victims engage with perpetrators more like equals, the perpetrators stop treating them as victims. To attempt this requires preparation, the right strategy and courage.

Perpetration: The Overall Conditions, the Specific Situation, the Persons Involved, and Their Roles

Most authors who write about group violence focus on the conditions that affect the group, on systems and institutions. Psychologists who describe violence in more limited circumstances, such as prisons like Abu Ghraib, or extermination camps, have also focused on the circumstances that lead people to violent action.[34] To a large extent, that has been my orientation as well, both in previous writings and in this book, and in writing about Abu Ghraib[35] or the My Lai[36] massacre perpetrated by American soldiers on several hundred unarmed Vietnamese civilians, including women, children, and old men.

Varied combinations can create a context that gives rise to group psychological and social processes leading to violence. Specific situations that develop or are created within such contexts, and occasionally outside of it, impact people and guide them to violence. Sometimes this specific situation becomes an "atrocity creating situation," a term coined by Robert Jay Lifton. Abu Ghraib was such a situation. In part because of the focus on the situation and its power, there has been much recent discussion of the "ordinary person" as the perpetrator. Implicit in this is the presumption that traditionally perpetrators of such evil were seen as different from other people, as having extraordinary characteristics, and that contrary to such a view certain conditions lead the "ordinary" person to engage in extraordinary, evil actions.[37]

While surrounding conditions are very important, how people respond to them is also affected by who they are. Social and personality psychologists have been concerned with how circumstances and personality join or interact—in determining how we see events, think about them, feel, and act. Some people will see threat, or danger, or insult, and respond with aggression when few other people would. Aggressive boys perceive actions as hostile that other people see as unintentional.[38] In the Milgram obedience experiments, participants with more of an authoritarian personality were more likely to administer the strongest shocks to the "learner." Those with more moral responsibility obeyed the experimenter less.[39]

Everything in this book so far suggests that people with little inclination for violence can get caught up in social processes that lead them to become followers of ideological movements and in the end perpetrators. However, while group violence is the outcome of *ordinary, normal psychological and social processes* that affect whole groups of people, people with certain characteristics and past experiences are more likely to end up as vanguards of a destructive ideological movement and perpetrators of mass violence.

Most perpetrators of genocide, of intense violence in the course of conflict between groups, or terrorists are not mentally ill, in the sense of diagnostic categories of mental illness. But such persons can have characteristics that make it more likely that they are attracted to destructive ideologies, that they will enter groups that have a violent potential or are violent, or that they are selected for violent roles by leaders.

Circumstances have powerful influence, but it is individuals who act, and their characteristics join with circumstances to shape their actions. I quoted from the account of Ilibigaza, a survivor of the genocide in Rwanda, describing how one man tried to save her brother, and that man's brother betrayed him. While the power of an already existing group or institution can be great, individuals can make the choice to participate or not even in an *igitero*, a killing group in Rwanda. To do that, sometimes they have to be willing to face ostracism or physical danger. In spite of the forces acting on people, still only a relatively small minority of male Hutus participated in the killings. Choice was also possible at Abu Ghraib, at My Lai, and even at Auschwitz.[40]

Behavior is the joint outcome of external influences and personality. Social conditions are an external influence, affecting people psychologically. Culture is partly an external influence. People know and live up to the expectations or norms of the culture, of their fellow group members. But it is also an internal influence, since to varying degrees people internalize the culture, which then shapes their thinking and feelings. Devaluation of others or respect for authority is absorbed.

The effects of a narrower social environment, a religious group, a gang, a group of friends, an ideological movement, and people who happen to be present at a certain time and place are initially external influences. However, children are born into particular environments which, like the larger culture, shape them. Moreover, people often join groups aligned with who they are. Even if initially there is a divergence, the views and perspectives of groups that people have stable associations with tend to become internalized. They become part of a person, and thus again the external and internal influence are aligned. For prevention it is important that people resist becoming socialized into and adopting the orientation of violence-inducing environments.

Personal characteristics in part derive from the general culture, and in part they are idiosyncratic, shaped by experiences in the family, with teachers and peers and through various group memberships, some of which may be at odds with the culture. They are also the result of powerful experiences such as being a victim of violence or undergoing a religious conversion. Among the especially important personal characteristics with regard to group violence are the way we evaluate people in general and members of certain groups in particular; hostility in general or toward particular groups; empathy and feelings of responsibility for other people's welfare and how inclusive these attributes are; the degree to which a person tends to obey and fear authority; the extent of personal strength or vulnerability (partly the result of past frustration or fulfillment of basic needs) that affects how a person is impacted by difficult conditions; moral values and moral sensitivity in relation to injustice to oneself, one's group, and others; the capacity for critical consciousness—to use one's own judgment and not only the guidance of others; and moral courage, the ability and willingness to act on the basis of moral values and caring about people even in the face of opposition and potential danger.

There is "self-selection" for perpetrator roles, and selection by people in authority, based on individuals' characteristics and actions. During the dictatorship of the colonels in Greece, those members of the military police were selected to be trained as torturers who showed especially strong obedience to authority and came from families with strong anticommunist views, which was the ideology of the colonels.[41] The Nazi doctors sent to Auschwitz were committed Nazis, presumably selected on the basis of their ideology.[42] The concept of the sleeper effect also suggests that certain people have an inclination to violence activated by extraordinary conditions, such as those that preceded the Holocaust. The combination of difficult life conditions and the Nazis allowing and encouraging violence activated inclinations that under normal conditions would remain dormant.

Sometimes people enter situations that change in ways that are difficult to predict or that require vigilance to do so. In Rwanda, many of those who became members of the Interahamwe initially joined youth groups associated with certain political parties. Young people in difficult economic times, many probably jobless, could gain both material and psychological benefits from joining. These parties, including the ruling party, were hostile to Tutsis and to various degrees were advocates of Hutu power. The groups were later turned into militias.

Many might not have foreseen at first the evolution from youth group members to killers, but given the party ideologies, there was likely self-selection.

At times people enter situations in which the use of certain kinds of force is required. The guards at Abu Ghraib chose to be soldiers and were members of the military police. Individuals who join the police tend to be more authoritarian, which means that they find satisfaction in submitting themselves to higher authority and using authority over others. Those who join a volunteer army are also likely to be different from the average person. Journalist Fareed Zakaria wrote about some soldiers in Iraq and Afghanistan who would "rather be in the war zone" than back home, who sign up for repeated deployments. He quoted a retired general saying, "Soldiers want to fight. That's why they signed up."[43] Obviously, not all soldiers are the same. But if people enter certain groups with some inclination to fight, this makes learning by doing and a personal evolution in violence easier.

The Stanford Prison study, set up by psychologist Philip Zimbardo of Stanford University,[44] is instructive about the role of circumstances and personal characteristics. College students were randomly assigned to be either prisoners or guards in a mock prison at Stanford. Before that they filled out personality tests aimed to establish that they were mentally healthy, normal individuals. The prisoners were then "arrested" by real police and taken to the mock prison. Immediately, the guards began to treat the prisoners badly, and the bad treatment escalated over time. A rebellion by the prisoners was forcefully repressed. During the night the guards conducted "counts," making naked prisoners stand in the corridor for hours, doing countless push-ups. The guards took away the prisoners' beds, put them into isolation in a small room as punishment, deprived them of sleep, verbally abused them, and harassed them in many ways. The emotional effects on the prisoners were intense. Five prisoners were released because of their severe distress or apathy, before the study was terminated after 6 days due to the impact on the prisoners.

This was a bad prison, in that the way it was set up and administered made the abusive behavior by those with power, the guards, more likely. The prisoners were intentionally degraded from the start. Their heads were covered with women's nylon stockings. They wore what looked like sack nightgowns, without underwear, so that "when they bend over their behinds show."[45] Day and night a chain was attached to each prisoner's ankle. Such conditions dehumanize people, making it more likely that those with power devalue them and abuse them.

The initial guidance by Zimbardo, acting as superintendent of the prison, emphasized the guards' power and could be seen as instruction for the negative treatment of the prisoners:

> You can create in prisoners feelings of boredom, a sense of fear to some degree, you can create a notion of arbitrariness that their life is totally controlled by us, by the system, you, me—that they'll have no privacy at

all....There'll be constant surveillance. Nothing they do will go unob-
served. They will have no freedom of action, they can do nothing, or say
nothing that we don't permit. We are going to take away their individuality in various ways. In general what all this leads to is a sense of powerlessness.[46]

Beyond this, there were no rules for the guards to follow. When they asked
how to respond to the prisoner riot, they received no advice. When they engaged
in abusive behavior, there was no limit set on them. In an extensive description
of the study, only one occasion is mentioned, when a guard used physical force,
that those in charge of the study (who could observe much of what was happening on video) discouraged such behavior. While Abu Ghraib was much more of
an atrocity-generating situation, in some important ways the situation created
at Stanford resembled that created at Abu Ghraib.

Normal college students as guards behaved in these abusive ways, and they
continued to do so in spite of the obvious distress and increasing passivity and
depression of the prisoners. Zimbardo believes that it was the power of the situation he created that explains their actions. It was his purpose to show this
power rather than the influence of the personal characteristics of individuals.
The dehumanized condition of the prisoners, the instructions to the guards,
and the absence of rules and of higher-ups to make sure that guards adhered to
rules of appropriate conduct certainly had a very significant role. Such conditions will tend to create abusive behavior.

But even all these conditions do not by themselves account for the behavior
of the guards. Psychologists Sam McFarland and his student Thomas Carnahan[47]
conducted a study to explore whether personal characteristics might have
played a role. They followed up a hypothesis I advanced in *The Roots of Evil* that
the people who respond to an ad about the study of prison life, which is how the
participants in the Stanford Prison Study were recruited, may have characteristics that would shape how they acted as guards in a prison like setting.[48]
McFarland and Carnahan put two types of ads into newspapers around Western
Kentucky University. In one type they were looking for participants in a "psychological study of prison life," while in the other they left out "prison life." They
had more trouble getting responses to ads for the study of prison life, already
indicating self-selection among those who did respond. Participants in the study
filled out questionnaires to assess personal characteristics the researchers saw
as relevant to dominant and aggressive behavior.

These researchers found that people who responded to ads about the study of
prison life were more aggressive, more authoritarian, more Machiavellian
(manipulative and with a negative view of human beings), more narcissistic,
and had higher scores on social power (believed more in the rights of those with
power to dominate) than those who responded to the ad looking for participants
in "a psychological study." The prison study respondents also had less empathy

and altruism. The findings of this study is only suggestive: its participants were not the actual guards in the Stanford Prison study, but people who volunteered for a prison study. However, the authors also note that the average level of authoritarianism of participants in the original Stanford Prison study, when this measure was administered to them in the course of their selection for the study, was similar to that of a "sample of 110 San Quentin male prisoners...."[49] Participants were randomly divided into prisoners and guards. The similar characteristics in the prisoners may have also affected their behavior and the development of the relationship between prisoners and guards.

To whatever degree participants in the prison study had certain personal tendencies, there had to be and was variation within the group. The imprint of the personality of both guards and prisoners is evident in the description of the original prison study. For example, one prisoner protested by refusing to eat and continued to do this in spite of intimidation, punishment, and under the instigation of the guards, pressure from the other prisoners, and even the attempt to force-feed him. Some of the guards were especially abusive, others simply enforced obedience to the rules they had created, and some tried to act in somewhat kinder ways and felt guilty about what was happening. However, none of the guards spoke out against the actions of the more abusive guards. Somewhat analogous variation in the behavior of guards and other personnel, such as Nazi doctors, has also been found in Auschwitz.[50]

The dynamics that were created by the actions of the more abusive guards also contributed to what happened at Stanford. The norms their actions established, the reactions by the prisoners and their responses to them, and competitive behavior by other guards appeared to contribute to the evolution of increasing aggressiveness.

One of the guards, whom the researchers came to refer to as John Wayne because of his toughness, on the first night came up "with a creative plan to teach Jerry-5486 (the prisoners had numbers on their "uniforms" and were addressed by those) his number in an unforgettable way. 'First five push-ups, then four jumping jacks, then eight push ups, and six jumping jacks, just so you will remember exactly what the number is, 5486.'"[51] One of the other guards on this shift competed with "John Wayne," which required him to be increasingly aggressive. I referred earlier to research showing that members striving for influence move groups in a more extreme direction. This phenomenon has been observed in varied settings, including mob violence[52] and terrorism.[53]

In summary, our earlier exploration of the impact of difficult life conditions and group conflict indicate that they frustrate basic needs and may lead to scapegoating and attraction to destructive ideological movements, even in people with less preexisting inclinations. But people with certain characteristics are more likely to enter aggression-generating situations, more likely to act aggressively in them, and more likely to be shaped and in turn shape a group and environment that promote aggression. For some people there may be a natural fit, a coherence between their personal dispositions and the requirements for aggression. Their evolution to increasing violence can be faster and more extreme.

Psychologists Donald Dutton and Christie Tetreault[54] call attention to "toxic situations," essentially what Robert Jay Lifton has called atrocity-generating situations. They suggest that in toxic situations some people go beyond their orders, even beyond killing that is the norm in the situation, and engage in extreme atrocities. In My Lai, in Vietnam, where U.S. soldiers expected resistance and found none, and proceeded to kill the villagers, one soldier later recalled killing about 25 people and mutilating them in horrendous ways. In the Nanking massacre, women were raped and then often mutilated; civilians were lined up and decapitated.[55] Richard Rhodes describes how a few men bludgeoned many Jews to death in a public square in a small town in Lithuania, while both the villagers and German soldiers watched.[56] I described scenes from Rwanda of such extremes, as well as brutal rapes in the Congo. Dutton and Tetreault write that in toxic situations such as massacres, genocides, prison riots, and lynchings, "the majority of men comply with orders to kill, a minority refuse, and another minority go well beyond what was ordered in the extent of their violence."[57]

Some of the characteristics that may contribute to an inclination to participate in group violence are the following. The absence of caring about other people and of moral values that prohibit harming others; a negative view of human beings, including devaluation of specific others and hostility; various forms of rigidity (authoritarianism, cognitive rigidity, black-and-white thinking); unfulfilled basic needs; and the fragility of the self, with sensitivity to threat and fear. Such characteristics can intensify the effects of threatening or frustrating conditions.

Dutton and Tetreault note that researchers have explored a narrow range of characteristics associated with extreme violence, and they suggest several more for study, such as narcissism and psychopathy. They also suggest, following others, that a "predation-behavior" brain system might exist that accounts for extreme violence. There is evidence, and theories about, a genetic contribution to individual violence that works through brain structures. To the extent there are genetic bases for it, their expression, and the readiness for activation of violence-promoting brain structures, is shaped and formed by experience. These experiences range from early diet to social experiences such as love and connection versus hostility and rejection.[58] Group violence is certainly greatly shaped by experience and environment.

Socialization can focus on external control of behavior by punishment. It thereby generates obedience to rules based on fear of and respect for authority. Such punitive and at times abusive socialization is likely to be experienced as hostile and rejecting. Instead of internalized values, it creates a combination of fear of the external consequences of one's actions, and fear of and hostility toward others.[59] But when circumstances not only free people of constraints but also give them license and reward violence, the combination of hostility and the newfound freedom to act with abandon may lead to satisfaction gained from extreme violence, or from others' suffering—and as violence evolves, from sadistic actions.

An essential aspect of prevention on the individual level, in the long run, is to inculcate both positive values and self-control, the capacity for positive self-guidance and self-regulation (see Chapter 22). This may lead people to resist entering destructive situations when possible, or when they find themselves in them, to act like the soldier at My Lai who, when ordered to shoot by another soldier, replied: "I can't, I won't."[60]

Different Personal Routes to Engagement with Movements, Especially Terrorism

Societal and world conditions, including repression, discrimination, low status, restrictions on a group' expression of identity, immigration, large numbers of refugees, and individuals moving from country to country as a result of globalization, impact people's lives and relationships, providing the initial impetus for the development of the ideologies and practice of contemporary terrorism. Oliver Roy,[61] a French scholar of Islam, writes about the deterritorialization of Islam and about deculturation, the loss of "pristine" cultures. Individuals and groups are affected both by great cultural changes in the world and by changes in their culture as they move from one society to another. As a movement evolves, the psychology of small groups and their impact on individual members has a powerful role in terrorism. But individuals have to join the group. How this happens has been learned to a large extent by court testimonies and newspaper accounts. Marc Sageman, Ariel Merari, and Jerrold Post all describe how people become involved through others already involved, through friends and family relations.

But who are those who initiate movements that become terrorist, and how do they get engaged? Who are those who get drawn in by people already involved? Not all friends and relatives of such people are attracted or join. Not everyone remains in an ideological movement as it becomes increasingly extreme and violent. Only a relatively small percentage of those attending training camps in Afghanistan became part of the global jihad. While many of them were not accepted into it, newspaper accounts indicate that an unknown percentage chose not to join.[62] Post describes the history of one young Palestinian who became a terrorist, while his many brothers did not.

I categorize those who initiate or join ideological movements or terrorist groups as idealists, responders, and lost souls. These are not mutually exclusive designations. A person can be an idealist, a respondent, and a lost soul at the same time, but often one can identify one or another personal route as more prominent. Within these larger categories, there are also subcategories.

By *idealists* I mean people who develop ideals and values that lead them to respond to others' needs and conditions by committing themselves to a cause. Ideals can be admirable, expressing positive visions about justice, better societies, and better lives for people. They can also be inherently destructive, or become destructive as people adopt destructive means to fulfill them. The idea of inherent superiority of some people over others, and the ideal of creating a world in which group relations are based on superiority and inferiority, is an inherently destructive idea. Social equality can be a positive idea, but it has been made destructive in various communist countries, such as Cambodia.

By *responders* I mean people who respond to their own personal experience or their group's experience. While groups of people who respond to difficult life conditions are respondents, the way I use the term here applies especially to people who respond to repression, injustice, bad treatment or violence that they themselves, or that people they are close to or a group they identify with have experienced. We might also call the latter *identifiers*. One's own suffering because of membership in a group, or the suffering of one's group is a powerful source of such identification. Many of the initial organizers of Al-Qaeda experienced repression. Some have had their own relevant personal experiences but were also identifiers, moved to action at least in part by what was happening to other Muslims.

By *lost souls* I mean people whose personal needs are frustrated or unfulfilled. This may be because of neglect or lack of guidance and support by their families, or their experiences as immigrants or minorities, or for other reasons. They are looking for connection, identity, security, a feeling of effectiveness, and a comprehension of reality.

The self-selection for becoming a genocide perpetrator or terrorist can be the result of accidental events, such as going to a radical mosque in which some people preach jihad, or having friends, relatives, or apartment mates who join ideological or terrorist groups. While many people who have such connection don't get involved, given an impetus born of past experience or current conditions, such connections can lead to engagement.

Certain conditions and experiences especially contribute to people becoming respondents or lost souls. They include living in social contexts such as repression in Egypt or the occupation in Gaza and the West Bank; direct personal experiences such as those of Palestinians who had their houses destroyed or family killed or placed in jail; prejudice and discrimination against Muslims in Europe and their disconnection from the society around them; abuse, neglect, and in general severely unfulfilled needs as a result of personal experiences in one's family or life; and displacement of individuals or whole communities and unfilled needs for identity, effectiveness, and connection. The impact of these experiences can be enlarged by the influence of family, friends, and teachers, by absorbing an ideology, and by membership in a group that helps fulfill needs. People for whom because of their background and experience violence is easier to contemplate and perform may be more likely to stay in a group that becomes violent.

Adventure seekers and other joiners.

Before I discuss in detail idealists, respondents, lost souls, and some other personal bases of involvement in terrorism, I want to note that once there is an attention getting world-wide terrorist movement, relevant to a very large group, such as Muslims (in contrast to a local one such as Basque terrorism in Spain), it can act as a magnet for varied kinds of people. Predominant among them my be the kind of people I already identified and will discuss further. But it may also include adventure seekers, people who have a need for attention at any cost, and perhaps others with attraction to extreme behavior. In the case of airplane hijacking, after the first instance, which attracted worldwide attention, there was a progressive, speedy and huge increase in the number of hijackings, until new policies brought them under control.

Idealists

People moved by ideologies, ideals about social reality, including religious ones, may be motivated to right what they regard as wrong and to create what they see as good. The development of their ideals may be the result of a combination of a societal context, the family context and influence, and partly accidental, partly intentional exposure to literature, people, and other sources of ideas and beliefs. The social contexts I have discussed in this book may then activate these beliefs. Sociologist Molly Andrews[63] interviewed long-term, committed socialists in England. These people did not engage in violence but were committed to and worked for a cause, often facing the opposition and hostility of the society around them. In their interviews they described how the world they saw gave rise to their concern about the way things were and motivated them to do something about it. Encounters with individuals who were the source of ideas, with books, as well as with groups shaped these people.

I have already mentioned individuals who were moved by ideologies of a different sort. Doctors were selected for Auschwitz because they were ideologically committed to Nazism. Self-selection, their joining the Nazi party and acting as committed Nazis, led to their selection for "working" at this extermination camp. One of their jobs was to do the "selections" of those to be exterminated. As people got off the trains that brought them to Auschwitz, some were sent to one line, to be immediately killed in the gas chambers, some to another line, to work as slave laborers. Some of these doctors were selected for Auschwitz on the basis of their earlier participation in the "euthanasia" program, where their job was to designate which Germans were to be killed, due to mental handicap or other reasons.[64]

The Greek torturers under the dictatorship of the Colonels between 1967 and 1974, were also selected by their superiors out of members of the military police. One basis of their selection was the ideology of their family, in this case strong anticommunism. Another was their strong tendency for obedience to authority, demonstrated while they were members of the military police. Once selected, they received further training in submission, including submission to their own physical abuse. They learned to be torturers by first observing others, then performing less intense torture, then more intense torture—a process of learning by doing.[65]

In a failed terrorist attack in London, two cars full of nails, explosives, and gasoline in a central area of the city failed to explode. Two of the planners of these attacks drove to Glasgow, found their way to the airport and set their cars on fire. To many people's surprise, the attack was planned by young doctors, engineers, and a medical technician from Muslim countries. Apparently such people have been in the vanguard of political engagement and part of militant Islam for some time.

A *New York Times* article described the background and history of one of them, Kafeel Ahmed.[66] He was the child of two doctors, the member of a very religious and wealthy family in India. When he was young, his family lived for a period of time in Iran and later in Saudi Arabia. Perhaps having been an outsider increased his capacity for empathy—with people he identified with. In India in the 1970s his father was jailed for a while for belonging to a Muslim group "deemed extremist by many Western observers." Ahmed was an excellent student and was not very political in college and while getting a master's degree in Northern Ireland.

During his doctoral studies in Cambridge, England, he got connected to people with strong political interests and radical views. According to those interviewed for the article, he discussed with them American imperialism, the merits of jihad, and "expelling American and British troops." He became concerned with the fate of Chechnyan Muslims, and in India in February 2006 he convened a group to mark what he called Chechnya Day. On returning from a stay in India, he appeared more deeply religious, with the beard of a religious Muslim. His story, to the extent we know it, combines strong religiosity, the influence of politically engaged companions, and concern about Muslims who have been the object of violence.

Some of the ideals that terrorist leaders—or individuals and groups—follow have been described as *messianic delusions*. Certain terrorist groups with messianic ideologies have been referred to as apocalyptic, for example, the Arum Shinrykio group in Japan,[67] which introduced poison gas into the Japanese subways in the 1990s. Jeff Victoroff writes that such groups "envision mass destruction as a path toward replacing the corrupt world with a pure new social order."[68] The theories of Qutb, which inspired Islamic terrorism and out of which Al-Qaeda evolved, advocate messianic transformation of the world.

There is much that we don't yet know. Who are the people who develop a sense that something is deeply wrong with the world, form a vision of a better world, and advocate violence as a way of creating this better world? What combination of personal and group experiences lead to it? Lifton,[69] who studied Aum Shinrykio, describes its members as characterized by absolutist/moralist or black-and-white thinking, a morality that sees everything as either right or wrong with no shades in between. It is possible to identify social conditions, educational and personal life experiences, and individual characteristics that contribute to a person becoming a terrorist. But this still is unlikely to enable us to predict whether particular individuals will become terrorists. From about 22.5 million people in Saudi Arabia, in a 2007 publication one author identified just 53 Saudis "who committed jihad-related suicide bombing in Iraq."[70]

Movements often start with intellectuals, individuals who put forth ideas and ideals, such as Marx and Engels in the case of communism, or Qutb whose ideas inspired Islamic terrorism. Often these ideals have to do with human welfare and with freedom from repression. Sometimes individuals both initiate ideas and act to execute them, such as Lenin or Hitler. In the case of joiners, the social context, accidental events, and associates all can have a role. Some joiners are perhaps specifically attracted to violence. But for many others constructive groups and movements might satisfy needs and ideals that could otherwise lead them to join destructive ideological movements.

Responders

Egyptian terrorists in the 1970s may have been both responders and idealists. They were religious in an Arab country that was both secular and repressive— of political opponents as well as religion. For example, although al-Zawahiri's family was not especially "pious," or intensely religious, he himself became religious when as a young boy he was influenced by an uncle who was a follower of Qutb. When al-Zawahiri was 15 years old, Qutb, who was (falsely) charged with actions to overthrow the Egyptian government, was executed. Al-Zawahiri was outraged, and as a secondary school boy, he joined with other boys his age in a group that wanted to overthrow the government. He became increasingly religious and soon joined the Egyptian Islamic Jihad, which engaged in terrorist actions. After Anwar Sadat was killed by terrorists associated with this group, he was imprisoned and probably tortured. He later became the leader of this organization. Some time after his release, he went to Pakistan and was part of the fight against the Soviets. He met Osama bin Laden there and was instrumental in the creation of Al-Qaeda. In his case, it was identification with a religious ideology and the repression of those who were followers of that ideology that was the impetus for his involvement in opposition to the government. This was followed by a history of evolution as a terrorist.

Painful experience may lead some respondents to a commitment to universal ideals such as justice and the protection of the life or well-being of all human beings. They may want to correct wrongs, to improve the world, to address social conditions by positive means. The violence of some responders evolves as they participate in movements that initially aim to bring about change by constructive means. Others may also hold ideals, but focus on the enemies of those ideals and the use of violence to fulfill them. Part of the ideology of Islamic jihad is to create a just system, guided by a strict form of Islam, Salafism. The ideology identifies the West as an enemy of such ideals, and of Muslims in general. Some followers of this worldview and ideology see violence as the only way to bring about desirable ends.

Responders may also be lost souls, born and raised in dire circumstances. Jerrold Post[71] described Palestinian terrorists as socialized into hostility and violence, with "hatred ... bred in the bone." He describes life histories that led to terrorism, starting with the expulsion of families from their homes at the time of the war of 1948, and continuing with life in refugee camps, usually under miserable conditions, with poverty and unemployment, and humiliation by an occupying power. Parents who continued to mourn their losses and blamed the Israelis, teachers who preached action against Israel, peers, youth camps, and organized fighting groups all had an influence. The reciprocal violence I described between Palestinians and the Israelis had a role as well.

In some cases the progressive change and evolution in people who came to be known for extravagantly violent terrorist actions can be traced, at least to some degree. One such case is Omar Rezaq, who had a central role in hijacking a plane in 1985. When during a stop in Malta he was refused fuel for the plane, he killed five hostages, one at a time, in the hope that the authorities would change their minds and fuel the plane. The plane then was stormed, resulting in the death of over 50 people. Post writes that "like his fellow terrorists, Rezaq believed that his actions were justified; they were not wrongful, but righteous acts in the service of the Palestinian revolution. He had been socialized to blame all of his and his people's difficulties on the enemy and to believe that violent actions against the enemy were justified."[72]

He was, however, the only one of eleven siblings to join the fight against Israel. It is likely that some combination of his home life and experiences outside the home led him to start on a road to terrorism. To Post, that combination was a harsh, physically punitive father, who opposed Rezaq's involvement, and a teacher who was a member of Fatah and told him that "the only way to become a man was to join the revolution and take back the land stolen from your parents and grandparents."[73] A young man, lost like many others in the camps, found a powerful role model who helped him imagine and enact a valued identity.

Some Muslim fighters in Afghanistan who became terrorists, certainly the Egyptian ones, also were both respondents and lost souls—uprooted, disconnected from their communities, with an unclear future. Palestinian suicide bombers lived under occupation, with limited opportunities, the life of their community disrupted by the conditions of the occupation. Post writes about a group of secular Palestinian terrorists who were interviewed between the two *Intifadas*, noting that "painful early experiences shaped identity and steered Palestinian children and youth onto the path of terrorism. Over 80 percent ... reported growing up in communities that were radically involved."[74] He also writes that while Palestinian families feared for their children's lives, and for what security forces might do to their families, they regarded those who joined the *Intifadas* as heroes. At least publicly, parents supported their sons' actions.

In research spanning over decades, Ariel Merari and his associates conducted a number of studies of Palestinian suicide bombers. In one study, family members, parents, and siblings of 34 Palestinian suicide bombers between 1993 and 1998 were interviewed. In another study, failed suicide bombers and organizers of suicide attacks were interviewed in prison.[75] Merari found that the suicide bombers had a higher educational level than Palestinians in general. Their economic status was at the average of Palestinians in the occupied territories. Consistent with the view of learning by doing and the evolution of violence, families described 19 of the "suicides" as very active and 8 as active in the *Intifada*, which included "stone throwing, demonstrations, distributing leaflets, painting graffiti and enforcing commerce strikes." However, studies show that during the first *Intifada* more than three-quarters of young Palestinians were involved in varied resistance activities, for example, stone throwing. While the behavior of this group does not differentiate them from other young Palestinians, given other elements in their background and personality, such involvement could change them in ways that increased their readiness for terrorism.

Many of these suicide bombers experienced the destruction of their houses as punitive measures by Israel, and they also experienced the killing of relatives and friends. Many spent time in Israeli prisons. In one case a close family member and in 11 cases friends had been killed prior to the suicide mission. In 7 cases a close family member had been jailed. In 15 cases the person had been beaten in the course of clashes with Israeli army during demonstrations, which in 11 cases resulted in injury.

Such experiences are likely to be traumatic, leading to feelings of loss and anger. In a study of Chechen suicide terrorists, family members, associates, and hostages who talked to some of them during a 3-day siege of a Moscow theater all said that these terrorists had had prior traumatic experiences, and that 27 out of 34 terrorists sought out extreme religious, radical groups after these traumas. They were secular Muslims before that. While the researchers had no information from the terrorists themselves, based on the interviews with others they believe that trauma was a crucial source of their motivation.[76] In contrast, in information compiled from public sources about 172 people engaged in "transnational" Islamic jihad against "far enemies," excluding people engaged in local jihads such as Chechens and Palestinians, Sageman[77] identified only one person with likely childhood trauma. However, the public information may have been inadequate to establish the presence of traumatic experiences.

With regard to Palestinians, the experiences I described earlier can certainly be traumatizing, perhaps especially so for people with certain personalities. Parents described 53.6% of the "suicides" as loners, as introverts. Like other researchers, Merari found no mental disorder. But in another study he and his associates studied terrorists themselves, not indirectly through interviews with others, but through "clinical psychological interviews" and tests given to 15 would-be suicide terrorists, 12 non-suicide terrorists, and 14 organizers of suicide attacks. They found differences in personal characteristics. Would-be suicide terrorists had less ego strength than the organizers of suicide attacks. Nine of the suicide bombers were assessed as having dependent (greatly needing others, afraid of having to care for oneself) and avoidant (socially inadequate, inhibited, and extremely sensitive to negative evaluation) personality styles.[78*] This would have made them vulnerable to public influence by their group and leaders. Four were found to be impulsive and emotionally unstable. More of them than those in the control groups showed symptoms of depression.[79]

Merari sees as the key explanation "that dependent types are more susceptible to social influence and find it hard to say 'no' to authoritative figures, such as the generally revered local commanders of the militant groups—the organizers of suicide attacks."[80] However, even suicide terrorists sensitive to social influence may have some larger motives; they may be more likely to be led to act on them under the influence of others. The experiences of young Palestinians are likely to also give rise to anger, and the desire to gain some control and empowerment, for themselves and their group.

Elia Awwad, a Palestinian mental health worker, writes in 1999 that "...Palestinians have been suffering for over 30 years from the loss of personal freedoms, humiliation, physical injuries, detentions, tear gas exposure, beatings, house demolitions, deaths, deportations, family disunions, and other forms of violence."[81] She writes that all the different segments of the Palestinian community have come together and participated in violent resistance in the (first) Intifada, between 1987 and 1992. Before that, there was helplessness and anxiety; the Intifada "had a healing effect as people began to feel empowered through taking action."[82] In a study of 900 Muslims in Gaza who were adolescents during the first Intifada, being exposed to violence was associated more with pride and social cohesion than with depression and antisocial behavior.[83]

The beginning of suicide attacks, the first one by Palestinians in April 1994, appears to have been an evolution from other forms of terrorism and then the Intifada, among the motives a desire for effectiveness in behalf of oneself and one's group, fighting the enemy and revenge. Such feelings are further shaped and developed in activist groups. In Merari's view the crucial elements were the decision by the terrorist group to use suicide, and the preparation by and power of the group over individuals. Suicide attacks increased in number and destructiveness over time. One hundred twenty Israelis were killed between 1994 and September 2000, and hundreds of Israelis in dozens of attacks each year between 2000 and 2005. After that an unofficial cease-fire began.[84]

Post summarizes the "suicide terrorist assembly line" described by Merari as having three key junctions: a volunteer or recruit is identified, usually by friends or relatives in the organization, receives indoctrination, and commits himself to becoming a suicide bomber; he is publicly identified as a "living martyr," which bring prestige to him and his family; and "he is videotaped reading his last will and testament, in which he explains his motivation and his goals...this makes it nearly impossible for him to back out..." without shame and humiliation, since the video is widely disseminated.[85] After that he is carefully supervised, so that he is unlikely to change his mind.

Selection by the group and self-selection must meet. Some individuals approach the group. Others are approached presumably if they seem likely candidates based on relationships, background, inclination, personality and previous engagement in anti-Israeli activities. Even then it is unlikely that everyone agrees to become a member and a suicide bomber. According to Merari, many youths with the kind of experiences I reviewed did not become suicide bombers. Identification with their community, witnessing actions against their group, friendship with members, adult models, childhood experience in the family, the family's history and how it is transmitted, the family's attitude toward Israel, ideology, personality, and orientation to authority can all contribute to self-selection and selection.

Lost (and Damaged) Souls

People often join groups because they feel lost, their needs unfulfilled. Some of the London terrorists, children of immigrants mainly from Pakistan, seem to have been lost souls in spite of having had jobs and seemingly normal lives. Raphael Ezekiel (1995, 2002) interviewed youths belonging to white supremacist groups in the United States, in particular a group in Detroit. Many of them experienced severe losses in childhood, often the loss of a father early in life who left the family and disappeared. They had no redeeming social contact with relatives or other caring adults. They apparently had no deep peer friendships, which can also be a source of resilience and healing. A number of them showed early interest in the Klu Klux Klan, writing to the Klan to ask for literature as early as junior high school. Ezekiel's description of their motivation for membership corresponds to what I see as the fulfillment of basic human needs: for connection, identity, security, and a worldview.

I see these young men as primarily lost souls, but they may also qualify as respondents, people who displace their angry response to their painful past onto vulnerable and accessible targets. The right-wing movements they joined, with their customary racist and anti-Semitic ideology, seemed to make them feel that by elevating white people and "reclaiming" the country for them they were going to right real wrongs that they themselves experienced, and imaginary wrongs that their group has suffered. Ezekiel described them as racist, but without the intense emotion of hate. However, leaders and groups can move people toward more intense hostility, and violence.

While idealists may respond to the conditions of other people and the world, and respondents to what they or their group have experienced, lost souls search for the fulfillment of important personal needs. They may adopt an ideology as they search for personal meaning in their lives, for identity, connection, and escape from loneliness. Many new recruits into the Reverend Moon's Unification Church did not initially believe in—or they even rejected—the ideology, but apparently hungry for personal connection, they moved in with the community because of relationships that group members had established with them. Similarly, Sageman, on the basis of his study of Al-Qaeda members, talks about isolated, lonely, and emotionally alienated young men. Young Muslims going to or living in Europe would experience prejudice and exclusion—and separateness. They find community at mosques, and build friendships, starting with a focus on their faith.

Adam Gadahn (aka Azzam al-Amriki), an American who became a propagandist for Al-Qaeda, speaking to Americans on videos prepared by Al-Qaeda, is an example of a lost soul. Journalist Raffi Khatchadourian[86] describes the likely isolating effects on Gadahn of the lifestyle his family chose. They lived on an isolated farm, surrounded by goats but not people to connect with, without running water and toilets, with his family living in the style of the 1960s counterculture. His attempts at connection are with people far away, with musical interests in "death metal," a somewhat marginal musical movement that is the descendent of heavy metal with a focus on the superficiality of the 1980s. "Gadahn wrote of a yawning emptiness, and he sought ways to fill that void."[87] He searched for connection mainly through telephone calls and CD exchanges with others interested in such music. He finally found the connection he sought by adopting Islam and engaging with a local Islamic Society. There he joined the evening discussion group of men who talked about the Koran and the wars in Bosnia and Chechnya. His evolution was gradual, from connections with others in the group, to moving in with them, moving to Pakistan, and getting increasingly embedded in Al-Qaeda.

The engagement with a certain ideological group may be partly accidental on the part of people I call lost souls, but there are likely to be elements in some young people's psychological makeup, derived from their history, that inclines them toward one group or another. For example, Adam's father had a religious epiphany, which Adam was well aware of, since he described it in an essay he wrote after his conversion to Islam. His rejection of the world around him also followed in his family's footsteps. But his family expressed this in their peaceful lifestyle. Rejecting both what his family rejected as well as his family may have been part of his road to a terrorist organization.

The journey to terrorism of Umar Farouk Abdulmutallab, the 23-year-old Nigerian who attempted to blow up an airplane over Detroit, may have also started as a lost soul.[88] One of sixteen children and one of the youngest of his father's two wives, he was a good, obedient boy, who during his adolescent years became intensely religious. It is unclear what led to this. Later, at a British style boarding school, teachers liked him, but he was called religious names, such as Pope, by fellow students. He wrote on an Islamic Web site: "I have no one to speak too (sic) ... no one to support me, and I feel depressed and lonely." Later, at the University College of London, he became the president of the school's Islamic Society. He organized a war-on-terror week, with speakers denouncing U.S. actions in the Middle East. He attended religious institutes, had training in Arabic in Yemen, and exposed himself to radical Imams, including lectures by Anwar al-Awlaki who has been associated with various terror activities. In 2009 he left graduate school in Dubai and went again to Yemen, at first to study Arabic, but wrote to his family that he found true Islam and won't come back. He apparently made connections to Al-Qaeda and Awlaki, and then went on his unsuccessful suicide mission. His seemed to be a process of self-radicalization, as he became extremely religious and exposed himself to radical/jihadist thinking. Already in 2005 he wrote on a website: "I imagine how the great jihad will take place, how the muslims will win insha Allah and rule the whole world, and establish the greatest empire once again!!!" And one of his classmates in Yemen in 2009 said: "He told me his greatest wish was for *sharia* and Islam to be the rule of law across the world."

For young Muslim men who are either respondents or lost souls, or both, turning to Islam, and Islamic groups, is a natural way to attempt to fulfill their needs. Moroccans in the Netherland, Pakistanis in England, or Algerians in France may respond to their experience in these countries as "others" by turning to the most easily available ideology and group for them, Islam and an Islamic group. So may a young Egyptian like Mohammad Atta, and some of his fellow 9/11 attackers who moved to Europe. People who become terrorists may come to see that the world is not as it should be, in general, or for them at least. They may find hope in an ideological vision, and both community and hope in an ideologically oriented group.

If young Muslim men searching for community or a vision of life go to mosques or study halls and engage with Islamic groups, some of them encounter a version of Islam that is very strict, allows little engagement with the rest of the world, and embodies anti-Western attitudes. In recent times some mosques have advocated violent jihad. Since in Islam the religion and the state and therefore politics are not separate, negative religious and political orientations to outsiders reinforce each other. However, alternative views of Islam have been emerging. Support by Muslim populations for terrorism has declined, especially since Muslims have also been frequent targets.

To reduce the likelihood of Islamic terrorism in the long run requires an emphasis on a peaceful form of Islam that is open to coexistence. It requires constructive ideologies, religious and secular, positive visions of how people can live together, and constructive groups and movements. It requires creating conditions, including economic development, that improve lives and enable Muslims to fulfill basic needs in constructive ways in both Islamic and non-Islamic countries. For all this, external parties need to thoughtfully support, inspire, and work with internal parties.

Hostile-Aggressive Terrorists

We saw in relation to genocide that some people who join perpetrators may be individuals for whom turning against a subgroup of society provides an opportunity to expresses hostile and aggressive inclinations. Some terrorists are also likely to be people like that. Some respondents or lost souls are likely to have developed an inclination for aggression that may be defensive (force is important in defending myself/my group), hostile (the desire to hurt), or dominant (a way of establishing superiority). Aggression for them can be a (destructive) way to satisfy basic needs. While observation suggests that some perpetrators are hostile-aggressive, we need more research to establish the extent that this is the case.

A social climate as a source of terrorism

Turning to violent movements, self-selection—or selection by authorities, leaders of movements—is only partly predictable. Prevention person by person is not practically possible. Even socialization that fosters moral values and caring can lead idealists to turn to violent action to correct injustice. While the mind of the terrorist is important to understand, while positive socialization and influences that prevent the development of "terrorist minds" are important, addressing the conditions that give rise to terrorism is essential. When these conditions exist, creating alternative responses to them, such as constructive visions and constructive internal communities within subgroups, is valuable. But these will not be sufficient in the long run without the availability of constructive avenues by less powerful parties to address grievances.

Under certain conditions a social climate can develop in which terrorist action, from the actors' perspective fighting an enemy, becomes a value and social norm, expressed in ways ranging from religious sermons to the games children play. Post[89] quotes a Friday sermon on June 8, 2001, on the Palestinian Authority Television: "Shame upon he who does not educate his children of Jihad...

blessings upon he who dons a vest of explosives on himself or his children..."
A political/social climate can create social contagion,[90] and according to terrorism
expert Jessica Stern, a tipping point that gives rise to a cult of suicide terror among
the youth. "Once this happens, the role of organization appears less critical: the
bombing takes a momentum of its own.... For example, on the streets of Gaza,
children play a game called shuhada, which includes a mock funeral for a suicide
bomber. Teenage rock groups praise martyrs in their songs."[91] This is an evolution in a whole society. Acts aimed at the enemy, whether soldier or civilian, are
accepted by the society, or more than that, seen as right, even as altruistic action
in behalf of the group. Group members, feeling diminished and powerless, can
give themselves over to this higher cause.

I have suggested early in the book that transcendence of the self is also an
important human psychological need. Elements of this need can arise in the
course of a person's development and emerge fully when other basic needs have
been fulfilled. In contrast, pseudo-transcendence, turning to religion, or giving
oneself over to ideals or causes, can be an escape from the self and from frustrated basic needs. In the case of Palestinian youth and some other terrorists or
people who join destructive movements, in addition to other motives, pseudo-
transcendence can have a significant role. To prevent such escape from the self
requires finding alternative avenues to satisfy needs.

Summary

In summary, many of the influences described in earlier chapters appear to
motivate perpetrators, including attitudes toward and devaluation of the
other, ideology, learning by doing and the evolution of violence, and the
mutual influence of perpetrators on each other. In some settings, such as
Rwanda, respect for, fear of, and obedience to authorities that guide and
order people had a significant role. While people in general are affected by
external conditions and the characteristics of the culture, and the appeal of
ideologies, varied personal characteristics also have a role in self-selection
for entering situations in which people ultimately become perpetrators, or
being selected by authorities for roles in which they are or become
perpetrators. With regard to terrorists, I suggested a classification of them
as idealists, responders, or lost souls. Some may also be guided by pseudo-
transcendence.

Notes

1 Hatzfeld, 2003
2 For example, des Forges, 1999
3 Straus, 2006

4 See also Gourevitch, 2009

5 Hatzfeld, 2003, p. 64

 6 Ibid, p.137

 7 Hatzfeld, p. 110

 8 Ibid, p. 133

 9 Ibid.

10 Ibid, p 166

11 Ibid, p. 167

12 Hilberg, 1961; Staub, 1989

13 Hollander, 2006

14 Hatzfeld, 2003, p. 159

15 Ibid, p. 163

16 Ibid, 240-241

17 Maguen et al., 2009

18 Ibid; on the mental health effects of killing, see also McNair, 2002

19 Mironko, 2004

20 Ibid, p. 184

21 Ibid, p. 198

22 Ibid, p. 198; see also Danzinger, 2004

23 People who have engaged in such terrible actions, without experiences that can help them heal and redeem themselves to some degree, especially as they face others who may judge them severely, may dissociate, or go numb. This can happen even as one deals with terrible events one has not caused. I was involved at age 25 in a tragic accident in which a dear friend drowned in the ocean. I was devastated. Two days later I met his parents, in the company of a number of other people. As I told them what has happened I felt completely numb. I talked in a flat, unemotional voice. I was young, I did not understand it, I was ashamed—I felt something was wrong with me that I had no feelings. But I had intense feelings—just not at that public moment. This was a hugely different situation from that of the killers, but perhaps some killers, even if they felt some regret, went numb in talking to an interviewer, or at other times to people in their former communities including relatives of people they have killed.

24 Ilibagiza & Erwin, 2006, p. 153

25 Ibid, p. 77

26 Panorama, 2004

27 Gettelman, 2007

28 Hatzfeld, 2003

29 Holly E. Hanson, African historian at Mount Holyoke College, personal communication, December 11, 2007

30 Quoted in Hochschild, 2009

31 Ingelaere, Havugimana & Ndushabandi, 2010

32 Human Rights Watch Report, 2007

33 Staub & Rosenthal, 1994

34 See Zimbardo, 2007; Lifton, 1986

35 Staub in press

36 Staub, 1989

37 See, for example, Browning, 1992; Waller, 2007

38 Dodge & Frame, 1982

39 Kohlberg & Candee, 1984

40 Lifton, 1986

41 Haritos- Fatouros, 2003

42 Lifton, 1986

43 Zakaria, 2009, p. 36, 39

44 The following discussion is based on Zimbardo, 2007, and on Staub, 1989, and 2007a

45 Zimbardo, 2007, p. 40

46 In Zimbardo, 1989, "Guard orientation," 1971

47 Carnahan & McFarland, 2007

48 Staub, 1989

49 Carnahan & McFarland, 2007, p. 611

50 Lifton, 1986

51 Zimbardo, 2007

52 Staub & Rosenthal, 1994

53 McCauley, 2004

54 Dutton & Tetreault, 2009

55 Chang, 1998

56 Rhodes, 2002

57 Dutton & Tetrault, 2009, p. 53

58 Raine, 2008

59 see deMause, 2008; Staub, 1979

60 Kelman & Hamilton, 1989, p.7

61 Roy, 2004

62 Sageman, 2008

63 Andrews, 2007

64 Lifton, 1986

65 Haritos-Fatouros, 2003; see also Staub, 1989

66 Girdiharadas, 2007

67 Lifton, 2000

68 Victoroff, 2009b, p. 73

69 Lifton 2000

70 Victoroff, 2009a, p. 397

71 Post, 2007

72 Ibid, p. 22

73 Ibid, p. 18

74 Post, 2007, p. 27

75 Merari, 2010

76 Speckhard & Akhmetova, 2005

77 Sageman, 2004

78 The descriptions in the parentheses of these personality styles are based on the American Psychiatric Association Diagnostic Manual, 1994.

79 Merari, 2010

80 Ariel Merari's e-mail to me on August 23, 2009

81 Awwad, 1999, p. 242

82 Ibid, p. 242

83 Bloom, 2009

84 BBC News, 2007

85 Post, 2007, p.182

86 Khatchadourian, 2007

87 Ibid, p. 56

88 The following material, including the first quote (p.10), comes from Hosenball, Isikoff, & Thomas, 2010, and from www.answers.com/topic/umar-farouk-abdulmutallab , including the other two quotes.

89 Post, 2009, p. 383

90 Bloom, 2009

91 Stern, 2004, p. 53

10

Understanding the Woundedness/ Psychological Transformation of All Parties in Mass Violence

Persistent hostility, discrimination, and violence tend to have powerful psychological impact, which in turn shapes future actions. Violence tends to create psychological wounds in all parties: victims or survivors, perpetrators or harm doers, and witnesses who are passive bystanders. The effects of victimization include the likelihood, under certain conditions, of unnecessary "defensive violence" by victims, as well as revenge and hostile violence. Violence by perpetrators brings about changes in them that can lead to the expansion of violence.[†*]

The Effects of Victimization and Long-Term Conflict

Whether victimization is one sided, one group harming another, or mutual, for many people it is traumatizing. One of its well-known effects is *posttraumatic stress disorder*. One element of this disorder is the avoidance of thoughts about or reminders of painful experiences. Another is intrusive imagery, including nightmares, about these events. A third is hypervigilance—a high level of activation, constant alertness, and easily activated startle responses.[1] Since for most people psychological healing requires engagement with the traumatic experience, avoidance prolongs symptoms and interferes with healing. The traumatic impact of violence can also manifest itself in a wide range of *symptoms*—psychological, somatic and behavioral, and spiritual. Among them are insomnia, problems with appetite, substance abuse, sexual issues, withdrawal, aggression, and other relationship difficulties. *Complex trauma responses* include bodily responses, and emotional problems such as depression and anxiety, as well as

---

† The material in Chapters 10 and 14 has been influenced by the work and ideas of Laurie Anne Pearlman. See References.

dissociation, which is a disconnection between experience and consciousness, or among elements of consciousness. This may mean not remembering painful events.

All of us dissociate sometimes. A common example is when a person becomes so completely absorbed in thought while driving that he or she does not remember getting from one place to another. This normal dissociation is different from dissociation that results from exposure to violence or victimization, which can interfere with everyday functioning. Judith Herman,[2] a trauma specialist, writes about a woman who as a child was repeatedly sexually abused by her father. During these times dissociation protected her psychologically from her painful experience, as she saw herself looking at the scene from the outside, floating above, suspended from the ceiling. Later in life, this person might spontaneously dissociate when stress or anxiety begin to arise.

Trauma and psychological woundedness do not necessarily lead to ineffectiveness. Survivors of mass violence often have quite varied experiences. Some felt they had no control at all over their lives. Other have shown great strength in trying to survive and survived due to their actions, or a combination of their efforts, help by others, and luck.[3] Afterward many showed great determination to rebuild their lives and reestablish their sense of worth. But nonetheless they still suffer, to various extents.

According to Yael Danieli, a trauma specialist who has treated survivors of the Holocaust and engaged with the traumas of many groups, survivors of the Holocaust "created families that tended to exhibit at least four adaptational identity styles: victim families, fighter families, numb families, and families of 'those who made it.'"[4] The last two, in particular, often kept their traumas to themselves, talking little about it. These adaptations were based on the parents' experiences during the Holocaust. While engagement with one's experience is generally believed as important to healing, according to Danieli it is also important to become aware of how one's experiences, both traumatic and in the course of survival, led to a later adaptational style, and how this shaped the life people lived. A fuller understanding of the experiences of victimization can help people lead fuller lives and help stop the transmission of the trauma to later generations.

Not everyone who has normally traumatizing experiences develops symptoms of trauma.[5] But part of the *psychological woundedness* that results from victimization is a changed orientation to self and others.[6] For many people there is a diminished sense of self; feelings of insecurity, danger, and threat; and an overall sense of vulnerability. There is also a negative view of other people, especially of those who caused the harm, but more generally of people outside the group, or of all people. In the case of group violence, members of other groups are seen as dangerous.[7] The consequences may include mistrust, fear, avoidance, hostility and aggression, and seeing the world as unjust.

My interview with a survivor of the genocide in Rwanda demonstrates the devastating effect genocide can have on trust. The survivor's husband had already been taken away and presumably killed when a Hutu man who had worked for her family, who was now going around with the killers, sent someone to her house to protect her. The man he sent arrived with a bible under his arm and stayed in her house until the genocide was stopped. He stayed in his own room, was never hostile to her, and never molested her. A couple of times when a group of men came to the door looking for the woman, he faced them down and persuaded them to leave. When the genocide ended, this man joined the exodus of Hutus leaving Rwanda. He was among many other Hutus who later returned, and he came to visit her. This survivor said to me: "What did he want from me? Why did he come? I knew that if I needed to, I could now ask the authorities to protect me from him."

This interview pointed also to another phenomenon: that some people were both killers and rescuers—in this case, an indirect rescuer, sending someone to help this woman. In another interview I talked both with a survivor and with a member of the family that saved her. For 3 months, they hid her in a hole dug in the ground on their property, bringing her food at night and removing her waste products. However, the head of the household, who had made the decision for the family to help her, was in prison at the time of this interview, accused of killing Tutsi children. In other genocides as well, for example, in Cambodia, there were people who were both killers and saved people.[8]

This shows, presumably, the joint influence of circumstances and personality. Different circumstances can activate different psychological needs, values, and personal goals, giving rise to the motivation by the same person to help or harm. Personal connections may lead to empathy and feelings of responsibility for the welfare of particular individuals, while the many influences we have discussed, including relationship to a violent group, the desire for belonging, and fear of not going along, can lead to violence.

While far from inevitable, victimization, feelings of vulnerability, and seeing the world as dangerous can to lead to the perception of hostility and threat by individuals and groups. As I will later discuss, healing and certain other experiences can lead people who have suffered to become caring and altruistic. But unhealed psychological wounds can, under certain conditions, lead some former victims to become perpetrators.[9] Members of groups that have been victims of violence may feel easily threatened and in a new conflict believe that they need to use force to defend their group, even if this is not the case. Unhealed wounds make it more difficult to take the other's perspective, to consider the other's needs, and to feel empathy for the other. Perceiving a threat, people may engage in what they believe is self-defense—but their "defensive violence" may be unnecessary or more forceful than necessary. Victimization can also generate hostility and anger toward other people and the world. A negative view of people, feeling threatened, hostility, and anger can also give rise to the desire to harm others.

The Persisting Effects of Traumas and Chosen Traumas

Deep injuries in the past often become a strong part of the individual's and group's identity. The group can define itself, see itself and the world, and interpret new events from the perspective of that past history and its meaning to the group. This is partly the result of the intergenerational transmission of trauma, experiences of woundedness handed down through the generations. Trauma is transmitted by the way children are treated, by a combination of what they are told by wounded parents and silence, and the way schools teach history.

It is also a result of the development of a culture of woundedness in which victimization and trauma can become central to the group's history, identity, and orientation to the world. Psychiatrist Vamik Volkan has called this a "chosen trauma." Trauma usually refers to the experience that is created by certain events; a chosen trauma can mean a focus on both suffering and the events that have created it. This is a valuable concept, although in one regard a misleading label, in that groups don't choose the trauma or the process by which they come to focus on it. It normally becomes central in the group's life as a result of a natural evolution. Carrying unhealed wounds, a society interprets new events from the perspective of the difficult past, thus maintaining vulnerability, the experience of danger, the need to defend oneself, or the desire for revenge. But in another regard the label is correct, in that groups can make intentional choices and create processes that help them heal and be less affected by past trauma. Awareness of the consequences of a chosen trauma is an important initial step. Knowledge of how traumas are "chosen" can help in prevention.

Unhealed historical wounds most likely contributed to Serb violence in the former Yugoslavia. The Serbs lost the battle of Kosovo in the fourteenth century. When people point to the Serbs with regard to a chosen trauma, they tend to disregard that after that loss the Serbs were ruled by Turkey for 500 years. They also suffered mass killing during World War II by Croatia, allied with Germany. After the war, during Tito's long rule, communist ideology, and perhaps Tito's Croatian heritage, led to a focus on moving forward, not looking back. Tito did not allow exploration of the past, which might have led to healing. Historian Michael Ignatieff wrote: "What seems apparent in the former Yugoslavia is that the past continued to torment because it is not the past... the past and present are continuous... (Reporters)....when they were told atrocity stories were occasionally uncertain whether these stories had occurred yesterday, or in 1941, or 1841, or 1441"[10] When I was in Belgrade in 1995, I spent time with an old and highly respected professor at the University who was railing against the Muslims in Bosnia because they converted to Islam. This happened centuries ago, under Turkish rule.

Leaders at times appear to use a chosen trauma as a way to manipulate the group to follow them and to accept their leadership and ideology. I say "appear to" because they may themselves react as members of a formerly victimized group that feels threatened by current events. For example, Milosevic incited Serbs using the historical meaning of Kosovo. But it is hard to know from the outside—and perhaps even from the inside—whether he just manipulated, or was himself affected by the country's circumstances, or how the two combined. Milosevic himself had significant traumatic experiences in his life. His father left the family. Both of his parents, as well as an aunt, killed themselves. There were suicides and people killed in his wife's family as well.[11] Personal traumas have similar effects to group traumas and will shape people's behavior as leaders. Personal traumas, group traumas, and wanting to gain supporters together shape leaders' behavior.

Stalin said: "The history of Russia consisted, among other things, in continuous beating due to backwardness. The Mongol Khans beat Russia. The Turkish nobles... The Swedish feudals... The Anglo-French capitalists... The Japanese barons... Everyone beat Russia due to its backwardness..."[12] Was he referring to Russia's past victimization because of his feelings about it, or the feelings he believed Russians had, which he then used to influence Russians? His own personal experience, having been regularly and severely beaten by his father, was also likely to influence his perspective.

Among the persistent effects of past victimization may be the attitudes of young African Americans toward school learning. At the time of slavery, blacks were severely punished for learning to read and write. After the abolition of slavery they were in danger of being lynched if they did well in business, which created competition for whites and challenged whites' beliefs of their superiority over blacks. Business competitors sometimes accused black men of sexual advances toward white women or of criminal activity, which led to their lynching.[13] The lingering effects of this past may shape attitudes toward education and achievement in "white domains." It may combine with poverty, which is associated for both black and white children with less early enrichment, and with still existing bias in schools, to limit African American students' interest in academic learning. Awareness of these connections between past and present may contribute to change—in both African American culture and the larger society.

The events surrounding Hurricane Katrina, the devastation of New Orleans and the region, and the delay in providing help to mostly poor African Americans who could not leave the city before the storm hit have been understandably and probably correctly interpreted by many African Americans in light of a history of prejudice and discrimination. Belief that black Americans have not been encouraged to return to the city and that some have wanted to reshape New Orleans as a white city has been cited as another example of discrimination and prejudice. Thus, past experiences of victimization can sensitize people to correctly perceive new ones, and they can create a bias to perceiving bad treatment or threat that does not exist. Addressing such biases can be challenging, but healing psychological wounds and reconciliation can reduce them, whether in New Orleans or Rwanda.

The Woundedness of Israeli Jews and Palestinians

While the Israeli–Palestinian conflict has material origins, the land, and has evolved into intense psychological conflict as well, the woundedness of Jews and Palestinians has certainly contributed to their difficulties in resolving it. The Jews, refusing to convert to Christianity, experienced centuries of persecution and violence in Europe. Discriminatory practices, such as those that barred them from owning land, and the prohibition against Christians handling money, guided Jews to activities such as commerce and money lending. They were welcomed to such activities, but people owing them money resulted in increased persecution of them. They were also forced to wear different clothing, which became another source of differentiation and persecution.

There was mass killing of Jews at different times, such as the time of the plague for which they became the scapegoats, partly because their hygienic practices led to less disease in their communities. During the Crusades as Christian armies moved through Europe, in pogroms in the Ukraine and Russia, Jews were killed in large numbers. In the end, the Nazi genocide aimed to exterminate all Jews and killed 6 million of them. The resulting woundedness among the Jews had to be reawakened and an intense feeling of endangerment created by Arab hostility and violence, by terror and suicide bombings, and by the often stated intention to eliminate Israel. At a talk as late as 2006, when young Palestinian men in the audience were asked what would happen to Israel if it lost a war, one of them answered with the old threat: "We would drive them into the sea." Although others said they no longer thought that way, this young man did, and many Israelis believe that many Palestinians and Arabs still think so as well.[14*]

The Palestinians also have a long history of suffering. They lived under oppressive occupation, first by Turkey, then Britain. They suffered as a result of the 1948 war, due to violence against them, and as a large number of them left their homes and became refugees. After that, many have lived for more than half a century in refugee camps. They were not admitted into Arab countries; they were used as pawns against Israel by Arab leaders. When the Palestinian Liberation Organization was allowed to settle in Jordan, it attempted to take over the country and was expelled. Its members and other Palestinians settled in Lebanon, continuing attacks against Israel. In response to Israeli retaliation against them and against Lebanon, they were also expelled from there. Palestinians living in the West Bank and Gaza have suffered greatly under Israeli occupation since 1967, as Israel has been responding punitively to terrorist attacks. There has been high unemployment in these territories, poverty, curfews and other restrictions imposed on people.

The past tends to create a lens through which the present is interpreted, shaping feelings and actions, magnifying the impact of new events. For Israeli Jews this lens is many centuries of persecution and killings, and then the Holocaust, brought alive by enmity from Arab and Muslim countries. For Palestinians it is a long history of occupation by various countries, the Nakba (tragedy)—as they call what they see as their expulsion from their homeland in 1948—followed by living under occupation by Israel.

Variations in the Impact of Victimization

While victimization and trauma can have devastating effects on people, a relatively new realm of work on posttraumatic growth has shown that trauma can have positive effects as well: It can strengthen a sense of self, relationships, and world views.[15] Research in this realm is still in its early stages, and the findings complex. For example, post-traumatic distress and growth often occur together.[16]

I and my students have been especially concerned with the phenomenon I named *altruism born of suffering*. When victimized/traumatized persons heal from trauma and have certain other constructive experiences, their pain and suffering can become a source of empathy and caring, and of motivation to help those who have suffered, or to prevent suffering. These constructive experiences include, among others described in Chapter 22, being helped by someone at the time of victimization and/or being able to help oneself or others, as as well as healing and support afterwards.[17] In one small study Holocaust survivors living in Israel were interviewed who either were or were not involved in the peace movement. The two groups differed both in the extent they or members of their families actively engaged in helping themselves, and in receiving help during the Holocaust. A woman involved in the peace movement described how her family moved from place to place and across borders to escape the Nazis, and how German soldiers allowed them to pass into the Soviet occupied part of Poland.[18]

Victimization and violence do not leave the same imprint on all individuals or groups, due to differences in temperament, in the specifics of the nature of persecution or of violence between groups, and differences in experiences before and after it. As a child I survived the Holocaust in Hungary. My mother and aunt got "letters of protection" for us from Raoul Wallenberg, the Swede who courageously helped tens of thousands of Hungarian Jews survive. A Christian woman who worked for my family stayed with us, helped us, and endangered her life to get food for us. My father escaped as his group from a forced labor camp was taken to Germany; he went into hiding and was the only survivor of that group. My family experienced losses under the communist rule that followed. The small business my parents rebuilt after the war was nationalized–taken away from them.

I ended up a politically liberal person. I believe in the use of force by nations only in extreme cases, in just, defensive wars, and for humanitarian reasons.

I have two friends, also survivors of the genocide in Hungary, who are politically conservative. Perhaps they shifted at the end, but overall they supported the Bush administration's policies (e.g., the "preventive war" against Iraq). One of my friends in a conversation asked me for one sentence I would use to summarize the lesson I took away from my experience in the Holocaust. I said, "People can be kind to others even under horrible conditions." His summary was, "The world is dangerous; you must be ready to defend yourself, using whatever means are necessary." When I asked my other friend, he said, "People will do terrible things to other people."

A useful concept is that of *victim beliefs*, "salient beliefs regarding the ingroup's victimization,"[19] which have been studied at the individual and group levels. The findings are consistent with the discussion here, showing, for example, that Israelis believe that the world is against them, and that reminders of past suffering lead people to endorse more aggressive policies toward the other group.[20] The concept of victim beliefs can be expanded to include not only beliefs regarding one group's victimization but also beliefs about human nature (as violent or potentially good), about safety, trust, and intimacy, and in general the possibility of fulfilling basic needs in the relations of individuals and groups.[21] Among Palestinians[22] and certainly also among Israelis, collective memory, a group narrative that is one type of group belief, focuses not only on victimization and suffering but also on heroism, such as Palestinians resisting Israel and Israelis creating and maintaining their state after the Holocaust.

As with individual experience, the specifics of a group's experiences before, during, and after violence against them matter. Leaders and members of groups can make conscious choices and use positive experiences to help the group heal from the past. They can create group experiences and shape institutions that build a constructive orientation to the future.

The Effects of Long-Term Conflict and Violence on Harm Doers

Usually, people harm others they have already devalued. They see them as lazy, unintelligent, or more often as morally deficient or bad and a danger to their own group. As they harm them, they justify their actions by devaluing them more. In the end, they exclude them from the moral realm and even see killing them as moral. In "intractable" violent conflict, this process can be mutual.

Both perpetrators and passive members of a perpetrator group will have less and less empathy for the victims. This reduction in empathy is likely to generalize to others, which is one reason that violence often veers off and is also directed toward new groups. In addition, research in the last decades indicates that engaging in violence is psychologically wounding and traumatizing. This is especially so when the violence is repeated and extreme. As I discussed before, American soldiers who killed in battle,[23] and those who committed atrocities in Vietnam[24] were more psychologically wounded than other soldiers there. But even the force used in maintaining the occupation in the West Bank and Gaza, by Israeli citizen soldiers, will tend to create psychological transformation and woundedness.

Perpetrators who have not been previously inclined to violence, as well as those who have been so inclined will change significantly as they engage in persistent, increasing violence. Although they justify the violence by increasing devaluation and by adhering to a destructive ideology, and receive support from comrades and the group, many perpetrators may feel guilt and shame. Since such emotions are in conflict with their actions and environment, they are kept out of awareness and/or are managed through dissociation, moral exclusion, the reversal of morality in relation to victims, a general lessening of empathy, and changes in identity or self-concept as people come to see themselves as capable of extreme violence—on behalf of a good, higher cause. Over time, as individuals and the group change in the course of the evolution of violence, shame and guilt may disappear. If and when the violence is stopped and perpetrators face the world's adverse reactions, guilt and shame may be reawakened, but paradoxically perhaps, remain still unacknowledged. At least some passive bystanders probably go through a similar process.

That perpetrators of great harm would be psychologically wounded, or feel shame, is difficult for many people to accept because most perpetrators don't show regret or acknowledge their responsibility. Their defenses against the enormity of the evil they have perpetrated are also enormous. One historian who has eloquently written about the survivors of genocide described at a conference I attended how he witnessed the trial of two men, in Germany in the 1960s, who were guards in an extermination camp. They engaged in animated conversation and laughed during the trial. He could not imagine that they were psychologically wounded. But such abnormal reactions and self-presentations, in people who are not mentally ill—as studies of perpetrators have shown—must arise out of defensive psychological processes.

The defensive stance that perpetrators and members of their group tend to adopt after their violence is stopped includes continued devaluation of their victims and justification of their harmful actions. But they also want to reestablish themselves and their group as moral, to be accepted or reincluded in the moral community.[25] They hope and expect this to happen as a result of the passage of time and due to their claims that what they have done was necessary, justified—and the responsibility of superiors. These beliefs and claims are slow to change, especially since they continue to serve a defensive function, against the world and against their own shame and guilt. Believing that what they have done was necessary and right creates resistance to change. It makes psychological recovery, healing, and renewed empathy for other people more difficult.

In our approach to reconciliation, we assume[26] that it is important that perpetrators heal. Healing can help them become aware of and acknowledge their shame and guilt, assume responsibility for their actions, show empathy to the survivors, express regret, and apologize. This can initiate mutual engagement and reconciliation. It can also lead to positive reactions to them from the world, helping them become psychologically, morally, and socially reintegrated, reducing the likelihood of their further violence. The psychology and actions of perpetrators and passive bystanders are to a substantial extent group processes. Therefore, the healing and recovery of victims/survivors and those of perpetrators—and passive bystanders—have to take place at least to a degree as part of group processes.

Receiving acknowledgment, expressions of regret, and empathy is important not only for survivors but also for their descendents. However, members of the perpetrator groups are reluctant in later generations as well to assume responsibility for the groups' actions. On the one hand, they have been usually socialized into a culture that denies responsibility. On the other hand, they want to distance themselves from a shameful past and the responsibility for the actions of past generations. But although they are not responsible as individuals, they are members of their group/society that carries this past culturally, psychologically, and materially.

Denying or not engaging with their group's responsibility to address the past, and withholding an empathic response to the victim group, contribute to the psychological difficulties of survivors, as in the case of Turkey's denial of the genocide of the Armenians. They also maintain the attitudes and beliefs that led to doing harm in the first place and that are often handed down through the generations, thereby contributing to the group's potential for renewed violence. For example, in East Germany, under communist rule, the Nazi past was presented as the responsibility of the leaders, of moneyed interests, not of *the people*. This denial of responsibility and inattention to the roots of violence was a likely contributor to violence in the eastern parts of Germany against foreigners (Turks and others living in Germany) after German reunification.

Later generations often also benefit materially from earlier generation's actions. In the United States, whites have continued to benefit financially and politically from the gains made by their slaveholding ancestors. This adds to their responsibility to engage with the past and its continuing impact.

The Effects on Bystanders

Bystanders are witnesses who are in a position to take positive, helpful action against harm doing. They usually remain passive, and often are complicit, at least in that they continue with business as usual as they participate in the life of the group that perpetrates harm doing. For example, Germans under Nazi rule did what they were told to do, boycotting Jewish stores and terminating relationships with Jews. Bystanders undergo psychological changes similar to but less intense than those experienced by perpetrators. They protect themselves from empathic distress as they see the suffering of victims and from their own internal conflict and distress about their lack of action. This makes it easier for them to avoid the psychological difficulty and danger of being at odds with their group. They distance themselves from victims, increasingly devalue victims, and deny their group's responsibility. Many of them increasingly align themselves with their group. Since passive (or complicit) bystanders are usually the substantial majority of a perpetrator group, for reconciliation to occur it is important that they heal and engage in the processes that lead to reconciliation.

Summary

Intractable conflict and violence have harmful psychological consequences, including changes in the nature of identity and self-concept (both individual and group) of many members of all parties. These changes for members of the victimized group (as well as some members of the perpetrator group) often include the experience of posttraumatic distress and psychological woundedness. Survivors also tend to feel vulnerable and to see other people and groups as threatening and dangerous. This can lead them to engage in unnecessary defensive violence. Harm doers increasingly devalue the scapegoated group or ideological enemy, which can lead to excluding the "other" from the human and moral realm and justifying greater violence. When the violence is stopped, perpetrators usually continue to devalue their victims and defend their actions, in part to defend against guilt, shame, and distress, and to maintain their moral standing in their own eyes and reestablish it in others' eyes. Bystanders change, through their passivity or complicit involvement, in ways similar to actual harm doers. To facilitate reconciliation, it is important for all parties to heal. This can move harm doers and bystanders to assume responsibility and feel and express regret. Victimized group at times focus on past trauma, which becomes a central aspect of their history, identity, and group life and guides perceptions and reactions to events. Group healing, and exploration of the group's culture that increases awareness, can lead to a more constructive orientation to the world.

Notes

1 American Psychiatric Association, 1994
2 Herman, 1992
3 Staub, 2008b.
4 Danieli, 1985, 2009

5 Bonano, 2004

6 Pearlman, 2003

7 Staub, 1998; Staub & Vollhardt, 2008

8 Ben Kiernen, personal communication, May 2009

9 Staub, 1998; Staub & Pearlman, 2006

10 Ignatieff, 1997

11 LeBor, 2004

12 Kiernan, 2007, p. 505

13 Brown, 1965; Ginzburg, 1988

14 In conversation I had in Israel in April and May 2010 many people said, in essence: "they" cannot be trusted, and they don't want peace. Others, committed to peace, were disheartened by this climate.

15 Tedeschi, Park, & Calhoun, 1998

16 Hobfoll et al., 2007

17 Staub, 2005c, Staub & Vollhardt, 2008; see Chapter 14

18 See description of the study in Staub & Vollhardt, 2008

19 Vollhardt, 2009, p. 135

20 For a review, see Vollhardt, 2009

21 See also Janoff-Bulman, 1992; McCann & Pearlman, 1990; Pearlman, 2003; Staub, 2003a

22 Khalili, 2007; Vollhardt, 2009

23 Maguen et al., 2009

24 McNair, 2002

25 See also Nadler & Shnabel, 2008; Nadler, Malloy, & Fisher, 2008

26 Staub, 2006a; Staub & Pearlman, 2006; Staub et al., 2005, 2010

Part II
Prevention and Reconciliation

11

Introduction and Late Prevention

We must aim at early prevention. But when there is already a crisis or actual significant violence, in progressive but speedy steps the involvement of international leaders in working with the parties to address issues, the attention of the world community and warning potential harm doers, sanctions and boycotts, a military presence, and military intervention can all be essential to prevent or halt violence. Offices in governments responsible for prevention can work with the U.N. to coordinate such actions.

Prevention, when it happens, is usually in response to already intense violence against a group. But ideally prevention of group violence will start early, before leaders and the population become committed to a destructive ideology and before there is a significant level of violence. Prevention can start in response to characteristics of a culture and to the emergence of social conditions (difficult life conditions, group conflict) that have the potential to generate violence. It can start later, when the processes that lead to violence, such as scapegoating and a destructive ideology, have begun to appear, or when harmful actions have begun. Early prevention is less costly, materially and in the potential loss of lives. When mass killing or genocide has already begun, usually forceful responses are required to stop it.

Early Prevention and Reconciliation

I strongly argue for the effectiveness of early prevention, although for two reasons this is not easy to demonstrate empirically. First, one cannot be certain that without prevention, group violence would have resulted. Second, the kind of systematic early prevention I will advocate has not been practiced. Indications that it can be effective come by extrapolation from research, from naturally occurring processes in societies that are analogous to what early prevention would look like, from limited interventions of the kind we have done in Rwanda and their evaluation, and from a limited number of relatively early preventive actions by the United Nations, international leaders, and other parties including nongovernmental organizations (NGOs).

The most important actors in early prevention are internal actors. They need to influence ideas, policies, and practices within a society. When there is conflict and violence between segments of a society—tribes, clans, political or ideological groups—other segments of the society can be active bystanders. However, external actors are crucial in providing economic and other kinds of assistance and in generating internal action and supporting internal actors. Although the international community has usually paid little attention when a society has begun to move toward violence, it can and does have a responsibility to notice the signs of this and to serve as an active bystander by addressing the threat of violence in collaboration with internal actors.

The signs indicating danger of violence between groups in a society may be difficult for members of that society to perceive or correctly interpret. How to effectively call it to their attention is a challenging matter.[1] Training of leaders about the origins and prevention of conflict and violence can help. In such training, as we did in Rwanda, examples can be used from other cases, with participants asked to apply what they have learned to their own countries. They can compare the conditions they identify in the country to general patterns. In addition, institutions that people in a country see as disinterested, possibly the United Nations, NGOs, or from a country allied with them, can analyze and identify the presence of violence-generating conditions. By providing their findings in ways that help people draw their own conclusions, they can limit resistance.

After group violence, reconciliation is important to create lasting peace. Most group violence in contemporary times takes place within countries. Whether it ends with the victory of one group or by a peace agreement, the hostility that led to the violence and increased in the course of it does not just disappear. It leads to new violence in a significant percentage of cases.[2] A primary aim of reconciliation is to avoid renewed violence and enable people to work together to build a peaceful society. When there is persistent, strong hostility, discrimination, and perhaps limited violence between groups, reconciliation can prevent greater violence. I am considering prevention and reconciliation together both because of this and because many of the same activities are required for both.

Some definitions of reconciliation include what it is, what leads to it, and what are its consequences. I and my associates at first defined reconciliation simply as mutual acceptance by two groups of each other,[3] which I still consider its essence. We later expanded this definition to encompass "mutual acceptance by hostile groups of each other and the societal structures and processes directly involved in the development and maintenance of such acceptance" and to clarify that "genuine acceptance means trust in and positive attitude toward the other, and sensitivity to and consideration of the other party's needs and interests."[4] Reconciliation also means that in people's minds the past does not define the future. It means that members of previously hostile groups can engage in actions that represent and further create positive coexistence.[5] These definitions and conceptions are consistent with those of others, like psychologists Everett Worthington and Dewitt Drinkard, who define reconciliation between individuals as the "restoration of trust in an interpersonal relationship through mutual trustworthy behaviors."[6]

However, lasting reconciliation between groups can also require political transformation and greater equality in access to power and wealth between previously unequal parties. The processes of reconciliation I will describe, combined with movement toward democracy and equitable relations between parties, can lead to what Nadim Rouhana, a social psychologist and conflict resolution expert, called *mutual legitimacy* that is gained within a new moral and political framework.[7]

Arie Nadler and Nurit Schnabel, Israeli psychologists, differentiate between instrumental and socioemotional reconciliation. Instrumental reconciliation involves building trustworthy relations so that groups can coexist. It can be promoted through "repeated acts of cooperation to achieve common *instrumental goals* (e.g., cleaner environment, better health.)"[8] Contact and joint projects I will later discuss should promote such reconciliation. Socioemotional reconciliation involves the admission of past wrongdoing and subsequent forgiveness. It centers on what Nadler and Schnabel call the apology–forgiveness cycle. In their view instrumental reconciliation changes relationships and comes about progressively, while socioemotional reconciliation changes the participants' identities and is relatively instantaneous and transformational. They suggest that when groups live separately, instrumental reconciliation may be sufficient for peaceful coexistence. When groups live together, socioemotional reconciliation is necessary to create integration.

This is a worthwhile distinction, when seen as relative, a matter of degree. For people who have been victimized, a limited form of instrumental reconciliation is not enough. They need emotional changes, both in relation to themselves and in relation to those who harmed them. Mutual acceptance, which requires changes in emotions, is important to make new violence between groups less likely. Furthermore, all forms of reconciliation and forgiveness after group violence tend to be *progressive.* Even great changes through apology and forgiveness can be temporary, with regression to old feelings and the need for renewed processes to move reconciliation further. In addition, the two types of reconciliation are intertwined. Instrumental reconciliation, as it progresses through contact, cooperation, and other influences, can create profound changes both in people's attitudes toward the other and in their identities, that is, their attitudes toward themselves. Working together in rebuilding lives and society is important for reconciliation. Engaging in activities that help with healing from the past and change attitudes toward the other make such cooperation more possible.

The psychology of individuals and groups, culture and structures all need to be addressed in prevention and reconciliation. Values, beliefs, interpretations of past and present, and attitudes toward members of another group can be psychological *characteristics of individuals*. But when they are widely shared, they are expressions of *cultural characteristics*, or the result of social conditions. Culture includes emotional orientation to others and beliefs about the nature of a shared future. The nature of institutions and established policies and practices are *structural characteristics*. Educational and religious institutions, the justice system and police, the political system, and the financial system are among the central structures of a society. The degree of equality or inequality in education of children belonging to different groups, in access to jobs, in living standards, in the application of justice, and in access to the public arena (e.g., media, participation in politics, positions in government), are all structural elements that have profound effects. Prevention and reconciliation can focus on psychological change or can directly aim at structural change. While each contributes to the other, psychological change may be a prerequisite in motivating people to bring about structural change.

For prevention and reconciliation we must identify the desirable outcomes to be created, such as positive orientation by members of groups toward members of other groups. We must also identify the activities or processes that bring these outcomes about, such as contact, and words and actions that humanize the other. The most difficult part is to actually bring about the activities or processes that can create the outcomes. Many things stand in the way: lack of "political will" by leaders is an important one. Author Samantha Power notes that leaders who take action to halt violence against people in other countries may take great risks in lives and money, without political gain.[9] Political scientist Robert Melson eloquently describes the problem: "A predicted event that fails to materialize is a non-event....politicians who spend lives and treasure to prevent catastrophes such as genocide are likely to be vilified, punished for their efforts: to the extent that their actions succeed ....there is no proof of their success, only the costs of their efforts."[10] However, early prevention requires less "treasure" than late prevention, and it rarely endangers lives.

Political will, often mentioned but not defined, has to be created for either halting violence or bringing about early prevention. I regard it as the willingness to forge ahead even if leaders have to convince the people of the value of their policy and actions, and the willingness to face, deal with, and accept adverse political consequences. Political will is enhanced, or less of it is required, if there is media attention to a problem situation, if citizens show caring about what happens to people in other countries and in that specific situation, and early actions are taken with limited costs. It also helps if awareness is developed in popular and political culture that helping another society in danger of violence can improve that society, even if violence would not have occurred.

The tasks of early prevention are demanding. Researchers/theorists do not always have direct experience with situations in the real world, which limits theory and the development of good practice. Experience in the real world, on the other hand, does not by itself make it possible to understand groups and their relations, which arise out of many complex events and processes. Government officials, diplomats, and other potential actors often lack the knowledge of relevant principles developed through research and theory, and the experience to translate them into practice. These different parties need to work together. But even with knowledge and experience, to see and act on the overall picture is challenging, made more so by the usually insufficient financial and human resources available for these activities.

David Hamburg[11] in his book on prevention focuses on a variety of important structural issues and on who can address them. Two are of special focus: building good governance, which can move a country toward democracy, and equitable socioeconomic development. Other authors, and the Genocide Prevention Task Force Report, also emphasize these. But democracy building and equitable development are hugely demanding, long-term activities. They require readiness on the part of the population and the elite to implement them. Those with power, wealth, and privilege have to shift from protecting their wealth and power and the legitimizing beliefs that support them, and allow and foster access by the rest of society to public discussion, political participation, economic opportunity, and education. Those without power have to learn to constructively engage in economic, social, and political activities. Countries have to move away from autocratic systems, and people have to turn away from destructive leaders. While I will discuss democracy building and the creation of just societies, this book focuses on creating psychological and cultural changes that make these possible.

The challenge may be clearer if we consider a specific realm: creating a system of equal justice. This does not exist even in the United States. How does one get people accustomed to power to allow one of their own to be equally punished for wrongdoing as the weakest in society? Or how can a government allow human rights organizations to research and report on injustice, unlawful or inappropriate discrimination and detention, torture and killing by the government or its agents? Healing from the past, humanizing others, and moderating authority change individuals and make institutional changes such as in the justice system possible. Changes in institutions further change people.

Just as a combination of influences leads to violence, so a combination is required for prevention. I will emphasize core principles and processes, which have to be applied in different combinations to different circumstances. Preventive efforts can address connections between events in different countries, such as Rwanda and the Congo. Addressing the presence and actions of former genocidaires and improving safety for Tutsis in the Congo could have led to greater political openness in Rwanda. Greater pluralism in Rwanda, with more possibility for Hutu voices, might have reduced violence in the Congo.

Late Prevention and Halting Mass Violence

A primary focus in this book is on early prevention. But late prevention is crucial as well, that is, addressing crises when violence is likely to be near or is already occurring to a significant extent. Later discussion will be relevant to this, but here I briefly focus on it. Some approaches to late prevention, listed in Table 11.1, have become international conventions, at least in conception. All too often not much is done in practice. They include warnings to countries and to their leaders, as well as sanctions and boycotts. When mass killing or genocide is in progress, usually military action is essential. But even if there is a significant crisis, but not yet systematic large-scale violence, more ought to be done that is personal, relational, and psychological, beyond material/instrumental actions such as sanctions and boycotts. At such times, some of what needs to be done comes under the heading of preventive diplomacy (see Chapter 13). Effective action at such times requires the participation of high-level leaders.

I have long believed that the involvement of high-level actors could help in many crisis situations. Their prestige and presence is meaningful to local actors and focuses the world's attention on them. In a rare example of this, a crisis was successfully addressed in Kenya in 2008. The claim by the government that it won the national elections, widely believed to be false, led to violence. The president who claimed victory belonged to a long dominant tribe, while his opponent belonged to a less privileged tribe.

Many important actors, including leaders from neighboring states, such as the President of Ghana, then head of the African Union, and the President of Tanzania, got involved. Their efforts were supported by other outside leaders, such as the foreign minister of Britain and the Secretary of State of the United States. Kofi Annan, the former Secretary General of the United Nations, became an intermediary and mediator between the government and the opposition. It also helped that internal parties, such as the Kenyan business community and church leaders, supported the resolution of the conflict through compromise. New organizations arose to press for reconciliation. A government including both sides was formed. This resolved the immediate crisis and brought violence to a halt. It is generally agreed, however, that it has not solved long-term problems, such as the difference between tribes in power, privilege, and access.[12] For lasting peace such issues must be addressed, and reconciliation between the groups must be promoted.

Kenya is a large country, with a more developed business community and civic society than most African countries, and it is seen as important by the international community, hence the motivation to act. But direct involvement and concerted effort by influential outside leaders can work at many places. It should be tried in the Congo, even if the difficulty there is enhanced by the many-sided nature of the conflict and violence and a weak central government. International meetings by the parties involved, along with the General Secretary

Table 11.1 Steps in Late Prevention of Genocide and Violent Conflict: Actions and Actors

General principles

- When a combination of predictive signs indicates significant danger of group violence, (late) prevention should begin, moving in steps of increasing intensity. There is no formula as to when to start; a reasonable judgment about it is more likely if made by officials who not only have knowledge and experience but whose position focuses responsibility on them to initiate preventive action. The longer the wait, the more difficult and costly is prevention.
- The direct involvement of high-level leaders—presidents, prime ministers, foreign ministers, the secretary general of the United Nations, leaders of neighboring countries—is crucial in late prevention. If there is time, leaders, regional organizations, and the United Nations should work together to develop a joint perspective and approach.
- Such leaders and their staff should meet and work with leaders of groups moving toward mass violence, and in group conflict help the parties engage with each other in dialogue, mediation, negotiation, and arbitration. Aspects of early prevention discussed later are relevant to this.
- When appropriate, when there is no ongoing significant violence, international working conferences of some duration should occur with the relevant parties and external bystanders.

Progressive steps

- As predictive signs of probable violence increase in a country, outside leaders should express concern and disapproval about internal policies and practices that move the group toward violence. To avoid creating resistance by autocratic leaders, these should initially be private communications.
- At the same time, help should be offered to address circumstances and issues involved in conflict.
- With an already existing crisis, the activities in this table should be initiated by high-level organizations within governments and the United Nations that are responsible for the prevention of mass violence, and executed by governments and the United Nations, with the assistance of nongovernmental organizations.
- The United Nations and many nations should issue strong expressions of disapproval of actions that promote group violence.
- Targeted sanctions and boycotts, focusing on major business enterprises, and on leaders, freezing their assets and their opportunity to travel, should be initiated.
- An extensive media and Internet campaign should be launched from the outside, aimed at the people and leaders within the country, calling for opposition and a change in direction.
- Peace-keeping missions should be used.
- Military action, including military exercises in neighboring countries, a military force gathered at the border, and if necessary military intervention should be used. A substantial U.N. rapid strike force should be created so that its existence, and especially its presence, can be a deterrent to violence.

of the United Nations and the Presidents and Prime Ministers of countries such as the United States, China, Japan, the European Union, and neighboring African countries, can initiate constructive engagement by warring factions that transforms the crisis. Leaders don't like to expose themselves to possible failure; they want background work to turn such high-level meetings into near certain successes. The meaning of leadership in such situations must be reformulated to define leaders as those who act with political and moral courage. This also requires changes in the media, which often shames leaders for lack of success in interceding in a crisis, rather than celebrating their willingness to try.

A different kind of engagement by external bystanders was successful in Macedonia, which declared independence from the former Yugoslavia in 1991 and managed to avoid involvement in the wars of the Yugoslav republics. But it has a number of ethnic groups, with a large Macedonian majority and a significant Albanian minority. After the violence in Kosovo in 1999, in 2001 there was a rebellion and fighting between the government and Albanians. International engagement brought the fighting to an end.

A significant aspect of this was U.N. peacekeeping. But under the influence of the international community, and perhaps due to some wisdom gained from seeing the consequences of violence surrounding the country, changes in the Macedonian constitution and laws were enacted, giving greater rights to the Albanian minority and more local autonomy. The hope of joining the European Union and NATO was also an important motivator for accommodation.

There was prior engagement by external NGOs in Macedonia that helped prepare the ground at the community level for these actions. Thus, early and late prevention joined. This included a project by the NGO Search for Common Ground. Journalists from the different ethnic groups worked together, interviewing and writing articles about the similar everyday lives, problems, and concerns of members of the different ethnic communities, which they published in each group's newspaper. In addition to the impact of such writing on the population, their shared work could develop relationships between and shape the perspectives of the journalists, in turn affecting their later writings (see Table 23.1 in Chapter 23). Among other active NGOs, one made recommendations for changes in laws to be enacted, many of which were accepted.[13]

The involvement of high-level leaders, including presidents, could have helped in other intense crises, for example, when the former Yugoslavia began to dissolve, violence began, and Serb artillery started to shell Dubrovnik. What might have happened if powerful outsiders, like President Clinton and leaders of neighboring countries, had brought together and met with the parties in Belgrade or a nearby location? In Rwanda, in the year before the genocide, there was an increasing crisis: the civil war, killings of Tutsi civilians, and intense hate propaganda. The French supported the Hutu government without objecting to what it did or allowed to happen in the country. What if President Clinton, and/ or top leaders of other countries, had called President Mitterand of France to discuss the situation and French actions? What if they had gathered some leaders from around the world and the region, accompanied by experts in negotiation and mediation, and engaged with the parties in Rwanda and helped them engage with each other?

Such international engagements would be more likely to happen if high-level government offices responsible for the prevention of mass violence, which I propose later in the book, existed in many countries. With access to heads of states, they would be in a position to initiate such actions. With such offices in different countries working in collaboration, governments that may oppose each other in other matters would be more likely to cooperate in preventing mass violence. If in addition a high-level system of mediation and arbitration was established, it could help the parties, once engaged, to work out practical matters. This is more likely to work, as I will stress, if psychological changes prepare the ground.

The international community also has to be ready for military intervention. Helen Fein noted that neighboring states have seldom intervened "for purely humanitarian reasons against states of genocide."[14] When they responded to mass violence, usually the genocidal states were also aggressors, and their neighbors acted to disable them in order to protect their borders or stop the flow of refugees. She mentions World War II as an example, as well as interventions, none of which were approved by the United Nations, in East Pakistan, Uganda, Cambodia, and Bosnia. She suggests that people at risk usually "have to rely on interested, not disinterested interveners." She notes, however, that "in the last decade of the 20th century more interventions were internationally mandated or approved than in the total of preceding four decades of the United Nations."[15] These included interventions in Liberia, Somalia, East Timor, Sierra Leone, Kosovo, and others.

Perhaps the world is changing, and the habitual tendency for passivity is lessening. Perhaps intervention for moral and humane reasons will become a standard. However, far from what is needed has been done in Darfur, in the Congo, or in civil wars like Sri Lanka. When military intervention is necessary, to limit suffering there should be a standing force that can be rapidly deployed. As Table 11.1 indicates, military action can begin with military exercises in a neighboring country that can intimidate would-be perpetrators or stop both sides in a violent conflict. Sometimes violence may be prevented or halted just by the presence of a military force of substantial size representing the international community. This most likely would have been the case in Rwanda. But often bystanders are still passive, and when there are interventions they usually follow the death of huge numbers of people and great suffering. The focus must be on early prevention. When intervention is needed, how can the international community join in action and who should make decisions about significant sanctions, boycotts, and military actions? The U.N. Security Council has failed repeatedly in this regard, spectacularly in Rwanda—where the genocidal government continued to represent the country and argued that a civil war was taking place and therefore no intervention was needed—in Darfur and other places. The Task Force Report suggests limiting veto power by the council's member countries. Instead, the system of high-level government offices I will suggest can be effective in developing international consensus (see Chapter 18). Involving many countries in working out and agreeing to what is to be done makes execution of an agreement more likely. A coordinating group from these offices, working with the Security Council, can increase the latter's effectiveness in prevention.

Even more than in relation to genocide or violent conflict, much of the practical focus in the prevention of contemporary terrorism has been on late prevention. Often the response is military, including targeted assassination of terrorists,[16] or police response and criminal prosecution. Martha Crenshaw[17] argues that when terrorist groups have substantial popular support, the use of force against them is unlikely, by itself, to stop them. It can even increase their determination, as well as popular sympathy with them. However, at times extremely violent acts by terrorists create aversion by sympathizers, and governments can actively use such acts to create or increase antagonism toward them.[18]

Terrorism arises from many of the same conditions that give rise to other mass violence, although it is conducted by less powerful groups. But in contrast to genocide, there has been less focus on identifying the societal and cultural roots of it. Moreover, since it is not necessarily a societal process in the same way as genocide, and since it can be perpetrated by a small number of people, it is less predictable. For both of these reasons, a focus on the late prevention of terrorism is more understandable than it is in the case of genocide and mass killing.

Still, military and police approaches to the prevention of terrorism are only part of the picture. Halting or preventing terrorism can include negotiating with terrorists; engaging with groups that have significant grievances, such as humiliating treatment, discrimination, economic inequality, and injustice; addressing conditions that are likely to give rise to group violence; allowing and encouraging groups to enter into the political process (either to end their terrorism or to prevent terrorism); engaging with individual terrorists and influencing them to abandon the group; and convincing populations which support terrorism that it will not benefit them. For example, both Venezuela and Colombia allowed violent opposition groups that agreed to stop violence against the government to enter the political process.[19] Early prevention can also address the personal orientations that lead people to terrorism, a long-term goal.

Renewed Invitation to Readers

In the rest of the book I will discuss principles and practices of prevention, with a focus on early prevention and reconciliation. I am repeating the invitation here to you, the readers, to post suggestions on a blog about ways/actions to prevent violence and promote reconciliation between groups. These suggestions can be for general principles/practices or for specific circumstances. You can also invite others to join in some action or to work on building an organization to promote prevention or reconciliation. As noted in Chapter 1, your suggestions will be gathered and studied by graduate students who specialize in the study of mass violence, supervised by faculty members. They will be summarized, integrated, and posted on the blog. I hope that there will be many contributions, making it possible for the students to write articles about them in professional journals. The blog can be accessed at http://overcomingevil.wordpress.com

Notes

1 Lund, 2009
2 Ibid; Long and Brecke, 2003
3 See Staub & Pearlman, 2001
4 Staub & Bar-Tal, 2003, p. 733
5 Staub, 2006a
6 Worthington & Drinkard, 2000, p. 93
7 See also Rouhana, 2010
8 Nadler and Schnabel, 2008, p. 41
9 Power, 2002
10 Melson, 2008
11 Hamburg, 2007
12 Carson, 2008
13 Burg, 1997
14 Fein, 2007, p. 230
15 Ibid, p. 228
16 Victoroff & Kruglanski, 2009
17 Crenshaw, 1996
18 McCauley, 2008
19 Crenshaw, 1996

12

Promoting Understanding, Healing, and Reconciliation in Rwanda

Understanding the roots and impact of violence, (and avenues to prevention), helps survivors, passive bystanders, and presumably also perpetrators to heal, brings about more positive attitudes toward the other group, and creates greater openness in each group toward reconciliation.

I stress in this book the importance, for both prevention and reconciliation, of people understanding the influences—the social conditions, culture, and psychological and social processes—that generate hostility and lead to the evolution of violence. Understanding can increase resistance to these influences. It can lead people to use their own judgment and oppose leaders who instigate hostility. It can lead to the belief that seemingly inexorable processes in a society can be halted and constructively addressed, and it can move people to active bystandership. Understanding the roots of violence may help prevent hostility from turning into violence, and it can lead to actions that mitigate hostility. Understanding the impact of harmful actions and violence is also important, that is, that intense emotional reactions and unusual behavior from victimized people/groups can be normal responses to their victimization. Understanding their vulnerability can create empathy and active bystandership on their behalf.

Understanding the influences leading to group violence can foster a "critical consciousness," the ability to notice instigation by social conditions, leaders, or the media. The practical problem is who will work on creating such understanding and how, especially in countries already engaged in violence, such as the Congo, where any action is dangerous and resources are limited. Radio is the primary media accessible to people in Rwanda, the Congo, and Burundi. Television can be used in more developed countries. Ideally these media will be combined with direct engagement with people.

Understanding is only one aspect of prevention, but it is an important starting point. To resist the destructive impact of difficult social conditions, to turn against destructive ideologies and resist rather than seek destructive leadership, people must have alternatives, constructive responses available to them.

These responses are psychological as well as behavioral. They include a constructive ideology and constructive groups that strengthen identity, feelings of effectiveness, connection, and hope. Ultimately, for the satisfaction of both basic material and psychological needs, social conditions and culture that give rise to violence must also be changed.

When people feel insecure, ineffective in influencing events, and diminished by circumstances, their ability to understand and critically evaluate what happens around and to them can temporarily stop them from destructive responses. But in the longer term, constructive actions are required. The more politicians, leaders, and citizens develop constructive avenues that satisfy basic needs, and change circumstances, and the earlier they do so, the less group violence will evolve.

After genocide or mass killing, seeing the many influences that have led to the perpetrators' actions can begin to help survivors heal and change their orientation to perpetrators and their group. It can also affect perpetrators' and bystanders' perception of themselves. Survivors may realize emotionally what they may struggle with in their minds, that they did not bring about and did not deserve what was done to them. By considering the influences that led to their actions, however horrible, the defenses of perpetrators' and members of the perpetrator group may ease enough to begin to feel and to deal with the shame and guilt associated with their own or their group's actions. Understanding can begin to create openness in each group toward the other and thereby start them on the road to reconciliation.

Our Work in Rwanda: An Overview

A primary aspect of our work in Rwanda has been to promote such understanding—of the roots of violence between groups, the influences that lead to genocide, and of the impact of the genocide on survivors as well as perpetrators and bystanders. We also included information in most of our work about avenues for the prevention of violence and reconciliation. We hoped to generate active bystandership in the service of prevention and reconciliation.[1]

Our work in Rwanda and subsequent work in Burundi and the Congo is an example both of external actors, in this case individuals with appropriate expertise, becoming active in reconciliation and prevention, and of collaboration between external and internal actors. The connections to Rwanda that led to this work began in 1995 when I was invited to a conference on how to rebuild Rwanda after the genocide. I was not able to go, but I invited Charles Murigande, a government minister who was an organizer of the conference, to a later conference I organized in collaboration with "The Friends of Raoul Wallenberg: Beyond Lamentation: Options for Preventing Genocidal Violence," which took place near Stockholm in 1997. By that time, Murigande was the president of the

National University of Rwanda. He subsequently became Rwanda's foreign minister.

He described at the conference the intense problems Rwanda faced in the aftermath of genocide and invited me and Laurie Pearlman to come to Rwanda to help. We applied for a grant, received funding, and went for the first time to Rwanda in January 1999. When we arrived, the horrors of the genocide were ever present. Whether standing, sitting, or walking on the streets, people seemed frozen, their faces unmoving masks. In a country where people were known for not showing their feelings and for talking about personal matters only to close relatives, many Tutsis we met immediately began to tell us how their relatives were killed, how they themselves survived, or where they were refugees before their return to Rwanda. This happened on the first night when walking from one hotel to another on dark and abandoned streets we asked a young man for directions. He told us his story as he walked with us, as did many people subsequently—whether taxi drivers, the staff of NGOs or government ministers.

I am writing this after 17 trips to Rwanda, most of them lasting for 3 to 3-½ weeks. In the course of 11 years many people wanted to work with us. Having limited funds and human resources, especially in the first few years, we could use the paid help of only a few, and the unpaid help of only a few volunteers. An important task for prevention and reconciliation is the creation of organizations and systems that have the capacity to use the energy and expertise of the people who want to help.

Moreover, it is essential that outsiders learn about the culture and develop relationships with and collaborate with local people. They should together decide what is most needed, whether at the community or national level. We spent a day in Boston in 1998 with a group of "cultural consultants," Rwandans and others who knew about the country. When we arrived in Rwanda, we planned to set up a freestanding project of our own. In January 1999, within a day of visiting and having discussions with the staff of a number of local organizations, we realized that doing so would mean that when we left, our work would disappear. At that time we did not know how long we would be working there, and we did not want to do what outsiders in postconflict situations sometimes do. An often used phrase to describe it is that they parachute in and parachute out, with little lasting impact from their presence.

We decided to enlist local organizations that could then carry on this work. We arranged a 1-day meeting with representatives of eight organizations. In the morning we described elements of the training we planned to do in the summer on our return to Rwanda and asked for their reactions. We spent the afternoon with the topic *they* thought would have especially great value: the origins of genocide. This became a central element of our training, with every group we worked with intensely engaged with it.

In collaboration with a local nongovernmental organization (NGO), we set up and then conducted a 2-week training in the summer of 1999 with 35 people from the staff of local organizations that were working with groups in the community. Working at first with this NGO, MUSECORE, and then with the National Unity and Reconciliation Commission, a government agency, in subsequent years we led workshops/seminars with journalists, community leaders, and high-level national leaders. We also trained people to be trainers in the approach we developed, which I will occasionally refer to as the Staub-Pearlman approach. In these workshops we talked about the following:

1. The origins of violence between groups (and soon added avenues to prevention and reconciliation)
2. The psychological impact of mass violence on the people involved, as well as avenues to healing
3. The nature of basic psychological needs; the role of their frustration in giving rise to psychological and social processes that lead to violence and in the psychological woundedness that results from violence; and the role of their constructive satisfaction in healing, reconciliation, and the prevention of new violence
4. Once trust developed among participants, and if there was enough time afterward to help people with the intense feelings that could arise, we also had people in small groups talk about their painful experiences during the genocide. We practiced with the group how they can provide empathic support to each other.

In these seminars/workshops, with both Tutsi and Hutu participants, we gave lectures on the first two topics, and sometimes also on the third topic, basic psychological needs. In examining origins, we used examples from genocides in other countries. This was a significant component of the training: Learning that similar violence had taken place elsewhere, that other people had similar fates, had special meaning to participants. We described pregenocide difficult life conditions, devaluation, and other cultural characteristics in Germany, Cambodia, Turkey, and other settings. The lectures were followed by extensive question-and-answer sessions and discussion. Rather than offering our own application of our conception of the origins of group violence, we always asked the participants to apply it to the genocide in Rwanda, based on their knowledge of their country and their personal experience.

The relationship of the concepts and examples to the participants' recent experience always led to their intense engagement with the material, with us, and with each other. In our large group, and then working in smaller groups that reported back to the large group, they discussed the origins of genocide, and in later workshops also prevention and reconciliation. For example, a small group might discuss creating a shared history in their society and report their ideas to the large group for general discussion. Our intention was to promote knowledge of what contributes to mass violence, and as an essential form of knowledge, an understanding of relationships between causes and effects, such as between difficult life conditions, the frustration of basic needs, and scapegoating and the creation of destructive ideologies, or between a history devaluation and the selection of a particular group as a scapegoat and ideological enemy.

I have found in a number of instances that providing information that people could apply to and confirm by their own experience had highly significant effects. For example, information about the characteristics of snakes (i.e., they flick their tongues to breathe, not in preparation to attack) enabled people extremely afraid of snakes to overcome this fear faster.[2] Information about the value of delaying gratification led children to wait for larger rewards rather than taking immediately available smaller rewards.[3] Information about the properties of electric shocks reduced both physiological reactions to and the experience of pain in response to mild electric shocks.[4] Information provided on television has changed beliefs and behaviour.[5] As participants in our workshops integrated information, concepts, and examples with their personal experience, with what happened to them, they seemed to gain an *experiential understanding*, a deeper from of knowledge, of the origins and impact of violence.

We conducted both formal and informal research to evaluate the impact of our first, 2-week-long training. In less formal research, we gathered information about its impact on the people we trained. Victims of violence, even if they know they are innocent, tend to feel that the violence must have happened because something is wrong with them. How could such horrible things happen otherwise? One effect of the training was to improve Tutsi survivors' image of and feelings about themselves. They said things like: "If this is a human process, if this has happened at other places, to other people, then it was not because God chose us for punishment." It also created feelings of effectiveness, of the possibility of prevention. Participants said that if we can understand how this happens, we can take action to prevent it. They seemed to feel reincluded in the realm of humanity and empowered to act to prevent new violence. It was partly their comments that led us in later training sessions to include more information about principles of and avenues to prevention and reconciliation.

The formal research we did to evaluate the training's impact was with people once removed, with members of mixed Hutu and Tutsi community groups we set up for this purpose.[6] One set of community groups was led by facilitators we trained, who integrated our approach and their own traditional approach in leading groups (*integrated groups*). This integration was part of our training. Another set of groups was led by facilitators from the same organizations but whom we did not train (*traditional groups*). They met for 2 hours, twice a week, for 2 months. Members of a third set of groups received no training (*control groups*) but were evaluated as the other groups at the times just before, immediately after, and on a "delayed posttest" 2 months after the training.

The groups that facilitators worked with were spread out over the country and had varied goals and activities. Some of them were agricultural groups.

Their members got together to talk about and organize their shared work in the fields. Other groups worked on healing from the effects of the genocide. Some of the groups had a religious orientation. In religious healing groups, the facilitators used passages from the Bible. Other groups were secular. All three of the conditions in our study, integrated, traditional, and control, had the same types and numbers of subgroups in them. Their activities and goals were similar to those the facilitators normally led as part of the organizations they belonged to. They included elements of our approach in these different contexts.

In groups led by facilitators we trained, on the delayed posttest there was significant reduction in trauma symptoms. There was a more positive orientation by Tutsis and Hutus to each other and a more complex understanding of the roots of violence. Both Tutsis and Hutus in the integrated group agreed more with statements that not all Hutus were perpetrators, that some Hutus saved lives, that it was "too dangerous for most Hutus to help Tutsis during the genocide," that "members of both groups are human beings, like everyone else," and that the genocide had complex origins.[7] These differences were both in comparison from before the training to the delayed posttest 2 months after the training, and in comparison to changes in members of the traditional and control groups.

Before we first went to Rwanda, we were told and read in reports that people there did not want to hear the word *reconciliation*. Right after the genocide in 1994, Westerners came and tried to get the groups to reconcile. Since people were not nearly ready, this experience created hostility to the concept. But by the time we arrived there, both the government and the people were talking about reconciliation. During the 1-day meeting in January 1999 I described earlier, as I walked into the lunch room, a woman standing there alone said to me, without preamble: "I could begin to forgive them if they acknowledged what they did." However, we did not assume that many people could have actually forgiven, and in evaluating the effects of our training we asked about what we regarded as "conditional forgiveness." Members of groups led by facilitators we trained agreed more with statements such as "I could begin to forgive members of the other group if they requested forgiveness of my group" and "I can forgive members of the other group who acknowledge the harm their group did."[8] The inspiration for our test included past research on forgiveness, the circumstances in Rwanda, as well as what Rwandans said to us.

In dialogue groups that are customary in conflict resolution and peace making between hostile parties, members of the opposing groups usually engage with their shared past, including the injuries they suffered at each other's hands. Intense emotions arise that can inhibit progress. Facilitators have tried to defuse these emotions in varied ways, by having members of the two groups first meet separately, communicating through intermediaries, third parties, or by having them meet in a peaceful natural setting. The approach we used, with a focus on knowledge and understanding, providing information about and participants engaging in discussion of the roots and impact of the violence participants experienced, or witnessed as bystanders (and if there had been perpetrators in our group presumably also violence they had perpetrated), helps limit the intensity of emotions. Such a process is likely to be a useful precursor to dialogue in conflict resolution.

It was in response to the positive effects of our first training that we expanded our project and conducted separate seminars/workshops with journalists, community leaders, and national leaders (government ministers, heads of national commissions, advisors to the president, members of parliament), using the Staub-Pearlman approach. Repeatedly, and especially in working with national leaders in 2001,[9] we were encouraged to expand the reach of our approach to the larger community. The leaders' group was concerned both about reconciliation and about the psychological impact of the *gacaca*, the community justice program. It was about to begin, at first in a number of pilot communities, and then all around the country. The whole population was going to be involved, exposed to testimonies about what people, including their neighbors, did during the genocide, as all around the country popularly elected judges were going to try perpetrators in weekly meetings in front of their local communities. The leaders' group thought that our approach, in addition to promoting healing and reconciliation, could modulate the retraumatizing and other potentially negative effects of the *gacaca*.

To reach the larger community, we invited a television and film producer based in Amsterdam, George Weiss, to join us in developing educational radio programs in Rwanda. He created an NGO, LaBenevolencija Humanitarian Tools Foundation, for producing them. Together we developed radio programs to promote understanding the roots of violence, as well as prevention, healing, and reconciliation, based on our prior research and theory and the Staub-Pearlman approach we developed in our work in Rwanda.

Our first program, a radio drama about two villages in conflict, began twice weekly broadcasts in May 2004 and has become extremely popular. An early survey in 2005 of listening habits involving all radio programs showed that 89% of the women and 92% of Rwandan men listened to it, a significant majority of them listening regularly. Since then the popularity of the program has increased. When Radio LaBenevolencija conducted public events, 6000 people came to one, 10,000 to another. As of 2010, the radio drama is expected to continue. I will describe it and the research evaluating its effects on listeners in Chapter 16.

In the fall of 2004, we also began monthly informational programs about the origins and prevention of violence, healing and reconciliation, and later added other programs. In 2005 LaBenevolencija began to broadcast the radio drama in Burundi, which has the same language as Rwanda and a history of intense violence between Hutus and Tutsis. In 2006 it started new radio dramas and other programs both in Burundi and in the Congo, applying our approach to the situation in that country. By 2007 the staff of this public education project was around 100 people. About 90 of them, including the writers, journalists, actors, and support staff, are local to the countries where the programs are produced and broadcast. The rest are Westerners—an executive team, producers, and an academic team. The latter is responsible for training the staff in the approach, collaborating on the development of the storyline, and editing and suggesting revisions in the weekly episodes and in the informational programs to make sure that the educational material is properly represented.[10]*

The core group that initiated the programs wrote the original storyline for the radio drama in Rwanda. After the first few years, further stories of the varied radio dramas have been developed in storyline workshops, including producers, members of the executive and academic teams, the writers, and "stakeholders," members of the local community as well as government officials. Sometime around 2008 this group also began to discuss what educational messages are important at the time, depending on what is happening in the country. However, the staff of the project decides on and develops the educational content. As a next step weekly episodes with educational content are written by the writers, overseen by producers, in the language of each country. They are translated into English for editing. The producers discuss proposed changes with the writers and then the final version of the program is prepared in the local language.

Summary

In training/workshops with varied groups in Rwanda, we have promoted understanding of the origins and impact of mass violence, as well as avenues to healing and reconciliation (which subsequent chapters describe). The evaluation of this work showed positive effects. As participants in our workshops applied the approach and concepts to their own experience, they seemed to gain experiential understanding, which may be a significant first step toward reconciliation—to openness to the "other," resistance to negative influences, and active bystandership. We then used our approach in educational radio programs in Rwanda, then in Burundi and the Congo.

Notes

1 See Staub, 2006a, 2008a; Staub & Pearlman, 2001, 2006, 2009; Staub et al., 2010; Staub, Pearlman, Weiss & van Hoek, in press

2 Staub, 1968

3 Staub, 1972

4 Staub & Kellett, 1972

5 Ball-Rokeach, Rokeach, & Grube, 1984; Bandura, 2006

6 Staub et al., 2005

7 Ibid, p. 316
8 Ibid, p. 316
9 Staub & Pearlman, 2006

10 The editing and training of staff was done in the first 3 years by me and Laurie Pearlman. After that increasingly a number of associates became involved, especially in editing, but also in staff training: Rezarta Bilali and Johanna Vollhardt since late 2005, Terri Haven in 2006, and Adin Thayer since 2007.

13

Constructive Responses to Difficult Life Conditions and Conflict, Preventive Diplomacy, and Dialogue

---

Dialogue between groups in a society (leaders as well as members of communities) can engage feelings and develop trust, address real problems and group differences, and create a shared vision for the future that makes violence less likely.

High level international leaders engaging with groups in conflict, especially at a time of crisis or the beginning of violence, can foster dialogue, negotiation, and inhibit or stop violence.

Early prevention ideally addresses life problems as they arise in a society and helps satisfy in constructive ways the basic psychological needs that these problems frustrate. This makes scapegoating and turning to destructive ideologies less likely. Group members and leaders have to identify the existing problems and work together to resolve them. This requires public discourse, dialogue, and inspirational leadership, which may be an outcome of public discourse. A constructive, inclusive ideology can provide hope and the belief that effective action can be taken. In the case of group conflict as well, early prevention requires addressing both psychological and "real" or material issues.

When a society is in extreme chaos, when it is becoming or has become a "failed state," it may not be able to address problems on its own. Similarly when there is conflict between groups due to great differences in power and wealth, the groups may be unable to resolve their problems. Help by external parties can be crucial to foster engagement and dialogue and the willingness by the powerful to lighten repression or promote enlightened economic, social, and educational policies. Interventions that promote positive attitudes and address material issues can support each other. In Northern Ireland, an important element in the resolution of centuries-old conflict was the improvement of the material situation of Catholics, such as living standards and schooling for the children.[1] Positive British policies, under "home rule," that is, rule by the British government, and financial aid by international institutions contributed to this improvement.

Franklin Roosevelt's action and policies during the Great Depression are an example of constructive response to difficult life conditions. Roosevelt took bad mortgages off banks' balance sheets, helping both home owners and banks, and making it possible for farmers to avoid foreclosure. In response to 26% unemployment and 75% decline in the stock market, his administration created extensive public job programs. Not only did these provide livelihood and thereby financial security, but they also strengthened people's identity, feelings of effectiveness, and experience of community. It took time and the beginning of World War II for the economy to work well again, but there were both economic benefits and substantial social benefits from these actions.

Poor countries cannot put a great deal of money into stimulating their economy by work programs. They need the help of the international community to respond early and effectively to serious economic problems. But even in poor countries, leaders can create a sense of community. Roosevelt provided a constructive vision, inspiring people to realize that they needed to face the difficulties together, as a community. His inspirational talks and policies drew the country together to attend to the needs of the varied segments of society affected by the Depression.[2] This was not an easy task. It has become no easier in subsequent years. For example, as the United States struggled to climb out of the economic crisis that began in 2007, a writer for the *New York Times* reported that on his blog, "readers have reacted angrily to my suggestion that we find ways to keep people from being evicted from their homes. 'It is not fair,' some wrote, since these people's mortgage problems were caused by their greed."[3] But many people may simply not have realized they could not afford the house they bought, especially in the face of seemingly generous offers by lenders. Whatever the reasons for the mortgage crisis, its victims still need help, both materially and psychologically by the support of their community.

In our educational radio drama in Rwanda called *Musekeweya* (meaning "new dawn"), a material cause of conflict, hostility, and violence between two villages is the result of authorities having given a fertile valley between them to one of the villages. When a draught strikes, this village has enough food, while the other is near starvation. The drama addresses devaluation, people following a bad leader, passive and active bystandership, and other issues. It also addresses how psychological changes are often necessary to enable people to work out and come to agreements about material issues. But both in public education and in the real world, stable improvement in the relations between groups ultimately requires the just resolution of conflict, in this case rights to the fertile valley.

Preventive Diplomacy and Negotiation

Constructive early responses to conflict include preventive diplomacy, such as mediation, dialogue, and negotiation that aim to address both material and psychological issues. The tools of preventive diplomacy are still broadly relevant but have a different meaning when there is no actual conflict, but where one party persecutes another, as in the case of the Holocaust, or in countries where the communists assumed power. In Cambodia the Khmer Rouge's ideological vision identified many kinds of people as enemies. Those who were educated were regarded as incapable of contributing to or living in the society the Khmer Rouge wanted to build. People who wore eyeglasses were targeted, since presumably they ruined their eyes by reading too much. Resolving the "conflict" in such cases requires change in the ideological vision and humanizing the other.

Conflict prevention/resolution and preventive diplomacy will be most effective if they can bring about "integrative solutions" that address both parties' interests. In the Israeli–Palestinian conflict, Israel wants a secure existence, while the Palestinians initially wanted to regain the land they considered their own. Over time there has been a shift. Many Palestinians accept Israel's existence, but they want their own state; many Israelis accept the Palestinians' right to have a state. But divergent interests remain, including the borders between the two countries, the rights to Jerusalem, the Israeli settlements on Palestinian land, and the return of Palestinian refugees. And many Palestinians still do not accept Israel's existence, and many Israelis still want a greater Israel that includes territories Palestinians live on. The ability to compromise and reach integrative solutions is facilitated by changes in emotional orientations and attitudes toward the other, and changes in ideologies.

Quiet diplomacy is important. Dialogue that takes place outside the public view limits the danger of either party losing face.[4] This is important for all leaders, perhaps especially autocratic leaders who have set themselves up as infallible. Private dialogue limits the danger of posturing and of the parties managing their image by hardening their positions. It makes it less likely that pressure is exerted on parties, such as angry reactions by members of their own group, which limits leaders' ability to negotiate. Leaders can endanger themselves and the success of any agreement if they greatly diverge from the perspective of their group. Prime Minister Netanyahu agreeing to even a limited halt to building settlements has evoked angry reactions among his supporters. As leaders move forward, it is essential for them to inform, educate, and help their group move along with them toward an acceptable solution.

Negotiation between parties can be advanced by "good offices," facilitation, and mediation. Good offices refer to influential outsiders engaging with a problem situation and working with the two sides, as in Kenya. Often this is in response to a crisis, but in the spirit of early prevention, it should often happen before a crisis develops. Influential outsiders can help the parties come together, and they or others can proceed to facilitate dialogue, negotiation, and act as moderators or mediators. The success of such efforts is enhanced if there is already ongoing early prevention, as there was in Macedonia.

When groups come together for dialogue and negotiation, they must first decide who is going to represent each side. Arriving at this decision can be problematic. Often there is conflict (and violence) *within* each side—less so on the side of an existing government, more among rebel or opposition groups—about who is going to represent it. Moreover, often each party attempts to influence who will represent the other, since that affects what substantive agreements can be reached. However, pressing for a certain negotiation party from the other side can compromise that party in the eyes of its group.[5] The mistrust and suspicion that each side in a conflict develops toward the other can make the resolution of conflict more difficult. Using real compromise proposals that Israeli and Palestinian negotiators have presented to each other, Ifat Maoz and her associates[6] assessed how Israeli Jews and Israeli Arabs responded to these proposals when they believed they came from their side or the other side. Each group saw the proposals as less fair, less effective, and less beneficial to its own side and more favorable to the other side when presented as coming from the other side. This tendency was stronger for Israelis who had a hawkish attitude and weaker for those with a dovish attitude.

Perhaps as problematic for the resolution of conflict is that the same tendency was present, Israelis seeing the proposals as more beneficial to the other side, when they were described as coming from a more peace-oriented Israeli government, the Rabin government. People not involved in the conflict showed only a very slight tendency to believe that the proposals were more beneficial for the party that presented them. Our work in Rwanda showing the value of understanding the influences that lead to violence suggests that education about the "cognitive biases" that people in conflict demonstrate, which distort their perceptions of the other (and of themselves, seeing themselves in a more beneficial light than warranted), may make negotiations more productive.

When chaos and violence are widespread, as in the Congo, creating security is an important step in resolving conflict. In the fall of 2008 as renewed violence raged in the Congo, with people dying and hundreds of thousands of new refugees, the Security Council engaged in lengthy discussions before expanding the peacekeeping force by 3000. But after so much violence, achieving security requires effective peacekeepers, a force that is not only present but will fight.

High-level, sustained diplomatic effort by influential third parties is worthwhile even under such conditions. To be successful it would have to go deeper than previous attempts at negotiation in the Congo. It would have to be sensitive to the impact of past history and the grievances of all parties. It would have to address the continued presence of and violence by former genocidaires, the hostile attitude toward Tutsis and Rwanda, the need for both Rwanda and the Congo to assume their share of responsibility, the lack of a political role of Hutus in Rwanda, and issues in the Congo ranging from land ownership and the distribution of power to ethnic attitudes and relations, woundedness, and identity.

Good offices, dialogue, and negotiations would have to be persistent, addressing material, political, as well as psychological issues.

Fast responses to crisis, as in Kenya, not only limit human suffering and the cost of rebuilding but may find the parties more open and willing to engage. Conventional wisdom is that later, especially after significant violence, parties are less willing to stop the conflict. They will do so only after much suffering and loss, when they reach a "hurting stalemate." Realizing that they cannot win is assumed to lead to "ripeness,"[7] a readiness for serious attempts to resolve the conflict. While this may be a result of natural progression, ripeness can be helped along. For example, in South Africa both sides, the African National Congress (ANC) and the government, came to realize they could not defeat the other without destroying the country—a condition of ripeness. Leading to this realization by the ANC was its awareness that the government was militarily strong. Internal actions by black South Africans were joined by boycotts, sanctions, and a searchlight directed at South Africa by the international community. This motivated white internal actors, such as the business community, to want a resolution with the ANC, contributing to ripeness on the government side.

Creating systems that routinely respond to the danger of violence avoids slow, cumbersome decision making at times of emergency that are often hostage to the vagaries of interests and inclinations of bystander nations. An example of one such system is the Organization of American States (OAS), which adopted a procedure requiring an automatic diplomatic response by its Secretary General and Permanent Council when there is a threat to democracy in one of the member states. This has led to diplomatic missions to mediate between the government and the opposition in Venezuela. The OAS also adopted a resolution to suspend member states if their democratically elected government is overthrown by force. It created special agencies to promote dialogue, oversee elections, and support democratic institutions.[8]

I will later describe problem-solving workshops and the training of leaders. I already mentioned "coercive" diplomatic approaches—threats of economic sanctions, and the use of force. Threats are more effective early, before violence, and when there is follow through, making threats credible. Threats against the Serbs in Bosnia did not work; only the actual use of force did.

Democracy, Development, and Creating Constructive Systems/Structures

Constitutional arrangements in multiethnic societies have been an important focus, as they shape how power is divided between groups.[9] On the basis of past history, it is assumed that there is no one arrangement that works. Arrangements that are not responsive to local conditions can destabilize the system and enhance conflict.[10] A straight majority rule has worked in South Africa but not in Northern Ireland. Power sharing is an approach that is often advocated. It attempts to represent each group in the power structure through its elites, and it ideally provides each with reasonable autonomy and with veto power over matters important to it. In contrast to divisions this approach maintains between groups, and separate identities, the pluralist approach promotes crosscutting relations, identities of groups not based on ethnicity but on shared interests.[11]

Many in the field of prevention consider democratization, and development practices that benefit all segments of society, essential. David Hamburg appropriately advocates "building effective systems that can help troubled or divided society move toward peaceful, mutually satisfactory ways of resolving conflicts and fostering democratic socioeconomic development."[12] Many conflict prevention efforts focus on changing structures, institutions, and/or their operations. They often focus on the level of the state and elites, government agencies, and the police, security, and justice systems. But changing local structures is also essential. In the Congo and many other places laws are needed that address conflicts over property rights. Land reform that redistributes land in a just manner and compensates those who lose land in the process is a component of peace making. So is a justice system that brings an end to impunity, to killing and raping without consequence.[13] In European countries, police that includes members of minority groups and is connected to the community rather than seen as hostile to it can reduce anger by and the "radicalization" of young Muslims. The 2005 riots in France started with a confrontation of young men with the police.[14] It was probably one of many, since it is usually a history of grievances against authorities and specifically the police that lead to riots in response to a specific incident.[15]

Such policies and institutions would decrease violence and begin to build trust in society. Outsiders can help generate them by engaging with and supporting moderate, constructive leaders within a troubled society. But this must be done with care so that these leaders are not undermined or endangered due to their positive views or relations to outsiders. Moreover, while the international community usually focuses on leaders, developing constitutions and furthering elections, for elections to be productive they require preparation in attitudes and civic institutions, addressing local grievances and unfulfilled needs. Otherwise people tend to disrupt movement toward democracy.

There are many local factors that have to be addressed in building real democracy and peace: land disputes, grievances against authorities, enduring hostilities between individuals and groups, jealousies, competition and power struggles, and corruption. They are activated at times of difficult life conditions and group conflicts, as they were in Rwanda and the Congo. In addition to being able to express and work to resolve grievances, local parties should be helped to "create enterprises, health centers, markets, schools in whose success all parties have a stake."[16] These are institutions of a civic society and their creation the opportunity for significant contact between groups, with "super-ordinate goals."

As a positive initiative with local focus in Rwanda, local officials have been appointed around the country to offer conflict mediation. If Hutus and Tutsis will go to them to help resolve everyday conflicts, this will improve intergroup relations. As part of our projects, LaBenevolencija has initiated a similar practice, which I will describe.

Economic development that improves the welfare of everyone reduces feelings of injustice and grievance. One reason for Islamic terrorism may be the lack of economic, as well as scientific and cultural development in Arab countries, as shown in the Arab Human Development report released by the United Nations in 2009. The report shows very little economic growth since 1980 and high unemployment compared to the rest of the world. Books from other languages, for example, English, are not translated into Arabic. Freedom is limited, women are not empowered, and there is little scientific research.

However, there has been improvement in life and in particular in economic conditions in the West Bank, with increased investment and trade. Twelve hundred new companies registered in 2008, almost 900 in the first 6 months of 2009. There seem to be two primary reasons for this. One of them is improved security, a result of the creation and training of four battalions of a new Palestinian National Security Force. They decrease lawlessness and increase order in Palestinian cities. They were trained in Jordan in a program initiated by Palestinian leaders and paid for by the United States. There is now less involvement by Israeli forces (and Palestinian gangs) in maintaining order, and by mid 2009 Israel eliminated two-thirds of the approximately 41 checkpoints around the West Bank.[17] Another apparent reason for the economic improvement in the West Bank is the leadership of the Prime Minister, a former International Monetary Fund economist and former finance minister, famous "for his incorruptibility" who says "he wants a government based on 'legitimacy by achievement.'"[18] The prime minister has also been building state institutions in expectation of a Palestinian state.

These developments make a potential Palestinian state more viable. They affirm the importance of both security and leadership in addressing conflict. In the Congo, effective and disciplined—in contrast to ineffective, undisciplined, and lawless—military and police could provide the basis for peaceful development. To create them requires outside leaders to engage and work with the leaders of states in need of such changes, and for their countries to provide appropriate assistance.

Another tool of prevention is the development of standards of conduct for states to abide by human rights conventions and international laws, and institutions and inducements/rewards to create compliance. A significant inducement for Eastern European countries for good behavior after the collapse of the Soviet Union was the possibility of joining the European Union. Regulating commerce in valuable natural resources, which are now bought by many companies however unlawfully they were obtained, would help reduce conflict in the

Congo and other places. In 2010 U.S. Senator Brownback added a provision to the financial regulation bill that requires publicly traded companies in their annual report to the Securities and Exchange Commission to indicate whether certain materials came from the Congo or neighboring countries, and if they did, "what steps the company took to ensure that the purchase of these minerals did not benefit armed groups in Africa."[19] An arms embargo in many places, and decreasing arms sales in general, would also help in prevention. Worldwide sales in arms were at about $1300 billion in 2008, and estimated to be $1500 billion in 2009. Punishing wrongdoers in international courts would be important.

David Hamburg sees as crucial the role of established democracies in preventing violent conflict. They can offer steady contact between opposing groups from the time problems emerge between them, contact that reflects "serious concern, sympathetic interest, empathy for suffering, respect for human potential, a vision of better opportunities, and the prospect of belonging in a valued group (such as the European Union)."[20] This is an ideal yet to be realized in practice. However, a number of European countries have been intensely involved in helping to resolve conflict around the world, with Sweden and Norway (e.g., the Oslo agreements between Israel and Palestinians) in the forefront of such efforts.

Engagement and Dialogue

A recurrent theme in this chapter is that dialogue is an essential tool of prevention. In the course of dialogue, the parties can come to understand and respect each other's needs. They can address the pain, mistrust, resentment, anger, and fear—and the belief in the rightness of one's own group and the wrongness of the other—that usually powerfully characterize the attitude of hostile groups toward each other. They can build relationships and trust, which make it possible for people to compromise, resolve practical problems, and address grievances.

While dialogue has great value, it does not simply and speedily resolve issues. There has to be persistent engagement, both at the level of the population and among leaders. It takes time before enough comfort and familiarity develop that trust is generated. It also matters what the dialogue is about. Engagement between parties can be a butting of heads, stuck in grooves. To be effective dialogue has to address feelings—of woundedness, hurt, pain, anger and hostility But talking about who did what to whom also does not work. It can lead to mutual accusations and angry feelings.

The kind of understanding of the origins and impact of hostility and violence that our work in Rwanda has promoted can be a good preparation for dialogue. As understanding develops, it can help Hutus and Tutsis to see the humanity of the other. In the course of discussing ideas about what leads to violence, how it affects people, and how it may be prevented, they develop some comfort with each other, become more open to each other, and become better prepared to address their own past and future.

Alastair Cooke, a former member of British Intelligence and then the head of Conflicts Forum that engages primarily with conflicts between Islam and the West, described an occasion in which the British put two opposing factions in Northern Ireland into a room to talk to each other. Instead of creating openness, talking reinforced their anger. The negotiators then asked each side to write down their history and vision for the future. It took them a long time after this to acknowledge the legitimacy of the other's history. Cooke reports that George Mitchell once told him, "You don't have a political process until you accept that the other side has a legitimate point of view."[21]

Such acceptance is the outcome of psychological changes in both groups, which are helped along by persistent engagement, effective preparation, and guidance by third parties. Dialogue can fulfill the need to be heard and to have one's suffering acknowledged. As the attitude toward the other changes, the willingness to compromise increases. Dialogue is an important form of *contact*. A great deal of research and practical experience, which I will review in the next chapter, has shown that contact helps to overcome devaluation/prejudice and humanize others.

It is likely that in Northern Ireland and between Palestinians and Israelis contact and dialogue limited the violence. Even in the midst of their conflict, some Protestants and Catholics came together to engage with each other. Palestinians and Israelis came together in many settings and formats. Even though as people return to their own communities and especially when violence has again flared up the changes in attitudes that resulted from contact are difficult to maintain, the memory of relationships can shape renewed peace efforts. Those who want to maintain or foster enmity often attempt to limit contact and dialogue. A somewhat absurd example of this was told by a Republican member of the U.S. Congress to a Brown University professor. He used to play basketball with Democratic members of Congress until Newt Gingrich, planning a Republican takeover of Congress, told him to stop it.[22]

I wonder what would have happened if the Belgians, who originally enhanced Tutsi dominance in Rwanda, instead of shifting to support Hutu rule after the 1959 Hutu revolt, had brought the parties together and facilitated dialogue between them. They still ruled the country, and they could have created a framework for significant, long-term engagement and the resolution of both practical and emotional issues. The British, while they ruled the region, could have made a concentrated effort to bring Arabs and Jews together for dialogue. These were hugely challenging situations, but little would have been lost if these powerful outside parties had facilitated dialogue about a joint future. While conflict resolution and preventive diplomacy have not yet been scholarly and practical disciplines, there was much diplomatic experience to draw on.

When a more powerful group persecutes and victimizes another, devalued group, it does not normally see a reason for dialogue. Why would the Nazi government in Germany have dialogue with Jews? The Hutu government in Rwanda might have seen reasons to negotiate with Tutsis, even before the invasion by the Rwandan Patriotic Front and its subsequent victories. But they devalued and were hostile to Tutsis, and they were in power, so they did not. For dialogue, the other has to be "humanized," seen as deserving consideration. This may often require external parties.

Groups abstain from dialogue and negotiating for varied reasons. In the Israeli–Palestinian conflict, Israel would often not negotiate because it held either that there was no one on the other side who was open to genuine negotiation or that the leaders didn't have the will, or the power, to fulfill agreements. The former claim was applied at various times to Arafat, and to Hamas, the latter sometimes to Arafat, and to Mahmoud Abbas, the Palestinian President after Arafat's death. Israel also demanded that before it negotiates, terrorist attacks—attacks on Israel—must stop. Israel would not negotiate with Hamas until it accepted the existence of Israel and gave up terrorism.

On the Palestinian side, for a long time the goal was to destroy Israel. Once Palestinian leaders, at least of Fatah, accepted that Israel was here to stay, they regarded various Israeli leaders as not open to their essential demands and not negotiating in good faith. Hamas and Fatah competing for political influence, and the absence of preparation of the population, also made leaders reluctant to engage in dialogue. In 2009 Palestinians refused to negotiate with Israel until they stopped all building of settlements. But neither party can expect that before it starts negotiation, the other party ceases to be an enemy. The thinking and behavior of the Palestinians may have been also shaped by political weakness and the belief that their only way to exert influence is through violence.

As a 37-year-old Palestinian, an NGO worker said:[23] "The issue is not should Hamas recognize Israel. The issue is that we are under occupation…We don't have a state yet, Israel does. They have embassies, offices, passports. We are the people who are neglected by Israel and the West. The basis for any solution is for Israel to recognize us." And a 50-year-old employee of the Palestinian authority said: "We are the ones who are oppressed, who need recognition, not Israel. It's for the occupier to recognize the oppressed, not for the oppressed to recognize the occupier. They have their own country, but we are still suffering to get our own."[24]

Israelis who have experienced terrorism, who for many years could not eat in a restaurant or travel in a bus without fear that they would be blown up, who experienced many wars, have a different perspective. But helping to reestablish the sense of dignity of a group makes it psychologically more possible for them to turn to dialogue. Perhaps this is especially true for groups with cultures in which respect and honor are what some call sacred values, which make certain kinds of compromises especially difficult, as Arab cultures seem to be. This makes it also important that dialogue, once begun, be respectful. But opportunities must be used to begin dialogue.

Hamas leaders talking about negotiating with Israel a permanent truce[25] seemed to have been, and probably still is an opportunity. According to President Jimmy Carter, Hamas leaders told him they would abide by an agreement negotiated by the President of the Palestinian Authority, Mahmoud Abbas, and approved by Palestinians in a plebiscite. Ethan Bronner, the New York Times reporter, found that it is possible to engage in reasonable discussion about the issues with Hamas political leaders in Gaza, although he is uncertain about how much power they have relative to the military leaders. The relative power of leaders in Gaza and leaders who live in Syria is also unclear. But according to a Special report by the United States Institute of Peace,[25*] Hamas has been carefully and consciously adjusting its political program for years and has sent repeated signals that it may be ready to move to coexistence with Israel.

According to its authors Hamas is not hostile to Jews because of their religion, but to Israel because it occupies land that is "inherently Palestinian and Islamic." Recognizing Israel is "indefensible under Islam" and would be a negation of Hamas' own cause. But Hamas has formulated mechanisms that make it possible to deal with the reality of Israel's existence, including the religious concepts of *tahadiya*, a short term calming period, and *hudna*, a truth for a specific period, and a concept Hamas developed, "Palestinian legitimacy." This is a concept that expresses the willingness to accept a binding peace treaty, as long as it is ratified by the Palestinian population. Hamas would not negotiate the treaty, but would be willing to be part of a coalition government with Fatah in which Fatah negotiates the treaty. Given past Jewish history and past history in relation to Palestinians and Arabs, it is not surprising that Hamas' refusal to recognize Israel's existence is difficult for Israelis to accept. But Hamas' position can be a starting point for the evolution of a relationship. Changes in the relationship and in realities on the ground—actual movement toward peace—can contribute to the evolution of Hamas.

Talking to a party with extreme views, a party that has a set position and seems firmly committed to its hostile principles and demands, *may* be fruitless. Some minds are closed; some people are true believers in a destructive ideology. Frontal attacks on extremist ideologies rarely work. But sitting together, *persisting* with dialogue, if necessary for extended periods, may bring about change, especially if dialogue also leads to constructive actions. But building relationships may have to be the first goal. Sitting at a table and talking, and ideally also eating and relaxing together, builds relationships. It can affirm the identity of the less powerful group, build trust and hope, create mutual empathy, and make compromise possible.

Thomas Pettigrew, a long-time researcher on the effects of contact, concludes that contact changes attitudes toward another group as people develop relationships and friendships with each other.[26] The positive feelings and trust that are generated can expand beyond specific relationships to others in the "outgroup." Deep and extended contact is usually necessary for this to happen. Extended contact is needed to develop relationships and trust both between leaders and populations. For example, after World War II Germany and France entered into practical arrangements, cooperation of varied kinds ranging from industrial projects to sister cities, that built ties. Extended contact and shared interests, as well as superordinate goals, transformed the relationship between two countries that had fought a number of bitter wars.

Third parties, impartial, knowledgeable facilitators, can be invaluable to dialogue. Progress usually requires that participants address past relations and mutual grievances. This is likely to reactivate hurt and anger. The power of listening, showing that one has heard the other, and of empathy are great. When feelings are intense, each party can first meet separately with facilitators, who carry messages between them or make videos that the parties send to each other.

Former Israeli fighter pilot Yohanan Shapiro is a member of *Combatants for Peace*, a group of Israelis and Palestinians who fought against each other. Now they see the violence as destructive to both groups. He was asked on a National Public Radio program[27] how the two sides manage to engage in dialogue after fighting each other. He said that when they get together they don't talk about the history of the two groups, but about their personal histories: their childhood, what has been their experience in growing up, and so on. By presenting themselves as individual human beings, they can empathize with each other, see each other's humanity, and work together for their shared cause.

Other groups of Israelis and Palestinians, whose children, sisters, brothers, and other relatives were killed by the other side, have also come together to work for peace. They have reached a realization of the futility of violence. Identification with their group and common fate as group members usually lead people to come together against an opponent or enemy. What might lead some people to act contrary to the usual tendency to turn against those who have harmed them and brave the disapproval of, and perhaps ostracism by, their group? The people on the two sides who fought against each other or lost loved ones also have a common fate. They must have had values, experiences, and at first, perhaps even by accident, associations with others that led them to turn to this sense of commonality and away from hostility and violence. Some may have been inspired by leaders. A large group of relatives of people killed who joined across group lines to work for peace was started by a charismatic Jewish Israeli, Yitzhak Frankenthal, whose son was killed. Loss of loved ones is traumatizing, and fighting (and killing) and being part of an occupying army can be traumatizing. The people involved in these activities were likely to have had additional experiences that lead to altruism born of suffering (see Chapter 22 and Fig. 22.1). Once they entered into such communities, their engagement in activities for peace would have further shaped them.

For many years, Herbert Kelman brought Palestinians and Israelis together in problem-solving workshops to work on the resolution of practical issues between them. He started doing this at a time when the two sides did not talk to each other. The identity of participants had to be kept a secret. Obviously, these were people open to working with the other group. Although the task set for the group was to address practical issues that needed to be resolved for the two groups to live peacefully together, at the start emotional issues, hurt, and anger had to be addressed. Kelman believes that his workshops contributed to the Oslo agreement. Palestinians from the workshops were among the negotiators. Israeli participants included members of the Labor party who became influential when the party regained power.

Kelman thinks that one reason the peace process did not progress beyond the Oslo agreement is that only leaders were involved, not the population.[28*] As I shall discuss later, reconciliation and prevention processes can be top down, bottom up, or focus at mid-level (such as the media) that can exert influence both on leaders and the population. The leaders, in Kelman's work mostly mid-level leaders, could nor or did not exert influence on the population, and it is unclear to what extent they exerted influence within the leadership of their countries.

What about dialogue with terrorists? The Bush administration considered such a thing morally repugnant—until as part of the "surge" in Iraq it began to engage with and pay Sunnis, who had previously attacked U.S. troops. There has been later public discussion in the United States about talking to the Taliban in Afghanistan. The Palestinian Liberation Organization was considered a terrorist organization when its members sat together with Israelis in Kelman's workshops, and now Fatah, its descendent, is the group Israel negotiates with. People once considered terrorists often become heads of state, as was the case with Menachem Begin in Israel. The African National Congress in South Africa was considered a terrorist organization, at least by the apartheid state.

Not all terrorists are criminals, and not all are such adherents to extreme ideologies that they can't change. Some fight against repression or other understandable causes. Many consider themselves freedom fighters. It was presumably her description of her reasons for her action generating empathy that led 60% of Israelis, who listened on Israeli television to an interview with a women suicide bomber whose mission has failed, to have positive feelings about her, some both positive and negative, some purely positive.[29]

Changing conditions, the realization that they cannot achieve their goals by fighting, and opponents reaching out to them can open terrorists to engagement. Jihadists in Egyptian prisons have undergone a transformation, publicly proclaiming that they were misled and expressing their opposition to terrorist violence. Dialogue with them, involving at least one prominent religious leader, had a role.[30] The extensive writings of these jihadists suggest a genuine change of mind.

The same change seems to have occurred among some members of the Red Brigade, an Italian terrorist organization that abducted and killed high-level military and government officials in the 1970s and 1980s. The Italian government succeeded in dismantling the Red Brigade by offering a program for those who "repented." The government promised to reduce sentences or forgive past actions in exchange for cooperation. The engagement between the parties included dialogue. Defections followed, and information by defectors led to the arrest of many members. Others relinquished the group when information provided by defectors was channeled back to the group and produced internal dissent.[31]

The above discussion of Palestinians in Gaza indicate that as the weak party, they may be open to Israelis and other countries reaching out to them. Opportunities to address grievances through political and diplomatic avenues can move people away from violence. Engagement and effective dialogue may be possible with at least those terrorists who aim at achievable goals. But under the right conditions, and with time, even impossible dreams may undergo a transformation into acceptable goals.

The Dangers of Nonengagement

Both exclusion and inclusion of potential "spoilers," radical parties, from dialogue can be dangerous. If they are excluded, they can subvert whatever agreements have been made. In the Arusha negotiations in Rwanda between the government, various parties, and the Rwanda Patriotic Front (RPF), the RPF insisted that the most radical Hutu power anti-Tutsi group not be included. That excluded group then sabotaged the peace agreement and led the country into genocide. The same thing happened as a result of the exclusion of Hamas from negotiations in Oslo. (However, in both cases, the parties involved in the negotiations also did not live up to agreements.)

But when extreme groups are included, they can sabotage negotiations. They can influence the stance of moderate parties and create strong reactions in the opposing side. Nonetheless, I see inclusion as less risky, and starting negotiations with the inclusion of all "stakeholders" as preferable. Preparation for dialogue may include discussion of the conditions under which parties would be excluded from further negotiation. In intractable conflict everything is difficult, and the parties need to experiment to find workable arrangements.

The consequences of the Bush administration's refusal to engage and negotiate are instructive. It refused to negotiate with Iran, which offered help after 9/11 and during the war in Afghanistan to capture Osama bin Laden. President Bush described Iran as one of the axes of evil. Iran has subsequently supported the violence in Iraq against the United States, provided refuge to Al-Qaeda leaders, opposed the United States on varied fronts, and has built facilities for enriched uranium.

For 6 years the Bush administration refused to continue with the policies and agreements the Clinton administration developed with North Korea and refused to directly engage with North Korea. By the time it entered into negotiation, in July 2007, losses due to its original policy were substantial. North Korea not only built nuclear weapons in the intervening period but also engaged in nuclear proliferation. It did not abide by the new agreements made after July 2007, and soon proceeded to underground testing of nuclear bombs and testing missiles. We will never know whether a consistent policy of engagement would have prevented this.

It is rare when dialogue between hostile parties, conducted in the right framework, is undesirable. Hillary Clinton and later John McCain criticized Barack Obama in the course of the U.S. presidential campaign in 2008 for saying that he would engage, without preconditions, in talks with leaders of countries hostile to the United States. Clinton said that she would be careful about direct talks with such leaders, because they can use them as photo opportunities with a U.S. President for propaganda purposes.

Caution, preparation, and safeguards are important. But courage in initiating and maintaining engagement is required to change relationships and resolve issues. It is true that the willingness to engage in dialogue can be abused. More important than propagandizing a photo opportunity, a party can draw out dialogue, engage in an extended process, using the time to further its goals. These may include continuing to enrich nuclear materials in the case of Iran, exploiting natural resources in the case of the Congo, or gaining territory before a peace agreement when parties are fighting for land. Prudence is essential. This may mean insistence on progress in the talks—ranging from signs of increasing mutual understanding and trust, to agreements and actions.

Who knows what might have happened if the first President Bush had acceded to Saddam Hussein's request/demand after Iraq's invasion of Kuwait that they appear together on television. Up to that point the United States supported Iraq, in spite of Iraq's aggression in starting a war against Iran, and its severe human rights violations in using chemical weapons both against Iran and against its own Kurdish citizens. According to media reports, the American ambassador to Iraq at the time even indicated to Hussein's representative acceptance by the United States of Iraqi plans for the invasion of Kuwait.

As an Arab man, leader, and a dictator Hussein needed to protect his image in front of his people. Would he have accepted a private meeting with Bush, with a brief television appearance, and then withdrawn from Kuwait? If so, could subsequent change in U.S. and Western attitude, from support for Hussein's actions to strong but nonviolent pressure, have changed his behavior? The combination of the first Iraqi war, U.N. sanctions and inspections, and U.S. bombing did lead Iraq to destroy its chemical and biological weapons and abolish its nuclear program, as we learned after the United States defeated Iraq in 2003.

But perhaps this could have been brought about with less cost to the world and to Iraqis.

Cooperation from Iraq might have been forthcoming if the United States had not pursued what became its policy aim after the first Iraqi war: regime change. This policy, Iraq's fear of its neighbors and of the United States, and the psychology of Hussein may explain two important matters relating to the run up to the 2003 Iraq war: why Iraq was not more forthcoming about the fact that it eliminated its weapons of mass destruction, and why the results of the U.N. inspections indicating the absence of these weapons were not believed. The support for Iraq was not followed by engagement, even after the first war against Iraq, which could have made these changes evident and brought further change.

The issue of engagement has been alive in relation to Iran. In a 2008 book, Robert Baer, a former CIA agent for 21 years whose assignments focused on the Middle East, claimed that bombing Iran, which the Bush administration and Israel have talked about, would lead to retaliation in the form of Iran bombing oil facilities and other sites. He believed, however, that Iran would be open to engagement and dialogue.[32] As often in real-world matters, events since shifted the landscape, with contested elections in Iran, widespread protests and violent government response, a new facility to process uranium discovered, and repeated threats to Israel. Constrained by these events, and probably also fearing Republican attacks, there seemed to have been only limited attempts at engagement by the Obama administration.

Correctly assessing and respecting a party's needs and interests is essential for effective dialogue. Like Iraq, Iran has faced a hostile United States interested in regime change. With the exception of Iraq after Saddam Hussein, it is surrounded by Sunni countries, with a long history of intense hostility between Sunnis and Shiites. Security is therefore an important consideration for Iran. Lifting boycotts and addressing commercial interests, gaining respect, having influence, and expanding its power[33] are all of concern to Iran.

Repression and violence against citizens in a country should be something that the world acts against in a united fashion. It should do so in every instance, not selectively. Along the way, however, persistent efforts at engagement and dialogue can work for change both within a country and in its relations to others.

Dialogue is more effective if there is relative equality between groups, at least within the dialogue. This is challenging when the groups have greatly unequal power in the real world. Having impartial facilitators and setting rules that ensure the rights of the less powerful group within the dialogue can help. Respect and equality make it less likely that the weaker group feels the need to assume a defensive posture or to balance power by resistance, refusal to cooperate, or aggression within or outside the dialogue. As I shall later discuss, bringing leaders together to develop relationships and learn effective interaction before entering dialogue can be helpful.

Summary

Structures, institutions and systems, are of great importance for the prevention of violence, both state structures and local ones. It is local institutions or structures that make up civic society, which is essential for democracy. In working with conflict and hostile parties, persistent engagement between them in dialogue, negotiation, and mediation can change hostile attitudes and develop trust, which makes compromise and the resolution of practical issues possible. High-level international leaders can provide good offices in bringing leaders together at times of crises. External parties, such as outside nations, international leaders and NGOs can foster early engagement both between leaders and populations.

Notes

1　Cairns & Darby, 1998
2　See Alter, 2006
3　Nucera, 2008
4　Ibid.
5　Anstey & Zartman, in press
6　Maoz et al., 2002
7　Zartman, 1989
8　Lund, 2009, p. 311
9　Chirot & McCauley, 2006
10　Ibid.
11　Burg, 1997
12　Hamburg, 2007, p. 99
13　Autesserre, 2008
14　Sageman, 2008
15　Staub & Rosenthal, 2004
16　Austessere, 2008, p.107
17　Friedman, 2009c
18　Friedman, 2009b
19　Wyatt, 2010, p. B8
20　Hamburg, 2007, p. 98
21　Worth, 2009
22　Described by this professor on PBS evening news, February 17, 2009
23　Quoted by Post, 2007, p. 190
24　Ibid.
25　Carter and Bronner said this on the NPR program Fresh Air, on January 27, 2009. See also Carter, 2009. For the USIP report, see Scham & Abu-Irshaid, 2009
26　Pettigrew, 1997
27　Morning Edition, 2007, November 20

28 This is based on a comment made by Herb Kelman at a conference
29 Maoz, 2008
30 Wright, 2008
31 Post, 2007, p. 250
32 Baer, 2008
33 Ibid.

14

Developing Positive Orientation to the "Other"

Humanizing and Contact with the Other

Creating a positive orientation to the "other"—as leaders, the media, and individuals humanize the other group by positive words and actions and by extensive, positive contact—makes violence against them less likely.

Central to harmful and violent actions against another group is people drawing a strong line between us and them, and devaluing the potential victim group. This also makes it more likely that witnesses remain passive when the group is harmed. Devaluation is psychological, but it is often institutionalized in the form of discrimination, which is structural. Central to prevention is developing a positive orientation toward particular, devalued groups and, beyond that, to human beings in general. We are not likely to harm those we value as human beings. Humanizing others, seeing them in a positive light, makes it possible to create constructive ideologies that consider the interests of all groups. Seeing the humanity of members of a group that has harmed one's own makes it possible to move toward reconciliation and forgiveness.[1]

Humanizing Devalued Groups

Seeing as similar to ourselves people who have been historically devalued or with whom our group is in conflict is an important condition for empathy. Empathy in turn inhibits aggression. Arab children who felt more empathy for Jewish children were less in support of aggression toward them.[2] In a study I will discuss later, contact between Tamil and Sinhalese students increased empathy for and donations to a charity to help the other group. In Northern Ireland as well, contact between Catholics and Protestants increased the ability to take the other's perspective and contributed to trust and forgiveness.[3]

The absence of empathy, according to psychologist Ralph White,[4] leads to war-promoting misperceptions. Writing about enemies, White notes that fear, and the beliefs that one's enemy is an inhuman monster and that one's group is always morally right, interfere with empathy. Knowing adversaries so as to accurately take their perspective, understanding their concerns and needs, and empathizing with them enables people to work on resolving conflict and overcoming hostility.

Positive information in the media and literature can humanize the other. It can point to similarity to one's own group (and to human beings in general) in basic needs, in love of family, and in suffering due to material deprivation or past victimization. Leaders can humanize the other group by what they say, and by having positive public contact with its members. Yasir Arafat and Yitzhak Rabin shaking hands at the White House would have positive impact on their followers.

As mentioned previously, the articles that journalists from different ethnic groups in Macedonia jointly wrote and published about families belonging to the different groups, based on interviews and observations of their lives, showed the everyday lives of people and their similarity to each other.[5] Becoming familiar with others' lives, their customs and habits, the challenges they face and how they address them and seeing similarities in needs and aspirations can increase acceptance. Journalists can also foster understanding of differences, as when the newspaper in Medellin, Colombia, *El Colombiano*, presented next to each other the perspectives of the guerrillas and right-wing paramilitaries.

Helping people understand the roots of devaluation can also humanize the other. These roots include the following: the tendency to categorize people as us and them; to label and devalue people based on their difference in physical appearance, customs, habits, and values, and their lower status; to justify by devaluation their bad treatment; and to scapegoat them in response to difficult life conditions or conflict. Such understanding can help people see the negative view as devaluation rather than an accurate description of the other, at the very least an exaggerated view of the other's characteristics, which is how the psychologist Gordon Allport defined a stereotype.[6]

Education in schools provides a natural opportunity to learn about the other. Humanizing the other can recast differentness, so that children can follow the human inclination of interest in and the desire to explore what is different, rather than see it as threatening and dangerous. Often, however, the other group has long been negatively represented in textbooks and literature. Humanizing the other requires rewriting textbooks—which requires a changed view by those who write them.

Education can also provide children with a functional understanding of other groups. Knowledge of the history and experiences of a group can show how difficult and demanding conditions and the choices they made in response to them led to the development of group characteristics, attitudes, and actions. For example, it can help people understand the psychological woundedness of both Israelis and Palestinians, and how combined with the ongoing threat they face from each other this has been affecting the groups' actions—and increasingly their culture and character. It can also help people understand German and specifically Prussian authoritarianism, which according to various scholars developed in response to destructive wars over the centuries on German territory, in which a substantial percentage of the German population died. People turned to authorities—rulers, princes, members of the nobility who had armies—for protection. Great scarcity has led people in some nontechnological societies to be scrupulous about sharing food, while it has led others to gorge themselves when they acquired food, so that they wouldn't have to share it.[7] Life conditions can lead to reactions and choices, which are starting points for the evolution of varying cultures. Understanding this can lead to empathy and begin to shift attitudes and actions.

Many of the processes of prevention and reconciliation I focus on in this book—such as understanding the roots of violence, establishing contact between opposing groups, creating a shared history, and forming just relations between groups—serve in part to humanize others. Our research in Rwanda found that helping people understand the influences that lead to genocide changes their view of perpetrators from seeing them as evil to seeing them as human beings who have engaged in horrible actions.[8] Our radio programs have resulted in increased empathy by listeners toward all groups—survivors, perpetrators, leaders, and others.[9]

Humanizing another group has to be done with sensitivity to the impact of past events. It is a great challenge for most survivors of genocide, or relatives of those killed in terrorist attacks, to see their shared humanity with killers. The initial focus should be on humanizing the group in general, not the perpetrators. This cannot be done after great violence, or even after a history of intense hostility, by simply saying nice things about the other group. Genuine information, such as the stories of rescuers or other evidence from history of positive actions by members of the other group, understanding the influences that led perpetrators to their actions, stories of suffering of members of that group, and working together to rebuild society can all help. Tutsi community members who after participation in groups led by facilitators we trained said that some Hutus saved lives, and that not all Hutu were perpetrators[10]—points that were factually correct but after the genocide did not receive much attention—showed that Hutus were humanized in their eyes to some degree.

Forgiveness, which I will discuss in Chapter 21, requires seeing the humanity of those who have done harm. Some Americans almost immediately after 9/11 said that they forgave the 9/11 terrorists. How deep-seated and lasting was this forgiveness is unclear.[11] Forgiveness, or at least a degree of acceptance of what has happened, is also shown by the relatives of Israelis and Palestinians killed by the other side who joined together to work for peace.

Significant/Deep Contact: Overcoming Prejudice and Humanizing the Other

I have already noted that deep engagement between people belonging to different groups can lead to experiencing the humanity of the other. A statistical summary of over 500 studies on the effects of contact shows that contact reduces prejudice. It creates a more positive attitude toward members of another group.[12] But superficial contact, people belonging to different groups living in the same neighborhood, seeing but not engaging with each other, will have limited effects. This was found in research conducted not long after World War II on black and white attitudes in New York City.[13] Limited contact can even reinforce prejudice. Tourists in far away countries, who travel there with already existing prejudices and who do not come to know anyone there, only seeing local people living with customs very different from their own, can come away with increased prejudice. Students who study in another country often spend time with other students from their own country. If they do not develop relationships with and come to know local people, they tend to develop negative attitudes toward them.[14] Deeper contact, more significant engagement, in which ideally people work together for shared goals, is more effective in overcoming prejudice and humanizing the other.

Gordon Allport[15] was the originator of the "contact hypothesis." He proposed several conditions as important for intergroup contact to be effective in reducing prejudice. There must be equality ("equal status" in Allport's terms) between parties in the course of their engagement. Otherwise contact may reaffirm group differences and the dehumanizing attitudes that have developed in the course of unequal relationships. Support by authorities, by leaders ("institutional sanction"), contributes to the positive effect of contact (and can determine whether there will be contact). Common goals ("pursuit of common goals"), especially those that are *superordinate* to often conflicting group goals, and cooperation between members of the groups to achieve them are important. So too are outcomes perceived as positive by members of the different groups.

Thomas Pettigrew and Linda Tropp[16] found that especially important for the positive effect of contact was support by authorities. Success also seemed important when contact involved cooperation. In general, contact had to have a positive quality for it to be effective. They found an "extended effect" of contact. When whites had contact with blacks, changes in their attitude extended to other blacks, as well as to members of other devalued groups, such as disabled people. An aspect of the positive change that resulted from contact was the reduction of anxiety about engaging with members of the other group. These research findings showed that the conditions Allport identified do not assure positive changes in attitudes, and that positive changes can occur in their absence. The latter is an important finding, since some of these conditions often do not exist.

When hostility is intense, leaders as well as the members of hostile groups do not encourage, support, or tolerate contact. This is why the names of participants in Herbert Kelman's interactive problem-solving workshops had to be kept secret. This can be balanced, to a degree, by the approval and support of those who arrange the contact and act as authorities in the course of it. They can help maintain equal relations in the course of it, even if relations between the groups in the real world are unequal.

People in contact can have experiences that lead them to dislike each other. In a demonstration project famous among social psychologists, the so-called Robber's Cove experiment, named after the location of the project,[17] boys were brought to two neighboring summer camps. The two groups had contact with each other mainly in competitive games, which one of the groups always won. This created hostility and fighting between them. It also led to disarray among the losers, with the boys who became leaders abandoning the group and trying to become friends with members of the winning group. As with larger groups, the persistent failure of the losers to fulfill important needs, in this case for effectiveness and positive identity, disrupted the group as a community. Such a situation often leads to destructive need fulfillment.

An accidental event in which a truck got stuck in the mud, which required the two groups of boys to join in pushing it out of the mud, began to ease relations. The adults in charge then designed activities that required the groups to join to accomplish shared goals, with very beneficial effects on group relations. This further developed and reinforced Gordon Allport's ideas about the value of common goals and cooperation in achieving them. The authors of this project and social psychologists subsequently emphasized the importance of superordinate goals, shared goals that override separate and potentially conflicting goals.

Although far removed from group relations among humans, a study with monkeys shows the effect of past cooperation on future relations. The researchers at first simply observed the frequency with which seven pairs of female macaques reconciled after conflict. They did this 25% of the time. The monkeys were then trained to cooperate for a shared goal. Only by working together could they get food. After this, when they had conflicts, they reconciled 50% of the time.[18]

A study of what happened in U.S. schools after desegregation demonstrates that being in the same life space is not enough, as well as the value of significant contact and shared goals. White children and black children continued to interact within their own groups. Black children had low self-concepts and did not live up to their academic potential. To address this problem, cooperative learning procedures were introduced. Children in mixed groups were led to cooperate on tasks that required real engagement with each other. For example, using what the designers of the project called a jigsaw technique, groups of six children had tasks that required each child to learn some material and teach it to the others. Each child was a teacher of and learner from the others. The completion of their task depended on their effective cooperation. In these and other projects attitudes toward members of the other group became more positive, social interaction increased, the self-concept and academic achievement of the minority children improved while that of white children did not decline.[19] Unfortunately, in the early twenty-first century American schools are to a large extent resegregated, mainly due to residential patterns.

In many societies members of different ethnic or religious groups have little contact. In India, where there is hostility and periodic outbreaks of violence between Hindus and Muslims, there is substantial segregation between the groups.[20] With already existing negative views, this lack of meaningful contact maintains devaluation. In the Netherlands there is substantial segregation between Dutch and Muslim children, due to residential patterns, with some increase in the segregation of neighborhoods in recent years. As a result of segregated housing in Amsterdam in 2004, only 10% of the Turkish and Moroccan population had a school nearby with a substantial percentage of Dutch children.[21] Dutch and Muslim adults have even less personal contact than children and youth. Most Muslims "know" the Dutch from the television programs they watch, a limited and even distorted picture.[22] Most Dutch know Muslims even less.

To create physical integration, in housing, the workplace, and schools, requires strong commitment by authorities and citizens. In the Netherlands the motivation to improve group relations substantially increased after the killing of Theo van Gogh in 2004 and the attacks on mosques, Muslim schools, and churches that followed. In response to this situation, and also to proposals I made to improve Dutch–Muslim relations based on principles I describe in this book,[23] a variety of actions were taken. Jeroen de Lange,[24] the assistant city manager at the time, lists the following:

- Organizing a festival during Ramadan, with many meetings and debates about Islam in the Netherlands and about what kind of city Amsterdam should be. Muslim families invited non-Muslims to share dinner with them after sunset.
- Scheduling days of dialogue during the year where citizens could talk about shared concerns
- Creating a council of young Amsterdam Muslims to facilitate giving voice to their needs and concerns
- Establishing a project called "welcome to my neighbourhood" to bring Muslim and Dutch children together who, because of a segregated school system due to residential patterns, have no contact with each other
- Creating an organization to advise teachers about the relations of children across group lines in the schools

- Pursuing a plan to create a debate, exhibition, and study center on Islam, to facilitate exploration of what it means to be a Muslim in a secular society

The greater birth rate of Muslims means that their percentage of the population will increase. To continue to improve group relations and prevent future violence requires the creation of a constructive ideology, a vision of how the Dutch and Muslims can live harmoniously.

The positive effects of limited engagement and contact are weaker in members of a minority group.[25] Most members of a majority, such as whites in the United States, have experienced little discrimination by members of the minority. It is not surprising that members of a minority who have experienced discrimination and bad treatment change less from limited contact, such as when people are brought together for a weekend. More experience in positive interaction would presumably have greater effects. Research findings also indicate that the effects of contact are modified by what happens in the course of the interaction. Especially in contact between members of natural, already existing groups, there is less control over what happens than in studies in which participants are brought together in a carefully arranged situation.

An Israeli researcher, Ifat Maoz, studied 47 "encounter programs" between Jews and Arabs, in which people ranging from preschool children to mostly college-age adults were brought together weekly or monthly for a period of 4 months to a year. One of the research questions was whether, given the greater power of Jews than Arabs in Israel/Palestine, this "asymmetry" was re-created among participants. While many of these programs (60%) aimed to engage participants with each other cooperatively (a coexistence mode), others (13%) aimed to address differences and hostility between the groups (a confrontational mode). Some groups operated in a mixed mode (27%) that included both approaches. Theories about contact provided the basis for the coexistence approach. The confrontational approach was developed in the field, especially initiated by Arab leaders of contact groups. It aimed both to create greater awareness in the parties of their relationship, including awareness by Israelis of their greater power, and to strengthen the identity of Palestinians. The confrontational mode was used only with older high school students and adults. It would have been inappropriate for younger children, given their cognitive and emotional level.[26]

When organizers attempted to establish equality in such contact situations, they usually focused only on equality in the number of participants on the two sides, and in their social and economic backgrounds. Although inequality in the outside world can be reproduced by inequality in power and influence exerted by participants, the research found substantial equality in the participation of group members, in 89% of the cases, regardless of the type of programs.

A substantial amount of the research evaluating the effects of contact has been conducted in the United States and other countries, where there may be devaluation and prejudice, but little active group violence, and in settings where usually there is limited aggression, such as schools and workplaces. But even though it is often assumed that reconciliation cannot begin until violence is over and people feel secure, as the discussion of contact and dialogue has shown, at least some people are willing to be in contact in the midst of violent conflict. This has been the case in Northern Ireland, the Palestinian Israeli conflict, Cyprus, Sri Lanka, and elsewhere. Some of the contacts have been organized by outside parties, others originated in the community, such as people meeting in church basements in Northern Ireland. Such contacts indicate that the society allows some freedom of action, some pluralism, and that some of its members harbor less hostility.

In Northern Ireland the government worked on boosting naturally occurring contact between Protestants and Catholics. While between 1968 and 1999 housing patterns, mixed marriages, and voting behavior did not improve significantly, public confidence in future positive relations between the groups has increased.[27] Probably improved economic circumstances and educational opportunities of Catholics[28] have contributed to this increase. Resolving long-standing conflict is more likely if many avenues are used to improve the relations of groups.

Examples and Long-Term Effects of Contact

Usually, studies on the effects of contact are assessed immediately after the contact ends, so that our knowledge of long-term effects is limited. In one study that evaluated long-term effects, individuals who were members of groups that have engaged in mutual violence in Sri Lanka for over two decades were randomly assigned to a contact and a control group. Specifically, 18- to 21-year-old students—Sinhalese who belong to the majority that rules the country, and Tamils who belong to the minority that has been fighting the government in a separatist movement—were brought together for 4 days. They participated in lectures, peace workshops, and visits to multiethnic villages. The researchers were especially interested in the extent this combined peace education and contact increased empathy. About a year later, they found that the students in the contact group expressed more empathy for members of the other group, and donated more money for poor children in the other group, than did comparable students who were selected in similar ways and did not have the contact experience.[29]

Another study by social psychologists Stephen Worchel and Dawna Coutant evaluated the long-term effects of contact between 14- to 16-year-old Israeli, Palestinian, Serb, Croatian, and Bosnian youth in a 3-week-long summer camp in Maine.[30] Like other researchers, they found that changes were greater in the participants of the stronger groups (i.e., Israelis, Serbs, and Croats). They studied changes both immediately after the camp, and with a small group of 18 participants 2–4 years later. The immediate changes were substantial. Among the lasting changes, the participants feared the "outgroup" less. They also perceived it as less homogenous—which means they applied stereotypes less to its individual members. While they continued to blame the other group for the conflict, belief in the responsibility of their own group increased. These young people showed increased self-esteem and increased belief in their effectiveness. The camp experience apparently affirmed and strengthened the participants, while changing their perception of both their own group and the other group. As in the study evaluating our intervention in Rwanda, these changes may indicate increased readiness for reconciliation.[31] However, without a comparison group, we don't know if the changes reflect only the camp experience, maturation and the impact of intervening events, or their combination.

Another project developed a community approach to improve education in a mixed Palestinian-Jewish city in Israel.[32] It introduced cooperative learning in the schools. Mixed parent groups participated in workshops on intergroup relations and jointly developed an educational plan for the city. Benefiting their children provides parents from different groups with a superordinate goal. Another mixed group consisting of school principals and community leaders advocated for educational change and worked to increase resources for the schools.

The Maoz research on symmetry in contact between Palestinians and Israelis found mostly equal amounts of participation by members of the two groups, but that in the confrontational programs, Jewish facilitators were more active than Arab facilitators. Similarly, Marc Gopin, a practitioner of such work, notes that Jewish participants, who are more fluent in English, have greater ease with verbal communication, and perhaps have a cultural background of greater verbal assertiveness, are frequently more active and forceful. This may limit the effectiveness of contact and dialogue.[33] Indeed, people from different cultures have different ways of thinking, relating, and communicating verbally and nonverbally. These differences can create misunderstanding, hurt feelings, withdrawal, and anger, and they can limit the development of relationships. One of my favorite examples comes from everyday interactions between white teachers and Mexican American children. The children learn in their culture to look down, rather than at an adult, when they are reprimanded. The teachers take this as resistance and insolence.

"Pretraining" in such cultural differences can reduce misunderstanding and can contribute to the success of engagement and dialogue. It has become a common practice in business. For example, Japanese executives coming to the United States learn to be more assertive in business meetings, so that they don't fade into the background. U.S. executives going to Japan learn to be less assertive, so that they are respected. Such training can help participants understand the other's culture and mode of relating, reducing negative perceptions and fostering acceptance. It can also help people to see themselves, their own customary way of behaving, both to understand their potential impact on others and to adjust their actions according to the demands of circumstance.

Structures That Create or Maintain Contact

As people return to their lives and are surrounded by those hostile to the other group, the psychological changes brought about by relatively brief contact tend to be overwhelmed by everyday realities. Certain measures to prevent or lessen this, "inoculation," should be part of the contact experience, including discussion of the difficulty of maintaining positive attitudes in home environments and identification of strategies to overcome this difficulty. If two or more people from the same side in each work or life setting are part of contact experiences, they can support each other's changed attitudes. This is especially important for leaders.

Structures or institutions that create, maintain, and enhance positive contact are especially useful. Schools, businesses, and religious and other community organizations are among important structures that can embed positive contact as part of their ordinary activities. Deep relations in structural contexts have inhibited violence between Hindus and Muslims in some Indian cities, and between Serbs and Muslims in some Bosnian cities. In India, a study by political scientist Ashutosh Varshney[34] compared three cities in which following instigating conditions there was violence between Hindus and Muslims, and three cities in which there was no violence. In contrast to the "violent cities," the cities without violence had chambers of commerce and other institutions in which Hindus and Muslims effectively worked together and to which they were committed. In response to the instigating conditions, they joined in exerting influence on the community, as well as on politicians to stop them from making inflammatory statements, even threatening to publicly speak out against them if they instigated violence.

Many of those engaged in peacemaking stress the importance of civil society, of institutions in which members of the different groups, including community leaders, are deeply engaged with each other. Sociologist Daniel Chirot and psychologist Clark McCauley note that Herbert Kelman's problem-solving workshops brought together Israeli Jews and Palestinians who were not part of existing institutions. They returned, instead, to communities that did not support their new ideas and attitudes. In addition, intercommunal cooperation between Jews and Palestinians was made impossible after 2000 by the second *Intifada*.[35]

Chirot and McCauley describe the creation of community-based institutions in the Ivory Coast as a means to prevent violence. The Ivory Coast had a political system that maintained peace by distributing resources—handing out material benefits and honors—from the top. With the increase in the population, economic problems, and the death of President Houphonet-Boigny in 1993, conflict between the primarily southern and Christian leadership, the northern and primarily Muslim communities, and the large number of immigrants came to the fore. It resulted in tainted elections, coups and countercoups, violence, and separate armies of the south and the north. While the problems were national and political, they were also local, with parts of the country, especially in the middle, ethnically and religiously mixed. In most places there were no local institutions to bring together members of the different groups. This was true in the Southwest, where land disputes led to many killings.

With limited funding from the World Bank, CARE encouraged local elites around the rebel capital, Bouake, to form a steering committee, with representatives of the highly varied ethnic and religious groups. They were to initiate similarly mixed local committees, in both rural villages and urban districts, that were to ask for "reconstruction funding to repair the damages of the civil war... ranging from ... repairing schools, dispensaries, and wells to providing small amounts of capital to get markets and small businesses functioning again."[36] The local groups submitted plans to the central regional steering committee. The winning proposals received small grants ranging from $2000 to $4000. Chirot and McCauley report that in just a few months these projects had significant benefits, although they don't describe how they were assessed.

Development assistance can effectively combine immediate help to people, community building, and reconciliation. In Sri Lanka, Tamil and Sinhalese farmers could make decisions about the use of funds provided for irrigation projects and were encouraged not to select leaders on ethnic/political grounds. The ethnic strife and violence that was widespread in the country did not engulf the area where this project was conducted.[37] Micro-lending and small grant programs that enable local people to start small businesses or rebuild communities can give rise to significant contact, superordinate goals in joint projects, and build civic society.

A research project in Rwanda also found a strongly positive effect from frequent, deep, and satisfying contact across group lines in a coffee collaborative. Members of the collaborative who were associated with a particular coffee washing station for a long time, and seemingly as a result experienced more economic satisfaction and generally were more satisfied with life, had more positive attitudes toward reconciliation. People who had more frequent work and social contact had more trust in members of the other group and expressed more "conditional forgiveness."[38*] The author of this project suggests that new commercial opportunities in Rwanda, specifically in this case a result of deregulation of the coffee industry by the government, have created structures that have made possible both increased economic well-being and opportunities for contact. Being part of a coffee collaborative was associated with economic and life satisfaction, which were associated with trust, positive attitudes, and seeing the other group as more heterogeneous and feeling less distance from it.

Some Limits and Challenges of Contact

If contact can have positive effects even in the midst of violence, how can we understand that people who have long lived together as neighbors, friends, or even spouses can seemingly speedily turn against each other? I wrote earlier that deep fissures often remain in the wake of past violence. Some individuals who have had painful life experiences mistrust everyone, including their families. The same can be true at the group level. Members of groups that have harmed each other can live next to each other and coexist—cooperate in everyday matters—and still maintain mistrust and negativity toward each other, and/or these can emerge in the context of a new threat to the group.

In many societies with deep past divisions there has been substantial inter-marriage. Deeper contact is difficult to imagine. But considering individual vio-lence, the majority of it occurs within families and among friends and associates. Someone who was "us" can become "them." Trust and caring can become dis-trust, anger, and hostility—brought about by real or presumed betrayal or threat. Threatening events can reassert the division between "us" and "them" and point to the other group as out to destroy one's own group; the past reemerges. Identity and loyalty shift to the group. As group attitudes shift, or authorities or paramilitary groups exert pressure (in places like Bosnia, destroy-ing civic institutions), fear of deviation from the group can shift attitudes, estab-lish new group norms, and create conformity.

Understanding how a new threat can transform attitudes can help with inoculation. People engaging with the past, talking about what has happened—for example, exploring what happened during World War II in the former Yugoslavia and assessing its impact on the present and its potential to disrupt relations—can address latent mistrust, inoculate against future divisions, and help with healing. Members of communities need to understand each other's psychological situation. In the former Yugoslavia, public discussion of the groups' past was not allowed. In Rwanda, before 1994, hostility toward Tutsis made such public discussion impossible, and now the new ideology of unity together with government actions prevent it.

Deep contact is powerful, but as later chapters show after past violence it also requires other influences/experiences to promote reconciliation, such as heal-ing, establishing the truth and justice, and creating a shared history. Moreover, to change group relations, in addition to citizens, there has to be persistent con-tact/dialogue at various levels: between leaders, and ideally between members of the media and other influentials.

Ongoing hostility and violence make effective contact challenging. In a meet-ing of a Palestinian—Israeli dialogue group, one Palestinian confessed that when rockets fell on Israeli cities he felt good about it. He tried to make the group understand what Palestinian life is like under Israeli occupation, and how this feeling arose from that. In this group, trust that had developed in an earlier meeting helped members of the group hear and deal with such truths.[39*] At times of intense hostility, facilitators and group members need to acknowledge the challenge of working together, and that hostile feelings are likely to arise and need to be addressed. It may help leaders who meet at such times to focus on their great and shared responsibility to stop violence and resolve the conflict.

When contact begins to develop more positive attitudes and norms of conduct, those with more negative attitudes will be threatened[40] and may attempt to reverse these changes. Some writers have attributed the increased anti-Semitism in Germany after World War I to a reaction to Jewish assimilation, with less ability to differentiate Jews from Germans, assuming that this made some Germans more open to Nazi ideology.

Even as devaluation and prejudice decline, some forms can persist for long periods. In the United States there is greater surveillance of black people in stores, and blacks are treated with suspicion in white areas.[41] The police stops black drivers more than whites, even if (or especially if) they drive expensive cars, and blacks receive more severe sentences than whites for similar crimes. These practices may be expressions of the remnants of old prejudice, and of anxiety or threat created by the changing position of African Americans in society. So may be the increase in the activities of white supremacist groups after the election of Barack Obama. Moving from devaluation, hostility, and discrimination to acceptance and structural changes requires substantial adjustment, including extensive public discussion of the challenges of change. Some of the aforementioned expressions of prejudice may be in line with contemporary research, much of it in the United States on black–white relations, which shows that current forms of prejudice are subtle, and are expressed in action under ambiguous circumstances, when there are no clear rules to guide interaction.[42]

Can ongoing positive contact have any harmful effects? Perhaps it can. Research findings have shown that positive contact leads members of minority groups to accept more the existing social arrangements, even if they are unequal and unjust. It reduces the motivation to work for social change.[43] Positive contact that involves a segment of a minority group, especially its elite, does not necessarily address the group's grievances. Over the long run, unjust social relations can turn into overt conflict and become an instigator for violence. Even positive contact at many levels of the group can, for some time at least, reduce dissatisfaction while allowing unjust conditions to persist.

Extended and Imagined Contact

The positive effects of direct contact with some members of an "outgroup" can generalize to other members as well. In addition, simply knowing that friends, people we value, have positive relationships with members of another group leads us to have a more positive attitude toward that other group. This has been called extended contact. It shows the power of our minds and imagination, which is further shown by the positive effects of "imagined contact." Researchers in England had people imagine scenes in which they interacted with a member of another group. They conclude, perhaps with some exaggeration, that "imagining a particular social situation can have the same effect as the experience itself."[44] Like actual contact, it creates a more positive attitude and reduces anxiety about interacting with members of the other group.

One social situation they asked each participant to imagine was of travelling on a busy train, finding a seat, and reading a novel. An older black man comes on the train at the next stop and sits down beside the person. He sees the book and says it is one of his favorites. The researchers tell each participant, "This begins a discussion in which you shared your thoughts on the book and what you both enjoyed about it." Then, before the person gets off the train in 30 minutes, the two of them "discuss a whole range of topics, from the stresses of having to commute to work every day, to what neighbourhood you live in, to what your children's favourite subjects are at school."[45]

The researchers found two crucial elements for imagined interactions to create positive attitudes. One is instruction to engage in "simulation." People cannot just think of an outgroup member; they have to run through in their minds an interaction with that person. Another is that like in actual contact, the interaction has to be positive. They note that guiding people to imagine a positive interaction can also guard against a negative tone that could emerge if people are left to imagine the interaction on their own, especially with members of a group they devalue or toward which they feel hostile.

Even imagining others having positive contact can generate positive attitudes. American children between ages 5 and 11 who were read stories about a member of their group and a refugee, and Finnish teenagers who read stories in school about peers of their age having close friendships with foreigners, had more positive attitudes toward refugees or foreigners.[46]

In many situations the opportunity for contact between socially segregated or hostile groups is greatly limited. A special value of imagined contact, or stories that connect people across groups, may be to prepare people for actual interaction and create a mental set that shapes the nature of actual contact and maximizes its benefits. The research has so far evaluated the effects of imagined contact only immediately after the interaction was imagined. Repeated or varied imagined interactions may be necessary for it to have lasting effects, and/or actual contact following it.

Summary

Developing positive attitudes toward members of another group is an essential aspect of preventing violence and promoting reconciliation.

This can be done by information that shows the other's humanity, including positive actions in the past. It can be done by extended positive contact, especially in the framework of cooperation in joint projects in the service of shared goals. Knowing that people we are close to have good relations with members of the other group, and even imagining contact with "others," can have positive effects. After past violence and extended hostility, contact must be combined with other aspects of prevention and reconciliation to bring lasting benefits, and it will ideally include "inoculation" to limit the impact of changing circumstances that may renew hostility.

Notes

1 Cairns, Hewstone, & Tam, 2006; Staub et al., 2005
2 Schechtman & Basheer, 2005
3 Cairns et al., 2005; Hewstone at al., 2008
4 White, 1984
5 Burg, 1997
6 Allport, 1954
7 Staub, 1978
8 Staub et al., 2005
9 Paluck, 2009a, Staub & Pearlman, 2009
10 Staub et al., 2005
11 McIntosh et al., 2006
12 Pettigrew and Tropp, 2006
13 See Deutsch, 1973
14 Stroebe, Lenkert, & Jonas, 1988
15 Allport, 1954
16 Pettigrew & Tropp, 2006
17 Sherif, Harvey, White, Hood, & Sherif, 1961
18 Cords & Thurnheer, 1993
19 Aronson et al., 1978
20 Guha, 2007
21 Diversiteists-en Integratiemonitor, 2004
22 Staub, 2007b
23 Ibid.
24 de Lange, 2007
25 Tropp & Pettigrew, 2005
26 Maoz, 2004
27 Cairns & Hewstone, 2002
28 Cairns & Darby, 1998
29 Malhotra & Liyanage, 2005
30 Worchel & Cotant, 2008
31 Staub et al., 2005
32 Stephan, 2008

33 Marc Gopin, personal communication, August 2008

34 Varshney, 2002

35 Chirot & McCauley, 2006

36 Ibid, p.194

37 Lund, 2009

38 Tobias, 2008. Conditional forgiveness was assessed using a variant of the measures developed and used by Staub et al., 2005.

39 I am not providing further information about the group to protect anonymity.

40 Dixon, Durrheim, & Tredoux, 2005

41 Ibid.

42 For a review, see Myers, 2010

43 For a review, see Dovidio et al., 2009

44 Crisp & Turner, 2009, p. 233

45 Ibid, p. 231–232

46 For a review of these studies, see Ibid.

15

Beyond "Us" and "Them"

Constructive Ideologies and Groups, Common Identities, Inclusive Caring, and Pluralism

---

The existence/creation of inclusive, constructive visions (ideologies) of the future of society, and constructive community groups, provide alternatives to destructive movements to fulfill basic needs in difficult times.

Caring that expands beyond one's own group, and common/or dual identities that include varied groups, make violence less likely.

People yearn for and seek hope in difficult times or in the midst of conflict and violence. Just as destructive ideologies have shared elements (i.e., a vision of a better future for the group, and the identification of enemies) but vary otherwise, so constructive ideologies have shared elements but vary otherwise. Constructive ideologies offer hope for increased security, strengthened identity, connection to other people, and in general the vision of a better future that is created by constructive means. Such ideologies will be inclusive, so that all groups can participate in the creation of social arrangements that address the needs and well-being of all groups. The ideology can give rise to shared goals and motivate members of different groups to join in their fulfillment.

Dialogue is essential to this process. In the case of group conflict, mediation, dialogue, and other conflict resolution processes can be used to develop a shared vision of society, and shared goals, which then can provide a framework for peace building. Such a process works best if not only leaders, but all members of society are involved. Dialogue between people can take place in schools, religious settings, homes, and the media. It can address material issues, divergent values and visions of society, past relations, and what a peaceful shared future might be like. Dialogue between leaders is essential to create peace agreements. But unless the population is involved, many may be dissatisfied with the agreement or remain hostile to a seemingly constructive ideological vision propagated by the government.

Persistent, intractable conflict, and extreme violence, are built and maintained out of many elements. Social psychologists Vallacher, Coleman, Nowak, and Bui-Wrzosinska suggest that the "pattern" itself resists direct influence.

Its elements need to be deconstructed or dismantled.[1]* The best approach to this is to develop new elements that replace the old ones, such as the more positive attitude toward the other group that I described in the previous chapter, and constructive ideology and constructive community groups that I describe in this one. Many means can be used in their service, such as humanizing members of the other group, contact and dialogue. The effects of such practices and constructive elements may not be immediately evident. However, after significant events, such as leaders reaching a peace agreement, their prior development makes genuine peace and reconciliation possible. The events in Macedonia that I described earlier are at least a partial example of this.

Rwanda's Ideology of Unity

The ideology of unity introduced by the Rwandan government after the genocide is seemingly constructive. According to this ideology, there are no Hutus and Tutsis, only Rwandans. The division between the groups was greatly enhanced by colonizers and this ideology claims that it was created by them. This simple ideology is inclusive. Everybody is part of the community and is to work jointly with others to create progress in Rwanda. However, the government labels deviation from the ideology and opposition to its positions as divisionism, sometimes as a genocidal ideology, and reacts punitively. The terms of a law that made "genocidal ideology" a criminal offense, punishable by 10–25 years in prison, passed in October 2009, are seen as "vague and ambiguous."[2] While especially in light of past history hate speech and incitement to violence should not be allowed, the way the law has been used inhibits public discourse and political processes.

The ideology of unity, imposed by the government, hides intense feelings by members of the groups toward each other. During a *gacaca* meeting, when someone stood up to speak, our interpreter immediately told us the person's ethnicity. This was also common in other settings. Discouraging talk about Hutus and Tutsis and other aspects of the ideology of unity make it difficult to discuss grievances, especially by Hutus, and to jointly engage with the past and resolve long-standing, intense feelings. When I was interviewed by the editor of an English language newspaper in Rwanda and expressed these views, the editor said: "I cannot print that; my prime minister would not like it." It told him to name me as the source, and then I would be responsible. He printed what I said, but Rwandans would not be able to do what I did.

In a short time this ideology came to be genuinely held by the leadership. I mentioned previously a seminar/workshop that we conducted with high-level leaders in 2001, and what happened when in discussing the origins of genocide I talked about divisions between us and them, and groups turning against each other. Seven years after the genocide the leaders said: 'but in Rwanda there are no groups.' Only after long discussion did the leaders overcome this ideologically created barrier and come to the view that there may not be biologically different groups in Rwanda, but there are socially constructed groups.

With intense hostility, civil war, and genocide in the recent past, it is understandable that the government wants to limit angry public debate that may incite violence. But if the suppression of public discussion is eased, if democratic institutions are allowed to operate, and if just social practices are maintained, over time people may make the ideology of unity now imposed on them their own. Before the elections of 2010 the government is moving in an opposite direction. Setting unity, a shared identity, as a goal to move toward and strive for, while allowing and even encouraging civil public discussion and debate, democratic processes, and if people insist, separate Hutu and Tutsi identities in the framework of this common identity, could serve as a constructive ideology.

Constructive Ideologies and Reflections on Islam

In the case of the Palestinian–Israeli conflict, a constructive ideology might stress the benefits of peace and security for both sides: avoiding the death, grief, and rage that the actions of each side create; improving the lives of Palestinians, their physical safety, economic well-being, and dignity; reducing the long-term danger to Israel's survival; and enhancing the moral stature of each people. It could also envision an economic community. Cooperation and collaboration between two independent states could lead to many benefits. The ideological vision might also stress that peace between the two groups would contribute to peace in the region and, in turn, peace in the world.

One way to combat destructive ideologies is by providing powerful alternative visions. A joint commission from the two groups could work on such a shared vision, continuously informing and inviting participation from the two populations. The resulting contact between the groups and dialogue in the service of a positive vision would help to overcome devaluation and destructive ideologies and promote reconciliation.

To inhibit Islamic terrorism outside Israel requires the dominance of positive Islamic ideologies or doctrines over the currently influential ones. There is a great deal of religious writing in Islam that can be used to advocate and incite violence, which is also true of the other major religions.[3] Inspired by these, contemporary terrorists have managed to interpret suicide as martyrdom, in the service of defensive jihad, even though killing oneself is prohibited in Islam. But there is also a great deal of religious writing that promotes caring and love, which can be used to develop a more moderate Islam, with a belief in a shared humanity and respect for all religions. This is a challenge for most religions.[4] While outsiders can help, such a shift has to come from within Islam.[5] It requires dialogue within Islam, the engagement of political and religious leaders, teachers in religious schools, as well as ordinary Muslims. This has been an ongoing process, gaining momentum. As an example, after initial silence there has been increasing although still insufficient reaction to killings by suicide bombers.

One of the great issues for the West is the role and treatment of women in Muslim societies and families: their subservient role, limited opportunities, and honor killings. For some, such as the Dutch, Muslim women's subservient position is one major hindrance to a positive vision of life together in the Netherlands. But even in this regard, there are complexities. While according to Herman Beck of the University of Tilberg in 2008, only two women were full professors at universities in the Netherlands, 20% of full professors were women at universities in Indonesia.[6] In Iran, the majority of undergraduate students are women. However, this represents a very partial emancipation of women in Iran, since they cannot get jobs after they graduate.

Why is there so much reluctance in Islam to modernize the role of women? People see their role as a central aspect of Islamic societies. The self-protective tendencies that have emerged in response to modernization and globalization, the uncertainty these have created, and the turn to fundamentalism can rigidify their role. The more Islamic countries develop the capacity to deal with change, the more changes in the world may bring about internal changes in Muslim societies in the role of women.

There are active efforts now to change Islam. Islamic principles about gender relations are reinterpreted by some Islamic scholars. Amina Wadud[7] uses the Koran, and fundamental principles of Islam, to challenge the views of women's role, the acceptance of gender inequalities, and historical practices in the treatment of women. She uses the texts of Islam to argue that these views and practices are incongruent with core principles of Islamic morality. Advocating a more peaceful and tolerant version of Islam seems to endanger its advocates less than before. As a more moderate Islam becomes influential, it will have to be introduced into those mosques and Islamic schools that have promoted fundamentalist or radical versions of Islam. Especially mosques had a significant role in moving young men to join violent jihad.

Many Western leaders have talked in the wake of terrorist attacks in derogatory and even apocalyptic terms about Islam. Verbal attacks on Muslims in Europe, for example, in the Netherlands, began before 9/11.[8] Political scientist Samuel Huntington had earlier declared that there is a war of civilizations, and some students of Islam consider the difference between Islamic and Western cultures and ways of life unbridgeable.[9] The reaching out by Barack Obama to Islam in 2009 seemed a new beginning, but without follow up. Ongoing dialogue is needed between political and religious leaders of Islam (who are often the same) and leaders of Western, non-Islamic nations, in addition to speeches, and brief, formal meetings between leaders such as the Pope and Saudi princes.

Changes within a group are influenced by new events. While the Saudi ruling family has established a very strict version of Islam and worked on promoting it in the rest of the world, as they themselves suffered terrorist attacks they have begun to take action to reduce the influence of radical Imams. They have also created a re-education program for terrorists in jail.

Changes within Islam can be helped by changes in Western policies that affect Muslim countries as well as minorities living in Western countries. Acceptance by the West of the result of democratically held elections that bring an Islamic party to power would show a more positive attitude toward Islam. Algeria's refusal to respect such election results—with support by the United States and other Western countries—led to great violence. In the Palestinian territories, where the United States exerted pressure to hold elections, the refusal to accept the victory of Hamas increased turmoil and violence between Hamas and Fatah, and Hamas and Israel. Waiting to see whether responsibility as a government and engagement with other countries moderate Hamas would have been wise policy.

Outsiders can support moderates within Islam, but with caution. Support from those regarded as enemies (or designated victims) can co-opt and reduce the influence of moderates.[10] Still, courage and positive initiatives by internal leaders can be supported and gently instigated by outsiders.

Ramadan, a Swiss Muslim philosopher, is one of the architects of "European Islam," the notion that Muslims living in Europe can create a form of their religion and culture that can coexist with Western democratic values. He has called for coexistence and civic participation, communities that concern themselves with the welfare of all members, and responsible relations between Muslims and non-Muslims.[11] Westerners question the degree of Ramadan's commitment to change in Islam. Some see him as a practitioner of *taqiyya*, an Islamic practice of saying different things to Arabs and Westerners.[12] This difference may be necessary so that he is not discredited in his group, which would eliminate his influence. There are many other Muslim leaders also working for change. In a meeting in Austria in 2005, 160 Imams called for gender equality. Meanwhile, some outsiders see the engagement by liberal Westerners with Muslims as naïve denial of the danger Islam represents,[13] while others see it as essential to facilitate change. Engagement is essential, with a combination of understanding the other, sensitivity, and holding on to core principles—a challenging task.

A natural and fundamental source of change is life experience. Living in pluralistic cultures has created substantial transformation in Muslims in Europe, especially in the younger generation.[14] One study in Rotterdam found that while young Muslims strongly identify with Islam, their Islam is individualistic and pluralistic, allowing internal debate, tolerance, and friendship across group lines. This was especially true, however, of more educated young people, especially females.[15] Such changes will be more widespread if Muslims are more accepted and integrated in European countries.

Europe has much less history of immigration than the United States, and accordingly it has less experience with immigrants who have a different religion, different values, and a different way of life. The Dutch want Muslims to be assimilated, while Muslims want to be integrated—to both maintain their identity as Muslims and become part of Dutch society. The French expect that minorities will submerge their identity in the larger identity of the nation.[16] Visions of social arrangements that allow minorities to maintain a double identity, identification both with their country, and with their group and culture, would contribute to peaceful relations.

While American Muslims are much better integrated and generally materially better off than European Muslims, this does not mean that the lure of fighting cannot reach them and appeal to them. The prejudice evoked by terrorism, and sometimes by different habits and customs (for example, Somali women in Minnesota tend to wear traditional dress) and due to the always existing divisions across group lines, the United States fighting wars in Muslim countries in the course of which many civilians are also killed, (see chapter 16), nationalism, personal life issues and the influence of recruitment probably all had a role in attracting 20 young Somalis in Minnesota to join a rebel group in Somalia associated with terrorism. In Somalia some of them were among the attackers of a U.N. compound. Part of the concern by U. S. authorities is that some may return to engage in terror attacks here.

Creating Constructive Groups or Alternative Communities

Ideological movements help people fulfill basic psychological needs. Sometimes they also help fulfill material needs, as in Rwanda, where young men who joined the youth arms of political parties, some of which later became the militia that killed people, also received food. Constructive groups, communities, and visions lessen the lure of destructive ideological movements. Groups that work together to create, promote, and fulfill constructive ideologies through concrete actions can satisfy needs for identity, connection, a feeling of effectiveness and control, and a new but positive comprehension of reality. Nonideological groups can also fulfill needs for connection, identity, and effectiveness, and they can provide a constructive alternative in difficult times.

What makes groups constructive is their values, purpose and goals, and internal organization. Ideally such groups will be inclusive in who is allowed in. They will not be strongly hierarchical. People need not deny important parts of who they are to be members. The limited relevant research shows that cooperating on positive tasks leads to positive attitudes to people both inside and outside the group.[17] Alternative communities, constructive groups, can be formed everywhere—schools, churches, and civic organizations.

Youth gangs have psychological value for young people. Arnold Goldstein, a psychologist who studied them, has proposed transforming them into prosocial gangs, instead of trying to eliminate them, which at any rate is a difficult proposition. Instead of selling drugs or engaging in violence, they can engage in legitimate business enterprises, such as owning Laundromats.[18] This would also serve the important function of providing jobs for young people.

A striking example of constructive groups is provided by a group of former child soldiers in Liberia.[19] Like many children in a number of countries in Africa, they were abducted by warring groups or enticed to join by the availability of food, protection, and community. Such children were often forced to kill people in their own villages, a practice used by guerillas and militias to cement their commitment to the group they fought with. When they managed to get free, reconnecting them to their villages was an important aspect of reconciliation.[20] The members of the group in Liberia have transformed themselves. They go to school, avoid the culture of drugs and alcohol of their former comrades, and devote themselves to serving their community. They call themselves "Future Guardians of Peace." In their late teens and early twenties, they act as big brothers and sisters to younger classmates, share their small allowances, and act as peacemakers in the community. They are active bystanders to conflict between children, as well as adults. They listen and engage in a mild manner.

How did such transformation come about? Nancy Myers,[21] who spent 3 weeks with them, writes that slowly, over time, because the emotional difficulty was too great to do it all at once, they had the chance to tell trusted listeners what they did and what was done to them. A U.S.-Liberian nongovernmental organization gave them food in exchange for doing chores and construction work, then gave them a permanent home and will pay for their education through college. Myers writes that the opportunity to be of service is an important element of their transformation. Healing, support, and the ability to help others are all experiences that help move people who have suffered away from aggression, to foster altruism born of suffering.[22]

Other examples of constructive groups for young people, even if temporary, are summer camps for youth from poor, violent neighborhood in Boston, and for Palestinian and Israeli children in Maine. In a project in Springfield, Massachusetts, young people receive pay for joining a group in which they are trained in agricultural work. On two small plots in the city they plant, grow, and harvest vegetables and fruits, which they sell at a roadside stand and a farmer's market.[23]* Church groups can serve both youth and adults. In Holyoke, Massachusetts, a city with a large Hispanic population, a pastor in a conservative church with primarily older Anglo members had social events that attracted large numbers of Hispanic youth. Starting with such events, joint activities and stable community groups can be created.

Micro-credits have gained worldwide popularity in promoting small-scale entrepreneurship. Small amounts of money can enable people in many parts of the world to start a small business, thus providing a livelihood. Such financial help is often accompanied by training and ongoing support by other people, thus providing community. In French suburbs, for example, 4.7 million people are primarily immigrants, many of them Muslims, with limited education. Fifty-six percent of them are unemployed. In recent years, they rioted a number of times, in 2005 torching thousands of cars.[24] Two young immigrant business-men, Abdellah Aboulharjan and Asis Senni, created an organization in 2002, Jeunes Enterpreneurs (young entrepreneurs), to help young immigrants in these communities. Since 2003, they have helped to start 50 projects. People come to them with a proposal, and both the proposal and the person's capacity to fulfill the proposal are evaluated. People who receive financial support are helped to create a business plan and are mentored by others who are also often of foreign origin and have their own businesses. Lawyers and accountants provide their services free of charge. The money for the start-up is provided by many sources, including wealthy donors who realize the value of these projects, as well as by municipalities. The recipients only have to pay back money as they make a sufficient profit. The businesses they open, such as garages, clothing companies, and home delivery services, also provide jobs for other people.[25*]

Whether enabling people through micro-credit and other support, or work projects such as those created during the depression by the Roosevelt adminis-tration, work can provide not only livelihood, but also community, identity, dig-nity, and feelings of effectiveness. The people who initiate such activities and provide support are fostering alternative communities.

In countries that are at risk for or have suffered violence, and that often have few civic organizations, outsiders who know the culture can initiate construc-tive groups or help with local efforts. In one town in Bosnia, people fought along group lines, and a great deal of hostility has remained. But the women had a shared interest in bartering with each other for household goods. Because of the hostility around them, they regularly met outside the town. Such an informal community can be one avenue for reconstructing relations. Outside organiza-tions could finance places for these women to meet—as they have provided money for hair salons in Bosnia for women to meet.

Constructive groups that engage in political activity could provide young Palestinians with alternatives to joining terrorist groups. In European countries constructive groups could help fulfill the needs of young Muslims for identity and connection, and foster a positive worldview. Such groups could be orga-nized around sports, cultural or intellectual activities, skills training, work, community affairs, and political activity. If they cut across group lines, they can improve group relations. Groups fostering social change could provide a combi-nation of a constructive ideology and community.

In the case of occupation or repression, constructive communities that fulfill the psychological and possibly material needs of people pose moral ques-tions if they make people accept the conditions their group faces. But instead of co-opting dissatisfaction and resistance, such communities can work on change by peaceful means. This issue has been addressed to some extent by Israeli and Palestinians students who have participated in Seeds of Peace, an organization that has promoted leadership programs for young people from various conflict-ridden regions in the world since 1993. They did not remain silent but expressed their views to each other on Listservs at times the conflict or violence escalated.[26]

In the midst of their hostile relations, many constructive Palestinian and Israeli groups have been emerging. They include children cleaning beaches together, adults trekking the desert together, development projects funded by the World Bank in which communities work side by side, and, again, the families of people killed by each side getting together to work for reconciliation. Some of these are more transient activities, and others qualify as constructive communities.[27] Such interactions may have prevented even greater violence. But the conflict is still ongoing. Peace would be served by extended engagement by leaders, as well as reconciliation processes.

At the conference on genocide prevention in Sweden that I co-organized, which inspired our work on reconciliation in Rwanda, a group of young participants, all under 30 years of age, created an organization called Global Youth Connect, with the help of an older participant who became the group's godfather, Frank Ochberg. It has been taking groups of young people to post-conflict regions ever since, such as Guatemala and Rwanda. They learn about the history of events and meet citizens and officials. Each of these groups is a constructive community, with its members inspired to act on others' behalf. I was delighted when one day in Rwanda, at a training session we conducted for the combined staff of the radio projects from Rwanda, Burundi, and the Congo, a group of young people, mostly Westerners, marched in, sat down, and listened to our discussions. We found out during a break that they were part of Global Youth Connect.

The reintegration of former perpetrators into the community is an important opportunity to create constructive groups. Every country where there has been internal violence has to deal with this issue. It is a great challenge in Rwanda, as killers are released from prison and sent back to live in their communities. Many of those who have returned from the Congo, where they fought in militias, do not go to prison at all. The younger ones among them were too young to have been genocidaires,[28] although they fought and most likely killed in the Congo.

Fighters who have returned from the Congo go into demobilization camps, where they are exposed to material similar to what released prisoners get in reeducation camps. They are taught about current life in Rwanda, including the new postethnic ideology. Many perpetrators who were old and sick, and who were very young at the time of the genocide, were released from jail in 2003; they went through reeducation camps before they were returned to their communities. When we worked with the Unity and Reconciliation Commission, which has been in charge of the reeducation camps, many of its staff participated in our trainings. They expressed the intention to introduce understanding the origins of violence and its impact into their work in the camps. Our radio programs provide such information to the general population. This kind of knowledge and understanding may help people deal with the challenges of everyday life, as former killers, their relatives, and survivors engage with each other. It prepares them to work together in groups on economic or building projects. Actively creating such groups would serve reconciliation.

As journalist Philip Gourevitch describes,[29] fighters who returned from the Congo also learn in reeducation camps how to form business collectives and work with banks. The government gives them several hundred dollars and "monitors regularly follow-up with them to insure that they are finding a place in civilian life." All this creates pain in the short run, as people have to face each other as neighbors in the villages, but it may help over time to pacify Rwanda and create a peaceful country. Unfortunately survivors, in this country of limited resources, receive less help. In Gourevich's words, President Kagame "favors political expediency over justice."[30] With the minority Tutsis in power, a combination of justice processes and attention to Hutu perpetrators may help with the reconstruction of the country.

Common Identities, Dual Identities, and Inclusive Caring

Humanizing the other, significant contact, and healing from the past can expand caring about people beyond "ingroups." Such inclusive caring is likely to be one of the most potent inhibitors of group violence. Learning in childhood to accept and positively value human beings in general is probably the most powerful root of inclusive caring.[31] Taking the perspective of others, walking in their shoes, which most people, especially leaders, tend not to do in highly antagonistic situations, can lead to empathy with *them*, and if their situation is difficult, to compassion or sympathy. This makes positive actions toward others more likely.

The psychologists Sam Gaertner and John Dovidio[32] have proposed that contact and other procedures between groups can help create a common ingroup identity, breaking down the separation between us and them and leading people to "recategorize" others, to see their own and the other group as part of a single, superordinate group. Recategorization involves "expanding intergroup boundaries."[33] As a result, favoring the ingroup also means favoring the former outgroup. Both intentional procedures, and naturally occurring conditions that create an overarching cause, such as being members of the same sports team or pulling together as members of a nation in response to threat, can give people a common identity.

Including another group in a common ingroup identity creates more positive attitudes toward that group. It also increases help for its members.[34] When people identify more with a larger community that includes the other group, they forgive more the harm that group has done to them. This was true of

Catholics in Northern Ireland who identified more with their country, but not of Protestants. When Jewish participants in a study were led to think about the Holocaust as Germans harming Jews, they were less forgiving of Germans than when the Holocaust was described as an example of violence by humans toward other humans.[35] Our procedures in workshops in Rwanda, with examples from group violence from around the world, were likely to have produced such a shift.

When groups are in intense conflict, or when there is intense devaluation and hostility, both creating such common identities and maintaining them over time are difficult. Social psychologist Marilyn Brewer's "optimal distinctiveness" theory suggests that people have competing motives; they want both to assimilate to and differentiate from others. Social identity theory suggests that as members of groups people prefer to differentiate themselves from others, especially when their group is threatened.

Emphasizing similarities between groups can sometimes intensify negative attitudes as a way of "reaffirming positive distinctiveness."[36] For example, emphasizing students' common university membership created more bias by humanities and math students against the other group than emphasizing their separate group memberships. I mentioned earlier that the assimilation of Jews in Germany, their greater similarity to other Germans, may have increased prejudice by some Germans. In fostering a common group identity, it is important therefore to acknowledge and recognize the nature, characteristics, and differences between the groups involved. Having their identity as members of their group affirmed can increase people's readiness to accept a common identity with another group. When it comes to groups in conflict, recognition of both groups' history and suffering is also important.

Dovidio and his colleagues[37] address this issue by proposing a "dual identity model," emphasizing both a common identity and separate subgroup identities. This makes a great deal of sense; as I suggested, it would be a constructive step in Rwanda to encourage people to regard themselves as Rwandans, as well as allowing them to identify themselves as Hutus or Tutsis. In the United States, people who hold dual identities, as both members of a subgroup and as Americans (e.g., Korean Americans), have more positive attitudes toward members of other racial and ethnic groups than those who define themselves only in terms their subgroup identity. However, stronger identification with America as a superordinate group predicted greater sensitivity to the just treatment of people both by minority and majority groups, regardless of how strong their identification was with their own group.[38] The examples of greater forgiveness cited earlier illustrate dual identity at work—people seeing themselves as both Catholics and Northern Irish, as both Jewish and human. But working to create or imposing dual identities can also create conflict, as among banking executives involved in a merger, and between members of blended families.[39]

What is the relationship between notions of a common or dual identity, and inclusive caring? A common identity means that at least at one level "we are one." A common identity can be the result of the influence of a situation, which can shift; however, it can also be socialized and become a stable personal disposition. Inclusive caring means "we care about the 'other.'" The other can be members of a devalued group, even an enemy, or human beings in general. Inclusive caring is a personal disposition that begins to develop in children as a result of guidance and experience. It can also develop through learning by doing. It may extend first to members of a particular outgroup and then evolve into caring about all human beings.

Inclusive caring requires that people see others as human beings to whom moral principles apply and who deserve consideration. It can mean that even if one does not include others in a specific common or shared identity, or even if one sees others in a negative way in certain regards, one grants them rights and consideration as human beings. This was presumably true of the small percentage of Christian rescuers in Nazi Europe who were anti-Semitic.[40]

Rescuers in Europe during the Holocaust who endangered their lives to save Jews tended to have had parents who treated them in a loving way and who had more positive attitudes toward and more actual engagement with people outside their own group, including Jews.[41] But having significant contact with others does not necessarily guarantee a common identity. In one study, Bosnian Muslims' reports of more contact with Serbs were associated with positive attitudes toward them, but not with greater identification with a shared larger group, Bosnia.[42] Contact with individuals may have led to more caring, but not to the experience of a common identity.

The Evolution of Caring and Positive Reciprocity

We have seen that learning by doing can be negative. But it can also be positive.[43] The attitudes and actions of the rescuers' parents provided guidance, models, and opportunities for learning by doing. Rescuers often started with limited action, sometimes in response to a request. Hiding a single person or family in their apartment or house, many became committed. They continued to hide people, often taking in more people. If they succeeded to help them move on to a safer place, some of them sought further opportunities to help.[44] Some of my research I describe in Chapter 22 also shows positive learning by doing.

People who help others focus their attention on the suffering and need of the people they help and become more concerned with their welfare. Progressively, their concern can extend to human beings in general. They may also come to see themselves as helpful people. Positive attitudes and actions by groups can also evolve over time.

Inclusive caring can also develop through positive reciprocity. The psychologist Charles Osgood, concerned about Soviet–U.S. relations in the 1960s, suggested that when hostile parties take small positive actions, which cost little, there would be likely reciprocation. He called this the principle of graduated and reciprocal initiative in tension reduction (GRIT).[45] There is experimental research with individuals that confirms this principle, as well as support in the relations of nations. For example, Israel allowed Egypt to open the Suez Canal, and in turn Egypt allowed ships to go to and from Israel through the canal.[46] This probably contributed to the reduction of hostility that eventually led to peace between the two countries.

Reciprocity in human relations is a universal norm and thus is found in every society.[47] The famous Swiss psychologist Jean Piaget considered reciprocity as the core logic of human interaction. It is probably in part genetically based. Considering positive reciprocity, people who mutually help each other are more likely to survive and pass on their genes to their offspring. Reciprocity is also shaped by and develops through experience, as children are taught to follow the norm, and as we appreciate those who are kind to us and therefore want to benefit them.

It is more likely that positive actions will be reciprocated if the actor's intentions are perceived as positive. Did the other intend to help, to gain something by reciprocation, or to manipulate? These interpretations depend on the circumstances and on the perceiver's personality and attitude toward the other. It is more likely that intentions will be perceived as positive if helpful actions address real needs and provide real benefits. It is also more likely if they respect the dignity of the recipient, rather than if they are provided in ways that assert, or are used to establish, the superiority of the provider.[48] Moreover, it is important that in the case of hostile relations positive actions not be interpreted as giving in, as a response to force, which then encourages the use of more force. This appeared to happen when Israel withdrew from Lebanon and Gaza, both unilateral actions that were interpreted as due to the actions of Hezbollah in Lebanon and Hamas in Gaza, that is, as defeat rather than based on positive intentions. Prior engagement, negotiation, and the insistence on mutual concessions may avoid this.

In addition to spontaneous acts, hostile parties can engage in a progressive exchange of beneficial actions, with the understanding that reciprocity is expected. Even if the actions of each party are the result of such explicit or implicit understanding, they can generate good feelings in the other party.

Naturally, negative responses inhibit a cycle of positive reciprocity. When the President of Iran, Mahmoud Ahmadinejad, appeared in a public forum in the United States in 2007, a positive initiative, there was intense criticism of Columbia University for inviting him. Presumably in response to this, the President of Columbia publicly derogated Ahmadinejad while introducing him to the audience. The effects of such actions may be enormous, in generating hostility. All too often between opposing parties positive actions are initiated with hesitance, ambivalence, and negative elements. This makes the development of a positive reciprocal cycle unlikely.

Perceptions of the other are also affected by what social psychologists have called the *fundamental attribution error.* People tend to explain their own behavior as a response to their circumstances. I hit him, a child might say, because he was mean to me, or because I was upset after a teacher shouted at me. However, they often explain others' behavior as due to their personality or character. She hit me because she is mean, or because she is a bad person. Assigning negative intention to the other would lead to more intense reciprocation of negative behavior. While the same is true of positive behavior, tending to see the actor as a good person or someone who cares about us, experience suggests that this may hold less in group relations. Perhaps people believe that positive actions by groups are less often based on selfless motives.

If we see harmful behavior toward us as deeply rooted in who the other party is, we assume that they cannot or will not change. We respond aggressively as a way of protecting ourselves. Understanding how life conditions and culture have influenced these actions may ease our reactions. Ralph White has power-fully argued for the importance of realistic empathy, seeing events through the eyes of an opponent. This makes it possible to see what led to these actions and to know what is required for making peace. Such role taking can also give rise to sympathy, if harmful actions arose out of loss, fear, humiliation, and suffering. Understanding the origins of others' actions and empathizing with them makes it more likely that we moderate our reactions, and reciprocate positive actions, so that a system of positive reciprocity can evolve. Immediately after one's group has suffered great harm, empathy with the harm doers is unlikely, but over time understanding and other processes can give rise to it.

What are some implications of this discussion for some of the cases in this book? In Rwanda the government could apply the ideology that "we are all Rwandans" by acknowledging harm done to Hutus in the past—before 1959, or when Hutu civilians or refugees in Zaire/Congo were killed. It could express empathy for past suffering by Hutus and engage in some kind of justice process. This could foster a common group identity. Hutus outside the country fully acknowledging the genocide, and showing empathy for Tutsis could also initiate a reciprocal process. In the Palestinian–Israeli conflict Israel could open more routes closed to Palestinians, move settlers out of Palestinian lands and giving their houses to Palestinians, engage with Gaza in a constructive manner. Palestinians could commit themselves to non-violence. Reciprocity by the two sides would avoid negative interpretations of such acts.

Promoting Pluralism and Democracy, Moderating Respect for Authority

Dialogue is also a key component of pluralism and an avenue for the creation of pluralistic societies. Pluralism needs to have two aspects: free expression of varied values and beliefs; and the right of all groups to a voice in the public domain and to political participation. Muslim participation has been limited in local elections in the Netherlands in the early years of this century, especially in Amsterdam, where there were no Muslim candidates. Turkish participation was greater in Rotterdam, where there were Turkish candidates for council seats.[49] Minorities often have limited access to media and the public space. Their inclusion and political participation is part of peace building.

Schools in which children are allowed and encouraged to express their views contribute to a pluralistic society. Social institutions that are less hierarchical and child rearing that is less autocratic allow and develop people's voices, which fosters pluralism and moderates respect for authority. Violence becomes less likely as people express, rather than act out, their grievances. The ability to do this is probably one reason for the near absence of mass killing and genocide in democracies,[50] at least in mature democracies[51] that have not only elections but also inclusive civic institutions.

Revolution, civil war, and system change, even moving from a one-party to a multi-party system, frustrate basic needs of both the population and elites, and/or raise issues of identity and justice in multiethnic societies. They make mass violence more likely. Competitive elections soon after violence, with winners and losers, increase the likelihood of renewed violence.

Effective prevention requires that societies give voice to every group, minimize discrimination, and respond to justified grievances. This is often not found even in mature democracies, leading to riots, such as those in U.S. inner cities in the 1970s. Extremism grows when there is inequality, repression, and the inability by groups to get a response to justified grievances. In many groups, such as "militant civil rights protagonists in the United States ... terrorist cells that advocated the political separation of Quebec from Canada..." and others, the extreme elements lost influence when the rest of the society appeared ready and "motivated to resolve intergroup issues."[52] Prevention is advanced when societies become not only democratic and pluralistic but have systems that are responsive to the needs and grievances of various subgroups.

Moroccans in the Netherlands, Algerians in France, and in general Muslims in European countries have limited public voice. Minorities who are residents of a country are not always granted citizenship, as in Germany today. The civil war in Rwanda, which then led to genocide, would probably not have happened if neighboring countries had given citizenship to Tutsi refugees from Rwanda. They did not do that even for Tutsis who lived there for decades, or for their children who were born there.

When laws do grant equal rights, lack of cultural knowledge and empowerment, discrimination, and differentness can severely limit participation. The culture, education, and ease of adjustment of Muslim minority groups vary with their national and class background. Helping them acculturate and develop the capacity to use the opportunities of their new societies, including the opportunity to advocate for themselves, would reduce the likelihood that they turn to fundamentalism and extreme ideological groups.

Pluralism is incomplete in most societies, and it is restricted in all our primary cases. Moderate Palestinians in the West Bank and Gaza, Hutu Rwandans or Tutsis who oppose government actions, Islamic moderates, even Palestinian citizens of Israel, have had often severe limitations placed on them, if not by authorities and institutions, then by their fellow group members and the psychological situation that exists in their societies or communities. Political scientist Carrie Wickham[53] writes that in some Sunni Muslim Arab states, "revivalist" political organizations advocate democratic elections, at times equating it with Shura, the Islamic principle of consultation. However, the policies, institutions, and social conservatism of the population limit how far they go. They reject practices that would lead to the free commingling of men and women or allow women to vote and run for elected office.

But reformist thinkers also advocate the principle of *ijtihad*, which gives Muslims the right to "reinterpret sacred texts in the light of new circumstances" and articulate new positions on "intellectual and political pluralism and the rights of women."[54] Reinterpreting sacred texts and revising principles related to historical practices—in her case, about the role of women—is easier for Amina Wadud, a professor in the United States. It is more difficult for those living in Islamic countries. But consistent with our discussion of learning by doing, Wickham suggests that participation in such activities can lead to further changes in political actors' values and beliefs.

To prevent group violence, people need to be able and willing to critically evaluate information communicated to them by leaders, to make judgments, and to challenge authorities that lead in destructive directions. A "critical consciousness" is important for such actions. A media that is legally free and not restricted by undue respect for authority, commercial interests that shape editorial policy, and self-censorship is necessary to provide the information that enables people to use their judgment. Self-censorship, the limits and biases of editors and reporters set by the culture and political climate, is a challenge to true pluralism. Sometimes such self-censorship is conscious, but often it is automatic and must be corrected by training.[55]

Many societies around the world, in Africa, Asia, and elsewhere, are highly collectivist. The group is primary. Respect by individuals for the needs of the group and for authorities, and obedience to leaders are paramount attitudes and values. Expressing views that are contrary to prevalent views and oppose authorities is especially difficult. Constructive communities can provide people with support in developing and expressing perspectives that diverge from those offered by authorities or are dominant in the group.

Democratization is a primary avenue to promote pluralism and moderate respect for authority. Not only free elections but also media that fairly represent political candidates must be supported. The Open Society Institute, created by the philanthropist George Soros, has promoted democracy by supporting the creation of civic institutions, local organizations, and nongovernmental organizations (NGOs), especially in East European countries. Financial support, help in developing expertise to fulfill needed functions in society, and engagement with constructive internal actors are all important. Agencies in governments that I will later propose as instruments of prevention can help develop civic organizations as well.

A good constitution can be a central element in building democracy and enabling people to live together without violence. It describes essential principles to guide public life. It sets the norms that members of a society are to live by. National laws, institutions like the justice system and free press, and practices that grow out of them are guided by constitutions. "When minority rights are enshrined in constitutions, and implemented through electoral, justice and education systems," it is probable that conflict might not occur at all and, if it does, that it will not fester and become intractable.[56] A good constitution is a constructive ideology. Its principles have to be translated into institutions and practices so that they actually guide life in the society.

Promoting democracy in dictatorial or highly autocratic political systems is a great challenge. Without press freedom people cannot evaluate the truth or falsity of information put out by the government. Propaganda by the government can lead people to turn against devalued groups and "internal enemies" and to support repression, violent attitudes, and actions. If the government describes some group as a threat, it is difficult for people to know otherwise. Information on the Internet can help to some degree. But external actors are crucial. This makes it especially tragic that powerful democracies, like the United States, often support repressive systems, guided by ideological reasons and a (narrow) view of national interest. A constructive policy for external actors is to patiently and consistently oppose the autocratic practices of governments. It is to encourage democratic reforms through both sanctions and rewards, and to help promote civil society by engagement and dialogue. Such actions strengthen internal actors who are motivated to oppose the authoritarian system they live in. Consistent policies of this kind, rather than support for armed rebel groups to further often misguided notions of one's national interest, is the ideal approach to "nation building."

Summary

A constructive ideology/vision for social arrangements that provide a better life for everyone can provide hope and motivate all groups in as society to work together to fulfill this vision. Constructive groups, whether people working to fulfill such an ideology or other goals, including economic ones, can provide alternatives to destructive ideological movement in fulfilling basic needs. Positive actions, especially when individuals and groups perceive the actors' intention as benevolent, can lead to a cycle of reciprocity and peaceful relations. Giving people a voice, as well as giving groups the opportunity and empowerment to engage in the public domain and express and address their grievances, is an important element of pluralism. Together with civic institutions it can lead to the development of a mature democracy, which makes violence between groups in a society unlikely.

Notes

1 Vallacher et al., 2010. Significant publications by these authors about a "dynamical systems" perspective appeared just before this book entered the final stage of its production, actual printing. Their conceptualization is consistent with my thinking.

2 Amnesty International Report for Rwanda, 2009, at www.thereport.amnesty. org/en/regions/africa/rwanda

3 Kressell, 2007

4 Ibid.

5 Aslan, 2005

6 Herman Beck, University of Tilburg, Netherlands. Personal communication, August 2008

7 Wadud, 2006

8 Fortuyn, 1997; Staub, 2007b

9 Lewis, 2005

10 Volkan, 1998

11 Ramadan, 2004

12 Bawer, 2009

13 Ibid.

14 Cesari, 2003

15 Phalet, van Lotrigen & Entzinger, 2004

16 Staub, 2007b

17 Deutsch et.al., 2006; Staub, 1979

18 Goldstein & Glick, 1994

19 Myers, 2008

20 Wessells, 2007

21 Myers, 2008

22 Staub, 2003a, 2005c; Staub & Vollhardt, 2008; see Chapter 14

23 Kristen Brennan is in charge of the group; on one occasion I have participated in their activities

24 Van Dijk, 2008

25 Ibid. See also Praszkier et.al, 2010. Writing from a "dynamical systems" perspective, they call the people who initiate such activities "social entrepreneurs." They appropriately stress their value, in my terminology as active bystanders, and social change agents.

26 Kuriansky, 2009
27 Ibid.
28 Gourevitch, 2009
29 Ibid.
30 Ibid, p. 46
31 Staub, 2005c
32 Gaertner & Dovidio, 2000
33 Dovidio et al., 2009, p. 5
34 Ibid.
35 Wohl & Branscombe, 2005
36 Dovidio et al., 2009, p.6
37 Dovidio et al., 2009
38 Huo, 2003, described in Dovidio et al., 2009
39 For references see Dovidio et al., 2009
40 Oliner & Oliner, 1988
41 Ibid.
42 Cehajic et al., 2008
43 Staub, 1979, 1989
44 Oliner & Oliner, 1988
45 Osgood, 1962
46 Pettigrew, 2003
47 Mauss, 1954
48 Nadler, 2002
49 Tillie & Slijper, 2005
50 Rummell,1999
51 Staub, 1999b
52 Taylor & Louis, 2003, p. 181
53 Wickham, 2005
54 Wickham, 2005, p. 3; see also Staub, 2007b
55 Staub, 1989
56 Baldwin, Chapman, & Gray, 2007, p. 2

16

Changing Hearts and Minds

Information, Peace Education, Deradicalization, and
Public Education in Rwanda and the Congo

Educational experiences can change people's attitudes toward a devalued
and hostile group; decrease negative emotions; increase positive emotions,
acceptance, and openness to the other's "narrative." They can lead to more
willingness to say what one thinks and believes and to change in behavior.

Education of many kinds can counteract devaluation and promote positive
ideas and caring. In the course of engagement with terrorists, dialogue and
information have been used to bring about change in them. Public education
through the media can influence large numbers of people. The Internet has
been used both to recruit terrorists and to foster positive change in them. "Peace
education" has been used to attempt to change attitudes toward the other
through instruction and other ways. Education in this realm needs to be not
only informational but also experiential emotional.

Some Positive Research Findings

In one study with 565 Palestinian and Jewish Israeli adolescents, half of them
who participated in a year-long peace education program were less likely to
believe that war was a way to achieve the group's goals and saw peace in more
positive terms. This study took place at the time of the second *Intifada*. Hostility
toward Israel by Palestinian students who did not participate in the program
increased, but not by Palestinians in the program.[1]

Promoting positive relations in the midst of hostility is challenging. Gavriel
Salomon, an Israeli educational psychologist, reports the failure of a pilot study
conducted at Haifa University at the height of the *Intifada* and Israeli military
responses to it. Two pairs of Israeli-Palestinian and Israeli-Jewish teachers were
to correspond over the Internet. They were to write about how the *other* side sees
events that were part of the conflict, for example, the 1948 war and the exodus

of Palestinians, and to receive reactions from the other side. A variety of projects have found seeing the past through the lens of the other group, its narrative of the past, especially challenging. The project was based on research on "induced compliance," that as people assume perspectives (or engage in actions) contrary to their position, their position changes. However, the teachers, all of them concerned with peace, were unable to see events from the other group's perspective. The Palestinian teachers were frustrated and angry. They said that they could not "step into the shoes of the oppressors of their brethrens."[2]

The work of Carol Dweck, a professor of psychology at Stanford, and her associates points to the possibility of using education to reduce hate. In her past work on how well children learn, Dweck has drawn a distinction between the belief that intelligence is an "entity," something fixed that you either have or don't have, and the belief that intelligence changes with experience. She found that students who hold an entity view of intelligence do worse academically than those who hold what she has called an incremental view. But she also found that education can develop an incremental view, leading to improved learning and performance. She applied her experience in this domain in attempting to change hate.

In research with Israelis, Dweck and her associates[3] found in one study that hearing a conflict-related text led some people afterward to check off hatred among the feelings this text evoked in them. These people were also more likely to express desire for violent action against, and the removal of, Palestinians. In another study with a national survey, they found that people who already had an incremental view of group relations, believing that groups can change, expressed less anger and hatred toward and less desire for strong actions against Palestinians and more readiness for compromise.

In a third study, they provided Israelis with information, supposedly based on basic research, to promote the view that groups can change. One part of it said, "The main finding of this research is that patterns of violence in groups changed dramatically over the years as a result of both changes in the character of the dominant leaders and changes in the environment of the group." Participants exposed to such an incremental view expressed less hatred of Palestinians and substantially more support for compromise, openness to positive information, and willingness to take risks in negotiation. This was true not only of the participants in the study as a whole but also of those identified as hawks, ideologically on the right.

This research is a beginning. Most people who on a questionnaire check off hate as one of several emotions in response to hearing or reading about threat to their group are unlikely to hate the way committed members of destructive ideological movements do. Their "hate" can be reactive and defensive, with the need for defense reduced by the belief that the other group can change. Whatever the nature of their hate, the limited information that ameliorated it is likely to have a temporary effect. But more in-depth information of this kind can have lasting effects. These research findings and our work and research findings in Rwanda seem consistent with and support each other. We told people what social conditions, cultural characteristics, and psychological reactions and actions by leaders, followers, and bystanders have led to violence[4]; both this and the discussion that followed implied that with changes in some of these elements people's behavior will change and violence will be prevented.

Information provided to people can affect their perspective, either temporarily or lastingly. Research studies have shown, for example, that telling people to *observe* (i.e., to take a disinterested perspective to) someone who is experiencing distress, to *imagine* what it is like for the person, or to imagine *themselves* in that situation has very different effects on empathy. Imagining the other creates the most empathy, imagining the self in the situation somewhat less, and taking the role of an observer substantially less.[5] Information about what others' suffering is like, including one's opponents in a conflict, may be an important way to generate empathy.

In a similar vein, researchers who lead people to think about death, activating "mortality salience," have found that by also activating compassionate values of the group that people belonged to transformed the usual effects of mortality salience from negative to neutral or even positive. For example, people holding more fundamentalist Christian values in the United States support the use of military force more. But when they were reminded of the compassionate teachings of Jesus (e.g., "Love your neighbor as yourself"), they supported the use of violence less. When this was combined with thinking about death, they came to support the use of military force at the same level as non-fundamentalist Christians.[6] In another study, the combination of making mortality salient and presenting compassionate verses from the Koran reduced hostility to the United States and other Western countries by Iranian Shiite students, in comparison to students who had not thought about death or were not exposed to compassionate verses. People who visualize accepting, warm interpersonal relationships showed similar effects.[7]

When people face intense threat to their group and themselves, it is rare that they are reminded of the compassionate values of the group. Those around them tend to draw on and propagate hostile perspectives. These findings point again to the importance of developing humane values through socialization and life experience, so that they are high in people's hierarchy of values and are activated even under hostile conditions and threat. They also point to the importance of constructive leaders who activate such values even in threatening times. Research in this tradition has also found that Americans who were both exposed to pictures of families from varied cultures and were led to think about death responded with less anti-Arab prejudice.

Awareness of others, and reminders of our shared humanity, matter. Sometimes people live next to each other, but still their knowledge of the other consists primarily of stereotypes. Education about each other—Europeans and

Muslims living in Europe, and of Israelis and Palestinians—can inform about the life, culture, and history of the other group, stress the other's positive qualities, show their past and current suffering, and generate empathy. Even people who have lived intertwined lives but have created psychological and social walls, like Hutus and Tutsis, can benefit from such education.

Deradicalization, Disengagement and Preventing Radicalization

In recent years programs to "deradicalize" captured or suspected Islamic terrorists, approximately 100,000 in custody in 2009, have been created at many places around the world.[8] A central component of deradicalization programs is religious authorities engaging in dialogue with detainees about their ideology, in this case the nature of their religious beliefs and their relationship to terrorist activities, and promoting a more tolerant and peaceful vision of "true" Islam. In some programs former "militants" do this.

Kruglanski and his associates[9] see terrorist ideology as consisting of a grievance, inherent in which is some form of injustice, a culprit or actor assumed to be responsible for the grievance, and a method, terrorism, that is considered morally justifiable because it addresses a great injustice. However, like other destructive ideologies, terrorist ideology can include an aspect that is positive, at least for those who hold them, sometimes specific (such as Northern Ireland uniting with Ireland), sometimes much less tangible (like creating a world consistent with God's design, or creating a Muslim Caliphate).

In Saudi prisons, moderate Muslim clerics engage prisoners in discussion in the attempt to change their understanding of Islam and their ideological views. There is also psychological counseling of prisoners. There is material help for families, at times with supplemental income, health care and schooling for the children. At the end of the program they assess the detainees' religious orientation to Islam. To prevent relapse, the program enlists families, holding them responsible for the released prisoners' actions.[10]

A project in Singapore also works with prisoners. It engages them around beliefs and ideologies, but it also helps their families—it supports the education of their children and offers professional training to their wives. It is hoped that such care for their families lessens the prisoners' anger and frustration so that they "open up to moderate religious interpretation and accept the notion that jihadism is contrary to the humane principles on which Islam is founded."[11] Helping families is hoped to address some of the emotional roots of commitment to an extreme ideology.

While anecdotal information indicates positive effects of deradicalization, these programs have not been evaluated in appropriate research. A test of religious beliefs can show knowledge of what is expected, not what people actually believe. While this does not mean that the program is ineffective, one graduate of the Saudi program was reported in 2010 to be a leader of Al Qaeda in Yemen.

The United States has a program in Iraq with 26,000 detainees. It offers "religious de-radicalization; coupled with vocational training; civic education; art programs; family and tribe and community engagement; counseling; medical (physical and mental) treatment; and job placement."[12] All of these elements are important for people to change and be able to reenter normal life and to reconnect with a larger community.

Developing an alternative religious/ideological view is crucial. Attempting to negate an ideology is less likely to change people strongly committed to it than offering an alternative that addresses the minds and hearts of people and fulfills the needs the original ideology has served. Belief in a more humane Islam moves in that direction. But the deradicalization programs only challenge and attempt to change belief in the use of violence, not beliefs relating to democracy or the role of women. This may make it easier for past or potential "jihadists" to accept them—or may offer too little of a changed world view to have long-term influence. Moreover, these programs don't provide people with means to address grievances—except when the grievance is their immediate life situation.

Earlier references to cases have shown that for many people, their motivation for entering terrorism is not their material circumstance. I have discussed the power of ideas (and feelings associated with ideas) in human life. Recently both in relation to terrorism and in relation to morality in general the concept of *sacred* (or protected) *values* has been used. These are values that are thought of as absolute, that possess a "transcendental" significance. Compromise, deciding about actions related to a sacred value depending on associated costs and benefits, is morally prohibited in the group that holds that value.[13] The rights of the refugees from 1948 might be such a sacred value for Palestinians. The sacred value need not prescribe solutions, but simply that the rights must be addressed. For some jihadists, violent jihad can be a sacred value. To the extent their views of what Islam holds about jihad and violence can be successfully redirected, it shows that sacred values, like most human thought and feelings, are not immutable.

But beyond such reformulation, to gain hope and inspiration, people facing complex circumstances need positive visions, constructive ideologies-relevant to their circumstances, grievances and values-and some sense that they can be fulfilled. For example, Muslim minorities in Europe need visions that realistically offer them connection to the democratic societies they are part of, as well as community practices that develop attitudes and skills to bring this connection about.

In contrast to deredicalization, at Guantanamo their severe treatment may have intensified the prisoners' enmity. According to Pentagon sources, at least 74 of the 534 inmates released as of May 2009 have gone back to fighting.[14] A couple of former inmates have turned up as terrorist leaders in Yemen.

To change course requires separation from one's former comrades; addressing or reformulating sacred values, finding new vision, meaning, and purpose in life; developing skills that make a new way of life possible; and reconnecting to a community. Approaches to reintegrating child soldiers into the community in African countries, which I have mentioned and will further discuss, provide some further suggestions for how to do this.

In addition to general approaches, idealist, respondents, and lost souls would best be deradicalized by different additional experiences. For idealists, a constructive ideological view would be especially important. For respondents healing from the effects of past victimization, whether personal or as group members, and coming to see constructive ways to address still existing grievances, would be important. For lost souls, connection, community, finding ways to fulfill basic needs would be paramount. For all of them, separating from a terrorist group and comrades in a dignified way, without feeling that they are betraying them, would matter. While connection to past comrades does present a danger of re-radicalization, engaging people to help their comrades move into the mainstream of society could serve this purpose. These considerations mean that the roots of engagement—the combination of personal history, the push of societal climate, social conditions, the pull of friends already involved—ought to be assessed and considered in approaches to deradicalization and prevention.

Independent of deradicalization programs, sometimes terrorists lose their motivation, become disillusioned, and disengage from their group. John Horgan, a political scientist, has studied 26 such people, former members of groups like the Irish Republican Army and Al Qaeda.[15] Some of them, while they accepted the necessity to kill, still found acts their group engaged in as morally difficult to accept, in Horgan's words as beyond their internal limit, such as killing a pregnant police officer, killing too many people, or forcing children and old people to fight with them—or robbing banks. Others were disillusioned when instead of the excitement of action in the service of improving the world they found boredom, as they sat around for interminable hours in safe houses, and competition and jealousy among members. Still others realized that the goals of the group are unattainable. However, some of those who stopped to engage in terrorist acts continued to serve their group in other ways.

Terrorist groups have intense hold on their members and leaving them is difficult. Still, what is learned from such research can be used to attract terrorists away from their groups, as well as in prevention. Members of communities from which terrorists recruit can be helped to understand, using the Internet, radio, and television programs, that this is not a glamorous life, that the group may not fulfill personal needs as much as they hope for, and that terrorist actions cross extreme moral limits, and do so without achieving worthwhile goals. Horgan also found that some disengaged because their life goals have changed with age, for example, wanting to get married and to have children. Educational influences can point out that life goals change.

Deradicalization and preventing radicalization involve similar processes. Some programs try to prevent terrorism by entering into dialogue on Islamist Web sites. In one project, supported by the foreign ministry of Saudi Arabia, Sunni clerics and other Islamic scholars, working with psychologists and sociologists, enter extremist Web sites and engage in discussion with participants. As in deradicalization programs, the aim is to move them from extremist to more tolerant forms of Islam.

Horgan offers a useful distinction between push factors and pull factors that lead to terrorism. In my terms the push factors include both the environmental conditions (such as repression, inequality, humiliation) and the psychological effects of the personal history of people, especially respondents or lost souls. The pull factors include the opportunity to live up to ideals, to right wrongs, to fulfill basic needs, community, for some the thrill of adventure. They include what some authors refer to as a sense of significance gained by people who want to "be somebody" and believe they can be by acting for an important cause—an ideology, their community and comrades.

Especially when their terrorism does not address a true grievance, understanding the influences that give rise to it can be helpful. It enables would be terrorists to see the guidance they receive from others as incitement, not truth, and terrorism as the outcome of psychological and social influences, not heroism. It can lead them to understand reciprocity, that violence begets violence.

A significant challenge is that for some terrorists, including cases I already mentioned, an important push factor seems to be outsiders attacking Muslims and the death of Muslim civilians in the course of fighting. The wife of a Jordanian double agent, Balawi, who killed a group of CIA operatives, claimed that the United States invasion of Iraq greatly transformed her husband. Faisal Shahzad, the would be Times Square bomber, repeatedly talked to family and friends about his anger about violence against Muslims in Afghanistan and elsewhere. In 2009 and the first half of 2010 about 25 American Muslims have been arrested as potential terrorists. A number of them reported that they were motivated by revenge for U.S. drone attacks in Pakistan on supposed Al Qaeda members, which at times also kills members of their families and civilians. We don't know all selective personal factors that determine who responds to this situation with turning to terrorism. Difficulties with jobs and family relations are likely to, and appear to have a role.[16]

It is challenging, in face of the reality of fighting between Westerners and Muslims in places like Iraq, Afghanistan and Pakistan, and the conflict between Israelis and Palestinians, to prevent the emergence of motivation to participate in fighting and revenge by education alone. Serious discussion of differences in beliefs and world views and ways of bridging them can be useful. Education can help justify the fighting, and its particular methods, to the extent they are justifiable from the perspective of Muslims. Convincing efforts to resolve conflicts in peaceful ways, when possible, even if they don't bring results, demonstrate good will.

Engaging with and helping to build communities can contribute to prevention, whether people's original communities or new, constructive groups. In Amsterdam, an idea important in working to prevent radicalization was that it is a result of social isolation. The mayor, Job Cohen, attempted to strengthen ethnic communities, in the belief that they reduce social isolation. His administration engaged with these communities and encouraged mosques, schools and community groups to watch out for their youths, to note changes in young people and engage with them.[17]

Preventive efforts should also expose people to the impact of terrorist violence on victims, their families and children, including Muslim victims. As I note elsewhere in the book, exposing harm doers to the *victims of others'* violence reduces defensiveness. People working in the field, with groups, have reported in conversation striking examples of how hearing some members of the group talk about how they were victimized in the past, led others in the group talk about how they victimized some people in the past, and express regret and the desire to seek forgiveness. However, I have encountered a few examples of terrorists/perpetrators who continue to believe that what they did was right. We don't know, how they would respond to such a process. Their proclaimed belief in the rightness of their action has implications for the notion, which I mention elsewhere, that perpetrators want to be reincluded in the moral realm. Whether theirs is a defensive stance or not, some seem to continue to believe that actions were moral.[18]

Prevention at the societal levels involves creating societal conditions that allow and empower all groups to participate in societal process—to express themselves in the public domain, to find ways to address grievances, to address inequality in group relations and have opportunities as individuals. In Amsterdam since 2004 more Muslims have become part of the political process. The current mayor of Rotterdam is a Moroccan immigrant. This is an important educational influence; alternative role models, who are part of society and act for the social good of the community.

Public Education: *Musekeweya*, an Educational Radio Drama in Rwanda

In societies where there is enough freedom to allow this, public education can help create resistance to violence and promote reconciliation and peace building. An important form of public education is the radio, especially in countries where radio is still the primary source of information and entertainment accessible to the population.

Our first and still ongoing educational radio program in Rwanda was the radio drama *Musekeweya* (meaning "new dawn"). We developed the educational content for all our radio programs on the basis of the Staub-Pearlman approach that we used in our trainings with groups in Rwanda, which I described earlier.[19]* We developed a "continuum," that described the principles of origins and prevention (called that way because of the progression in the course of the evolution of violence). The approach was then translated into 12 "communication messages" (see Table 16.1), which guided the writers in including educational content into the radio drama from May 2004, when it began to broadcast, until 2007. In 2007 we expanded the communication messages to 35, to include more on prevention and reconciliation. Some of the statements at the beginning of the chapters in this book are revisions from this longer list. The radio dramas and other programs now cover the whole range of principles and issues (except terrorism) that this book engages with. We have continuously trained writers and producers in the educational material they are to convey in the radio programs.

As I wrote earlier, the radio drama became extremely popular in its first year, and from every indication, it has become more popular since. Most people in the country have been listening to it. It is a story of two villages in conflict. We learn early in the drama that some time in the past the authorities gave a fertile valley lying between the villages to one of them, Bumanzi. There is a drought, and

Table 16.1 "Communication Messages" of the Rwandan Radio Drama

1. Life problems in a society frustrate basic needs and can lead to scapegoating and destructive ideologies.
2. Genocide evolves as individuals and groups change as a result of their actions.
3. Devaluation increases the likelihood of violence, whereas humanization decreases it.
4. The healing of psychological wounds helps people live more satisfying lives and makes unnecessary defensive violence less likely.
5. Passivity facilitates the evolution of harm doing, whereas actions by people inhibit it.
6. Varied perspectives, open communication, and moderate respect for authority in society make the evolution of violence less likely.
7. Justice is important for healing and reconciliation.
8. Significant connections and deep engagement between people belonging to different groups help people overcome devaluation and hostility and promote positive relations.
9. Trauma can be understood.
10. It is important to tell one's trauma story, and there is a way to tell it that is emotionally safe and constructive.
11. People can help their neighbors heal and help them tell their stories as part of the healing process; everyone can participate in and can contribute to healing.
12. Healing is a slow process.

Source. Reprinted from the Staub & Pearlman, 2009. We are grateful to the American Psychological Association for permission. These messages, based on the Staub-Pearlman approach, were developed in collaboration with George Weiss and the staff of LaBenevolencija.

people in the other village, Muhumuro, go hungry. A man instigates hostility and violence. He attracts followers and is elected the leader of Muhumuro. They attack the well-to-do village and steal the harvest.

The radio drama moderates respect for authority, one of our goals, by showing the complexity of the motivation and character of the destructive leader, Rutanagira, and by dramatizing the behavior of bystanders. He responds to the conditions in his village, the drought and scarcity of food. He blames the other village, Bumanzi. But he also acts out of personal grievances and animosities. His father had a second wife in Bumanzi. The father, when he died at the beginning of the story, contrary to tradition, appointed his son in Bumanzi as the head of the family, even though Rutanagira is the oldest son. He cannot accept this. In the dark of a night he attacks and beats up his half brother. His mother, Zaninka, driven by jealousy, instigates him against the other village. In addition, in a storm, his daughter falls off a small bridge, which the two villages built together in a period of cooperation, and drowns in the creek. For this also he blames the other village.

The villagers in Muhumuro are affected by the injustice that the fertile land was given to the other village, which makes them permanently poor, and by the current drought and scarcity. The frustration of their material and psychological needs makes them vulnerable to instigation. The instigator's influence in this authority-oriented culture greatly increases when he is elected village headman.

In the course of the conflict, active bystanders speak out against the leader and the faction that incites and engages in violence. Some older people maintain friendships across village lines. One man courageously goes to and speaks against violence at a meeting of the leader with his followers, and he continues to speak out after his house is burnt down. The most powerful example of a positive bystander is Batamuliza, the sister of the destructive leader. There is a love story between her and a young man, Shema, from the other village. Over the years of the program, the two of them are central in the activities of the young people of the two villages who organize and speak out against the violence.

Batamuliza and Shema undergo many trials. One of them is her kidnapping by one of her brother's followers, a man to whom her brother had promised her as a wife, without her knowledge. She manages to free herself and continues to defy her brother and mother. Many of the characters in this radio drama have become immensely popular, and when after many challenges Batamuliza and Shema are married in one of the episodes in February 2009, people were sending in real presents for the couple.

Other characters in the radio drama provide models of active bystandership as well. A young boy encourages another boy who is about to be sent home from his secondary school, because his family cannot pay the tuition, to ask the principal to allow him to stay. In Rwanda, where decisions by authorities are customarily not questioned, such an action demonstrates and encourages more moderate respect for authority. There is a village "fool," in fact a wise man in the mold of a Shakespearean fool, who, in his foolish way, says things to the leader and his followers that show how wrong their actions are. The drama explores justice processes, including its imperfections. It shows corruption and bias by officials.

In the first 3 years of the story, there is hostility, attacks, and counterattacks. When Bumanzi, the wealthier village, counterattacks, the inhabitants of Muhumuro become refugees. They leave their village and live under very poor conditions. There is continued hostility, with factions in both villages that persist in advocating against the other village. Some sympathizers from Bumanzi join and live with the refugees. They, and others who speak for reconciliation and peace, are the objects of suspicion and hostility. But slowly, opinions turn, and reconciliation begins. At a later time, when there is the threat of new violence in the region, the two villages join, using their past experience to stop the violence by nonviolent means. There is a transformation in some important characters, such as Rutanagira, the bad leader. He is tried, there is increasing hostility to him by "bystanders," and slowly over time he changes, joining those who work for reconciliation and peace.

Rwandan leaders advocate reconciliation, but at the same time they also limit open discussion and political processes. But this public education program that, among other things, encourages moderate respect for authorities and pluralism, people speaking their minds, has been allowed to broadcast each of its episodes twice a week.

Evaluations and Further Story Content of *Musekeweya*

We placed great importance on assessing the impact of our educational interventions. Our research evaluating our earlier work in Rwanda showed that it had highly positive impact. The effects of the radio drama were also carefully evaluated, in experimental research in the first year and then by research using other methods. As in our earlier work, it is on the basis of the positive effects that the evaluation showed that we continued with our programs.

The evaluation covered the period of hostility and attacks, with resistance by active bystanders, but not the programs on reconciliation. It included individual interviews with participants, their responses to questions about program effects, focus group discussions, and an "unobtrusive" measure when participants did not know they were evaluated. I will describe the evaluations in the first and second year separately, except when a later finding clarifies an earlier one.

Before the broadcasts began, "listening groups" were set up around the country and were visited each month to assess their reactions first to pilot programs and, during the first 3 years, to actual programs. Their reactions were used to shape program content.[20]* Following this model, as part of her doctoral dissertation research, Elizabeth Levy Paluck set up, during the first program year, groups in six communities (identified as treatment or reconciliation groups) that listened together once a month, on audiotapes, to the four weekly programs of *Musekeweya*. In six comparison (control or health) groups, people listened together to a radio program about health practices. There were a total of 480 people in the study.[21]* These were mixed groups of Tutsis and Hutus, but there was also one group in each condition made up of survivors only, and one group of prisoners. Health group members were promised a small reward and agreed not to listen in the course of the year to *Musekeweya* broadcasts. If they listened in spite of their agreement, one would expect smaller differences between the groups.

After the assessment of the effects of the radio drama at the end of the first year, members of the comparison or health group could also listen to the program. Another group was added to the evaluation, elites in the communities where the first-year participants were located. The effects of the radio drama were evaluated in the second year by comparing former reconciliation and health group members, as well as assessing differences among all participants as a function of how much they listened to the programs. In addition to self-report, knowledge of drama content, which corresponded well with participants' reports, was used to indicate amount of listening. People who in the previous year were treatment group members listened more to the program. Not surprisingly, people who listened more showed greater changes.[22]

The evaluation showed that the program has affected both attitudes and behavior. Among varied effects, listeners to *Musekeweya* were more likely than members of the comparison group to believe in speaking their minds and to actually do so, to express controversial views, and to show independence from authority.

Effects on Behavior

At the end of the first year, at a party to acknowledge their participation, each group received audiotapes of the whole year's *Musekeweya* programs and a tape recorder. In every one of the six health groups, participants decided, after very little discussion, to have the village headman be in charge of them. In each case one person suggested this, and it was agreed to without further discussion. In all six of the reconciliation groups, participants engaged in long discussion of where they should keep the materials they received and who should be in charge of them. They decided that either the group jointly would be in charge or one of its members would be in charge and make them available to the others. Usually, in the reconciliation groups, one person suggested that they give the material to the village headman to manage, but others disagreed, and a long discussion followed.[23] In this unobtrusive measure, at a time when participants thought the project had ended, people who listened to the radio drama showed freedom to express their views and independence of authority.

In individual interviews, listeners to *Musekeweya disagreed* more with the statement, "If I disagree with something that someone is saying or doing, I keep quiet."[24*] This was one of the strongest effects of the radio drama. Listeners' behavior was consistent with this in the unobtrusive measure. In addition, in individual interviews, participants in both health and reconciliation groups agreed that there was mistrust in their communities. When this was later discussed in focus groups, those who listened to *Musekeweya* were much more likely than participants in the comparison groups to express this view, countering a cultural tendency to hold such opinions privately.

The Effect on Empathy

In individual interviews, people who listened to *Musekeweya* expressed more empathy for varied groups of Rwandans: people in prison because of their role in the genocide, survivors, poor people, and political leaders. This is consistent with what we found in our earlier study, that members of community groups guided by facilitators we trained in our approach, on which the radio drama was based, had a more positive orientation to people in the other ethnic group.[25]

It is likely that one source of empathy and positive orientation to others was increased understanding of the influence of events on people, their psychological impact and effects on behavior. Understanding how personal experiences, the conditions in the society, and the influence of other people jointly lead to actions, including extremely harmful ones, is a form of cognitive empathy that can foster at least some openness to harm doers—whether direct perpetrators or leaders—and to passive bystanders. The programs also showed the trauma and psychological wounds resulting from the attacks, this presumably increasing empathy with survivors of the genocide. Perpetrators, and many passive members of a perpetrator group, stop thinking about the victims' suffering. They tend to minimize what they (or their group) did and its harmful effects.[26] The radio drama increased awareness of pain and suffering created by violence, as people in the village that was attacked struggled with anxiety, sexual difficulties, and intimacy.

Understanding the influences leading to and the effects of violent actions presumably joined with identification with positive characters in the story and the values they expressed in creating empathy.[27] A Penal Reform International (PRI) report on rescuers in Rwanda concludes that "belief in values that affirm the humanity of the victims, creating a deep empathy with them ....as well as the existence within their social environment, particularly within the family, of positive examples of interethnic coexistence" were the primary characteristics of the "righteous" who saved Tutsi lives during the genocide.[28] Their feelings of empathy, beliefs, and values enabled them to deviate from then dominant norms of conduct.

Other Changes

The changes I just described and those that follow suggest that the radio drama affected beliefs and values, that listeners came to see certain outcomes (such as less dependence on and subservience to authorities) and actions (speaking what one believes) as desirable. This is an especially impressive finding in that during the first year of the radio drama the words and actions of active bystanders did not stop hostility and violence. In some cases there were negative consequences to them.

Research studies have shown that the example of models can lead to imitation, even if their actions are not rewarded. This does not happen, however, if the models' actions lead to negative consequences for them, and it is unlikely to happen if their behavior is evidently ineffective. But in the radio drama the active, positive bystanders were guided by strong values that served positive ends. The rewards to them were intrinsic, as they lived up to these values. They were also "rewarded" by good relationships to each other, even across village lines. And they acted in the context of understanding the importance of resisting influences that move people to violence.

The radio drama also showed trauma. The invaders intruded into people's houses during the night, attacked them, and stole their crops. One character later struggled with giving testimony at a trial, finding it difficult to talk about her experience, as traumatized individuals often do, the difficulty intensified by an initially insensitive judge. Another character began to avoid his wife, avoiding intimacy and sexual relations. She began to suspect that he had another woman in his life. Slowly she learned that his behavior was the result of the attack, which created difficulty in his sexual functioning; this made him ashamed and led him to avoid her. Educational radio dramas need to entertain to be effective. The writers have infused the story with a great deal of humor, for example, when the wife follows the suggestions of a village healer to regain her husband's affections by stealing one of his pubic hairs—before she understands that he has been traumatized. In this and other cases of trauma, other characters invite traumatized people to talk about their experiences. Those who listened to the program were more likely to believe that one should talk about painful, traumatic experiences (see Chapter 19).

Rwandans experienced great violence in their society, in spite of intermarriages, and neither evaluation group believed that marrying across group lines contributes to peace, although listeners to *Musekeweya* believed slightly more that it does. However, while in a small number of instances participants talked about intermarriages ending in bloodshed, more often they mentioned Tutsis who were saved through their connection to Hutus. The PRI report about rescuers found that a majority of those who saved Tutsis were connected to them through intermarriage.[29] Asked about their personal preferences, reconciliation group members were more likely than health group members to believe that intermarriage should be allowed in their family and that children should not be advised against it. In individual interviews and focus groups, they said that it can be a force for good, creating bonds and reducing division and discord between groups. Both the discrepancy between their belief based on past experience that intermarriage does not contribute to peace and their belief that it should be allowed and can create bonds, and some other findings suggest that the program has generated hope, an expectation and belief that people can take effective action to make the future better. Both values that motivate people and such positive expectations are necessary for people to take action.[30]

While the majority of the participants in both groups believed that trust can be rebuilt in their communities, a compelling difference was in the ways people thought about rebuilding trust. For those in the reconciliation group, interaction was one avenue, such as engaging with people, socializing, and sharing resources. Another was mutual forgiveness, asking pardon, and establishing the truth about the past. Those in the health groups emphasized these less, and government policies more, such as government information programs (called sensitization in Rwanda) and laws prohibiting divisionism and political favoritism.[31]

The differences between groups in beliefs, values, and behavior showed substantial changes in listeners. But there was no difference on some dimensions. One of them was that neither group agreed with the view that violence evolves gradually. One explanation is participants' own experience, the way they perceived the genocide. Although they could see the progressive increase in tension and hostility in the country, they experienced the beginning of the genocide as sudden and surprising. This was also reported by others.[32] People get accustomed to gradually increasing hostility and violence and are surprised when there is a great shift in intensity. There was also no difference, probably again due to the constraining effect of personal experience during the genocide, in reactions to the statement, "If I stand by while others commit evil actions, I am also responsible." Members of both groups agreed somewhat with this statement. But they said that during the genocide it was not possible to intervene. Once the genocide began, intervening did mean significantly endangering one's life.

The lack of difference on some items at the end of the first year could also be due to members of the comparison groups actually listening to a limited extent, which brought them some knowledge but not enough to change deeper attitudes and actions. Even more likely was the spread of the effects of the educational radio drama through public discussion. Past research has found that the effects of programs about HIV/AIDS and reproduction spread through discussion between spouses and in the community.[33] Both participants in the reconciliation groups and others who were interviewed in the second year reported extensive discussion of the programs. Reconciliation group members talked about them to others, and they were discussed in families and among community members. Children and adolescents, who have been avid listeners, often initiated discussion with their parents.[34]

People in the community in Rwanda often listen to the radio together; their discussion of the programs is likely to enhance their effects. This was probably the case with people listening together in the evaluation study. In the second year, elites in the communities where the study took place reported that members of these groups continued to have strong ties, and that the study had a positive effect on their communities.

Another explanation for the absence of some differences may be that, depending on particular issues, creating change may require more exposure to influential content. This is especially so if change goes contrary to recent powerful experience, such as the perceived sudden beginning of the genocide. In the second-year evaluation, there was again no difference between the two groups on the question about the evolution of violence. But people from either group who listened more to the radio drama, as measured by the number of characters they could name, disagreed more with the view that violence comes about suddenly.

Participants expressed views about a couple of matters contrary to what we expected. This was most likely due to actual program content. Contrary to our intention to communicate that violence is a societal process and the importance of followers, people who listened to *Musekeweya* agreed more that "evil people cause violence." Given the strong prevailing view in Rwanda that genocide was the result of bad leaders, and given the cultural emphasis on authorities, our attempt to change the perspectives of the writers of the radio drama, through training and editing their work, proved difficult. In the first year the writers continued to emphasize the role of the bad leader in the poor village, and his mother who exerted a strong negative influence on him. But the way they depicted the character of the bad leader, and the role of his personal/family relations in his actions, helped moderate respect for authority, as the behavior of listeners showed.

The joining of cultures, as external and internal parties work together, can be challenging. At a staff meeting a member of our academic team realized that the writers resisted the concept of moderating authority because they thought it meant that children need not obey their parents. We clarified that what we meant was that children and adults should learn to judge if their elders, leaders, or society engages in harmful, immoral action, and people should speak out against and attempt to correct such actions.

On another item, those who listened to *Musekeweya* were less likely to believe that trauma recovery is possible. The radio drama was planned to last for a number of years, with evolution in its content. Some of the items in the evaluation assessed the program's intended effects as indicated by communication statements, not its likely effects based on its actual content. The radio drama in the first year showed people traumatized by conflict and attacks, and others encouraging them to talk about their painful experiences. We did not yet show healing and recovery, in part because we were intent to truthfully represent what Rwandans also know from personal experience, the difficulty of recovering from the trauma of victimization (see message 12 in Table 16.1).

The Effects of the Radio Drama in the Second Year

In the second year, when everyone could listen to the program, some of the differences between reconciliation and health group members disappeared. For example, all groups said that they supported intermarriage, and that they would speak up if they disagreed with something someone did or said. But the amount of listening was important. Regular listeners believed more in speaking what they believed and expressed their views and concerns more.

The major conclusion suggested by the research findings in the second year is that people who listened more to *Musekeweya* were more ready, willing, and able to express their views. Reflecting a widespread cultural fear in Rwanda about poisoning, regular listeners expressed more concern about drinking a beer with a member of a group that has offended them, if this person opens the beer out of their sight. They were more likely to say that there is mistrust in their village, in keeping with what both observers and surveys authorized by the Unity and Reconciliation Commission indicated—that there is mistrust in Rwanda, due to the genocide and reawakened by the *gacaca*. They expressed more concern about the return of prisoners who perpetrated violence and who were released into their communities. Given the other effects of listening to Musekeweya, it is unlikely that listeners developed a more negative view of the world. It is much more likely that *Musekeweya* contributes to people using their judgment and expressing their views.

Everyone in the second year reported that they participated in reconciliation activities; those who were in the reconciliation group during the first year participated in these activities slightly more, and regular listeners substantially more. Members of the former health groups reported more that they encouraged others to reconcile: helping neighbors resolve conflicts at home, encouraging forgiveness, or talking to people about the *gacaca*. Regular listeners reported more directly engaging in activities promoting reconciliation. They shared land with people who killed their family, talked to returned prisoners who killed members of their family, returned goods stolen by a son to a survivor and asked for forgiveness. The evaluator concluded that" The actions of Musekeweya listeners are exceptionally personal."[35]

The Value of Public Education

Public education can take many forms: trainings in seminars and workshops, courses in schools and universities, radio and television programs, and information disseminated in newsprint and on the Internet. Longer exposure matters, especially when the goal is to change deep-seated beliefs, attitudes, norms, and behavior. As these change, slowly the culture changes, including the standards of acceptable conduct. The idea of changing another group's culture may seem arrogant. But Rwandans themselves agree that there is too much respect for authority, not enough pluralism, and a history of devaluation. To moderate orientation to authority requires a focus on the merits of authorities, and reevaluation of the relationship between leaders and citizens.

The trainings we conducted with groups in Rwanda, described in Chapter 12, affected understanding of the roots of the genocide, created more positive orientation by members of the two groups toward each other, and conditional forgiveness.[36] The radio drama seemed to contribute to a "critical consciousness" by listeners, to their use of their own judgment, and greater willingness to engage in discussion and publicly express views. It also affected behavior, some self-reported, some observed. There are public education projects of many kinds, and they show that public education can have what seems not only a statistically significant but also a practically significant impact. In the complex and difficult social world of post-genocide Rwanda, the changes our programs produced provide hope for more active bystandership on behalf of reconciliation and peace.

Audience Feedback

At some point audience members began writing letters with their thoughts and feelings about the programs, and when LaBenevolencija provided a telephone number, they began to call in large numbers. Their reactions were highly positive and also informative about program content. Later, to further involve the audience, there were poetry competitions with themes related to *Musekeweya*, with small awards given to the winners. Starting in 2008, some letters that reinforced program messages were read on the radio. I quote and paraphrase a few letters in one week in early May 2009, some responding to the preceding week's drama episode:[37]*

- "Hello you teachers of hearts filled with hatred...you have not stopped teaching us in Rwandan society. The importance of *Musekeweya* is inexpressible." Speaking to Zaninka, the mother of the bad leader, the writer admonishes her for her bad behavior in relation to her daughter and wants to exile her. "Good riddance." He also advises Shema to let his wife, Batamuliza, go work in the village that now has problems. "That will bring good results."
- "The seed you have planted has begun to grow. The intelligence and wisdom that you have used to teach us is of great value. *Musekeweya* is a boat, where all of us who are listening are together. Shema, Batamuliza, (Kigingi, Hirwa—other characters in the drama) have the techniques rowing us, and we are sure to arrive at a good port." This writer also speaks directly to the characters and says to Zaninka, "Where has your soul gone?" He also admonishes Shema not to get angry at Batamuliza,

if she goes to the other village to help—"You and others have much to gain, and you can also go to help.... I am resolved to be your ambassador among us."

- "... the seed you have sown in the heart of the afflicted ...has given the fruits of humanism, tolerance, love, and unity. In the fashion of Shema and Batamuliza, we are ready to give testimony of what we have pulled from this tree."
- "I am thanking you for showing the hearts of people directed by hatred, rancour, and wrath..."
- "Please read this message to the listeners.... For those who have not won a prize in the poetry competition, try to find some reward for them— they have participated. That would make them happy."
- One letter asked that the programs cover rape (which has been done in the radio dramas in Burundi and the Congo but not in Rwanda) and that Batamuliza be a counselor to rape victims.

Ongoing Program Development

In developing the radio programs there has been an increasingly deep and equal relationship between internal and external parties. There are training workshops on the underlying conception and approach, and design and storyline development workshops. These bring local staff, producers, and some members of the academic team and the executive team together. Stakeholders—representatives of local organizations and leadership groups—are often included for part or all of them.

In February 2009, at one of these workshops, there was discussion of the communication messages that the programs would focus on in the following year. One of these was "establishing the complex truth about past group relations and about conflict and violence and developing a shared view of history are important for reconciliation." In the course of the discussion, participants commented that the notion of "shared history" should reflect not only two versions of what happened in Rwanda, as represented by the two main groups, Hutus and Tutsis, but many versions. In real life there are not only the two primary groups but also divisions by region, status and wealth, and others, each with their own perspective on history. (One of these other divisions is between Tutsi survivors and "returnees," Tutsis whose families were refugees in neighboring countries and returned after the genocide. It was primarily refugees in Uganda who fought the civil war and then ended the genocide.)

The educational content aims to promote knowledge, attitudes, and actions in relation to each communication message. The following guidance to producers and writers (and for evaluators) for the message described earlier was drafted by a member of the "academic team" and then developed further in the January workshop. It specifies the aims of the programs that are to be developed.

KNOW:

- That establishing the complex truth about past group relations is a difficult task, since the two parties in the conflict have different perspectives
- The importance of having a shared history, including both sides' experiences, the two versions of the conflict, rather than having a history presenting the perspectives of one side

DO:

- Have an overall view of the past, always engage to confront one-sided versions of history
- Continue to discuss the past conflict with others, with a mind open to various perspectives and ready to understand that those various visions can complete each other (even when there are disagreements)

HAVE AN ATTITUDE OF:

- Eagerness to understand the past conflict between the two groups
- Willingness to make others question their exclusive version of history[38*]

A Grassroots Project and Further Evaluation of *Musekeweya*

Using the radio drama as a base, LaBenevolencija created a companion project to engage citizens in reconciliation. It trained "agents of change" in communities to notice and address problems between people before they become severe, help resolve conflicts, and foster peaceful relations. Thirty-seven communities were identified that were especially strongly impacted by the genocide, and where recovery, in terms of social cohesion, the absence of conflict, and economic activity, was slow. With the help of local officials, LaBenevolencija staff selected, for training as agents of change, highly diverse groups of people in each community, with varied backgrounds and positions in society. They included genocide survivors, prisoners returned to the communities, poor people, people with some "deviant" behaviors, elected and appointed officials, pastors and teachers, and agricultural and health advisors. The aim was not to duplicate the activities of local officials, but to help people with social cohesion, with problems that affect people's everyday relations.

Those selected received 5 days of training in the Staub-Pearlman approach, by staff that was previously trained in and had been using the approach in creating the radio programs. The training focused on the communication messages, used segments from *Musekeweya*, and included role playing. After the training, local and national coordinators worked with the local agents. The team engaged by LaBenevolencija to evaluate the effects of the program wrote: "The grassroots programme has the objective to amplify the messages through a direct intervention on the ground in localities that encounter serious problems in the domain of conflict resolution, prevention and reconciliation."[39]

This team first evaluated whether the agents of change understood the communication messages. When shown varied segments from *Musekeweya*, they were substantially better at identifying their meaning—for example, a segment showing passivity by bystanders—than other people from the same communities. They were then asked to describe the type of conflicts they encountered and identify the most important ones. Theft and internal household problems were frequent. Land redistribution was in progress and the government had people stop growing their customary crops and replace them with different crops. Land conflict, and conflict related to the *gacaca*—both in a general sense and specifically in terms of returning property—were both frequent and described as the most important.

The evaluators compared communities with change agents to others in the same area. They concluded that while "gacaca-related conflicts receive the highest ranking overall ...(they) are not ranked highest in the grassroots sites...." They speculated that "this might be due to the grassroots activities since they have the objective of conflict resolution (especially related to issues dealt with in gacaca) and fostering social cohesion and reconciliation issues that are apparently most negatively affected by the introduction of the gacaca in rural life."[40]

People have become less fearful of cohabitation, living their everyday lives together—sharing a beer, attending a wedding, helping to take a sick person to the hospital. But interpersonal reconciliation, a "matter of the heart," trust and confidence in neighbors, in members of the other ethnic group, is more challenging. The evaluators regard this as the realm of social cohesion. In open questions, when people can say whatever they want, community respondents identified *Musekeweya* (25%), or LaBenevolencija in general (23%) and activities organized by it, and the agents of change in particular (10%) as sources of increasing cohesion over the past 2 years. In this open format, 54% of respondents identified LaBenevolencija-initiated activities as sources of social cohesion. Local community gatherings organized by officials were identified by 25% of the respondents. When asked a direct question, "Did LaBenevolencija play a role in the increase of social cohesion in your community over the past 2 years?" 96% said it did.[41]*

In 2008, to create cohesion among the change agents and make their activities more sustained, the coordinators helped them develop associations around agricultural activities, initiated by small grants to the groups. People who normally would have little contact coming together in associations, especially after the genocide, seemed to have special value. However, in an in-depth look at two associations, the evaluators found that only one had a highly mixed membership. In that community, agents of change were highly active. Not surprisingly, in that community they received more credit for social cohesion.

Reconciliation activities have often focused on national processes, such as truth commissions, tribunals to bring about justice, or political arrangements. But reconciliation at the local level, between parties who have harmed each other and now have to rebuild their lives living next to each other, such as former prisoners living next to survivors in Rwanda, is crucial. Mozambique has moved from violence to relative peace without a national reconciliation process, but with reconciliation activities at local levels.[42] The aim of Musekeweya was to reach the population, and the grassroots project, engaging with people directly, seemed to have enhanced its influence.

Musekeweya and the Democratic Forces for the Liberation of Rwanda (FDLR)

We began to hear reports that members of the FDLR in the Congo, the militia led by former genocidaires, have been listening to *Musekeweya*. Some of them left their group and returned to Rwanda, and according to these reports, they were influenced by *Musekeweya*. LaBenevolencija commissioned the same researchers who evaluated the grassroots project, and they conducted interviews in Rwanda with ex-rebels in a demobilization and reintegration camp and on a rural hill. They interviewed 101 ex-rebels in the course of several weeks.[43]

The FDLR members in the Congo have listened a great deal to radio stations such as the BBC, Voice of America, and Radio Rwanda. They listened to Radio Rwanda to keep up with the developments in the country and to understand what might be the situation of family and friends. The most popular programs were *Urunana* and *Musekeweya*, both radio dramas. Most of 101 ex-rebels followed the weekly broadcasts of *Musekeweya*, and according to them most of the Kinyarwanda speakers in the Congo, regardless of ethnicity, listen to the program. For the former members of FDLR, the theme of reconciliation between the villages was especially striking. The change in Rutanagira, the bad leader, made a strong impression on them, as he became active in working for reconciliation and peace.

Coming to learn about the changing nature of Rwanda, mainly from telephone conversations with family in Rwanda and visitors from Rwanda played a role in their return. So did issues within the FDLR, such as lack of objectives, conflicts and incompetence of leaders, the hard life in the Eastern Congo, and separation from families in Rwanda. While *Musekeweya* is an educational radio drama, a story, the researchers write that "It is evident that radio broadcasts have played a major role in the spread of" a new image of Rwanda. "The theme of reconciliation underlies a great number of the striking episodes mentioned by the ex-rebels." Although there is no evidence that it "played a decisive role in their final decision to return home... the radio soap is somehow at work in a dynamic of competing ideologies and mindsets."[44] Interestingly, in addition to getting trustworthy information about Rwanda, a main obstacle to return was a practical one, finding demobilization points in the Democratic Republic of Congo.

Other Radio Programs

Like all forms of prevention and reconciliation, to be effective educational efforts must be informed by the actual conditions of group conflict, history, and culture. The radio dramas for Burundi and the Congo were guided by the same conceptual approach as *Musekeweya*, but their content was adjusted according to differences in conditions from Rwanda. The differences are especially great with the Congo, where more groups are involved in the conflict and in addition to tribe or ethnicity, conflicts over local (and national) power and material resources have significant roles.

Broadcasting from October 2004 until 2008, another radio program engaged in direct education in Rwanda. Called *Kuki* (Why?), it provided information about the concepts embodied in the communication messages. This program meant to reach Rwanda's educated population and leaders. Journalists posed questions and local experts answered them on the air. A weakness of this program was that while the journalists leading the broadcasts were trained in our approach, the local experts were not, and most of them were not scholars of genocide.

Nevertheless, an evaluation showed positive effects. People who listened to the programs did not change their opinions related to the content of the messages in comparison to people who agreed not to listen for a year. However, everyone was sympathetic to the messages, and listening affected behavior. Those who listened discussed the messages with family and friends. They became more inclusive, inviting members of the community to a public dialogue on reconciliation and the healing of trauma.[45] Increased engagement by opinion leaders with the larger community on these issues is a valuable outcome.

Summary

Public education, especially if it involves extensive exposure, can and has been found to change attitudes, beliefs, and behavior. It can include lectures and workshops, literature, various media, and the Internet. Public education has to consider local conditions, as we did in applying the same conceptual approach to Burundi and the Congo. Listening to our educational radio drama in Rwanda, developed on the basis of the Staub-Pearlman approach, made it more likely that people use their judgment about the meaning of events and act on their beliefs. The grassroots projects, building on the radio drama, and other radio programs, also had positive effects.

A striking real world effect of Musekeweya was reported to me in August 2010. Members of a predominantly Hutu village, many of whom were perpetrators of violence against the inhabitants of a predominantly Tutsi village living on another hill, approached the Tutsi survivors. They came with their implements to help work the field. After a while the survivors engaged with them, the two groups created a ceremony of forgiveness and have increasingly reconciled. Both groups reported that they were inspired by Musekeweya. (As one man said, it was messages on the radio that led him to ask for forgiveness.) [46]

Notes

1 Biton & Salomon, 2006

2 Salomon, 2004

3 Dweck, 2009, describing studies by Halperin, Russell, Dweck, & Gross on the Israeli-Palestinian Conflict

4 Staub et al., 2005; Staub & Pearlman, 2006

5 Aderman & Berkowitz, 1970; Stotland, 1969

6 Pyszczynski, Rothschild & Abdollahi, 2008, p. 320. See this article for an overview of such research

7 Ibid.

8 Horgan & Braddock, 2010; Kruglanski, Gelfand, & Gunaratna, 2010, in press

9 Kruglanski et al., in press

10 Kruglanski et al., 2010; Horgan & Braddock, 2010

11 Kruglanski et al., 2008, p. 118

12 Kruglanski et al., 2010, p. 21

13 See, for example, Tetlock et al., 2000

14 Kruglanski et al., 2010

15 Horgan, 2009

16 Hosenball & Thomas, 2010

17 Shorto, 2010

18 Nadler & Shnabel, 2008

19 For a detailed description of the radio drama and its development, see Staub, Pearlman, Weiss, & van Hoek, in press; see also Staub, 2008a; Staub & Pearlman, 2006; Staub, Pearlman, & Bilali, 2010.

20 The listening groups were designed and organized by Suzanne Fisher, the first local producer of Musekeweya.

21 The evaluation research was done by Elizabeth Levy Paluck, at the time a graduate student in psychology at Yale, working with an advisor who specialized in evaluation research. We (Staub, Pearlman, and LaBenevolencija) invited applications by individuals and organizations to do the evaluation and selected her from several interested parties. The findings of the first year evaluation is described in Paluck & Green, 2005, the second year evaluation in Paluck, 2006. The results of

the first-year evaluation were published in Paluck, 2009a. See also Staub & Pearlman, 2009; Paluck, 2009b.

22 Paluck, 2006

23 Paluck, 2009a, b; Staub & Pearlman, 2009

24 This is the version of the statement that is reported in the original evaluation report for LaBenevolencija by Paluck & Green, 2005. In Paluck, 2009a, the statement reads: "If we disagree with something that someone is doing or saying, we should keep quiet." I assume the original version was used in the study. We disagree with Paluck's interpretation of the findings; she sees the changes in listeners as indicating that their beliefs about what are the social norms in their society have changed (Paluck, 2009a, b). This seems highly unlikely to us; instead we interpret the results as changes in individuals' understanding, personal beliefs, and values, which are then expressed in some behaviors. Changes in norms would follow as a sufficient number of people in the group express or enact change. See Pearlman & Staub, 2009, and later discussion in this chapter.

25 Staub et al., 2005

26 Baumeister, 1997

27 Paluck, 2009a, b; Staub & Pearlman, 2009

28 PRI, 2004. p. 3

29 Paluck & Green, 2005; PRI, 2004

30 Staub & Pearlman, 2009

31 Paluck & Green, 2005

32 Ilibagiza & Erwin, 2006

33 Bandura, 2006; Staub et al., in press

34 Paluck, 2006

35 Ibid, p. 42

36 Staub et al., 2005

37 The letters were translated from Kinyarwanda into French, and then English, and paraphrased in part. Some of their content may be motivated by the hope that they will be read on the radio

38 From Musekeweya workshop, February 16–21 2009. Design, storyline and message sequencing document for Rwanda. Episodes 247–300, March 2009–April 2010. Prepared by Johan Deflander.

39 Ingelaere, Havugimana, & Ndushabandi, 2009a

40 Ibid.

41 However, such a direct question can elicit the tendency of people in Rwanda to say what they think others expect.

42 Broneus, 2008a

43 Ingelaere, Havugimana, & Ndushabandi, 2009b

44 Ibid, pp. 1–2

45 Paluck, 2008

46 Aimable Twahirwa, the producer of LaBenevolencija in Rwanda in, 2010was approached by the villagers who told him about this. Maggie Ziegler, who in 2010 worked at the Kigali Genocide Memorial and visited the villages with him, sent me the draft of a story she is writing about it.

17

The Potential and Power of Active Bystanders

Citizens, Leaders, Nations, and the International System

Active bystandership, that is, positive and continuous actions by individuals and groups, inhibits the evolution of violence and helps to build a peaceful society.

To inhibit the evolution of violence requires members of society to join together and be active bystanders who oppose destructive policies and practices, as well as leaders who advocate them. Acting early, people can constructively address these and other conditions so that destructive processes do not gain strength. Actions by outsiders are essential to this effort, particularly in autocratic societies in which insider action is difficult and dangerous. Outsiders can join with, help, support, and generate active bystandership within a society. Part I of this book surveyed the many conditions and events, and especially their combinations, that can alert witnesses/bystanders about the dangers of violence and indicate that action is needed to inhibit its evolution. These conditions are summarized in Table 17.1.

Active bystanders have power. I will later describe examples of amazing actions by individuals and actions by groups that had significant effects, from Ron Ridenhour persisting until people in the United States knew about the massacres at My Lai, to Baha'i communities around the world stopping the killing of Baha'i in Iran, to the boycott of apartheid in South Africa. To become active requires that people focus their attention on a problem, so that their values or feelings of empathy are activated. For some people, knowing that large numbers of people are severely harmed or killed, or are in danger, is enough. They are capable of feeling empathy with distant others, have strong principles of morality, and believe in their responsibility for others' welfare. But most people need what the late Amos Tversky and Nobel recipient Daniel Kahneman, both psychologists, called "availability heuristics," information that is specific enough to engage their imagination. The numbers of people killed may not evoke empathy; the suffering of one person, a child or a family, may bring home to people the tragedy of the many.

Table 17.1 Summary of Indicators of the Need for Active Bystandership*

- *Instigating conditions.* The presence of difficult life conditions (e.g., a deteriorating economy, political disorganization, great social-cultural-technological changes); conflict between groups (e.g., over land, inequality, privileged groups responding forcefully or violently to the demands of the less privileged for more opportunity, rights, and power); and war of any kind.
- *Cultural/societal characteristics.* Especially a number of them together, make it more likely that in response to instigating conditions an evolution begins that can lead to extreme violence. They include historical devaluation, past group trauma, authority orientation, absence of pluralism, an autocratic political system.
- *Increase in devaluation.* Increase in negative/devaluative statements, in the media and by leaders, about a historically devalued group, which is described as bad, immoral, treacherous, and/or as a danger to one's own group.
- *Scapegoating.* The target group is scapegoated, incorrectly and unfairly blamed for problems in the society.
- *Destructive ideologies.* An ideology develops, is created or adopted (e.g., a vision of a desirable future for the group or for all humanity) that identifies usually a previously devalued group as standing in the way of the fulfillment of this vision, and that increasingly asserts that to create the better future the other group must be neutralized, "dealt with," or eliminated.
- *Groups develop destructive characteristics or new ideological movements are formed.* People turn to existing groups (ethnic, religious, political parties) or new groups that are guided by ideology or enmity. Leaders emerge who emphasize the importance of the group, nation, or movement; identify one or more minorities as outside this community; and advocate scapegoating or a destructive ideology.
- *Increased focus on past group trauma (and at times on past glory).* There is increasing reference to past suffering by the group due to violence against it or other misfortunes. This is used to introduce and justify harsh policies and practices as necessary for protecting the group. Separately, or jointly with the trauma, there may be a focus on past glory and greatness—and future glory.
- *Progress in the evolution of violence.* There are acts of violence against the other group, which over time increase in frequency and/or intensity. This can be an increase in violence by individuals against members of the other group, or violence by spontaneously formed, or semi-organized or organized groups, or initiated by the government.
- *Justification of harmful actions; propaganda and hate speech.* Harmful actions against the designated victim group are justified by a negative view of that group, by reference to their behavior or nature—their harmful actions, immorality, the threat they represent. There is progressive increase in the frequency and intensity of devaluative, hostile statements, of hate speech.
- *Grievances of the target group receive no response.* The targeted group has no public voice, no means to express its concerns and grievances, or to defend itself. Noticing this requires special vigilance, since what people need to notice is the absence of public participation by the target group. When this group finds ways to express grievances related to discrimination, injustice, or violence, it receives no appropriate response or a punitive response.

Table 17.1 continued

- *The absence of public discussion of or opposition to the evolution of hostility and violence.* There is little or no public discussion of the preceding processes. There is no significant opposition or resistance. Those who speak out against them are vilified or silenced by forceful means.
- *Institutions are established to serve the system of discrimination, persecution, and violence.* These may include government offices, paramilitary groups, and media whose function is to attack the group.
- *Further harmful actions and isolation.* In some cases the target group may be impoverished through special taxes, and their property may be confiscated. At times, the group is segregated.
- *The actions/events/conditions listed above become part of normal life.* Such actions become part of the flow of everyday life—and are paid decreasing attention. Witnesses/bystanders may hope that each small increase in harmful attitudes and actions will be the last one, take no action, and get accustomed to the progressive evolution of the psychological, institutional, and societal bases of mass violence and of the violence itself.
- *History of the use of violence to resolve conflict, and especially of mass violence.* A past history of violence against the perpetrator group, or by the perpetrator group, or between two groups, makes the proceeding conditions more dangerous.
- *Limited mass killing* of the target group changes the perpetrator group and increases the possibility of large-scale mass killing and genocide.

When people were exposed to television images of human suffering due to drought and starvation in Ethiopia in 1984–1985, there was an outpouring of response. The protest of the Vietnam War was a response, in part, to young men being drafted to fight the war but also to the images of violence and suffering that the war inflicted on Vietnam. The unforgettable picture of a young Vietnamese girl, burned by napalm, running down a road screaming, with others running behind her, or of a police chief holding a gun to a man's head about to shoot him, were images that created empathy, anger, outrage, and protest. If people saw similar images about the war in Iraq, that war would also have generated significant protest. But with little mention in the media of Iraqi casualties, mostly hiding injuries to and even the bodies of dead American soldiers, and focusing on 9/11 and problems at home, Americans have mainly ignored the war.

Of course, bystander action does not always achieve its intended effects. Whenever harmdoers receive support, or acceptance by significant others, the power of other bystanders diminishes. Russia's sympathy to the Serbs during the violence in Bosnia, and China's unwillingness to speak or act against the Sudan with regard to Darfur, reduced the impact of other active bystanders. This is also relevant to terrorism. Some terrorist groups are not only accepted, and ideologically supported, but receive material support and encouragements by nation states. Pakistan has used terrorists as proxies in fighting India. Iran and Syria have supported Hezbollah and Hamas. Countries may sometimes regard the terrorists they support as fighting for their legitimate rights, at others times use them to fight on their behalf.

It is essential that the international community engage with these countries to stop their support, while also working to resolve the conflict situations involved. Actions by citizens before the 2008 Olympics in China, including prominent individuals like the filmmaker Steven Spielberg who publicly withdrew from his involvement as artistic adviser to the Olympics due to Chinese passivity in relation to violence in Darfur by Sudan, brought about some change in these polices.

As described in Chapter 7, Rwanda was an extreme example of bystander failure. Romeo Dallaire, the Canadian general in charge of U.N. peacekeepers in Rwanda, warned of preparations for the genocide, but his superiors at the United Nations instructed him not to act. Once the genocide started, he asked for additional troops in order to stop it. Instead, soon after, when Belgian peacekeepers were killed, the United Nations withdrew most of the peacekeepers.[1] Dallaire believes that U.N. officials simply discounted him, interpreting his warnings not as a response to the actual situation, but due to an overwrought personality. Some in the U.S. state department saw him as simply inexperienced.[2]* Neither the United Nations nor the United States wanted to act, after what they saw as the failure of intervention in Somalia.[3] When people do not want to act, they are inclined to ignore, avoid, or resist the validity of information that indicates the need to act.

Prevention requires active bystandership. Individuals with values of caring and responsibility, empathy, and feelings of competence, or who are in positions of responsibility to act, or who have allies to support them, are more likely to act. But groups of citizens need to influence their governments, international organizations, and nongovernmental organizations (NGOs) to act. Pressure by people can overcome others' resistance to attend to information and take action. Sometimes pressure by events will do so, although the killing in Rwanda of hundreds of thousands of people evidently wasn't pressure enough.

Helping after Violence

After a crisis the international community often provides humanitarian assistance and other kinds of help. In Rwanda, under the auspices of USAID, a former representative in the New Hampshire legislature worked for years after the genocide to help the Rwandan parliament develop effective processes. Attorneys from the U.S. justice department provided legal expertise and training to rebuild the justice system. U.S., British, Dutch, and other funding agencies have supported development and reconciliation. The United States after World War II, while occupying parts of Germany, helped to rebuild Germany (and Europe) economically through the Marshall Plan. It helped to design constitutions and build institutions in both Germany and Japan.

Another example of a benevolent role comes from peacekeeping operations in Bosnia. After the Dayton agreements, elections in Bosnia led to separate and highly partisan republics. This has interfered with reconciliation. But the status of Brcko, a town of about 100,000 people that is located at the intersection of Serbia, Croatia, and Bosnia, was undecided. It was administered by the Office of the High Representative, the chief civilian peace implementation agency in Bosnia and Herzegovina. The town saw a lot of fighting, with concentration camps around the town set up by Serb occupiers. Later the town did well economically, with cooperation among the ethnic groups living there. The Serbs who occupied Muslim houses were made to leave them, but they received help to build new houses in other parts of the city. While the election in the rest of region was affected by the "... memories of the fury and agony of the fighting still fresh, elections in Brcko... (were held several years later.)... Instead, successive US supervisors plucked well-intentioned moderates from the non-fanatical political parties to create an assembly, and presented them with the basic building blocks of brotherhood and unity, the rules of the game which a just, multi-ethnic state ought to play. When finally the Americans grasped the nettle and called elections, the winners were the moderates."[4]

Help can also be psychological, introducing practices that help a traumatized population heal, or working with leaders to promote understanding the roots of violence and avenues to their prevention. It can also take the form of capacity building, training people in skills that strengthen the society. But countries and their citizens can interpret even genuinely useful help as interference in their internal affairs. This is especially so when outsider actions aim to change elements of culture or societal processes, in order to decrease the potential for violence. Such actions need to be sensitive and skillful, and even more than other help they require collaboration with internal parties.

Active Bystandership by Individuals: Inhibitors and Motivators of Action

Individuals are inhibited from action, or moved to action, by a combination of their personal characteristics and the influence of circumstances, including the words and actions of other people. I described before several specific inhibitors of action. One of them is diffusion of responsibility,[5] people feeling less responsible when there are other witnesses present, or other people who because of their expertise or positions of authority can be expected to take action.[6*] However, in the case of mass violence, it is often those with authority who move the group to harmful action, and outside leaders remain passive. Prevention requires citizen action.

The personal characteristics that move some people to take action—such as a sense of responsibility for others' welfare, or empathy for others in need or distress—are the result of the way the children are socialized and of life experience (see Chapter 22). In my research, people who had a stronger "prosocial value orientation," a combination of a positive view of human beings, concern about others' welfare, and most important, a feeling of personal responsibility for others welfare, were more helpful than people who had less of this characteristic. In a study with men, those with a stronger prosocial orientation helped more when they heard sounds of distress from an adjoining room. Whether they went into that room, or if they did not the distressed person came into their room, more of them made phone calls or went to fill a prescription for him even though they had to leave the task they were working on.[7] In two studies with women, the stronger their prosocial orientation, the more they shifted their attention from what they were working on to listen and show interest when another woman began to tell them about a recent distressing life event.[8] A sample of 2000 people who had more of this characteristic reported that they helped more under a variety of circumstances in everyday life.[9] Competence, both actual and believed, is also important. Helping was greater by people who in addition to having prosocial values believed that they had the capacity to improve others' welfare.[10] Rescuers of Jews in Nazi Europe had more of a characteristic like prosocial orientation than people who did not help.[11] People feeling responsible for others' welfare also helped more when another witness to an emergency was present, a situation that normally leads to diffusion of responsibility.[12]

People also help more if they have responsibility focused on them, for example, by the situation when there is no one else present, or by a position of leadership. Other people can also focus responsibility on a person. In a PBS film around 1970 on real-life heroes, people stand in front of a burning building with a child trapped inside. They turn to a man apparently known for his courage and say: "Are you going in?" And he does. In one of my studies, we either told a young child that he or she was "in charge, if anything happens" or just left the child working on a task. First graders who were "in charge" helped more when they heard sounds of distress from another room.[13]

Some roles, such as policeman or fireman, focus responsibility on the people who occupy them. The role requires them to act under certain conditions. But responsible parties, such as governments and the United Nations, often do little or nothing in the face of genocide or mass killing, and they rarely act early to prevent violence. Creating awareness of this can increase a feeling of responsibility by average citizens to be active bystanders. Creating offices that focus responsibility on people in particular positions in governments would also help.

Another inhibitor of action that I identified earlier is "pluralistic ignorance."[14] It is created by the absence of reaction to events, for example, the media and other people acting unconcerned about injustice, hostility, or violence against a group at home or in far away countries. Social reality is socially defined. The interpretation of the meaning of events is affected by other people. If they seem unconcerned, there must be no need to act. Euphemistic language used by perpetrators and justification by devaluation and ideology further reduce the perception that action is needed. As the persecution of Jews became intense in Germany in 1938, anti-Semitism reached its highest level in the United States. Lack of information, others' seeming lack of concern, and justification of harmful actions combine with costs such as time, effort, or danger to create bystander passivity.

The media has a crucial role in generating attention, concern, and feelings of responsibility in the case of a destructive evolution. But if media in a particular country fail to cover harmful actions, the worldwide media almost certainly does. Pluralistic ignorance can be reduced and empathy and responsibility increased by information on the Internet.

Concerned individuals can call attention to events. The words or actions of each person can influence others—whether among ordinary citizens, members of elites, or government officials, whether in countries in danger of violence or potential bystander nations. In research the uniform actions of a number of people can create conformity, but a single dissenting voice or act greatly decreases conformity. In Stanley Milgram's obedience experiment, what one observer says can stop "teachers" from obeying the experimenter.

In one of my studies, when two people who are together in one room hear sounds of distress from another room, *how one person interprets the meaning* of the sounds and the *appropriate action* greatly affects whether the other person takes action. When the first person says it is nothing to be concerned about, the other person goes into the adjoining room 25% of the time. When the first person says, "This sounds bad, maybe we should do something," even if this person remains passive, about 75% of the time the other person takes action. If the first person adds, "I'll go and find the person in charge, you go into the other room to see what happened" and then leaves through another door, the other person goes into the adjoining room 100% of the time.[15*]

In Chile, a simple but nonetheless dramatic action overcame pluralistic ignorance. It provided information about opposition to General Pinochet, and started the country on the road to ending his rule. Miners planned to strike, but they were surrounded by the military and knew that if they did strike, they would be killed. Instead, they mobilized people to show their support by either walking slowly at a designated time or flicking their car lights. People did this on a very large scale.[16]

Joining together can increase motivation and give people a sense of potential power. Information by the media generates shared knowledge and enables people to more easily mobilize each other. A single bystander will normally feel powerless to subvert a societal process. However, as we shall see, sometimes even a single person can initiate powerful societal processes that serve the prevention of violence.

Active bystanders can humanize members of a devalued group. This is important, since even in everyday situations people who are devalued are helped less. They are even less likely to be helped when helping requires going against one's own group. Active bystanders can speak out against practices, policies, and specific acts. They can question a destructive ideology and offer alternative visions. They can shape others' interpretation of events. They can turn to others and initiate with them efforts to influence the way institutions work—such as children belonging to different groups treated the same way in schools, and people treated equally in the justice system.

Opposing one's own group, especially under difficult social conditions, is especially challenging in collectivist or interdependent (in contrast to individualist or independent) cultures, where people are more embedded in their group and have learned to hold the group's goals as especially important. External actors can provide information and perspectives that may lead people even in collectivist cultures to question their group's harmful actions and the authorities' explanation of them. For this, actors credible to a particular group need to be involved—for example, not only CNN but also Al Jazzera presenting information that challenges jihadist beliefs and actions.

Moral Courage, Motivation, and Action

Opposing the direction of a group requires not only empathy, feelings of responsibility and moral values, but also *moral courage*: the courage to act on one's values even in the face of potential or actual disapproval, or ostracism. In autocratic, repressive systems, or even in a democracy moved by ideological fervor, it also requires physical courage. Early opposition is usually less risky and therefore requires less courage than opposition later in the evolution of hostility and violence.

Moral courage, too, is partly the result of socialization. Children (and adults) have to be allowed, or guided, to express their views, in the home and in schools, to develop confidence, and the habit to act. Since moral courage means acting in opposition to other people or the group, it requires the capacity to form one's own judgment. Understanding the influences that lead to group violence adds to common sense in enabling people to do that.

Research has shown that people who strongly identify with their group are more likely to conform to its norms and standards. They want to elevate their group and promote its goals. As I already suggested, when people shift to a collective identity, they put the group's interests ahead of their personal interests; they act in the best interests of the group, even if it harms them personally.[17] Strong identification makes it difficult to have an independent perspective and to follow personal values, to be able to decide that the group's current actions are contrary to important values or to the group's best interests.

In addition to strong values and trust in one's judgment, opposing a primary group is made more possible if people belong to varied groups, which makes them less dependent on the identity, connection, and fulfillment of basic needs that one group provides. Opposing the group's current direction may be especially difficult for leaders who have helped shape it, are strongly identified with the group, and whose followers expect them to be true to their ideology and goals. It is admirable when leaders who have been part of a system shift a group in a more positive direction, like Gorbachev in the Soviet Union, Sadat in Egypt, and de Klerk in South Africa.[18]*

For individuals to feel that they can make a difference and to be effective actors requires support from and cooperation by like-minded others. Political scientist Kristina Thalhammer and her associates use the term "network" to describe associations they consider crucial for "courageous resistance."[19] In the village of La Chambon, in Southern France, during World War II, the Huguenot residents hid thousands of refugees, mainly Jews, the majority children. Their pastor and other village leaders provided strong leadership and the village was a powerful network. In addition, Quakers and other organizations helped to move refugees to safety, mainly to Switzerland. The Mothers of the Plaza del Mayo in Argentina began to march around the Plaza, in front of government offices, to demand information about their children who had disappeared. They endangered their lives, some of the mothers themselves disappeared, but they formed a powerful community and network. Western humanitarian organizations helped the mothers buy a place to meet; this is an example of practical help that also reminds people that they are not alone.

Networks can motivate, support, and empower active bystandership in response to social injustice or harmful actions. Individuals, local and international organizations, and outside governments can provide ideological, emotional, and material support. As repression increases in the course of the evolution of violence, internal opposition and human rights groups usually disappear, making external actors especially important.

People who oppose a violent system desperately need connections. After the talk I gave in Belgrade in 1995, the members I met from a group that opposed the Serbian government and its nationalist policies, as well as others I met individually who were working for peace, were all eager to talk to a like-minded outsider about their country and their situation in it. It was such people who created and participated in the widespread nonviolent resistance that led to the fall of Milosevic, the president of Yugoslavia and a central instigator of the violence toward Bosnia.

The Nazis were ruthless against individuals and groups they considered their enemies. In one instance when German students tried to generate opposition to the regime, the so-called White Rose movement, they were executed. Participants in a plot to kill Hitler were also executed. But I have previously described two instances of protest, which were directed not at the existence of the government but its *policies*, that were successful. One was opposition to the euthanasia killings. Relatives, lawyers' groups, and some Catholic bishops protested.[20] Together, they represented a substantial network. The other instance, the only known effort to support the Jews in Germany, was when German wives protested in front of government buildings against the deportation of their Jewish husbands. They were each other's "network." After several days, the government yielded.

Heroes and Other Committed Individuals

The actions of single individuals sometimes have wide-ranging consequences. Major Schmelling, a German, informed the villagers of La Chambon about impending raids, through anonymous telephone calls.[21] He also persuaded a superior not to destroy the village. Although he acted alone, he may have felt confident because of his relationship to a leading general.[22] A number of Westerners who stayed in Nanking after the Japanese invasion of China in World War II acted with determination and courage to save lives during the massacre there. One woman missionary, the dean of a girls' college, transformed the college into a sanctuary for the Chinese. A German businessman, a member of the Nazi party, hid 600 people in his home. He was also instrumental in establishing a safe zone, a large area in the city, in which tens of thousands of Chinese survived. He continuously protested the killings at the Japanese embassy. After he returned to Germany, he wrote to Hitler with dismay about what happened in Nanking. But Japan was Germany's ally, the Germans were even more violent, and the Gestapo came to his house and told him to not talk about it again.[23]

Armin Wegner was a volunteer medical nurse in the German army in World War I. He heard about the killing of Armenians and during a leave traveled to areas where the genocide of the Armenians was taking place. In spite of strict orders of both the Turks and the German army, he took many photos—of women and children marching to their death, of dead Armenians, of orphaned children. He was arrested, many of his pictures taken away, but he hid and smuggled others to Germany and the United States, this material of great value in calling attention to the fate of the Armenians. In the 1930s, he spoke out against the persecution of Jews. He was detained and tortured, but he survived and went into exile in Italy.[24]

Joe Darby, the guard who put a disk with the Abu Ghraib pictures under a superior's door, also acted alone, although he first sought the advice of a friend, and his former, trusted commander. Aware of the ostracism and danger he faced, he sought their advice in a veiled manner, by describing to them a hypothetical situation.[25] The abuse of prisoners was widespread in American prisons in Iraq. The shocking pictures and subsequent investigations of Abu Ghraib at the very least lessened the abuse in these prisons and prevented the evolution of greater violence.

Ron Ridenhour was a U.S. soldier in Vietnam. He was not at My Lai, where several hundred civilians were killed by American soldiers, but learned about it from fellow soldiers he trained with. He completely invested himself in finding out what happened at My Lai from fellow soldiers and friends who were there. He searched out a soldier who was reputed to have been there but not to have participated in the shooting. He found him in a hospital. According to the soldier, his superiors, aware of his nonparticipation, kept him at the front and constantly sent him on dangerous missions. They did not allow him to leave even though he had jungle rot, a serious condition, but he hopped on a nearby helicopter and had himself taken to a hospital.[26]

After he collected all possible information, Ridenhour consulted relatives and friends at home, who advised him to forget about it. It was not his business. Instead, he wrote many letters to Congress about My Lai. In one letter, explaining his reason for writing, he quoted Winston Churchill: "A country without a conscience is a country without a soul, and a country without a soul is a country that cannot survive."[27] He did not rest until one Congressman, Mo Udall, held hearings on the massacre. Then journalist Seymour Hersh wrote about it in the *New York Times*. Public knowledge about My Lai, and the trial of Lt. William Calley in charge of the troops there, were important in making such actions less likely in the future and affecting attitudes toward the Vietnam War. Another courageous resister—a much more appropriate term than "whistle blower"—was Daniel Ellsberg, who passed the Pentagon Papers, the top-secret government history of U.S. involvement in Vietnam, to the *New York Times*, publicly revealing the extent to which several presidents had misled the nation about their intentions in the war. While he had help, he made the decision and took action. What these heroic individuals did had important social consequences.

Institutions, and their members, often protect their own even if they act contrary to proclaimed values of the institution. But they turn against their own if they perceive them as harming the institution. Darby and Ridenhour became the targets of intense anger by other soldiers. General Taguba, who was appointed by the army to provide the first report on the Abu Ghraib abuse of prisoners and wrote a truthful report, apparently ruined his career by doing so. The army, and defense secretary Rumsfeld, wanted a whitewash, not the truth.[28]

Another courageous person, Matthew Diaz, was part of the Navy judicial system, the JAG corps. He sent the list of prisoners at Guantanamo Bay, which the government kept secret, to a human rights lawyer. He dearly paid for this—the lawyer gave it to a judge, who sent it to the military. Dias was court-martialed, spent 6 months in jail, and had difficulty finding a job afterward. The psychological challenge in acting as he did is indicated by contrasting statements he made. At his trial he said he was ashamed of his actions. After his release, when he received an award for what he did, he said he was guided by the U.S. Constitution, by a Supreme Court ruling that the inmates had a right to representation, and by his ethical/moral compass.[29] Different values, morality and the rule of law, versus loyalty, were apparently activated by the different social contexts.

The story of Leyman Gbowee of Liberia was told in the documentary film *Pray the Devil Back to Hell* and described by columnist Bob Herbert in the *New York Times* in January 2009. The film shows the horror of the Liberian war between the dictatorial president Charles Taylor and a brutal rebel army, with civilians running from gunfire, children "paralyzed with fear by nearby explosions; homes engulfed in flames."[30]

A single individual can inspire many people to act together. Leyman Gbowee first inspired the women at her Lutheran church to pray for peace, then she organized them for action, involving both other Christian churches and Muslim women. To prayer they added demonstrations, involving more people and becoming the movement Liberal Mass Action for Peace. Thousands of women joined them to demonstrate for peace at the marketplace, which was their headquarters, in response to their call broadcast over Catholic radio stations. As their public support grew, first Charles Taylor and then the rebel leaders met with them. Their actions contributed to pushing the parties to negotiate. When the peace talks held in Ghana seemed to break down, about 200 of the women staged a sit-in at the site of the talks. Their continued engagement had a role in bringing about at first a tentative peace, and then Charles Taylor's exile from the country. The women remained active. In 2006 Liberia elected the first woman president of an African country.[31]

Ralph Lemkin, an attorney, a Jewish refugee from Poland, worked tirelessly for many years to create what became the U.N. Genocide Convention. At the start he was a lone voice in the wilderness; slowly he gained the support of influential people, including Eleanor Roosevelt.[32] In a number of other instances a few individuals managed to create institutions to protect human rights. Amnesty International and Human Rights Watch were started by a few dedicated people.

The empowerment of people under difficult conditions who feel helpless, diminished, frustrated in both their material and psychological needs, is especially valuable in preventing violence. Otherwise, like the men in the Congo, they empower themselves through violence. Social entrepreneurs, effective social change agents, are people who with ingenuity and commitment generate activities in communities that build connections and create opportunities. As one example, a woman in Poland, Dagmara Bienkowska, engaged with people in a highly divided community. One part of the community has taken "possession of all the economic assets...the other left without any financial capital,"[32b] a real world version of the story in our radio drama in Rwanda. She lived in the community for 1 month, talking to people. She learned that two groups in particular were excluded from the life of the community, senior citizens and aggressive "wayward" youth, "local bullies." She involved the two groups in a joint undertaking: the young people gathering recipes of regional dishes from the old people, and putting them together in a cookbook. The unedited version of this was a great success. A professional edition that followed was even more success-ful. Through further entrepreneurial activities of the youth group, the County experienced substantial economic development. Such social change agents are heroes of a different kind, as they use their substantial creativity for the social good.

Much of the literature on preventing mass violence has focused on sanc-tions, boycotts, or military action once there is a crisis, on changing the institu-tions of society, democratization and economic development as means of prevention, and on external pressure on leaders as a society moves toward violence. But the role of individual actors within a society is also of great impor-tance. However, during the evolution of destructiveness that culminates in genocide, there is frequently limited opposition and resistance, or active bystand-ership generating positive processes. But once a genocide has begun, often a small number of people take action to save lives. The characteristics of such rescuers, like inclusive caring, independence in values and judgment, and the ability to deviate from the society around them[33] could also lead them to engage in resistance and prevention. Rescuers often had support from other people to save lives. To change the course of a destructive evolution in a society, it is neces-sary to develop strategies of people joining in early action.

Learning by Doing: The Evolution of Positive Bystandership

Just as violence evolves, so does helping and the motivation that leads to it. My research with young children shows that getting them to engage in helping others leads them to be more helpful at later times (see Chapter 22). Many rescu-ers of Jews, people who endangered their lives to save Jews during the Holocaust in Europe, only intended to help to a limited degree, for example, to hide a person for a few days. Many of them—in one study about 50%—responded to a request for help either by a Jewish person they knew, or by an intermediary, including influential people such as priests. But after they began to help, they continued. Some hid people for years, adding new people to those they were hiding. Others, if they managed to move people they hid to safer places, looked for more oppor-tunities to save lives, connecting up with other rescuers, entering or creating a network.[34] Positive actions often start an evolution.

Small positive acts can transform individuals—and groups. Oscar Schindler, a German who grew up in Czechoslovakia, was a member of the Nazi party, an opportunist who took over a Jewish factory in Poland to enrich himself. He started with small acts of kindness toward his Jewish slave laborers and ended by sacrificing everything he had, and repeatedly endangering himself, as he saved the lives of the people who worked at his factory. Before they began to hide refugees in La Chambon, the villagers, under the influence of their pastor Andre Trocme and other leaders, engaged in small acts of resistance, such as not ringing the bell in the church tower to celebrate a Nazi event. Both resistance and helpful acts can change individuals and communities.

Helpful acts tend to both increase helpers' caring for those they help and to lead them to see themselves as helpful and willing to take risks for the sake of others. Both research and life examples also show that helping acts provide an example that others imitate.[35] The German major Schmelling was inspired by the village doctor of La Chambon, and by his explanation at his trial for why he acted to save Jews.[36] In our radio programs in Africa, listeners' emotional engagement with active bystanders in the programs is one likely source of change in them.

Creating Networks of Active Bystanders

While one person can have significant impact, effective bystandership to prevent group violence requires allies, connecting to or building networks. Values and concerns don't turn into motivation and action unless people believe that their actions can make a difference, which may require a group of like-minded people. Individuals can influence others by defining situations and events as requiring action, just as the person did in my study upon hearing sounds of distress from another room.

Even in a repressive and punitive system, conversations among members of churches and other small communities can become a starting point for action. In the United States and other democratic countries, people can advocate in words and by nonviolent actions positive bystandership of their country without danger to themselves. Organizations with shared values can join in active bystandership. Members of churches, or civic groups like Rotary clubs, can engage with other groups and develop joint actions.

Thalhammer and associates[37] argue that a positive context helps bystanders resist unjust and harmful practices. Such a context is created by humanitarian principles and laws the United Nations advanced and by institutions and structures like Amnesty International. These also provide a positive context for people in government. As I discuss elsewhere in this book, government officials, like other people, are shaped by their contexts. Their predominant goals may become loyalty to party, government policy and ideology, obedience to leaders, and concern for their careers. A context created by humanitarian principles, and connection and dialogue with like-minded colleagues, can join to activate values that otherwise remain dormant. They can overcome loyalty and narrowly defined "national interest" that often limit action on behalf of endangered people.

Bystanders can engage in actions to prevent violence, advance principles, and build institutions. They can even engage in citizen diplomacy, what has been called Track Two diplomacy, to facilitate communication between adversaries and build peace. People living everyday lives with jobs and families can also do a great deal. They can help reduce pluralistic ignorance and shape public opinion in conversations and in discussions in local institutions. They can join or participate in creating institutions, demonstrate, and demand that their governments create institutions that will do the work of prevention. Even limited engagement by many people can have a powerful impact. Imagine the effect of 50 million people writing to the U.S. President, their Congressional representatives, and the media, or to Chinese and other prime ministers to demand preventive action.

The Importance of Self-Awareness

I discussed why past victimization and psychological woundedness can lead to unnecessary "defensive" violence (and also to hostile violence). Groups can also use their victimization as an excuse and justification for violence. The belief in the need for self-defense, and the use of past victimization as a justification, can go together in ways that are difficult to separate, even by the actors. This seems true of Palestinians and Israelis, in some of Rwanda's actions in the Congo, and U.S. actions following 9/11.

Self-awareness and "group awareness" can help in prevention. A critical consciousness needs to be applied to one's own beliefs and emotional reactions, as well as to those of one's group, to the way that history both motivates and is used to justify the group's behavior toward another group. Understanding the impact of victimization and how it can lead to violence can have a corrective influence. It makes possible a more accurate assessment of the meaning of others' actions as well as a more reasoned reaction. It can increase people's ability to live with uncertainty, to listen to others, to take risks for peace, and to make concessions and compromises.

People tend to perceive unfavorable reactions to their group as incorrect, biased, or hostile. As a result, the informational value of others' reactions is lost. Discounting media reports as unfavorable to or slanted against one's group is common. A study following a contentious football game between Dartmouth and Princeton found that fans on each side, looking at the same film, thought their opponents had been violent and blameworthy. Another study found that when pro-Arab and pro-Israeli students saw a television series on the 1982 killing of hundreds of Palestinians in two refugee camps in Beirut by Christian militias that were allowed into the camps by the Israeli military, each group of students saw the program slanted against the group they identified with.[38]*

There are many avenues, starting with socialization, for promoting a critical consciousness that makes it possible to see the actions of one's group that are contrary to important values and principles. Socialization can promote what I have called "constructive patriotism." In contrast to blind patriots, constructive patriots care more about and have stronger feelings of responsibility for others' welfare, and they believe that love of their country requires that they respond when their country acts contrary to essential values. The college-age constructive patriots we studied also informed themselves more about events in the world.[39]

"Instigation" of Bystander Action in Dangerous Situations

What is right and moral for outsiders to encourage people to do in autocratic systems and violent settings, where resistance and opposition can result in getting killed? Should external bystanders incite resistance, opposition, and rescue? Should my associates and I, for example, provide models of active bystandership in radio programs in the Congo, and if so what kind, given that many participants in focus groups said that reporting human rights violations, or resisting the various forms of violence against other people or themselves, can get them killed?[40]

It is the responsibility of external witnesses to be informed, to learn about local conditions, and to use good judgment. They should certainly advocate and support early prevention and reconciliation. It is principled, moral, and to the benefit of everyone to resist an evolution of increasing violence and to promote reconciliation by providing information and support for those who act internally— a supportive network and positive context for action.

Educational programs and other interventions can, for example, help people take an independent perspective, enabling them to see what is wrong in their society and activating moral values and empathy for those who are harmed. They can show what is required for people to act, ranging from an independent perspective to feelings of responsibility and moral courage. These programs can provide guidance to potentially effective actions, to ways of finding and creating support from like-minded individuals and organizations. But it does not seem morally right to advocate actions, or suggest that it is a moral obligation to take actions, that would greatly endanger the actors' lives. Instead, educational programs—if they are allowed to operate—can provide examples of people struggling with the issue of whether to act and how to act. They could include examples of people in other settings who decided to act (e.g., the villagers of La Chambon), with honest depictions of both the dangers of action and the benefits, if not immediate, then long term.

In addressing leaders, such programs can show them struggling with questions about what to do to protect people, address injustice, or to create a more accepting climate in society, in the face of political and sometimes physical danger.

They can show that while such actions can be contrary to short-term political or material interests, they can create long-term benefits for society, and even for the leaders who act in these ways. Leaders can struggle, in a radio drama, with values and moral courage, recruit allies and create networks of support, and build positive institutions. Those speaking to the people of a country in which there is an evolution toward group violence, whether internal or external parties, must show a delicate balance: Avoid pressuring people to endanger themselves and yet help them become aware of what is happening and the need for active bystandership.

Constructive bystanders' aim can be to influence the population, a *bottom-up approach.* They can aim to create resistance to destructive leaders, change culture (humanize the other, promote contact, and so on), inspire people to become active bystanders, and generate action to influence leaders, institutions, and policies. Some of our workshops in Rwanda and the radio programs aimed to influence the population. Pluralism, access to media, and the freedom to organize make a bottom-up approach more possible and effective.

When constructive bystanders aim to influence leaders and the elite, they are engaging in a *top-down approach,* addressing parties that can in turn affect the population. The trainings we conducted with leaders in Rwanda to foster their awareness of what choices and policies would make violence more or less likely was a top-down approach. Such training, as I'll discuss in the next chapter, can provide leaders with knowledge and tools and encourage them to act contrary to short-term political or material interests in order to create long-term benefit for the group. We have also conducted workshops with members of the media in Rwanda. The media can exert influence both upward, at leaders, instigating them to act and generating support for them, and downward at the population, promoting culture change and active bystandership.[41]

Summary

Information in the media, people talking to each other, and seeking information (for example, on the Internet) can overcome pluralistic ignorance, the belief that there is no need for action. Awareness by people that those in positions of authority often don't act can increase their feeling of responsibility to act. An independent perspective, empathy, personal responsibility for others' welfare, and moral courage can lead people to act to inhibit the evolution of destructiveness. Courageous, heroic actions by some individuals have had important social effects. But to be motivated to act and feel effective people need support and empowerment by joining with others. External (and internal) parties can help generate self-awareness about what inhibits action, and exert influence to promote action, but they must do so in a responsible manner, acknowledging when there is significant danger to actors.

Notes

1 Dallaire, 2003

2 Dallaire is highly regarded as an active bystander who attempted to take action. Still, two students in a large lecture course I used to teach at the University of Massachusetts at Amherst, "Cruelty and Kindness: The psychology of good and evil", had a different perspective. In the course of questions and answers during a lecture, these students, who said they were former US soldiers, asked: Why did he not disobey his orders? At a conference during the 10th anniversary commemoration of the genocide, at least some people in Rwanda asked the same question. Actually Dallaire did disobey, but too late. When he was told to evacuate the last 250 peacekeepers left in the country, he refused. With such a small contingent, there was little he could do.

3 Dallaire, 2003; Fein, 2007

4 Popham, 2005

5 Latane & Darley, 1970

6 See Myers, 2010; Staub, 1978, for a review of studies on this phenomenon

7 Staub, 1974

8 Feinberg, 1978; Grodman, 1979; Staub, 1978, 1980

9 Staub, 2003a, 2005c

10 Staub, 2003a

11 Oliner & Oliner, 1988

12 Schwartz & Clausen, 1970

13 Staub, 1970a

14 Latane & Darley, 1970

15 Staub, 1974, 2003a. The person who speaks is a confederate.

16 Merriman & DuVall, 2007

17 For a recent discussion of these issues see Packer, 2008

18 However, the subsequent role of De Klerk was less constructive. Together with other past leaders, as Donald Shriver (2005) notes, he refused to accept his party's or the nation's responsibility, or acknowledge any personal responsibility for the misdeeds of the apartheid regime.

19 Thalhammer et al., 2007

20 Lifton, 1986

21 Hallie, 1979

22 Ibid.

23 Chang, 1998; see also www.irischangthemovie.com

24 http://www.armenian-genocide.org/wegnerbio.html

25 Thalhammer et al., 2007

26 For Ridenhour's account on collecting information about My Lai see http://www.law.umkc.edu/faculty/projects/ftrials/mylai/Myl_hero.html#RON

27 See the letter at http://www.law.umkc.edu/faculty/projects/ftrials/mylai/ridenhour_ltr.html

28 Zimbardo, 2007

29 NPR, 2008

30 Herbert, 2009

31 Ibid.

32 Lemkin, 1944; See also Power, 2002

32b Praszkier at al., 2010, p. 161

33 Oliner & Oliner, 1988; Staub, 1997; Tec, 1986

34 Oliner & Oliner, 1998; Staub 1989, 1997

35 Staub, 1978, 1979, 1997, 2003a

36 Hallie, 1979

37 Thalhammer et al., 2007

38 For a description of these studies see Pettigrew, 2003

39 Schatz et al., 1999; Staub, 1997

40 Oxfam, 2008

41 See also Lederach, 1997

18

Generating Constructive Action by Leaders and Citizens, Creating Structures for Prevention

---

Constructive leaders affirm the humanity of all groups, offer positive visions (constructive ideologies and shared goals), and help shape institutions and generate concrete actions to fulfill these visions.

Constructive leaders are important in mobilizing active bystanders. A constructive leader would consider peaceful alternatives under violence-generating conditions, and would work for reconciliation and peace after violence. In the case of 9/11, the outpouring of sympathy and caring for the United States created an opportunity, albeit a missed one, for such leadership on a global scale—the potential for a worldwide alliance to fight terrorism in a coordinated manner, the potential to create a more harmonious international community, and the potential to constructively address worldwide problems. Such leadership affirms the humanity of all members of a society, and even of enemies in a conflict, and recognizes the importance of all parties working together.

Nelson Mandela did this in South Africa, as did Abraham Lincoln in the United States before his assassination. Under Lincoln most Confederate soldiers received full pardon and were even honored by Union soldiers. The "conciliation of difference" was a high priority for him. He engaged in symbolic acts, such as having the White House band play "Dixie," the battle song of the South, when Lee's surrender brought the war to an end.[1] Mandela, echoing Lincoln's words, made "binding the wounds of the country" his mission. He also engaged in significant symbolic acts, such as beginning his first presidential address with a poem by an Afrikaner poet, and appearing at a 1995 World Cup Rugby game wearing the jersey of a formerly all-white team that stood as a symbol of apartheid.[2]

Constructive leaders will work with all segments of society to identify real problems and develop strategies to address them. They will work to generate a sense of shared community, what might be called a *positive collectivism*. Understanding and addressing differences, focusing on commonalities between groups, and identifying and working for shared goals—an important aspect of an inclusive, constructive vision or ideology—are all important.

The Roosevelt administration's response to the Great Depression was also an example of constructive leadership. But it had limitations. Perhaps due to the hostility of the population to immigrants, who were seen as taking away jobs in economically difficult times, the government did not admit Jews seeking refuge from Nazi Germany into the United States. Creating new legislation to admit more refugees might have been difficult in the political climate of the times, although Roosevelt had taken on many politically difficult issues. But even the admission of Jewish refugees under existing legislature was sabotaged. Author Dan Wyman eloquently described how the United States kept out about 90% of those who could have been admitted under already existing quotas.[3] In addition, the United States and its allies refused to bomb the railroad that carried people to Auschwitz. Even constructive leaders can draw lines around their group and do not necessarily create policies that are inclusively caring.

Commitment to destructive ideologies, devaluation, or vested interest in maintaining hostility may lead people to strike out at visionary leaders and peacemakers. The murders of Lincoln, Gandhi, Martin Luther King, Jr., Anwar Sadat, and Yitzhak Rabin attest to this. But many other lived, and at least the partial success of most of them, except Rabin who was killed before peace could be solidified, attest to what such leaders can accomplish. External bystanders, whether leaders or citizens, may face opposition, but little physical danger.

South Africa provides a valuable example of what might facilitate constructive leadership. As Benjamin Pogrund[4] notes, the African National Congress (ANC) had a cohesive leadership, which neither Israel nor the Palestinians have. Arafat was a powerful leader, but his aims and motives were questionable. And even under him the division between Hamas and Fatah was great. The ANC also had visionary leaders. In addition to the personal characteristics and beliefs that led Nelson Mandela to promote cooperation and peace, he had the tradition of these leaders (one of them, Chief Albert Luhuli, was awarded the Nobel Peace Prize in 1960), and the ANC ideology and beliefs, which were influenced by Gandhi, to guide him. The traditional Ubuntu culture prevalent among black people in South Africa may also have had a role. It promotes, among other values, forgiveness between rivals. It probably contributed to the relative success of the country's Truth and Reconciliation Commission. South Africa also had the Afrikaner leader F.W. de Klerk, who had the wisdom to realize that white rule could not be sustained and had the courage and skill to move the population to accept a "controversial compromise."

The following are a few of the lessons related to leadership, intermingled with my comments and extensions of them, that Benjamin Pogrund describes. He draws on sociologists Heribert Adam and Kogila Moodley,[5] who see these lessons from South Africa as relevant to the Israel–Palestinian conflict. They are relevant to most, if not all, violent conflicts.

- "An end to violence is the outcome of negotiations but should not be a precondition for their start." Often a government or an opposition, rebel, or terrorist group has no control over some of those under its aegis who engage in violence. Or the group strategically engages in violence, even as it wants peace. Waiting until violence stops to initiate negotiations does not make sense.
- "Only a relatively unified, not a fragmented, adversary guarantees adherence to controversial compromises and prevents populist outbidding." It is misguided to believe that Israel could make peace with Fatah, without including Hamas. The continued conflict in Darfur, with great loss of lives and hundreds of thousands of people driven from their homes by the government aided by so-called Arab militias, and by rebel groups, is difficult to resolve in part due the disagreements and conflict among "rebel" groups, and by 2008 also among the Arab militias.
- "...bottom-up involvement through voter education must parallel top-down leadership deals." Cultural change involving the population, which in turn can influence leaders, prepares the ground for its acceptance of compromises, and moves people to active bystandership.
- "Each side has to understand the problem of its partner with his or her constituency and should empower the antagonists to deal with it." As Vamik Volkan also writes, leaders of another group can only be partners in resolving conflict if they remain connected to their populations. External actors, such as leaders of a group, can delegitimize leaders of another group by having too friendly relations with them.

An example of this last point is provided by Jan Egeland when as a high official of the United Nations he spearheaded a creative attempt to resolve the many decades-long fighting between guerillas and the government and right-wing paramilitaries in Colombia.[6] This fighting has profoundly affected life in Colombia, a country that until recently had the highest rate of kidnapping people for ransom—almost 50% of all the kidnappings in the world. Egeland and his team went into the territory held by guerillas, met with their top leaders, and established a relationship with them. Some of these men agreed to come to Norway, together with government officials, to visit the country and its Parliament, as well as to Sweden and other neighboring countries. Disconnected from their home environment, never having been anywhere else, the guerillas were introduced to socialists and conservatives working together in Parliament, and to countries in which many of the goals they have been fighting for were achieved. During the trip, while traveling, learning, eating, drinking, and singing songs with their hosts, they established relationships with government officials.

However, on their return home, their fellow commanders were enraged about the positive press releases their colleagues issued jointly with government officials. They insisted on burning all the presents their colleagues received, fearing that they hid instruments to spy on the guerrillas. They had had such experiences before with paramilitary groups. The change in a few leaders, without any commensurate change in the leadership group, had no lasting effect on the policies and actions of the guerillas.

In hindsight, what might have made this venture more successful? Obviously, the press releases were a mistake. After his admirable success in establishing a relationship and working with a few guerilla leaders, together with them Jan Egeland might have tried to meet again with the group of top commanders, as few or as many as their security considerations would allow. They could have reported on their mission and discussed the ideology, policies, and practices of the countries the group visited and their meaning for the guerillas. Such dialogue could have engaged more leaders of the guerillas and led to an evolution in their thinking and actions.

While group values, the culture, and social conditions will influence constructive leadership, the characteristics of the leaders are important. Daniel Lieberfeld[7] describes the qualities of Lincoln and Mandela as self-control, forgiveness, empathy, cognitive complexity, and optimism about others' capacity for change.

Both Lincoln and Mandela were able to rise above feelings of personal hurt. While an associate described Mandela in the mid 60s as "quickly stung to bitterness and retaliation," at a later time a fellow prisoner described him as someone who had "consciously mastered his anger and impulsivity."[8] A biographer also described him as harboring great bitterness about how he was treated but able to hide it and show the smiling face of reconciliation.

Both men had great ability to put themselves in the place of others and to show respect for other people. In a letter from jail to then President Botha, Mandela identified as central issues to discuss: "firstly, the demand for majority rule in a unitary state; secondly, the concern of White South Africans over this demand."[9] Both Mandela and Lincoln were able to see the world in differentiated and complex terms, the very antithesis of authoritarians. Both possessed the ability to adjust their thinking in response to new and complex situations. Mandela believed that even confirmed racists were educable. He saw human beings as good, and when they err, an aberration. He expressed this view in many speeches and forums. He specifically applied it to the former enemies, the Afrikaners, and thereby humanized them in the eyes of black South Africans.

Group members can look for such characteristics and turn to constructive rather than destructive leaders. But leaders also evolve. Both Lincoln and Mandela were shaped by life experience, ranging from personal losses—each lost a parent at age 9, and later lost two of their children—to experiences they created, for example, by successfully influencing others for the better. Among the influences that can change leaders are educational experiences, the influence of others, their own actions (learning by doing), and their results.

The Training of Leaders and Peacemakers

It is important to provide information and education/training to government officials that will help them take positive action in difficult times. I created the first version of Table 4.1 (in Chapter 4) for working with mid- and high-level national leaders in Rwanda, to show them influences that make group violence probable, and opposing influences that make it less likely. After discussing these, we had leaders engage in an exercise. In groups of three, they considered the extent to which recent government policies and practices would be likely to increase, or to prevent, renewed hostility and violence. They considered, for example, the potential psychological and social impact of aid given to Tutsi survivors, but not to poor Hutus, a policy that was just introduced. Involving very high-level leaders in such training is especially important in countries with autocratic regimes or strongly hierarchical cultures.

This training should create awareness of the effects of a group's past victimization on the leaders and on the population. It should further knowledge about how they themselves and their populations might heal, and it should include experiences that further healing. Just like citizens, people in government also need to become aware of the influences on them, and within them, that may make them passive bystanders or potential perpetrators. Awareness of how their situation can lead them to act in conformity with superiors and government policy can reduce the power of that situation.

Some of this influence is fairly straightforward. Opposing superiors or a whole leadership group, speaking out, or acting against policies tends to have adverse consequences. In some countries, like the United States, these may be loss of opportunities for career advancement and loss of jobs. In autocratic countries, the consequences can be more severe. Even if it had no practical consequences, it is very difficult to again and again advocate positions contrary to the rest of the group, a situation that a few people in the Bush administration—such as Paul O'Neil, the treasury secretary, and Colin Powell, the secretary of state—apparently found themselves in.

But the influences of circumstances on officials can be more insidious. Circumstances shape and activate values and goals. As I discussed before, basic needs evolve into values and goals that vary in their importance for us, forming a hierarchy. This hierarchy is changeable. We are not acting out of the same values and goals when we interact with our children, work in our jobs, or vacation at the beach. People in government and in leadership roles are embedded in a system that focuses on and elevates the ideology of that system, political considerations, and loyalty. The close ties they develop to others in the system—for example, to a president and his policies—and a sense of group cause, as well as but also beyond desire for personal success, enhance the power of the system. Circumstances can powerfully activate particular values or goals and thereby change their place in the hierarchy, their relative importance at that time.

The U.S. government supported Iraq, even though it was the aggressor, in the Iran-Iraq war during the 1980s, presumably due to a belief that the Islamic revolution and the government in Iran were contrary to our national interest (and most likely to Iran holding the staff of our embassy hostage in 1979). During the war, Iraq started to use chemical weapons against Iran. Then it turned against its own population, using chemical bombs to kill Kurds and destroy their villages. Samantha Power[10] described the slow awakening of Peter Galbraith, a member of the State Department at the time, to what was happening. Our government's attitude, its support of Iraq, and Galbraith's embeddedness in the system, combined with the ambiguity of media reports and claims that Iran was the culprit in the war, made this a difficult process for him. Assessing what is really happening is a difficult but essential task—and a moral obligation—of a government in a situation like that of the United States at that time. By neglect or design, the government avoided making an accurate assessment. When the truth became evident, it avoided acting as a moral bystander, continuing to support Iraq.

The influence of the system they are part of affects the members of every leadership group, whether potential perpetrator, bystander, or victim. It can create a shift away from previously dominant values and goals even in people with strong moral values. It can activate and elevate values and goals normally lower in their hierarchy, create conformity to the group, and lead to groupthink. The processes that take place in small groups, such as "polarization," moving toward the extreme, also apply to leaders. Consistent with the approach we have used in our trainings in Rwanda, the Genocide Prevention Task Force report suggested that information about the conditions that lead to mass violence should be included in the training of "the front lines of American foreign policy apparatus." Early warning and prevention should also get into the DNA of policy analysts.[11] In addition, training and workshops can help both internal and external leaders become less embedded in the systems they are part of, to understand the influence of the system on them, and to hold an independent perspective and use their own judgment. The "system" may resist this because it reduces loyalty. But such changes in individuals can transform the system.

Barack Obama promised during his campaign both a leadership group whose members hold a range of perspectives and an environment that encourages their expression. It may not be the case that he did the former in all domains, for example, in the financial domain, where his advisors seem tilted toward business interests. But with regard to the latter, the media has reported that as president, before he expresses his views, he often asks everyone in a group he has gathered to state his or her views. Such an approach reduces groupthink.

Creating a system in which prevention is the central responsibility of some high level officials can help overcome inhibitors of action. Jon Western, a former diplomat who wrote National Intelligence Estimates, found that officials in the State Department who had experience in particular local settings were usually unwilling to make the judgment that mass violence was probable in those settings. This happened, for example, with regard to an assessment of Serb violence in Bosnia.[12]* His experience and my experience in Rwanda both suggest that close relationships to a group, and to influential people in them, make it difficult to see or acknowledge their negative intentions or actions, and even more difficult to address it with them. I did speak what I regarded as the truth to high officials in Rwanda, in particular that the ideology of unity and not allowing Hutus a voice is a problematic policy, this making my relationships with some more challenging.

Jon Western also said that in making judgments about likely violence, human rights people and neo-conservatives were on the same side, believing that violence in Bosnia was likely. Centrists, whether Republicans or Democrats, resisted this assessment. In Western's view, one reason was that they did not want to agree with neo-cons. Not only relationships to people in local settings but also relationships between government officials and their reactions to each other's ideologies affect judgment.

Howard Wolpe, former director of the Project on Leadership and Building State Capacity at the Woodrow Wilson International Center for Scholars,[13] and his associate Steve McDonald, have been working with leaders in Burundi, the Congo, and elsewhere. They aim to enable leaders of hostile groups to work with each other. They write that institutions depend on "...the individuals that comprise their constituent elements. Indeed, institutional transformation requires, in the first instance, the personal transformation of individual leaders—in the way they understand their conflict, in how they relate to each other, and in their capacity for collaborative decision-making."[14] Wolpe believes that after conflict and violence, without enabling leaders to work together across lines of ethnic and political divisions, institutional transformation will have little substance and long-term effect. Consistent with my view, he suggests that without changes in people that create the motivation to transform institutions, institutional change is not likely to take place.

Wolpe and McDonald argue that a competitive political process with national elections, which for many in the West is the definition of democracy, is incomplete. Democracy depends on a shared or common vision of the "rules of the game," of how the national community is to be constituted, how leaders are to relate to each other, and so on. That is, democracy depends as much on cooperation as on competition. This common vision they refer to is, in my terms, a constructive ideology. Unfortunately, in divided societies the different groups usually don't see themselves as members of a national community, with a shared vision of social arrangements. To resolve conflict and create a peaceful society, attention must be paid to developing this shared vision. Attitudes and perceptions must change to enable leaders to work together. They need to move beyond a zero-sum attitude—that only one party can win. They need to develop the ability to hear each other, to enter the other's perspective, and accept the legitimacy of the other's needs. They need to develop the capacity to focus on what their group needs, not insist on what their group wants, and to see the needs of the other party. They need to realize that their enlightened interests are best served by understanding and considering shared interests with the other party—corresponding to what psychologists have called superordinate goals.[15]

Consistent with the view that my associates and I have arrived at in our workshops in Rwanda, Wolpe and McDonald[16] believe that when leaders of hostile groups meet, having them engage at the start with the issues between the groups gives rise to powerful feelings and makes progress difficult. We have found that by first helping leaders understand the origins of violence and avenues to prevention and reconciliation, their attitudes shift, making it possible for them to engage with issues more positively. Wolpe and his associates focus on the development of role taking—seeing the perspective of the other, effective communication, and trust, all skills and attitudes necessary for collaborative relationships. Participants engage in simulations, role plays, and other experiential activities that aim to develop collaborative capacity. By presenting this activity as technical capacity building, it is easier for leaders from the two sides to enter into it. They get to know each other, develop some comfort with each other, as well as skills, before they engage with substantive matters, ideally in "interest-based" negotiations. They learn that for durable solutions to issues they have to include all relevant parties. Participants are brought together repeatedly; extended engagement is important for building relationships.[17] One of the early beneficial effects of their leadership training in Burundi was agreement on the long-standing issue of the ethnic composition of the army.[18]

One challenge is to find the right leaders and have them be willing to enter this process. External parties such as the United Nations, the World Bank, particular countries, or trusted individuals can initiate the process. The leaders, however, must be chosen by the parties as genuinely representative of them. Afterwards, collaborative decision making must be constantly reinforced, in the face of the challenges in the real world, the significant issues between parties, and the people who have not participated in the process. This can be done by "the practice of skills learned, the strengthening of relationships, and actual collaborative initiatives."[19]

Being in or visiting certain settings might be useful. One training for mid-level leaders from a number of countries was conducted in 2008 at Auschwitz.[20]* Bringing participants into contact with victims' suffering can create empathy, moral outrage, and the motivation to act. Walking along the ramp where the selections took place, seeing the remnants of the building where people were sent to the "showers" and where they were immediately killed by gas, or seeing the barracks where slave laborers were crowded onto wooden planks to sleep, participants can imagine what it was like to be treated that way. Going into a church or school where thousands of Tutsis sought refugee but were killed can do the same. Seeing both the suffering of Palestinians, and the grief of Israelis in the wake of suicide bombing, can create empathy for both sides and motivate action for peace.

Varied programs around the world offer training for peacemakers whose activities range from local communities to distant conflict regions. One example is the Conflict Transformation across Cultures (CONTACT) program at the School of International Training in Vermont. Out of about 200 applicants, they admit between 60 and 70 people from 25 to 30 countries to a 3-week summer program. Usually participants are from different sides of a conflict and from many professions, including law, education, social work, nongovernmental organizations (NGOs), management, academics, psychology, religion, engineering, and business. Many sign up for a certificate program and continue their engagement over the Internet, and every January a group of those who were trained before go on a trip to Rwanda.

The substantive knowledge such training provides is important; the deep engagement with other participants is crucial. Paula Green, the creator of this program, writes: "Shifts in attitude and behavior cannot be 'taught' intellectually; they are learned through encounter. We observed religious, racial and ethnic stereotypes and prejudices replaced by genuine relationships...(Participants) learned to see their lives in the context of a universal tragedy of ethnic warfare currently tearing apart the world."[21]

In addition to helping participants with peacemaking activities in their home countries, this experience sometimes leads to collaborative projects. One of them sought to advance reconciliation in Rwanda by acknowledging and celebrating rescuers during the genocide. In January 2009 an exhibit opened about rescuers in Rwanda at the genocide museum in Kigali, created by two previous participants in CONTACT, one of them a Rwandan survivor.

Leaders and the Population

For societal transformation to take place, there has to be change in both the leaders and the population. When leaders bring a violent conflict to an end by negotiating and signing peace agreements, one reason that violence often restarts is that the attitudes of the populations have not changed. Their hostility and anger must be addressed. "Middle-level" processes such as the media and truth commissions, as well as reconciliation at the grassroots level, are all important. As part of our work in Rwanda, we trained trainers from many organizations, so that they could train others. We also worked with members of the media, who enthusiastically participated in workshops and in exercises in creating news articles and programs that would promote peace. But they expressed frustration that their freedom to use their new knowledge would be limited.

Leaders often don't prepare the population for peace, perhaps because they are ambivalent or afraid to challenge the hostility of the population to the other group. Since each party carefully monitors the thoughts and acts of the other, continued devaluation in the schoolbooks, in the media, and negative statements about the other by leaders to their own people maintains mistrust and fuels hostility in both groups. Training can help leaders understand the importance of humanizing the other group in the eyes of their population, thereby creating sound underpinnings for peace agreements. The leaders' words and the example of their actions, educational media, and school curricula are among the tools for humanizing the other.

The Role of External Bystanders in Prevention: Governments, the United Nations, and Citizens

My associates and I are outsiders, as we work on reconciliation in Rwanda, Burundi, and the Congo. So was Jan Egeland in Colombia. So are outside NGOs and even the United Nations as it works in many countries.

External bystanders can help strengthen the positive capacities of a society. In Africa and around the world, unemployed and uneducated young men have had a major role in conflict and violence, which in turn has halted economic and social progress. Outsiders can help with establishing local industries, training in skills, and building capacity for what has been called social capital. In Rwanda, Palestine, and elsewhere, they can work with governments, businesses, and other local organizations to create structures that improve economic well-being for everyone. In the Eastern Congo, to create a normal society, the men who have been part of the many fighting groups will have to learn skills and to have opportunities for work. They will also have to heal, reconnect with the rest of society, and develop the psychological capacity for self-discipline and a normal life.

In various places, for example, in South Africa, the existence of a business community, for which a relationship with the outside world was important, had an important role in preventing further violence. It may be that helping to develop a middle class in the Muslim world that is interested in economic success and the well-being of people will be an important force turning Islam away from religious extremism.[22] To accomplish such goals, outside and inside actors have to join to create civic and commercial institutions. The Open Source Society Foundation created by George Soros has helped build civic institutions in Eastern Europe. While Russia under President Putin has moved back toward authoritarian rule, these activities helped Eastern European countries establish democracies.

I have stressed the need for cultural knowledge and sensitivity all along. Let's assume that outside parties want to help improve the educational system of a country. They can use their experience in developing the design of an educational system and introduce it to the government, administrators, and teachers. But the motivation of these insiders to work with a system designed by others may be limited. They need to be involved in developing the system from the ground up. This also is challenging, since effective educational practices, such as students as active participants in learning, are often contrary to the traditional practices in which students are passive recipients of information. Outsiders can help insiders understand why certain things are important, as we have done, for example, by showing the importance of moderating "authority orientation" in preventing mass violence. In a different realm, Elinor Ostrom, a 2009 economics Nobel Prize winner, and her students have shown that exhaustion of commonly shared environmental resources can be much more effectively prevented when local communities design their own systems of the use of these resources. Outsiders can initiate this process, but imposing rules from the outside makes it less effective.[23]

In this and many other realms, outsiders can impart relevant technical/scientific knowledge. Especially when such knowledge is required, local control needs to have limits. For example, in our educational radio programs, it would not be appropriate for local actors without a background in the study of group violence to determine the educational content of the program. But local actors have a variety of important roles, such as how information can be effectively communicated to a local audience, how educational material that is in some ways at odds with the culture is best communicated, and others. Moreover, they will only be effective if they make the perspective they aim to develop in the programs their own. What this and many other projects require is effective collaboration among various actors.

By improving life and reducing the difference in the material conditions of groups, material help produces significant psychological benefits. It affirms the identity and self-worth of the less privileged group, lessens feelings of injustice, creates hope, and builds connections. Given that genocidal societies tend to be less connected to other countries, external bystanders can reduce the likelihood of violence by simply engaging with a country/group economically.[24] Social connections also helps, reducing the country or group's sense of isolation and increasing its concern for what others might think about its internal activities.

But material help must be contingent. Providing economic support that strengthens destructive leadership is a form of complicity. One criticism of Western economic support for Rwanda preceding the genocide was its mindless nature.[25] It was given regardless of what was happening. When at one point the European community suspended its aid because of human rights violations, the impact was widespread, with community discussions even at the village level.[26] However, aid was resumed without a change in Rwandan policy. Balance is important; help should be provided without inappropriate strings attached, but those who provide help should insist on moral practices in the country they help.

Outsiders can foster ripeness for conflict resolution by engaging in dialogue with each party, carry information between them, help the parties see that violence will not resolve matters, and prepare the way for negotiation and compromise. Bystanders can influence other bystanders. In the Middle East, with Shiite Iran in ascendance, and with the threat of it developing nuclear weapons, Sunni countries are more amenable to peace with Israel. Arab countries have put forth proposals to create a Palestinian state, combined with recognition and peaceful relations with Israel. The Israeli attack on Gaza in late 2008 and early 2009 created a strong reaction in many Arab countries, especially in the population, but the leaders were ready to continue with this policy. Diplomacy and active, positive bystandership by the United States and others can help bring this about. Pressure by President Obama led the Israeli prime minister to say in June 2009 that he accepted a two-state solution, and later to halt the building of some settlements.

Early in the evolution of destructiveness, privately rather than publicly expressed disapproval and behind-the-scenes diplomacy are important starting points for preventing or halting violence. Autocratic leaders, out of pride and a need to maintain their image, want to show that they will not be affected by outside pressure. In some cultures, saving face is an especially important value. It is essential that the diplomats who engage with such a situation know the country's culture, its history, as well as past relations between hostile groups. Since past victimization and historical traumas may have an important role in leaders' behavior, diplomats should also have training in and staff that has experience with trauma, and in ways to constructively engage psychologically wounded leaders and populations.

Potential perpetrators tend to develop a self-righteous and ideological view, convincing themselves that they have good reasons for what they are doing and that others see their actions as right. Reactions by outsiders might correct this view. These reactions might be expressed in the course of preventive diplomacy, not only by proclamations but with influential parties engaging with the situation, as in Kenya.

As I have written earlier in the book, this might have helped in the former Yugoslavia. A gathering of relevant actors could have offered support, help, and reassurance to Serbs threatened by the collapse of communism, by a greatly deteriorating economy, by the disintegration of their country, and by the already shown hostility toward them by the newly created Croatia, a country that during World War II perpetrated mass murder against the Serbs. It could also have offered the Serbs material help. And it could have made clear that force would be used to stop further Serbian aggression.

If such actions do not bring about change in policies, the next step can be targeted sanctions and boycotts. The experience with boycotts, especially of Iraq where it created great suffering and many deaths, especially among children,[27]* led to the belief that sanctions and punitive actions should as much as possible focus on leaders.[28] Confiscating their foreign bank accounts, not selling luxury items to the country, and not allowing leaders and members of the elite into other countries except for diplomatic missions are possible actions. Diplomatic missions should be allowed because, in the perspective of this book, dialogue should not stop. When a general boycott of a country is instituted, its effects on the population ought to be monitored. Its effectiveness depends on how unified the international community is in instituting it, and whether a middle class and civic institutions exist that can use its influence to change policies.

A new principle of *responsibility to protect*, adopted by the United Nations in 2005, states that "mass atrocities that take place in one state are the concern of all states." This principle makes it the obligation of states to protect their own citizens, to reject and prohibit genocide, ethnic cleansing, or other atrocities. However, if they fail to do so, it makes it the responsibility of other states to protect citizens in any and all countries. The primary aim of responsibility to protect, or R2P as it is often called, is less to promote humanitarian intervention than to motivate countries to protect their citizens. It should also motivate the international community to engage in early prevention. But neither the mechanisms for early prevention nor for intervention, if required, has been created. Without these, R2P, like other human rights conventions, will have limited effect.

International conventions that affirm the sovereign right of states to deal with their internal affairs, originating from the treaty of Westphalia in 1648, helped to prevent wars among European countries, but they have inhibited intervention in cases of mass violence. States also want to avoid precedents, which would allow intervention in their own internal affairs. The responsibility to protect addresses this, clearly stating that states do not have the sovereign right to harm their citizens, and if they do not protect them, others have the obligation to intervene. Francis Deng, the Special Representative of the United Nations for the prevention of genocide and mass atrocities, reported in 2008 that he stressed in his discussions with leaders that by protecting their citizens, they protect their sovereignty.[29] Such persuasion is useful but often will not be sufficient. Both Darfur and the Congo show that the principle is not easily translated into practice.

R2P requires that the international community balance the right to sovereignty with the value of human lives. Unfortunately, as Madeleine Albright, the U.S. secretary of state under President Clinton, has argued, the Bush administration's invasion of Iraq, along with its rhetoric about preemption, "has weakened support for cross-border interventions even for worthy purposes...the concept of humanitarian intervention has lost momentum."[30] At a time when the United Nations promotes the concept of responsibility to protect, as she further writes, "many governments, especially in the developing world, are now determined to preserve the principle of sovereignty...."[31]

Given how much harm is done to people in many places, that is unacceptable. The principle of responsibility to protect should become a new, revised treaty of Westphalia for the modern age. What should happen when a society is on a path toward mass killing or genocide, whether the government harms people or does not protect them from harm? The principle itself and when and how it becomes active must be further developed, together with the mechanisms to act on it. This will contribute to the will to act.

Leaders in the United States and elsewhere can facilitate this effort by instituting policies that convince the international community that the only aim of future intervention in other countries will be to protect people or defend against aggression—which very few believe was the case in the invasion of Iraq. However, waiting until the principle is applied in a given country means that much harm will already have been done. Without early prevention, emotional-ideological forces will still lead to violence—and to the need to intervene. Intense hostility and enmity, once they develop, are not easily restrained by the knowledge that negative consequences might follow.

When dangerous conditions have already developed, in recent times the United Nations has been active in peacekeeping. In 2008, in 17 peace operations, over 100,000 personnel were deployed.[32] But peacekeeping in the tradition of the United Nations—peacekeepers not allowed to fight, even to defend themselves, and at times withdrawn when fighting begins—has been inadequate in a number of situations. While new rules give peacekeepers greater leeway, they are still far from the fighting force needed to prevent or stop mass killing or genocide. In addition, when the urgency for action is great, it may not work to have as peacekeepers rotating military units from member countries, since states are often reluctant to provide military for U.N. purposes. Thus, a U.N. rapid deployment force should be created.

The Genocide Prevention Task Force Revisited

In Chapter 2, I introduced the 2008 report issued by the Genocide Prevention Task Force that Madeleine Albright and William Cohen chaired, and I analyzed some of its strengths and limitations. I'll briefly summarize that discussion here in preparation for additional details that relate to this chapter's focus.

The report sees a moral and humane obligation for prevention, while clearly showing the lack of preparedness by the United States to engage either in actions to halt already occurring mass violence, or in early prevention. It calls on the president and the secretary of state to increase focus on prevention and to be more directly involved, but the manner of their involvement is not spelled out. It suggests that the actions of our top leaders can contribute to prevention becoming the norm and suggests training government officials in relevant knowledge. Such training can also develop emotional orientations and enhance caring for the welfare of human beings in far away places.

In discussing origins and prevention, the Task Force report[33] focuses almost entirely on external, environmental factors, not on culture and the psychology of the people and their leaders. It states that genocide usually occurs in the context of violent conflict and major political instability, in very poor countries where ordinary citizens lack economic opportunities. But these conditions do not inevitably lead to genocide or extreme mass killing. If they did, we would have many more of them. They are starting points, instigators. Culture, the psychological effects of these conditions and societal responses to them by the population and leaders, past relations between groups, and the behavior of external parties all affect the course of events.

The Task Force report also notes the role of grievances about the inequitable distribution of resources, and opportunistic elites exploiting these situations to amass power and "eliminate competitors" (p. 36).[34] It suggests "promoting economic development and strengthening capacities to prevent instability and violent conflict of all kinds" (p. 35) as important elements of prevention. It does not spell out, however, how to strengthen these capacities and how to create engagement by outside parties.

Among environmental factors that the report considers as triggers for violence are unfair or postponed elections, assassinations, battlefield victories, and anniversaries of "traumatic and disputed events." In each situation, according to the report, prevention must match its tools to the salient factors, the particular conditions and triggers. As a general principle, though, the report suggests targeting leaders and their resources, with negative and positive inducements. The report notes the value of early warning if it is reliable, if its language is effective in communicating with policy makers, and if it is linked to possible mechanisms for preventive action. Systems to be created within the government can be responsible for designing preventive actions. It suggests finding appropriate channels to communicate early warning so that it is not lost in bureaucracy and amid varied tasks. The report indicates that early warning should not be expected to predict violence or its timing, but at the same time should take into account that if violence does not occur, the credibility of early warning is diminished. However various events and processes, naturally occurring or intentional, such as bystander actions, can avert violence. And even if violence would not occur in spite of the conditions for it present, preventive actions improve a society in danger of violence.

I am advocating early prevention that according to what is needed provides material help, engages in preventive diplomacy, and addresses culture, group psychology and beliefs about, attitudes toward, and relationships with the other group. Prevention should start automatically when the available information (see Table 17.1 in Chapter 17) indicates the *likelihood* of group violence. The cost of such action is sufficiently low that it can be conducted in many countries at the same time, especially when compared to the costs of dealing with violence and its aftermath.

The report stresses that international norms, which were created by humanitarian principles that have been developed within the United Nations and outside of it (e.g., the Geneva accords), are likely to reduce mass violence. So far the United Nations and other international bodies have developed principles, but the norms (widely held expectations of appropriate actions) are only slowly developing. The Task Force sees successful early action as depending on the ability and willingness of indigenous leaders to act. But this often requires outside support and resources, and knowledge and skill in effective help by outsiders.

The report focuses on changing the direction of potentially destructive leaders through positive and negative inducements. Trade incentives and increased aid are positive inducements. Aid that is conditional, threats of moral and legal accountability, public shaming, and sanctions against specific industries, imports or exports, are negative inducements. So are interdicting funds and arms. These are worthwhile recommendations, but instrumental gain and the threat of material loss must not be the only inducements.

The report mentions the leadership program in Burundi I described, in which through shared experiences leaders from different sides come to see each other's humanity. In addition to changing potentially or actually destructive leaders, it is important to help positive leaders emerge, through training of mid-level and community leaders, and when they are willing, high-level leaders. Outside leaders personally engaging and developing relationships with internal leaders can also be a very important force in bringing about change in them and their policies.

Another focus is on developing institutions in countries in danger of violence. Establishing the rule of law, with independent judiciary and prosecutorial systems, would eliminate impunity. Land reform is important in many settings. Seeing grievances over power sharing and resource distribution as the most important precursors of genocide and mass atrocities, the report stresses creating transition to democracy and power sharing. By providing incentives for collaboration, the formation of identity-based political parties can be avoided. The report describes many worthwhile ends, but little about the means to accomplish them. It mentions education in general, for women in particular, and for peace. These can affect group psychology and culture.

Security forces and paramilitary groups associated with them have often been involved in perpetration. The report suggests reforming security forces, so that they are comprised of all elements of a society, trained to protect rather than destroy life, and legally accountable to civilian leadership. Creating military to military relationships is important, such as ongoing programs that bring foreign military for training to the United States. Whether this stops them from becoming perpetrators depends on their attitudes, ideology, and the training they receive. In the infamous School of the Americas, for many years the United States trained South American military in counterinsurgency techniques.

In their home countries, many of them became perpetrators of torture and of mass killing through death squads, disappearances, and other ways.

The Task Force report is useful on military intervention, especially in noting that military action is not an either/or matter, and offering distinctions among different kinds of actions. For example, as part of prevention, "...exercises could be held in neighboring countries..." Such exercises warn would-be perpetrators; they might have deterred them in Rwanda. The report distinguishes between stability operations (such as peacekeeping), and military action that aims to protect people or to defeat perpetrators. Considerations that make the military unwilling to intervene include the assessment that it might increase violence and harm to civilians, fear of "mission creep," and the absence of an exit strategy. Post conflict reconstruction is essential to enable the military to leave after intervention. Effective post conflict reconstruction requires reconciliation as it is discussed in this book.

As with other aspects of prevention, the Department of Defense has not developed specific tools or strategies for preventing genocide. Plans for action are currently event driven. However, according to the report, policy is shifting toward greater preparedness. The North Atlantic Treaty Organization (NATO) and the European Union are both developing forces that can be deployed fast. The United States should help enhance the capacity of the United Nations, the African Union, and other regional bodies to militarily prevent and halt genocide and mass atrocities, and develop the capacity of the United Nations and NATO to help other organizations as needed. Different processes would be required if genocide develops quickly and suddenly (volcanic) or slowly and gradually (rolling). While this is a valid distinction, it is a relative matter, since even in the former case, there is a progression toward violence. With appropriate assessment, a seeming eruption would usually seem less volcanic. As in other realms, the report stresses greater military coordination with international partners.

In summary, this valuable but incomplete document calls for much more effort in prevention. Its relative focus is still on late prevention, but it does consider early prevention. It suggests that in deciding on action the following need to be considered: static risk factors; potential triggers; whether leadership in a country has the means and motives for violence; and whether the United States has effective levers to influence behavior in a given context. The report provides lists of the goals of prevention but gives insufficient attention to how to bring about these desired outcomes. It identifies positive and negative inducements, or payoff structures, to change the motivation of leaders, and it focuses on changing institutions. But it does not concern itself with the ways people's thoughts, feelings and attitudes toward each other need to change, so that they are ready to create a more equitable distribution of power and wealth, more equal justice, build positive institutions, or resist movement toward destruction when those institutions do not yet exist. It also pays limited attention to avenues or methods to bring change about.

Creating Internal and External Structures to Prevent Mass Violence

It is essential to create structures and institutions that promote positive psychological changes, together with other aspects of prevention. They can foster opportunities for dialogue, promote healing, enhance pluralism, work for access by all groups to the public domain, build civil society, and foster social justice. Such structures include an effective justice system; anti-discrimination laws; the operations of the schools, police, and the military; nongovernmental institutions that engage people in civil society; and so on. Without these structures, psychological changes are likely to be temporary; without psychological changes, such structures will not develop and may not persist or be effective. However, once they operate effectively, they create further positive change.

To create structures of prevention and reconciliation requires changes in the psychology (thinking, feelings, values, and worldviews) of people who are maintaining existing structures and are in a position to change them or to create new ones. It is also important that potential agents of change understand the interplay between psychology, culture, and institutions.

The absence of appropriate structures limits action by the U.S. State Department,[35] and government leaders in general, in times of crises in other countries. The Task Force report describes many and varied institutions within the U.S. government that have a potential role in information gathering and initiating action, but it shows that no office has direct responsibility for prevention. Responsibility is diffused.

At this time, political will to act depends on the personality, values, and inclinations of specific officials. I asked a member of the National Security Council after about 2 years of concentration camps, fighting and killing in Bosnia, Sarajevo shelled, and ethnic cleansing—the removal of Muslim from certain areas—why President Clinton does not do more to stop the violence. I knew this man; he was thoughtful and decent. He said the president cannot act because people in the country would not accept it. Such an attitude at the top, whether it is a genuine feeling of helplessness or a cover for inaction, shapes the perspective of other officials. Action will only be reliably generated by the right system, which includes high-level officials with access to the top leadership and with the knowledge and values that lead them to inform, advocate, and initiate action.

I have advocated for a number of years, in publications[36] and talks at conferences with U.S. government officials,[37]* the creation of very high-level offices, both in the U.S. State Department and in the foreign ministries of other countries, with the responsibility to initiate and coordinate preventive responses when there is a danger of mass violence anywhere in the world. Only when their position directly focuses responsibility on them can we expect the relevant values of busy government officials to become active and for their attention to focus on prevention. With all the focus on early warning, when there was early information about impending violence, in Rwanda and elsewhere, or even clear evidence of intense ongoing violence, often no action or only very delayed action has been taken. Our focus must be on *early action*.

The Task Force report on prevention advocates institutions similar to, but not identical with, what I had in mind. It advocates the creation of an *Atrocities Prevention Committee* (APC), with representatives from a number of relevant government agencies, all assistant secretaries. Its work is to be coordinated by a National Security Council *Directorate for Crisis Prevention and Response*. The Task Force suggests that these arrangements are better than a single, stand-alone office, which experience has demonstrated can easily be marginalized.

The members of the Task Force's commission, former members of the cabinet or Congress, would know what type of government institutions would be effective. But they may not appreciate enough the psychology of the actors. Members of the APC would have other primary duties. Both what I have written earlier about the way people's circumstances activate different goals, and my experience in less august bodies, suggest that results in one realm are not inspiring when people have primary duties and concerns in other realms. In this case, the APC's function would be secondary to the members' main jobs. The report suggests that an assistant secretary of state for democracy, human rights, and labor, a person with many responsibilities, should be the lead person for prevention. My analysis of the psychological forces, the activating potential of the contexts in which government officials operate, suggests that there should be a group of officials whose *only* responsibility is to work on prevention. With the APC having the responsibility the Task Force suggests, and this group a part of its meetings, they would not be marginalized.

The creation of what might be called the *Central Office for the Prevention of Mass Violence* (perhaps COPV), with its own assistant secretary of state who would be the lead person in the APC, and with the new NSC Directorate, diffusion of responsibility would be limited. Inspiring other countries to create similar offices would provide for effective collaboration. I noted earlier that a crucial challenge in times of crises is outside parties making speedy collaborative decisions. A coordinating group of representatives of these Central Offices for Prevention, working with the Security Council, would facilitate this.

While such systems are lacking as yet, there are communities of engaged professionals. The U.S. Holocaust Museum's Committee on Conscience, the United States Institute for Peace, the Woodrow Wilson Center, and the U.S. State Department and CIA have been bringing together scholars, diplomats, and other professionals to engage with matters of group conflict, genocide, and its prevention. Some of these institutions, as well as USAID (aid for international development) support or initiate activities aimed at prevention.

In his book *Preventing Genocide*, David Hamburg proposed *International Centers for the Prevention of Genocide*, one in the United Nations and one in the European Union. He sees these centers as organizers of early warning and prevention. Their staff would include people with varied expertise, such as scientists, diplomats, and military people. One of their functions would be to "formulate preventive measures at various levels of danger and feasible contingency plan."[38] This would avoid improvising in crises. The Hungarian government is establishing the European center, to begin operation in 2011.

In Hamburg's vision, the Centers would integrate warning functions and work on development aid, trade agreements, investment, education, and prejudice reduction. They would work with authorities to neutralize and block media incitement, foster cooperative networks of institutions of civil society, heighten public awareness, and build constituencies for prevention. They would offer training to professionals and provide grants and technical assistance to strengthen relevant education and stimulate research. They would regularly convene varied experts as well as leaders in business, religions, and media. They would disseminate their findings and recommendations to policy makers and policy advisors, and to the general public to build support for the prevention of mass violence.[39]

Hamburg also proposes that these Centers would coordinate work of the appropriate ministries of supporting nations. In my view this requires a powerful executive group, such as the Central Offices for Prevention located in foreign ministries that I am proposing. A number of other functions that he proposes for the Centers, for example, development aid and trade agreements, require the power of governments and should involve these Central Offices.

Hamburg is concerned both with short-term "operational prevention (preventive diplomacy of foreseeable crises) and...structural prevention (democratic socioeconomic development)."[40] While this book is concerned with both, it is greatly concerned with a third type, essential for the other two: *sociopsychological prevention.* This refers to prevention that addresses the psychological effects of social conditions and culture, and brings about psychological changes that give rise to and motivate constructive social processes and the creation of constructive institutions. This crucial and necessary aspect of prevention usually receives little attention.

There are also institutions now in varied countries that aim to deradicalize captured or suspected terrorists. Since a central thesis of this book is that there are shared principles of origins and prevention of different forms of mass violence, I see it appropriate for subgroups in the Central Offices for Prevention to work on the prevention of terrorism. Addressing instigating conditions and cultural characteristics can prevent all forms of mass violence. In addition, those involved in the U.S. government with preventing mass violence can monitor U.S. policies and attempt to limit support for autocratic and repressive systems. Such systems can give rise to terrorism, as in Egypt, engage in mass killing, as in Guatemala, Chile, and Iraq, or give rise to revolution, as in Iran under the Shah, all countries the United States supported and most of them under governments the United States had a role in creating.

What Can Citizens Do?

I have emphasized in this and the previous chapter the importance of individuals becoming active bystanders. Table 18.1 summarizes the ways in which people can move themselves to active bystandership. Governments remain passive in part because the events at far away places, however tragic, remain only at the periphery of leaders' attention, and because they believe that at best their citizens are unconcerned, or at worst any action demanding sacrifice would be unpopular and politically harmful to themselves. But if leaders explained to their citizens why they act, make them aware of the human suffering, the economic costs of mass violence, its impact on the international system and their own countries, and the morality of action, citizens would usually follow.

Often the opposite needs to happen: Citizens need to explain all of this to leaders and let their governments know that they expect them to act. A substantial number of letters to leaders, whether in the United States or elsewhere, is likely to have influence. Thousands of letters to the editors, even if most of them are not published, will lead newspapers to do what they often do not do: cover the news about mass violence at far away places. There is a Catch 22 here—how are citizens to know, and to come to care, without good news coverage? Citizens must use the limited information in the media, enlarge their imagination about the danger or suffering it reports, and use the Internet for more research. A search in Google on the "prevention of genocide," or about events in particular countries, will provide a wealth of information.

Citizens can organize discussion groups at their churches and other civic organizations, even at their workplace. They can inform themselves and offer to come to their children's schools, making age-appropriate presentations to children— and their teachers—about the suffering of people in other countries and the need for action. They can call in to talk radios and introduce these issues, even when the topic is only tangentially relevant.

Citizens can also support or when possible join as volunteers civic organizations that are active in this realm, such as the International Rescue Committee, Doctors without Borders, Oxfam, Save the Children, or religiously based organizations such as World Vision. These organizations mostly attempt to help in the wake of mass violence. They are active in postconflict societies, providing humanitarian assistance. However, these and other organizations are also involved in development assistance, democratization, and institution building. There are many activist organizations that work on reconciliation and peace building. The Darfur Coalition is probably the largest assembly of citizens ever to work on halting mass violence. Citizens can also work with businesses so that they influence the policies of countries that harm their citizens. Such citizen actions led to the boycott of South Africa by many corporations, which led its business community to support a shift away from apartheid.

Table 18.1 How Individuals Can Become Active Bystanders—Internal or External

Learning about inhibitors of action to counteract their influence

- Individuals, the media, and leaders show no concern and act as if there were no problems (this creating pluralistic ignorance and the perception that nothing is wrong).
- Diffusion of responsibility: Since there are many potential actors, each thinks that others can take action or that influential individuals would or should, and all remain passive.
- Concern about others' disapproval if one takes action.
- Other costs: effort, time, stress, and danger
- Other people defining the meaning of events as requiring no action, or that there are good reasons for the hostility and violence against a group and opposing them is wrong
- Preoccupation with one's own goals and needs, especially in difficult times. (An examination of these can provide perspective, activate moral values and caring, and shift concern to the great danger for victimized people.)

Cultivating personal inclinations that make action likely

- (Inclusive) caring about others' welfare
- Empathy, sympathy, feelings of personal responsibility, and moral values (justice, the sanctity of human life)
- Resistance to the substitution of other values, such as obedience and loyalty to leaders and one's group, regardless of their actions, for essential moral values
- An independent perspective/judgment, a critical consciousness in evaluating events, including the words and actions of leaders and other authorities
- Moral courage, the willingness and capacity to act out of caring or according to one's values, in spite of potential opposition and negative consequences
- Feelings of effectiveness, whether due to skills or confidence in one's ability to develop and execute plans of action, or support by others
- The knowledge of social norms that guide helpful action, but not being bound by norms that inhibit action (for example, in some societies, as standing out, being too visible)

Prior actions that can develop positive active bystandership

- Collecting information about significant events—from national and international media, the Internet, and other sources
- Resisting alignment with or joining groups that can subvert one's values
- Initiating conversations and expressing concerns that may lead to a shared definition of the meaning of events—shared concerns and actions
- Engaging in limited actions at first
- Developing flexible plans and strategies of action
- Collecting information about and joining communities, organizations, or small groups that share concerns and are engaged in action
- Initiating individual and group activities; promoting active bystandership by others

Citizens groups can also follow the example of Baha'i communities. In 1979, after the revolution led by Khomeini in Iran, the new government started to kill Baha'i. The Baha'i, who observe a peaceful religion, have communities around the world, which made presentations to their governments and the United Nations, asking for help. After protests by some governments and the United Nations, the killings stopped.[41] People can join together and do this for any mistreated and endangered group. The faith communities are natural places for organizing such actions. Catholics, Protestants, Evangelical Christians, Jews, Muslims, Unitarians, and Buddhists can all join in this truly holy cause.

Summary

Leaders, citizens, and those who can influence both such as the media, are all important in prevention. Constructive leaders have characteristics such as cognitive complexity, seeing the humanity even of the enemy, and empathy. The training of leaders at varied levels, of citizens, and the media can all develop the sociopsychological conditions that contribute to constructive leadership, active bystandership, effective interaction with members of the other group, and the building of institutions that help in prevention and promote reconciliation. Preventing violence and reconciliation requires changes in both leaders and citizens. External actors can initiate and support change processes, but a central role for internal actors and, when possible, local control are important. High-level institutions in governments whose members are responsible to assess the need for and initiate preventive actions would make diffusion of responsibility and a shift away from relevant values less likely.

Notes

1 Lieberfeld, 2009
2 Ibid, pp. 32-33
3 Wyman, 1984
4 Pogrund, 2007
5 Adam & Moodley, 2005
6 Egeland, 2008
7 Lieberfeld, 2009
8 Ibid, p. 36
9 Mandela, quoted in Lieberfeld, 2009, p. 39
10 Power, 2002
11 Albright & Cohen, 2008, p. 55
12 Jon Western, personal communication, January 13, 2009
13 Starting in 2009 as Special Envoy to the Great Lakes region in Africa, as he was under President Clinton

14 Wolpe & McDonald, 2008, p. 138

15 Ibid.

16 Ibid.

17 Ibid.

18 Albright & Cohen, 2008

19 Wolpe & McDonald. p. 143

20 This training was initiated by Fred Schwartz, a retired business man and activist—I participated in developing its design. He was at the conference in 1997 that led me to begin work in Rwanda.

21 Green, 2002

22 Nasr, 2009

23 Hess & Ostrom, 2007

24 Harff, 2003

25 Uvin, 1998

26 des Forges, 1999

27 However, as we found out, the actions by the international community— U.N. resolutions, inspections, the boycott, the bombing of Iraq by the U.S. during the 1990s—did lead Iraq to get rid of its chemical and biological weapons and dismantle its nuclear program.

28 Carnegie Commission on the Prevention of Deadly Conflict,1997

29 Deng, 2008

30 Albright, 2008, p. A29

31 Ibid.

32 Albright & Cohen, 2008

33 Ibid.

34 Albright & Cohen, 2008, p. 36

35 Power, 2002

36 Staub, 1999b

37 I did brief workshops for Africa analysts at the CIA and spoke at a number of conferences on the prevention of genocide organized by the State Department

38 Hamburg, 2007, p.284

39 Ibid, pp. 284-285

40 Ibid, p.284

41 Bigelow, 1993

19

Healing/Psychological Recovery and Reconciliation

Healing by survivors, as well as perpetrators and bystanders, makes reconciliation more likely. Healing by survivors of mass violence reduces their vulnerability and perception of the world as dangerous, and the likelihood of unnecessary "defensive violence," hostile violence, or revenge. Healing by perpetrators, as well as passive members of the perpetrator group, can reduce their (often unacknowledged) shame and guilt to more manageable levels and make it more likely that they can engage with the consequences of their actions and assume responsibility for them, feel empathy, and express regret.

Everyone can participate in and contribute to recovery by empathic listening and demonstrating compassion and tolerance, respecting others' experiences, creating ceremonies together, and by inviting neighbors into daily activities.

I have suggested that working with leaders has a top-down influence: They can create policies and practices that affect the whole group. Working at the community level affects the population; its members can influence leaders, a bottom-up process. Paul Lederach, a practitioner of reconciliation in many settings, distinguishes between top-level, middle-range, and grassroots-level practices.[1] Top-level practices include training, working with and influencing leaders, as well as international and national criminal tribunals that promote justice. Middle-level practices can influence both leaders and the population. He considers the media, as well as truth commissions, as middle level. We intended our educational radio programs as primarily a bottom-up influence, because while the small elite in East Africa has access to television and print media, the great majority of the population gets its news and entertainment from radio. However, they may be a middle-level "practice," since Rwandan government officials, diplomats, various practitioners, and students, some of whom I met at events outside Rwanda, all know and say they listen to *Musekeweya*.

By grassroots level Lederach means targeting the population, for example, schools, with reconciliation practices. Its targets also include local leaders and focuses on creating dialogue between them. In our work in Rwanda and the Congo, using the radio dramas and their approach as a base, people were selected and trained as agents of change in their communities (see Chapter 16).

These various concepts of top-down, bottom-up, and other levels of intervention apply to both prevention and reconciliation. Indeed, most of what I have discussed with respect to prevention is important for reconciliation as well (humanizing the other, contact, constructive ideologies, and so on). Table 19.1 shows some of the main processes/activities that I regard as especially important for reconciliation and the prevention of new violence. I will explore these various processes in this and the next few chapters.

Although physical and economic security are not identified in the table, they are essential. Without them, it is difficult and sometimes impossible to address psychological and structural elements of reconciliation. David Whittaker, an

Table 19.1 Reconciliation and the Prevention of New Violence

Inhibitors (←):	Promoters (→):
Lack of understanding the roots of violence	Understanding and actions guided by it
Lack of understanding the impact of violence	Understanding its impact on survivors, perpetrators, bystanders
Lack of Truth	Truth (complex: shared)
Lack of Justice	Justice
Unhealed wounds of survivors, perpetrators, bystanders	Healing of wounds by all parties
Lack of acknowledgement of their responsibility by perpetrators and their group	Acknowledgment, apology, regret, empathy
Conflicting views of history	Shared views of history/ Shared collective memories
Lack of contact, superficial contact	Deep contact, shared goals
Lack of acceptance of the past (lack of forgiveness by survivors)	Increasing acceptance (and forgiveness)
Raising children as obedient followers	Raising inclusively caring children with moral courage (positive socialization)

Source. Revised and expanded from Staub, 2006a.

expert in international relations, commented that "no feelings of reconciliation would ever take root without a secure economic base."[2] Rebuilding an economy after great violence, in a country with strong human capital, a trained and motivated workforce, as in Germany after World War II, can be relatively fast, especially with external help such as the Marshall Plan. Probably surprising to government officials not usually concerned with psychology, it can be faster than addressing the psychological impact of violence. However, the material rebuilding of a country does require developing a supporting culture, and individual preparedness—social capital or skilled, educated people. Rwanda and more recently Palestinians in the West Bank have made progress in building this element for reconciliation.

Healing/Psychological Recovery by Survivors[†]

Under certain circumstances, for example, Jews scattered around the world after the Holocaust, individual healing through psychotherapy, counseling, and even medication (both initially and when necessary) is valuable. However, survivors of the Holocaust have often joined in small groups to engage with the past and its effects on them. After group violence—in all the primary cases in this book— collective trauma may best heal through group and community processes. Group healing is important for several reasons: *(1)* People were harmed as a group, and because they were members of a group. *(2)* Group recovery processes are more appropriate to "collectivist" as compared to "individualist" societies (and since individualist societies tend to be democratic, group violence is less frequent in them). *(3)* Community healing processes may more readily convey the fact that the problems (symptoms) and psychological wounds people have are "normal," natural consequences of violence, rather than implying that people's problems are due to individual weakness or personal vulnerability. *(4)* With many people affected, infrastructure and resources are usually not available to provide help for individuals. *(5)* Very importantly, people assume that others (at least members of their own group) would understand (and empathize) with their experience. *(6)* When members of perpetrators and victims groups work on healing together, their contact may reduce the experience of threat, which helps with healing. In intractable conflict, victims/survivors can include members of both groups.

One avenue for healing by victimized people is for them to learn and understand the short- and long-term impact of their painful experiences. What are

---

[†] The material on trauma and healing in this book has been strongly influence by the work of Laurie Anne Pearlman, and my exposure to it in working together in East Africa.

the effects of violence on them as individuals, and on their group and its culture? Addressing that question can help people see the changes in themselves, and in the people around them, and understand these changes as *the natural consequences of extreme events*. They can come to understand, for example, that children who become resistant and disobedient, or "regress," acting as they did at a younger age, are not bad or sick but show the effects of traumatizing events, or are impacted by the actions of traumatized adults. Such understanding can help survivors accept themselves, and it can promote empathy and patience for self and others. These are elements of healing. It can help people know that they are traumatized, not crazy. It can help them learn that despite their trauma they can be effective, contributing members of the community and that there is hope for recovery.

Survivors can also learn how psychological woundedness is maintained and transmitted to future generations. A combination of awareness of this process and their own healing makes such transmission less likely. Transmission happens partly within families, by what adults say and by how they act toward their children, and by the models they provide. Both talking too much about and overwhelming children with the parents' suffering and hiding it from them create problems. I mentioned previously that "knowing but not knowing" has been one condition that had a negative effect on children of Holocaust survivors: knowing that something very bad happened to the parents, with what happened held back or hidden from them. Parents talking to children about their experiences, but to a moderate extent and in an age-appropriate manner, can help children construct a meaningful understanding of their family—and the world.

The adults' feelings of vulnerability, understandable as that is, their fears and strong reactions even to mild threat, their inappropriate anger, or their tendency to be overly protective, all affect children. So does the way that a group deals with the past, such as a focus on its trauma. Transmission of trauma also occurs in schools, directly through teaching of history from a particular perspective, and indirectly through teachers' attitudes and behaviors. When trauma has become "chosen," embedded in the culture, it is important for people to understand and become aware of how it shapes perceptions and actions. This may be a first step in moving beyond a chosen trauma.

Another avenue to healing is *engagement with the group's trauma and with personal experiences in the course of traumatic events*. This can happen in small groups, with people talking to each other about their experiences and empathically listening to and supporting each other. Solace Ministries in Rwanda, a Christian organization, helps widows and orphans, including members of "child-headed households" (in many cases parents had been killed and the older children assumed the responsibility to care for their younger siblings). One of their activities is to gather people together to offer testimonies—describe what has happened to them and their families during the genocide. Giving testimony is intensely emotional, and the rest of the group, themselves survivors, can empathically support the person doing it.

People can also express their experiences by creating (and enacting) drama, or through dance, music and song, poetry, visual art, or other forms that fit the culture and the person. People need to engage not only with experiences of violence against them but also with those of violence by them (see later discussion), with their passivity in the face of violence against others, and with painful experiences that have resulted from the group trauma in the relations of individuals, including parents and children. *Group healing* means that people in the community help each other heal by talking about their experiences to each other, listening to each other, and empathically supporting each other. It also means that the group as a whole heals by understanding violence and trauma, by establishing the truth of what happened to them, and by working together to forge a shared history. Healing stories also include stories of small or large acts of heroism or courage witnessed, experienced as recipient or actor, or told by others.

The stories people tell, ideally in a safe setting to empathic listeners, can help them realize that the present is not the past and can diminish the power of painful past events. Since the loss of control over what happens to oneself is a central aspect of trauma, having control over telling one's story—when, how much, how—is important.[3] While stories can engage with the responsibility of perpetrators and bystanders, and with the person's own role in the violence, whether actual or perceived, the purpose of a healing story is not to affix blame, but to engage with experiences and feelings, and create meaning. The stories and the experiences that surround telling them are ways to re-create a sense of connection with—rather than alienation from—one's experiences, feelings, and self, as well as a basis for reconnection with other people.

Stories go beyond remembering; they are creations that help people make some sense of their past experiences. Specialists working with traumatized individuals stress the importance of this process.[4] Even among people who simply write about painful experiences for a brief period, those who construct more meaning out of their experience benefit more.[5] But what meaning can be found in having been the victims of group violence? A possible meaning is the belief that what has happened to them should not happen to other people, and this can give rise to a commitment to try to prevent such suffering and help those who have suffered. Such meaning is one root of altruism born of suffering.

Acknowledgment from others of one's past suffering is important for healing. Not only actual perpetrators but also other members of the perpetrator group and external parties often fail to do this. This is another form of passive bystandership. As Yael Danieli says, what happens after traumatizing events shapes people's psychological experience and the nature of their trauma. Empathic engagement with traumatized people by the community furthers healing, as the trauma and mourning become shared rather than stigmatizing.

Acknowledgment, support, care, and help can mitigate trauma and its long-term effects. Even acknowledgment of past suffering unrelated to a current conflict seems to enable people to acknowledge the suffering of their opponent in the conflict.[6]

It is acknowledgment when a government officially declares the violence against a group as genocide or some other form of human rights violation. Testimonials, ceremonies, commemoration, dialogue, or simply what other people say can offer acknowledgment of suffering, connect survivors to each other, to other people, and even to perpetrators. In the course of group events people can mourn the loss of loved ones, homes, one's old self, community, spirituality, and optimism about life.

Commemorations and group ceremonies often focus on victimization, pain, suffering, and loss. This can maintain vulnerability and create or maintain a chosen trauma. They will be most healing and will help most with reconciliation if they include a turning toward or imagining of a positive future. Their optimal forms will depend on how close people are to the violence and original trauma and who the participants are. Including all parties in commemoration—bystanders, rescuers, even former perpetrators when it emotionally becomes possible, and caring outsiders—is psychologically untenable right after intense violence. But later on, this inclusive approach can build community as it helps people connect a painful past with the vision of a hopeful future.

In Rwanda, the commemoration of the genocide every April is a highly significant event. An important part of it is the reburial of the bodies of Tutsis taken out of mass graves. I know from conversations with people in Rwanda that the commemoration is a painful and difficult day not only for Tutsis but also Hutus, who feel both excluded and reminded of their group's actions.

For commemorations to be inclusive requires that survivors allow members of the perpetrator group to participate, and that the two groups open themselves to connection with each other. In Rwanda there is some attention now in commemorations to Hutus who saved lives. This started after the publication of a book about these rescuers.[7] It may also be partly the result of our advocacy; the person in charge of planning the commemorations at the time we conducted trainings in Rwanda participated in two of our workshops where we discussed the value of doing this. Hutus who were killed because they opposed the genocide should also be commemorated, and those who joined the Rwanda Patriotic Front in fighting against the government honored. Acknowledging that not all Hutus were perpetrators or indifferent bystanders can foster the vision of a peaceful future.

While this is a difficult challenge for both Tutsi leaders and survivors, including in the commemoration of the genocide or having a separate commemoration for Hutus who were not perpetrators, who were killed by the RPF and RPA during and after the genocide, would publicly acknowledge that such killings happened. It would provide Hutus with an opportunity to mourn, to begin to heal, and for Hutus and Tutsis to connect with each other. It could be done in a way consistent with government policy, saying to people that terrible things happen when Hutus and Tutsis become separate, hostile, and violent against each other.

I have already noted that apart from its other benefits, *understanding the origins of violence* against one's group, or by one's group against another, also contributes to psychological recovery. Understanding that many influences led to extreme violence does not mean that harm doers had no choice and have therefore no responsibility. But awareness of what contributes to violence, and examples from other places, can help victimized groups feel less alone, more part of humanity, and can help both groups see the perpetrators as human, not simply evil creatures. Both make reconciliation more possible.

All forms of violence can be analyzed and to some degree understood. Slavery can be understood as a product of self-interest, the devaluation of black people as inferior and less human, and the use of ideology—even using parts of the Bible to provide justification. In Jewish history, the great suffering of Jews at the hands of Christians in Europe, and then finally the Holocaust, led them to want to create a land of their own and the creation of Israel. For some, the history of ancient Israel and the religious tradition of praying for return to Jerusalem was an added motivation. This past, combined with Arab hostility and Palestinian terrorism, has to lead to intense insecurity among Israelis. Israel's severe policies of occupation in the West Bank and Gaza both expressed this insecurity, and increased it, since violent responses followed. Evolution in individuals and groups has a role in every instance. Past woundedness may also have led to a feeling of entitlement, one possible result of victimization and trauma.

Sometimes actions by victimized groups have contributed to the violence against them; exploring this helps groups find the complex truth of the past. In Rwanda, Tutsi dominance before, and increased dominance during, colonial rule were instrumental in creating a difficult life for Hutus. The exploration of their group's past role by victims of genocide or mass killing, and by participants in mutual group violence, goes contrary to the intense need of group members to focus on their own suffering and pain. It is likely to take place only after some healing, and perhaps in the context of justice processes. When it does, it can help with changing collective memories. It can also reduce the defensiveness of perpetrators and open them to acknowledge their actions. Understanding how their own actions may have joined with other influences in contributing to violence against them may also, perhaps paradoxically, empower victims—to take a step from victim to survivor role, and to work on building a better future.

The group healing I am advocating involves both healing by individuals and changes at the level of the whole group—in group self-concept (even though we were harmed because we are members of a group, nothing is wrong with our group and the harm did not happen because we as a group are bad people)— group attitudes toward others, and so on. One approach that can provide core concepts for group healing is RICH —Respect, Information, Connection, and Hope—developed by Kay Saakvitne, Laurie Anne Pearlman, and their associates.[8]

Respect includes respect for the need of victimized people to maintain control about when, how, and to whom they talk about their experiences. The experience of control facilitates healing especially in cases of trauma, given that its central aspect is the loss of control. Information about the origins and impact of violence and avenues to prevention and reconciliation fit the information component of the RICH approach. Understanding that violent events are not inevitable parts of human life, and gaining empowerment for preventive action, provide hope. Talking about one's experience to others, getting support from others, and participating with others in ceremonies and commemorations foster connection. In the next chapter I will discuss how people can create a shared narrative that helps put their experiences into a context. This blends the information and connection aspects of the RICH approach.

Understanding basic psychological needs and their role in the origins of group violence, woundedness, and healing has special value. The frustration of these needs, and the destructive psychological and social reactions that emerge to satisfy them, are starting points on the road to intense group violence. Intensely painful experiences that result from victimization deeply frustrate basic needs. Healing involves the constructive (nondestructive) satisfaction of these needs—for security, positive identity, feelings of effectiveness and control over important events, and positive connections to other people built on mutual trust, justice, and a new, hopeful vision of the world and one's place in it.

The beliefs people develop, their ideologies, can give them strength. This can be strength for destruction, for opposition, or for resuming life. Psychologist Stevan Hobfoll and his associates[9] found in studying people exposed to terror attacks in Israel that greater psychological growth in the course of these highly stressful events is often associated with greater posttraumatic stress disorder (PTSD), suggesting that perhaps what looks like growth is psychological defense—positive thoughts protecting people from fully experiencing their pain. While not very likely, it could also be that more distress leads to more psychological growth. They also studied a group of Israeli settlers in Gaza as settlements were demolished, who chose to stay and oppose the soldiers evacuating the settlements. In this group those who reported more psychological growth had fewer symptoms of PTSD. A likely reason for the difference is that these people had intentionally exposed themselves to stressful confrontation, led by strong values that guided both their actions and their interpretation of events. People who join in group healing activities may gain understanding and develop beliefs, values, and a worldview that gives them strength to renew their lives.

Genuine growth may occur in people when cognitive changes, such as renewed meaning, are transformed into action, such as helping others, resistance, or building peace.[10] In German extermination camps slave laborers could help others through small acts, and at the very least it helped them maintain their feeling of dignity.[11]

Contributing to other people or the group's recovery, whether in a kitchen table conversation, working together in the fields, or working for social change, can strengthen self-worth, connection, and meaning, and help people heal. Other processes of reconciliation, as I'll discuss later, also foster healing. Truth and justice, for example, acknowledge past suffering. They imply or directly express that the violence was wrong and unacceptable and promise the re-creation of a moral order that provides safety.

I have been using both the terms *psychological recovery* and *healing* as though they are interchangeable. They are nearly so, but psychological recovery is a more inclusive term. In the course of the evolution of violence, there are changes in the personalities of all involved, such as decreased capacity for empathy by perpetrators and bystanders. I use the term *psychological recovery* to refer to recovery from all harmful changes, both in the personality of victims, perpetrators, or bystanders, and as a result of psychological wounds due to victimization or perpetration. I use *healing* to refer to recovery from trauma and the particular psychological wounds it causes.

Healing/Psychological Recovery by Perpetrators and Passive Members of a Perpetrator Group

The processes I just described can be applied to healing by perpetrators and other members of the ethnic, religious, or political group they come from. Like survivors, they need to understand the causes and effects of conflict and violence. The findings of our research in Rwanda[12] have suggested that such understanding created in Hutus a more positive view of Tutsis. Their greater openness to others may be partly the result of empathy with themselves. Understanding the influences that led to the genocide may have reduced their guilt and shame to more manageable levels. Understanding the suffering of the victims and survivors is also essential.

Perpetrators and members of their group need to be guided to see in their mind's eye and empathically experience the effects of their actions on their victims, which they most likely tuned out at the time of their harm doing. They can be guided to imagine what it would be like to have the victims' experiences, in line with research that found that imagining others' experience promotes empathy.[13] They can imagine their lack of control and helplessness, the force used on them, and the loss of loved ones. One way to generate empathy with their victims is to expose perpetrators to the trauma and pain of the victims of others' harmful actions, which is less likely to create defensive reactions. I discussed this earlier in relation to the deradicalization of terrorists.

Like survivors, perpetrators and bystanders also need to engage with their own experience. It can be extremely useful to help them consider the effects on themselves of their past actions. Repeated empathic engagement by a psychologist interviewer with De Kock,[14] one of the most notorious perpetrators of violence again black South Africans, helped bring about a transformation in him (see Chapter 21). Showing empathy to perpetrators, or even passive bystanders, is challenging, but it can bring about changes in them. Empathy with them requires responding not to their defensive and sometimes belligerent attitude, the hard shell they have developed, but to the fear and shame underneath.

If and when perpetrators or members of a perpetrator group express empathy and regret, atone, and make amends, they contribute not only to survivors' healing but also to their own. Experience shows that some and possibly many people who have been harmed can forgive, or at least accept harm doers and let go of their anger, to a surprising extent.[15] Forgiveness is greatly facilitated by, and often requires, that harm doers acknowledge what they have done and express regret, show empathy, ideally apologize, and engage in positive actions. Such words and feelings have to be expressed in ways that are perceived as genuine, to bring forth positive responses. While it is not possible to restore a life, by such words and actions perpetrators, enablers, and passive bystanders can progressively reclaim their humanity.

Trauma recovery by victimized people is a long, slow process. This is true for individual trauma, and certainly for the extreme traumas created by mass violence. They require reconnecting with experience, mourning huge losses, rebuilding the self and relationships, feeling less vulnerable, trusting other people and feeling less endangered, and creating meaning. Helping people to understand this and to be patient with themselves and tolerant of others who cannot easily let go of grief, rage, and terror has been one of the goals of our radio projects. Once changes in their circumstances, such as loss of power and the world's reactions, and lessening of their own denial opens perpetrators to their own trauma, healing for them as well is a long, slow process.

Engagement between members of a perpetrator group and victim group can serve healing and provide contact that promotes reconciliation. Engagement is challenging between people who are wounded, have harmed each other, and usually hold incompatible views of the past. It often occurs in the course of dialogue in the service of conflict resolution. We have created it in a different context in Rwanda, in the course of promoting understanding. Engagement can start with discussion about concepts and influences leading to violence, creating readiness to explore the past and to begin to acknowledge responsibility for the suffering one's group has caused.

When people belonging to hostile groups discuss their past history and relationship, intense feelings tend to arise. In contrast, focusing not on each other but on concepts that offer understanding can defuse these feelings to some degree. It can create, and in our groups it has created, some openness to the other. In Rwanda, Hutu and Tutsi participants in our educational workshops were able to engage with each other constructively around concepts and issues, join in applying their understanding of the roots of violence to their own history, and subsequently, in small groups, talk about their painful experiences.[16] All this prepares people to constructively think about a shared future.

Summary

Recovery from the psychological impact of the evolution of violence and of extreme violence, and healing from trauma (by victims/survivors, harm doers, and bystanders) are helped by understanding the immediate and long-term impact of painful experiences, as well as the origins of or the influences leading to harmful, violent actions. They are helped by engaging with and talking about traumatizing events and the experiences and feelings they generate. They are helped by empathy from others and their acknowledgment of one's experience and suffering. Engagement with such experiences can take place as people tell—and create meaning from—the story of what has happened to them, as well as through ceremonies and commemorations, and through poetry and art. Respect, Information, Connection, and Hope are concepts that are useful in summarizing important elements of healing. Healing by perpetrators and bystanders also takes place through atonement and positive actions in helping others heal and working to rebuild society. In wounded societies, healing should be a community process. Everyone can participate in and contribute to recovery by empathic listening and demonstrating compassion and tolerance, respecting others' feelings, creating ceremonies together, and inviting neighbors into daily activities. Healing is fostered by establishing truth, justice, and other elements of reconciliation described in the next chapters.

Notes

1 Lederach, 1997
2 Whittaker, 1999, p. 15
3 Pearlman & Caringi, 2009
4 Newman, Riggs, & Roth, 2007
5 Pennebacker, 2000
6 Bar-On, 2000
7 Africa Rights, 2002
8 Saakvitne, Gamble, Pearlman, & Lev, 2000; see Pearlman, 2001; McCann & Pearlman, 1990; and Pearlman & Saakvitne, 1995 for the theoretical basis of the approach
9 Hobfoll et al., 2007
10 Ibid.

11 Frankl, 1984

12 Paluck, 2009a; Staub et al., 2005; Staub & Pearlman, 2009

13 Aderman & Berkowitz, 1970; Stotland, 1969; see also work with sex offenders, Carich, Melgger, Baig, & Harper, 2003; and with other violent people, Meichenbaum, 2001

14 Gobodo-Madikezela, 2003

15 O'Connell Higgins, 1994; see Worthington, 2005 for a review of forgiveness research; see also Chapter 21 on forgiveness

16 Staub, 2006a; Staub et al., 2005; Staub & Pearlman, 2006

20

Other Elements of Reconciliation

Complex Truth, Collective Memory, Shared History, and Justice

---

Establishing the complex truth about past group relations and about conflict and violence, and moving toward a shared view of history are challenging but important for reconciliation.

Justice is important for healing and reconciliation, with retributive justice (punishment), restorative justice (compensatory actions), procedural justice (an effective justice system), and just relations (fair access for everyone to societal resources) all important aspects of justice.

Establishing the (Complex) Truth

Establishing what has happened in group violence, who did what to whom and why, is important for victims/survivors. It provides acknowledgment of their suffering and fosters healing. Knowing what has happened is also necessary for justice. The truth is also important because if a society, or a dominant group in it, does not look at itself, at its culture, its ways of seeing the world, its past behavior, its chosen traumas, and how they guide its perceptions of the world, it is likely to re-create mistakes of the past. For example, in East Germany, under communist rule, the actions of Nazi Germany were interpreted as due to "them," to corruption by money, capital, nationalism, and nothing to do with *the people* who were now presumably leading the country. This probably had a role in the violence, after the reunification of Germany, in the Eastern parts of the country against those who were not of ethnic German origin.

However, establishing truth and having it be accepted by all the parties is difficult. Survivors of intense violence are focused on their suffering. They usually see themselves as innocent and the other group as completely responsible and evil. Perpetrators often deny what they did, or at least justify their actions, which is a form of denial of the truth. For reconciliation the truth has to recognize the injuries that each side has suffered at the hands of the other.

In Rwanda, part of the truth is the harsh rule by Tutsis over Hutus before 1959, under Belgian colonial rule.[1] Another part is that Hutus, when they took power in 1959, and then officially in 1962 when the country became independent, did not create a more equal society but instead discriminated against the Tutsis and engaged in frequent violence against them, repeatedly on a scale of mass killing. A major part of the truth is the horror of the genocide. For reconciliation the truth must also recognize the killing of Hutus by the Rwandan Patriotic Front (RPF) during the civil war and the Rwandan Patriotic Army (RPA) afterward; the killing of Hutu civilians as the Rwandan army fought infiltrators from the Congo in the second half of the 1990s; and the killing of Hutu refugees by the Rwandan army in the Congo.[2] All this was not comparable to the genocide, but it is highly significant and part of the truth.

Both perpetrators of mass violence, and parties in a more balanced but violent conflict, hold on to their own truth. They often disagree about actual actions and events. Perpetrators tend to deny that a genocide has taken place. Even more frequently they interpret them differently, seeing their own actions as defensive and just, as a response to the other's actions and intentions, and the actions of the other as aggressive and immoral. In formal research, with harm doing of much lesser magnitude than in the cases addressed in this book, harm doers usually blame the other party or the circumstances.[3] They also see the harm as less severe than the victims do.[4] These different views interfere with reconciliation. Each party continuing to see the other as blameworthy and a threat makes it probable that, with new societal problems or new threat, violence will reemerge.

Experiencing collective guilt about one's group's actions[5], seemingly a precondition for acknowledging it, requires that people see it as unprovoked and morally unjustified. This is a difficult requirement, especially for people who were in some ways involved, even if just as passive bystanders.

Truth commissions have become a favorite method of establishing the truth. About 25 of them have been created up to 2009. They have operated in varied ways. An early one, Nunca Mas (meaning "never again"), in a searing report based on many interviews, laid out the violence perpetrated during the disappearances in Argentina. It described the many methods of torture used, the presence of priests during torture, the ways in which people were killed, and the taking of the children of parents who were kidnapped and killed and giving them to loyal members of the regime.[6]

In South Africa, many testimonies before the Truth and Reconciliation Commission (TRC) were public and televised, for the population to have direct access to what happened during apartheid. In Rwanda, the *gacaca* aimed to establish the truth, but it was also a court in which people were judged, which changed the meaning and psychological impact of the proceedings. Truth commissions can be a valuable tool, but how they are constructed can shape the extent to which they inform, shape attitudes, and contribute to reconciliation.

Establishing the truth makes it more difficult for perpetrators to continue to blame victims and to refuse to accept responsibility. Society establishing the truth and, through a combination of truth and justice, making it evident that it considers such conduct unacceptable increases feelings of safety by survivors. But truth requires truth tellers. What is the impact on those who help establish the truth? What is the impact on society?

The Impact on Truth Tellers and Society

It has been assumed that survivors of mass violence would benefit from engaging with the truth of what has happened to them. This would only be the case if they can do it under safe conditions, with support by and empathy from other people. Traumatized people can heal in therapy, as they tell the truth of their trauma and experience to an empathic and supportive person, with whom they have developed a relationship and when the telling of their story is under their control.[7] Presumably they can also heal as they tell their stories to empathic people in their community. But serving as witnesses to establish the immorality and criminality of perpetrators, reliving their traumatic experiences in front of impartial (which can be perceived as indifferent) judges, or even worse in front of hostile perpetrators and defence attorneys, and exposing themselves to potential condemnation and danger of retaliation can be extremely stressful, however important their testimony is for truth and justice.

The difficulty was especially great in Rwanda, at the *gacaca*, which not only established the truth but tried perpetrators. Witnesses had to say what they knew about the crimes of perpetrators in front of the local community that was predominantly Hutu and included the relatives of the perpetrators. It is not surprising that psychologist Karen Brounéus[8] of Sweden found, in a large study of 1200 members of the Rwandan population, that while posttraumatic stress disorder (PTSD) was about the same and depression was significantly elevated in comparison to that found in another study 7 years earlier, people who testified before the *gacaca* had substantially higher rates of PTSD and depression than others.

She also found that both PTSD and depression were even greater among witnesses who were the neighbors of survivor witnesses—that is, among Hutu witnesses. Testifying against members of one's own group must have been especially difficult, dangerous, and traumatizing, the witness feeling that he or she betrayed the group or would be seen as a traitor. Possibly shame about the group's actions and their own passivity at the time also affected these people. Trauma and depression were also substantially elevated among the elected judges of the *gacaca* courts. Their difficult task was made even more difficult for many in that they were elected from and by a predominantly Hutu population and were likely to be predominantly Hutu, with the responsibility to judge and sentence other Hutus.

Contrary to earlier assumptions, even in truth commissions individuals who give testimony about their own or their group's extreme victimization appear to suffer from this experience, at least at first. The small amount of relevant research shows negative emotions associated with such experiences, but with indications of positive emotions as well. For example, in one study of 30 South Africans who were interviewed about their testimony in front of the TRC, 80% reported that it was a painful experience, although the rest reported that the experience was positive and helpful.[9] In another study, participants in the *gacaca* reported negative emotions such as anxiety and anger. But Tutsi survivors also reported a decrease in shame.[10] Similar to our findings that understanding the roots and impact of violence may lead survivors to see that they are not to blame, exposure to testimonies in the *gacaca* may have done the same.

But what is the time course of negative emotions? Talking and hearing about terrible acts against oneself or one's group would be expected to have immediate negative effects. But under supportive and safe conditions, over time healing may result from such experiences, as it does in the course of therapy. In our study in Rwanda,[11] exposure to information and discussion of the roots of mass violence and engagement with painful experiences had somewhat negative effects on Hutu and Tutsi participants immediately after the end of twice-weekly meetings over a 2-month period. But 2 months later there was a reduction in trauma symptoms, and an increase in positive orientation to members of the other group and in conditional forgiveness. However, since in Rwanda all members of the community were expected to attend *gacaca* meetings, everyone was continually exposed to stories of great violence. This would have made recovery by former witnesses difficult.

Security for those who testify, acceptance and empathy as people describe heart-rending experiences of suffering and loss, and limiting exposure are all important. The supporting elements usually do not exist. Truth commissions and justice processes should do the utmost to provide them before and during testimony. The challenge is even greater after testimony, as people may turn against those who testify. Those who testified in front of the TRC were stigmatized, and those who testified at the International Tribunal on the former Yugoslavia were afraid on their return home and were stigmatized.[12]

Brounéus[13] conducted a small in-depth interview study of 16 survivor women, 14 of whom testified in front of the *gacaca*. Most if not all their family members had been killed during the genocide, and several of these women had been raped. In addition to reliving during their testimony what happened to them, the "witnesses were threatened before the *gacaca* to deter them from giving testimony, during the hearings to quiet them, and after, as punishment."[14] People tried to interrupt their testimony, stopped talking to them afterwards, and threw rocks at their houses.

While testimony in truth and justice processes, especially the latter, can be painful and difficult, it can contribute to societal healing and reconciliation.

James Gibson, a political scientist, found that in South Africa truth telling by victims in front of the TRC did not contribute to reconciliatory attitudes by them. However, members of the society who were less involved, who were neither perpetrators nor victims, had more reconciliatory attitudes after hearing the testimonies.[15]

These members of the population would have already known what happened, but only in a limited way. Even high-level government officials claimed ignorance about death squads and other violent practices of the apartheid regime.[16] Some of the violence was hidden, and people tend to screen out what makes them uncomfortable, when knowledge would burden their conscience or require difficult action. The testimonies, after the events past, could create emotional engagement and generate empathy. Members of a society learning about and engaging with the truth may be vital for national/societal-level reconciliation. Survivors, even if testifying is painful, can benefit if there is affirmation of their truth, and of them, by society, and if society changes as a result of their testimony.

Part of the beneficial effects to society may come from changes in participants that go beyond the emotions they experience at the time. A study that found negative emotions associated with participation in the *gacaca* by both survivors and accused perpetrators, also found that in both groups positive stereotypes of the other group increased and negative stereotypes declined, the latter change especially substantial among survivors. In both groups, members of the other group were seen as less homogeneous. A more differentiated view of members of another group, seeing them more as individuals, is usually associated with less prejudice. In both groups, again more in survivors, identification with one's own group declined.[17]

In addition to establishing the truth by the testimony of witnesses, sometimes a great deal of what has happened, who was harmed, by whom, and why, can be established by the documents perpetrators have created. The Germans maintained meticulous records of confiscation of property, lists of inmates of concentration camps, dates when they were killed, and films of many of their violent actions. Some other perpetrator groups have also maintained records.

With regard to witnesses, it is the responsibility of society to create the right circumstances for testifying. Witnesses need support by judges, court personnel, or truth commission members. It may be possible to train such people using educational media, and to train witnesses what to ask for and demand. In our radio drama in Rwanda, we show an insensitive judge who causes distress in a traumatized witness by treating her without respect and consideration. She then refuses to return to testify. We also show transformation in the judge, who becomes more sensitive as he comes to understand trauma to some degree.

Witnesses also require preparation, which can serve as inoculation. This may include discussion of the difficulty of testifying, and preparation for the insensitivity of some judges and the antagonism of members of a perpetrator group.

Witnesses can gain strength if they focus on the important contribution their testimony makes, its value to society. Prior healing and coming to understand the influences that lead to mass violence can reduce the impact on survivors of revisiting extremely traumatizing events. The emotional impact can also be mitigated by someone accompanying and providing support to each witness during testimony, and being available to share feelings afterwards.

The benefit to society of public testimony and survivors' needs can be balanced by giving survivors the choice to testify in front of a small group of sympathetic people, their testimony later made public, when and in a manner that is appropriate. The same applies to perpetrators. Giving testimony in front of members of one's village (in the *gacaca*) about one's violent acts, or about planning or ordering cruel acts, has social value. But both this public testimony, and talking in front of television cameras, can numb feelings, which onlookers see as indifference or even pride by perpetrators in their actions.

This discussion also applies to people visiting memorial sites and participating in commemorations. This can traumatize or retraumatize and create or re-create hostility, or it can contribute to understanding, healing, and reconciliation. One time I was asked to help prepare, accompany, and debrief a large group of high school students who visited the Holocaust Memorial Museum in Washington DC. After seeing the exhibit, a number of the students were visibly impacted. Some did not feel well and had headaches. Debriefing should have been a crucial part of this experience, but time ran out, the buses arrived, and the debriefing consisted of a hurried few minutes of discussion.

Large national surveys conducted on behalf of the Unity and Reconciliation Commission showed a complex picture of changes in people, probably a combined effect of the *gacaca* and the general social situation. Comparisons between 2002 and 2006 showed a more positive view of *gacaca* judges and proceedings in 2006, and increased belief that the *gacaca* contributed to reconciliation and lessened people's tendency to categorize each other by ethnicity. But there was also an increase in fear. Specifically, prisoners believed that those who were accused would feel threatened during the *gacaca*, and those who confessed would be threatened and experience retaliation from their accomplices. Survivors believed that they themselves would feel threatened. Fifty-three percent of respondents believed that "it is naïve to trust others," and a large majority thought that perpetrators still continued to hold the ideas that led to their actions.[18] The still recent genocide, the *gacaca*, and the government talking about the presence of "genocidal ideology" are all likely to have contributed to this belief.

Truth Telling: Challenges and Mistakes

Attempts to foster more complex truth require sensitivity by outsiders, and sensitivity and courage by insiders. Perhaps the only time in Rwanda that I encountered strong disagreement was when, early in our work there in 2000 and during the one time we worked with a Tutsi-only group, made up of community leaders, I suggested that there was some Tutsi repression of Hutus *before* colonial rule. This was contrary to the prevailing view among Tutsis that bad treatment of Hutus by Tutsis was entirely due to colonial policies. To support my suggestion, I read a couple of paragraphs from the book *When Victims Become Killers* by Mahmood Mamdani,[19] a professor at Colombia University of South African origins. The group rejected the writing of this "outsider"—and what I said.

In subsequent seminars/workshops, I was able to state challenging ideas in ways that were apparently more sensitive and thoughtful. For example, in a seminar with a large group of national leaders, in response to a comment that there was already a genocide in 1959, I said that I regarded what happened then as a rebellion against Tutsi oppression, under Belgian rule, that unfortunately rebellions often get out of hand and become violent, and what happened may have been a mass killing but was not genocide.[20] (A recent account gives a much smaller number of people killed in 1959 than the many thousands reported in earlier accounts.)[21] This seemed to be accepted by the group.

I mentioned the leaders' workshop, when in divergence from our usual practice, in response to the group's request I applied my conception of the origins of genocide to Rwanda. There was one other time when I did not follow the principle to invite Rwandans to apply this conception. In 2004 I was the opening speaker at a conference in Rwanda commemorating the 10th anniversary of the genocide. There were 600 invited guests, the leaders of the country and the international community, with President Kagame and I sitting on a platform; I was the first speaker and he followed me. I was overcome with "greed," the opportunity to "educate" Rwanda's leadership, hoping to influence policies in ways that contribute to reconciliation. In a 45-minute talk I summarized the origins of mass violence, avenues to prevention, and how this applied to Rwanda. I stressed the importance of pluralism and the dangers of unnecessary "defensive violence" by a victimized group. I used the term "defensive superiority" to characterize Rwanda's approach to threat (a term that is also applicable to Israel). Contrary to our usual work settings in Rwanda, there was no opportunity for questions and answers, much less extensive discussion.

While many people responded enthusiastically, it raised questions for others. The next day Jeannette Kagame, the first lady, approached me to ask whether the Tutsis, by contributing before 1959 to the woundedness of the Hutus, *caused* the genocide. The answer to that question is no. Many influences contribute to genocide. The actions of Hutus, discrimination and intense violence against Tutsis after 1959 when Hutus had the power, greatly contributed to maintaining and increasing hostility between the groups, the creation of the RPF, and the civil war.

However, without the victimization of Hutus under Belgian rule, the relations between Tutsis and Hutus would most likely have developed differently.

Belgians bear substantial responsibility for that victimization. It perhaps never happened that an overlord, like the Belgians in Rwanda, had an already dominant group rule on its behalf, giving it both power and an ideology of superiority, and this group refused to be elevated and insisted on the kind treatment of a subordinate group. Still, the Tutsis bear responsibility for their actions; assuming responsibility for them, and for later actions, could contribute to reconciliation.

Jeannette Kagame showed understanding of another important implication of victimization: that Tutsis have to be careful so that their victimization does not lead them to unnecessary violence. If members of the audience came to see that, perhaps my abandonment of the principle I advocate had value.

Changing Collective Memories, Creating a Shared History

The truth about the past is usually complex, and such truth may be resisted by all parties to group violence. Catherine Newbury writes about Rwanda that "With an intensity that surpasses the normal clichés, there is no single history: rather, there are competing histories."[22] There are divergent narratives, even within the same group, even about events that just took place. At the beginning of June 2010 Israeli soldiers shot at and killed 9 people on the board of a ship of activists that tried to bring supplies and break the Israeli blockade on Gaza. Some parties, including Israelis, for example, Amos Oz, the famous Israeli writer and peace activist, accused Israel of having acquired the habit of using force, now uses it mindlessly. The Israeli government has claimed that the peace activists on board were really provocateurs, that they attacked the Israelis after they boarded the ship, who shot in self-defense. Even videos, taken by each side, were interpreted differently—or used to support different interpretations. An important aspect of the truth lies in the larger picture—that the conditions were created and allowed to unfold under which such a confrontation would take place.

Difficult as it is, working toward and approximating and if necessary negotiating a complex truth about a history of conflict and violence, and the parties creating some form of a shared view of history, shared collective memories, is important for long-term peace. Collective memory has been defined as "the collective representations of past events ... that are shared by the vast majority ... (and) is seen by them as valid accounts."[23] The vast majority are members of the same group.

The challenge to creating a shared history is shown in the brief but eloquent summary, by Ethan Bronner, a reporter for the *New York Times*, of the two sides' position in the Palestinian–Israeli conflict. "One side says that after thousands of years of oppression, the Jewish nation has returned to its rightful home. It came in peace and offered its hand to its neighbors numerous times only to be met with a sword. Opposition to Israel, this side argues, stems from Muslim intolerance, nationalist fervor and rank anti-Semitism, all fed by envy of the young state's success....The other side tells a different story: There is no Jewish nation, only followers of a religion. A group of European colonialists came here, stole and pillaged, throwing hundreds of thousands off their land and destroying their villages and homes. A country born in sin, Israel built up an aggressive military with the help from Washington in the grips of a powerful Jewish lobby."[24] For one side there was the War of Independence in 1948, for the other side, Nakba, the Catastrophe. Bronner wrote that whenever he writes a story, unless he affirms a side's narrative, that side sees him as failing to do his job and thus untrustworthy.

We present this "truth," that there are divergent views of history and it is difficult to discuss them, in our radio drama *Musekeweya*, in Rwanda. The following is a brief excerpt:

> THE TEACHER: (Moderately) Mugenga, without defending yourselves, don't you know that it is you the people of Bumanzi who are the culprits for the disaster? (The conflict with and the attack by the other village, Muhumuro, on Bumanizi.)
>
> MUGENGA: (Angry) How should we be held responsible when the land was officially given to us!
>
> THE TEACHER: Even though you didn't take it by force, you should have shared it with the people in Muhumuro with whom you shared it before! I say it impartially as I hail from neither Muhumuro nor Bumanzi.
>
> MUGENGA: (Indignant) You don't deserve being listened to! Fabiya, I won't talk to you anymore! Our children are in trouble if you teach them such things!
>
> THE TEACHER: Look! Why do people call a spade a spade and you get angry and start insulting them! Does being at loggerheads with someone give you the right to insult them?

Change in the collective memory of each group is usually required as part of the path toward the creation and acceptance of a shared view of history. Creating an acceptable shared history requires historians, politicians, representatives of the community, psychologists, and active external bystanders. But it also requires the population. This is true of peacemaking in general, and of this important aspect of peacemaking, working for and moving toward recognizing and acknowledging each other's narratives.

In an article about the conflicting narratives of Israelis and Palestinians, Paul Scham, an expert in conflict resolution, writes that Israeli and Palestinian intellectuals made a major effort to reach out to each other during the Oslo period and notes "the difficulty of making peace when peace oriented intellectuals and academics [*as well as politicians—my comment*] are too far from the mainstream of their own societies...." Both groups believed that "their counterparts on the other side represented a far greater portion of their society than was actually the case ... and both were angry and disillusioned [even before Camp David but especially after the second Intifada began] when both sides rallied around their own flag to some degree."[25]

Like all history, a shared history is a re-creation and creation. It is likely to require dialogue, compromise and sometimes acceptance of aspects of the other's narrative, in place of agreement on "objective" events and their interpretation. This is demanding, since in conflict and violence usually both the other, and its views of events are devalued. It can be necessary, in part, to let the two narratives stand side by side, so that each group is heard and its truth taught to children. Truth commissions have been useful in establishing actual events, which can form a basis for a shared history. There are exceptions to the notion of accepting the other's history, as there are to most generalizations—one does not accept narratives of evil, destructive systems and their ideological justifications.

To consider changes in a group's collective memory, I will use Israel as the primary example. As I have briefly discussed in Chapter 3, its collective memory has changed, and relevant information about the change exists. A long-held view, propagated by state agencies and in textbooks, had been that Israel was not responsible for the exodus of Palestinians from Israel, which turned them into refugees. This "Zionist" view held that when Arab armies invaded in 1948, after the state was established, the Palestinians left for reasons unrelated to Israeli actions. The primary reasons given were the following: for their own safety and so as not to hinder the war effort, the invading Arab countries encouraged them to leave temporarily, for the duration of the war, which Arab leaders believed was going to be short and victorious; the Palestinians had great and unjustified fear, created to a large extent by Arab leaders, of what the Jews would do to them if they stayed; and there was a collapse of the Palestinian society and leadership—the leaders themselves leaving, and the people following them.

While some of these appear to be aspects of the truth, slowly, in the 1980s, publications appeared by "new historians" in Israel, at first Benny Morris, which on the basis of the documents from the period of the war have shown that the Palestinians were partially expelled.[26] Just prior to the war, the massacre at one Palestinian village, Deir Yassin, became widely known, which would have made Palestinian fear of the Jews understandable. According to Paul Scham,[27] Morris had more influence than some other new historians because he exposed the problems of the "Zionist" narrative, but in contrast to these others, he did not throw it out. He became, however, a complex figure, after a later, famous interview in the Israeli newspaper *Ha'aretz*, in which he argued that the expulsion was necessary. Some have interpreted his argument as due—whether consciously or unconsciously—to his initial difficulty of finding a job in the wake of his "new history." Groups are often hostile to messengers of truth.

One of the other new historians is Ilan Pappe, who makes more extreme claims about the expulsion of Palestinians. He wrote that it was ongoing to a very significant extent before the invasion of the Arab armies in 1948, and that it was done with great cruelty. His history is controversial: By his own admission, it is ideological and guided by his sympathy for the oppressed. Such sympathy is admirable, but one-sided sympathy can interfere with complex truth. He believes that only the return of all Palestinian refugees could bring peace.[28]

In the official version of history, the massacre at Deir Yassin was described as the action of right-wing military groups, not the Israeli army, and its influence was underplayed. The new version of history used documents showing that although it was militias like the Stern gang and not the army that were involved at Deir Yassin, the army did have a plan to clear Palestinians from areas of the country and did engage in expulsion.[29]* This new version slowly spread. Between the mid 1980s and 2000, many Israeli school textbooks included both the old version and some form of the new version.[30] But even with the new Israeli collective memory, a divergence with Palestinian collective memory has remained. The dominant Israeli view has now been that only acts of violence represented expulsion. The Palestinian view has been that there were other, less extreme forms of intimidation in the service of expulsion, such as leaflets encouraging Palestinians to leave. That such actions have contributed to the Palestinian exodus is accepted by some Israelis.

Some authors[31] see Israel as a colonial enterprise, in the same vein as the conquest of colonies by European powers. Such a view seems incorrect, at the very least on the grounds that Jews did not plan to settle in the area to exploit the local population and natural resources (the latter barely exist), or to convert them to their religion, which were dominant motives of colonial powers. However, they did plan to create a country on territories where the Palestinians lived.

Changing conditions of society, for example, a more positive attitude toward Palestinians during the Oslo peace process in 1993, and a more questioning attitude toward the government, may have allowed the new history to take hold. They also brought forth memoirs written by people involved in events at the time, especially soldiers, which supported this new version of history. Earlier memoirs of this kind did not surface, partly because their authors did not want to be disloyal to the country, and partly because of government censorship.

A famous case was an early memoir by Yitzhak Rabin, the chief of the army and later prime minister, in which he wrote about the army's role. It was not allowed to be published.[32] While loyalty to a country in a violent conflict is natural and common, a more open society, and more truthful collective memory— and openness to the other's truthful collective memory—can contribute to the resolution of conflict. The power of the state to control collective memories has been somewhat reduced by the communication explosion, especially the Internet.

Although the new version of history over time entered the media, public discourse, and eventually school textbooks, collective memory, people's narrative of the past, is affected not only by what is known but also by shifting attitudes toward the other and feelings of security and insecurity. Especially as a new collective memory is formed, it can be unstable. Public opinion surveys of Israeli Jews have shown the influence of changing circumstances. By 1999, 31% of the Israeli-Jews believed that "the *main* reason for the exodus was expulsion." In 2003, after the second *Intifada* by Palestinians began, only 17% agreed with this statement.[33] Renewed fear of and anger at Palestinians may have led to this shift by Jewish Israelis away from acknowledging their country's role in the Palestinians' situation.

What happened after the second *Intifada* was also likely to reduce Israelis' openness to seeing their role. Hamas won the Palestinian elections and then took over Gaza, with continuous rocket attacks on Israel from Gaza. Israel had a relatively unsuccessful war against Hezbollah in Lebanon, an Iranian and Syrian supported militant group created to fight Israel, with increasing political influence in Lebanon. The Iranian President denied the Holocaust and threatened to wipe Israel off the face of the earth, at a time of worldwide concern about Iran developing the capacity to build nuclear weapons.

Israelis had good reasons to feel under attack, with suicide bombings, the shelling from Lebanon and the West Bank, Hamas refusing to accept Israel's existence, and Iran's expressing the intention to destroy it. Palestinians had good reason to feel badly treated by Israelis, enduring their occupation, punitive practices, attacks on terrorist leaders that also killed civilians, settlements in lands that should be the Palestinians' in a two-state solution, and cumbersome travel in the area for Palestinians, with often long waits at Israeli checkpoints. Conditions that intensify hostility are likely to create resistance to collective memory that points to one's own responsibility.

A public opinion survey explored the content of the collective memory of Israeli Jews in 2008, before the new fighting in Gaza. In response to a question about the Israeli–Palestinian conflict overall, the survey found that 43% of the respondents claimed that the Arabs/Palestinians hold the main responsibility (which the authors call the Zionist narrative), 46% claimed that both parties are equally responsible (critical narrative), while 4% claimed that the Jews hold the main responsibility (Palestinian narrative), and about 7% did not know. With regard to the 1948 Palestinian refugees, 41% claimed that the refugees left due to fear and calls by the Arab/Palestinian leadership to leave (Zionist); 39% said they left due to fear, calls of the leadership to leave, as well as expulsion by Jews/Israelis (Critical), while 8% claimed they were expelled (Palestinian), and 12% did not know.[34]

Older and more religious people held the Zionist narrative more, younger people less. The stronger people's memory was of Jewish persecution, of anti-Semitism, and of the Holocaust, the more they held the Zionist narrative. Those who held this narrative had more negative views of Arabs and were less willing to support peace agreements between Palestinians and Israelis. The authors of this report see Israel's increased power, greater individualism and more willingness to criticize the government, the work of the new historians, less active conflict (at the time of the survey), and the growing up of a new generation as accounting for the level of agreement with the "critical" view.[35] Presumably, had violence between groups remained low and relations improved, the Israelis would have increasingly accepted the new narrative. Instead, the war in Gaza and in 2009 a less peace-orientated government in Israel followed.

The return of the refugees is one major practical issue between the two sides. But the issue of refugees is also a psychological matter. The Israelis are likely to allow only a token return of a small number of refugees, presumably willing to compensate the others. The Palestinians supposedly know this and the majority accept it. But the Palestinians very much want acknowledgment of Israel's role in what they call the *Nakba*, their disaster, what they hold as their expulsion by Israel from their homeland and homes.[36]

Each side also wants and needs the acknowledgment and acceptance of its nationhood.[37] And more than acknowledgment is needed. The Zionist vision of the creation of Israel ignored the people who already lived there. This is not surprising; a persecuted and long victimized people that has just suffered a horrible genocide, even a people normally concerned with ethics and morality as Jews have been, will tend to focus on its own powerful needs. Also, the historical/religious Jewish collective memory has focused on a return to historical Israel. But the resolution of the conflict, and reconciliation between the two groups, require addressing both groups' material and psychological needs. The Israelis will not and cannot give up their home, their state, which is now a long-established reality. But the Palestinians lost their home. Both acknowledging their loss of home, their suffering since then, and helping them create a home for themselves are central to change the groups' relationship.

To create a shared history, Palestinians also need to change their collective memory. A changed collective memory might acknowledge that apart from expulsion, Palestinians left in 1948–1949 because of the influence of their leaders' words and actions, to escape the war, and due to the mutual influence of people on each other.

Nets-Zehngut[38] examined Palestinian autobiographical memory about why Palestinians left, based on 4 oral history projects, conducted by both Palestinians and Israelis between 1978 and 2005, involving 38 communities, with Palestinians participants who lived at the time of these studies in many parts of the region.

The oral histories show several causes of Palestinian exodus. Two primary ones were expulsion, Palestinians ordered or forced to leave their locality by

Jewish/Israeli military, and fear of attack or actual fighting where they lived or near to them during the war. Some of the testimonies were presented in their more original forms, others in a more academic form. Nets-Zehngut gives the following examples of the former: "Why did the people of A'Jalil leave from here? Not far from here six people of the Shubacky family were murdered, but Arab propaganda made it seem as if the entire family was murdered, about 100 people. So everyone ran away from here in fear. Everyone ran away in every direction"; and of the latter "...the Jews ordered all the Arabs to leave, carrying them in trucks to the river and forcing them to cross to Transjordan."

The official Palestinian historical/collective memories stress expulsion. But in the autobiographical memories expulsion was not a primary reason for leaving; many of them don't mention it. It is given as the exclusive cause in one community, and one of the causes in 13 (34%) of the communities. Fear of attack or actual fighting are additional reasons in these communities, and prominent reasons in the others. In 7 localities, or 18 per cent of the cases, respondents gave Arab orders as a primary reason for leaving. Morris,[39] on the basis of government documents, described the reasons for Palestinians leaving in individual communities all around the country. According to Nets- Zehngut there is good correspondence between these reasons and the autobiographical accounts. In 10 percent of the localities, respondents reported that they were approached by Jews asking them to remain and live in coexistence.

The Palestinian collective memory would ideally come to acknowledge Arab rejection of and violent attacks against Israel, the harm done to Israelis, the loss and disruption of lives first by terrorism and then by suicide attacks on buses, restaurants, the marketplace, and at weddings. It could and should include the role of the Arab states, which with the exception of Jordan refused to take in Palestinians.

It interferes with the resolution of the conflict and the beginning of reconciliation that the Israeli and Palestinian societies have not done "the essential preliminary work" required for "getting their societies to compromise on the fundamental issues that divide them."[40] Humanizing the other, and actions that build trust, such as moving toward a complex, and hopefully shared truth, and each side acknowledging the harm it has done to the other, would be such "preliminary work." Working for change in collective memories may be a piecemeal process, looking at major events in groups' relations and considering the role of each side in them. Examining the start of the 1948 war, of the 1967 war, the punitive practices in the occupation of the West Bank and Gaza, Palestinian acts of violence, and to the extent each side responded to the other, may create changes in narratives and changed attitudes toward the other.

Collective memories serve basic needs. They help protect self-image or identity, the group's view of itself as good, worthy, and moral. A view of the other as responsible for all that happened and as evil can also enhance feelings of both security and connection, as it creates cohesion and readiness by the group to protect itself. Collective memories also provide a comprehension of reality, by explaining why one's group has acted as it did. But collective memories that more accurately represent what has happened serve the group better. They don't give rise to unnecessary violent self-defense or revenge, which brings about retaliation and continues a cycle of violence.

Official collective memories propagated by leaders and collective memories of the population tend to go together, since leaders have the media and other tools to propagate their views. But as the research on autobiographical memories shows, this is true only to a degree. Moreover, as our work with public education suggests, there can be cultural change that starts with the population. The work of the new historians may be regarded as influence in the middle, exerting influence "upward" on official memory and "downward" on the population.

Daniel Bar-Tal and Gavriel Salomon write that collective narratives are an expression of the human need "to live in an environment that is meaningful, comprehensible, organized and predictable."[41] Narratives, another way to talk about collective memory, screen information to make it confirm to the already existing story. The negative view of the other in conflict narratives, and narratives about a dangerous world, lead to suspicion of positive initiatives by the other group. In a number of instances in the Israeli–Palestinian conflict, positive gestures by either side were interpreted as political maneuvers.[42] This has been true of most conflicts, including in U.S.–Soviet relations.

Dan Bar-On, an Israeli psychologist who studied the children of Nazi perpetrators, realized that they have also been traumatized.[43] What I wrote earlier about perpetrators is also true of their children, that the moral meaning of their suffering is not the same as of survivors. While their suffering was real, it is unlikely that the children of Nazi perpetrators would have suffered psychologically if Germany had won the war, or even if Germany had not been shamed for its terrible actions.

But Bar-On, and later others, began to bring children of perpetrators and of survivors together for dialogue and a joint exploration of their history. The exchange of experiences had healing power for both groups. They created constructive communities, one of them One by One, and talked to groups about their experiences, inspiring these groups by the emotional connection that they have developed.[44]

Later Bar-On and his Palestinian colleague Sami Adwan developed a curriculum for schools to teach students about the narratives, or collective memories, of both Palestinians and Israelis. On one side of the page was the narrative of one group, on the other side, the narrative of the other group. Teachers have tested the material and together with the investigators have revised it based on their students' and their own reactions. This material and approach have been used in some Israeli and Palestinian schools.[45]

How can members of groups in conflict shift their focus to the joint or "collective future" of the groups? This requires some degree of acceptance of the past, a letting go: "This is what happened to us, this has been our life. Now we must focus on the future." Individuals who have suffered victimization or other trauma are often able, as their primary task after their victimization, to attend to the demands of life. But to accept the past and genuinely move toward the future requires some degree of healing, security, and some level of trust. Acknowledgment of harm done to the other party and expressions of regret should also make acceptance and a vision of a collective future more possible.

Changes in collective memories and moving toward a shared history contribute to reconciliation, but in many cases, and probably in Rwanda, a truly shared history may not be reached for a long time. To move toward it, beyond the *gacaca* and other courts judging perpetrators, they, and/or influential Hutus both inside and outside Rwanda, need to clearly acknowledge the genocide and their group's actions and responsibility. Tutsis leaders need to acknowledge violence by the RPF/RPA and allow some form of a justice process.

Beyond the challenge of this for leaders—it may require some guarantees for a degree of protection of leaders who had a role in the violence—it may be highly problematic for Tutsis that the focus might shift from the genocide to the RPF and RPA violence. Many authors already emphasize the past violence and current actions of the RPF to an extent that the genocide appears secondary. This makes the move toward greater openness less likely. For complex truth and a shared history, there must be two perhaps contradictory processes: first, acknowledging the suffering of each side but not equating them, and second, moving beyond a comparison of how much each group has suffered. Rwanda has been successful in attending to the present by creating stability and effective development policies. It has the capacity to move to address the past in full,

Creating Openness to Change in Collective Memory

As is already evident, collective memory of a society is not monolithic. There are significant variations within groups. In the fall of 2007, after the U.S. House of representatives discussed a resolution to acknowledge the Armenian genocide in Turkey, which Turkey denies, there was such intense and hostile Web site discussion among members of the Turkish students' association at the University of Massachusetts at Amherst that the Web site was closed down for a while. The students were affected, presumably, by the varied ways Turks interpret their group's violence against Armenians: "blaming the Armenians of treason, claiming that violent acts were in self-defense, shifting responsibility to Turkey's difficult position during World War I, claiming responsibility for their group's massacres, denying the massacres altogether, etc."[46]

Many of the students' passionate views expressed the official Turkish view. But living in another country may have exposed some of them to a different view of their history, or it may have changed the degree and nature of their identification with their group. Recasting the meaning of attachment to the group and shifting to constructive patriotism, which in contrast to blind patriotism allows questioning and the desire to change the group when it deviates from important human values, can help people assume responsibility for their group's actions.

How might revisions of collective memory come about? The preceding discussion shows that the work of historians, information collected from individuals who were present at historical events, and the media publicizing new information can help. Using an "understanding" approach, about the origins and impact of violence, as we did in Rwanda, can also increase openness to change in collective memory. This is suggested by our findings of positive attitudes toward members of the other group, decrease in trauma, more empathy and what I interpreted as greater independence of authority.

At a 4-day national leaders' seminar/workshop in Rwanda in 2001, we had participants discuss important issues, first in small groups, and then in a larger group of about 35 participants. One small group of high-level leaders, including government ministers and an advisor to the president, discussed the possibility of creating a shared history for Hutus and Tutsis. They recognized the great importance of this goal but believed that given the recent genocide it was not yet possible to achieve it. However, simply discussing the possibility of change in collective memory, and a shared history, can create awareness that the way a group sees history is not immutable.

In the midst of ongoing conflict, shifting the focus away from one's own conflict, examining the history and collective memories of people in a different conflict, can help, as Lustig, one of Gavriel Salomon's students, found.[47] Half of a group of 68 Israeli 12th grade students studied the Northern Irish conflict, exploring the perspectives/narratives of both sides, and half of them did not. (Originally Palestinian schools also agreed to participate, but in 2001 they pulled out because of the second *Intifada*.) There was no mention during this time of the Israeli–Palestinian conflict. The students were then told to write two essays, one describing the conflict from the Palestinian perspective and one from the Israeli perspective. Ninety-four percent of those who studied the Northern Irish conflict wrote full-length essays from the Palestinian perspective, while only 25% of those who did not study that conflict were able or willing to describe the conflict from the adversary's perspective. Those in the former group used many more positive words, such as compromise and negotiation; those in the latter group used more negative ones, such as war, death, and deportation. In the former group, blaming the Palestinians for the conflict was unrelated to belief about Israeli responsibility; in the latter group, the more students blamed the Palestinians, the less they believed in Israeli responsibility.

Focusing on similarities in each other's history may also be beneficial. The perception of similarity is a major contributor to empathy. The current suffering of Palestinians has to do in part with their commitment to their identity and to the land that is part of this identity. The persecution of Jews over the centuries was due to their commitment to their faith and identity. There are also intersecting points of Jewish and Muslim history and suffering. At the time of the Crusades' war against Muslims to "free" Jerusalem, as the crusaders repeatedly marched across Europe on their way to the Holy Land, they killed Jews along the way.

Justice Processes

Justice is also of special importance for reconciliation. People who have been greatly harmed yearn for justice. Truth, which is required for justice, and justice itself[48] provide acknowledgment of a group's suffering and show that the community holds unacceptable the harm done to them. They make it less likely that the past will be repeated. Truth makes it more difficult for perpetrators to blame the victims. Truth and justice help people heal, fulfill basic needs, repair connection to the community, repair worldviews, and prepare the ground for a shared history.

One of the criticisms of the war on terror has been that since terror is a strategy that can be adopted by any individual or group, it cannot be defeated.[49] An alternative would have been to deal with terrorist acts as they have often been dealt with in the past, as criminal actions to be addressed by police and the justice system. This issue is also relevant to the Palestinian–Israeli conflict, which has been guided by some combination of the rules of war and punishment for criminal action, mainly of Palestinians by Israelis. The occupation of the West Bank and Gaza, problematic as it has been, may have been less violent had relations been guided more by justice proceedings.

Justice takes a variety of forms, all of which are important. *Retributive justice* is the punishment of perpetrators. This is essential, but when punishment extends to too many people, the former perpetrator group comes to see itself as the victim, potentially starting a new cycle of violence. Another form or avenue to justice is *restorative justice*. One meaning of this term is that harm doers contribute to the restoration of the life of victims and the rebuilding of community. They provide compensation, in money, or more often (since often perpetrators, once stopped, don't have money) in service. The sentence of many perpetrators in Rwanda includes service to the community. Helping to rebuild the community also provides opportunities for contact between groups. Another meaning of restorative justice is helping to restore the emotional well-being of victims and the relationship between them and perpetrators, by having them engage with each other.

Procedural justice is the creation of justice processes and institutions that give people confidence that past harm doing will be appropriately dealt with, and future harm doing will not go unpunished. It shows a commitment to a moral society, and when it comes to international justice, a moral world. It provides a context in which trust between groups can develop.

Professionals working in the fields of "transitional justice"—a term used to refer to restorative processes in postconflict societies, especially but not only justice—and those working on peacemaking tend to be at odds about the punishment of perpetrators. The latter believe that punishing perpetrators risks renewed hostility. I see justice as an aspect of reconciliation and peace building. When perpetrators go unpunished after horrible deeds, insecurity and mistrust remain, and healing by survivors (and psychological recovery by perpetrators) is retarded. Justice that assigns reasonable punishment, that does not go to extremes, does not become vengeance, with a focus on leaders and the worst perpetrators, can advance reconciliation and peace building. So can compensation in money and service to the community by perpetrators, both to help victims and to restore society. And so can the creation of fair procedures to judge and punish future harm doing. Justice and other aspects of reconciliation and peacemaking should go forward as the same time.

It is realistic to fear when the perpetrator group is a majority, or when violence was perpetrated by the military, that they will resist punishment, possibly by resuming violence or authoritarian rule. But psychological-societal wounds fester. Even if not immediately, when maintaining peace and rebuilding society may require all available energy, they need to be addressed. In Argentina, when a democratically elected government replaced the architects of the disappearances, laws were passed that limited the prosecution of those involved. For example, the Law of Due Obedience allowed obedience to orders as a viable defense. In 1990, under President Carlos Menem, an amnesty freed all members of the military who were in prison. The absence of just punishment of perpetrators left serious unresolved emotional and social aftereffects.[50]

In response to demands by many segments of the society, including the Mothers of the Plaza del Mayo who originally began to turn the country against the military as they protested the disappearance of their children, Argentina returned to the issues of the past. The amnesty law was annulled in 2005, and the other laws that interfered with prosecution were struck down, with new trials starting in 2006. These new trials brought to the fore old wounds and hostilities, with witnesses and judges threatened, and at least one witness disappearing.[51] But Argentina has developed into a stable enough democracy that it is able to address the past. The issues of the past are also reemerging in Spain, a country that avoided an examination of the extremely violent civil war and subsequent rule by Franco. Society must not be vengeful; justice must be measured and even merciful in order to avoid renewed violence, but just punishment helps to heal society. The opposite claim, that justice has to take precedence over everything else, is also problematic.

Existing circumstances must be considered in these and other reconciliation efforts. Explanation by authorities and societal dialogue can create public support and some degree of consensus about necessary actions, even by some who have originally supported the perpetrators. Some actions require courage, by leaders and citizens—both moral and physical courage. Some are best done after the passage of time.

International tribunals have become an avenue to pursue justice after mass violence. The first such tribunal was at Nuremberg after World War II. The evidence, hundreds of thousands of pages of documents and films, most of them material created by the Nazis themselves, together with the testimony of witnesses, powerfully presented the history of Nazi atrocities. Even more than punishing perpetrators, establishing the truth was the tribunal's great achievement.

The tribunals for Rwanda and the former Yugoslavia had similar roles. The International Criminal Court is a new instrument of justice to deal with human rights violations and atrocities. The United States has refused to ratify it, mainly so that U.S. nationals won't be subject to it. The proposed indictment by the Court in 2008 of the President of Sudan because of Sudanese actions in Darfur has created controversy, some claiming that it reduces his incentive to go along with the international community—which he did not do anyway. If this supposed pragmatism had trumped principles, it would have undermined the Court's usefulness.

The President of Sudan was indicted in February 2009. The immediate, but short-term reaction of Sudan was to interfere with humanitarian aid to refugees. In July 2009 the United Nations reported that while the situation of civilians "remains dire," "government cooperation with peacekeepers in Darfur has improved and major violence there is now uncommon."[52] In January 2010 the situation has further improved, with no government and janjaweed attacks on the population, and the rebel groups inactive. Huge numbers of people are still in refugee camps, but there is no organized violence.[53] Contrary to predictions about issuing the arrest warrant, if anything, it has helped to stop violence.

Restorative justice, focusing on restoration rather than retribution, is a movement of increasing force. In the form of it that aims to serve the emotional needs of victims/survivors, and to restore the relationship between the parties,[54] victims and harm doers meet and talk, usually in the presence of people important in their lives. So far its focus has been on harm done to individuals, but it can be extended to group violence and serve both justice and peacemaking. The engagement between perpetrators and victims can be through letters, or through a mediator carrying information between the parties. But much of the time it is face to face, in a meeting between the victim and perpetrator, with a mediator or facilitator present. Or in a "conference" or family conference, victims, offenders, family members, and close supporters—friends, co-workers or other relevant persons—are present. Another form, the circle, also includes members of the community. In every form, all participants have the opportunity to talk. The talk continues until people have said what they needed to say. Participation in restorative justice programs improved the psychological and physical health of victims as well as perpetrators.[55] It was associated with substantially less fear and anger by victims, and more sympathy for perpetrators, in comparison to victims who had not participated in such programs.[56]

Restorative justice has been used either after the conviction of offenders or after their admission of guilt. As part of the process offenders frequently apologize and express remorse.[57] In the case of mass violence, direct engagement with members of the victimized group might lead perpetrators to acknowledge responsibility and show regret. Admission of guilt might be an outcome, rather than a precondition. However, a danger is that perpetrators who continue to be hostile will harm the victims during the engagement. Here again, understanding the roots of mass violence, and healing experiences, may be helpful in preparing both parties for constructive engagement.

The Gacaca, Justice, Truth, and Complex Truth

Sometimes justice is especially difficult because of the huge number of perpetrators. This was certainly true in Rwanda. The *gacaca*[58] was a creative attempt to try the majority of over 120,000 people who had been in jail, accused of perpetrating the genocide, with more people subsequently accused as well. The *gacaca* had elements of both retributive and restorative justice. Its basis was an ancient local practice. A person accused of wrongdoing met with his or her accusers, and with relatives of each party to support them, in front of the whole community, to be heard and judged by the village elders. The elders decided whether the accused was guilty, and what this person had to do to be reinstated as a member of the community.

In its new form, the *gacaca* proceedings, which ended in Rwanda in 2009, took place in front of a panel of judges, members of the community who were elected to serve and received limited training. The local community gathered weekly, and went through steps from specifying who lived in the community the day before the genocide began, to establishing what crimes were committed by and against whom, to the judgment of perpetrators. The proceedings were often moving, as members of the community, all of whom could and were expected to participate, told what they knew. Often women who testified broke down in tears and were unable to speak, then recovered and continued their testimony. Sometimes people admitted their crimes and showed remorse; at other times they did not. At one *gacaca* meeting I attended, a man stood up and said, "I have a burden in my heart" and confessed his crime. At another meeting, someone accused a man of a killing another man during the genocide. The accused claimed that he only escorted the man out of the village. Another community member spoke up: He saw the accused return wearing the clothes of the person he took away.

As I described earlier, being a witness, testifying in front of relatives of the accused and the Hutu majority, was difficult. Potential witnesses I talked to, who had left their original communities, were afraid to return to the place where their families were killed and they themselves barely survived. The witnesses didn't have sufficient emotional support before, during, and after their traumatic memories and feelings were reactivated. A few potential witnesses were killed. With its challenging combination of truth commission and court, of punitive and restorative justice, the *gacaca* created turmoil and instability.

But the *gacaca* also provided benefits, such as some degree of justice, and the beginning of the reintegration of many people into the community. In addition, while their immediate psychological effects on many individuals were negative, one study I mentioned indicated societal benefits, such as less stereotyping of the other group. Its overall impact is as yet difficult to evaluate. With no justice system in Rwanda after the genocide, limited resources, and so many perpetrators, no alternatives were evident. Before the *gacaca* began, a high-level government official wondered in a conversation with me whether it might be better not to prosecute perpetrators. I thought that some punishment was essential.

The *gacaca* did create perhaps *needed* disruption. Before it began, communities started to reestablish the coexistence that characterized the society before. This was a natural result of again living together, near each other, in an interdependent manner. This led to a certain degree of amnesia about the past.[59] This amnesia was similar to that preceding the genocide, a period about which people could say that they lived together harmoniously—in spite of the hostility, discrimination, and violence against Tutsis. For a while the need to restart life, to work the fields, meet each other at the store, and so own, made such amnesia useful. But amnesia in the long run is not healthy; the memories are there and create a roadblock to reconciliation.

The *gacaca* had many challenges, with the insecurity of survivors in the midst of the majority Hutus, the absence of defense attorneys, the fear of Hutus about retribution, the focus on punishment, and limited dialogue. Although punishment was often relatively mild given the magnitude of the crimes, Bert Ingelaere[60] believes that the *gacaca* did not provide the truth, or empathy with the other, because of its focus on punishment. The local authorities, mainly RPF members and primarily Tutsis, shaping the process from the background and thereby reminding people of the old days of Tutsi rule, also did not help. The government worked to improve the process, but a perfect process would be difficult to imagine with so many accused and in prison, new accusations emerging in the course of the trials, and untrained judges, even if many were committed to justice. The International Court for Rwanda, working in Arusha, was certainly also imperfect; it was very slow, handling a very small number of cases, ineffective and even corrupt, and provided little psychological protection to witnesses.

While the *gacaca* may not have always brought forth the specific truth in individual instances, it did provide part of the overall truth. But reconciliation requires the complex truth. It requires leaders to acknowledge the violence against Hutus. It may make it easier to present the complex truth, and the population to accept it, to begin with our approach—to help people understand how the actions that have taken place have come about, by the genocide perpetrators, and by the RPF/RPA.

By apologizing for their role leaders could facilitate forgiveness and reconciliation, and provide an example for Hutus to stop all forms of the denial of the genocide and apologize for what they have done. But apology can be cheap, and it must be backed up with just and fair practices, especially the opening up of the political process for everyone. For this to happen, Tutsis, including leaders, would have to see that acknowledgment, apology, and the positive process it can generate is in their long-term self-interest as well as in the national interest. For such a process to evolve it would have to be reciprocal, with positive responses from Hutus, both inside and outside the country, and from the international community. But it could start with dialogue involving all segments of society and involved parties.

Addressing Economic Distress and Inequality as an Aspect of Justice

Mass violence destroys lives and devastates the survivors materially. An aspect of justice is to improve survivors' material conditions. One of the first actions of the Unity and Reconciliation Commission in Rwanda was to meet with different groups of survivors and ask them what they needed for reconciliation. At a meeting in Kigali, women dressed in colorful local dresses for this public event said, one after another, that to reconcile they must have help with core necessities. They wanted help to feed surviving members of their families and to send children to school, which at that time required paying tuition (now education is free up to secondary school). As one woman whose husband was killed said: "How can I forgive ...if I cannot even pay for the schooling of my children?"[61] In South Africa, a problematic aspect of the TRC's work has been that survivors were promised but received little compensation. While most perpetrators, by testifying to what they did, received pardons, survivors received much less compensation than what they were initially promised.[62]

Perpetrators can atone and to a small degree compensate survivors by their actions, even if their actions can rarely balance the harm they have done. There is a story about Gandhi, near death as he refused to eat until the intense rioting and killings between Hindus and Muslims that had flared up all around the country stopped. Authors Gary Zukav and Linda Francis describe a scene in which Gandhi is lying in bed, surrounded by friends, when a Hindu man storms into the room, throws some food at him, and shouts, "Eat! I am going to hell anyway. I won't have your death on my head too!" The man had killed a Muslim boy, crushed his head against a wall, and is now desperate about his deed.

"Nothing can help me," he says. Gandhi points him to "a way out of hell." He tells the man to find a Muslim boy whose parents have been killed, and raise him as his own son—but raise him as a Muslim.[63] But even simpler actions, such as helping to rebuild houses, or speaking out for better relations, can offer some combination of atonement and compensation and contribute to reconciliation.

Addressing the poverty and economic disparity between groups is another aspect of justice. Equitable economic development is an oft-mentioned aspect of early prevention. This requires an effective educational system, so that the less advantaged can gain the benefits of our technological world. Even in a society with relatively good resources, as in South Africa, creating such a system is a great challenge. In 2010 South Africans see one of their greatest problems to be the inadequacy of the educational system to give people the skills required to improve economic conditions in general, and to fulfill the hopes and expectations generated among the many poor South Africans after the shift in power. In South Africa and elsewhere, some redistribution of wealth may also be essential. In El-Salvador a small number of white landowners owned most of the land. After the end of the civil war, in the early 1990s, the land was redistributed, and poor people, mostly native Americans, received some land.[64]

In newly developing countries the difference in the economic conditions of people often increases. A country like Rwanda needs to pay attention that there is no de facto discrimination, and that the situation of the poor improves. In a study of people in the countryside who mostly work in agriculture, participants reported improvement in their economic situation in recent years but also that their economic well-being was way below what it was before the genocide.[65] In the West Bank, there has been recent improvement in economic conditions, but not in Gaza. Allowing and fostering economic development there would contribute to peace.

Increased economic equality usually requires changes in political arrangements and institutions. As I have stressed, this requires changes in attitudes, beliefs, and the willingness of the more powerful to yield some of their power, to build democratic institutions. Sometimes circumstances create ripeness for such actions. External parties can work with internal groups to thoughtfully foster the changes required for this.

Contact and Postconflict Reconciliation

I have emphasized previously contact between groups as a way to humanize the other. Through contact, especially working for shared goals, in joint projects, people can form relationships that help overcome hostility and promote reconciliation. Members of hostile groups often have little direct contact with each other—for example, Muslims and the original inhabitants in many European countries. In the Netherlands, there is only limited opportunity for contact between the Dutch and Muslim minorities. But in mixed neighborhoods, when children and youth spend time on the streets and interact with each other, attitude toward the other group is more positive.[66]

Sometimes contact between groups occurs naturally, but especially for reconciliation after great violence the intentional, purposeful creation of contact is necessary. An example of naturally occurring contact, which seemed to have significantly contributed to reconciliation, was millions of Poles working in West Germany after World War II. This was mutually beneficial, providing employment for Poles and contributing to Germany's economic recovery. An example of planned contact was the cooperation between Germany and France, important for reconciliation between countries that had many wars over the centuries. This included relationships between twin cities starting soon after the war, with about 2300 of them in 2003, and school partnerships, about 5500 in 2003.[67]

Consistent with earlier discussion, a barrier to engagement can be the reluctance of perpetrators to acknowledge harmful actions. Japan was not ready to acknowledge and express regret for its violent actions in South Korea during World War II, and correspondingly not willing to pay reparations to Korean women forced to serve Japanese soldiers sexually. However, in 1965 the two countries established diplomatic relations and began to develop commercial and security relations.[68] Such steps can lead to a positive evolution that progressively improves relations.

Joint commissions can further contact and address important issues between groups. After World War II a joint commission of French and Germans worked on a shared history to show aspects of the groups' relations that were peaceful, and a Czech-German commission worked on issues that needed to be resolved to promote reconciliation.[69] In Rwanda, a joint commission could work on creating a constructive vision for living together. It could specify steps toward accomplishing what the government ideology proclaims, that the people are all Rwandans rather than members of different groups. What kind of dialogue, what social policies—some already existing in principle and laws, such as equality of education—are required? Another commission may address education in the schools and the teaching of the history of the relationship between the groups. Working on this could foster the creation of a shared history.

Israelis and Palestinians could create a joint commission of government officials, academics, and community leaders who would work on proposals about the resolution of material issues that divide them. Another commission could work on the joint economic development of Israel and a future Palestinian state, and of the region. They could create a joint commission on tourism—in Jerusalem, a holy place for Islam, Judaism, and Christianity, and in the region. Such commissions could further contact by engaging their populations in the issues they are addressing.

Summary

Establishing the complex truth, which represents both groups' "truth," is essential for reconciliation. It usually requires changes in both groups' collective memories and the development, if necessary through compromise, of some form of shared history. Justice is also essential. One aspect of this is punishment, especially of primary perpetrators. Another is establishing just procedures, for the present and the future. Another is restorative justice, leading perpetrators to engage in actions that help survivors and society, improving survivors' material existence, and having victims and perpetrators engage with each other. Truth commissions, international tribunals, and other justice processes such as the gacaca in Rwanda, contact between groups, and commissions that work on resolving issues and building relationships are among the practices to advance the reconciliation processes described in this chapter. Since being a witness in truth and justice processes can have positive social effects, but negative effects on the witness, the physical and psychological protection of witnesses is important.

Notes

1 Mamdani, 2001
2 des Forges, 1999
3 see Branscombe & Miron, 2004; Herbert & Dunkel-Schetter, 1992
4 Baumeister, 1997
5 Miron & Branscombe, 2008
6 Nunca Mas, 1986
7 Herman, 1992; Pearlman & Saakvitne, 1995
8 Brounéus, 2008b
9 Byrne, 2004
10 Rimé, Kanyangara, Yzerbyt, & Paez, 2009
11 Staub et al., 2005
12 Backer, 2007; Stover, 2004
13 Broneus, 2008c
14 Ibid, p.21
15 Gibson, 2004
16 Shriver, 2005
17 Rime et al., 2009
18 The survey results are summarized in Ingelaere, Havugimana, & Ndusha-bandi, 2009b
19 Mamdani, 2001
20 Staub, 2006a
21 Straus, 2006
22 Newbury, 1989

23 Nets-Zehngut & Bar-Tal, 2007

24 Bronner, 2009, p. 4

25 Scham, 2006

26 Morris, 1989, 2004, 2008a

27 Scham, 2006

28 For example, Pappe, 2006

29 These events took place very soon after the Holocaust, with survivors of extermination camps among members of the Stern gang and the army. The impact of victimization and unhealed wounds giving rise to aggression, which I discuss in Chapter 10, may have contributed to perpetrating such violence—especially under threatening conditions.

30 Nets-Zehngut, 2008

31 Pappe, 2006; Prior, 2005

32 Nets-Zehngut, 2009b

33 Nets-Zehngut, 2009a

34 Nets-Zehngut & Bar-Tal, in press; see also press release, http://www.tc.columbia.edu/news/article.htm?id=6811

35 Nets-Zehngut & Bar-Tal, in press

36 Scham, 2006

37 Kelman, 1992

38 Nets-Sehngut, in press

39 Morris, 2004

40 Scham, 2007

41 Bar-Tal & Salomon, 2006, p. 20

42 Ibid.

43 Bar-On, 1989

44 Bar-On, 2000

45 Adwan & Bar-On, 2003; For material on this project see also http://prime-peace.org/tmp/articles.php.

46 Bilali, 2009

47 In Salomon, 2004; see also Salomon, 2006

48 Proceedings, 2002

49 Richardson, 2006

50 Burchianti, 2004

51 Ibid.

52 Reuters, 2009

53 Gettlemen, 2010a

54 Maiese, 2003

55 Rugge, 2007

56 Strang et al., 2007

57 Ibid.

58 See Clark & Kaufman, 2009; Honeyman et al., 2004; Staub, 2004

59 Ingeleare, 2009a

60 Ingelaere, 2008, 2009b

61 Staub, 2000, p. 379

62 Kaminer, Stein, Mbanga, & Zungo-Dirwayi, 2001

63 Zukav and Francis, 2007
64 Mason, 1999
65 Ingelaere, 2009c
66 Phalet et al., 2004
67 See Nets-Zehngut, 2007
68 Kang & Kadesa, 2002
69 Handl, 1997

21

Forgiveness, Healing, and Reconciliation

Forgiveness, when it happens, is usually progressive. It can reduce the distress of people who were harmed and make revenge less likely. But one-sided forgiveness can further reduce the status of victims, and lead to additional harmful action against them. The ideal is mutuality, harm doers acknowledging their actions, showing regret and empathy. This, together with healing and other processes contributes to *mutual acceptance*—which is reconciliation.

Another element of reconciliation is forgiveness. One hindrance to both, which I have repeatedly stressed is common after violence between groups, is each side focusing on its own suffering and even in the case of mutual and relatively equal violence believing that its suffering has been greater than the other side's. Research conducted in Chile and Northern Ireland found that empathy and trust were associated with forgiveness, but what these researches called "competitive victimhood" was negatively associated with it.[1] Learning about the other's history and experience, and understanding the roots of violence and healing, may reduce competition in victimhood. Stronger identification with one's group is also associated with less forgiveness.

Catholic identification with Northern Ireland, as a common "ingroup," was associated with empathy for the other group. But Protestants who identified with Northern Ireland were less forgiving. Perhaps they saw it as their country, and the Catholics as not really part of it because historically they have been intent on joining Ireland.[2]

Forgiveness has become a fashionable concept. Its study has focused on individuals forgiving other individuals who have harmed them, but it is increasingly applied to relations between groups. What is required for forgiveness? What are the benefits to individuals who barely survived and whose relatives have been killed to forgive their victimizers, or the victimizing group? What are the meaning and benefits of groups forgiving other groups? Forgiveness can reduce the suffering of victims, uplift them spiritually, reduce the likelihood of retaliation or revenge, and open people to engage in other processes of reconciliation. But forgiveness is not without dangers.

There are many definitions of forgiveness, based on research and theory about individuals.[3] To me it means letting go of anger, of the desire for revenge; it means an increased acceptance of and more positive attitude toward the party that has caused harm to us (or others). Theologian and political psychologist Donald Shriver describes forgiveness in the political realm as a "collective turning from the past that neither ignores past evil nor excuses it."[4] A survivor of the Rwandan genocide, Immaculee Ilibagiza[5] said that forgiveness for her includes wishing "them" and their children well. This refers, in her case, to the people who killed so many, including all but one member of her family, and who intended to kill her. We may regard forgiving actual perpetrators as an extreme form of inclusive caring. It extends the boundary of people we accept and include in the realm of humanity even to those who have done extreme harm to us. However, forgiveness is a matter of degree and, like reconciliation, a process rather than a specific outcome.

Forgiveness in the case of genocide or mass killing is regarded by some scholars, some practitioners of peace building, sometimes by governments, and by some religions as healing and transformative. But some victims, and people sympathetic to them, find the idea of forgiving the planners of and killers in mass violence, at least forgiving them unconditionally, as inconceivable and even appalling. The president of a survivor group in Bosnia said: "The word 'forgiveness' insults me. ...Nobody has a right to demand from the victim to forgive or to reconcile with the offender. ...It is a shame to talk about forgiveness while the main perpetrators who have killed our children and husbands still have not faced legal persecution."[6]

Forgiveness cannot be required of people, but can it be fostered? Does it in fact further reconciliation? As social psychologist Morton Deutsch writes, "Forgiveness, of course, is not to be expected in the immediate aftermath of torture, rape or assault. It is unlikely, as well as psychologically harmful, until one is able to be in touch with the rage, guilt, fear, humiliation, hurt and pain that has been stored inside. But nursing hate as well as 'competition for victimhood' between the conflicting parties keeps the injury alive and active in the present instead of permitting it to take its proper place in the past. Doing so consumes psychological resources and energy that are more appropriately directed to the present and future."[7] Nursing hate also maintains the danger of new violence. But healing and other experiences are needed for forgiveness. Deutsch sees forgiveness as accepting the other into the moral community, and as contributing to reconciliation, which he sees as going beyond forgiveness by establishing or reestablishing a positive or cooperative relationship.

Since reconciliation means mutual acceptance, both parties letting go of anger and coming to accept the other party more, forgiveness is by definition an aspect of, and some degree of it even a requirement for, reconciliation. Research with individuals has focused on the benefits of forgiveness to the forgiver. It has shown that those who forgive, either naturally or as a result of various procedures or interventions, feel less distress, less pain. Their trauma is diminished. In these studies, friends forgive friends, rape victims forgive perpetrators.[8] Rape is an extreme harm, but in many studies of individual forgiveness, the harm done was quite limited. Formal research has not focused on people who as children suffered physical or sexual abuse over long periods of time, which is closer to the experience of people who have been the victims of a history of discrimination, violence in extreme conflict, or survived a genocide.

In mass killing or genocide, and in terrorism, while the victims are harmed, the perpetrators are usually angry at and feel injured by their victims, both before they have harmed them and afterwards, if they are stopped and taken to account. The anger and feeling of injury may come from their past history of relations, as in the case of Hutus and Tutsis, or from an ideology as in the case of Germans, or both. There is also anger and a sense of injury between Muslims living in Europe and the ethnic populations that surround them, with Europeans feeling that Muslims have been benevolently treated but feel and show no gratitude, and Muslims feeling devalued and excluded. Scapegoating and destructive ideologies create anger both in those who enact them and in those who are victims of them. Hostility becomes more intense both in the people who loot, destroy, and kill and in victims/survivors. It is maintained in the aftermath of violence, as the perpetrators are accused and judged but continue to blame the victims for their own actions. Whatever the source of the wisdom that "it is hard for perpetrators to forgive the victims for what they, the perpetrators, have done to them" seems true. The mutuality of anger and the sense of injury, and often the desire for revenge, is more natural in violent group conflict in which both parties are victims and both are perpetrators.

Mutual acceptance, or reconciliation, is the ideal. Moving toward forgiveness is more likely when both parties contribute, in which case they are in the process of reconciliation. In our study of the impact of our training in Rwanda, participants expressed conditional forgiveness. They needed members of the other group to tell the truth and assume responsibility for what they or their group did. The more harm doers, or at least members of their group, acknowledge what they or their group have done, express regret, apologize, show understanding of the pain they have caused and are empathic, and the more they are perceived by the victims to experience distress about their own or their group's actions, the more likely that survivors of violence forgive. This means that in the usual process that brings about forgiveness, there is mutuality. Apology by itself can be cheap, self-serving, and not genuine. But if perpetrators or the group they come from genuinely acknowledge their responsibility and show regret, it means at the very least that they have let go of anger and accept the people they or their group have harmed.

But perpetrators and their groups tend to deny their responsibility. I was the moderator of the section on healing and reconciliation of a 1995 *The New York Times* Conference on peace in Bosnia, which was conducted on the Internet.[9]

I initiated the discussion with a statement, and then occasionally entered to guide the exchange among participants from around the world, including Serbs, Croats, and Bosnian Muslims. There was only one person who acknowledged some of his group's responsibility for the violence in Bosnia. Everyone else blamed the other groups. In a study in Bosnia, Serbs expressed low levels of shame and guilt about the violence there. They were unwilling to acknowledge that members of their group committed atrocities.[10] This may be one reason that Bosnian Muslims are not inclined to forgive the Serbs.[11]

The likely reasons for perpetrators' unwillingness to acknowledge responsibility include both their long-held negative view of members of the other group and their ideology. In addition, shame and guilt are difficult emotions, and people protect themselves from them. Acknowledging responsibility is also risky: It can lead to punishment and demands for compensation. Perpetrators may fear that they will be shunned even more than before. Small steps on both sides can lead to a reciprocal process of increasing repentance and forgiveness.

Just as violence evolves, and caring and helping evolve, so forgiveness and reconciliation can evolve. The need for a gradual process is indicated by research showing that when trust between groups is low, apology by perpetrators is not accepted. It is seen as a ploy and increases tension between groups.[12] Apology may be genuine, and perceived as genuine, if it comes about in the course of a relationship, if it makes sense given the context, and if it is credible that the perpetrators have come to realize and regret the suffering they have created.

Significant contact may show people the humanity of the other. Bosnian Muslims who reported more contact with Serbs, especially those who felt close to their Serbian friends and saw them as similar to themselves, perhaps because they had deeper contact, had more empathy toward and trust of Serbs. These feelings were associated with forgiveness. Those who had more contact also didn't lump all Serbs together; they saw them as more heterogeneous, more varied as individuals. We don't know, however, whether contact created these effects, or whether those Muslims who had more empathy with and trust in Serbs engaged in more contact with them and forgave them more. The actual level of forgiveness was relatively low, presumably because of the unwillingness of Serbs to accept responsibility and show regret.[13]

Pumla Gobodo-Madikizela,[14] a member of the Truth and Reconciliation Commission in South Africa, writes that what was done to victims says to them that they do not matter, that the moral obligation extended to others does not apply to them. This creates a crack in their psyche. She proposes that they can seal this crack by forgiving—when a person who represents their pain drops his façade and expresses contrition. The perpetrators' contrition validates the victims' pain and frees them. In turn, they can forgive, which affirms their efficacy and increases their sense of power, which was diminished by the violence against them.

She describes a meeting between six mothers and a black policeman who lured their sons into a trap, where the police of the apartheid system brutally murdered them. At first, the mothers angrily denounce him. But he had approached them to ask for their forgiveness, about 10 years after the event, and he showed great pain and contrition. The mothers told him that they forgave him. The first mother who expressed forgiveness apologized for their anger at him. She said that their pain had been sitting inside, they needed to get it out to have peace, and they had nowhere else to throw it.

It may be that seeing his pain and being able to express anger empowered these mothers to some extent, and that this freed them to feel empathy for him. But we don't know how each of the mothers felt. The public statement of forgiveness by one mother, who assumed the role of speaking for them, may have inhibited the other mothers. Their hurt and anger, probably reduced in intensity over the years and perhaps lifted in the moment, may not be gone. This encounter may have been one step on the long road to forgiveness.

After great violence, forgiveness or reconciliation is progressive, a matter of degree, a process rather than an event. When a person says to another, "I forgive you," this can be an important point on a long road with gradual internal changes. But what happens in the world, or within that person, can lead to reversals. Even more than with collective memory, there are likely to be relapses, especially if there is new threat from a party one has forgiven, or perhaps new threat of any kind. The dark night of the soul is likely to emerge at times, plunging people into memories of their victimization, helplessness, and loss of loved ones. Nonetheless, under the right conditions, the ability to let go of anger and accept members of the other group is likely to grow over time and lessen the psychological burden of victims. As pain diminishes, people slowly become open to varied relations across group lines,[15] from commerce to friendship, with mutuality that represents reconciliation.

Private and Public Forgiveness, and Their Consequences

Forgiveness can be private. Immaculee Ilibagiza,[16] while hiding from the killers in Rwanda in a small bathroom with six other women, prayed constantly. This helped her take her mind away from the constant threat. From a psychological perspective she seemed in a state of dissociation; from a spiritual perspective she was uplifted in the midst of discomfort and danger, and she felt connected to and protected by God. With her life still in great danger, she began to pray that she be able to forgive the killers. She experienced forgiveness, which she later lost when the threat was intense, and then again when she was visiting her village where her family had been killed. But each time she recaptured the experience of forgiveness.

Private forgiveness has psychological benefits to the forgiver and also creates benefits in making violence by them less likely. When it is expressed in action, it can contribute to reconciliation.

An important but so far unanswered question is the response of perpetrators, or their group, to words and acts that publicly express forgiveness toward them. The benefits of public forgiveness certainly depend on its context. If Immaculee Ilibagiza had stepped out of her hiding place as a throng was shouting "kill them, kill them, kill them all," and was specifically looking for her, and if she had told the people who already killed many that she forgave them, she quite certainly would have been killed. But under other conditions forgiving may elicit positive responses.

After perpetrators are stopped, and their actions are identified as immoral and criminal, forgiveness may reduce their defensiveness and lead them to acknowledge their responsibility and express regret. I have talked to eyewitnesses of meetings arranged in Rwanda between survivors who expressed forgiveness and perpetrators who responded this way. In such encounters, however, we don't know how genuine this response is, given that for perpetrators, it is important to appear in a positive light, especially in a public setting with witnesses. When the response is genuine, and is perceived as such, it contributes to reconciliation. An experiment with individuals who were led to mildly harm another person found that, when they received forgiveness, they were less likely to repeat their harmful actions and more likely to cooperate.[17] But the harm done was limited. The participants were not in an antagonistic relationship; there had been no evolution of harm doing and therefore no justification of it by increasing devaluation and ideology.

There are potential dangers to one-sided, unconditional public forgiving after mass violence. Violence creates an imbalance, diminishing those who are harmed. When perpetrator and survivor groups continue to live together, as in Rwanda, the imbalance is enhanced if survivors show forgiveness by words and actions, but perpetrators do not apologize, express regret, or receive punishment and make compensatory acts. Imagine an abused child or spouse, or a survivor in Rwanda whose family was killed by a neighbor, forgiving the perpetrating relative or the neighbor if they act as though nothing had happened. Perpetrators may continue to devalue their victims and/or feel free to harm them again,[18] perhaps even more than before.

There is another danger, not only in unconditional forgiving but also at times in forgiving in response to appropriate words and actions by perpetrators or their group. If violence against them makes people feel diminished, to feel "less than" those in the perpetrator group, they may forgive in an attempt to gain the good graces of these others. They may be unaware, however, of their reasons for forgiving, which, arising out of woundedness and the imbalance in the relationship, can further diminish the forgiver.

Need Fulfillment and Reconciliation

Nurit Schnabel and Arie Nadler[19] have proposed that in order to reconcile, victims who have been disempowered need to have their sense of power restored. They also proposed that perpetrators' primary need is to have their moral image restored. Victims need empowerment, and perpetrators need acceptance. In one study they assigned to people in dyads the roles of victims or perpetrators; in another participants read a vignette about a person who was harmed by another; in a third study they had them recall personal experiences in which they hurt or were hurt by a significant other. They found that perpetrators felt greater threat to their moral image and greater need for social acceptance, while victims felt greater threat to their sense of power and greater need for power and justice.

In subsequent research, again assigning to people roles of victims and perpetrators, messages to victims that they were competent led them to feel more powerful and more ready to reconcile. Messages to the perpetrators that they were socially acceptable led them to feel more moral and more ready to reconcile. To a degree the latter finding is consistent with my view that anything that moderates the shame and guilt feelings of perpetrators (of which they may be unaware) makes it more likely that they acknowledge their responsibility and open themselves to reconciliation.

A limitation of this research is that role playing, or reading about victims and perpetrators (for example, that the position of a person in an organization is taken over by another person, or in another study that a request to work on a certain shift is declined by a superior) is far removed from the reality of intense group violence.[20]* Another limitation is that in real life people rarely see themselves or acknowledge that they were perpetrators. Moreover, while Schnabel and Nadler are correct that effectiveness and control are crucial for victims, all basic needs are frustrated by victimization. Victims of extreme violence tend to also feel that something must be wrong with them, that such horrible things were done to them. They also need security, a positive identity, connection to other people, and to rebuild a positive worldview.

One of the important needs of perpetrators is likely to be to have their moral image restored. But real perpetrators cannot simply be told that they are socially or morally acceptable. The community also has needs. Healing/psychological recovery may be important way stations, enabling perpetrators to feel and express shame and guilt, and then progress to regret and assume responsibility for their actions. This makes empathy with and acceptance of them by victims, and the world, more possible. Over time, their identity, self-image, and connection to others can be restored.

Michael McCullough[21] has argued that both forgiveness and revenge are part of our evolutionary heritage, our genetic makeup. Revenge serves to deter future aggression and to make sure that other people do not think a person is an easy mark, which would lead them to take advantage of him or her. One experiment showed that a provoked or abused victim retaliated more if an audience witnessed this, and especially if it let the victim know that he or she looked weak or vulnerable. However, aggressive responses to aggression are not necessarily protective. As we have seen, reciprocal aggression can lead to continuing cycles of violence. We can make forgiveness/reconciliation dominant over revenge by creating the conditions that lead to it.

Feelings of insecurity, humiliation, ineffectiveness, and the frustration of other basic needs of those who were harmed can persist if the relationship with the harm doers remains unbalanced. The relationship can be balanced by revenge, or to varying degrees by the positive words and actions of the harm doers, other members of their group, and even outsiders, society, or the world. Since the essence of victimization and trauma is loss of control, victimized people do need both their effectiveness and identity strengthened. They need acknowledgment, evidence of regret, and justice. Forgiveness without justice can be morally repugnant to victims, as well as to witnesses outside the group. Justice can serve as acknowledgment, balancing the relationship to harm doers and making forgiveness more likely.

Ways to Promote Forgiveness after Group Violence

To some extent, beliefs about when forgiveness is acceptable and ideal differ according to the religious background of people and their own past history of victimization. In Rwanda, people are religious, most of them Catholic, and feel the pressure of their faith to forgive. The same is true of other countries in the region. In the Congo, girls who were raped are quoted as saying "...it is more important that they forgive their rapists rather than wait for justice."[22]

Sometimes secular authorities at least implicitly pressure people to forgive. As I discussed forgiveness with Rwandans, some have offered the view that many people feel pressure to forgive and express forgiveness, but that it is often on the surface, not genuine and deeply held.[23] In Northern Ireland, researchers collecting information in focus groups and questionnaires found that members of both groups, Protestants and Catholics, believed that imposing intergroup forgiveness is likely to be counterproductive. Instead, they believed that contact between groups, and joint ceremonies in which people can remember together and share loss, would make forgiving easier.[24]

Understanding the influences that have led perpetrators to their actions may be an important way station to forgiveness. In a case study, a man whose parents had severely abused him from an early age gained relief and was able to have a relationship with them by coming to understand them. He came to see his father's rage as arising from childhood neglect. The father's mother had died when he was an infant, leaving him with a father who was extremely preoccupied with work, and this person imagined his father as an infant standing in his crib, screaming for attention and help without getting a response.[25] Among its many benefits, understanding may help to accept one's past suffering, one's life, which makes moving forward possible.

As mentioned, our intervention to promote in Rwanda an understanding of the varied influences that lead to genocide, and of its impact on people, increased conditional forgiveness, expressions of the willingness to forgive if the perpetrators acknowledged what they had done or asked for forgiveness. Other effects were also consistent with forgiveness: a more positive attitude toward the other group. People agreed more with statements that members of the other group were not all perpetrators, and Tutsis agreed more that some Hutus tried to save lives.[26] Seeing some members of a perpetrator group as caring human beings may bring people closer to forgiving the group as a whole. People also expressed more willingness to work with members of the other group for the benefit of the whole society. Trauma symptoms also diminished.

Confession, the acknowledgment by perpetrators of what they have done, can imply a request for forgiveness. However, confession can be purely instrumental. In Rwanda the sentences of those who confess are reduced. Similarly in South Africa, in front of the Truth and Reconciliation Commission, perpetrators had to confess, to describe what they had done, to make them eligible for amnesty. They learned to tell the truth, as early in the process some who did not were confronted by the testimony of witnesses. Circumstances may also lead perpetrators who feel no regret to apologize, such as being called on at public events to do so.

In Rwanda sometimes confession and apology, in front of communities, with perpetrators showing little emotion and seeming to speak in an arrogant manner, created pain and anger in survivors. The same was true when perpetrators in South Africa testified in front of the Truth and Reconciliation Commission. Genuine regret and apology require emotional transformation, through perpetrators engaging with their own woundedness and having experiences that can generate empathy with victims. Moreover, the act of describing their very violent actions in the presence of an audience can lead perpetrators to freeze, go numb, and look as if they do not care.

Forgiveness after genocide is excruciatingly difficult, and it is made more so when, as it is often the case, the perpetrators- or members of the perpetrator group- are perceived as not feeling genuine regret. After he interviewed the group of Rwandan killers he called the Kibungo gang, Jean Hatzfeld was unsure about what they felt, but he believed that they did not feel regret. He describes their attitude toward forgiveness as "a sort of bargain, a trade-off—so many confessions for so much forgiveness—or a formality. Since I have been punished, I have been pardoned, because the hardship of my sentence brings proportionate forgiveness. Or forgiveness vaguely represents an opportunity: forgiving is forgetting, the best way for everyone to return to the good old days and start over as if nothing had ever happened."[27] And he writes, "they ask for pardon with certainty that this request, because it is humiliating and expresses sympathy, deserves in itself a positive response."[28] Law professor Martha Minow writes: "Observers of South Africa's Truth and Reconciliation commission note that although many who were victimized are prepared to forgive or reconcile with police officers and government officials from the apartheid regime, the survivors recoil when perpetrators greet victims with open arms and handshakes. In these cases forgiveness is assumed, rather than granted...Forgiveness is a power held by the victimized, not a right to be claimed."[29]

Both forgiveness and reconciliation may be fostered by acknowledgment not only by perpetrators but also by formerly passive bystanders. The Truth and Reconciliation Commission invited the submission of comments by people who were neither victims nor perpetrators. Many of the early comments were by bystanders expressing something like: "I should have done more to fight the atrocities."[30] Such words are likely to be experienced as acknowledgment of one's suffering, perhaps as support and caring. Any human being, if credible to the recipient, can help survivors heal and generate faith in the potential of human beings for goodness and love. Even if the direct perpetrators are not forgiven, such experiences can advance reconciliation *between groups*, which is of primary importance for the prevention of future violence and the creation of peace.

Perpetrators can protect themselves psychologically in the course of a justice process by interpreting their situation as victory by the other side that is now extracting revenge. This interpretation allows them to maintain a belief that they were right in what they did. It may be especially likely to form in prison, where the perpetrators are in the company of other perpetrators. One of the killers Hatzfeld interviewed said that what some of the prisoners thought about was "finishing the job."

Once their moral cover of ideology and group solidarity is pulled and they face the disapproval of the world, perpetrators and their supporters need to protect themselves from guilt and shame. Even those who feel regret, until further transformation in them may need to defend themselves from empathy with deeply wounded survivors. Perpetrators "don't use the questioning language of self-examination,"[31] and they don't know how to behave. "The killer does not understand that in seeking forgiveness, he is demanding that the victim make an extraordinary effort, and he remains oblivious to the survivor's dilemma, anguish and courageous effort... and that his attitude increases the victim's pain...."[32]

It is due both to the nature of the violence against them and to the attitude of perpetrators that survivors in Bugesera where the Kibungo gang killed were unanimous in saying to Hatzfeld that they could not forgive those who tried to exterminate them. One of them said: "A man may ask for forgiveness if he had one Primus (a Rwandan beer) too many...but if he has worked at killing for a whole month, even on Sundays, whatever can he hope to be forgiven for?"[33]

A contrast to this is the experience of a Rwandan boy whom the Swedish psychologist Suzanne Kaplan interviewed.[34] He was a street child, taken in and cared for in Kigali, together with other boys, by a German doctor. He talked about wanting revenge, but this shifted in the course of the interview as he described a woman who was kind to him. She listened to him talk about his desire for revenge, later looked for him again, and gave him food. Kaplan interviewed him a year later, when he was still living with the German doctor. This time he was talking about wanting to help Rwanda become a peaceful country. The kindness of people such as the German doctor and the woman who provided him with the opportunity to talk about his feelings and express his anger and who took care of him, and probably also his interviews with Kaplan, contributed to this shift.

I have stressed that the conditions surrounding people, including the behavior of other people, society, and the world, can facilitate or hinder forgiveness and reconciliation. As women in Kigali said, people need to feel that their lives, destroyed by the violence, can be rebuilt. The conditions that hinder them in Rwanda may include painful experiences during *gacaca* proceedings; instead of support, many witnesses experienced hostility, exclusion, and retaliation afterward. But developments in the society until recently may have had positive effects, such as the perception by Tutsis that some degree of justice was served by the *gacaca*, increasing stability and economic and physical security. However, Hutus feeling that their losses have not been addressed and their voice and political opportunities are limited is likely to interfere with reconciliation.

Education about the influences leading to genocide can suggest to both parties that in spite of what they have done, perpetrators are human beings, and their actions were the result of human processes. Educating perpetrators and formerly passive bystanders about trauma as well as about the psychological impact of their actions on themselves, helping them both see the deep suffering of survivors and engage with their own experience and woundedness, may lead them to empathize with survivors and ask for forgiveness, in words and by their actions. All this can prepare the ground for dialogue about past relations. But for such dialogue more open public processes are needed in Rwanda, and more security is needed in the Congo.

All the processes of reconciliation I have discussed—such as understanding the roots of violence, fostering healing, establishing truth and justice, and bringing about contact between opposing groups—can contribute to forgiveness. They all take place in *relationships*, usually to other individuals and to community. But Immaculee Ilibagiza in her private forgiveness in the small bathroom where she was hiding did not talk to the other women. She experienced forgiving in the course of her praying, in relationship to God, a relationship that was deeply fostered in her family. Forgiveness always has an element of transcendence, and this was especially so in her case, with killers all around, and in the absence of human relational influences—except that she was in the company of others, and someone took the great, everyday risk of hiding her.

Not only perpetrators but also their descendants often refuse to acknowledge their group's actions or responsibility, as in the case of Turkey with regard to the Armenian genocide and Japan with regard to the mass killing at Nanking and the sexual slavery of Korean women. When they do acknowledge their responsibility, what is said is often limited and is accompanied only by limited actions to address consequences, as in Australia with regard to the treatment of aborigines in spite of apology by the government for taking aboriginal children from their parents, or in the United States with regard to slavery and later discrimination and persecution of African Americans. Words alone, especially when they seem insincere, can reawaken the pain of survivors.

We need to learn more about what can move perpetrators to acknowledge their responsibility. Their engagement with what they have done, their healing, others' empathy with them, and exposing them to the suffering of people who are harmed through actions like their own but who are not their own victims may all help. While he was in jail after the end of apartheid, De Kock, perhaps the most infamous of the South African perpetrators of government violence, talked about seeing the eyes and faces of his victims, the fear and pain in them.[35]

How can we understand this? Possibly, our mind "takes a picture" and retains the memory of what people look like as we harm, torture, or kill them. The meaning of this picture depends on the context and our state of mind. When De Kock "took this picture," he was serving a violent system, working with and leading a group of killers of black South Africans. His job was to get rid of these enemies. Instead of empathy, his victims' terror and pain was likely to give rise to psychological defenses. Killing them evoked no guilt, at least not to a degree that would have lead to a change his behavior. But the picture is retained, and if and when the harm doer has certain experiences, or events create a different context, the picture comes up again in the mind's eye, and the person's reaction can be different. It can be regret and sorrow.

Minimally, the change in context for De Kock was that his cause was discredited. He was also in jail, awaiting punishment. Perhaps he experienced some doubt before, since he said that after one of his killing missions in a neighboring country he had the thought of not continuing. In jail he had a series of conversations with Pumla Gobodo-Madikezela. In spite of her at least initial aversion to him, they developed a good connection. She was empathic with him, and in the course of repeated conversations, he had the opportunity to engage with and examine his actions and his life.

But when perpetrators do not acknowledge their responsibility, as is often the case, survivors can avoid being victimized by them again by finding other avenues to healing. Coming to understand the origins of the perpetrators' actions, testimonials, and commemoration *within* their group, and together with caring outsiders, can help survivors accept the past and move toward a constructive future.

Group-Level Forgiveness and Reconciliation

Forgiveness and reconciliation can be between victims and the perpetrators who harmed them or their families, between victims and the perpetrator group as a whole, and between groups both as collections of individuals and as entities involving leaders, institutions, and systems. It is easier to forgive those members of the group who were not involved in the violence. But usually the perpetrators are seen as deeply tied to and representing their group. Survivors blame the whole group—and to some degree correctly, as violence between groups is usually a group process.

In Germany the whole system was geared toward the perpetration of the Holocaust and other atrocities. In Rwanda as well the genocide was a group process with very many "ordinary" people as perpetrators. Still, perpetrators and bystanders are not the same, and peace can prevail if the groups reconcile, even if perpetrators are not forgiven. For most people, peace and friendship with the hundreds of millions of Muslims in the world should be possible, even if they do not forgive Muslim terrorists.

Often discussions of forgiveness between individuals and groups are intermixed. The elements of forgiveness and reconciliation I have discussed are relevant at both levels. For the group level, public gestures by leaders are likely to make a difference, such as Willy Brandt, Chancellor of Germany in the 1970s, tearfully kneeling at Auschwitz and asking for forgiveness. His gesture seemed, and given his anti-Nazi past most likely was, genuine, but such words can also be empty rhetoric. There must be policies that go beyond words. Germany provided monetary compensation to many Jewish survivors. This cannot make up for the Nazi violence, but it has emotional and symbolic meaning, as it acknowledges the suffering and German responsibility and may provide needed help to people whose prior existence has been destroyed. The response of leaders and members of a victim group to such words and actions can be various degrees of acceptance. When leaders respond, they must take care not to forgive in the name of those survivors who cannot, which is likely to backfire.

Donald Shriver sees forgiveness in the political realm as having four elements: moral truth—a form of shared truth; forbearance, which does not mean the abandonment of justice but means not seeking revenge; empathy, which involves understanding and acknowledging a former enemy's humanity in spite of the enemy's deeds; and a commitment to repair human relationships, which involves creating a shared political community.[36] Audrey Chapman's views of national reconciliation include much of what I have already discussed, including envisioning a shared future. She writes, in addition, that "adversaries need to make a commitment to repairing and reestablishing their relationship." Such a commitment develops out of the processes that I have discussed. She also writes that "...members of the communities should explicitly establish the terms of the new and common future."[37] This can partly be done by a new constitution, which as I wrote is a kind of constructive ideology. They also need to address tensions and problems that have led to violence, including past inequalities, and set goals and policies that are supported by the varied social groups in the society. As in the case of destructive ideologies, constructive ones can generate goals derived from them, or that are consistent with them.

A Few Examples of Reconciliation Projects

I have mentioned a few of the many projects around the world that aim to promote reconciliation, some very local, others more encompassing. Our work in Rwanda with facilitators who then worked with groups in the community is one example of a local project. Here I will describe a few projects from around the world as examples.

One of them is private effort that offers an example. A South African, Mark Solms, whose family has owned a large farm for centuries, went to live in London when apartheid ended. He later returned with the intention to contribute to the new South Africa, to help create a more equitable society. He met with each of the seven black farmers who have long lived on and worked his family farm and asked them what ideas they had for doing things differently. These people, never before asked their opinions and having lived in submission to the owners of the farm, did not even look into his eyes, much less say anything. One man afterward wrote him a letter saying he understood they will now have a safer life with him. Solms decided to build better houses for them, in place of their shacks, but his neighbor told him he is crazy—according to current South African law, if for any reason his workers move, he would have to build equivalent houses for them wherever they move to.

Solms wanted to build a swimming pool for his children, but thought, how could he do that without the children of his black farmers having a place to swim. He did not want, however, to share his pool. He decided to build a pool for them, but his manager told him that all the children from the nearby school would come to swim there. So he offered the school principal to build a pool for the school. After some time the principal said we need other things more— teachers, school supplies, computers.

Solms then decided to create a local history of the farm. He was also a psychoanalyst, had academic connections, and called in specialists like an archeologist and an anthropologist. But everyone on the farm participated in creating this history, telling their stories. The archeologist found that the tribe the farm's manager came from had lived on that land for hundreds of years. Among the many stories collected about people who lived on the farm was that of a black woman accused of wrongdoing, and a German who came to South Africa because he could not afford to buy land in Germany. In the course of creating what may be regarded as a shared history, connections were built and people found their voice.

As a farmer/psychoanalyst, Mark Solms talked about the importance of facing reality, such as the current reality in which South Africans are working to build a new country, and of moving feelings up to the level of consciousness, which can transform them and lead to realistic solutions. He came to believe that whites cannot just hold on to their land, that the inequity cannot continue. He asked banks to give black farmers a loan so that they could buy a neighboring farm. The banks said we must have collateral, and he put up his farm as collateral for a loan well in excess of a million dollars. Now his farm, the neighboring farm owned by black farmers, and a third farm, all winemakers, work cooperatively, sharing equipment, and the process of turning their grape into wine.[38] Starting with good intentions, engagement, creating a shared history, building relationships, and a personal evolution are all part of this story.

Another reconciliation project has been developed around the Tribunal in Cambodia which, with the help of the United Nations, was established to try Khmer Rouge leaders. In 2006 the "Extraordinary Chambers in the Courts of Cambodia" were formally established, and the trials are in progress. Theary Seng, president of the Center for Justice and Reconciliation in Phnom Penh, says that while as a court of law the Tribunal is limited, its activities and the presence of the international community can be a catalyst for conversation about the genocide, create a safer place for dialogue about it, and call attention to its traumatic effects. Seventy percent of the population of Cambodia was born after the genocide. Children have a hard time believing their parents' stories—and as I wrote earlier, survivor parents often don't tell them.

Her organization has created public forums on justice and reconciliation, with about 150 people each time, inviting local authorities, teachers, and young people. They take them on tours of a prison where people were tortured and killed, a genocide museum, and a place where people were killed. About a week later, on Forum Day, they meet with judges, prosecutors, and lawyers from the tribunal. What follows is a conversation among those present, a dialogue. This is recorded and later put on the radio. With testimonies from the tribunal previously broadcast on the radio, this process adds to the national conversation.[39] It can help shape the kind of traumatic memories that society carries.

In various community rebuilding projects after violence, one element of the rebuilding is the reintegration of child soldiers. In Angola and other places sometimes Westerners have been involved, developing with the community a combination of traditional and Western psychological practices to help child soldiers reconnect with their communities. As I have mentioned, children are sometimes enticed with food, but they are often abducted, and often forced to kill people in their own communities, sometimes their own parents and siblings. This both commits them to their guerilla group or militia and makes them violent. The practices of reintegration have included engaging with the spirit of ancestors to gain forgiveness for violent acts, Western practices of healing, and connection with others in the course of shared projects such as building houses and building community.[40]

In Sierra Leone, one project[41] involved meeting with people in different regions, initiating conversations about the times before the violence began, when people got along, and asking them, "Do you want to reconcile?" The project designed "Family Talk" as a way of engaging people with each other. Under a tree, or in other settings, organizers, ex-combatants, and victims/community members sit around a bonfire. Religious leaders start the meeting, saying, "If you have done something wrong, come forward, tell about it, apologize to the family of the people harmed, and the whole community." Confess to a person who never knew who killed his or her son that you did it. The spirit of these meetings is that the truth is cleansing and can be the beginning of reconciliation.

This is followed by engaging people, killers and survivors, in varied activities. Some are recreational, such as a soccer match, followed by dialogue. In others people work together, for example, to replenish stock. Others are community forums that people initiate. In still others, sitting under a tree, they talk through how to engage in acts that contribute to reconciliation—such as having worn a blue shirt while killing someone's parents, and not wearing blue when visiting that person. The leaders of the project see both such talk and acknowledging wrongdoing as essential, since without that, those who are returning to the community are not accepted.

In another approach Charles Rojzman[42*], a French psychologist, developed and has used in trainings—in France to address violence in cities, with Israelis and Palestinians, in Rwanda, in Russia after terror attacks there, in Chechnya, in the U.S. with regard to race relations--what he calls Transformational Social Therapy. Rojzman meets with a varied group of people separated by dislike, prejudice, hate, to prepare them to work on a project that aims to improve community relations and reduce violence. On the basis of information he collected, he proposes a project to improve the system—such as reducing violence in the schools. Early in the meeting, he asks group members to express any suspicions, doubts, apprehensions about the project, everything that stands in their way. In the course of the meeting, which occasionally lasts for a few hours but usually several days, a week, or more, the project is reshaped. The group develops a common goal that satisfies everyone.

The group leaders' tasks include accepting group members, regardless of what they say or do (except physical violence), and providing a feeling of security, that he himself will not attack them. Paradoxically, to develop trust in the group, the leader encourages participants to express their fears and negative feelings about each other: that someone (or a particular person) will criticize them, dislike them, talk too much or not participate. Group members than explore violence they have experienced in their lives. This includes concrete examples of violence by the other group against them—which helps the other party understand them. But what normally happens between hostile groups or segments of a community (such as police and young people belonging to a minority) is that they focus on the hostility and violence of the other group. Rojzman has group members also talk about the violence they have experienced in their own group, whether in the family, workplace, school, and personal relationships. People talk about physical violence, humiliation, verbal abuse, neglect, and abandonment they have suffered. People then talk about harm they personally have done to others in all the contexts of their lives.

People in the group air their "secrets," get rid of their masks. They become more conscious of who they are, develop a more complex view of human relationships, and very importantly an increased willingness to assume responsibility for what they do. The project aims to reduce personal suffering, and to enable participants, even if they still see the other group as an enemy, to see each other's humanity and to work together for shared goals.

Finally, an integrated approach that can move reconciliation forward is under development in Rwanda. It was described to Adin Thayer by Suzanne Ruboneka of ProFemmes, an umbrella organization that coordinates organizations addressing the needs of Rwandan women. The project involves three Rwandan organizations working with International Alert.

Thayer wrote to me:

"The government has provided a structure (in the *gacaca*) for Rwandans to collectively tell the story of what happened, person by person, body by body, stolen cow by stolen cow, and an astonishing number of people have stood up in their local assemblies to tell and to listen … . (but) ….what will happen … . when ex-combatants and ex-prisoners have completed their penance, and are back in the house next door, right where they lived when they turned on their neighbors, next door to what's left of those neighbors?"

This project sets up income-generating activities for local people working in mixed groups, for which micro-credit is provided. It sets up trauma-healing activities: individual and group counseling, training in active listening so that people can help each other as they share their stories, and training community leaders to support people in distress and direct them to resources, and to examine their own experiences as part of their preparation for supporting others. ProFemmes, through its Committee of Coordination, will provide community leaders (selected by community members), survivors, ex-combatants, and ex-prisoner participants a 3-day training, on the prevention, management, and transformation of conflict, gender equality, and nonviolent communication. Following this the community leaders will organize local debates-discussions, suggesting topics for each, like forgiveness. The project will also work in schools.

Harmdoers will be encouraged to approach and seek forgiveness from those they have harmed. Ruboneka said, "this person or that person has apologized to the state via *gacaca*, but what about the person he/she harmed? This is the sole human being who can further the process of acquittal by offering forgiveness, if it is emotionally possible." Ex-prisoners are given the opportunities for role playing, to prepare them for this critical encounter. They are encouraged to visit the national genocide memorial museum, accompanied by someone who can support them. When they approach the person(s) they harmed and initiate a dialogue, someone from ProFemmes accompanies and supports them.

This project integrates several avenues to reconciliation. It helps people to improve their lives economically, to listen to and support each other, and to learn how to communicate and resolve conflict in a nonviolent way. Its communal approach, bringing Hutus and Tutsis together in all these domains, can create deep contact.

Summary

What is required by those who have been harmed to heal, forgive and reconcile? Understanding the influences that have led harmdoers to their actions, engaging with their painful experience with empathic support, acknowledgement by harmdoers and/or their group of their responsibility and showing regret and empathy, constructive commemoration, support and caring by others can all contribute. What is required by perpetrators of harm to heal, forgive and reconcile? A nonthreatening environment so that defenses are not activated, engaging with their harmdoing, ideally at first through understanding the influences that have led to it, engaging with their experience with the help of empathic others that can lead to empathy with themselves, and or conditions generating empathy with their victims (which may be made more possible after empathy with themselves), and the resulting ability to assume responsibility and feel regret all contribute. Healing, forgiveness and reconciliation can also take place at the group level.

Notes

1 Noor et al., 2008
2 Cehajic et al., 2008
3 McCullogh, 2008; McCullough, Finchman, & Tasang, 2003; Worthington, 2005
4 Shriver, 1995
5 Ilibagiza & Erwin, 2006
6 Subasic, 2005, quoted in Cehajic et al., 2008, pp. 351–352

7 Deutsch, 2008, p. 478

8 For reviews, see Worthington, 2005; McCollough, 2008

9 New York Times on the Web, 1995

10 Brown & Cehajic, 2008

11 Cehajic et al., 2008

12 Nadler & Liviatan, 2006

13 Cehajic et al., 2008

14 Gobodo-Madikizela, 2008

15 See also Cairns et al., 2005

16 Ilibagiza & Erwin, 2006

17 Wallace, Exline & Baumeister, 2008

18 Staub, 2005a

19 Schnabel & Nadler, 2008; see also Nadler & Schnabel, 2008

20 A number of authors, for example, Dutton and Tetrault, 2009, argue that we need to be very cautious in interpreting studies that create a laboratory analogue to real world events. This is especially so when the real world events are as intense and extreme as group violence.

21 McCullough, 2008

22 Rath, 2003

23 Staub, 2005a

24 Cairns et al., 2006

25 O'Connell Higgins, 1994

26 Staub et al., 2005

27 Hatzfeld, 2003, pp. 198-199

28 Ibid, p. 200

29 Minow, 1998, p.17

30 Ibid, p.19

31 Hatzfeld, p 198

32 Ibid. p. 199

33 Ibid. p. 196

34 Kaplan, 2008

35 Gobodo-Madikezela, 2003

36 Shriver, 1995

37 Chapman, 2001

38 Solms, 2009

39 Seng, 2009

40 Wessells, 2007; Wessells & Monteiro, 2001

41 Described by John Caulker, Executive director of Fambul Tok, Freetown, Sierra Leone, at the Course Design Seminar on Reconciliation and Coexistence, December 7–9, 2009, Stellenbosch, South Africa.

42 The following is based on Charles Rojzman describing his work to me in July, 2010. In 2004 I observed part of a training of trainers (facilitators) that he conducted in his approach.

22

Raising Inclusively Caring, Morally Courageous Children and Altruism Born of Suffering

Raising inclusively caring children with moderate respect for authority is important for a peaceful future.

Certain experiences can help people who have been victimized and are psychologically wounded to become caring and helpful, motivated to prevent others' suffering.

There are two outcomes of child rearing that can affect group violence: the kind of persons children become, and the kind of group members they will be. Raising children so that they become adults who care about the welfare of other people, who feel empathy and responsibility for others' welfare, and whose caring extends to people outside the boundaries of their own group makes group violence less likely. So does helping them develop a moderate, rather than overly strong respect for authority.

Children also need to become sensitive to devaluation or dehumanization; it is important that they learn that it is usually in people's minds, not inherent in its objects. They need to be taught the value and habits of active bystandership, as well as the potential people have and the power they can gain to influence events positively, especially as they join with other people. Active bystandership requires feelings of responsibility, caring values and empathy, a sense of effectiveness, and often moral courage as well. It also crucially requires the capacity to use one's judgment in assessing the meaning of events. Children should learn about the conditions that generate group violence, including knowledge about and awareness of how groups operate and how they influence individuals. This increases the ability to judge the meaning of events, and it inoculates people to some degree against the harmful influence of social conditions, culture, and the dynamics of groups.

The expression of moral values, responsibility, or empathy in action also requires what I have called a connected self. In individualistic societies many people develop autonomous selves, an extreme version of which I call the "disconnected self," a very autonomous and possibly emotionally cut-off person.

Psychologists have contrasted the autonomous self with the relational self, deeply rooted in relationships to others and community. This is more character- istic of people in collectivist societies, and it is found more in women than men in Western societies. But at the extreme, people can be so embedded in rela- tionships to individuals and in their group that they are incapable of indepen- dent judgment and opposition to their group's activities. What I have called a connected self is balanced, capable of entering into connections with other people, but also capable of independent judgment and, when appropriate and necessary, opposition to the other people and to the group's activities and direction.[1] A self so constituted contributes to, and may be a prerequisite for, moral courage.

Socialization for Caring and Helping

Two core aspects of such socialization are love and affection for and experienced by the child, and guidance that promotes the values of caring and helping. Children who are loved and nurtured will feel good about themselves and trust other people. In contrast, children who are harshly treated, who experience neglect and frequent punishment, will feel vulnerable, mistrust other people, and tend to see people and the world as dangerous. Unfortunately, in many cul- tures, severe physical punishment of children is the standard practice. In the United States "each year 3 million children ...are reported to Child Protective Services for child abuse and neglect."[2] Research has also shown that emotional neglect and disinterest in and unresponsiveness to children can have even greater negative emotional impact than physical abuse, perhaps because it is more relentless.

Love and nurturance must be accompanied by positive guidance, with appro- priate rules and values, and models of caring. Guidance that promotes caring and helping includes explaining to children the consequences of their actions on other people[3]—both their harmful actions that diminish others'physical or emotional well-being or hurt their feelings, and their helpful actions.[4] It includes adult and peer models of caring and helping. The beneficial influence of this is shown both in academic research and in the study of rescuers in Europe. Rescuers often had at least one humanistic parent who cared about and helped people. The parents also engaged with people outside the group.[5] If children are to develop inclusive caring, the concern with others'welfare that adults show, including their examples of caring actions, must extend to people outside their own group.

Leading children and youth to engage in helpful action, learning by doing, increases later helping.[6] As we help people, as we engage with their needs, pro- tect them, reduce their distress, or improve their welfare, we come to feel more responsible for them and value their well-being more. We also come to see ourselves as helpful people. Progressively, our caring can extend to the welfare of people in general.

In nontechnological societies, children participate in significant ways in maintaining the family, for example, by caring for younger children and tending farm animals. They tend to be more altruistic and less egoistic than children who have no responsibilities or have limited responsibilities they would not see as being of significant value to others, such as cleaning up their rooms. They offer help more, actually help more, and ask less for help than children in societies where they don't engage in such helpful activities.[7] Research has also shown that children who take care of pets are more helpful.[8] Children who are oldest siblings respond more to an emergency than same-age younger siblings, perhaps because they have responsibilities at home, including taking care of younger siblings.[9]

In my research, children who were led to make toys for poor, hospitalized children were later more helpful, especially if the benefits of their actions, such as the good feelings their actions produced in the recipients, were pointed out to them. Older children were more helpful after they spent time teaching younger children, whether they taught them skills in helping others, such as first aid, or how to make toys. The more cooperative the relationship between the teacher and the child they taught, the more it increased later helping by the teacher. Teaching is an inherently helpful activity, and these children learned by doing.[10] When children are led to engage in a helpful activity, if they are then called helpful by an adult, this further increases their later helping.[11]

On the basis of her research on parenting, developmental psychologist Diana Baumrind described authoritarian families, in which reasons for rules are not explained and children must obey these rules without questioning, and permissive families, in which parents do not provide guidance. They either don't set rules or don't insist that the children follow the rules.[12] In contrast to these is "authoritative" child rearing, the adults both setting rules and explaining to children the reasons for them. In these families parents exercise sufficient control so that children act according to essential values, and the rules that express these values. Baumrind regards "firm control" as an aspect of this kind of parenting. Firm control is not harsh control. It works best when it is in a context of love and caring, with adults talking with children, listening to them, and when it is reasonable and appropriate, yielding to them. Harsh control has contrary effects.

Effective control in important domains must be balanced by giving children a voice in their families and schools. Children ought to learn that they can use their judgment, express their positive values in words and action, and if necessary challenge authority. They need to feel empowered to express their ideas and act according to their values even in the face of opposition, and within limits, even in the face of potential threat, at least the threat of unpopularity and exclusion. This empowerment can be fostered by allowing and encouraging children to participate in decision making in the home, and in expressing their ideas in discussions with teachers and peers about rules for the classroom and about life in their school. Such encouragement, together with respect for their ideas and beliefs, can give children confidence and develop the habit of expressing and acting according to their beliefs. When adults support children in having a voice, and in acting according to their values even when doing so may be unpopular, they promote moral courage. They also moderate respect for authority and help develop critical consciousness—children thinking for themselves about the meaning of events.[13]

Positive socialization practices develop caring values, empathy, and responsibility. They fulfill basic needs constructively. Negative practices frustrate and can transform basic needs and their expression. In place of the need for effectiveness and control, they can develop a need for, or at least special satisfaction in, having power. For children and adults who have not been able to satisfy their basic needs constructively, power offers security and effectiveness, and it strengthens identity. But a strong need for or satisfaction in having power makes destructive need satisfaction more likely. It can lead to manipulation, domination, or aggression.

The need for power can develop not only through deprivation but also through encouragement and reinforcement. Adults can encourage, reward, or at least accept a child's use of power over others. Successfully dominating others, by taking other children's toys, or getting recognition for becoming a leader even if it is through psychological or physical force, can turn the child's need for effectiveness into a need for power.

However the need for power develops, as with any need once it becomes an important personal goal, high in a person's hierarchy of goals, it is difficult to change it. But a practice we have successfully used with aggressive boys is worth trying. One of my students Darrell Spielman and I[14] worked with small groups of boys who were rated aggressive by their teachers and received frequent in-school suspensions. Session by session we described to them basic human needs, as well as constructive and destructive ways to fulfill them. In each session we also had them role play everyday situations in which they might frequently use aggression. We provided the first such situation; they were usually able to provide others. In one situation, for example, a boy put his school bag on a chair at a table in the school cafeteria where he was going to have lunch with his friends. While he went back to the classroom to get something, another boy removed his bag and took his seat, with no seat left at the table.

The boys first role played each scene the way they would normally act, that is, aggressively. Then they role played it by engaging in constructive actions to both accomplish their immediate goals and fulfill basic needs—for connection, effectiveness, and positive identity. They role played each scene several times, shifting actors for the roles of the aggrieved boy, the opponent, and bystanders. They also videotaped each performance and then watched and discussed it. In a school with a problematic social climate, aggressive boys in a comparison group who participated in an alternative activity became more aggressive over time, as

measured by teacher ratings and detentions. The boys who received this training became slightly less aggressive over time and were in the end significantly
less aggressive than those in the comparison group.[15]

The practices of positive socialization, especially those that moderate respect
for authority and allow children "voice" and participation in decision making,
demand transformation by parents and teachers, even in Western individualist
cultures. They would be especially challenging for parents and teachers in collectivist, authority-oriented societies, as they are contrary to cultural modes of
conduct. To develop the use of such practices, adults need to understand their
value and to receive training in necessary skills.

It may seem presumptuous to advocate what are essentially Western ideals.
But rather than showing disrespect for others' culture, advocating for changes
in cultural characteristics and practices that can contribute to hostility and violence between groups, or passivity in the face of it, shows respect for people's
lives and well-being, and for peace. That said, practices that are contrary to a
culture must be introduced in respectful and culturally sensitive ways.

Altruism Born of Suffering

Research on altruism has focused on its positive roots, such as love and positive
guidance. Research on victimization, whether by physical or sexual abuse or
group violence, has focused on its negative effects, including aggression, mental
health problems, and difficulties in functioning. But many people who have suffered are concerned with and act to protect and help others. In 1989 I developed
a questionnaire on values and helping for the magazine *Psychology Today*. Over
7000 people filled out and returned it, and many wrote accompanying letters in
response to my request to do so. Some people wrote that because of the way they
suffered in their own lives, they wanted to do all they could to help others who
have suffered and to prevent suffering.[16*]

Case studies, autobiographies, media stories, and sociological/demographic
data show that many Holocaust survivors are in social service professions.[17]
Both such evidence and anecdotal information indicate that many people who
have been victimized or have suffered greatly through loss or in other ways are
highly altruistic.[18] Somewhat surprisingly, given the past emphasis on the negative effects of victimization and suffering, college students in the United States
who have experienced bad treatment in their families; suffered discrimination,
persecution, and violence as members of their group (a good number of the
latter students were born in other countries); or suffered in natural disasters
reported on the average more empathy with and more feelings of responsibility
to help victims of the 2004 Asian tsunami than did students who indicated that
they had not suffered in these ways. The former were also more likely to agree to
participate in collecting money for tsunami victims.[19]

How do people move from suffering to caring about and helping others? How does this happen, especially in the case of victimization, which often creates a negative orientation to other people that is antithetical to caring about their welfare? On the basis of research in psychology, my observations while working in settings where people have been victimized, my own personal experiences,[20] and the research we have conducted, I believe that a number of experiences— before, during and after victimization—promote altruism born of suffering (see Fig. 22.1).

Positive socialization before victimization, which provides the experience of caring connections, can remind people in the wake of victimization that others can be caring and life can have meaning. Such experiences enhance resilience. During victimization, there may be two primary protective influences. One is action by the targets of victimization to help themselves, to whatever limited extent this is possible, or to help family members or other people. A 7-year-old child in Holland during World War II remained in the hospital after she recovered from an illness because a neighbor who brought her clothes told her it was safer and that by staying there she would delay the deportation of her family. When German soldiers came and began to gather people, she put on her clothes, walked out of the hospital, and walked 10 blocks to the neighbor's house.[21] Such an action can affirm a sense of effectiveness and the ability to improve one's life—and the life of others.

Receiving help from people at the time of victimization also promotes altruism born of suffering. Such help was reported by Holocaust survivors in Israel who were part of the peace movement, in contrast to those who were not.[22] This means that active bystanders, helpers, and rescuers not only save people from suffering and death but also help save them psychologically. By experiencing goodness, people become more able to live goodness in their later lives.

After victimization, one primary contributor to altruism born of suffering is healing—through therapy, talking and writing about one's experiences (ideally in the company of others), societal processes that seek truth and justice, understanding the roots of violence and avenues for the prevention of future violence, and connections to other people. A second primary contributor is support by and connections to caring people. People who come from difficult backgrounds or have been abused and are resilient, or altruistic, often talk or write about a relative, a teacher, or a neighbor who took interest in them and provided support or help.[23] A third contributor, which is likely to enter especially after some degree of healing, is to actually begin to help other people. Helping others can help with further healing and facilitate learning by doing. It can transform pain and suffering into empathy and increased caring for other people's welfare. It can re-create lost meaning in life. A fourth influence is the example of models of caring and helping. Most of these influences are important at all three points, before, during, and after suffering. They strengthen the self and create a more positive view of the world and other people.

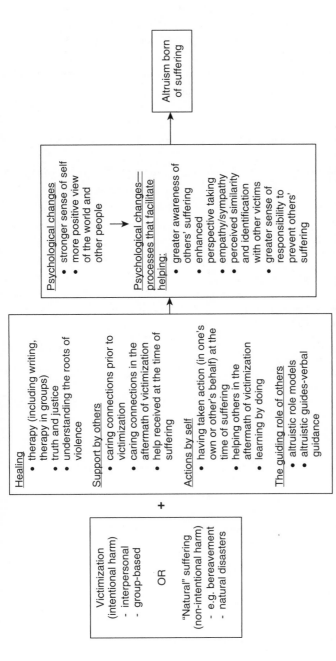

Figure 22.1. *Experiences and psychological changes leading to altruism born of suffering.* (from Staub & Vollhardt, 2008).

All that I have written about healing applies to both victimized children and adults. However, for children, healing practices have to be particularly sensitive to their age and vulnerability. Engagement with their experience needs to be less direct. With very young children, it may be through play. With teenagers it may be through reading about and writing stories about others' painful experience. Older children, when they are psychologically ready, may be encouraged to write about their own experiences and to talk about them with adults or youth of their own age who have had similar experiences.

Summary

The experience of nurturance and affection, guidance by positive values and rules that express them, pointing out to children the consequences of their behavior on other people, and guiding them to engage in helpful action jointly contribute to the development of empathy, a feelings of responsibility for others' welfare, moral values, and caring and helping. Guiding children to learn to fulfill basic needs in constructive ways also contributes. Positive models are important, and when they show caring about people outside the group, they contribute to inclusive caring. People who have been victimized or suffered for other reasons can become caring and helpful through a variety of experiences, such as being helped by others, helping themselves and others, healing, understanding, and receiving support from other people. Coming to understand the influence of groups on oneself and others is also important.

Notes

1 Staub, 1993
2 van der Kolk, 2009, p. 455
3 Eisenberg, Fabes, & Spinrad, 2006; Hoffman, 2000; Staub, 1979, 2005c
4 Staub, 1971b
5 Oliner & Oliner, 1988
6 Eisenberg et al., 2006; Staub, 1979, 2003a, 2005c
7 Whiting & Whiting, 1975
8 Murphy, 1937
9 Staub, 1970b
10 Staub, 1979, 2003a
11 Grusec, Kuczynski, Rushton, & Simutis, 1978
12 Baumrind, 1971, 1975
13 see Staub, 2005c
14 Spielman & Staub, 2000
15 Ibid.

16 A report on the results of this survey is in Staub, 2003a, Chapter 9. The magazine Psychology Today suspended publication for about two years the month they were to publish a report on the survey

17 Valent, 1998

18 O'Connell Higgins, 1994; Staub, 2003a, 2005c, Staub & Vollhardt, 2008

19 Vollhardt & Staub, 2009

20 Staub, 2008b

21 Ibid.

22 Staub & Vollhardt, 2008

23 Ibid; O'Connell Higgins, 1994

23

Recommendations and Conclusions

I discussed some successes in prevention; in all cases there was already ongoing violence, at times mass killing or genocide. The violence in Bosnia and Kosovo was stopped by military action. The relatively low level of violence that occurred over many years in Northern Ireland was limited by British troops maintaining order in their fortress-like vehicles. The resolution of the conflict was helped by policies that improved the economic and social situation of Catholics, as well as by the work of many intermediaries, including Tony Blair as British prime minister, Bill Clinton, George Mitchell, and others, working with local actors. It was helped by some Catholics and Protestants engaging in dialogue all along. It was also helped by each group having political representation, so that they could move from terrorist acts to political processes. The repression and violence in South Africa was stopped and the conflict resolved as a result of internal resistance by the black population, probably also both by violence by the opposition, the African National Congress, and that the violence was limited, by the actions by the international community, ostracism and boycotts, activated by internal resistance and violent reactions to it by the government, and by the development of support among some white South Africans for policy change. In Kenya, the violence was halted by the engagement of very high-level intermediaries. In Macedonia, a combination of U.N. peacekeepers, prior work done by international organizations, and actions by politicians who responded to grievances of the Albanian minority by changing the constitutions and laws prevented further violence.

Some elements of reconciliation I have described were present, but most of them were not introduced in most of these cases, and it is unclear to what degree real reconciliation has taken place. The Northern Ireland peace was made uncertain by recurring violence in late 2009, although in January 2010 the Ulster Defense Association, the major Protestant paramilitary group, announced that it fully disarmed, fulfilling one of the last requirements of the 1998 peace accord. The group also apologized for killing in the course of the conflict 400 people, mostly Catholic civilians. In a number of other situations, for example, in Kenya, significant issues of group relations and power differences were not addressed. In Bosnia they were mainly addressed by the groups separating. While halting violence prevents even greater violence, both early prevention and reconciliation must be our goal.

In this chapter I summarize actions to take in the primary cases in this book. I then discuss what is required to create a harmonious world with less, little, perhaps someday no mass violence. First, however, I will consider the what, how, and who of prevention.

How and Who: Actions and Actors

The primary focus in this book has been on *what* needs to be accomplished, the outcomes that in turn prevent violence between groups or lead to reconciliation (e.g., humanizing the other/developing positive attitudes toward the other, inclusive caring, truth, justice, healing, equitable economic development) and the *actions* needed to bring them about (e.g., contact, positive socialization, truth commissions, justice processes). But describing desirable outcomes and actions is easier than the how and the who—how to bring about the activities that lead to these outcomes, and who is to engage in the actions needed and to create the systems required for consistent action.

In Table 23.1, I summarize some of the "how and who."[1] The table addresses the "how," which itself constitutes action, by focusing largely on training various parties in prevention and reconciliation. Those who are trained, the essential "who's," are the primary actors. Some of the actions listed in Table 23.1 have been taking place, but to a limited extent and haphazard manner, with nongovernmental organizations (NGOs) and international nongovernmental organizations (INGOs) as the main actors. They develop new knowledge and practice, but they also rediscover old ones and engage in overlapping work. Some of this is good; many parties are needed to address these huge problems. But the power of prevention and reconciliation will increase if training potential actors becomes a standard and if actions that flow from it are organized and coordinated to a reasonable extent. This requires the creation of proper structures. Our knowledge of what to focus on to prevent violence (the outcomes, such as healing, positive attitudes toward the other and a constructive ideology), what actions to take to bring these outcomes about (such as engagement with painful experience, contact, dialogue to create a shared vision), how to bring these actions about, and who are the individuals and organizations to do it, is still developing.

Table 23.1 Early Prevention and Reconciliation: Some Actions and Actors

The following should be activities that regularly take place in every country, and internationally, since every country is either in the danger of violence at some point or a potential bystander that can help to prevent violence.

- Working with/training members of the media:
  - To promote knowledge and understanding of the origins, and the impact/consequences of hostility and violence between groups, as well as avenues to prevention and reconciliation. For example, the media need to understand the psychological woundedness of groups and how this is expressed in policies and practices, and to understand that violence and its psychological and institutional bases evolve progressively, so that they can notice and point to small changes and their dangers.
  - To promote knowledge and skills in writing about events in ways that avoid dehumanization, humanizes each group, and presents issues between them in constructive ways.
  - To become aware of: how a group's culture, including their own, affects policies and practices; the tendency for self-censorship, to not deviate from the climate or ways of thinking that is becoming dominant in the group;[a] and the importance of their role in enabling the population to use their "critical consciousness" in assessing the meaning of events and to become active bystanders.
  - To generate media that educate people and promote culture change. The media can promote understanding (as identified above), present wide-ranging discussion of issues from varied perspectives (pluralism), and moderate respect for authority so that authorities can be challenged and are judged on the basis of their actions.

Who should do this work:
  - Schools of journalism, whose faculty ought to include people who are knowledgeable in these matters or are willing to receive training in them.
  - Organizations and foundations concerned with issues of group violence can set up media-training programs. For example, the Dart Foundation has a program of training journalists how to write about trauma, offering fellowships and seminars to journalists from around the world. This program partly works through journalism departments at universities. The nongovernmental organization (NGO) Radio LaBenevolencija, my partner in our radio projects in East Africa, is working on developing an academic program at a university, in collaboration with other universities that have programs related to group violence (and with me), to train people in the media to create public education programs.
  - The United Nations, governments and their institutions, academic institutions, and NGOs ought to create training programs for members of the media. Organizations already engaged with these issues should start this effort, such as the United States Institute for Peace, The U.S. Holocaust Museum, the Woodrow Wilson Center, and comparable organizations around the world, for example, the Folke Bernadotte Academy in Sweden.

(Continued)

Table 23.1 continued

- Activist citizen groups working for the prevention of mass violence should exert influence on governments and relevant institutions to set up training programs for media (as well as leaders—see below). They should engage in advocacy with media outlets to generate, and with funding organizations to fund, relevant programs.
- Working with mid- and high-level national leaders and community leaders, in both endangered countries at risk for violence, and bystander nations:
  - To promote understanding of origins, prevention, and reconciliation (as in the first point under media). When appropriate, this should include leaders' understanding of their own psychological woundedness as members of their group, due to past historical events, and understanding groups they are in conflict with, their woundedness and needs, the importance of a complex truth, and so on.
  - To develop the knowledge and skills to create policies, practices, and institutions to prevent violence and promote peace; for example, how they might create constructive ideologies; and the ability to judge the impact of their policies on other parties.
  - To develop skills in bringing about contact, engagement, and dialogue with leaders of hostile groups that can increase understanding and trust.
  - To develop awareness of the important role of nations as bystanders and how to be effective bystanders.
  - To become aware of the pressures of the contexts in which they as leaders operate and how these may change the hierarchy of their values and goals, and to learn ways to inoculate themselves against undesirable changes—such as finding like-minded others.[b]
  - Often in the United States, analysts gain knowledge and then provide information and analysis to decision makers. It is important for decision makers themselves to develop knowledge and skills in prevention.

Who should do this work:
- There have been varied but not regular trainings. One of them is the leaders' training used mainly in Burundi developed by Howard Wolpe and associates at the Woodrow Wilson Center. My associates and I have trained leaders in Rwanda. Occasional training has been provided by a program at Columbia and George Mason Universities on Engaging Government in Genocide Prevention.[c] However, ongoing programs are needed.
- There should be widely available trainings, participation becoming a standard practice for leaders from all over the world. Agencies responsible for or engaged in work on prevention, such as the United Nations and the United States Institute of Peace, and others to be created such as the Central Offices for the Prevention of Mass Violence, and International Centers for the Prevention of Genocide, should be among the institutions organizing these training programs.

(Continued)

Table 23.1 continued

- Training diplomats, the staff of international NGOs and NGOs, academics, and practitioners:
  - Similar to training in the other groups. Also learning how group traumas and leaders' traumas affect emotions, perceptions, and actions; the characteristics of cultures that affect leaders' and followers' behavior such as devaluation, pride, and face saving; and histories of group relations. Training in skills to effectively engage with leaders and citizens in varying contexts.

Who should do this training:
  - The same agencies that provide the leadership trainings.
- Providing public education.
  - Government agencies, NGOs, and universities should engage in wide-spread public education, along the same lines as the trainings, through television, radio, print media, books and pamphlets, lectures, discussions, and "town meetings." Like the training of leaders and diplomats, this should become a standard process everywhere. It can generate societal dialogue, promote and facilitate dialogue between leaders and group members, and encourage dialogue across group lines. It can activate and support internal and external bystanders.
- Providing material but contingent aid:
  - By outsiders to help address the economic aspects of a country's difficult life conditions.

Who should do this work:
  - The international community has been helping countries with economic problems through direct aid and through the International Monetary Fund and the World Bank. At times of intense crises, such aid is essential. Even then, but certainly under more normal conditions, aid should be contingent on the recipient countries moving toward pluralism and democracy, ceasing repression and discrimination against subgroups, and reducing inequality. According to some critics, the International Monetary Fund and the World Bank often demand that countries they help enact measures that create a market economy in ways that increase the wealth of some and the poverty of others.[d]
- Other countries creating commercial and cultural ties to isolated countries, especially when the predictors of group violence are present.
- Providing capacity building in countries at risk of or recovering from violent conflict: that is, training in constitutional, parliamentary, power-sharing processes and security; and knowledge and skills to promote economic development, education, and to build constructive institutions.

(Continued)

Table 23.1 continued

Who should do this work:
  - — Constitutional lawyers, former and current members of parliaments, economists, educators. The United States, among others, has provided such training and expertise to Rwanda since 1994.
  - — Such activities should be organized and funded by governments, the United Nations, foundations, and NGOs. They should be coordinated and made into standard operating procedure.
- Helping to develop schools that treat children equally, promote inclusive caring and moral courage, and teach history that is respectful of all subgroups of society. Teaching about past instances of mass violence can help students understand the importance of active bystandership.

Who should do this work:
  - — A few educational organizations, such as Facing History and Ourselves in the United States, have extensive international experience in teacher training and curriculum development in this realm.
  - — To develop systematic, ongoing training requires creating organizations central to prevention and reconciliation focused on children, and consistent funding for them.
- Meetings by diplomats and external leaders with leaders of at-risk countries to help them shift course.
- Exerting influence on the United States and other governments to create the structures required to initiate, organize, and systematize prevention activities.

Who should do this work:
  - — In addition to actions previously listed in this table, citizen action is required, people joining in advocacy groups, which can be organized as NGOs, and supported by individuals and foundations. Churches and secular organizations should be involved both as allies and as independent advocacy groups.

[a]Staub, 1989.
[b]For an outline of one possible curriculum for such a training, see www.ervinstaub.com.
[c]The engaging governments program was initiated by Andrea Bartoli. See also http://www.auschwitzinstitute.org/ for a program that was conducted at Auschwitz
[d]Klein, 2007.

Summaries of What Might Be Done in the Primary (Contemporary) Cases

Terrorism

There are varied causes of terrorism and varied reasons that individuals are attracted to it, or engage in it. On a group level they include repression and other harmful actions against groups; discrimination; conflict among subgroups in a society over rights, autonomy, and exclusion from public processes and the response of the weaker party to these; great changes in the world in culture, technology, and ways of life; inequity and unfavorable comparison by groups between their own situation and that of others; and injustice or the perception of injustice. All of these frustrate basic needs. Ideology (including religion-based ideology) and indoctrination of people in it are further contributors. These can lead individuals to create and join terrorist groups. At times a societal climate develops in which terrorism against outsiders is accepted, tacitly or actively supported, even celebrated.

Sometimes the impact of social changes and states redirecting hostility away from themselves join in ways that generate terrorism against outgroups. When changes in culture, technology, and mores intrude from the outside and are not digested or integrated, especially in traditional/repressive societies, outsiders may be blamed for corrupting religion and indigenous culture. Sometimes states sponsor terrorism or create or support terrorist groups, using them as proxies to fulfill their aims. When there is a visible and widespread terrorist movement, individuals who seek adventure or escape from their lives and a burdensome identity, may also be attracted.

Commentators refer to humiliation of Arabs/Muslims as a contributing factor in Muslim terrorism. Humiliation is "real" in Palestinians, many of whom have lived in refugee camps and under occupation for many years. If other Muslim groups feel humiliation it may be partly the result of a past history of greatness and lost greatness, as Muslim countries have fallen behind the West in technology and intellectual and cultural evolution, and the West continues to dominate in these domains.

Resentment, anger, and humiliation also have to do with colonial domination, Western interference, including support for repressive governments, and Western economic policies. All of these have been significant in the Middle East. Antipathies toward the West have to do with Muslim ethnocentrism as well, and with Muslim religion, which like other religions claims superiority. The intermixture of religious and political life in Islam makes it understandable that religion would become a source of a nationalistic vision of a global Muslim society, the Umma, and a caliphate, a joining of religion, community, state, and power.

Terrorism may also be a response to recent and ongoing Western actions, such as unwillingness of the United States and the West to effectively engage with the Israeli–Palestinian conflict so that it is resolved, the war in Iraq and Afghanistan, exploitative business practices, and more. Unfortunately, even positive actions have downsides. Many European countries have allowed a large inflow of Muslim immigrants, who have been provided substantial material (and social) support when their jobs disappeared. But life changes associated with their dislocation, in addition to their experiences of prejudice and discrimination in these countries, frustrate psychological needs and give rise to resentment and anger.

As with genocide, a combination of influences generates terrorism, but even under activating conditions, it usually involves only a small minority of individuals. In those individuals, apart from experiences as group members, family and other personal experiences, and current circumstances that may frustrate basic needs, can draw them to ideologies and groups that provide potential meaning to life, connection and community. Idealist, respondents and lost souls may become involved through friends-associates, pushed by a societal climate and pulled by the attraction of an active movement. Certain cognitive styles (such as a need for "cognitive closure"), and an authoritarian personality also make involvement more likely.

Who are the people who start terrorist movements? Sometimes they are idealists, who adopt others' ideals and ideologies, transforming them into violent action. This was the case with Al-Zawahiri, who came from a well to do family but was inspired by the ideas of Qutb, and responded to the hostility to Islam by the Egyptian government. Sometimes terrorism begins as people fight against powerful others for freedom and rights, their own or others'. But often terror is a the result of a simple understanding of the complex world people live in, as destructive ideologies and a violent group help fulfill basic needs destructively.

How can Al-Qaeda, Palestinian terrorism, and other future terrorism be prevented? Using force, and killing and punishing perpetrators have been the primary methods. Jerrold Post[2] stresses the importance of inhibiting people from joining terrorist groups, as well as helping them exit, and reducing support for such groups by delegitimizing their leaders. All these are useful. But it is crucial to lessen the motivation for terrorism to arise.

Western countries must stop supporting nations with repressive governments. They must do more to address problem situations and conflicts of interest in non-violent ways. In the material realm, they need to help economic development in vulnerable nations and work to make it equitable. This contributes to just group relations and provides ordinary people with opportunities for constructive employment, a decent material existence and a sense of dignity. In this process connections can develop between groups, and countries, that overcome isolation and us-them differentiation. External parties need to collaborate with internal parties in fostering equitable development and democratization, in ways consistent with indigenous culture and religion.

People, young and old, need hope. Young people who might be attracted to ideologies and groups that move them to violence need alternatives. These can be provided by constructive communities, youth organizations and civic institutions, and schools that build connections between students. Connections to peaceful groups and society make it unlikely that the motivation to create or join violent groups arises. They help prevent radicalization. People also need to be sensitized to the suffering violence creates, in a concrete manner, involving real people. Influential people who are appropriate role models and ideals for youth speaking out against terrorist acts also helps prevent radicalization.

We must work to generate a shared global vision. Technology, business, and communication are globalized. People move around the world with ease. All countries must address prejudice in their attitudes and practices toward their own people, including immigrants. Societies must humanize all their people and create institutions that support people. The power of ideas is great, and ideologies can generate a spirit of inclusiveness, a vision of human beings across the globe thriving together. A global vision of interconnection and community would be an important part of the prevention of all forms of mass violence. But such a vision must be followed by action. The United States is one of a number of powerful countries that can use its power and influence to propagate this vision, followed by actions that make it real.

A significant challenge is to address the pain and anger of young Muslims who respond to the suffering of other Muslims in wars fought against them by the United States, as well as Russia and other countries. It is difficult to see how they can address their grievances in this realm by constructive means. If the international community works hard and with some success to resolve such conflicts by peaceful means, that can lessen the anger of some potential terrorists. It would make it possible for them to join groups that work to promote such peaceful resolution of conflicts.

Rwanda

There is stability, substantial security, and significant economic development in Rwanda. People have gained confidence that enables them to work hard and to create their own and their country's future.[3] The laws dictate equal access to education and jobs, and to the extent they are followed this will improve group relations. But political freedom is limited. The prospect of being charged with divisionism and genocidal ideology eliminate dissenting voices. Potentially constructive leaders leave the country—as did, for example, Joseph Sebarenzi, a Tutsi survivor who was the speaker of Parliament.

The psychological situation is problematic. Posttraumatic distress is high, and depression has increased. The passage of time allows trauma and grief to come to the fore, and the *gacaca* was likely to activate them. Fear remains. The victim group in power is a small minority and not surprisingly continues to feel endangered.[4] Paradoxically perhaps, the government limiting open discussion can increase fear, since Tutsis and Hutus don't know what the other party is thinking and feeling and cannot work on their relations.

Helping Tutsis heal seems of genuine concern to the government, but while many we have worked with have come to understand that Hutus are also wounded, their need to heal has not received attention. The *gacaca* focused on truth and justice, matters of great importance. Now the time has come to facilitate reconnection between groups: establish the complex truth, acknowledge harm done to Hutus as well, celebrate "righteous" Hutus who were active bystanders during the genocide, and create shared commemorations so that people can remember and grieve together. The time has come to move toward creating a shared history that acknowledges legitimate Hutu perspectives (not the perspective of Hutus who hate or deny the genocide). It has come to allow the expression of varied views, which would also moderate respect for authority, and political freedom with the participation of all political groups that do not promote hate and violence. The time has come to see unity as something to be achieved over time by engaging the varied segments of society in the shared goal of creating it.

An important issue in building the future is addressing the violence against Hutu civilians in Rwanda and the Congo in the course of the civil war, fighting the genocide, and afterwards. This is a challenging matter, given the responsibility of the current leaders in it. Acknowledgment, as well as expressions of regret and apology, is crucial. With care so that it does not negate them, these should be accompanied by helping people understand the conditions under which the violence took place: the psychological impact of the genocide, the role of the war between Hutus and Tutsis, the continuing threat posed by genocidaires— and the sad but real human inclination for revenge. It is unclear whether punishment is practically possible, given the political conditions and that some of the violence was presumably part of RPF and RPA policy. But even limited justice would serve reconciliation; its form could be jointly developed by the international justice system and Rwandans. The government ought to acknowledge the violence and begin such a process. A justice system that gives people confidence that future violence by either group will not be tolerated should help.

Our work in promoting reconciliation and prevention, such as emphasis on a pluralistic society and active bystandership, and the political situation are at odds with each other. But the changes our work creates, which since it reaches most of the population may represent culture change, can begin to manifest themselves with a change in the political situation.

Israel–Palestine

In January 25, 2009, after the powerful Israeli military response to the thousands of Hamas rockets and Hamas' refusal to renew a cease-fire, *The New York*

Times columnist Thomas Friedman summarized the urgency and great challenge of bringing peace: "It is five to midnight and before the clock strikes 12 all we need to do is rebuild Fatah, merge it with Hamas, elect an Israeli government that can freeze settlements, court Syria, and engage Iran—while preventing it from going nuclear—just so we can get the parties to talking. Whoever lines up all the pieces of this diplomatic Rubik's Cube deserves two Nobel Prizes."[5] A year and a half later there is relative calm, but the core challenges remain.

The new Israeli prime minister in 2009, Netanyahu, at first did not accept the idea of an independent Palestinian state. Israelis certainly would not accept a one-state solution, that is, Jews and Palestinians in a single state. What would this leave, other than permanent occupation? Under U.S. pressure Netanyahu changed his "public" mind, with the condition that the Palestinian state be demilitarized. Apparently he came to accept a two-state solution. U.S. suggestion for some Arab gestures, such as allowing Israeli flights over Arab territory, was firmly rejected by Saudi Arabia, wanting Israel to take steps first to resolve the Israeli–Palestinian conflict.

To resolve the conflict, motivated and wise leaders on both sides have to consider each other's circumstances: the political situation, the psychological situation, and the cultural, security, and practical issues to be resolved. Consider the rockets that Hamas shot into Israel, a self-defeating enterprise from a pragmatic point of view. They did little physical damage, yet generated much hostility. But this practice may have had cultural, psychological, and political meaning. "Saving face" is important in Arab culture, and given Israeli power and the humiliation of occupation, the rockets could maintain Palestinian pride, saying, "we are here; our shoulders are not pinned to the ground." With the rockets Hamas could make a statement to itself, to Israel, to other Palestinians and the Arab world. It could maintain the image of itself as a fighter, and serve, at least in Hamas' view, to maintain its influence among Palestinians. It may have also have been attempting at the time to maintain its role as the primary opposition to Israel, in its competition with Hezbollah.

The "asymmetry" between Israelis and Palestinians may make the resolution of the conflict more difficult. Hamas' situation as the weaker party, its proclaimed ideology, its conflict with Fatah, and saving face make it difficult for it to change directions. But as I discussed it in Chapter 13, according to a number of observers, Hamas has moved significantly from its original positions, and would be ready to abide by a peace agreement negotiated by Mahmoud Abbas and approved by a Palestinian plebiscite.[6] Positive engagement initiated by Israel might not only improve relations with Hamas, but also between Hamas and Fatah.

To the extent Israelis believe that Hamas—and Palestinians in general—are a mortal and *unchangeable* enemy, negotiation makes no psychological or political sense. But the Palestinian Liberation Organization once had a similar ideology and Fatah has changed, although its members sometimes make contrary statements, possibly in the face of the pressures of circumstance, such as the

Israeli attack on Gaza in 2008–2009. In 2009 and 2010, there has been collaboration between Israel and the Palestinian Authority in maintaining security in the West Bank, and Israel has been dismantling checkpoints.

Negotiations also don't make sense for people committed to a Greater Israel. Their ideology makes them blind both to the danger of continued conflict for Israel's long-term survival and to Palestinian suffering. But courageous Israeli leaders, supported by external parties, especially the United States, could initiate a reciprocal process. Initial success would highly likely bring support from substantial segments of both populations. Positive actions can start with words, in dialogue between leaders and people, including acknowledgment of harm done, regret about the losses of the other side, and acknowledgment of the many people on both sides who have worked for peace. Leaders on the two sides have not said such things. If the parties can move to concessions and agreements about practical issues, that would further affect the psychological situation.

For Israel to initiate such a process requires that Jews understand how past wounds have shaped their orientation to security, to be gained by power and force. It is an orientation of not only never again a Holocaust, but never again the weakness and vulnerability that made it possible. Given Jewish history, and that Jews misjudged Hitler's words and the beginning of the persecution under the Nazis, many believing that like earlier persecutions this would pass,[7] Israeli response to the words and actions of Hamas, Palestinians, and Arabs is understandable. This joins with the success, or seeming success—since Israel is still not secure— in the use of force since 1948.

But lessons from the past cannot be transferred in a direct manner to the present. Israeli Jews and their supporters need to see both how past Jewish suffering intensified their experience of collective threat and how their responses have maintained the threat. Such self-exploration, which can be led by intellectuals, political leaders, and the media, could help Israel reformulate its approach to security as something that can be better gained by taking risks for peace. I could also open more Israelis to empathy with Palestinian suffering.

Palestinians are also focused on their own suffering, past and current. Positive Israeli actions can create hope among Palestinians, whose attitudes have shifted at times of hope. Renewed hope may enable Palestinians to consider and come to understand both Israel's psychological situation and its real situation, the threat to it by Hamas, Hezbollah, Iran, and Syria, by terrorism, and by Arab hostility in general (and by the likelihood that by 2040 or 2050 Arabs will constitute the majority of Israel's citizens).[8] It may open them to Jewish suffering and to accepting responsibility for the suffering Palestinians have created. It may enable them to move from an orientation to the past, to what they have lost, to one in the present and future. For such change in psychology and behavior Palestinians will have to overcome psychological barriers intensified by occupation and difficult lives.

Positive actions, combined with ongoing dialogue between decision makers, can develop relationships and trust. This makes it possible to effectively address practical issues. But assuming that a Palestinian state comes into being, that does not dissolve mutual devaluation and hostility. Reconciliation can be furthered by acknowledgment of each others' narratives and by some form of a shared history. This may start with a commission—of historians, politicians, members of the media, and the population. A related commission can work on what to teach children in schools, in both groups, about the other group and shared history, to avoid indoctrination in devaluation and hate.

Creating a constructive ideology about life together is crucial, in place of the two destructive ideologies: the Hamas vision of life without the state of Israel, and the vision of a greater Israel that makes Palestinians an obstacle. Destructive ideological visions are best fought by an alternative, hopeful vision. Its central elements can be the economic development of the two countries, and friendly relations and peace between the two countries and in the region. A vision and practice of working together, collaboration, could replace enmity. Israel can make many contributions to joint economic development. But a constructive vision must also identify the contribution of the Palestinians, not just by providing labor, but in ways that affirm their identity and dignity. A constructive vision of the future could inspire Palestinians to initiate and engage in reconciliation processes, in the service of improving the welfare of the Palestinian people and of all people in the region.

To address divisions not only between but within the groups, concentrated action is needed by many external bystanders. Bystanders have helped create security by contributing to the training of Palestinian police. They may need to persuade the parties to use peacekeepers, ensuring that the United Nations provides them. As the journalist Stephen Kinzer wrote in relation to the Congo, "Security is the essential factor in nation-building. It cannot be an end in itself, nor should it be so overbearing that people feel repressed. Without security, though, there can be no development and no progress."[9] External parties need to work on reducing support for the use of force by Hezbollah and Hamas and on transforming these groups into constructive social organizations, which is part of the history and practice of both groups. Committed and determined, in place of halting and ambivalent, U.S. and international engagement could move the parties to engage in ongoing, persistent, rather than on and off dialogue. Important external bystanders include Arab and other Muslim countries, and Jews outside Israel.

Significant actions in creating a system of positive reciprocity can include, on the Israeli side, building no more settlements, and beginning to withdraw from those that cannot be part of a territory exchange—and giving the vacated buildings to the Palestinians rather than destroying them. There is great resistance to suspending the building of settlements in influential political groups, more than in the public in general. A partial suspension by the Netanyahu government created vocal opposition among his supporters. But according to news reports, only a minority of the settlers are in the West Bank because they are motivated to create a Greater Israel. On the Palestinian side, renouncing and stopping all attacks and changing Hamas ideology would presumably contribute to positive reciprocal actions. With a reciprocal process, the other's positive actions would not be interpreted as originating in weakness.

What could the Israeli government do to make peace? In February 2009 Kadima, one of the three major parties in Israel, won the most seats in parliament. Netanyahu invited Kadima and the Labor party to join the government, both more peace oriented than his Likud party, but did not agree to the condition set by Tzipi Livni, the leader of Kadima, to alternate in the position of prime minister.

He could reverse course, agree to this condition, and form a unity government. (Another future government could also form a unity government). But whether he does that or not, he could exchange Israeli territory for the territory some of the settlements occupy, and dismantle the rest. This would make reasonable boundaries between the states possible. He could agree to East Jerusalem as the capital of the Palestinian state. All this was agreed to in 2000 in the Clinton-led negotiations. He could propose and develop an economic zone for the two countries and, as part of it, create joint projects. Israel could offer training in technical realms to Palestinians. Israel could acknowledge its role in the dispersal and suffering of the Palestinians, and work with them and the international community on a reasonable arrangement for Palestinian refugees, primarily a combination of compensation and resettlement in the West Bank. As I proposed, joint commissions could be created to address a variety of issues.

As part of the agreement to create the Palestinian state, there would have to be a commitment by Palestinians to prevent violence against Israel. As for Israel, so for Palestinians, violence has become a hindrance rather than help for security and well being. Suicide on behalf of the group by members of the population could be replaced by moral and physical courage in working for peace, both by leaders and members of the community. Israel cannot expect perfect success in preventing violence, but international monitors should evaluate whether the Palestinian police do everything in their power, and substantial failure could invalidate the agreement. The recent success of Palestinian police units in maintaining security in the West Bank is promising. A timeline would need to be negotiated to fulfill these agreements and to assess whether the security needs of Israel are satisfied.

In working for regional peace, Israel should return the Golan Heights in exchange for a stable peace with Syria. This would require suspension by Syria of support for military actions by Hezbollah and Hamas. Syria could provide "good offices" between Israel, and Hezbollah and Hamas, and it might act as an intermediary to Iran.

In summary, constructive leadership on both sides would mean initiating and reciprocating positive actions. It would mean fostering more positive attitudes toward the other in their populations. It would mean engaging in persistent dialogue, using outside parties as needed to maintain positive contact and help develop agreements, as the two groups create a shared vision and resolve practical issues.

The Democratic Republic of the Congo

Although it has been receiving much less attention than any of the other tragic situations in the world, such as Darfur, the situation in the Congo has been the most challenging and damaging in the world in the first decade of the twenty-first century. Security is very important to address the influences leading to violence, although taking action cannot wait until security is established. Security requires an effective fighting force. Hutu militias continue to kill, rape, and abduct people. Congolese interviewed by Oxfam[10] have reported that the army rapes, loots, and kills, and U.N. peacekeepers with MONUC (mission of the United Nations in the Congo) are nowhere to be seen. Many members of the army are from militias integrated into it. Those who have remained violent, and violent members of the army, ought to be discharged. Healing, job skills, and reintegration into their original communities could prevent future violence by them.

The army and police both need training and supervision, which probably can only be provided by outsiders. They would need to convince the government to allow and invite such help, a government that in 2010 wants to reduce the number of peacekeepers in MONUC, which it regards as infringement on its sovereignty. Outsiders could also provide training in government operations, which might change the corrupt culture and ineffectiveness of the government, and in creating a functional justice system that would increase the capacity and will to punish perpetrators.

The Hutus militia (FDLR) that are led by and in part consist of former genocidaires in Rwanda must be dissolved. "Without progress on ending the FDLR problem once and for all, their presence in eastern Congo will contribute to regional instability .... and the promising Congo-Rwanda entente will be at risk."[11] A joint Congo-Rwanda military operation and subsequent Congo military operation has not eliminated this force. There should be engagement and negotiation with this group, offering the possibility for its members of reintegration into the community; followed as necessary by negotiation supported by a military/peacekeeping force; and military force against them as a last resort. As I have noted earlier, some members of this group have returned to Rwanda, in part due to communications from family there about the conditions in Rwanda, in part to radio programs like ours which gave them the vision of a different kind of life. This suggests that dialogue and engagement with them can make a difference.

Many members of the FDLR are too young to have been perpetrators during the genocide in Rwanda.[12] Who should be punished and to what degree is an important issue. But both those who are punished and who are not, and those who return to Rwanda and those who remain in the Congo, need healing, understanding their group's past actions, training in job skills and life skills, and reintegration into communities.

Much is needed in the Congo: healing and reconciliation, security, dialogue and negotiation between groups, contact across ethnic lines in working for shared goals, the development of the knowledge and practices of effective government, and the building of civic institutions. In Rwanda, many Western organizations and individuals have provided expertise, training, and consultation to build and rebuild societal institutions. They must develop relationships in the Congo, with the government, with NGOs, help create new NGOs, and do the same there.

Training leaders, the media, and influential parties from various ethnic groups and political factions could be of great benefit, making it more likely that they can create a shared vision for society and cooperate in working for its fulfillment. A constructive vision, societal institutions and practices that engender trust (such as policies involving land), developing natural resources for everyone's benefit, and equitable economic development would set the conditions for harmonious relations between groups.

Two other kinds of outsider actions are important. One is international agreements, and their enforcement, to stop companies outside the Congo from buying the minerals that are looted from the Congo. Not having markets would diminish the fighting that revolves around minerals. A step in this direction that I mentioned earlier was a provision about this included in the financial reform bill in the U.S. Senate. The other is Rwanda becoming a constructive actor in relation to the Congo. Rwanda has been engaged there since 1996, at first for justifiable reasons but increasingly in problematic ways. As of 2010, it appears much less engaged.

The Congolese and outside parties must also address the problem of the FDLR, thereby making sure that Rwanda has no reason to be involved—except in positive ways, to develop a peaceful relationship with the Congo. Rwandan policies that address the concerns and political role of Hutus in Rwanda would also help.

Conclusions: Creating a Less Violent, Harmonious World

Positive social conditions make group violence less likely. So do just social relations between groups and social processes through which grievances can be effectively addressed. These are crucial aspects of prevention. I have proposed in this book principles and practices of prevention and presented them as generally applicable. But I have also stressed that they have to be applied as a function of existing conditions. However valuable dialogue is, persisting at attempts at it makes no sense in a repressive system where people who step forward or are put forward by community groups to dialogue and negotiate with those in power are put in prison or killed. Assessing conditions, deciding what should be done, and by whom, as much as possible by nonviolent means, are crucial aspects of prevention.[13]*

The reasoning and suggestions in this book are consistent with the characteristics and ways of functioning that anthropologists have identified in peaceful societies, most of them small and nontechnological. As Douglas Fry described them,[14] they hold and propagate beliefs, values, and attitudes of nonviolence. They emphasize cooperation and peacefulness, and they reject violence. Conflict seems natural and probably unavoidable among living creatures, but these groups have conflict resolution mechanisms, often involving third parties, mediation, arbitration, and social institutions, to deal with conflict. The Semai of Malaysia, for example, call a conflict resolution assembly. The headman and elders address the group. As with the original version of the *gacaca*, the intention is to bring the disputants back into the community. Many of these groups have rituals of apology and reconciliation. They often have "peace systems" with neighboring societies. In some groups, aversion to violence is so great that their members flee rather than attack enemies. In most of these groups, children are not physically punished. Adults convey to them beliefs in and model nonviolence and harmony.

Living in large, complex societies, with varied subgroups, makes peaceful relations more challenging. But Fry argues that these examples show that people can live in peace. These examples, and what we saw about the role in group violence of relationships within small communities, whether in Rwanda or Poland, also point to the importance of community processes in building peace. Individuals, community organization, local NGOs are essential to create an attitude that "we are all in this together," and to address social problems and build positive relations and institutions. Even in the midst of conflict, they can create the underpinning for resolving differences and peaceful relations.[15]

In difficult times or when groups are in conflict, whether in less peaceful, small societies or in complex and heterogeneous societies with competitive values and practices, and often without effective protective values and institutions, people get caught up in ordinary, normal psychological processes of devaluation, scapegoating, and habituation to small acts of discrimination and violence. Their moral values and caring can get circumvented and subverted. Without conscious deliberation and resistance, they may develop a new morality, in which killing some people for real or imagined reasons is right. Internal bystanders are to various degrees also caught up in events. Most do not resist the immorality and violence around them. When large-scale killings begin, only a few become rescuers.

Children can be socialized, however, to become people who develop constructive responses to difficult social conditions or conflicts, and do not get caught up in an evolution that leads to violence. Educational experiences in schools and in the home can develop moral values and inclusive caring. Moral values refer to *principles* that people hold, such as the sanctity of human life and justice, or the greatest good for the greatest number. Caring refers to *feelings of connection* to and empathy or sympathy with other people. Prosocial orientation, with its central components of concern about and feelings of responsibility for others' welfare, has elements of both.

But other aspects of personality are also crucially important, such as the ability to use one's own judgment and to think about complex life issues in complex ways. So is moral courage. Educational experiences to help develop persons with these attributes have to be emotional, not only conceptual. They have to include personal experiences of being cared for, and guidance that develops caring toward others.

After she heard me give a talk, the American social psychologist Marilyn Brewer asked: "Of the many influences leading to mass violence, do you consider any one especially crucial?" One influence does not create, or prevent, mass violence. But a central influence is looking at people as "them" and devaluing them. If we see people as having the same needs and hopes and aspirations as we do—needing to eat, to protect their families, wanting to be respected— it becomes more difficult to harm them, easier to feel caring and empathy for them and to help them. If Al-Qaeda saw Americans this way, 9/11 would not have happened. If our soldiers had seen the Vietnamese this way, they would not have massacred the people in the villages of My Lai. They expected enemies to fight, but when they got there, they found only women, children, and old men, whom they killed.

Much of individual violence is within families. We can also devalue people who are close to us, when we are or feel diminished, frustrated, threatened, or attacked. The challenge is to maintain our awareness of others' humanity even at such times. If we can take each other's perspective, feel empathy for each other, and feel responsible for each others' welfare, we will avoid actions that contribute to the evolution of hostility and violence. It is part of being human to feel anger at those who thwart or threaten us, and even to want to strike out at them and those connected to them. The great challenge is to limit our actions to genuine self-defense.

We can dehumanize even those who are part of our group by turning them into abstractions. Leaders would be much less ready to send young men into war if they paid attention to them as persons. Our love, commitment, loyalty to the idea and abstract concept of our group can overwhelm our love of concrete human beings. They can also become slogans that mislead us. A second core influence leading to violence is another kind of abstraction, an ideology that promises a better world or better life for the group. It leads some people to justify any means by the supposed ideals or vision, and to not see the humanity of those who are identified as the enemy standing in the way.

Can we humans develop as persons, relate to others in ways, and create cultures, societies, and international systems that are inherently preventive? To limit violence in the world requires certain values and societal arrangements. It requires less hierarchy in social relations and between groups. It requires that garbage collectors and teachers, who do essential jobs, are respected as are doctors and bankers. This means addressing legitimizing ideologies that support great inequality. Severe material deprivation is unacceptable; great poverty must be addressed. But research has shown, again and again, that when people have reached even a modest level of material well-being, their satisfaction in life, their happiness, is barely affected by further material gain, by possessions and wealth. We need to bring such understanding home to people so that they focus less on gaining or glorifying privilege and wealth. This must not be a matter of individual perspective, but become cultural values that shape social climate.

Our culture and institutions are crucial. If the systems of a society help people fulfill basic material and psychological needs by work and through positive relations, if group relations (between subgroups of societies and between nations) are reasonably equitable, if people trust that conflict between individuals and groups will be justly resolved, and if values that promote inclusive caring are dominant, there will be little violence. Just as certain social conditions and climates make terrorism and other violence more likely, there can be social conditions and climates that make harmonious and peaceful relations likely.

We need to work to create societies in which people value not only their own but also others' well-being and happiness. Understanding the influences that lead to harm doing, establishing positive contact across group lines, pursuing cooperative actions in the service of shared goals, creating constructive ideologies, and fostering dialogue and active bystandership will not only prevent violence but also generate a positive evolution and societal transformation.

There are moments in history that offer opportunities for improving the world. There was such a moment after World War II. It was fulfilled at least to a degree by the Marshall Plan and the creation of the United Nations, the European Union, and a democratic, peaceful Japan. In contrast, the opportunities offered by the collapse of the Soviet Union, and by the outpouring of sympathy for the United States after 9/11 and the seeming readiness for cooperation by much of the world, at least in fighting terrorism but with the potential for more, have not been fulfilled. Positive leadership by the United States after 9/11 could have contributed to an international community in which nations focus less on their individual interests and more on worldwide, communal well-being.

The worldwide financial/economic crisis at the end of the first decade of the new century, great changes in the world, even terrorism and the widespread concern about it, represent both danger and opportunity. They can lead people to turn to destructive ideologies and movements and governments to destructive actions. But it is in such times that entrenched views and practices loosen; and people yearn for constructive visions and actions. This makes a shift possible from the pursuit of wealth at any cost, from politics dominated by self-focus and narrow business interests, to enlightened and humane policies. Leaders and followers can influence each other and call forth each others' best inclinations.

The opportunity for positive change, specifically in the United States, has been enhanced by the evidence of failed policies of the past and by Barack Obama's election. But this opportunity is endangered by a highly adversarial political and media culture, an intensely competitive view and practice of democracy. Many of the leaders, the elected representatives in the United States, and influential segments of the society and media, seem to see the "rules of the game," the rules of the democratic system, as using all opportunities to gain advantage for themselves. Making the other party fail, even if it harms the common good, is seen an advantage—a characteristic of the ideology of antagonism (see Chapter 5.) This has a destructive effect internally and reduces the capacity of the United States for positive leadership in the world, a collaborative leadership much needed in a world of many challenges. The opportunity for positive change presented by crises and challenges is also endangered by their impact as difficult life conditions. It is endangered by failed policies that threaten the identity of the United States as a great power and the belief by leaders and citizens in its superiority which must be maintained.

As in preventing mass violence, positive change, especially in difficult times, requires effective engagement, active bystandership by many people. I have stressed the great power of ideas in human life. The inspiration and motivation for change must come from a positive vision. A first task of people concerned with the prevention of violence and the creation of a harmonious world is to propagate such a vision or combination of visions—like Islam, Christianity, and Judaism living harmoniously together, and/or the vision I briefly touch on here, a collaborative view of life. A second task is for many people to initiate activities that would contribute to its fulfillment. Over time a social climate can develop which prizes individual initiative, but also stresses exercising it not only in one's own behalf, but also in behalf of the common, shared good. What we know about happiness, and a meaningful life, suggests that this is more satisfying than acquiring unnecessary wealth. The fulfillment that results from joining others this way will be much greater than any fulfillment people gain in destructive movements.

Their active participation in such a societal evolution would help people to move away from a defensive posture toward life, from fear and anger about its difficulties, to accept its real and inevitable challenges such as illness and unfulfilled expectations, and open themselves to its positive possibilities and to other people. Working together for the common good can fulfill our psychological needs as well as our spiritual need for transcendence. Moving beyond ourselves will then mean committing ourselves to shared humanity, inclusive caring, and the desire to bring benefit to everyone.

Notes

1 For further discussion of organizations as potential actors, especially the U.N., EU and regional organizations, see Hamburg, 2007

2 Post, 2007, p. 246

3 Kinzer, 2007

4 Ingelaere, 2009c

5 Friedman, 2009a

6 See Carter, 2009; Scham & Abu-Irshaid, 2009

7 Hillberg, 1961

8 Morris, 2008b

9 Kinzer, 2007

10 Oxfam, 2008

11 International Crisis Group Report, 2009b

12 Gourevitch, 2009

13 A variety of scholars/practitioners stress this, one of them Jan Oberg, in a talk at a conference on conflict in Aarhus, Denmark, June, 2008

14 See, for example, Fry, 2007

15 See also Vallacher et al., 2010

References

Abel, T. (1938). *The Nazi movement: Why Hitler came into power.* Reprinted, 1966. Englewood Cliffs, NJ: Prentice-Hall.

Aciman, A. (2009, June 9). The exodus Obama forgot to mention. *The New York Times,* pp. A23.

Ackerman, P., & Du Vall, J. (2000). *A force more powerful.* New York: Palgrave.

Adam, H., & Moodley, K. (2005). *Seeking Mandela: Peacemaking between Israelis and Palestinians.* Philadelphia: Temple University Press.

Aderman, D., & Berkowitz, L. (1970). Observational set, empathy and helping. *Journal of Personality and Social Psychology, 14,* 141–148.

Adwan, S., & Bar-On, D. (2003). Shared history project: A PRIME example of peace-building under fire. *International Journal of Politics, Culture and Society, 17,* 513–521.

Africa Rights. (2002). *Tribute to courage.* Kigali, Rwanda.

Ajami, F. (2009, August 2). Strangers in the land. [Review of the book Reflections on the revolution in Europe: Immigration, Islam and the West, by C. Caldwell], The New York Times Book Review, pp. 1, 7.

Albright, M., & Cohen, W. (2008). *Preventing genocide: A blueprint for U.S. policy makers.* Washington, DC: U. S. Holocaust Museum.

Albright, M. K. (2008, June 11). The end of intervention. *The New York Times.* http://humanrightsactioncenter.org/blog/2008/06/end-of-intervention.html

Allport, G. W. (1954). *The nature of prejudice.* Reading, MA: Addison-Wesley.

Altemeyer, B. (1996). *The authoritarian spectre.* Cambridge, MA: Harvard University Press.

Alter, J, (2006). *The Defining Moment: FDR's Hundred Days and the Triumph of Hope.* New York: Simon and Schuster.

Al-Zawahiri, A. (2001, December 2). *Knights under the Prophet's banner.* Serialized in eleven parts in Al-Sharq al Awsat (London), Part 11.

American Psychiatric Association. (1994). *Diagnostic and statistical manual of mental disorders: DSM-IV.* Washington, DC: Author.

Andrews, M. (2007). *Shaping history: Narratives of political change.* Cambridge, England: Cambridge University Press.

Anstey, M., & Zartman, I. W. (in press). External efforts to promote negotiation in identity conflicts. In M. Anstey & I. W. Zartman (Eds.), *Reducing identity conflicts and preventing genocide*. New York: Oxford University Press.

Arendt, H. (1963). *Eichmann in Jerusalem: A Report on the Banality of Evil*. New York: Viking Press.

Armstrong, K. (2001). *Battle for God*. Ballantine Books.

Aronson, E., Stephan, C., Sikes, J., Blaney, N., & Snapp, M. (1978). *The jigsaw classroom*. Beverly Hills, CA: Sage.

Asch, S. E. (1956). Studies of independence and conformity: I. A minority of one against a unanimous majority. *Psychological Monographs*, 70 (9, Whole No. 416).

Aslan, R. (2005). *No god but God: The origin, evolution and future of Islam*. New York: Random House.

Autessere, S. (2008). The trouble with the Congo: How local disputes fuel regional conflict. *Foreign Affairs, 87*(3), 94–110.

Awwad, E. (1999). Between trauma and recovery: Some perspectives on Palestinian's vulnerability and adaptation. In K. Nader, N. Dubrow & B.H. Stamm, (Eds). *Honoring differences: Cultural issues in the treatment of trauma and loss*. Philadelphia: Brunner/Mazel, pp.234–267.

Backer, D. (2007). Victims' responses to truth commissions: Evidence from South Africa. In M. Ndulo (Ed.), *Security, reconstruction and reconciliation: When the wars end*. London: University College London.

Baer, R. (2008). *The devil we know: Dealing with the new Iranian superpower?* New York: Crown Publishers.

Baldwin, C., Chapman, C., & Gray, Z. (2007). *Minority rights: The key to conflict prevention*. London: Minority Rights International.

Ball-Rokeach, S., Rokeach, M., & Grube, J. W. (1984). *The Great American Values Test: Influencing behavior and belief through television*. New York: The Free Press.

Bandura, A. (1999). Moral disengagement in the preparation of inhumanities. *Personality and Social Psychology Review*, 3, 193–209.

Bandura, A. (2006). Going global with social cognitive theory: From prospect to paydirt. In S. I. Donaldson, D. E. Berger, & K. Pezdek (Eds.), *Applied psychology: New frontiers and rewarding careers*. (pp. 53–79). Mahwah, NJ: Lawrence Erlbaum.

Bandura, A., Underwood, B., & Fromson, M. E. (1975). Disinhibition of aggression through diffusion of responsibility and dehumanization of victims. *Journal of Research in Personality*, 9, 253–269.

Bar-On, D. (1989). *Legacy of silence: Encounters with children of the Third Reich*. Cambridge, MA: Harvard University Press.

Bar-On, D. (2000). *Bridging the gap: Storytelling as a way to work through political and collective hostilities*. Hamburg, Germany: Koerber.

Bar-Tal, D. (2000). *Shared beliefs in a society: Social psychological analysis*. Thousand Oaks, CA: Sage.

Bar-Tal, D. (2007). Socio-psychological foundations of intractable conflicts. *American Behavioral Scientist, 50*, 1430–1453.

Bar-Tal, D., & Salomon, G. (2006). Israeli-Jewish narratives of the Israeli-Palestinian conflict: Evolvement, contents, functions and consequences. In I. R. Rothberg

(Ed.), *History's double helix: The intertwined narratives of Israel and Palestine* (pp. 19–46). Bloomington: Indiana University Press.

Bartov, O. (2003). Seeking the roots of modern genocide: On the Macro-and micro-history of mass murder. In R. Gellately, & B. Kiernen (Eds.), *The specter of genocide: Mass murder in historical perspective* (pp. 75–97). New York: Cambridge University Press

Bauman, Z. (2000). *Modernity and the Holocaust*. Ithaca, NY: Cornell University Press.

Baumeister, R. F. (1997). *Evil: Inside human violence and cruelty*. New York: Freeman and Co.

Baumrind, D. (1971). Current patterns of parental authority. *Developmental Psychology, 4*, 1–101.

Baumrind, D. (1975). *Early socialization and the discipline controversy*. Morristown, NJ: General Learning Press.

Bawer, B. (2009). *Surrender: Appeasing Islam, sacrificing freedom*. New York: Doubleday.

BBC News (2007, January 29). Analysis: Palestinian suicide attacks. http://news.bbc.co.uk/2/hi/middle_east/3256858.stm

Becker, E. (1975). *Escape from evil*. New York: The Free Press.

Beschloss, M. (2009, April 12). We are still one. *The New York Times Book Review*. pp. 11.

Bigelow, K. R. (1993). A campaign to deter genocide: The Baha'I experience. In H. Fein (Ed.), *Genocide watch* (pp. 189-196). New Haven, CT: Yale University Press.

Bilali, R. (2009). The Effect of Group Identity on Memories of Past Conflicts. Unpublished Dissertation, University of Massachusetts at Amherst.

Biton, Y., & Salomon, G. (2006). Peace in the eyes of Israeli and Palestinian youths: The effects of collective narratives and peace education program. *Journal of Peace Research, 43*, 167–180.

Bloom, M. (2009). Chasing butterflies and rainbows: A critique of Kruglanski et al.; "Fully committed: Suicide bombers' motivation and the quest for personal significance." *Political Psychology, 30* (3), 387–395.

Branscombe, N. R., & Miron, A. M. (2004). Interpreting the ingroup's negative actions toward another group: Emotional reactions to appraised harm. In L. Z. Tiedens & C. W. Leach (Eds.), *The social life of emotions* (pp. 314–335). New York: Cambridge University Press.

Brewer, M. B. (1978). Ingroup bias in the minimal intergroup situation: A cognitive-motivational analysis. *Psychological Bulletin, 86*, 307–324.

Brewer, M. B., & Pierce, K. P. (2005). Social identity complexity and outgroup tolerance. *Personality and Social Psychology Bulletin, 31*, 428–437.

Bronner, E. (2009, January 25). The bullets in my in-box. *The New York Times, Week in Review*, pp. 1, 4.

Brounéus, K. (2008a). Analyzing reconciliation: A structured method for measuring national reconciliation initiatives. *Peace and Conflict: Journal of Peace Psychology, 14*(3): 291–313.

Brounéus, K. (2008b). *Rethinking reconciliation: Concepts, methods, and an empirical study of truth telling and psychological health in Rwanda* (Doctoral dissertation). Department of Peace and Conflict Research, Uppsala University: Uppsala.

Brounéus, K. (2008c). Truth telling as talking cure? Insecurity and retraumatization in the Rwandan gacaca courts. *Security Dialogue, 39*(1), 55–76.

Brown, R., & Cehajic, S. (2008). Dealing with the past and facing the future: Mediators of collective guilt and shame in Bosnia and Herzegovina. *European Journal of Social Psychology, 38,* 669–684.

Brown, R. W. (1965). *Social psychology.* New York: Free Press.

Browning, C. R. (1992). *Ordinary men: Reserve battalion 101 and the final solution in Poland.* New York: HarperCollins.

Burchianti, M. E. (2004). Building bridges: The mothers of the Plaza del Mayo and the cultural politics of maternal memories. *History and Anthropology, 15*(2), 133–150.

Burg, S. L. (1997). Preventing ethnic conflict: Macedonia and the pluralist paradigm. Presentation at the Woodrow Wilson Center, February 19. Retrieved June, 2009, from http://www.wilsoncenter.org/index.cfm?fuseaction=topics.print_pub&doc_id=18947&group_id=7427&topic_id=1422&stoplayout=true

Burton, J. W. (1990). *Conflict: Human needs theory.* New York: St. Martin's Press.

Buss, A. H. (1966). The effect of harm on subsequent aggression. *Journal of Experimental Research in Personality, 1,* 249–255.

Buss, D. (2009). The great struggles of life. *American Psychologist, 64,* 140–149.

Byrne, C. (2004). Benefit of burden: Victims' reflections on TRC participation. *Peace and Conflict: Journal of Peace Psychology, 10*(3), 237–256.

Cairns, E., & Darby, J. (1998). The conflict in Northern Ireland. *American Psychologist, 53,* 754–776.

Cairns, E., & Hewstone, M. (2002). Northern Ireland: The impact of peacemaking in Northern Ireland on intergroup behavior. In G. Salomon & B. Nevo (Eds.), *Peace education: The concept, principles and practices around the world* (pp. 217–228). Mahwah, NJ: Lawrence Erlbaum Associates.

Cairns, E., Hewstone, M., & Tam, T. (2006). Forgiveness in Northern Ireland. In *Forgiveness: A sampling of research results* (pp. 20–23). Washington D.C: American Psychological Association.

Cairns, E., Tam., T., Hewstone, M., & Niens, U. (2005). Forgiveness in Northern Ireland. In Worthington, E. L. (ed.), *Handbook of forgiveness* (pp. 461–476). New York: Routledge.

Campbell, N. (2008, November 8). DR Congo: "Feeding on War". International Herald Tribune. Retrieved November 14, 2008, from http://www.crisisgroup.org/home/index.cfm?id=5771&l=1

Caplan, G. (2009). Review of the book After genocide: Transitional justice, postconflict reconstruction and reconciliation in Rwanda and beyond, P. Clark & Z. D. Kaufman (Eds.). London: Hurst. Retrieved from the Pambazuka News Web site: http://pambazuka.org/en/category/books/57932

Caplan, G. (2010, June 11). The law society of Upper Canada and genocide denial in Rwanda. *Globe and Mail Update.* www.theglobeandmail.com/news/politics/the-law-society-of-upper-canada-and-genocide-denial-in-rwanda/article1601215/

Carich, M. S., Melgger, C. K., Baig, M., & Harper, J. J. (2003). Enhancing victim empathy for sex offenders. *Journal of Child Sexual Abuse, 12*(3/4), 255–259.

Carnahan, T., & McFarland, S. (2007). Revisiting the Stanford Prison Experiment: Could participant self-selection have led to the cruelty? *Personality and Social Psychology Bulletin, 33*, 603–614.

Carnegie Commission on the Prevention of Deadly Conflict. (1997). *Preventing deadly conflict: Final report.* New York: Carnegie Corporation of New York.

Carson, J. (2008, October 30). Ambassador Carson speaking on the panel "What went right, what went wrong in Kenya" at the Conference on the Prevention of Genocide, organized by the State Department, Washington D.C.

Carter, J. (2009). *We can have peace in the Holy Land: A plan that will work.* New York: Simon & Schuster.

Castano, E., & Giner-Sorolla, R. (2006). Not quite human: Infrahumanization in response to collective responsibility for intergroup killing. *Journal of Personality and Social Psychology, 90*(5), 804–818.

Cehajic, S., Brown, R., & Castano, E. (2008). Forgive and forget? Antecedents and consequences of intergroup forgiveness in Bosnia and Herzegovina. *Political Psychology, 29*(3), 351–369.

Cesari, J. (2003). Muslim minorities in Europe: The silent revolution. In J. Esposito & F. Burgat (Ed.), *Modernizing Islam: Religion in the public sphere in the Middle East and in Europe* (pp. 251–269). Camden, NJ: Rutgers University Press.

Chalk, F., & Jonassohn, K. (1990). *The history and sociology of genocide: analyses and case studies.* New Haven, CT: Yale University Press.

Chang, I. (1998). *The rape of Nanking.* Penguin Books.

Chapman, A. R. (2001). Truth commissions as instruments of forgiveness and reconciliation. In S. J. Helmick & R. L. Petersen (Eds.), *Forgiveness and reconciliation: Religion, public policy and conflict transformation* (pp. 205–229). Radnor, PA: Templeton Foundation Press.

Chirot, D., & McCauley, C. (2006). *Why not kill them all: The logic and prevention of mass political murder.* Princeton, NJ: Princeton University Press.

Clark, P., & Kaufman, Z. D. (Eds.). (2009). *After genocide: Transitional justice, post-conflict reconstruction and reconciliation in Rwanda and beyond.* London: Hurst

Colby, A., & Damon, W. (1992). *Some do care.* New York: The Free Press.

Coleman, P. T. (2006). Intractable conflict. In M. Deutsch, P. T. Coleman, & E. C. Marcus (Eds.), *The handbook of conflict resolution: Theory and practice* (pp. 533–560). San Francisco: Jossey-Bass.

Cords, M., & Thurnheer, S. (1993). Reconciliation with valuable partners by long-tailed macaques. *Ethology, 93*, 315–325.

Craig, G. A. (1982). *The Germans.* New York: The New American Library.

Crandall, C. S., Eidelman, S., Skitka, L. J., & Morgan, S. S. (2009). Status quo framing increases support for torture. *Social Influence, 4*, 1–10.

Crenshaw, M. (1995). *Terrorism in context.* University Park, PA: Penn State University Press.

Crenshaw, M. (1996). Why violence is rejected or renounced: A case study of oppositional terrorism. In T. Gregor (Ed.), *A natural history of peace* (pp. 249–272). Nashville, TN: Vanderbilt University Press.

Crenshaw, M. (2000). The psychology of terrorism: An agenda for the 21st century. *Political Psychology, 21*, 405–420.

Crisp, R. J., & Turner, R. N. (2009). Can imagined interactions produce positive perceptions? Reducing prejudice through simulated social contact. *American Psychologist, 64*(4), 231–240.

Cutler, I. (2009, March 20-22). Comments at the conference, "Remembering Rwanda 15: Lessons learned/not learned." University of Toronto, Toronto, Ontario.

Dallaire, R. (2003). *Shakes hands with the devil: The failure of humanity in Rwanda.* New York: Carroll & Graf Publishers.

Daly, M., & Wilson, M. (1988). *Homicide.* New York: Aldine de Gruyter.

Danieli, Y. (1985). The treatment and prevention of long-term effects and inter-generational transmission of victimization: A lesson from Holocaust survivors and their children. In C.R. Figley (Ed.), *Trauma and its wake* (pp. 295–313). New York: Brunner/Mazel.

Danieli, Y. (2009, Winter). Conspiracy of silence. A Conversation with Dr. Yael Danieli (Aron Hirtman). *Reform Judaism, 51*–53.

Danziger, N. (2004). In pictures: Remembering the genocide. BBC News. Retrieved June 30, 2004, from http://news.bbc.co.uk/1/shared/spl/hi/africa/04/photo_journal/rwanda/html/9.stm

Davies, J. L. (1969). The curve of rising and declining satisfactions as a cause of some great revolutions and a contained rebellion. In H. D. Graham & T. R. Gurr (Eds.), *Violence in America* (pp. 671–709). New York: Bantam Books.

De Lange, J. (2007). The impact of the Staub model on policy making in Amsterdam regarding polarization and radicalization. *Peace and Conflict: Journal of Peace Psychology, 13*(3), 361–364.

DeAngelis, T. (2009). Tools for tough times. *Monitor on Psychology, 40*(1), 32–35.

deMause, L. (2008). The childhood origins of WWII and the Holocaust. *The Journal of Psychohistory, 36*(1), 2–30.

Deng, F. (2008, February 11). Speech given at the Conference on Modern Genocides and Global Responsibilities, California State University, Long Beach.

Dentan, R. K. (1968). The Semais: A non-violent people of Malaysia. New York: Holt, Reinhart & Winston.

Des Forges, A. (1999). *Leave none to tell the story: Genocide in Rwanda.* New York: Human Rights Watch.

Deutsch, M. (1973). *The resolution of conflict: Constructive and destructive processes.* New Haven, CT: Yale University Press.

Deutsch, M. (2008). Reconciliation after destructive intergroup conflict. In A. Nadler, T. Malloy, & J. D. Fisher (Eds.), *Social psychology of intergroup reconciliation* (pp. 395–423). New York: Oxford University Press.

Deutsch, M., Coleman, P. T., & Marcus, E. C. (2006). (Eds.). *The handbook of conflict resolution: Theory and practice.* San Francisco: Jossey-Bass.

Dickey, C. (2010, January 11). *A thousand points of hate.* Newsweek, http://www.newsweek.com/id/229078/page/1

Diversisteits-en Integratiemonitor. (2004). The city of Amsterdam, The Netherlands.

Dixon, J., Durrheim, K., & Tredoux, C. (2005). Beyond the optimal contact strategy: A reality threat for the contact hypothesis. *American Psychologist, 60*(7), 697–711.

Dodge, K. A., Bates, J. E., & Pettit, G. S. (1990). Mechanisms in the cycle of violence. *Science, 250*, 1678–1683.

Dodge, K. A., & Frame, C. L. (1982). Social cognitive biases and deficits in aggressive boys. *Child Development, 53*, 620–635.

Dollard, J., Doob, L., Miller, N., Mowrer, O., & Sears, R. (1939). *Frustration and aggression*. New Haven, CT: Yale University Press.

Dovidio, J. F., Gaertner, S. L., & Saguy, T. (2009). Commonality and the complexity of "we": Social attitudes and social change. *Personality and Social Psychology Review, 13*, 3–20.

Dreber A, Rand, D. G., Fudenberg, F., & Nowak, M. A. (2008). Winners don't punish. *Nature, 452*, 348–351.

Dutton, D., & Tetreault, C. (2009). Who will act badly in toxic situations. *Journal of Aggression, Conflict and Peace Research, 1*, 45–56.

Dweck, C. (2009, February 6). *Changing the world like a social psychologist*. Campbell Award Address, Meetings of the Society for Personality and Social Psychology, Tampa, Florida.

Egeland, J. (2008). *A billion lives: An eyewitness report from the frontlines of humanity*. New York: Simon and Schuster.

Eisenberg, N., Fabes, R. A., Spinrad, T. L. (2006). Prosocial development. In W. Damon (Ed.), *Handbook of child psychology, Volume 3: Social, emotional, and personality development* (5th ed., pp. 646–718). New York: Wiley.

Epstein, S., & Taylor, S. (1967). Instigation to aggression as a function of degree of defeat and perceived aggressive intent of the opponent. *Journal of Personality, 35*, 265–289.

Erlanger, S., & Kersinger, I. (2008, March 7). Gunman kills 8 and is shot dead at Israeli Yeshiva. *The New York Times*, p. A1, A8.

Erlich, V. (1966). *Family in transition—A study of 300 Yugoslav Villages*. Princeton, NJ: Princeton University Press.

Evans, G. (2008, November 10). *Preventing and resolving deadly conflict: What have we learned?* Talk by Gareth Evans, President, International Crisis Group, to Issam Fares Institute for Public Policy and International Affairs, American University of Beirut, Lebanon. http://www.humansecuritygateway.com/showRecord. php?RecordId=27224

Ezekiel, R. S. (1995). *The racist mind*. New York: Penguin Books.

Ezekiel, R. S. (2002). The ethnographer looks at Neo-Nazi and Klan groups: The Racist Mind revisited. *American Behavioral Scientist, 46*(1), 51–57.

Fein, H. (1979). *Accounting for Genocide: Victims and survivors of the Holocaust*. New York: Free Press.

Fein, H. (1993a). Accounting for Genocide after 1945: Theories and some findings. *International Journal of Group Rights, 1*, 79–106.

Fein, H. (1993b). *Genocide: A sociological perspective*. London: Sage.

Fein, H. (1994). *The prevention of genocide. A working paper of the Institute for the Study of Genocide*. City University of New York.

Fein, H. (1999). Testing theories brutally: Armenia (1915), Bosnia (1992) and Rwanda (1994). In L. Chorbajian & G. Shirinian (Eds), *Studies in comparative genocide* (pp. 157–164). New York: St. Martin's Press.

Fein, H. (2007). *Human rights and wrongs: Slavery, terror, genocide*. Boulder, CO: Paradigm Publishers.

Feinberg, J. K. (1978). *Anatomy of a helping situation: Some personality and situational determinants of helping in a conflict situation involving another's psychological distress* (Unpublished doctoral dissertation). University of Massachusetts, Amherst.

Fiske, S. T. (2004). *Social beings: A core motives approach to social psychology*. New York: Wiley.

Fortuyn, P. (1997) *Tegen de Islamisering van Onze Cultuur. Nederlandse Identiteit als Fundament.* [Against the Islamization of our culture: Dutch identity as a foundation]. Utrecht, The Netherlands: Bruna.

Frank, R. (1985). *Choosing the right pond: Human behavior and the quest for status*. New York: Oxford University Press.

Frankel, G. (2006, July 16). A beautiful friendship? In search of the truth about the Israel lobby's influence on Washington. *Washington Post Magazine*, p. W3.

Frankl, V. (1984). *Man's search for meaning* [originally published in 1958]. New York: Pocket/Simon & Shuster.

French, H. W. (2009, September 24). Kagame's hidden war in the Congo, *New York Review of Books*, 56(14). http://www.nybooks.com/articles/archives/2009/sep/24/kagames-hidden-war-in-the-congo/

Friedlander, S. (2007). *The years of extermination: Nazi Germany and the Jews, 1939–1945*. New York: HarperCollins Publishers.

Friedman, M., & Rholes, S. W. (2007). Successfully challenging fundamentalist beliefs results in increased death awareness. *Journal of Experimental Social Psychology, 43*, 794–801.

Friedman, T. L. (2002, January 27). The 2 domes of Belgium. *The New York Times*, p. 13.

Friedman, T. L. (2009a, January 25). This is not a test. *The New York Times, Weekly Review*, p. 10.

Friedman, T. L. (2009b, August 5). Green shoots in Palestine. *The New York Times*, p. A17.

Friedman, T. L. (2009c, August 9). Green shoots in Palestine II. *The New York Times, Weekly Review*. p. 8.

Fry, D. P. (2007). *Beyond war: The human potential for peace*. New York: Oxford University Press.

Gaertner, S. L., & Dovidio, J. F. (2000). *Reducing intergroup bias: The common ingroup identity model*. Orlando, FL: Academic Press.

Gelb, L. (2009). *Power rules: How common sense can rescue American foreign policy*. New York: HarperCollins.

Gerald, J. B. (1995). *Is the U.S. really a signatory to the U.N. genocide convention. An essay against genocide.* Retrieved June 2009, from http://www.serendipity.li/more/genocide.html

Germert, F. van. (2004, August). *Youth groups and gangs in Amsterdam: An inventory based on The Eurogang Expert Survey.* Paper presented at the congress of the European Society of Criminology, Amsterdam, The Netherlands.

Germert, F. van, & Fleisher, M. (2005). In the grip of the group: Ethnography of a Moroccan street Gang in the Netherlands. In F. Weerman & S. H. Decker (Eds.),

European street gangs and troublesome youth groups: Findings from the Eurogang Research Program. Walnut Creek, CA: Altamira.

Gerner, P. J. (2003). The Middle East: The Palestinian issue. In J. R. Rudolph, Jr. (Ed.), *Encyclopedia of modern ethnic conflict reader.* Westport, CT: Greenwood Publishing Group.

Gettelmen, J. (2007, October 7). Rape epidemic raises trauma of Congo War. *The New York Times,* http://www.peacewomen.org/news/Africa/GreatLakes/October07/DRCrape.html

Gettelmen, J. (2009a, January 25). With leader captured, Congo rebel force is dissolved. *The New York Times,* p. A10.

Gettelmen, J. (2009b, March 4.), In Congo, with rebels now at bay, calm erupts. *The New York Times,* p. A6.

Gettelmen, J. (2010a, January 2). After years of mass killing, fragile calm holds in Darfur. *The New York Times,* p. A1, A8.

Gettelmen, J. (2010b, April 30). Rwanda Pursues Dissenters and the Homeless. *The New York Times.* http://www.nytimes.com/2010/05/01/world/africa/01rwanda.html

Gibson, J. L. (2004). Does truth lead to reconciliation? Testing the causal assumptions of the South African truth and reconciliation process. *American Journal of Political Science, 48*(2), 201–217.

Gibson, J. L. (2006). Do strong group identities fuel intolerance? Evidence from the South Africa case. *Political Psychology, 27*(5), 665–706.

Ginzburg, R. (1988). *100 Years of Lynching.* Baltimore, MD: Black Classic Press.

Girdiharadas, A. (2007, July 15). A clearer picture emerges of suspect in bomb plot. *The New York Times,* p. 10.

Gobodo-Madikezela, P. (2003). *A human being died that night: A South African story of forgiveness.* Boston: Houghton-Mifflin.

Gobodo-Madikezela, P. (2008). Trauma, forgiveness and the witnessing dance: Making public spaces intimate. *Journal of Analytical Psychology, 53,* 169–188.

Goldberg, J. (2009, May 24). No common ground. *The New York Times Book Review,* p. 12.

Goldhagen, D. J. (1998). *Hitler's willing executioners: Ordinary Germans and the Holocaust.* New York: Knopf.

Goldstein, A. P., & Glick, B. (1994). *The prosocial gang: Implementing aggression replacement training.* Newbury Park, CA: Sage.

Gourevich, P. (1999). *We wish to inform you that tomorrow we will be killed with our families.* New York: Farrar Straus and Giroux.

Gourevitch, P. (2009, May 4). The life after. *The New Yorker,* pp. 37–49.

Green, P. (2002). Contact: Training a new generation of peacebuilders. *Peace and Change,* p. 5–6.

Grille, R. (2005). *Parenting for a peaceful world.* Alexandria, Australia: Longueville Media.

Grodman, S. M. (1979). *The role of personality and situational variables in responding to and helping an individual in psychological distress* (Unpublished doctoral dissertation). University of Massachusetts, Amherst.

Grusec, J. E., Kuczynski, L., Rushton, J. P., & Simutis, Z. M. (1978). Modeling, direct instruction, and attributions: Effects on altruism. *Developmental Psychology, 14,* 51–57.

Guha, R. (2007, August 15). India's internal partition. *The New York Times,* p. A25.

Gurr, T. R. (1970). *Why men rebel.* Princeton, NJ: Princeton University Press.

Gurr, T. R., & Harff, B. (1994). *Ethnic conflict in world politics.* Boulder, CO: Westview Press.

Hagan, J., & Rymond-Richmond, W. (2008). *Darfur and the crime of genocide.* New York: Cambridge University Press.

Hagee, J. (2007). *Jerusalem countdown: A prelude to war.* Lake Mary, FL: FrontLine.

Hallie, P. P. (1979). *Lest innocent blood be shed. The story of the village of Le Chambon, and how goodness happened there.* New York: Harper and Row.

Halperin, E., Canetti-Nisim, D., & Hirsch-Hoefler, S. (2009). The central role of group-based hatred as an emotional antecedent of political intolerance: Evidence from Israel. *Political Psychology, 30,* 93–123.

Hamburg, D. (2007). *Preventing genocide: Practical steps toward early detection and effective action.* Boulder, CO: Paradigm Publishers.

Handl, V. (1997). Czech-German declaration on reconciliation. *German Politics, 6,* 150–167.

Harff, B. (2003). No lessons learned from the Holocaust? Assessing risks of genocide and political mass murder since 1955. *American Political Science Review, 97*(1), 57–73.

Harff, B., & Gurr, T. R. (1990). Victims of the state genocides, politicides and group repression since 1945. *International Review of Victimology, 1,* 1–19.

Haritos-Fatouros, M. (2003). *The psychological origins of institutionalized torture.* London: Routledge.

Hatzfeld, J. (2003). *Machete season.* New York: Farrar, Straus and Giroux.

Helson, H. (1964). *Adaptation Level Theory: An experimental and systematic approach to behavior* New York: Harper & Row.

Herbert, B. (2009, January 21). A crazy dream. *The New York Times,* p. 19.

Herbert, T. B., & Dunkel-Schetter, C. (1992). Negative social reactions to victims: An overview of responses and their determinants. In L. Montada, S. Filipp, & M. J. Lerner (Eds.), *Life crises and experiences of loss in adulthood* (pp. 497–518). Hillsdale, NJ: Erlbaum.

Herman, J. (1992). *Trauma and recovery.* New York: Basic Books.

Hess, H., & Ostrom, E. (Eds.). (2007). *Understanding knowledge as a commons: From theory to practice.* Cambridge, MA: The MIT Press.

Hewstone, M., Kenworthy, J. B., Cairns, E., Tausch, N., Hughes, J., Tam, T., Voci, A., von Hacker, U., & Pinder, C. (2008). Stepping stones to reconciliation in Northern Ireland: Intergoup contact, forgiveness and trust. In A. Nadler, T. Malloy, & J. D. Fisher (Eds.), *Social psychology of intergroup reconciliation* (pp. 199–227). New York: Oxford University Press.

Hiebert, M. S. (2008). Theorizing destruction: Reflections on the state of Comparative Genocide Theory. *Genocide Studies and Prevention, 3,* 309–339.

Higginson, J. (2008, April 3). *The bullet and the chicotte are the children of Bula Matadi: The problem of violence and popular intervention during the transition from the Congo*

Free State to the Belgian Congo, 1895–1913. Paper presented at the conference on Landscapes of Violence: Conflict and Trauma through Time, University of Massachusetts at Amherst.

Hilberg, R. (1961). *The destruction of the European Jews.* New York: Harper & Row.

Hitler, A. (1925). *Mein Kampf* (R. Manheim, Trans.). Boston: Houghton Mifflin.

Hobfoll, S., Hall, B., Canetti-Nisim, D., Galea, S., Johnson, R., & Palmiari, P. (2007). Refining the understanding of traumatic growth in the face of terrorism: Moving from meaning cognitions to doing what is meaningful. *Applied Psychology: An International Review, 56,* 345–366.

Hochschild, A. (2009, August 13). Rape of the Congo. *New York Review of Books.* Retrieved from http://www.nybooks.com/articles/22956

Hoffman, M. L. (2000). *Empathy and moral development.* New York: Cambridge University Press.

Hogg, M. A. (2007). Uncertainty-identity theory. *Advances in Experimental Social Psychology, 39,* 69–126.

Hollander, P. (2006). Editor's introduction: The distinctive features of repression in communist states. In P. Holander (Ed.), *From the Gulag to the killing fields.* Wilmington, DE: ISI Books.

Honeyman, C., Hudami, S., Tiruneh, A., Hierta, J., Chirayath., L., Iliff, A., & Meierhenrich, J. (2004). Establishing collective norms: Potentials for participatory justice in Rwanda. *Peace and Conflict: Journal of Peace Psychology, 10,* 1–24.

Horgan, J. (2009). *Walking away from terrorism: Accounts of disengagement from radical and extremist movements.* New York: Routlege.

Horgan, J. & Braddock, K. (2010). Rehabilitating the terrorists?: Challenges in assessing the effectiveness of deradicalization programs. *Terrorism and Political Violence.22.*1–25.

Horowitz, D. (2008, April). *The structure and strategy of ethnic conflict.* Paper presented at the Annual World Bank Conference on Development Economics, Washington D.C.

Hosenball, M., Isikoff, M., & Thomas, E. (2010, January 11). The radicalization of Umar Farouk Abdulmutallab. *Newsweek,* pp. 37–41.

Hosenball, M. & Thomas, E. (2010, June 21). Blowback: The Obama administration faces a dilemma: how to battle Muslim extremists without creating more at home. *Newsweek.* pp. 26–29.

Human Rights Watch Report. (2007). *Renewed crisis in North Kivu.* Vol. 19, No. 17(A). http://www.hrw.org/de/reports/2007/10/22/renewed-crisis-north-kivu-0

Human Rights Watch (2010). World Report, 2010. Events of 2009.

Human Security Center. (2006). *Human Security Brief.* New York: Oxford University Press.

Ignatieff, M. (1997 September/October). Articles of Faith, Index of Censorship, *Harper's Magazine,* pp. 15, 16–17.

Ilibagiza, I., & Erwin, S. (2006). *Left to tell: Discovering God amidst the Rwanda Holocaust.* Carlsbad, CA: Hay House.

Ingelaere, B. (2008). The Gacaca Courts in Rwanda. In L. Huyse & M. Salter (Eds.), *Traditional justice and reconciliation mechanisms. After violent conflict: Learning from African experiences.* Stockholm, Sweden: International Idea.

Ingelaere, B. (2009a). *Do we understand life after genocide? Centre and periphery in the knowledge construction in/on Rwanda.* Institute of Development and Policy Management, University of Antwerp, Belgium.

Ingelaere, B. (2009b). Living the transition: Inside Rwanda's conflict cycle at the grassroots. *Journal of Eastern African Studies, 3*(3), 438–463.

Ingelaere, B., Havugimana, J., & Ndushabandi, S. (2009a). *LaBenevolencija grassroots project—evaluation.* Research report. Radio La Benevolencija – Humanitarian Tools Foundation. http://www.ua.ac.be/main.aspx?c=bert.ingelaere

Ingelaere, B., Havugimana, J., & Ndushabandi, S. (2009b). *Musekeweya in the Congo: Radio listening habits of ex-FDLR combatants in Eastern-DRC.* Research report. Radio La Benevolencija – Humanitarian Tools Foundation. http://www.ua.ac.be/main.aspx?c=bert.ingelaere

Ingelaere, B., Havugimana, J., & Ndushabandi, S. (2010). *All Congolese women are ready ....to be raped: Ex-FDLR combatants on sexual violence in eastern DRC.* Research report. Radio La Benevolencija – Humanitarian Tools Foundation.

International Crisis Group Report. (2009a, May 11). *Congo: Five priorities for a peacebuilding strategy.* http://www.cfr.org/publication/19433/advanced_search.html

International Crisis Group Report. (2009b, July 9). *Congo: A comprehensive strategy to disarm the FDLR.* http://www.cfr.org/publication/19813/advanced_search.html

Iyer, A., Leach, C. W., & Crosby, F. J. (2003). White guilt and racial compensation: The benefits and limits of self-focus. *Personality and Social Psychology Bulletin, 29,* 117–129.

Janis, I. (1972). *Victims of groupthink; a psychological study of foreign-policy decisions and fiascoes.* Boston: Houghton Mifflin.

Janis, I. (1973). Groupthink. *Yale Alumni Magazine.* New Haven, CT: Yale Alumni Publications.

Janoff-Bulman, R. (1992). *Shattered assumptions.* New York: The Free Press.

Jones, A. (2006). *Genocide: A comprehensive introduction.* New York: Routledge.

Jost, J. T., Banaji, M. R., & Nosek, B. A. (2004). A decade of system justification theory: Accumulated evidence of conscious and unconscious bolstering of the status quo. *Political Psychology, 25,* 881–920.

Kaminer, D., Stein, J. D., Mbanga, I., & Zungo-Dirwayi, N. (2001). The truth and reconciliation commission in South Africa: Relation to psychiatric status and forgiveness among survivors of human rights abuses. *The British Journal of Psychiatry, 178*(4), 373–377.

Kang, E., & Kadesa, Y. (2002). Confidence and security building between South Korea and Japan. *Journal of Political and Military Sociology, 28* (1), 93–108.

Kaplan, S. (2008). *Children in genocide—extreme traumatization and affect regulation.* London: IPA Publications.

Kelman, H. C. (1990). Applying a human needs perspective to the practice of conflict resolution: The Israeli-Palestinian Case. In J. Burton (Ed.), *Conflict: Human needs theory* (pp. 283–297). New York: St. Martin's Press.

Kelman, H. (1992). Acknowledging the other's nationhood: How to create a momentum for the Israeli-Palestinian negotiations. *Journal of Palestine Studies, 22,* 18–38.

Kelman, H. C. (2007). The Israeli-Palestinian peace process and its vicissitudes: Insights from attitude theory. *American Psychologist, 62*(4), 287–303.

Kelman, H. C., & Fisher, R. J. (2003). Conflict analysis and resolution. In D. Sears, L. Huddy, & R. Jervis. (Eds.), *Political psychology.* Oxford, England: Oxford University Press.

Kelman, H. C., & Hamilton, V. L. (1989). *Crimes of obedience: Toward a social psychology of authority and responsibility.* New Haven, CT: Yale University Press.

Khalili, L. (2007). *Heroes and martyrs of Palestine—The politics of national commemoration.* New York: Cambridge University Press.

Khatchadourian, R. (2007, January 22). A reporter at large. Azzam the American. The making of an Al Qaeda homegrown. *The New Yorker,* pp. 50–63.

Kiernen, B. (2007). *Blood and soil: A world history of genocide and extermination from Sparta to Darfur.* New Haven, CT: Yale University Press.

Kilcullen, D. (2009). *The accidental guerrilla: Fighting small wars in the midst of a big one.* New York: Oxford University Press.

Kinzer, S. (2007, December 13). The current wave of violence in DRC has its roots in the Rwandan genocide. *The Guardian,* http://www.guardian.co.uk/commentisfree/2007/dec/13/worldsapart

Kinzer, S. (2008). *A thousand hills: Rwanda's rebirth and the man who dreamed it.* Hoboken, NJ: John Wiley and Sons.

Klein, N. (2007). *The Shock Doctrine: The rise of disaster capitalism* New York: Picador.

Kohlberg, L., & Candee, L. (1984). The relationship of moral judgment to moral action. In W. M. Kurtines, & J. L. Gewirtz (Eds.), *Morality, moral behavior, and moral development* (pp. 52–73). New York: Wiley.

Konner, M. (1978). Social and personality development: An anthropological perspective. In M. Lamb (Ed.), *Social and personality development.* New York: Holt.

Kressel, N. J. (2007). *Bad faith: The danger of religious extremism.* Amherst, NY: Prometheus Books.

Kriesberg, L. (1998a). *Constructive conflicts: From escalation to resolution.* Boulder, CO: Rowman & Littlefield.

Kriesberg, L. (1998b). Intractable conflicts. In E. Weiner (Ed.), *The handbook of interethnic coexistence* (pp. 332–342). New York: Continuum.

Kristof, N. D. (2009, May 21). After wars, mass rapes persist. *The New York Times,* p. A27.

Kristof, N. D. (2010, January 31). Orphaned, raped and ignored. *The New York Times, Week in Review,* p. 11.

Krueger, A., & Maleckova, J. (2003, June 6). Seeking the roots of terror. *Chronicle of Higher Education, 49,* p. B10.

Kruglanski, A. W., Chen, X., Dechesne, M., Fishman, S., & Orehek, E. (2009). Fully committed suicide bombers motivation and the quest for personal significance. *Political Psychology, 30*(3), 331–359.

Kruglanski, A. W., Crenshaw, M., Post, J. M., & Victoroff, J. (2008). What should this fight be called: Metaphors of counterterrorism and their implications. *Psychological Science in the Public Interest, 8*(3), 97–133.

Kruglanski, A.W., Gelfand, M., & Gunaratna, R. (2010, January). Detainee deradicalization: A challenge for psychological science. *American Psychological Society Observer, 23*(1), 19–22.

Kruglanski, A.W., Gelfand, M., & Gunaratna, R. (in press). Aspects of deradicalization. In Gunaratna, R., Gerard, J. & Rubin, L. (Eds.), *Terrorist rehabilitation: A new frontier in counterterrorism.* New York: Routledge.

Kuehne, T. (2009). Male bonding and shame culture: Hitler's soldiers and the moral basis of genocidal warfare. In O. Jensen, C. W. Szejnmann, & M. L. Davies (Eds.), *Ordinary people as mass murderers. Perpetrators in comparative perspectives* (pp. 55–77). Houndmills, UK: Palgrave Macmillan.

Kuehne, T. (2010). *Belonging and genocide. Hitler's community, 1918–1945.* New Haven, CT: Yale University Press.

Kuriansky, J. (2009). Moving forward: A renewed approach to the Israeli-Palestinian conflict. *Peace Psychology, 18*(1), 15–18.

Latane, B., & Darley, J. (1970). *The unresponsive bystander: Why doesn't he help?* New York: Appleton-Crofts.

LeBor, A. (2004). *Milosevic.* New Haven, CT: Yale University Press.

Lederach, J. P. (1997). *Building peace: Sustainable reconciliation in divided societies.* Washington, DC: United States Institute of Peace Press.

Lemarchand, R. (2008). Reflections on the crisis in Eastern Congo. http://wilsoncenter.org/topics/docs/lemarchand%20article.pdf. Retrieved on January 5, 2010.

Lemarchand, R. (2009). *The dynamics of violence in Central Africa.* Philadelphia: University of Pennsylvania Press.

Lemkin, R. (1944). *Axis Rule in Occupied Europe: Laws of Occupation - Analysis of Government - Proposals for Redress,* Washington, D.C.: Carnegie Endowment for International Peace.

Lerner, M. (1980). *The belief in a just world: A fundamental delusion.* New York: Plenum Press.

Lerner, M. J., & Simmons, C. H. (1966). Observer's reaction to the "innocent victim": Compassion or rejection? *Journal of Personality and Social Psychology, 4,* 203–210.

Lewis, B. (2005). *From Babel to Dragomans: Interpreting the Middle East.* Oxford, England: Oxford University Press.

Li, Q. (2005). Does democracy promote or reduce transnational terrorist incidents. *Journal of Conflict Resolution, 49,* 278–297.

Lieberfeld, D. (2009). Lincoln, Mandela, and qualities of reconciliation-oriented leadership. *Peace and Conflict: Journal of Peace Psychology, 15,* 27–47.

Lifton, R. J. (1986). *The Nazi doctors: Medical killing and the psychology of genocide.* New York: Basic Books.

Lifton, R. J. (2000). *Destroying the world to save it: Aum Shinrykio and the new global terrorism.* New York: Holt.

Lifton, R. J. (2003). *Superpower syndrome.* New York: Thunder's Mouth Press/Nation Books.

Lillie, C. (2004). Unpublished research. Department of Psychology, University of Massachusetts, Amherst.

Lindner, E. G. (2006). *Making enemies: Humiliation and international conflict.* Westport, CT: Greenwood Press and Praeger Publishers.

Lindner, E. G. (2008, March 7-9). *The relevance of humiliation studies for the prevention of terrorism*. Paper presented to the NATO Advanced Research Workshop 'Indigenous Terrorism: Understanding and Addressing the Root Causes of Radicalisation among Groups with an Immigrant Heritage in Europe,' Budapest, Hungary. http://www.humiliationstudies.org/documents/evelin/Preventionof TerrorismBudapest08.pdf

Lippitt, R., & White, R. K. (1943). The "social climate" of children's groups. In R. G. Barker, J. S. Kounin, & H. F. Wright (Eds.), *Child behavior and development* (pp. 485–508). New York: McGraw-Hill.

Long, W. J., & Brecke, P. (2003). *War and reconciliation: Reason and emotion in conflict eesolution*. Cambridge, MA: MIT Press.

Lowery, B. S., Chow, R. M., & Crosby, J. R. (in press). Giving to those who have less or taking from those who have more: How inequity frames affect correction for inequity.*Journal of Experimental Social Psychology*.

Lund, M. S. (2009). Conflict prevention: Theory in pursuit of policy and practice. In W, Zartman, V. Kremenyck, & J. Bercovitch (Eds.), *Handbook of conflict resolution* (pp. 285–321). Thousand Oaks, CA: Sage.

Maguen, A., Metzler, A. J., Litz, B. T., Seal, K. H., Knight, S. J., & Marmar, C R. (2009). The impact of killing in war on mental health symptoms and related functioning. *Journal of Traumatic Stress, 22*(5), 435–443.

Maiese, M. (2003). Restorative justice. In G. Burgess & H. Burgess (Eds.), *Beyond intractability*. Boulder: Conflict Research Consortium, University of Colorado. Retrieved June 30, 2007, from http://www.beyondintractability.org/essay/ restorative_justice/

Malhotra, D., & Liyanage, S. (2005). Long-term effects of peace workshops in protracted conflicts. *Journal of Conflict Resolution, 49*(6), 908–924.

Malik, S. (2007, June). My brother the bomber. *Prospect Magazine*, http://www. prospectmagazine.co.uk/2007/06/mybrotherthebomber/

Mamdani, M. (2001). *When victims become killers: Colonialism, nativism, and the genocide in Rwanda*. Princeton, NJ: Princeton University Press.

Mandel, D. R. (2002). Instigators of genocide. Examining Hitler from a social-psychological perspective. In L. S. Newman & R. Erber (Eds.), *Understanding genocide: The social psychology of the Holocaust* (pp. 259–285). New York: Oxford University Press.

Maoz, I. (2004). Coexistence is in the eye of the beholder: Evaluating intergroup encounter interventions between Jews and Arabs in Israel. *Journal of Social Issues, 60*(2), 437–452.

Maoz, I. (2008). "They saw a terrorist"—Responses of Jewish-Israeli viewers to an interview with a Palestinian terrorist. *Peace and Conflict: Journal of Peace Psychology, 14*(3), 275–291.

Maoz, I. & McCauley, C. (2005). Psychological correlates of support for compromise: A polling study of Jewish-Israeli attitudes toward solutions to the Israeli-Palestinian conflict. *Political Psychology, 26*, 791–807.

Maoz, I., Ward, A., Katz, M., & Ross, L. (2002). Reactive devaluation of an "Israeli" vs. "Palestinian" peace proposal. *Journal of Conflict Resolution, 46*, 515–546.

Maslow, A. H. (1955). Deficiency motivation and growth motivation. In M. R. Jones (Ed.), *Nebraska symposium on motivation* (Vol. 3, pp. 1–30,). Lincoln: University of Nebraska Press.

Maslow, A. H. (1971). *The farther reaches of human nature.* New York: Viking.

Mason, T. D. (1999). The civil war in El-Salvador: A retrospective analysis. *Latin American Research Review, 34*(3), 179–196.

Mauss, M. (1954). *The gift: Forms and functions of exchange in archaic societies.* Glencoe, IL: Free Press.

McCann, I. L., & Pearlman, L. A. (1990). *Psychological trauma and the adult survivor: Theory, therapy, and transformation.* New York: Brunner/Mazel.

McCauley, C. (2004). Psychological issues in understanding terrorism. In C. E. Stout, (Ed.), *Psychology of terrorism* (pp. 33–67). Westport, CT: Praeger Publishers.

McCauley, C. (2008). Group desistance from terrorism: A dynamic perspective. *Dynamics of Asymmetric Conflict, 1*(3), 269–293.

McCullough, M. (2008). *Beyond revenge: The evolution of the forgiveness instinct.* New York: John Wiley & Sons.

McCullough, M., Finchman, F. D., & Tasang, J. (2003). Forgiveness, forbearance, and time: The temporal unfolding of transgression-related interpersonal motivations. *Journal of Personality and Social Psychology, 84*(3), 540–557.

McGregor, I. (2006). Offensive defensiveness: Toward an integrative neuroscience of compensatory zeal after mortality salience, personal uncertainty, and other poignant self-threats. *Psychological Inquiry, 17,* 299–308.

McGregor, I., Gailliot, M. T., Vasquez, N., & Nash, K. A. (2007). Ideological and personal zeal reactions to threat among people with high self-esteem: Motivated promotion focus. *Personality and Social Psychology Bulletin, 33,* 1587–1599.

McGregor, I., Haji, R., Nash, K. A., & Teper, R. (2008). Religious zeal and the uncertain self. *Basic and Applied Social Psychology, 30,* 183–188.

McIntosh, D., Kline, G., Wadsworth, M., Ahlkvist, J., Burwell, R., Gudmundsen, G., Raviv, T., & Rea, J. (2006). Forgiving the perpetrators of the September 11th attacks: Associations with coping, distress, and religiousness. In *Forgiveness: A sampling of research results* (pp. 17–20). Washington D.C: American Psychological Association.

McNair, R. M. (2002). *Perpetration-induced traumatic stress.* London: Praeger.

Meichenbaum, D. (2001). *Treatment of individuals with anger-control problems and aggressive behaviors: A clinical handbook.* Clearwater, FL: Institute Press.

Melson, R. (1992). *Revolution and genocide: On the origins of the Armenian genocide and the Holocaust.* Chicago: University of Chicago Press.

Melson, R. (2008). Churchill in Munich: The paradox of genocide prevention. *Genocide Studies and Prevention, 3,* 297–308.

Melvern, L (2000). *A people betrayed: The role of the West in Rwanda's genocide.* London: Zed Books.

Melvern, L. (2004). *Conspiracy to murder: The Rwanda genocide.* London: Verso.

Merari, A. (2005). Suicidal terrorism. In R. I. Yufit & D. Lester (Eds.), *Assessment, treatment, and prevention of suicidal behavior* (pp. 431–453). Hoboken, NJ: Wiley.

Merari, A. (2010). *Driven to death: Psychological and social aspects of suicide terrorism.* New York: Oxford University Press.

Merkl, P. H. (1980). *The making of a stormtrooper.* Princeton, NJ: Princeton University Press.

Merriman, H., & DuVall, J. (2007). Dissolving terrorism at its roots. In R. Summy & R. Senthil (Eds.), *Nonviolence: An alternative for countering global terror(ism)* (pp. 221–234). Hauppauge, NY: Nova Science Publishers.

Midlarsky, M. (2004). *The killing trap: Genocide in the 20th century.* New York: Cambridge University Press.

Milgram, S. (1965). Some conditions of obedience and disobedience to authority. *Human Relations, 18,* 57–76.

Milgram, S. (1974). *Obedience to authority: An experimental view.* New York: Harper and Row.

Miller, A. (1983). *For your own good: Hidden cruelty in child-rearing and the roots of violence.* New York: Farrar, Straus, and Giroux.

Minow, M. (1998). *Between vengeance and forgiveness: Facing history after genocide and mass violence.* Boston: Beacon Press.

Miron, A. M., & Branscombe, N. R. (2008). Social categorization, standard of justice, and collective guilt. In A. Nadler, T. Malloy, & J. Fisher (Eds.), *The social psychology of intergroup reconciliation* (pp. 77–96). Oxford, England: Oxford University Press.

Mironko, C. K. (2004). Ibitero: Means and motive in the Rwandan genocide. In S. E. Cook (Ed.), *Genocide in Cambodia and Rwanda: New perspectives* (pp. 173–201). Yale Center for International and Area Studies. Genocide Studies Program Monograph Series No. 1.

Mitchell, G. (2008, October 25). Talk on Foreign Policy Issues, at the Commonwealth Club of America. Presented on C-Span.

Modenos, L. (2008, April 3). *A peaceful conflict: The paradox of peacebuilding in Cyprus.* Presentation at the Conference on Landscapes of Violence: Conflict and Trauma through Time, University of Massachusetts at Amherst.

Moffatt, G. (2008). *Stone cold souls: History's most vicious killers.* Retrieved from http://www.mysteriousplaces.com/mayan/BallCourt.html

Montville, J. V. (1993). The healing function in political conflict resolution. In D. J. D. Sandole & H. Van der Merve (Eds.), *Conflict resolution theory and practice: Integration and application* (pp. 112–128). Manchester, England: Manchester University Press.

Morris, B. (1989). *The birth of the Palestinian refugee problem, 1947–1949.* Cambridge, England: Cambridge University Press.

Morris, B. (2004). *The birth of the Palestinian refugee problem revisited.* Cambridge, England: Cambridge University Press.

Morris, B. (2008a). *1948: A history of the First Arab-Israeli War.* New Haven, CT: Yale University Press.

Morris, B. (2008b, December 30). Why Israel feels threatened. *The New York Times,* p. A21.

Mortenson, G., & Relin, D. O. (2007). *Three cups of tea. One man's mission to promote peace, one school at a time.* New York: Penguin Books.

Moscovici, S., & Zavalloni, M. (1969). The group as a polarizer of attitudes. *Journal of Personality and Social Psychology, 12,* 125–135.

Murphy, L. B. (1937). *Social behavior and child personality: An exploratory study of some roots of sympathy.* New York: Columbia University Press.

Myers, D. (2010). *Social psychology.* New York: McGraw Hill.

Myers, N. (2008, June). Peace breaks out. *Ode*, p. 25.

Nadler, A., (2002). Postresolution processes: Instrumental and socioemotional routes to reconciliation. In G. Salomon, & B. Nevo (Eds.), *Peace education*. Mahwah, NJ: Lawrence Erlbaum Associates.

Nadler, A., & Liviatan, I. (2006). Intergroup reconciliation: Effects of adversary's expressions of empathy, responsibility, and recipients' trust. *Personality and Social Psychology Bulletin, 32*, 459–470.

Nadler, A., Malloy, T., & Fisher, J. D. (Eds.). (2008). *The social psychology of intergroup reconciliation*. New York: Oxford University Press.

Nadler, A., & Shnabel, N. (2008). Instrumental and socioemotional paths to intergroup reconciliation and the needs-based model of socioemotional reconciliation. In A. Nadler, T. Malloy, & J. D. Fisher (Eds.), *The social psychology of intergroup reconciliation* (pp. 37–57). New York: Oxford University Press.

Nasr, V. (2009). *Forces of fortune: The rise of the new Muslim middle class and what it will mean for our world*. New York: The Free Press.

New York Times, (July 13, 2007) Editorial: The land of opportunity?

New York Times on the Web (1995). Bosnia: Uncertain paths to peace. www.nytimes.com/specials/bosnia

Nets-Zehngut, R. (2007). Analyzing the process of collective reconciliation. *International Journal on World Peace, 24*(3), 53–81.

Nets-Zehngut, R. (2008). The Israeli National Information Center and collective memory of the Israeli-Arab conflict. *The Middle East Journal, 62*(4), 653–670.

Nets-Zehngut, R. (2009a). Determinants of War Veterans' Documentary Literature—The Israeli Case regarding the 1948 Palestinian Refugee Problem. Unpublished manuscript.

Nets-Zehngut, R. (2009b). Collective memory of conflicts—The impact of the phase of the conflict. Unpublished manuscript.

Nets-Zehngut, R. (in press). Palestinian autobiographical memory regarding the 1948 Palestinian exodus. *Political Psychology*.

Nets-Zehngut, R., & Bar-Tal, D. (2007). The intractable Israeli-Palestinian conflict and possible pathways to peace. In J. Kuriansky (Ed.), *Psychotherapy in a turmoil region: Reconciliation between Palestinians and Israelis from a psychological perspective* (pp. 3–13). Westport, CT: Praeger.

Nets-Zehngut, R., & Bar-Tal, D. (in press) The Israeli-Jewish popular collective memory of the Israeli-Arab/Palestinian conflict. In N. Gertz (Ed.), *Identities in transition in Israeli culture*. [In Hebrew]. Ra'anana: The Open University.

Newbury, C. (1998). Ethnicity and the politics of history in Rwanda. *Africa Today, 41* (1), 7–24.

Newbury, D., & Newbury, C. (2000). Review essay: Bringing the peasants back in: Agrarian themes in the construction and corrosion of statist historiography in Rwanda. *American Historical Review*, 832–878.

Newman, E., Riggs, D. S., & Roth, S. (2007). Thematic resolution, PTSD, and complex PTSD: The relationship between meaning and trauma-related diagnoses. *Journal of Traumatic Stress, 10*(2), 197–213.

Noor, M., Brown, R., Gonzalez, R., Manzin, J., & Lewis, C.A. (2008). On positive psychological outcomes: What helps groups with a history of conflict to forgive and reconcile with each other? *Personality and Social Psychology Bulletin, 14*(6), 819–833.

NPR. (2008, April 10). Ex-Navy Lawyer Explains Guantanamo Leak. *All Things Considered.* http://www.npr.org/templates/story/story.php?storyId=89538109&ft=1&f=1001

Nucera, J. (2008, November 8). 75 years later, a nation hopes for another F. D. R. *The New York Times*, p. B3.

Nunca Mas. (1986). *The report of the Argentine National Commission on the disappeared.* New York: Farrar, Straus, Giroux.

Nusseibeh, S., & David, A. (2007). *Once upon a country: A Palestinian life.* New York: Farrar, Straus and Giroux.

Oberschall, A. (2000). The manipulation of ethnicity: From ethnic cooperation to violence and war in Yugoslavia. *Ethnic and Racial Studies, 23,* 982–1001.

O'Connell Higgins, G. (1994). *Resilient adults overcoming a cruel past.* San Francisco: Jossey-Bass.

Oliner, S. B., & Oliner, P. (1988). *The altruistic personality: Rescuers of Jews in Nazi Europe.* New York: Free Press.

Opotaw, S. (Ed.). (1990). Moral exclusion and injustice. *Journal of Social Issues, 46* (1), 1–20.

Oren, N., & Bar-Tal, D. (2007). The detrimental dynamics of delegitimization in intractable conflicts: The Israeli–Palestinian case. *International Journal of Intercultural Relations, 31,* 111–126.

Osgood, C. E. (1962). *An alternative to war or surrender.* Urbana: University of Illinois Press.

Oxfam. (2008). *Report on the Democratic Republic of the Congo.* London: Author.

Packer, D. J. (2008). On being with us and against us: A normative conflict model of dissent in social groups. *Personality and Social Psychology Review, 12*(1), 50–72.

Packer, G. (2010, February 1). Letter from Dresden. Embers: Will a prideful city finally confront its past. *The New Yorker*, pp. 32–39.

Paluck, E. L. (2006). The second year of a "new dawn": Year two evidence for the impact of the Rwandan reconciliation radio drama Musekeweya. *LaBenvolencija evaluation report.* Unpublished manuscript.

Paluck, E. L. (2008). Kuki evaluation, 2007–2008. Final report. *LaBenevolencija evaluation report.* Unpublished manuscript.

Paluck, E. L. (2009a). Reducing intergroup prejudice and conflict using the media: A field experiment in Rwanda. *Journal of Personality and Social Psychology, 96,* 574–587.

Paluck, E. L. (2009b). What's in a norm? Sources and processes of norm change. *Journal of Personality and Social Psychology, 96,* 594–600.

Paluck, E. L., & Green, D. P. (2005). LaBenevolencija's reconciliation radio project: Musekeweya's first year evaluation report. *LaBenevolencija evaluation report.* Unpublished manuscript.

Panorama. (2004, April 4.). *BBC News.* Retrieved June 25, 2004, from http://news.bbc.co.uk/nol/shared/spl/hi/programmes/panorama/transcripts/killers.txt

Pappe, I. (2006). *The Ethnic Cleansing of Palestine.* London: Oneworld.

Pearlman, L. A. (2001). The treatment of persons with complex PTSD and other trauma-related disruptions of the self. In J. P. Wilson, M. J. Friedman, & J. D. Lindy (Eds.), *Treating psychological trauma & PTSD* (pp. 205–236). New York: Guilford Press.

Pearlman, L. A. (2003). *Trauma and attachment belief scale (TABS) manual.* Los Angeles: Western Psychological Services.

Pearlman, L. A., & Caringi, J. (2009). Living and working self-reflectively to address vicarious trauma. In C. A. Courtois & J. D. Ford (Eds.), *Treating complex traumatic stress disorders: An evidence-based guide* (pp. 202–224). New York: Guilford Press.

Pearlman, L. A., & Saakvitne, K. W. (1995). *Trauma and the therapist: Countertransference and vicarious traumatization in psychotherapy with incest survivors.* New York: W. W. Norton.

Pennebaker, J. W. (2000). The effects of traumatic disclosure on physical and mental health: The values of writing and talking about upsetting events. In J. M. Violanti, D. Paton, & C. Dunning (Eds.), *Posttraumatic stress intervention* (pp. 97–114). Springfield, IL: Charles Thomas Publisher.

Peraino, K. (2008, April 28). The Jihadist riddle: Destination martyrdom. *Newsweek,* pp. 24–30.

Pettigrew, T. (1997). Generalized intergroup contact effects on prejudice. *Personality and Social Psychology Bulletin, 23*(2), 173–185.

Pettigrew, T. (2003). People under threat: Americans, Arabs and Israelis. *Peace and Conflict: Journal of Peace Psychology, 9,* 69–90.

Pettigrew, T., & Tropp, L. (2006). A meta-analytic test of intergroup contact theory. *Journal of Personality and Social Psychology, 90,* 751–783.

Pew Global Attitudes Project. (2006, June 22). *The great divide: How Westerners and Muslims view each other.* Washington, DC: Pew.

Phalet, K., van Lotrigen, C., & Entzinger, H. (2004). *Islam in the multicultural society: The views of young people in Rotterdam.* Utrecht: ERCOMER. http://www.ercomer.org/publish/reports/EN_Rot_Islam.html.

Piliavin, I. M., Rodin, J., & Piliavin, J. A. (1969). Good samaritanism: An underground phenomenon. *Journal of Personality and Social Psychology, 13,* 289–299.

Pogrund, B. (2007). South Africa is not a model for us. *Palestine-Israel Journal, 14*(2), www.pij.org/details.php?id=1067

Polgreen, L. (2008a, November 16). Congo's riches, looted by renegade troops: Militia's grip on tin mine reflects history of exploitation. *The New York Times,* p. A1, 14–15.

Polgreen, L. (2008b, December 20). Congo warlord, linked to rights abuses, seeks a bigger stage. *The New York Times,* p. A1, A9.

Popham, P. (2005, November 18). Winning the peace in the Balkans: Risen from the ashes of war. *The Independent,.* http://www.independent.co.uk/news/world/europe/risen-from-the-ashes-of-war-winning-the-peace-in-the-balkans-515791.html

Post, J. M. (2007). *The mind of the terrorist: The psychology of terrorism from the IRA to Al-Qaeda.* New York: Palgrave Macmillan.

Post, J. M. (2009). Reframing of martyrdom and jihad and the socialization of suicide terrorists. *Political Psychology, 30*(3), 381–385.

Post, J. M., Sprinzak, E., & Denny, L. (2003). The terrorists in their own words: Interviews with 35 incarcerated Middle Eastern terrorists. *Terrorism and Political Violence, 15*, 171–184.

Power, S. (2002). *A problem from hell: America and the age of genocide.* New York: Basic Books.

Praszkier, R., Nowak, A., & Coleman, P. T. (2010). Social entrepreneurs and constructive change: The wisdom of circumventing conflict. *Peace and Conflict: Journal of Peace Psychology, 16*, 153–174.

PRI. (2004, November). *Report on monitoring and research on the gacaca. The righteous: Between oblivion and reconciliation? Example of the province of Kibuye.* Retrieved from http://www.penalreform.org/resources/rep-2004-gacacaKibuye3-en.pdf

Prior, M. (2005). Zionism and the challenge of historical truth and morality. In M. Prior (Ed.), *Speaking the truth: Zionism, Israel, and occupation.* Northampton, MA: Olive Branch Press.

Proceedings of Stockholm International Forum: A conference on Truth, Justice and Reconciliation, April 23–24, 2002. Stockholm, Sweden: Regeringskanliet.

Prunier, G. (1995). *The Rwanda crisis: History of a genocide.* New York: Columbia University Press.

Prunier, G. (2009). *Africa's world war: Congo, the Rwandan genocide, and the making of a continental catastrophe.* New York: Oxford University Press.

Pyszczynski, T., Abodllahi, A., Solomon, S., Greenberg, J., Cohen, F., & Wise, D. (2006). Mortality salience, martyrdom, and military might: the great Satan versus the axis of evil. *Personality and Social Psychology Bulletin, 32*, 525–537.

Pyszczynski, T., Greenberg, J., Solomon, S., Arndt, J., & Schimel, J. (2004). Why do people need self-esteem: A theoretical and empirical review. *Psychological Bulletin, 130*, 435–468.

Pyszczynski, T., Rothschild, Z., & Abdollahi, A. (2008). Terrorism, violence and hope for peace: A terror management perspective. *Current Directions in Psychological Science, 17*, 318–322.

Quabbin Mediation & Staub, E. (2006). Training active bystanders: A curriculum for school and community. Unpublished manuscript.

Ragasuguhanga, Y. (2008, March 27). Lecture given on the U.N. panel "Eliminate Racism: Prevent Mass Atrocities" organized by The Office of the High Commissioner of Human Rights, New York, and Sub-Committee of the Elimination of Racism of the NGO Committee on Human Rights, New York City, New York.

Raine, A. (2008). From genes to brain to antisocial behavior. *Current Directions in Psychological Science, 17*, 323–329.

Ramadan, T. (2004). *Western Muslims and the future of Islam.* Oxford, England: Oxford University Press.

Rath, T. (2003, April 27). In war-riddled Congo, militias rape with impunity. *WE News.* Retrived April 18, 2010 from http://www.womensenews.org/story/030427/in-war-riddled-congo-militias-rape-impunity

Remnick, D. (2008, May 5). Blood and sand: A revisionist Israeli historian revisits his country's origins. *The New Yorker*, pp. 72–77.

Report of the International Commission of Inquiry on Darfur to the United Nations Secretary-General, 2005.

Reuters (2009). Sudan: Cooperation better, U.N. finds. *The New York Times*, July 18, 2009, p. A6.

Reyntjens, F. (2004). Rwanda, ten years on: From genocide to dictatorship. *African Affairs, 103*, 177–210.

Reyntjens, F. (2009, November 17). Talk at Smith College, Northampton, MA.

Rhodes, R. (1999). *Why they kill*. New York: Knopf.

Rhodes, R. (2002). *Masters of death: The SS-Einsatzgruppen and the invention of the Holocaust*. New York: Alfred Knopf.

Richardson, L. (2006). *What terrorists want: Understanding the enemy*. New York: Random House.

Ricolfi, L. (2005). Paletinians, 1981-2003. In. D. Gambetta (Ed.), *Making sense of suicide missions* (pp. 77–129). New York: Oxford University Press.

Rimé, B., Kanyangara, P., Yzerbyt, V., & Paez, D. (2009). Emotional, social, and inter-group consequences of participation in a truth and reconciliation process after a genocide: Assessing the effects of gacaca tribunals in Rwanda. Unpublished manuscript.

Rouhana, N. N. (in press). Key issues in reconciliation: Challenging traditional assumptions on conflict resolution and power dynamics. In D. Bar Tal, (Ed.), *Intergroup conflicts and their resolution: Social psychological perspective* . New York: Psychology Press.

Roy, O. (2004). *Globalized Islam: The search for a new Ummah*. New York: Columbia University Press.

Rubin, Z., & Peplau, L. A. (1973). Belief in a just world and reactions to another's lot: A study of participants in the national draft lottery. *Journal of Social Issues, 29*, 73–93.

Rugge, T. (2007). The impact of restorative justice practices on participants. *Dissertation Abstracts. Section B: Science and Engineering, 67*(10–B), 6076.

Rummel, R. J. (1994). *Death by government*. New Brunswick, NJ: Transaction Publishers.

Rummel, R. J. (1998). Macht und Gesellschaft. Volume 2. Statistics of democide: genocide and mass murder since 1900. Berlin-Hamburg-Münster: LIT Verlag.

Rummel, R. J. (1999). *Statistics of democide: Genocide and mass murder since 1900*. New Brunswick, NJ: Transaction Publishers.

Saakvitne, K. W., Gamble, S. G., Pearlman, L. A., & Lev, B. T. (2000). *Risking con-nection: A training curriculum for working with survivors of childhood abuse*. Lutherville, MD: Sidran Foundation and Press.

Sageman, M. (2004). *Understanding terror networks*. Philadelphia: University of Pennsylvania Press.

Sageman, M. (2008). *Leaderless jihad: Terror networks in the twenty-first century*. Philadelphia: University of Pennsylvania Press.

Saguy, T., Dovidio, J. F., & Pratto, F. (2008). Beyond contact: Intergroup contact in the context of power relations. *Personality and Social Psychology Bulletin, 34*, 432–445.

Salomon, G. (2004). Does peace education make a difference? *Peace and Conflict: Journal of Peace Psychology, 10*, 257–274.

Salomon, G. (2006). Does peace education *really* make a difference? *Peace and Conflict: Journal of Peace Psychology, 12*(1), 37–48.

Sanday, P. R. (1981). The socio-cultural context of rape: A cross-cultural study. *Journal of Social Issues, 37*, 5–27.

Schachter, S. (1959). *The psychology of affiliation*. Stanford, CA: Stanford University Press.

Scham, P. (2007). Annapolis, November 2007: Hopes and doubts. *Middle East Institute Policy Brief. No. 2*. Retrieved from http://www.mideasti.org/policy-brief/annapolis-november-2007-hopes-and-doubt

Scham, P. L. (2006). The historical narratives of Israelis and Palestinians and the peacemaking process. *Israel Studies Forum, 21*, 58–84.

Scham, P., & Abu-Irshaid, O. (2009). Hamas. Ideological rigidity and political flexibility. United States Institute of Peace Special Report. Washington DC: United States Institute for Peace.

Schatz, R. T., Staub, E., & Lavine, H. (1999). On the varieties of national attachment: Blind versus constructive patriotism. *Political Psychology, 20*, 151–175.

Schechtman, Z., & Basheer, O. (2005). Normative beliefs supporting aggression of Arab children in intergroup conflict. *Aggressive Behavior, 31*, 324–335.

Scheff, T. J. (1994). *Bloody revenge: emotions, nationalism, and war*. Boulder, Co: Westview Press.

Schnabel, N., & Nadler, A. (2008). A needs-based model of reconciliation: Satisfying the differential needs of victim and perpetrator. *Journal of Personality and Social Psychology, 94*(1), 116–132.

Schwartz, S. H., & Clausen, G. T. (1970). Responsibility norms and helping in an emergency. *Journal of Personality and Social Psychology, 16*, 299–310.

Scoliano, E., & Schmitt, E. (2008, June 8). A not very private feud over terrorism. *The New York Times, Week in Review*, . http://www.nytimes.com/2008/06/08/weekinreview/08sciolino.html?_r=1&ref=world

Sebarenzi, J. (2009). *God Sleeps in Rwanda: A Journey of Transformation*. New York: Atria.

Segev, T. (2006). *1967: Israel, the war and the year that transformed the Middle East*. Northampton, MA: Metropolitan Books.

Semelin, J. (2007). *Purify and destroy: The political uses of massacre and genocide*. New York: Columbia University Press.

Seng, T. (2009, December). Description of this public education project at the "Course design seminar on reconciliation and coexistence." Stellenbosch, South Africa.

Sereny, G. (1974). *Into the darkness: From mercy killing to mass murder*. New York: McGraw-Hill.

Shamir, J., & Shikaki, K. (2002). Self-serving perceptions of terrorism among Israelis and Palestinians. *Political Psychology, 23*, 537–557.

Shavit, A. (2008). The big Yudkovsky. *Haaretz*. Retrieved from http://www.haaretz.com/hasen/pages/ShArtStEngPE.jhtml?itemNo=996630&contrassID=2&subContrassID=14&title='The%20big%20Yudkovsky%20'&dyn_server=172.20.5.5

Sherif, M., Harvey, D. J., White, B. J., Hood, W. K., & Sherif, C. W. (1961). *Intergroup conflict and cooperation: The robber's cave experiment*. Norman: University of Oklahoma Book Exchange.

Shorto, R. (2010, May 30). Can a Jew who reaches out to Muslims be the next Dutch prime minister—and a model for Europe? *The New York Times Magazine*. pp. 24–29.

Shriver, D. (1995). *An ethic for enemies: Forgiveness in politics*. New York: Oxford University Press.

Shriver, D. (2005). *Honest patriots: Loving a country enough to remember its misdeeds.* New York: Oxford University Press.

Sidanius, J., & Pratto, F. (1999). *Social dominance: An intergroup theory of social hierarchy and oppression*. New York: Cambridge University Press.

Sidanius, J., Pratto, F., Martin, M., & Stallworth, L. (1991). Consensual racism and career track: Some implications of Social Dominance Theory. *Political Psychology, 12,* 691–721.

Smith, C. S., & Myre, G. (2007, June 17). Hamas may find it needs its enemy. *The New York Times,* http://www.nytimes.com/2007/06/17/weekinreview/17smith.html?ei=5090&ex=1339732800&amp=;en=65f6de66c692109a;amp=&pagewanted=print

Smith, R. W. (1999). State power and genocidal intent: On the uses of genocide in the twentieth century. In L. Chorbajian & G. Shirinian (Eds.), *Studies in comparative genocide* (pp. 3–14). New York: St. Martin's Press, Inc.

Solms, M. (2009). Facing up to intergenerational cycles of violence: Psychological reflections of a South African land owner. Plenary address at the conference, "Beyond Reconciliation," University of Cape Town, South Africa, December 2–6.

Solzhenitsyn, A. (1973). *The gulag archipelago* (Vol.1). New York: Harper & Row.

Speckhard, A., & Akhmetova, K. (2005). Talking to terrorists. *Journal of Psychohistory, 33,* 125–156.

Spielman, D., & Staub, E. (2000). Reducing boys' aggression. Learning to fulfill basic needs constructively. *Journal of Applied Developmental Psychology, 21*(2), 165–181.

Stanton, G. (n. d.). *Factors facilitating and impeding genocide.* Retrieved from http://www.armeniaforeignministry.com/conference/gregory_stanton.pdf

Staub, E. (1968). The reduction of a specific fear by information combined with exposure to the feared stimulus. *Proceedings, 76th Annual Convention of the American Psychological Association, 3,* 535–537.

Staub, E. (1970a). A child in distress: The effects of focusing responsibility on children on their attempts to help. *Developmental Psychology, 2,* 152–154.

Staub, E. (1970b). A child in distress: The influence of age and number of witnesses on children's attempts to help. *Journal of Personality and Social Psychology, 14,* 130–140.

Staub, E. (1971a). The learning and unlearning of aggression: The role of anxiety, empathy, efficacy and prosocial values. In J. Singer (Ed.), *The control of aggression and violence: Cognitive and physiological factors* (pp. 93–125). New York: Academic Press.

Staub, E. (1971b). The use of role playing and induction in children's learning of helping and sharing behavior. *Child Development, 42,* 805–817.

Staub, E. (1972). The effects of persuasion and modeling on delay of gratification. *Developmental Psychology, 6,* 168–177.

Staub, E. & Kellett, D. S. (1972). Increasing pain tolerance by information about aversive stimuli. *Journal of Personality and Social Psychology, 21,* 198–203.

Staub, E. (1974). Helping a distressed person: Social, personality and stimulus determinants. In L. Berkowitz (Ed.), *Advances in experimental social psychology* (Vol. 7., pp. 203–342). New York: Academic Press.

Staub, E. (1978). *Positive social behavior and morality: Vol. 1. Personal and social influences* New York: Academic Press.

Staub, E. (1979). *Positive social behavior and morality: Vol. 2. Socialization and development* New York: Academic Press.

Staub, E. (1980). Social and prosocial behavior: Personal and situational influences and their interactions. In. E. Staub (Ed.), *Personality: Basic aspects and current research* (pp. 237–294). Englewood Cliffs, NJ: Prentice-Hall.

Staub, E. (1985). The psychology of perpetrators and bystanders. *Political Psychology, 6*, 61–86.

Staub, E. (1989). *The roots of evil: The origins of genocide and other group violence.* New York: Cambridge University Press.

Staub, E. (1993). Individual and group selves, motivation and morality. In G. G. Noam & T. E. Wren (Eds.), *The Moral self* (pp. 337–359). Cambridge, MA: MIT Press.

Staub, E. (1996). The cultural-societal roots of violence: The examples of genocidal violence and of contemporary youth violence in the United States. *American Psychologist, 51*, 117–132.

Staub, E. (1997a). Blind versus constructive patriotism: Moving from embeddedness in the group to critical loyalty and action. In D. Bar-Tal and E. Staub (Eds.), *Patriotism in the lives of individuals and groups.* Chicago: Nelson-Hall Publishers.

Staub, E. (1997b). The psychology of rescue: Perpetrators, bystanders and heroic helpers. In J. Michalczyk (Ed.), *Resisters, rescuers and refugees: Historical and ethical issues* (pp. 137–147). Kansas City, MO: Sheed and Ward.

Staub, E. (1998). Breaking the cycle of genocidal violence: Healing and reconciliation. In J. Harvey (Ed.), *Perspectives on loss* (pp. 231–241). Washington, DC: Taylor and Francis.

Staub, E. (1999a). Aggression and self-esteem. *American Psychological Association Monitor, 30*, p. 6.

Staub, E. (1999b). The origins and prevention of genocide, mass killing and other collective violence. *Peace and Conflict: Journal of Peace Psychology, 5*, 303–337.

Staub, E. (1999c). The roots of evil: Personality, social conditions, culture and basic human needs. *Personality and Social Psychology Review, 3*, 179–192.

Staub, E. (2000). Genocide and mass killing: Origins, prevention, healing and reconciliation. *Political Psychology, 21*(2), 367–382.

Staub, E. (2001). Ethnopolitical and other group violence: Origins and prevention. In D. Chirot & M. E. P. Seligman (Eds.), *Ethnopolitical warfare: Causes, consequences and possible solutions* (pp. 289–304). Washington, DC: American Psychological Association.

Staub, E. (2002). Understanding and preventing genocide: a life's work shaped by a child's experience. In S. Totten & C. Jacobs (Eds.), *Pioneers of genocide studies: Confronting mass death in the century of genocide* (pp. 479–507). Westport, CT: Greenwood Publishers.

Staub, E. (2003a). *The psychology of good and evil: Why children, adults and groups help and harm others.* New York: Cambridge University Press.

Staub, E. (2003b). Understanding and responding to group violence: Genocide, mass killing, terrorism. In A. J. Marsella & F. Moghaddam (Eds.), *International terrorism and terrorists: Psychosocial perspectives* (pp. 151–169). Washington, DC: American Psychological Association.

Staub, E. (2004a). Justice, healing and reconciliation: How the people's courts in Rwanda can promote them. *Peace and Conflict: The Journal of Peace Psychology, 10,* 25–32.

Staub, E. (2004b). Preventing terrorism: Raising inclusively caring children in the complex world of the 21st century. In C. E. Stout (Ed.), *The psychology of terrorism.* (pp.185–199). Westport, Connecticut: Praeger.

Staub, E. (2005a). Constructive and harmful forms of forgiveness and reconciliation after genocide and mass killing. In E. Worthington (Ed.), *Handbook of forgiveness* (pp. 443–461). Brunner-Routledge.

Staub, E. (2005b). The origins and evolution of hate, with notes on prevention. In R. Sternberg (Ed.), *The psychology of hate* (pp. 51–67). New York: Cambridge University Press.

Staub, E. (2005c). The roots of goodness: The fulfillment of basic human needs and the development of caring, helping and nonaggression, inclusive caring, moral courage, active bystandership, and altruism born of suffering. In G. Carlo & C. Edwards (Eds.), *Moral motivation through the life span: Theory, research, applications* (pp. 33–73). Nebraska Symposium on Motivation. Lincoln: Nebraska University Press.

Staub, E. (2006a). Reconciliation after genocide, mass killing or intractable conflict: Understanding the roots of violence, psychological recovery and steps toward a general theory. *Political Psychology, 27* (6), 865–895.

Staub, E. (2006b). The cultural and psychological origins of war with notes on prevention. In M. Fitzduff & C. E. Stout (Eds.), *The psychology of resolving global conflicts, vol. 2.* Praeger.

Staub, E. (2007a, August). Evil: Understanding bad situations and systems, but also personality and group dynamics. [Review of the book, The Lucifer Effect: Understanding how good people turn evil, by P. Zimbardo]. *PsychCritiques.*

Staub, E. (2007b). Preventing violence and terrorism and promoting positive relations between Dutch and Muslim communities in Amsterdam. *Peace and Conflict: Journal of Peace Psychology, 13*(3), 333–361.

Staub, E. (2008a). Promoting reconciliation after genocide and mass killing in Rwanda—and other post-conflict settings. In A. Nadler, T. Malloy, & J. D. Fisher (Eds.), *Social psychology of intergroup reconciliation* (pp. 395–423). New York: Oxford University Press.

Staub, E. (2008b). The heroism of survivors: Survivors saving themselves, its impact on their lives, and altruism born of suffering. In D. C. Berliner & H. Kupermintz (Eds.), *Fostering change in institutions, environments, and people: A festschrift in honor of Gavriel Salomon.* (pp. 211–219). New York: Routledge.

Staub, E. (2008c). The origins of genocide and mass killing, prevention, reconciliation and their application to Rwanda. In V. M. Visser & R. A. Vernon (Eds.),

The breakdown of ethnic relations: Why neighbors kill (pp. 245–269). Malden, MA: Blackwell Publishing.

Staub, E. (Ed.). (in press a). *The panorama of mass violence: Origins, prevention, reconciliation and the development of caring and active bystandership.* New York: Oxford University Press.

Staub, E. (in press b). Understanding the violence by guards at Abu Ghraib—and in other prison settings. In E. Staub (Ed.). *The panorama of mass violence: Origins, prevention, reconciliation and the development of caring and active bystandership.* New York: Oxford University Press.

Staub, E., & Baer, R. S., Jr. (1974). Stimulus characteristics of a sufferer and difficulty of escape as determinants of helping. *Journal of Personality and Social Psychology, 30,* 279–285.

Staub, E., & Bar-Tal, D. (2003). Genocide, mass killing and intractable conflict: Roots, evolution, prevention and reconciliation. In D. Sears, L. Huddy, & R. Jervis (Eds.), *Handbook of political psychology* (pp. 710–754). New York: Oxford University Press.

Staub, E., & Feinberg, H. (1980, August). *Regularities in peer interaction, empathy, and sensitivity to others.* Presentation at the Development of Prosocial Behavior and Cognitions symposium, the meetings of the American Psychological Association, Montreal, Quebec.

Staub, E., & Pearlman, L. (2001). Healing, reconciliation and forgiving after genocide and other collective violence. In S. J. Helmick & R. L. Petersen (Eds.), *Forgiveness and reconciliation: Religion, public policy and conflict transformation* (pp. 205–229). Radnor, PA: Templeton Foundation Press.

Staub, E., & Pearlman, L. A. (2006). Advancing healing and reconciliation. In L. Barbanel & R. Sternberg (Eds.), *Psychological interventions in times of crisis* (pp. 213–245). New York: Springer-Verlag.

Staub, E., & Pearlman, L. A. (2009). Reducing intergroup prejudice and conflict: A commentary. *Journal of Personality and Social Psychology, 96,* 588–594.

Staub, E., Pearlman, L. A., & Bilali, R. (2008). Psychological recovery, reconciliation and the prevention of new violence: an approach and its uses in Rwanda. In B. Hart (Ed.), *Peacebuilding in traumatized societies* (pp. 131–155). University Press of America.

Staub, E., Pearlman, L. A., & Bilali, R. (2010). Understanding the roots and impact of violence and psychological recovery as avenues to reconciliation after mass violence and intractable conflict: Applications to national leaders, journalists, community groups, public education through radio, and children. In G. Salomon & E. Cairns (Eds.), *Handbook of peace education* (pp. 269–287). New York: Psychology Press.

Staub, E., Pearlman, L. A., Gubin, A., & Hagengimana, A. (2005). Healing, reconciliation, forgiving and the prevention of violence after genocide or mass killing: An intervention and its experimental evaluation in Rwanda. *Journal of Social and Clinical Psychology, 24*(3), 297–334.

Staub, E., Pearlman, L. A., Weiss, G., & van Hoek, A. (in press). Public education through radio to prevent violence, promote trauma healing and reconciliation, and build peace in Rwanda and the Congo. In E. Staub (Ed.), *The panorama of* mass violence: Origins, prevention, reconciliation and the development of caring and active bystandership. New York: Oxford University Press.

Staub, E., & Rosenthal, (1994). Mob violence: Social-cultural influences, group processes and participants. In L. D. Eron, J. H. Gentry, & P. Schlegel (Eds.), *Reason to hope: A psychosocial perspective on violence & youth* (pp. 281–315). Washington, DC: American Psychological Association.

Staub, E., Tracy, S., &Wallace, S. (in press). Training active bystanders. In E. Staub (Ed.), *The panorama of mass violence: Origins, prevention, reconciliation and the development of caring and active bystandership.* New York: Oxford University Press.

Staub, E., & Vollhardt, J. (2008). Altruism born of suffering: The roots of caring and helping after experiences of personal and political victimization. *American Journal of Orthopsychiatry, 78, 267–280.*

Steiner, J. M. (1980). The SS yesterday and today: A socio-psychological view. In J. Dimsdale (Ed.), *Survivors, victims and perpetrators: Essays on the Nazi Holocaust* (pp. 405-457). New York: Hemisphere Publishing Company.

Stephan, W. G. (2008). The road to reconciliation. In A. Nadler, T. Malloy, & J. D. Fisher (Eds.), *Social psychology of intergroup reconciliation* (pp. 369–395). New York: Oxford University Press.

Stern, J. (2004). *Terror in the name of God.* New York: HarperCollins.

Sternberg, R., & Sternberg, K. (2008). *The nature of hate.* New York: Cambridge University Press.

Stotland, E. (1969). Exploratory studies of empathy. In L. Berkowitz (Ed.), *Advances in experimental social psychology* (Vol. 4). New York: Academic Press.

Stover, E. (2004). Witnesses and the promise of justice in the Hague. In E. Stover & H. A. Weinstein (Eds.), *My neighbor, my enemy: Justice and community in the aftermath of mass atrocity.* Cambridge, England: Cambridge University Press.

Strang, H., Sherman, L., Angel., C., Woods, D., Bennett, S., Newbury-Birch, D., et al. (2007). Victim evaluations of face to face restorative justice conferences: A quasi-experimental analysis. *Journal of Social Issues, 62, 281–307.*

Straus, S. (2006). *The order of genocide: Race, power, and war in Rwanda.* Ithaca, NY: Cornell University Press.

Stroebe, W., Lenkert, A., & Jonas, K. (1988). Familiarity may breed contempt: The impact of student exchange on national stereotypes and attitudes. In W. Stroebe, A. W. Kruglanski, D. Bar-Tal, & M. Hewstone (Eds.), *The social psychology of intergroup conflict: Theory, research and application.* New York: Springer-Verlag.

Subasic, M. (2005). President of the Association of "Mothers of Srebrenica and Zepa Enclaves". Presentation at the Pathways to Reconciliation and Global Human Rights International Conference, Sarajaveo, Bosnia Herzegovina.

Suedfeld, P., & Schaller, M. (2002). Authoritarianism and the Holocaust: Some cognitive and affective implications. In L. S. Newman, & R. Erber *Understanding genocide: The social psychology of the Holocaust* (pp. 68–91). New York: Oxford University Press.

Tajfel, H. (1978). Social categorization, social identity and social comparison. In H. Tajfel (Ed.), *Differentiation between social groups* (pp. 61–76). London: Academic Press.

Tajfel, H. (1982). Social psychology of intergroup relations. *Annual Review of Psychology, 33,* 1–39.

Tajfel, H., Flamant, C., Billig, M. Y., & Bundy, R. P. (1971). Societal categorization and intergroup behavior. *European Journal of Social Psychology, 1,* 149–177.

Tajfel, H., & Turner, J. C. (1979). An integrative theory of intergroup conflict. In W. G. Austin & S. Worchel (Eds.), *The social psychology of intergroup relations.* Monterey, CA: Brooks-Cole.

Tajfel, H., & Turner, J. C. (1986). The social identity theory of inter-group behavior. In S. Worchel & L. W. Austin (Eds.), *Psychology of intergroup relations.* Chicago: Nelson-Hall.

Taylor, D. M., & Louis, W. (2003). Terrorism and the quest for identity. In A. J. Marsella & F. Moghaddam (Eds.), *International terrorism and terrorists: Psychosocial perspectives* (pp. 169–187). Washington, DC: American Psychological Association.

Tec, N. (1986). *When light pierced the darkness: Christian rescuers of Jews in Nazi occupied Poland.* New York: Oxford University Press.

Tedeschi, R. G., Park, C. L., & Calhoun, L. G. (Eds.), (1998). *Post-traumatic growth: Positive transformations in the aftermath of crisis.* Mahwah, NJ: Erlbaum.

Tetlock, P. E., Kristel, O. V., Elson, S. B., Green, M. C., & Lerner., J. S. (2000). The psychology of the unthinkable: Taboo trade-offs, forbidden base rates, and heretical counterfactuals. *Journal of Personality and Social Psychology, 78,* 853–870.

Thalhammer, K. E., O'Loughlin, P. L., Glazer, M. P., Glazer, P. M., McFarland, S., Shepela, S. T., & Stoltzfus, N. (2007). *Courageous resistance: The power of ordinary people.* New York: Palgrave Macmillan.

Tilllie, J., & Slijper, B. (2005). *Immigrant political integration and ethnic civic communities in Amsterdam* (Unpublished manuscript). Institute for Migration and Ethnic Studies, Department of Political Science, University of Amsterdam.

Tobias, J. (2008). Intergroup contact caused by institutional change. An exploration of deregulation in Rwanda's coffee sector and attitudes towards reconciliation (Unpublished doctoral dissertation). Washington State University, Pullman.

Totten S., Parsons, W. S., & Charny, I. W. (Eds.). 1997. *Century of genocide: Eyewitness accounts and critical views.* New York: Garland Publishing.

Triandis, H. C. (1994). *Culture and social behavior.* New York: McGraw-Hill, Inc.

Tropp, L. R., & Pettigrew, T. F. (2005). Relationships between intergroup contact and prejudice among minority and majority status groups. *Psychological Science, 16,* 951–957.

United Nations Convention on the Prevention and Punishment of the Crime of Genocide, Article 2. (1948).

United States Holocaust Memorial Museum Alert. (2008, October, 28). *Responding to the threat of genocide. Congo: Civilians Caught in Violent Crossfire.* Washington, DC: U.S. Holocaust Memorial Museum.

Uvin, P. (1998). *Aiding violence. The development enterprise in Rwanda.* Sterling, VA: Kumarian Press.

Valent, P. (1998). Child survivors: A review. In J. Kestenberg & C. Kahn (Eds.), *Children surviving persecution: An international study of trauma and healing* New York: Praeger.

Valentino, B. A. (2004). *Final solutions: Mass killing and genocide in the 20th century.* Ithaca, NY: Cornell University Press.

Vallacher, R.R., Coleman, P.T., Nowak, A.& Bui-Wrzosinska, L. (2010). Rethinking intractable conflict: The perspective of dynamical systems. *American Psychologist.* 65, 262–279.

Van der Kolk, B.A. (2009). Afterword. In C. A. Curtois & J. D. Ford (Eds.), *Treating complex traumatic stress disorders* (pp. 455–466). New York: Guilford.

Van Dijk, P. (2008, April). Open for business. *Ode*, pp. 34–38.

Varshney, A. (2002). *Ethnic conflict and civic life: Hindus and Muslims in India.* New Haven, CT: Yale University Press.

Verwimp, P. (2004). Peasant ideology and genocide in Rwanda under Habyarimana. In S. Cook (Ed.), *Genocide in Cambodia and Rwanda: New perspectives.* Yale Center for International Area Studies: Genocide Studies Program Monograph Series No. 1.

Victoroff, J. (2009a). Suicide terrorism and the biology of significance. *Political Psychology*, 30(3), 397–400.

Victoroff, J. (2009b). The mind of the terrorist: A review and critique of psychological approaches. In J. Victoroff & A. W. Kruglanski (Eds.), *Psychology of terrorism: The best writings about the mind of the terrorist* (pp. 55–87). New York: Psychology Press.

Victoroff, J., & Kruglanski, A. W. (Eds.), (2009). *Psychology of terrorism: The best writings about the mind of the terrorist.* New York: Psychology Press.

Volkan, V. D. (1997). *Blood lines: From ethnic pride to ethnic terrorism.* New York: Farrar, Straus and Giroux.

Volkan, V. D. (1998). Tree model: Psychopolitical dialogues and the promotion of coexistence. In E. Weiner (Ed.), *The handbook of interethnic coexistence.* New York: Continuum.

Volkan, V. (2004). *Blind trust: Large groups and their leaders in times of crisis and terror.* Charlottesville, VA: Pitchstone Publishing.

Vollhardt, J. (2009). The role of victim beliefs in the Israeli-Palestinian conflict: Risk or potential for peace? *Peace and Conflict: Journal of Peace Psychology*, 15(2), 135–159.

Vollhardt, J., Coutin, M., Staub, E., Weiss, G., & Deflander, J. (2007). Deconstructing hate speech in the DRC: A psychological media sensitization campaign. *Journal of Hate Studies*, 5(1), 15–37.

Vollhardt, J., & Staub, E. (2009). *Altruism born of suffering: The effects of past suffering on prosocial behavior toward outgroups* Unpublished manuscript. Department of Psychology, University of Massachusetts.

Wadud, A. (2006). *Inside the gender jihad: Reform in Islam.* Oxford, England: One World Publisher.

Waldorf, L. (2007). Ordinariness and orders: Explaining popular participation in the Rwandan genocide. *Genocide Studies and Prevention*, 2(3), 267–270.

Wallace, H. M., Exline, J. J., & Baumeister, R. F. (2008). Interpersonal consequences of forgiveness: Does forgiveness deter or encourage repeat offenses? *Journal of Experimental Social Psychology*, 44, 453–460.

Waller, J. (2007). *Becoming evil: how ordinary people commit genocide and mass killing.* (2nd ed.), New York: Oxford University Press.

Weimann, G. (2006). *Terror on the internet: The new arena, the new challenges.* Washington, DC: United States Institute for Peace Press Books.

Weiner, T. (2008, December 7). The Kashmir connection: A puzzle. *The New York Times. Week in Review*, p. 3.

Wessells, M. (2007). *Child soldiers: From violence to protection.* Cambridge, MA: Harvard University Press.

Wessells, M., & Monteiro, C. (2001). Psychosocial interventions and post-war reconstruction in Angola: Interweaving western and traditional approaches. In D. J. Christie, R. V. Wagner, & D. D. Winter (Eds.), *Peace, conflict and violence* (pp. 262–277). Upper Saddler River, NJ: Prentice Hall.

White, R. K. (1984). *Fearful warriors: A psychological profile of U.S.-Soviet relations.* New York: Macmillan.

Whiting, B. B., & Whiting, J. W. M. (1975). *Children of six cultures: A psycho cultural analysis.* Cambridge, MA: Harvard University Press.

Whittaker, D. J. (1999). *Conflict and reconciliation in the contemporary world.* London: Routledge.

Wickham, C. (2005, June). *Debates on democracy, pluralism, and citizenship rights.* Paper presented at the PISAP/NESA Annual Conference: Political Islam: Critical and Emerging Ideologies and Actors.

Will, G. F. (2009, April 20). The what of nations? *Newsweek*, p. 64.

Wolpe, H., & McDonald. S. (2008). Democracy and peace building: Rethinking the conventional wisdom. *The Round Table, 97*(394), 137–145.

Worchel, S., & Coutant, D. K. (2008). Between conflict and reconciliation: Toward a theory of peaceful coexistence. In A. Nadler, T. Malloy, & J. D. Fisher (Eds.), *Social psychology of intergroup reconciliation* (pp. 423–447). New York: Oxford University Press.

Worth, R. F. (2009, May 2). Ex-spy turned negotiator sits down with Islamists and the West. *The New York Times*, p. A5.

Worthington, E. (Ed.). (2005). *Handbook of forgiveness.* New York: Routledge.

Worthington, E., & Drinkard, D. T. (2000). Promoting reconciliation through psychoeducational and therapeutic interventions. *Journal of Marital and Family Therapy, 26*, 93–101.

Wright, L. (2008. June 2). The rebellion within: An Al Qaeda mastermind questions terrorism. *The New Yorker*, pp. 37–53.

Wyatt, E. (2010, May 21). Congo Minerals Provision Becomes Part of Financial Bill. *The New York Times.* http://www.nytimes.com/2010/05/22/business/22congo.html?ref=edward_wyatt

Wyman, D. S. (1984). *The abandonment of Jews: America and the Holocaust, 1941–1945.* New York: Pantheon Books.

Zakaria, F. (2008, June 2). The only thing we have to fear. *Newsweek*, p. 37, quoting a study done at Simon Frazer University in Canada.

Zartman, I. W. (1989). *Ripe for resolution, conflict and intervention in Africa.* New York: Oxford University Press.

Zimbardo, P. G. (1969). The human choice: Individuation, reason, and order versus deindividuation, impulse and chaos. In Arnold, W.J. & Levine, D. (eds). *Nebraska symposium on motivation*. Lincoln: University of Nebraska Press. pp. 237–307.

Zimbardo, P. G. (1989). *Quiet rage: The Stanford Prison study* [video]. Stanford, CA: Stanford University.

Zimbardo, P. G. (2007). *The Lucifer effect: Understanding how good people turn evil*. New York: Random House.

Zinn, H. (2003). *A people's history of the United States: 1492–present*. New York: HarperPerennial.

Zukav, G., & Francis, L. (2007). *Soul to soul: Communications from the heart*. New York: Free Press.

Author Index

Gobodo-Madikezela, P., 441n14, 488n14, 488n35
Goldberg, J., 98n119
Goldhagen, D. J., 164n43, 194n70, 237n55
Goldstein, A. P., 360n18
Gomaa, G. M. A. A., 161
Gonzalez, R., 163n11
Gopin, M., 335
Gorbachev, Mikhail, 395
Gourevich, P., 97n73
Gray, Z., 361n56
Green, P., 429n21
Green, D.P., 386n21, 386n24, 386n29, 386n31
Greenberg, J., 130n29, 130n32
Grille, R., 24n23, 237n47
Grodman, S. M., 404n8
Grube, J. W., 307n5
Grusec, J. E., 496n11
Gubin, A., 236n36
Guha, R., 341n20
Gurr, T. R., 129n2, 131n62, 163n4

Habyarimana, Juvenal 155, 201
Hagan, J., 236n8
Hagee, J., 165n79, 207n21
Hagengimana, A., 236n36
Haji, R., 165n82
Hallie, P. P., 404n21, 405n36
Halperin, E., 236n28
Hamburg, D., 46n11, 95n2, 131n53, 164n51, 164n61, 299n11, 325n12, 325n20, 429n38, 517n1
Hamilton, V. L., 272n60
Handl, V., 469n69
Hanson, H. E., 271n29
Harff, B., 129n2, 131n48, 131n67, 163n4, 193n45, 236n23, 237n65, 237n81, 238n87, 429n24
Haritos-Fatouros, M., 193n12, 272n41, 272n65
Harper, J. J., 441n13
Harvey, D.J., 341n17
Hasan, Nidal, 93
Hatzfeld, J., 131n51, 236n4, 236n29, 270n1, 270n5, 271n7, 271n14, 271n28, 488n27, 488n31

Haven, T., 95n1, 308n10
Havugimana, J., 271n31, 386n39, 386n43, 467n18
Helson, H., 193n15
Herbert, B., 404n30
Herbert, T. B., 467n3
Herman, J., 284n2, 467n7
Hersh, Seymour, 397
Hess, H., 429n23
Hewstone, M., 163n11, 341n1, 341n3, 341n27
Hiebert, M. S., 236n1, 236n9
Higginson, J., 236n37
Hilberg, R., 24n13, 165n66, 271n12
Himmler, H. 141, 149
Hirohito, emperor, 179
Hirsch-Hoefler, S., 236n28
Hitler, A., 146, 149, 150, 154, 164n57, 171, 176, 190
Hobfoll, S., 165n78
Hochschild, A., 131n82, 271n30
Hoffman, M. L., 496n3
Hogg, M. A., 130n27, 163n19, 164n21, 164n24, 164n25
Hollander, P., 24n10, 164n31, 271n13
Honeyman, C., 468n58
Hood, W.K., 341n17
Horgan, J., 46n7, 46n10, 385n8, 385n10, 385n15
Horowitz, D., 95n2, 96n24
Hosenball, M., 273n88, 385n16
Houphonet-Boigny, President, 337
Hume, 171,
Hussein, Sadam, 85, 91, 203, 323

Ignatieff, M., 285n10
Ilibagiza, I., 271n24, 386n32, 487n5, 488n16
Ingelaere, B., 96n41, 96n53, 97n74, 97n75, 271n31, 386n39, 386n43, 467n18, 468n60, 469n65, 518n4
Isikoff, M., 273n88
Iyer, A., 95n7

Janis, I., 164n63
Janoff-Bulman, R., 285n21
Jonas, K., 341n14
Jonassohn, K., 129n3, 164n28

Rothschild, Z., 130n29, 130n33, 130n35, 385n6
Rouhana, N.N., 25n26, 299n7
Roy, O., 272n61
Rubin, Z., 95n12
Ruboneka, Suzanne, 486
Rugge, T., 468n55
Rummel, R.J., 24n22, 25n25, 97n62, 97n63, 97n64, 237n64
Rumsfeld, Donald, 38
Rushton, J. P., 496n11
Rymond-Richmond, W., 236n8

Saakvitne, K.W., 24n19, 95n1, 130n17, 440n8, 467n7
Sadat, Anwar, 395, 159, 262
Sageman, M., 46n5, 46n10, 98n129, 98n130, 131n58, 164n53, 165n80, 165n83, 194n65, 194n76, 194n79, 236n15, 236n33, 272n62, 272n77, 325n14
Saguy, T., 95n8, 97n79
Salomon, G., 385n1, 385n2, 468n41, 468n47
Sanday, P.R., 237n49, 237n83
Sau'ud, King of Saudi Arabia, 157
Savimbi, Jonas, 77
Schachter, S., 163n17
Schaller, M., 164n23, 237n56
Scham, P., 325n25, 468n25, 468n27, 468n36, 468n40, 518n6
Schatz, R.T., 207n29, 405n39
Schechtman, Z., 341n2
Scheff, T.J., 130n41
Schimel, J., 130n29
Schindler, Oscar, 399
Schlesinger, A., 151
Schmelling, Max, 396, 400
Schmitt, E., 99n136, 99n139
Schnabel, N., 285n25, 299n8, 488n19
Schwartz, S.H., 193n23, 404n12
Scoliano, E., 99n136, 99n139
Sears, R., 130n23
Sebarenzi, J., 97n69, 97n75
Segev, T., 98n114
Semelin, J., 126, 131n76, 192n3
Seng, T., 484, 488n39
Senni, Asis, 350

Sereny, G., 193n31
Shamir, J., 95n23
Shapiro, Y., 320
Sharon, Ariel, 23, 183
Shavit, A., 236n25
Sherif, C.W., 341n17
Sherif, M., 341n17
Shikaki, K., 95n23
Shorto, R., 385n17
Shriver, D., 404n18, 467n16, 487n4, 488n36
Sidanius, J., 95n9, 95n11, 237n74
Simmons, C.H., 95n12, 193n20
Simutis, Z.M., 496n11
Slijper, B., 361n49
Smith, C.S., 98n121
Smith, R.W., 95n17, 164n32
Solms, M., 483–84, 488n38
Solomon, S., 130n29, 130n32
Solzhenitsyn, A., 164n27
Soros, George, 359, 415
Speckhard, A., 272n76
Spielberg, Steven, 390
Spielman, D., 496n14
Spinrad, T.L., 496n3
Sprinzak, E., 165n87
Stalin, Joseph, 8, 143
Stallworth, L., 95n11
Stanton, G., 193n39
Staub, E., 24n1, 24n9, 24n12, 24n15, 24n16, 24n17, 25n24, 25n31, 25n32, 46n10, 46n15, 46n19, 46n23, 46n24, 46n26, 46n27, 46n28, 46n29, 46n30, 46n31, 46n33, 47n35, 47n36, 47n37, 95n2, 95n13, 96n44, 98n126, 98n127, 99n142, 103t, 130n5, 130n7, 130n8, 130n10, 130n14, 130n17, 130n18, 130n19, 130n22, 130n36, 130n42, 131n43, 131n50, 131n54, 131n63, 131n68, 131n70, 139n52, 163n2, 164n26, 164n30, 164n56, 164n59, 165n64, 165n66, 165n91, 165n92, 169n34, 169n40, 192n1, 192n6, 192n9, 192n11, 193n22, 193n25, 193n27, 193n28, 193n38, 193n44, 193n47, 193n48, 193n55,

Victoroff, J., 24n7, 46n10, 98n129, 237n69, 272n68, 272n70, 299n16
Volkan, V., 131n55, 360n10
Vollhardt, J., 46n27, 130n17, 193n27, 237n50, 285n7, 285n17, 285n18, 285n19, 285n20, 285n22, 360n22, 495f, 497n18, 497n19, 497n22

Wadud, A., 360n7
Waldorf, L., 237n53
Wallace, H.M., 488n17
Wallace, S., 47n36
Wallenberg, R., 280
Waller, J., 163n16, 192n10, 271n37
Wegner, Armin, 396
Weimann, G., 164n54
Weiner, T., 99n138
Weiss, G., 25n32, 193n27, 285n19, 307n1
Wessells, M., 46n9, 360n20, 488n40
Western, Jon, 412
White, R. K., 164n26, 327, 341n4, 356
White, B.J., 341n17
Whiting, B.B., 496n7

Whiting, J.W.M., 496n7
Whittaker, D.J., 440n2
Wickham, C., 361n53, 361n54
Will, G.F., 46n12
Wilson, M., 193n50
Wise, D., 130n32
Wolpe, H., 25n28, 429n14, 412, 429n19
Worchel, S., 341n30
Worth, R.F., 325n21
Worthington, E., 41n15, 299n6, 487n3, 487n8
Wright, L., 98n130, 165n77, 165n88, 326n30
Wyatt, E., 325n19
Wyman, D.S., 428n3

Yzerbyt, V., 467n10

Zakaria, F., 99n134, 272n43
Zartman, I.W., 164n58, 325n5, 325n7
Zavalloni, M., 194n64
Ziereis, F., 170
Zimbardo, P.G., 163n15, 194n68, 207n9, 207n10, 236n14, 271n34, 272n44, 272n45, 272n46, 272n51, 404n28
Zukav, G., 469n63
Zungo-Dirwayi, N., 468n62

Subject Index

Note: Page numbers followed by "*n*" denote notes.

Arab states, 86
Argentina, 58, 145, 174, 228, 233, 395
   mass killing in, 38
Armenians, genocide of, 34, 38, 44, 457 (*see also* Turkey)
Arusha peace accords, 63, 147, 184, 322
atrocities, 30, 43
Atrocities Documentation Survey, 211
Atrocities Prevention Committee (APC), 424
attitudes and actions of the rescuers' parents, 354
attitudes
   developing positive, toward other, 327 (*see also* contact; humanizing)
   positive, between groups, 14, 29
Aum Shinrykio group, 261, 262
Auschwitz, 176, 201, 215, 252
   Nazi doctors at, 253, 256, 360
   self, 109
Australia, 123, 150
Austria, 154, 204, 231, 347
Autesserre, S., 124
authoritarian political system, 18
authority
   excessive respect for, 18, 42
   respect for and obedience to, 20, 222–25, 257
authority orientation, 225
autobiographical memories, 455, 456
autocratic/authoritarian government, 13
autocratic and democratic political systems, 227–30
autogenocide, 8, 178
autonomus self, 189
autonomy, 56, 105, 108, 117, 138
availability heuristics, 387
awareness of others, 364

Baader-Meinhof gang, 187
Baha'i, 387, 428
Balfour declaration, 81
Bali
   2002 incident, 7
banality of evil, the, 34
Banyamulenge, 67, 74
Barbary Wars, 220

Battle for God, 159
Basic psychological needs
   See frustration of; psychological needs
BBC, 383
Belgium, 55, 449
biological difference claim and mass violence, 62
blind patriots, 206
blood feuds, 183
Bolshevism, 141
Bosnia, 191–92, 203, 205, 215, 267, 297, 389, 473
   constructive groups in, 350
   ethnic cleansing in, 27, 38
   and Serbs, 354
Boston, 349
Brazil, 217
Brcko, 391
Britain, 69, 81, 92, 120, 154, 204, 268, 279, 294, 340
Bugesera, 479
bureaucracy, 10
   and Holocaust, 9
Burundi, 76, 110, 244, 300, 301, 306
Bush administration, 23, 410
Bystanders and bystandership (*see also* active; constructive; passivity; positive)
   active, 5, 20, 41
   effects of, 283–84
   external bystanders, 18, 59, 200–204, 207, 228
   inhibitors of, 195–98
   instigation of action, 402–3
   internal bystanders, 18
   networks of, 395
   opposition and nonviolent resistance, possibility of, 198–200
   passivity and complicity of, 5, 18, 56, 59, 146, 173, 176, 195, 196–98, 200–204, 206–7, 220, 274, 282, 283–4, 297, 300, 310
   United States as bystander, 204–6

Cambodia, 6, 10, 117, 118, 143, 144, 156, 168, 178, 215, 232, 297, 303, 311, 484
   civil war of, 55
Camp David accords, 202
Canada, 231

conflict (*cont.*)
  unjust social arrangements and, 230
  as zero sum situation, 59, 80
Conflicts Forum, 317
Conflict Transformation across Cultures (CONTACT), 414
Congo, 3–4, 8, 27, 31, 64, 117, 119, 128, 134, 144, 178, 201, 204, 219, 232, 244, 247, 293, 297, 300, 301, 306, 312, 314, 323, 512–13
  fighters returned to Rwanda from, 351–52
  killing and raping in, 248–51
  violence in, 65–68, 75–80
connected self, 189–90, 489, 490
connection, (see disconnection; psychological needs)
consciousness, (*see* critical)
constitution
  and democracy, 359
constructive bystander, 403 (*see also* active bystandership)
constructive fulfillment, 107, 108
constructive groups,
  creation of, 20, 348–351
constructive ideologies, 343, 367, 509–10
  alternative communities and, 348–52
  alternative groups and, 359
  in Palestinian-Israeli conflict, 345–48
  creation of, 20
constructive leadership, 406–9, 511
constructive patriotism, 206, 402
constructive responses and structures, 309
  and democracy and development, 313–16
  engagement and dialogue, 316–24
  preventive diplomacy and negotiation, 310–13
contact, positive effects of, 28
contact and humanizing
  devalued groups, 327–29
  extended and imagined contact, 339–40
  limits and challenges of, 338–39

prejudice, overcoming through, 330–36
  structures creating and maintaining, 336–37
contact, between groups, 473
  Israelis and Palestinians who fought against each other, 320
  and reconciliation, 465–66
contagion, 187
continuum of destruction, 125, 139, 168, 177–79, 192n3, 199
Convention against Torture, 101
Convention on the Elimination of Discrimination against Women, 101
Convention on the Rights of the Child, 101
Convoy of Mercy, 192
cooperation, 139, 186, 324
corruption, 128
counterinsurgency, 125
  campaigns, 205
counterterrorism, 7–8 courage, (*see* moral courage, heroes)
"critical consciousness," 300, 378–79
Croatia, 181, 277, 417
Cuba, 151, 152
cultural and societal
  characteristics, 208
  autocratic and democratic political systems, 227–30
  compliance and, 223–24
  devaluation and discrimination, 208–18
  fear of consequences, 225
  group beliefs, 230–31
  group self-concepts, 231–32
  harsh child rearing and family systems, 220–22
  isolation of state, 234
  obedience and, 222–25
  pluralism, absence of, 226
  psychological and social wounds and, 218–20
  rape, in violence between groups, 233–34
  respect for authority and, 222–26
  socialization, 234
  unjust social arrangements, 230

discrimination, 52, 88–89, 105, 106,
120, 167, 208, 209, 213, 218,
235, 268, 278, 279, 290, 298,
327 (*see also* devaluation)
  adaptation to, 171–72
  as instigation, 121, 214–15
  against Jews, 173, 176, 210
  against Muslims in the Netherlands,
    88–89
  against Tutsis, 62, 115, 123, 175,
    177, 181, 215, 216
disengage, from terrorist groups,
  367–68
disillusion, 367–68
dislocation, 191, 204, 214
  personal, and societal change,
    117–21
  due to migration, 18
dissociation, 246, 275
divisionism, 70, 343, 376, 506
Doctors without Borders, 426
dual identity model, 353
  and inclusive caring, 354
Dutch bureaucracy, 10
Dutch–Muslim relations, 60, 88–89,
  213 (*see also* the Netherlands)
  Proposals to improve, 39
"dynamical systems" theory, 59

early prevention, 28, 420
  democracy promotion, 29
  economic development, 29
  humanizing, 29
  just social relations, 29
  participants in, 30
  positive attitude between
    groups, 29
  and reconciliation, 289–93
East Timor, 200, 297
economic deterioration, 116, 117
economic development, 29
economic inequalities, 12
education, 362–63, 364–65, 368, 480,
  514 (*see also* Radio
  LaBenevolencija; public
  education)
  radio programs for, 416
  educational radio drama in Rwanda,
    369–377
  educational programs, 402

effectiveness and control, need for, 105,
  10 (*see also* psychological needs)
Egypt, 8, 13, 85, 90, 91, 157, 159,
  160, 202, 205, 227, 259, 355
Egyptian Islamic Jihad, 262, 263
Einsatzgruppen, 189
El Colombiano newspaper, 328
El Salvador, 13, 205, 465
embedded self, 189
emotions, strong, 175
empathy, 191, 192, 197, 212, 222,
  244, 253, 261, 276, 283, 320,
  321, 327, 439, 470, 482
  creating it by bringing perpetrators
    into contact with victims'
    suffering, 414–15
  reduction in, 281
Encyclopedia of the Orient, The, 161
energy crises, 4
engagement between perpetrator and
  victim groups, 439–40
England. *See* Britain
entitivity, 137
equal justice, 293 (*see also* justice)
Ethiopia, 74, 389
ethnic conflict, 57, 58
ethnic minorities, 8
"ethnic-nationalist-separatist"
  terrorism, 7
ethnic polarization, 128
ethnocentricity, 230, 231
European countries
  constructive groups in, 350
European Islam, 162, 347
European Muslims, 124, 213
European Union, 28, 422
euthanasia, 199, 260, 396
evil, 32–34
evolution (*see also* learning by doing)
  of violence, 17–18, 167–177
  of caring/helping, 354–56
excessive respect for authority,
  18, 42
exclusion, 191, 214, 267
  of group members, 167, 172
  of Jews, 173
  moral, 139, 168, 172, 281
  of other, 168, 175, 284
  of women, 234
  of potential spoilers, 322

expansionism, 144
  Japan and, 179
exposing harm doers to the *victims of
    others'* violence, 369
expulsion
  of Germans, 68–9
  of Palestinians, 451–55
extended contact, 340
"extended effect" of contact, 330
extermination camps, Nazi,
    174, 199
external bystandership, 200–204, 296
    (*see also bystanders and
    bystandership*)
  role in prevention, 415–19
Extraordinary Chambers in the
    Courts of Cambodia, 484
extreme repression, 32

fanaticism, 158
Fatah, 23, 84, 85, 86, 157, 184, 185,
    263, 318, 319, 321, 508
FDLR. *See* Democratic Forces for the
    Liberation of Rwanda (FDLR)
fear, 66, 80, 114, 134, 224–25,
    246–47, 327
  creation of, 81–82, 104, 110–11,
    126, 181, 257
  of consequences, 225
  of groups, 57, 88, 127, 167, 197
  of life, 152, 159
  and reconciliation, 87
  of retribution, 71
  of Tutsis, 64, 216
feminism, 118
Festinger, L., 133
financial crises, 4
Finland, 231
food supply crises, 4
forbearance, 482
forgiveness, 21, 329, 439, 470–72
  conditional forgiveness, 305, 337,
    472, 478
  culture's impact on, 11
  dangers in, 475
  definitions of, 471
  group-level forgiveness, 482–83
  perpetrators denial of responsibility,
    472–73
  private forgiveness, 474–75

promotion of, 477–81
public forgiveness, 475
France, 64, 67, 117, 126, 154, 190,
    201, 204, 231, 268, 314, 320,
    348, 350
Friends of Raoul Wallenberg, the, 301
frustration, 52, 117, 120, 250
  of basic needs, 57, 91, 100, 104,
    105–6, 108, 110, 111, 114,
    116, 118, 121, 124, 125–26,
    140, 143, 191, 214, 228, 232,
    256, 270 (*see also* psychological
    needs)
frustration-aggression hypothesis, 110
frustration and fulfillment. *See*
    psychological needs
Fuhrerprinzip, 223
fulfillment, of universal psychological
    needs, 106 (*see also*
    psychological needs)
fundamental attribution error, 356
Future Guardians of Peace, 349

gacaca, 3, 12, 73, 223, 306, 382, 443,
    444, 447
  benefits, 463
  challenges to, 463
  complex truth, 463–64
  proceedings of, 462, 480
  witnesses, 462–63
gang rape, 249
Garumba refugee camp massacre,
    73–74
Gaza, 23, 83, 85, 126, 156, 157–58,
    183, 185, 206, 259, 270, 279,
    282, 319, 322
genocidal ideology, 343 (*see also*
    ideology; destructive ideology)
genocide, 6, 34, 101–2 (*see also* mass
    violence; mass killing)
  definition of, 100
  during war, 126
  evolution to, 174–79
  governments planning for, 55–56
  ideological, 142
  monopolistic, 142
  routinized, 55
  in Rwanda, 61–75
  types of, 142
Genocide Convention, 100–101

inclusive caring, 352
 common identity and, 353–54
 dual identity and, 354
 and positive reciprocity, 354–56
incremental view, 363
India, 94, 153, 192, 199, 261, 332, 336, 390
indiscriminate killing, 33
indiscriminate state violence, 8
individuals, active bystandership by, 391–94, 427
 heroes, 396–99
indoctrination, 170, 217, 234–35, 266
Indonesia, 59
inequalities, 12–13, 61, 230, 346, 483
information provided to people, 363–64
infrahumanization, 211
ingroup, 133 (see also common ingroup identity)
injustice, 52–55, 106
 perception of, 52
 unequal power and wealth, 230
 unjust social arrangements, 54, 230
insecurity, 128, 137
Inside Terrorism, 93
Instigation for violence100 (see also psychological and societal groups and processes; difficult life conditions; conflict)
 difficult life conditions, types of, 115–21
 group violence and international system, 100–104
 mass violence, and conflict, 121–25
 state failure and, 128–29
 universal psychological needs, 104–15
 war and revolution and mass violence, 125–27
institutional genocide, 142
institutions, 5, 12, 14, 17, 22, 28, 29, 30, 43–44, 71, 72, 118, 124, 128, 148, 166, 222, 230, 231, 251, 281, 290, 309, 313–315, 325, 336, 357–360, 397–403, 412, 415, 425, 506, 513
 and culture, 14
instrumental reconciliation, 291
instrumental violence by groups, 15

integrated approach, to reconciliation, 485–87
intelligence, 363
Interahamwe, 63, 64, 65, 117, 170, 224, 241, 244, 253
internal bystanders. See passivity, bystanders
International Centers for the Prevention of Genocide, 424
international community, 390
 (see also active bystandership, passivity)
 unwillingness to engage in prevention, 27, 28
International Criminal Court, 69, 79, 102, 461
International Crisis Group,11
International Rescue Committee, 426
Internet, 45, 121, 199, 217, 226, 359, 362, 367, 393, 414, 426, 453, 472
 and jihad, 148
Intifadas, 15 82, 86, 185, 264, 265, 336, 362, 453
intimate genocide in Rwanda, 64
intractable conflict, 32, 51, 58, 59, 60, 80, 124, 169, 182, 184, 322
invitation to readers, 45
Iran, 13, 86, 91, 94, 203, 205, 227, 261, 322, 324, 390
Iran-Iraq war
 U.S. government support to Iraq, 411
Iraq, 4, 59, 91, 93, 125, 159, 197, 203, 220, 232, 254, 262, 323–24
 suicide bombings, 7
Irgun, 81
Irish Republican Army (IRA), 184
Islam, 267–69 (see also European Islam, Muslim minorities)
 and constructive ideologies, 345–48
 and United States, 91–93
 Islamic Forum, 268
Islamic fundamentalism, 144
Islamic Group, 161–62
Islamic Society, 267, 268
Islamic terrorism, by Al-Qaeda, 8, 262, 315, (see also Al-Qaeda, suicide terrorism/bombings)

Legitimizing ideologies, 53, 54, 230
Liberal Mass Action for Peace, 398
Liberia, 168, 297
    child soldiers in, 349
    active bystandership in, 398
Libya, 219, 232
Libyan Islamic Fighting Group, 219
limited rights, 7
Lithuania, 189, 257
London transit bombing, 7
lost souls, terrorists as, 259, 263,
    266–69

Macedonia, 296, 311, 328
madrassas, 125, 148, 217
Madrid
    2004 incident, 7
majority group
    against minority group, 7
Malaysia, 57, 180
Malta, 263
Marshall Plan, 36, 204–5,
    391, 516
mass killing, 6, 100 (*see also* genocide;
    mass violence; violence)
mass violence, 6, 109, 173, 181, 211,
    215, 221 (*see also* genocide;
    mass killing; violence)
    difficult life conditions as
        instigators of, 115–21
    conflict as instigator of, 121–25
    halting, and late prevention and,
        294–98
    primary examples of, 60–62
    war and revolution as
        contributors to, 125–27
material conflict, 55–56
Mayi Mayi militias, 75
media, 19, 358, 393
    access to, 403
    actions and actors in, 500–501
    educational radio drama in Rwanda,
        369–377
    public education using, 362
Mein Kampf, 149, 150
Men's Resources International,
    237n85
messianic delusions, 261
Mexico, 152
micro-credits, 349–50

Middle East (*see also* Israeli-
        Palestinian conflict, Iraq)
    suicide bombing wave, 15
middle-range practices, 430
MidEastWeb, 185
migration, 18
military intervention, 422
minorities, 357 (*see also* Muslim
minorities)
    as victims, 7
mistrust, 56, 57, 59, 80, 84, 85, 114,
        124, 127, 181, 184, 186, 218,
        275, 312
mob violence, 54
modernity, and Holocaust, 9, 10
monolithic society, 18, 208, 226
monopolistic genocide, 142
MONUC (mission of the United Nations
        in the Congo), 512
moral agents, 200
moral courage, 394–95 (*see also*
        heroes)
moral disengagement, 172
moral exclusion, 139, 168, 172, 281
        (*see also* exclusion).
morality, 262
    definition of, 32
    reversal of, 168, 172, 245
moral obligation, 31
moral realm, 168, 172, 175,
        281, 284
moral reasoning, 225
moral responsibility, 252
moral truth, 482
moral values, 118–119, 172, 189,
        206, 248, 253, 269, 394, 402,
        411, 489, 496, 514
    values, principles and evil, 10, 13,
        15, 19, 32–35, 89–91, 109,
        111–112, 114, 118, 291, 328,
        366, 392, 493, 496,
        514–516,
    and goodness, 35
Morocco, 88, 190
mortality salience, 111–12,
        130n34, 364
mosques, 148, 190, 191, 217, 220,
        228, 259, 267, 268, 346
Mothers of the Plaza del Mayo,
        395, 460

positive orientation toward the "other," 19–20

positive reciprocity, 354–56 (*see also* reciprocity)

positive socialization, 494 (*see also* socialization)

postethnic ideology, 351

posttraumatic stress disorder (PTSD), 218, 246, 274, 437, 444

poverty, 80, 106, 115–16

power
  importance of, 29
  inequalities, 12
  and opportunity, competition for, 51–55

power principle, 227

Power Rules, 28

"predation-behavior" brain system, 257

prejudice, 58, 210–11, 216, 267, 268, 278 (*see also* devaluation; dehumanization; infrahumanization)
  in the Netherlands, 88–89
  overcoming , 330–36press freedom, 358–59

pretraining and cultural differences, 335

prevention, 11, 289, 357, 412
  early prevention, 26–29, 289–93
  external bystanders role in, 415–19
  inhibitors and promoters of, 431
  late prevention, 26–29, 294–98, 295
  structures in, 423–25

preventive diplomacy and negotiation, 310–13

price crises, 4

principles
  of origins, prevention, reconciliation, 11–12
  overview of , and practices, 16–22

"prisoner's dilemma" game, 186

prisoners, 365

private forgiveness, 474–75

privilege, justification of, 54

procedural justice, 459

ProFemmes, in Rwanda, 486

proportional representation and governmental system, 229–30

prosocial value orientation, 392

Protestants, 12, 135, 152, 214, 317, 327, 334, 353, 470, 477, 498

pseudo-transcendence, 106, 270

psychological and behavioral evolution, 168 (*see also* evolution, learning by doing)

psychological and societal groups and processes (*see also* instigation)
  Al-Qaeda terrorism, 158–62
  collective identity, shift to, 132–37
  German Nazi ideology, 153–55
  ideologies
    of antagonism, 162–63
    in Israeli–Palestinian conflict, 156–58
    in Rwandan genocide, 155–56
  leaders and followers, 145–51
  nature of groups and people, 137–39
  power of ideas, 151–53
  scapegoating and ideologies, 139–45

psychological changes, 423 (*see also* evolution, learning by doing)

psychological characteristics
  of perpetrators, 253–258
  of active bystanders/helpers, 391–2
  (*see also* rescuers)

psychological needs, 104
  basic needs, 108–9
  destructive fulfillment of, 107, 111
  fulfillment of, 14
  group formation to address, 17
  humiliation and multiple influences in group violence, 112–15
  and mortality salience, 111–12
  and personal goals, 109
  threat to, 110–12
  uncertainty, 110–11, 112

psychological recovery, 438 (*see also* healing)
  by survivors, 432–38
  by perpetrators and bystanders, 438–40

psychological woundedness and victimization, 275–76
  (*see also* wounds)

psychology, culture, and structures, 12–14

public discourse, 453

survivors (*see also* healing)
  of the Holocaust, 71, 80–81, 235, 275, 280–81
  healing of, 432–38
suspicion, 111, 186, 312, 339
Sweden, 231, 316, 351
Switzerland, 196
Syria, 82, 94, 319, 212, 298, 390, 511
system justification theory, 53, 171–72

tahadiya, 319
Taliban, 93, 125, 321
Tanzania, 294
teacher-learner setup, 168–69 (*see also* obedience to authority experiments)
technological changes, 4
terrorism, 6, 7–8, 27, 32, 33–34, 504–6
  acceptance and support of surrounding community, 18
  and counterterrorism, 7–8
  nations' support for, 389–90
  origin of, 505
  push and pull factors in, 368
  social influence in, 18–19
  suicide terrorism (*see* suicide terrorism/bombings)
terrorist ideology, 365
terrorists, 6, 18 (*see also* perpetration and perpetrators, personality and perpetration, radicalization)
  Al-Qaeda, 8 (*see also* ideology)
  disengagement of, 367–68
  Hezbollah, 7
  motivations, 7
  Salafi Jihad, 8
  targets of, 7
  violence, 4
terror management theory, 111
testimony, 445–47
Thayer, A., 70, 238, 308n10
third parties, 20
threat, 55, 87, 94, 128, 129, 138, 162, 167, 210, 257, 313 (*see also* fear)
  collective, 110, 111
  continued, 67
  creation of, 100, 104, 114, 126
  ideology and, 59

increase in, 56
to living, 79, 80, 112
mortal, 212
of mortality, 112, 130n34
new, 136, 175, 218, 338
old, 279
perceiving of, 276
real, 74, 133
and research, 137, 159
to self-respect and dignity, 105
top-level practices, 430
torture, (see Convention against)
toxic situations, 257
Track Two diplomacy, 401
training, leaders, 22, 410–14
  actions and actors, 502–3
transcendence, of self, (and pseudo-transcendence), 106, 270
transitional justice processes, 27, 460 (*see also* truth commissions)
transnational terrorism, 265
  and democratic systems, 229
trauma, 277–79 (*see also* chosen, complex, healing, personal;, posttraumatic stress disorder, psychological woundedness,psychological recovery, wounds)
treaty of Westphalia (1648), 418
Treblinka extermination camp, 174
trial massacres, 178
Tribunal in Cambodia, 484
truth about past, establishing, 21
Truth and Reconciliation Commission (TRC), South Africa, 407, 443, 444–45, 464, 407, 478–79
truth commissions, 443–44, 451
truth establishment, 21, 442–43
  challenges and mistakes, 447–48
  impact on truth tellers and society, 444–47
  shared history, 449–57
Turkey, 58, 88, 117, 118, 122, 126, 127, 143, 168, 177, 178, 211, 215, 232, 277, 279, 303
  Armenian genocide in, 457
Tutsis, 10, 76, 78, 146, 224, 344–45, 356 (*see also* Hutus and Tutsis, conflict between; Rwanda)
Twa, 61